About Osho

Osho defies categorization. His thousands of talks cover everything from the individual quest for meaning to the most urgent social and political issues facing society today. Osho's books are not written but are transcribed from audio and video recordings of his extemporaneous talks to international audiences. As he puts it, "So remember: whatever I am saying is not just for you... I am talking also for the future generations." Osho has been described by *The Sunday Times* in London as one of the "1000 Makers of the 20th Century" and by American author Tom Robbins as "the most dangerous man since Jesus Christ". *Sunday Mid-Day* (India) has selected Osho as one of ten people – along with Gandhi, Nehru and Buddha – who have changed the destiny of India. About his own work Osho has said that he is helping to create the conditions for the birth of a new kind of human being. He often characterizes this new human being as "Zorba the Buddha" – capable both of enjoying the earthy pleasures of a Zorba the Greek and the silent serenity of a Gautama the Buddha.

Running like a thread through all aspects of Osho's talks and meditations is a vision that encompasses both the timeless wisdom of all ages past and the highest potential of today's (and tomorrow's) science and technology. Osho is known for his revolutionary contribution to the science of inner transformation, with an approach to meditation that acknowledges the accelerated pace of contemporary life. His unique OSHO Active Meditations are designed to first release the accumulated stresses of body and mind, so that it is then easier to take an experience of stillness and thought-free relaxation into daily life.

OSHO books also published by Watkins Publishing

Living Dangerously (Masters of Wisdom)
When the Shoe Fits
The Buddha Said
Meetings with Remarkable People
Tantra: The Supreme Understanding
The Art of Living and Dying

thesecretofsecrets

On *The Secret of the Golden Flower*

TAOIST TEACHINGS ON LIFE AND EXISTENCE

OSHO

WATKINS

Sharing Wisdom Since
1893

This edition first published in the UK and USA 2014 by
Watkins Publishing Limited, PO Box 883, Oxford OX1 9PL, UK

A member of Osprey Group
For enquiries in the USA and Canada:
Osprey Publishing, PO Box 3985, New York NY 10185-3985
Tel: (001) 212 753 4402   Email: info@ospreypublishing.com

Design and typography © Watkins Publishing Limited 2014

Original English title: *The Secret of Secrets – On the Secret of the Golden Flower*

This book is a transcript of a series of original talks, *The Secret of Secrets* by Osho,
given to a live audience. All of Osho's talks have been published in full as books, and are
also available as original audio recordings. Audio recordings and the complete text archive
can be found via the online OSHO Library at www.osho.com

1 3 5 7 9 10 8 6 4 2
Designed and typeset by Luana Gobbo
Printed and bound in China
A CIP record for this book is available from the British Library
ISBN: 978-1-78028-997-7

Watkins Publishing is supporting the Woodland Trust, the UK's leading woodland
conservation charity, by funding tree-planting initiatives and woodland maintenance.
www.watkinspublishing.co.uk

Contents

Preface

Life is the way. Life has no goal.

That's why I love the word *Tao*. *Tao* means the way, with no goal. Simply *the way*. It was courageous of Lao Tzu, twenty-five centuries ago, to tell people that there is no goal and we are not going anywhere. We are just going to be here, so make the time as beautiful, as loving, as joyous as possible. He called his philosophy Tao, and Tao means simply "the way."

Many asked him, "Why have you chosen the name Tao? Because you don't have any goal in your philosophy..."

He said, "Specifically for that reason I have chosen to call it 'the way,' so that nobody forgets there is no goal, but only the way."

And the way is beautiful, the way is full of flowers. And the way goes on becoming more and more beautiful as your consciousness goes on becoming higher. The moment you have reached the peak, everything becomes so sweet, so ecstatic, that you suddenly realize that *this* is the place, this is home. You were unnecessarily running here and there.

Never think of going somewhere. Think in terms of transforming yourself *here*.

"There" is a cunning strategy of the mind to deceive you. The mind always makes you interested in things far away, *there*, so that you can be led away from *here*. Or at least your attention is no longer here, it is there. And you will never *be* there. Going from here to there, slowly, slowly you acquire the habit of always looking *there*, so wherever you reach, that place is no longer in your focus – your goal has shifted somewhere else.

In India there is an ancient proverb – *diya tale andhera* – "there is darkness under the lamp." The lamp gives light all around, and just exactly underneath it there is darkness. This is the situation of man. You are capable of seeing everywhere, all around, but you are incapable of seeing where you are, who you are.

So cancel all the tickets you have booked! There is nowhere to go; just being here is so blissful. Close your eyes, so that you can see the reality of the *here*. There and then are only fictions.

Here and now are the only realities.

Osho, *Sermons in Stones*

CHAPTER 1
The Secret of the Magic of Life

Master Lu-tsu said:

That which exists through itself is called the Way, Tao. Tao has neither name nor shape. It is the one essence, the one primal spirit. Essence and life cannot be seen. They are contained in the light of heaven. The light of heaven cannot be seen. It is contained in the two eyes.

The Great One is the term given to that which has nothing above it. The secret of the magic of life consists in using action in order to attain nonaction.

The Golden Flower is the light. One uses the Golden Flower as a symbol. The phrase "The lead of the water-region has but one taste" refers to it.

The work on the circulation of the light depends entirely on the backward-flowing movement, so that the thoughts are gathered together. The heavenly heart lies between sun and moon.

The Book of the Yellow Castle says: "In the square inch field of the square foot house, life can be regulated." In the middle of the square inch dwells the splendor. In the purple hall of the city of jade dwells the God of Utmost Emptiness and Life. Therefore when the light circulates, the energies of the whole body appear before its throne, as, when a holy

*king has established the capital and has laid down the fundamental
rules of order, all the states approach with tribute; or as, when the
master is quiet and calm, manservants and maids obey his orders of
their own accord, and each does his work.*

*Therefore you only have to make the light circulate; that is the deepest
and most wonderful secret. The light is easy to move, but difficult to fix.
If it is made to circulate long enough, then it crystallizes itself. It is the
condition of which it is said: "Silently thou fliest upward in the morning."*

*In carrying out this fundamental principle you need to seek for no other
methods, but must only concentrate your thoughts on it. By collecting
the thoughts one can fly and will be born in heaven.*

*The Golden Flower is the Elixir of Life. Although it works very
accurately, it is yet so fluid that it needs extreme intelligence and clarity,
and the most complete absorption and tranquility. People without this
highest degree of intelligence and understanding do not find the way;
people without this utmost capacity for absorption and tranquility
cannot keep fast hold of it.*

A parable.

Once there was a very rich magician who had a great many sheep. But at the
same time this magician was very mean. He did not want to hire shepherds, nor
did he want to erect a fence about the pasture where his sheep were grazing. The
sheep consequently often wandered into the forest, fell into ravines, and so on,
and above all they ran away, for they knew that the magician wanted their flesh
and skins, and this they did not like.

At last the magician found a remedy. He hypnotized his sheep and suggested
to them first of all that they were immortal and that no harm was being done to
them when they were skinned, that on the contrary, it would be very good for
them and even pleasant.

Secondly, he suggested that the magician was a good master who loved his
flock so much that he was ready to do anything in the world for them. And in the
third place, he suggested to them that if anything at all was going to happen to
them it was not going to happen just then, at any rate not that day, and therefore
they had no need to think about it.

Further, the magician suggested to his sheep that they were not sheep at all. To some of them he suggested that they were lions, to others that they were eagles, to others that they were men, and to others that they were magicians.

And after this, all his cares and worries about the sheep came to an end. They never ran away again but quietly awaited the time when the magician would require their flesh and their skins.

George Gurdjieff loved this parable very much. His whole philosophy is contained in this small parable. And this parable represents man in the ordinary state of unconsciousness. It is one of the most beautiful illustrations of man as he is: man is a machine.

Man is not born to be a machine, but man lives like a machine and dies like a machine. Man has the seed of a great flowering of consciousness, man has the possibility to become God. But that doesn't happen. It does not happen because man has been hypnotized – by the society, by the state, by the organized church, by the vested interests. The society needs slaves, and man can remain a slave only if he is not allowed to grow into his uttermost flowering. The society needs your flesh and your skins and naturally nobody likes it. Hence the whole process of socialization, of civilization, is nothing but a deep hypnosis.

Man is being hypnotized from the very moment he is born. He is being hypnotized: that the society exists in his favor, for his good. That is utterly wrong. He is being hypnotized: that he is immortal. He is not. He can be, but he is not. And if the hypnosis persists he will never be immortal.

You live only as a mortal being because you live in the body. The body is going to die. That which is born is bound to die; birth is the beginning of the body and death the end. Do you know anything more than the body in you? Have you experienced anything higher than the body, deeper than the body? Have you seen anything in you which was even before you were born? If you have seen that, then you *are* immortal. If you know your face, your original face, the face that you had before you were born, then you know you will be there after death too; otherwise not.

Man can be an immortal, but man lives surrounded by death because man lives identified with the body. The society does not allow you to know more than the body. The society is interested only in your body; your body can be put to use, your soul is dangerous. A man of soul is always dangerous because a man of soul is a free man, he cannot be reduced to slavery. A man who has an immortal soul in him has a deeper commitment to existence itself, to God himself. He does not care a bit about the man-made structures of society, civilization and culture;

these are prison cells for him. He does not exist as a Christian or a Hindu or a Mohammedan. He cannot be part of a crowd. He exists as an individual.

The body is part of a crowd, your soul is not. Your soul is deeply individual. Its flavor is that of freedom. But your soul cannot be put to any use in the marketplace. The society needs only your body. And it is very dangerous for the society if you start striving for the soul, because then your interest changes. You turn from being an extrovert into an introvert; you start moving inwards. The society is outside, the society wants you to remain an extrovert – interested in money, power and prestige – so that your energy goes on moving outwards. If you start moving inwards, that means you have become a dropout, you are no more part of the game that is being played on the outside. You don't belong to it. You start diving deep within your own being. And there is the source of immortality.

The society prevents you from going inwards. And the best way is to give you a false idea that you are going inwards. The magician told the sheep that they are lions, suggested to them that they are immortals, hypnotized them into believing that they are not only men but they are great magicians.

When you go to a church you are not going inwards, when you go to the temple you are not going inwards. But the society has hypnotized you to believe that if you want to go inwards, go to the church. But the church is as much outside as anything else. The society has hypnotized you to believe that if you want to go inwards, go to the priest. And the priest is an agent of the state and the society. The priest has always been against the mystics, because if you go to a mystic you will start moving inwards.

A mystic lives in a totally different way. His energy has a different gestalt: his river moves inwards. So one who comes to a mystic, falls in tune with the mystic, will start moving inwards naturally, simply, spontaneously. That is the whole purpose of being with a master, with a mystic.

The Secret of the Golden Flower is one of the most esoteric treatises in the world. It will show you the way to become more than the body. It will show you the way to go beyond death. It will show you the way to bloom – how not to remain a seed but to become a golden flower – what in India we have called the one-thousand-petaled lotus, in China they call the golden flower. It is a symbol.

The flower represents perfection, totality. The flower represents the uttermost expression of the potential, the actualization of the potential. The flower represents the beauty, the grandeur, the splendor of being. And unless you have become a thousand-petaled lotus or a golden flower...

Remember, you have to go far. Remember, that you have to get out of the traps that the society has put around you. Do not forget, you have not yet done the work for which you have come to the earth. Remember, you are just a seed, not yet a soul.

This treatise, *The Secret of the Golden Flower*, is very ancient – possibly one of the most ancient treatises in the world – certainly twenty-five centuries old, but the possibility is that it is older than that. But twenty-five centuries can be traced back very easily. And this treatise is also a great synthesis of all the great religions. That is rare, unique. The Bible belongs to the Christians, the Talmud belongs to the Jews, the Vedas belong to the Hindus, the Dhammapada to the Buddhists, the Tao Te Ching to the Taoists. But this small book, *The Secret of the Golden Flower,* belongs to no one in particular, or it belongs to all.

It is deeply based in Taoist teachings, it is a flowering of the Taoist approach to life and existence. But it is not only that – Zarathustra has played a role; Zarathustra's teachings have been incorporated in it. Buddhist teachings have also been incorporated in it, and a certain esoteric school of Christians, the Nestorians, they have also played their part. So Christianity and Judaism also have become part of it.

It is one of the most synthetical approaches. It combines all that is beautiful in all the traditions of the world. For centuries it was only transmitted orally and the book remained esoteric. It was not available to the public because it has something very secret to teach; it was available only to the disciples. The master would tell it to the disciple only when the time was ripe, because it gives you such a potential secret that if you don't understand rightly, if you do something wrong with it, there are bound to be harmful effects from it. It has to be understood rightly, and it has to be worked at only in the presence of a master. It is a powerful method – it is as powerful as atomic energy.

Now the secrets of atomic energy are kept hidden from the public. Once they start leaking out to the public there is going to be great danger. If people can manufacture atom bombs privately, there is bound to be great chaos. Great secrecy is maintained about atomic research. Exactly in the same way this book teaches you one of the most potential methods of inner explosion. For centuries the secrets were guarded – only given to the disciples in privacy, in intimacy – and the people who followed this particular esoteric school resisted all temptations to write the book. In fact, all the religions of the world have long resisted writing their spiritual teachings.

There is some beauty when something is transferred orally. It is alive, one thing – the master is behind it. It is not a dead word, the word has soul, wings.

The experience of the master supports it, the master is a witness to it. It is not just speculation, not only a philosophy, but something existential, experienced, lived. And the master has traveled the path – he knows the dangers of the path, he knows the pitfalls, he knows the points at which people go astray – and he will take every care so that the disciple cannot go astray.

The closer you come to the truth, the more is the possibility of going astray, because when you come closer to the truth, you can become very egoistic, thinking that, "Now I know," that "Now I am." And if the ego exploits the situation you will fall back to your old dark valley, you will lose the peak. When you come closer to the truth, a great desire arises to share it with people. But you have not attained it in its wholeness and it is dangerous to share half-truths because half-truths are more dangerous than lies, because they are powerful. Lies are impotent. Sooner or later people will themselves find that it is a lie. But the half-truth can persist for centuries, can have effects for centuries.

Nobody can reach through the half-truth. And the person who travels half the way will belong neither to this world nor to the other. He will be in a limbo, and that is a very strange situation to be in: you lose the old and you don't gain the new; you become a chaos. The old order is gone and the new has not happened. You become a cloud, you become confusion. Rather than becoming more clear, rather than becoming more alive, rather than becoming more light-full, your life becomes a conflict between two polarities. You are pulled apart, you start falling into pieces. Half of you belongs to the earth and half of you belongs to the sky. Now you are nowhere. Now you are nobody. This can create madness. So for centuries *The Secret of the Golden Flower* was only conveyed orally.

Furthermore, with an oral tradition the book remains always alive. That's how it became a synthesis. Basically it was born in the Taoist climate of China. But then Bodhidharma reached China – a new master, with a new message from India, Buddha's message. And the people who were following *The Secret of the Golden Flower* were very open people; they were not part of any established church. They could immediately see that Bodhidharma also has it – it was so apparent, so manifest. They allowed Bodhidharma's teachings to be part of their teaching. And the same happened with Zoroastrian masters, with Nestorian Christians: again and again something came to China, and if it was worthwhile it was incorporated.

An oral teaching remains alive, growing, like a river. New streams of water come and become part of it. Once a teaching is written, then it cannot incorporate anything anymore. Then it becomes rigid, it loses fluidity; it becomes dead, it is a corpse. Now *The Secret of the Golden Flower* is not growing; for centuries it has not grown. Since it has been written it has not grown. Why have I chosen to speak on it? – so that it can still grow. It is such a beautiful message to the world, it should not die. I would like to revive it. And now I can talk to people who are disciples, who have come to me and who are ready to die in order to be reborn, who are ready to die for flowering. The seed has to die, only then can it grow; the seed has to disappear, only then can the tree happen.

I will be speaking to you on this small but immensely valuable book so that the book can become alive again. It can become alive between me and you. It can again start flowing. And it has something of immense importance. If you understand it and if you practice it, you will be enriched.

But the first thing to understand is: remember that you have been hypnotized, and you have to go through a de-hypnotizing process. Remember that you have been conditioned and you have to be unconditioned. You must remember that death is coming. Don't think that it is not going to happen today; it can happen any moment.

In fact, all that happens always happens now. The seed dies now, the bud becomes the flower now, the bird starts calling now. All that ever happens happens only in the space made available by now, this moment. Nothing ever happens in the past and nothing ever happens in the future. All that happens always happens in the present – that is the only way for things to happen because the present is the only time there is.

Past is just your memory and future is just your imagination. But you have been hypnotized to live in the past and you have been hypnotized to live in the future: Choose, either past or future. But no society allows you to live in the present.

Christians and Hindus and Mohammedans – they condition you to live in the past. Their golden age was in the past. Communists, socialists, fascists – they condition you to live in the future, their golden age is in the future, the utopia is coming: when the revolution comes, then you will be able to really live, then there will be a golden age. Either you are taken to the past, which is false, or to the future, which is again false. No society tells you to live in the present, in the here and now.

To be a sannyasin, to be a real seeker, means to live in the here and now – and there is no other life. But for that you will have to de-automatize yourself, you will have to become a man and not a machine. You will have to become a little more conscious. You are not conscious.

Once I was sitting by the side of a dying man – he was a professor in the same university where I was a professor. He was at the pinnacle of his successful career and then came the heart attack – which always comes when you are at the pinnacle. Success is always followed by a heart attack. What else can you have after it? So he had a heart attack and he was dying. I went to see him. He was very sad – who wants to die? – and he was in great despair and anguish. I told him, "You need not worry. You are not going to die."

He said, "What are you saying? But the doctors…all the doctors say that there is no possibility of my survival. On what grounds are you saying that I am not going to die?"

I said, "In the first place you cannot die because you never lived. You have not fulfilled the first requirement for dying. For these fifty-five years you have been sleepwalking, you have dreamed; you have not lived. I have watched you for years."

He was shocked, he was angry – so angry that for a moment he forgot all about death. His eyes were aflame with anger and he said, "Is this the way to treat a dying man? Can't you be a little courteous? Why are you so hard on me? I am dying and you are talking such great philosophy – 'You never lived.' Is this the time to say such things?"

I listened silently. I just became absolutely silent. Then the rage disappeared and he started crying, and great tears came to his eyes. He held my hand with great love and then he said, "Maybe you are right. I never lived. Maybe you are not rude, you are just being true. And I know nobody else would have said this to me." And then great gratitude, and for a moment he became so conscious that one could have seen the light on the face – it was there, he was all aura. And he thanked me. That night he died. I remained with him to the last moment.

And he said, "If you had not been here I would have missed my death too, as I have missed my life. But I am dying consciously. At least one thing I am happy about – I am not dying unconsciously."

And his death was beautiful. He died without any regret, he died in a relaxed way. He died almost with a welcoming heart. He died full of gratitude. He died prayerfully. His next life is bound to have a different quality.

If death is so beautiful it brings a new life to you.

But one has to live each moment, whether it is of life, of love, of anger, of death. …Whatsoever it is, one has to live each moment as consciously as possible.

A peasant, carried away by his imagination, found himself in a vegetable garden stealing cucumbers.

"I'll carry off this sack of cucumbers," he thought, "and with the money I get for them I'll buy a hen. The hen will lay eggs, she will sit on them and hatch a brood of chicks, and I'll feed the chicks till they grow, then I'll sell them and buy a suckling pig. I'll feed the suckling pig till it grows into a sow, I'll breed her, and she'll have a litter of pigs and I'll sell them. With the money I get for the pigs I'll buy a house with a garden; I'll plant cucumbers in the garden, and I won't let anyone steal them – I'll keep guard over them. I'll hire a strong watchman, and from time to time I'll go out to the garden and shout, 'Hey, you! Take care!'"

The peasant was so carried away by this thought that he shouted at the top of his voice. The watchman heard him and came running. He caught the peasant and gave him a good thrashing.

But this is how man lives: in dreams, in imagination, in projections. This is how *you* live, and this is not the way to live this beautiful, tremendously valuable life – this is sheer wastage. You have to become more attentive to the moment, to the present. You have to gather your consciousness. Consciousness is your treasure, and all the methods that have been invented, devised down the centuries, are nothing but ways to create more consciousness in you, to create more fire in you, to make your life a passionate affair, a flame. People are living dull lives, people are living absent-mindedly, people are living inattentively. How can you live with so much inattention around you? Inattention is darkness, attention is light. And this treatise will teach you how to create more light in you, so that one day the golden flower will blossom.

Two psychiatrists met on the street. "You are feeling fine," said one. "How am I doing?"

People are asking each other. Nobody knows how they are doing, they are looking into each other's eyes, gathering information about themselves from others. That's why the opinion of others has become so important. If somebody says you are a fool, you become angry. Why? Or you become sad. Why? You are shattered. You were thinking you are a wise man because others had told you that you are wise. It was the opinion of others that you depended on. Now somebody else says you are a fool. He can easily shatter your wisdom, very easily. He has thrown a stone and you had made a palace with playing cards. Now all is shattered. That's why one becomes so angry, so enraged, so violent, and one becomes so worried, anxious. You are continually looking for what others are thinking, because you know only that which others think about you, you don't know anything about yourself. Now what kind of situation is this? If I cannot know about myself, who else can know about me? From the outside nobody can watch me, I am not available that way. From the outside only my body can be watched. From the inside I can know my consciousness.

Even when you stand before a mirror you see only your body, you cannot see your consciousness in the mirror. Even you cannot see it in the mirror – your own consciousness. You have to see it directly. It is never mirrored, it is never reflected in anything; it is invisible. You have to close your eyes and be it. And that is the only way of knowing it. But people live so unconsciously. They simply live by the opinion of others. What others say becomes their soul. Others can take it away any moment. People remain beggars.

Have you known anything about yourself directly? Have you ever encountered yourself directly without bringing the opinion of others into it? If you have not done it, you have not yet lived. Life starts only by encountering oneself, by seeing oneself directly, immediately. Life exists only when you are capable of seeing yourself as you are, not as others think about you. What can they think about you? What can they say about you? They can watch your behavior, they cannot watch you. If you want to watch yourself, only you can do that, nobody else. It cannot be done by servants, it cannot be delegated to somebody else. It cannot be done by the experts either. But we are so much interested in the opinions of others because we are absolutely absent, there is nobody awake inside – deeply asleep, we are snoring inside.

The absent-minded professor went in for a haircut. He sat down in the barber's chair, but didn't remove his hat.

"I'm afraid you will have to take off your hat," said the barber.

"Oh, I'm sorry!" said the professor, "I didn't know there were ladies present."

Watch your own absent-mindedness. Watching it will create attentiveness in you. Watch what is happening within you: thoughts passing, memories arising, a cloud of anger, a dark night of sadness, or a beautiful morning of joy. Watch all that passes in you, become more and more watchful. Slowly, slowly you will develop an integrated watchfulness. And the method taught by *The Secret of The Golden Flower* is how to become integrated in your inner light. This is the story of this book before we enter into the sutras.

The book comes from an esoteric circle in China. The founder of this esoteric circle is said to have been the well-known Taoist adept, Lu Yen. Where did Lu Yen get this secret teaching? He himself attributes it to Master Kuan Yiu-hsi, for whom, according to tradition, Lao Tzu wrote down his *Tao Te Ching*.

Lao Tzu never wrote a single word in his whole life. He declined again and again, to write anything. He conveyed to his disciples what he had come to know, but he was not ready to write because he said, "The Tao which can be said is not the true Tao." The Tao which can be expressed is already falsified. It can be learned only in intimate contact with the master. There is no other way of communicating it. It can only be learned in a deep communion where the disciple and the master meet, where the disciple holds nothing back, where the disciple and the master overlap, where their consciousnesses merge into each other. Only in such a meeting, in communion, can Tao be conveyed. So he refused again and again.

He lived a long life. But when he was going to die he left China on a water buffalo. Why on a water buffalo? His whole teaching had been the teaching of the watercourse way.

He said: "One should be like water – flowing, fluid, fresh, always moving towards the ocean and one should be like water – soft, feminine, receptive, loving, nonviolent. One should not be like a rock. The rock appears to be very strong but is not, and water appears to be very weak but is not. Never be deceived by appearances. Finally the water wins over the rock and the rock is destroyed and becomes sand and is taken to the sea. The rock disappears finally – against the soft water."

The rock is masculine; it is the male mind, the aggressive mind. Water is feminine, soft, loving, not aggressive at all. But the nonaggressive wins. The water is always ready to surrender, but through surrender it conquers – that is the way of the woman. The woman always surrenders and conquers through it. And the man wants to conquer and the ultimate result is just a surrender and nothing else. Hence, Lao Tzu chose a water buffalo when he left the country. Where was he going? He was going to the Himalayas to die into that eternal beauty.

A real man knows how to live and how to die. A real man lives totally, dies totally. A real man lives in benediction and dies in benediction.

He was going into absolute aloneness in the Himalayas, but he was caught on the border. And the man who caught him on the border is Master Kuan Yiu-hsi. He was a guard at the last post of the Chinese border. Lao Tzu had to pass that post; there was no other way to get out of the country. And Kuan Yiu-hsi persuaded him: "You are going to die, you are leaving the country forever, and soon you will be leaving the body. Please write just a few words. And I won't allow you to get out of the land if you don't write them. This price you have to pay." And Lao Tzu had to sit in Kuan Yiu-hsi's hut for three days, and there he wrote the *Tao Te Ching*. Kuan means "the Han-ku pass"; hence he is called Master Kuan, that is "Master of the Han-ku pass." And he must have been a great adept, otherwise it would have been impossible to persuade Lao Tzu to write – his whole life he had declined. He could not decline the invitation of this man. This man must have had something that it was impossible even for Lao Tzu to say no to.

This is how the tradition of *The Golden Flower* is connected with Lao Tzu. But it didn't start with Lao Tzu. Lao Tzu himself says that whatsoever he is saying has been said before, again and again, down the centuries. He is not bringing a new truth in the world but only a new expression. It is always so: truth is the same, only expressions differ.

What Lao Tzu said is the same as what Krishna had said before him. What Krishna said is the same as what Buddha said later on. What Buddha has said is the same as Mohammed, as Jesus, as Zarathustra have said, although their expressions are so different that you will need great intelligence to see to the very core. The structure is different, the language is different, their ways of saying it are different; naturally, because they are different persons, different individuals, with their own uniqueness. But truth is neither new nor old and wherever truth is, it is eternal.

The book *The Secret of the Golden Flower* is one of the eternal sources where one can again become alive, one can again find the door to the divine.

The sutras:

> *Master Lu-tsu said:*
> *That which exists through itself is called the Way, Tao.*

The word *Tao* essentially means "the Way." Nothing can be said about the goal. The goal remains elusive, inexpressible, ineffable. But something can be said about the Way. Hence, Taoists have never used the words *God*, *truth*, *nirvana*; no, they simply use the word *Way*. Buddha says: "Buddhas can only show you the Way. If you follow the path, you will reach to the truth."

Truth will have to be your own experience. Nobody can define the truth, but the Way can be defined, the Way can be made clear. The master cannot give you the truth, but the master can give you the Way. And once the Way is there then all that is needed is to walk on it. That has to be done by the disciple. I cannot walk for you and I cannot eat for you. I cannot live for you and I cannot die for you. These things have to be done by oneself. But I can show the Way, I have walked on the Way. Tao simply means "the Way."

That which exists through itself is called the Way.

And the definition is beautiful. Lu-tsu says, "That which exists by itself, that which needs nobody else's support, that which has always existed whether you walk on it or not..."

Whether anybody walks on it or not does not matter, it always exists. In fact, the whole existence follows it unknowingly. If you can follow it knowingly your life will become a great blessing. If you follow it unknowingly, then you will go on stumbling, then you cannot enjoy it as it should be enjoyed.

A man can be brought into the garden and he may be unconscious; he may be drunk or he may be in a coma or under the impact of chloroform. He can be brought into the garden, he is unconscious, the songs of the birds will be heard by his ears, but he will not know. The fragrance of the flowers will come riding on the breeze to his nostrils, but he will not know. The sun will shine on him and will shower light on him, but he will not know. The breeze will caress him, but he will not know. You can put him under the shade of a big tree and the coolness of it, but he will not know. That's how man is.

We *are* in Tao, because where else can we be? To live is to be on the Way. To live is to live in God, to breathe is to breathe in God. Where else can we be? But just as the fish lives in the ocean and is completely oblivious of the ocean, we are living in Tao and are completely oblivious of Tao. In fact it is so obvious, that's why we are so oblivious. The fish knows the ocean so well…the fish is born in it, the fish has never been out of it, the fish takes it for granted, hence the fish is not aware of it. We are on the Way, we are in God, we live in Tao, through Tao, but we are not aware of it. The Tao exists, because without the Tao trees will not grow and stars will not move and the blood will not circulate and the breath will not come in. Life will disappear.

Life is possible only if there is a fundamental law holding it. Life is possible only if there is something that supports it. Look at the immense order in existence. It is not a chaos, it is a cosmos. What makes it a cosmos? Why is there so much harmony? There must be a law that keeps the harmony going, flowing, keeps everything in accord. But we don't know about it. We don't know anything about our own being, and we are joined through our being with Tao.

Tao has neither name nor shape. It is the one essence, the one
primal spirit.

It is the ocean of life that surrounds us, it is within and without – the pure essence. It is existence, it is the primal spirit. No name can contain it. All names are its name. And no shape is particular to it, because all shapes are Tao's shape. Tao exists in millions of forms. In the tree it is green, in the flower it is red, in man it is man, in fish it is fish. It is the same law. You can replace the word *Tao* with God and it will be the same. What Christians and Mohammedans call God, Taoists call Tao, Buddhists call *dhamma*, Jews used to call it "Logos," but they mean the same thing. No name can contain it, or, it can be expressed by any name.

> *Essence and life cannot be seen. They are contained in the light*
> *of heaven. The light of heaven cannot be seen. It is contained in*
> *the two eyes.*

You can see the form, you can see the body – the body is the form, the substance that surrounds the essence – but you cannot see the essence. The essence is invisible to the eyes, unapproachable by the senses. It has to be felt immediately, not through any media.

You see my body, I see your body – it is through a medium. My eyes are telling me you are here, your eyes are telling you that I am here, but who knows? – the eyes may be deceiving, they do deceive sometimes. In the night, in the dark, you see a rope as if it were a snake, and when you see it as a snake it affects you as a snake: you are afraid, you start running. Or you can see in the desert an oasis which is not there, which is only a projected phenomenon because you are so thirsty that you want it to be there, so you create it there. Eyes deceive many times, so who knows?

If truth is known through a medium then it will always remain suspect, doubtful; it can't have any certainty – absolute certainty it can't have. And a truth which is not absolutely certain is not truth at all. The truth has to be absolutely certain, it cannot be only approximately certain. Then there is only one way: it should be known without a medium, one should know it directly, immediately, one should know it without any senses. And that's how it is known: you cannot see life, but you can feel it. It is a subjective experience, not an object.

> *Essence and life cannot be seen. They are contained in the light*
> *of heaven. The light of heaven cannot be seen. It is contained in*
> *the two eyes.*

You have these two eyes. These two eyes for the Taoist are very significant. Only modern science has been able to see the truth of it. These two eyes are not only the visible eyes. These two eyes represent the male and the female in you. Now modern science says that the mind of man is divided into two hemispheres, and one hemisphere is male, the other is female. The right side of your mind is feminine, and the left side is masculine. So your one eye represents the male in you and your other eye represents the female in you. And when your male and female meet inside you, that meeting is what is called heaven – that meeting, that inner communion of your male and female.

Jesus says: "When your two eyes become one, there will be light." He is talking like a Taoist alchemist: When your two eyes become one there will be light. When your two eyes become one – when your male and female disappear into each other – that is the ultimate orgasmic experience. What you feel making love to a woman or to a man is only a glimpse of it, a very fleeting glimpse. It is so momentary that by the time you become aware of it, it is already gone. You become aware of it only in the past – it is so fleeting. But it is a glimpse, a glimpse of the meeting of the man and the woman.

This is an exterior meeting. It is a miracle that it happens even for a single moment. But there is a deep possibility and this has been the work of Tantra, Tao, yoga, and all the great secret teachings of the world: to help you become aware of your feminine and your masculine inside. It is what Tantrikas call Shiva and Shakti and Taoists call yin and yang – the polarity of positive and negative, the day and night in you – will meet.

The light of heaven cannot be seen. It is contained in the two eyes.

But unless they become one you will not become aware of it.

It is contained in the two eyes.

But you cannot see it unless they become one. Then it is released, then there is a great explosion of light. Zarathustra calls it "explosion of fire," Lao Tzu calls it "explosion of light." It is the same.

You must have come across the statement of John the Baptist. He used to say to his disciples, "I baptize you with water. After me shall come one who will baptize you with fire." That's what he meant – "After me there will come one who will baptize you with fire" – the baptism of water is an outer baptism; to John the Baptist, water represents the outward flow. Remember this, that the outward and the downward are synonymous and the upward and the inward are synonymous; whatsoever goes downward also goes outward and whatsoever goes upward also goes inward, and vice versa. Water always goes downward, hence it represents an outward flow, it goes away from itself; its journey is an exterior journey. Fire goes upward, always upward, and upward is synonymous with the inward; its journey is always interior.

John the Baptist is saying: I am baptizing you with water, I am giving you the outer body of religion. After me will come Christ who will give you the inner baptism, the baptism of fire.

Jesus himself again and again says, "Repent. Repent ye!" and the word has fallen into a wrong interpretation with the Christians. They have made it repentance for misdeeds. It has nothing to do with misdeeds. The word *repent* actually means return, go in, go back. It means turning back: restore your originality. The word *repent* means *metanoia*, turning back – a one-hundred-and-eighty-degree turn. If you go on flowing outwards you remain water. If you turn in you become fire.

And when the two eyes, when these two flames, when these two hemispheres of your consciousness join together, are absolutely bridged and you become one flame, that one flame is what Plotinus calls the "flight of the alone to the alone."

The Great One is the term given to that which has nothing above it.

And if you can become that one, you have become the Great One. This is the Taoist way of saying something about God without using the word *God*: if you become one, you have become God.

The secret of the magic of life consists in using action in order to
attain nonaction.

These are potential words. What is the secret of making these two eyes one? How to make the male and the female one in you? How to let your woman and man dissolve into each other so that you are no more a duality, so that you are no more a divided house, against yourself, so that there is no longer any conflict and tension, so that all is one? In that oneness is bliss because all tension disappears, all conflict disappears, all anxiety disappears. How to become that one?

The secret of the magic of life consists in using action in order to
attain nonaction.

Man represents action, woman represents nonaction. You have to use action to attain nonaction, you have to make effort to become effortless. You have to go and put in all your energies, you have to become so active that nothing is left behind – all energy becomes involved in that creativity – and then suddenly, when all energy is involved, there happens a transformation. Just as at a hundred degrees water evaporates, action when it becomes total evaporates and nonaction is left behind.

First you have to learn how to dance, and you have to put all your energies into dancing. And one day that strange experience happens when suddenly the dancer disappears in the dance and the dance happens without any effort. Then it is inaction. First you have to learn action to go into inaction. That's what meditation is all about.

People come and ask me why I teach active meditations. Because that is the only way to find inaction: dance to the uttermost, dance in a frenzy, dance madly. And if your whole energy is involved in it, a moment comes when suddenly you see the dance is happening on its own, there is no effort in it – it is action without action.

> *The Golden Flower is the light. One uses the Golden Flower as*
> *a symbol. The phrase "The lead of the water-region has but one*
> *taste" refers to it.*

The golden flower is a symbol, the symbol of when your energies are no longer dual and have become one: great light is released, and the light is golden. It is as if a flower of golden light has opened inside of you. And it is not just a symbol. It is a symbol but it is almost literally true; it happens exactly like that. Right now you exist as a darkness, as a dark night. Then you exist as a sunrise. You cannot see the sun anywhere but the light is there. There is no source to it – it is a sourceless light. But once you have known that golden light in you, you have become an immortal. Then there is no death because the light never dies.

The whole life, the whole existence consists of nothing but of light – all are forms of light. You can ask modern physics too, and modern physics is in perfect agreement with Tao, that all is light; forms go on changing, but the light continues. Light is eternal.

Many scriptures of the world begin with the word *light*. "In the beginning God said, 'Let there be light.'" That is the beginning. If there had ever been a beginning, it cannot be otherwise; it had to have been with light. But there has never been a beginning; this is just a parable! Light has existed always. The Koran says God is light. One of the names of God given by the Sufis is *Noor*. *Noor* means light.

And the taste is the same – whether it happens in me or in you, the taste is the same. The taste of buddhahood is the same. Buddha has said: "The taste of buddhahood is like the ocean. You can taste it from the north or south, or from this part or that part, from the shore or from the middle, but the taste of the ocean is the same. So is the taste of buddhahood." The moment a person attains to this eternal light, his life has a single flavor. That flavor is contained by absolute awareness: his unconscious has disappeared, there is no longer any dark part in his being.

Now if a Freudian looks into such a man, he will find only consciousness, *only* consciousness; he will not find the unconscious. If a Freudian looks into you, only one part is conscious, against this one part there are nine parts which are unconscious – only one-tenth of your mind is conscious. A buddha is one hundred percent consciousness.

> *The work on the circulation of the light depends entirely on the backward-flowing movement, so that the thoughts are gathered together. The heavenly heart lies between sun and moon.*

The sun represents the male energy, the moon represents the female energy. And the heart lies between the two. The heart is neither male nor female and that is the beauty of the heart: the heart is divine and it lies exactly between the two.

If you are leaning too much towards the male energy, you are too active and you don't know how to be passive. That's what has happened in the West: the West is sun-oriented – too much activity. People are driving themselves mad with their activity. Too much speed – everything has to be done immediately – no patience, no waiting. They have forgotten how to be passive, how to be patient, how to wait for things. They have lost all capacity to be inactive. They don't know how to go on a holiday. Even if they go on a holiday they are more active than ever.

More people have heart attacks on Sundays in the West than on any other day, because it is a holiday and people are too occupied. During the entire working week they think they will rest when the holiday comes, and when the holiday comes, they have a thousand and one things they have planned to do. Not that they have to do them, that they are needed – no, not at all – but they cannot live in rest. They cannot just lie down on the lawn and be with the earth, they cannot just sit silently under a tree and do nothing. No, they will start doing a thousand and one things around the house to fulfil this need to stay busy. They will fix this and unfix that, they will open their car engines and start doing things to it. They will do something rather than stop and enjoy just being. They will remain active.

Their whole life people think that when they are retired then they will enjoy. But they cannot enjoy, they cannot rest. People die very fast once they become retired. Psychologists say they die ten years premature because they don't know what else to do. Death seems the only way to get rid of a life which has become meaningless, which has always been meaningless, which has just been a rush. People are rushing, not knowing where they are going. All that they know is they have to go faster and faster and faster without ever being worried: where exactly are you going? You may be running in a circle. That is exactly what is happening: people are running in a circle.

The West is sun-oriented, the East is moon-oriented. The East has become too passive, too fatalistic: "Nothing has to be done. Simply wait, God will do it." This is another kind of foolishness and stupidity. The East is poor, lazy, lousy, and people are not worried by anything. The misery all around, the poverty, the beggars, the illness – nobody is worried, everything is accepted. "What can you do? It is God's will. We have to accept. We have to just wait. When things are too much, God will come. What else can we do?" This is the feminine mind.

The Secret of the Golden Flower says you have to be exactly in the middle – neither male nor female, no leaning to any extreme – then there is balance. Then one is active and yet remains inactive deep inside, then one is inactive and yet remains active on the outside. On the outside be sun-oriented, on the inside be moon-oriented. Let sun and moon meet in you and be exactly in the middle. And in the middle is transcendence.

> *The work on the circulation of the light depends entirely on*
> *the backward-flowing movement, so that the thoughts are*
> *gathered together.*

Man is a center and also a circumference. If you move towards the circumference, then you will have many thoughts. The circumference consists of many, the center is one. If you move towards the center, thoughts start disappearing. At the very core all thoughts disappear – there is only awareness. That's what this secret treatise says:

> *…so that the thoughts are gathered together.*

The light has to move inwards. When you look at a tree, your eyes are throwing their light on the tree – the light is moving outward. When you close your eyes, the light starts turning inward – metanoia, repent, return. And when the light falls on your own being, there is self-knowledge, self-knowing. And that self-knowing brings you freedom – freedom from all entanglements, freedom from all attachments, freedom from death, freedom from body. It creates the soul in you. That's what Gurdjieff used to say to his disciples: that you are not born with a soul, you have to create it by metanoia.

> The Book of the Yellow Castle says: "In the square inch field of the
> square foot house, life can be regulated."

In this small temple of your body life can be regulated.

> In the middle of the square inch dwells the splendor. In the purple
> hall of the city of jade dwells the God of Utmost Emptiness and Life.

Just see the contradiction: emptiness and life. Life is male, emptiness is female. Life and emptiness – both are two aspects of the inner God. When you have not chosen either in preference to the other, when you have not chosen at all – you have been just a watcher – you become that God whose one aspect is life and whose other aspect is death, whose one aspect is perfection and whose other aspect is nothingness.

> Therefore when the light circulates, the energies of the whole body
> appear before its throne…

And when the light moves inwards and circulates inside your being, because there is no outlet left – that's what meditation is, that's what Buddha is doing under the *bodhi* tree – you sit silently and patiently, you close all the doors and allow the light to circulate within. Then for the first time you become aware of the body and all that the body contains – all of its mysteries. This small body contains all the mysteries of the universe. It is a miniature cosmos.

> Therefore when the light circulates, the energies of the whole body
> appear before its throne, as, when a holy king has established the
> capital and has laid down the fundamental rules of order, all the

states approach with tribute; or as, when the master is quiet and
calm, manservants and maids obey his orders of their own accord,
and each does his work.

And when this light is there moving inside you, the body becomes a servant, the senses become obedient servants, you need not try to control them. Of their own accord they follow you.

This is the beauty of Tao: it never enforces anything, it does not want to cultivate any character. It says: Simply become full of light and all else will follow.

Therefore you only have to make the light circulate; that is the
deepest and most wonderful secret. The light is easy to move,
but difficult to fix. If it is made to circulate long enough, then it
crystallizes itself. It is the condition of which it is said: "Silently
thou fliest upward in the morning."

A very significant thing is being said in this sutra: The light is easy to move; it is difficult to fix it, so don't try to fix it.

That's where yoga tries to do something which cannot be done easily. Hence, the difficulty, the arduousness of yoga: yoga tries to fix the light. It also tries to fix the light between the two eyes, just exactly between the two eyebrows at the third eye center. Yoga tries to fix it. That is the difference between Tao and yoga: yoga wants to fix it – concentrate on the third eye. In a nutshell, that is the whole philosophy of yoga: if you can concentrate your whole consciousness on the third eye you will be transformed, your two eyes will become one and you will be full of light.

And just beyond the third eye – the third eye is the sixth center in the yoga map of consciousness – beyond the sixth is the seventh. The seventh is called the one-thousand-petaled lotus. If the light is concentrated at the third eye, when it becomes too much, it will give a push to the seventh center, it will start rising like water in a reservoir. And the push to the seventh center will open the bud that has remained a bud for centuries, for millions of lives.

Tao works from a different route. Tao says: To fix the light is very difficult. Don't become concerned with fixing it. The easy way is to circulate it.

Mind always finds circulation easy: it is mind's nature to move; mind always finds it difficult to concentrate. So why not use mind's capacity? Why not ride on it?

Tao is a spontaneous science: Don't cultivate, don't force, don't create unnecessary troubles for yourself; use the natural capacity of the mind – that it moves, that it likes movement, that it is a wanderer. Use it, let light circulate. We will come to know how to circulate it later on – find paths, and let it circulate.

Through its circulation, Taoists came to discover the seven hundred points of acupuncture. Circulating it all over the body, they became aware that there are seven hundred points where light becomes very, very aflame, and they counted them exactly. Now science corroborates it: there are exactly seven hundred points. Now even machines have been invented which can just picture your seven hundred points, and where the light is missing in your points, where the energy is not moving in the right meridians. How did the Taoists come to know about it? They had no machines, no technology. Their only technique was to go in and circulate the light.

We will come to know about the actual method – how to circulate it. This is just to make a background so you understand what exactly their approach is.

They say if you circulate the light and go on circulating it, at a certain point it crystallizes on its own, you need not worry about fixing it. Circulating, circulating, circulating, one moment, suddenly, you find all has stopped, and the thing has happened that yoga tries to *make* happen. In Tao it is a happening, in yoga it is a hard, long journey of effort. Yoga is male-oriented.

Tao is not female-oriented, Tao is both – a synthesis. Circulation is masculine energy and fixation is feminine energy. Reach to the nonactive, reach to the passive through action, through effort attain effortlessness.

> *In carrying out this fundamental principle you need to seek for no other methods, but must only concentrate your thoughts on it. By collecting the thoughts one can fly and will be born in heaven.*

> *The Golden Flower is the Elixir of Life...*

It is the secret of all immortality. This is what the Western alchemists used to call the philosopher's stone, what in India is called *amrit,* elixir, nectar. This is an alchemical treatise: it gives you the secrets for transforming your chemistry into alchemy, for transforming the baser metal into gold. Right now you are only a baser metal, but you contain the secrets. If those secrets are worked out, you are transformed into gold. The gold is immortal.

> *The Golden Flower is the Elixir of Life. Although it works very accurately, it is yet so fluid that it needs extreme intelligence and*

clarity, and the most complete absorption and tranquility. People
without this highest degree of intelligence and understanding do not
find the way; people without this utmost capacity for absorption and
tranquility cannot keep fast hold of it.

Two requirements... First, one needs intelligence and clarity. Don't be worried about it. Don't start thinking that if you are not intelligent, then what? Everybody is born intelligent. Intelligence is an intrinsic quality: just as everybody is born breathing, everybody is born intelligent. The idea that a few people are intelligent and a few are not is utterly wrong and has been de-humanizing many people – it is very insulting, degrading.

All are born intelligent, although their intelligences may differ in their expressions. One is intelligent in music, another is intelligent in mathematics, but if you make mathematics the criterion then the musician looks unintelligent. If you put them both into one examination where mathematics is the criterion, the musician fails. Let music be the criterion and put them both into the examination where music will decide, then the mathematician looks stupid.

Because we have chosen certain criteria, that's why many people have been condemned as stupid – they are not. I have never come across a single person who is stupid – it does not happen – but his intelligence may be a different kind of intelligence. Poetry needs a different kind of intelligence than being in business. A poet cannot be a businessman and the businessman will find it very difficult to be a poet. One kind of intelligence is needed in being a politician, another kind of intelligence is needed in being a painter. And there are millions of possibilities.

Remember, everyone is born intelligent, so that is not debarring anybody. You just have to find your intelligence – where it is. And once you have found your intelligence you will be clear. People are living without clarity because they are living with wrong ideas about themselves. Somebody has told you – a schoolmaster, a headmaster, a university – that you are not intelligent. But their criterion is only a chosen criterion, their criterion is not applicable to all. The universities are not yet universal: they don't allow every kind of intelligence, they don't accept all manifestations of intelligence. Once you have accepted your intelligence and you start respecting it, you will become clear, there will be no problem.

The poet feels stupid because he cannot be a good businessman. Now this creates confusion. He becomes inferior in his own eyes, disrespectful, condemning.

He tries to succeed in business but he cannot. This creates great smoke around him. If he simply understands that he is a poet and he is not meant to be a businessman, and to succeed as a businessman will be a suicide to him – he has to succeed as a poet. That is his intelligence, and his intelligence has to flower in his own way. He has not to imitate anybody else. Maybe the society will not pay for it, because poetry is not needed as much as bombs are needed, love is not needed as much as hatred is needed.

That's why in the movies, on the radio, on the television, murder is allowed; it is not called obscene. But lovemaking is not allowed; it is called obscene. This society lives through hate not through love. If somebody is murdering, it is perfectly okay. If somebody puts a dagger into your heart and the blood rushes like a fountain, it is perfectly okay. But if somebody hugs you, kisses you, loves you, the society is afraid. This is strange, that love is obscene and murder is not, that lovers are condemned and soldiers rewarded, that war is right and love is wrong.

If you accept your intelligence, if you accept yourself, you will become clear, absolutely clear; all clouds will disappear.

And the second thing: you need absorption and tranquility. Intelligence and clarity are part of the male mind, absorption and tranquility are part of the female mind. Only a woman can absorb, that's why she becomes pregnant – she has the womb.

These two things are needed together. If you are not intelligent you will not be able to understand what is being said to you, you will not understand what the master is imparting to you. And if you are not feminine, you will not be able to absorb it, you will not be able to become pregnant with it. And both are needed: you have to be intelligent, utterly intelligent to see the point, and you have to be utterly absorptive to keep it in you, so that it becomes part of you.

This is just a background. Slowly, slowly we will go into the techniques of how to circulate the light. Listen attentively, intelligently. Absorb it. It can be one of the greatest experiences of your life.

Enough for today.

CHAPTER 2
Empty Eyes

The first question:

> *Osho,*
> *Lately several friends have asked me if I was skeptical towards*
> *sannyas, the ashram and you. I had to admit to the truth and said,*
> *"Yes, at times I am." This left me with a feeling of guilt. Have I*
> *committed some unforgivable, sacrilegious crime or is it natural*
> *to be skeptical rather than being sure? I do not know if you are*
> *enlightened. I can only feel your beauty and trust.*

Faith is afraid of doubt – afraid because it has repressed it. And whatsoever you repress you will remain afraid of, because it is always there deep inside you, waiting to take revenge, and whenever the opportunity arises it is going to explode in you with a vengeance. Faith is sitting on an earthquake and every day the doubt becomes stronger, because every day you have to repress it. Sooner or later it is more than you can repress, it is more than your faith. Then it simply throws your faith away.

But trust is not afraid of doubt because trust is not against doubt. Trust uses doubt, trust knows how to use the energy contained in doubt itself. That's the difference between faith and trust. Faith is false; it creates a pseudo kind of religion, it creates hypocrites. Trust has a sublime beauty and truth about it. It grows through doubt, it uses doubt as manure, it transforms doubt. Doubt is a friend, doubt is not the enemy.

And unless your trust has moved through many doubts it will remain impotent. From where will it gather strength, from where will it gather integration? If there is no challenge it is bound to remain weak.

Doubt is a challenge. If your trust can respond to the challenge, can befriend your doubt, it will grow through it. And you will not be a split person, deep down doubting and just on the surface faithful, believing; you will have a kind of unity, you will be an individual, undivided. And that individuality is what is called "soul" in the old religions.

The soul is arrived at through doubt, not through believing. Belief is just a mask: you are hiding your original face. Trust is a transformation: you are becoming more illumined. And because you are using doubt as a challenge, as an opportunity, there is never any repression. Slowly, slowly doubt disappears because its energy has been taken by trust.

Doubt, in fact, is nothing but trust growing; doubt is trust on the way. Always think of doubt in such a way: that doubt is trust on the way. Doubt is inquiry and trust is the fulfillment of the inquiry. Doubt is the question and trust is the answer. The answer is not against the question – there will be no possibility of any answer if there is no question. The question has created the occasion for the answer to happen.

So please, never feel guilty around me. I am utterly against any kind of guilt. Guilt is absolutely wrong. But it has been used by the priests and the politicians and the puritans down the ages – for centuries. Guilt is a strategy, a strategy to exploit people: make them feel guilty. Once you have succeeded in making them feel guilty, they will be your slaves. Because of the guilt they will never be integrated enough, because of the guilt they will remain divided. Because of the guilt they will never be able to accept themselves, they will be always condemning. Because of the guilt they will be ready to believe in anything. Just to get rid of guilt they will do anything. Any nonsense, any nonsense ritual they will perform just to get rid of the guilt.

Down the centuries the priest has made people guilty. All the so-called religions exist on your guilt, they don't exist on the existence of God. They have nothing to do with God and God has nothing to do with them; they exist on your guilt. You are afraid, you know that you are wrong: you have to seek the help of somebody who is not wrong. You know that you are unworthy: you have to bow down, you have to serve those who are worthy. You know that you cannot trust yourself, because you are divided.

Only an undivided person can trust himself – his feeling, his intuition. You are always shaking, trembling inside; you need somebody to lean on. And once you lean on somebody, once you become dependent on somebody, you remain childish, you never grow. Your mind age remains that of a child. You never attain to any maturity, you never become independent. And the priest does not want you to become independent. Independent and you are lost to him, dependent and you are his whole marketplace, his whole business.

I am utterly against any kind of guilt. Remember it always: if you start feeling guilty about something around me, then you are doing it on your own. Then you are still carrying the voices of your parents, the priests within you; you have not yet heard me, you have not yet listened to me. I want you to be totally free of all guilt. Once you are free of guilt you are a religious person. That's my definition of a religious person.

Use doubt – doubt is beautiful – because it is only through doubt that the trust attains to maturity. How can it be otherwise? It has to be beautiful – it is only through doubt that the trust becomes centered, it is only through doubt that the trust flowers, blooms. It is the dark night of doubt that brings the golden morning closer to you. The dark night is not against the dawn, the dark night is the womb for the dawn. The dawn is getting ready in the very being of the dark night.

Think of doubt and trust as complementary – just as man and woman are, just as night and day, summer and winter, life and death. Always think of those pairs, inevitably, in terms of complementariness; never think in terms of opposition. Even though on the surface they seem to be opposed, deep down they are friends, helping each other.

Think of a person who has no trust: he will not have any doubt either, because he has nothing to doubt about. Just think of a person who has no trust at all – how can he doubt, what has he to doubt? Only a man of trust has something to doubt. Because you trust, hence you doubt. Your doubt proves your trust, not otherwise. Think of a man who cannot doubt – how can he trust? If he is even incapable of doubt, how can he be capable of trust? Trust is the highest form of the same energy; doubt is the lowest rung of the same ladder and trust is the highest rung of the same ladder. Use doubt, use it joyfully.

There is no need to feel guilty at all. It is perfectly human and natural to feel great doubts about me sometimes and great doubts about what is going on here. It is perfectly human – there is nothing extraordinary in it. If it doesn't happen, then something seems to be abnormal. But remember that one has to reach to trust: use doubt, but don't forget the goal, don't forget the highest rung of the ladder. Even if you are standing on the lowest, look at the highest – you have to reach there. In fact, doubt is pushing you towards that because nobody can feel at ease with doubt.

Have you not watched it? When there is doubt there is uneasiness. Don't change that uneasiness, don't interpret that uneasiness as guilt. Yes, uneasiness is there, because doubt means you are uncertain of the ground you are standing on. Doubt means you are ambiguous, doubt means you are not yet a unity – how can you be at ease? You are a crowd: you are not one person, you are many persons – how can you be at ease? There must be great noise inside you, one part pulling you in this direction and another part in that direction. How can you grow if you are pulled in so many directions simultaneously? There is bound to be unease, tension, anguish, anxiety.

Nobody can live with doubt and in doubt. Doubt pushes you towards trust. Doubt says, "Go and find a place where you can relax, where you can be, totally." Because doubt is your friend. It simply says, "This is not the home. Go ahead – search, seek, inquire." It creates the urge to inquire, to explore.

Once you start seeing doubt as a friend, as an occasion, not against trust but pushing you towards it, suddenly guilt disappears, there is great joy. Even when you doubt, you doubt joyously, you doubt consciously, and you use doubt to find trust. It is absolutely normal.

You say, "I do not know if you are enlightened." How can you know it? There is no way to know it unless you become enlightened. How can you know what has happened to me unless it happens to you too? It is absolutely right to feel that you cannot trust me sometimes. The miracle is that sometimes you can trust: just those few moments will be enough. Don't be worried: trust has such infinite power. Trust is just like light and doubt is like darkness. Just a small candle of trust is enough to destroy the darkness of ages.

The darkness cannot say, "I have lived in this place for so long, I cannot leave so easily. And I cannot leave only because of this small candle." Even a small candle has more potential than the darkness of ages, of centuries, of thousands of lives. But it will have to go…once the light is there it has to go.

Those few moments of trust – let them be few and far between, don't be worried – they are enough to destroy all your doubts slowly, slowly. And by "destroying" I mean just releasing the energy contained in doubt. Just breaking the shell called doubt…and deep inside you will find the pure energy to trust. Once it is released more and more trust will be available to you.

You say, "I do not know if you are enlightened." Good that you don't believe. If you start believing you will stop seeking. A believer never moves – he has already believed. That's why there are millions of people worshipping in the churches, temples, mosques, *gurdwaras,* but their worship is out of belief. Because it is out of belief, those millions of people remain irreligious: they don't search for God, they don't seek God – they have already accepted. Their acceptance is lame; they have not struggled for it, they have not earned it.

You have to fight, you have to struggle, you have to earn. Nothing is without a price in life; you have to pay the price. They have not paid the price – and they think that just by worshipping in a temple they will attain? They are utter fools, they are wasting their time. All their worship is just an illusion.

The really religious person cannot believe; he searches. Because he cannot believe, he remains in doubt, and nobody can be at rest with doubt. One has to seek and search and to find. Doubt goes on gnawing at your being, goes on goading you: "Search, seek, find, and don't be contented before you have found."

Good that you cannot believe. Only remember: there is no need to believe and there is no need to disbelieve. And that's happening. And I am happy.

You say, "I can only feel your beauty and trust."

That's all that is needed. That's enough, more than enough. That will become the boat to the other shore – if you can feel my love, if you can feel my trust in you, if you can feel my hope in you, if you can see that something beautiful has happened – although you don't know what exactly it is. You cannot define it and you cannot explain it, but if you can even feel that something of the beyond... That's what beauty is. Beauty is always of the beyond.

Whenever you see a roseflower and you say, "It is beautiful," what do you mean? You are saying that you have seen something of the beyond, something invisible has become visible to you. You cannot prove it. If somebody else standing by your side denies seeing any beauty in the rose, you cannot prove it to him – there is no way. You will just have to shrug your shoulders. You will say, "Then nothing can be done about it. I see and you don't see, and that is that."

You cannot go to the scientist to dissect the rose and find whether it contains beauty or not – it does not contain it. The beauty is not contained in the rose. The beauty is from the beyond, it simply dances on the rose: those who have eyes will see; those who don't have eyes will not see. You can take the rose to the chemist – he will dissect it, he will find everything that is in the rose – but beauty is not *in* the rose. The rose was just an occasion for beauty to descend from the beyond. The rose was just a screen for beauty to play upon it. The rose was just a stage for the drama to happen. It is not the drama itself. You take the rose away, you dissect the rose, you cut it into pieces, you find all the constituents – but beauty is not a constituent of the rose, although without the rose the beauty cannot descend.

It is just like the sun rises in the morning and the rays are dancing on the lotus pond. You don't see the rays themselves, you can't see. That's what *The Secret of the Golden Flower* says: You can't see essence, you can't see life; all that you see are only consequences.

Have you ever seen light itself? No, you have never seen it. If you think you have seen light itself, you have not thought about it, you have not pondered over it. You have seen illuminated things, you have not seen light itself. You have seen the glistening pond, you have seen the glowing lotus, you have seen the radiant face of your woman or man or your child. You have seen the luminous world, but have you seen the light itself? If there is nothing for the light to play upon, you will not be able to see it.

That's why the moment the astronauts go away from the earth, even in the daytime, the sky is dark, utterly dark, because you cannot see light itself and there is nothing there for the light to play upon. Hence the infinite sky is dark. You see light on the stars because stars become the playground for the light, but surrounding the stars it is all darkness because there is nothing to obstruct the light. And unless light is obstructed you cannot see it.

You cannot see enlightenment, you can see only the consequence of it. You cannot see what has happened to me, but you can see something has happened; something like X. There is no need to call it enlightenment either, just X will do. Something mysterious has happened. And the more you feel me the more you will become aware of it, and the more you become aware of it something inside you will start responding to it. What has happened to me can trigger a process in you. It cannot be the cause of your enlightenment, remember. Your enlightenment will not be the effect of my enlightenment. There is no cause and effect relationship between the master and the disciple; there is a totally different kind of relationship.

Just in this century, Carl Gustav Jung was able to penetrate into the mystery of that different kind of relationship. He calls it "synchronicity." Cause and effect is a scientific relationship, synchronicity is a poetic relationship. By synchronicity what is meant is that if something has happened somewhere and you become available to it, you remain vulnerable to it, something can start responding in you parallel to it. But it has not been the cause of it, it cannot cause it.

It is just like somebody is playing beautiful music and a great desire arises in you to dance: it is not caused by the music, it is a parallel response in you.

Something that was fast asleep in you – the energy to dance – has been hit; not caused, just hit, provoked, inspired. It is synchronicity. If it is a cause then it will happen to everybody.

For example, you are here, three thousand sannyasins are present. I am available to all of you, but all of you are not available to me or, even if you are available to me, you are available in different ways. The quality differs, the quantity differs. If I can be a cause of your enlightenment, then all three thousand of you will become enlightened. But I am not the cause, I can only become a catalytic agent. But for that you have to be open towards me. If I were a cause, there would be no need for you to be open to me. Fire burns whether the wood is open to it or not – it is a cause. Water evaporates at hundred-degree heat; whether it is open to the heat or not doesn't matter.

Cause and effect is a blind relationship; it is materialistic, it is between matter and matter. But synchronicity is not material; it is spiritual, it is poetic, it is a love affair. If you become open to me, something will start happening to you. And remember, I am not the cause of it. You need not thank me, you need not be grateful to me, I am not the cause of it. If anybody is the cause of it, it is you, because you opened towards me. I could not have done it alone. There is no doing on my part. All that is needed is for me to be present, and for you too to be present. Then something will start happening. And nobody is doing it – neither I am doing it nor are you doing it. I am available, you become available, and these two energies fall into a love affair, they start dancing together.

So don't be worried that you cannot know about my enlightenment. This is enough – you say, "I can only feel your beauty and trust." This will do. And once it has happened in you, you will know. To know a Buddha one has to become a Buddha, to know a Christ one has to be a Christ.

The second question:

> Osho,
> In the past few weeks, just when I am feeling overwhelmed with the
> mystery and miracle of life and this world, I suddenly feel everything
> outside me descending closer and closer until it goes inside my eyes. I then
> find myself looking at what seems like a one-dimensional screen sitting
> just at my eyes. It seems as though there is nothing but me and I am so
> alone. But then people are on the scene interacting with me and I become
> confused. And what about you? You also seem just part of the painting.

Even though this lasts only a few seconds, I become so terrified when
this happens. Is this my mind playing with me? How could I really
be so alone?

One is alone. Aloneness is ultimate – but aloneness is not loneliness. You
are not lonely. And that's where the whole misunderstanding lies and that's what
makes you so terrified. To be lonely means you are missing the other. To be lonely
is a negative state. To be lonely means you are feeling empty, you are searching
for the other: you believe in the other, you depend on the other – and the other
is not there. And because the other is not there, there is great nothingness, but
that nothingness is a kind of negative nothingness. You are groping for the other,
and you cannot find the other, and everything starts disappearing. And when
everything starts disappearing, the *real* problem is: *you* cannot remain yourself.

When everything else has disappeared, you will have to disappear too, because
you depend on others, you are just a reflection of the others. You have seen your face
in the eyes of others; they have been mirrors. Now there are no longer any mirrors –
who are you? All has disappeared, then how can you remain in this loneliness? You
also start evaporating and that creates great fear – the fear of death.

The ego starts dying and the ego starts searching somewhere for somebody
to cling to. And that's why soon you start interacting with people. Out of the fear
of death you start getting occupied with others again. And then great confusion
is bound to be there, because your natural being was moving into a deep
nothingness. But you became frightened and you pulled yourself out of it. You
created a contradiction in the energy: the energy was going in and you jumped
out, hence the confusion.

But aloneness is ultimate. And when I say aloneness is ultimate, I mean
that there is only one, there are not many. You are not separate from existence.
Nobody is separate from anybody else, existence is utterly one. The very idea of
separation is our misery, the very idea that "I am an island" creates hell. Nobody
is an island, we belong to the continent; we are part of this oceanic existence.
Past, present, future, in all directions and all dimensions, it is all one. In fact, the
word *alone* means all-oneness – that is aloneness. All-one is alone.

But for that, you will have to go a little more into this nothingness. First the
nothingness is negative; the negative is its outermost core, the shell part. If you
go a little deeper you will find the positive negativeness. The positive negativeness
is what Buddha calls nirvana, enlightenment, *shunya*. When you move deeper
and you have crossed the shell part – the hard negative part, the dark part –

suddenly there is light, the night is over. And then you feel a totally new kind of aloneness which you have never felt before, and then you know the distinction between loneliness and aloneness. In loneliness you were searching for the other, in aloneness the other has disappeared and so has the ego disappeared. Now there is nobody inside and nobody outside, and all is one.

This unity, this absolute oneness brings benediction. Then there is no fear, there cannot be, because now there can be no death – how can there be fear? The death has already happened, that which could die has died. Now you are in the world of immortality, you have found the elixir. This is the nectar we will be talking about again and again in these sutras of *The Secret of the Golden Flower*. This is the nectar, *amrit*. This is the elixir, the philosopher's stone. Once you have tasted of it, all death has disappeared, all time has disappeared, all distinctions have disappeared. Now you will see the tree as your extension, the cloud as your extension, or you as the extension of the tree. Now the center is everywhere and nowhere. The "I" does not exist anywhere anymore. The very word has become utterly false.

Once a Christian missionary asked a Zen master, "Isn't the end-point of man's journey the union with God?"

The Zen master said, "The end-point of man's journey is *not* union with God, because there has never been a separation. All that is needed is the flash of insight that makes one see it."

Tao, Zen, Tantra – their insight is far deeper than the so-called religions of the marketplace. Christianity thinks in terms of joining with God, of being one with God, but the Zen master's insight is far more penetrating and deeper. He says: "But where has there been a separation? When? It has not happened at all, you have been dreaming that you are separate. Just come out of the dream! There is no union, you have *always* been one with existence. Not for a single moment has there been a separation, there is no possibility of separation."

You are coming to a very important and significant insight. If you don't get frightened and run out of this experience, you may attain the flash of insight that makes one *see it*: that all is one.

But fear always comes. It is not new. Each seeker has to go through it. And it is really so much that before you have thought about it you have already run out of it. It is so frightening that it does not give you time, space, to ponder over it – what to do? It is like the house is on fire – you don't think anymore: "Should I get out or not?" There are no more alternatives left; you simply run out of the house without thinking. There is no time to think. Later on you can think: when you are outside the house, sitting under a tree, you can think and ponder in luxury. But when the house is on fire, how can you think? Action is needed immediately, and thought is never immediate. That's the problem.

When you go into your aloneness at first it is very lonely, because you have lived with the idea of the other. It was a dream idea; the other is not there. "I" and "thou" – both are false. Martin Buber says that the ultimate quality of prayer is a dialogue between "I" and "thou." That's where Judaism got stuck: the ultimate prayer is not a dialogue at all, the ultimate prayer is a monologue because the other is not there.

A Zen master used to call his own name in the morning; every morning. He would shout his own name and say, "How are you?" And he would answer, "I am perfectly well, sir."

You will think he is mad – but this is prayer. There is no "I," there is no "thou"; you have to play the part of both. It is a game, it is a play. Prayer is a play – playing with your own self. There is no "other."

But Judaism got stuck there with the idea of "I" and "thou." That's why they were so much against Jesus, because he declared – although not in such a drastic way as a Zen master declares... It was not possible to be more drastic than he was in his situation. But still he said, "I and my father are one." But that was enough to infuriate people: "What is he saying? Declaring himself God?"

He is not saying anything, he is not declaring himself God. He is simply saying there is no God and no devotee, there is only one. You can call it devotee in a certain situation, you can call it God in another situation. That's why he says, "I and my father are one. If you look at my body I am the son, if you look at my soul I am the father. If you look at my form I am a man, son of man, if you look at my essence I am son of God." That's why he goes on repeating it again and again. Sometimes he says, "I am son of man," and sometimes he says, "I am son of God." It looks contradictory but it is not.

You say, "In the past few weeks, just when I am feeling overwhelmed with the mystery and miracle of life and this world, I suddenly feel everything outside me descending closer and closer until it goes inside my eyes."

All that you see is a projection of your eyes. The world, as it is, you have not seen yet. What you have seen is just a projection, so when you start moving inwards, everything that you have projected on the world will come closer and closer and closer to the eyes and will disappear into your eyes. This world is a projection of your eyes. You don't see that which is, you project a dream upon it.

For example, there is a great diamond, the Koh-i-Noor. Now, it is just a stone like any other stone, but we have projected so much value on it. Many people have died because of the Koh-i-Noor; whosoever possessed it was killed. Now see the whole nonsense of it: just that stone has proved very murderous – because of the projections of people. It is one of the most precious things in the world, the costliest thing in the world, but if man disappears from the earth will it be anything more than any other pebble? It will be just lying there with other pebbles, in the same way. There will be no distinction, no difference.

From where does the difference come? Our eyes project, we make it special. We go on pouring our desire, greed, onto it. It becomes very precious, and very dangerous too. If you are meditating on the Koh-i-Noor – silently seeing it – one moment will come when you see that something from the Koh-i-Noor is coming closer and closer to your eyes and then it disappears into the eyes. Then you open your eyes, the Koh-i-Noor has disappeared: there is something, but you had not known it before and the one that you had known before is no longer there.

A beautiful experience, tremendously significant; go into it, go deeper and deeper into it. Let the whole world disappear. Yes, I will also disappear into that, because that which I am you have not seen yet, and that which you see is your projection. Your projection will disappear, and when all your projections have disappeared, then the world comes in its nakedness, as it is.

And the wonder of it! Then small things are so wonderful, then ordinary pebbles are so wonderful. Because of the Koh-i-Noor they cannot be wonderful; you have projected all on the Koh-i-Noor, you have not left any love for anything else. Once the projection disappears and you open your eyes, empty eyes – not projecting anything at all, just seeing whatsoever it is, with no idea what it is, with no names, no labels, no interpretations, just seeing, emptied, passive – the world comes to have a totally different meaning and significance.

"I suddenly feel everything outside me descending closer and closer until it goes inside my eyes. I then find myself looking at what seems like a one-dimensional screen sitting just at my eyes."

Perfectly good and perfectly right. This is the way one finds himself able to move deeper into meditation.

"It seems as though there is nothing but me and I am so alone."

The only problem is that you are still there, that's why you feel so alone.

You mean lonely. The "I" remains alone, "thou" has disappeared, and without the "thou" the "I" is lonely. The "I" exists only in relationship; the "I" is not an entity but a relationship – it cannot exist without the "thou," it needs the "thou." How can the lover exist without the beloved? Once the beloved is not there the lover starts disappearing. You need the beloved, love is a relationship. So is the "I" a relationship. And because you are still protecting the "I" somehow, you have not yet been courageous enough to let it go too.

Just as the whole world has disappeared, let this "I" also disappear. It will be frightening in the beginning; it will be a death process – it *is* a death process. It will look as if you are committing suicide, it will look... Who knows where you are going, whether you will be coming back again or not? As if madness is exploding in you, great fear will arise and in that fear you will be thrown out again and again. It will happen many times. Slowly, slowly you will have to learn not to be so afraid – there is nothing to fear: you are very close to the treasure.

These are the moments when a master is needed to help you, to give you courage, to hold your hand, to say to you, "All is perfectly right. Go in!"

I had to pass through the same and I was also as much afraid as you are. And many times I came out just as you are coming out. And you are more fortunate than me because I had no master – nobody to give me courage, nobody to hold my hand. I was simply struggling with myself. There was nobody who could tell me what was going to happen ahead. I had to grope and go into it – and it was dangerous, it was maddening. And the people who were around me in those days had already started believing that I had gone mad. Everybody who loved me was worried. My friends were worried, my teachers, my professors in the university were worried, my parents were worried, everybody was worried. But I had to go. Many times I went out, the fear was so much. I am perfectly acquainted with the fear.

But one day one has to face it and go through it, because again and again you fall upon it and you rush out and the out is not meaningful anymore. The out is all empty, and you come inside and the fear – you have to choose between the two. The outside is no more relevant. You can go on making empty gestures, but how long can you deceive yourself? You know the screen is empty and all your projections are dead and you go inside to the fear, a great storm of fear arises. But there is no other way – one has to go through it to know exactly what happens after this death. The sooner you gather courage the better.

And I say again, you are more fortunate, because I am standing ahead of you in that utter emptiness, calling you forth: "Come on! Come ye all. Come again, and again!" And I go on calling you forth just as Christ called Lazarus from the grave: "Lazarus, come out!" In fact, that parable is not a historical fact. It is a parable. It is a parable of moving from the outside to the inside.

The outside becomes a grave when it loses meaning. The outside becomes just a futility, a wasteland, a grave. Nothing grows in it anymore, nothing flowers in it anymore – no possibility of any song and dance – and you live only in empty motions, empty gestures.

But the master is standing where you are afraid to go and he calls from there. I am not only standing outside you; you will meet me in that innermost nothingness – not as me, of course – not as a person but as a presence, not separate from you but one with you.

That's why I insist so much on sannyas. Unless you are a sannyasin it will be difficult for me to call you from the inside. I can call you from the outside, but then you remain just a student. I can teach you a few things – that will become knowledge – but I cannot call you from your inside, from your very heart. And the need is there. That is possible only if you become a disciple, if you are a sannyasin, if you are ready to go with me, if you are ready to trust me, at least in some moments. I will use those "some moments" and sooner or later they will become your very state of being.

So go on. Let this "me," this "I" also disappear. And once this "I" disappears there is no loneliness, there is aloneness. And aloneness is beautiful, aloneness is freedom, it is a very positive feeling of wellbeing, a positive feeling of great joy. It is a very great, festive moment. It is celebration.

"It seems as though there is nothing but me and I am so alone." Yes, if "I" remains you will remain lonely.

"But then people are on the scene interacting with me and I become confused. And what about you? You also seem just part of the painting."

Allow me to become part of the painting on the outside, only then can I start working from the inside. Let me disappear from the outside so that you can see me inside. And that will be my truth. And that is the truth of Christ and that is the truth of Buddha and Krishna. That is the truth of all the masters, of all those who have become awakened.

"Even though this lasts only a few seconds, I become so terrified when this happens." It is natural, but gather courage. I am with you. Go in.

"Is this my mind playing with me?"

No, not at all. Mind creates the fear, not this experience. Mind is playing when it creates the fear. It is not mind when you see all your projections coming closer and closer and disappearing into your eyes, it is not mind when everything becomes a white empty screen. It is not mind, it is meditation: it is movement towards no-mind. Mind creates the fear – when it comes very close to the no-mind, it becomes so afraid of death that it creates fear – and in that fear you rush out again.

Next time it happens, go in, in spite of the fear. Just be like the elephant who goes on moving although the dogs go on barking. Let the dogs of the mind bark, go on moving like an elephant. Don't care at all about the mind – what it is saying.

The third question:

Osho,
What happens when an enlightened man slides back into delusion?

Fallen flowers don't jump back to the branches. That is not possible. The enlightened person cannot slide back into illusion. There is no way; for many reasons there is no way.

The first reason: the enlightened man is no more – who will slide back? Enlightenment is; there is nothing like an enlightened person. Enlightenment is perfectly there, but there is nobody who is enlightened. That is just a way of speaking, a linguistic fallacy. Who will slide back? The one who could have slid back has disappeared. And where can one slide back? Once you have found it is illusion, it is no more there. Once you have seen it is no more there, it is finished. Where can you go back? It is not possible.

But the idea arises in our mind because in life we have never seen anything like that. We attain one thing and we fall back: we are in love and then we fall back out of it, we fall in love and we fall out of it, we are happy and then we become unhappy, we are feeling good and then we start feeling very bad. We know the duality, the duality never disappears, so we naturally think about enlightenment also as if one can slide back.

Enlightenment is the realization of the non-dual. That's why Zen masters say samsara is nirvana – the very illusion is truth. There is no distinction left. It is not that this is truth and that is illusion. All is truth, only truth is. Where can you fall back? You have gone beyond the point of no return. Nobody has ever fallen back. And don't be worried about these people – you should worry about yourself.

First become enlightened and then try to slide back. And then you will see: it is easier to become enlightened, it is very difficult to slide back. I have tried, but I have not been successful.

The last question:

Osho,
Please explain about bliss and misery, for whenever I encounter
love or beauty, I only feel tremendous pain but not bliss, and I don't
understand this.

You have been told again and again, you have been taught again and again that to be joyous is wrong and to be miserable is right. You may not have been told so directly, but indirectly you have been conditioned and hypnotized for misery. You have started believing that misery is natural. You see misery all around, misery abounds, everybody is miserable. It seems to be the way things are.

When you were born, you were a happy child – as every child is happy. It has not happened otherwise – never. Whenever a child is born he is happy, utterly happy, and that's why children look very selfish: they only think of themselves, they are not worried about the world, and they are happy about small things. For example, a butterfly in the garden, and the utter joy and their wonder. They notice small things, nothings, but they are happy, they are naturally happy.

But slowly, slowly we cripple their happiness, we destroy it. We cannot tolerate so much happiness. The world is very miserable and we have to prepare them for the world. So indirectly we start indoctrinating them that, "The world is misery. You cannot afford to be happy. Happiness is just a hope. How can you be happy? Don't be so selfish! There is so much misery all around – feel for others, consider others." Slowly, slowly the child gets the feeling that to be happy is a kind of sin. How can you be happy when the world is in such misery?

People write letters to me asking: "How can you teach people meditation when the world is in such a misery? And how can one be happy when people are starving?" As if by being unhappy you will help them! As if by not being meditative you will be of any kind of service to them. As if wars will disappear if you don't meditate, and poverty will disappear if you are not happy. But misery has been put on a pedestal, misery has been worshipped.

I always suspect that Christianity became the greatest religion because of the cross. It represents misery, suffering. Krishna could not become a great religion because of his flute, because of his dance. Even those who worship him feel a little guilty about him. "How can you be so happy and dancing with girlfriends? And not just one – thousands! And singing and playing on the flute! People are dying and there is death and starvation and war and violence and all kinds of things are going on all around. It is hell, and you are playing on your flute! It seems callous, it seems you are cruel." Jesus seems to be more suitable, dying on the cross. Look at the face of Jesus. The way Christians have painted him, his face is very long, sad; he is carrying the whole burden of the earth. He has come to take all the sins of all the people on himself. He seems to be the greatest servant – very unselfish. But my feeling is that Christians have depicted Christ wrongly.

This Christ is a myth; the real Christ was more like Krishna. In fact, if you go deep down into the word *Christ* you will be surprised: it comes from Krishna, its root is Krishna. Jesus must have been a very joyous man; otherwise how can you think of him eating, drinking, merrily? There are so many scenes where friends have gathered and they are eating and drinking and gossiping. He is not always "gospeling," sometimes he is gossiping too! And he seems to be the only messenger from God who drinks and eats well and enjoys the small pleasures of life.

My feeling is that if Zen masters were to create a religion out of Jesus, they would make him laugh on the cross – a belly laugh. Jesus would have as big a belly as Bodhidharma and the belly would be shaking like an earthquake with great laughter! And that would have been far more, far more true.

Even in Japan and China the statue of Buddha is made with a big belly. In India they don't make that big belly – no, not at all. The Indian concept, the yogic concept, is that the belly has to be very small and the chest has to be big, because the yogic breathing is a false breathing, it is not natural. It can make a Muhammad Ali out of you but not a Buddha. It will give you the shape of a Mr Universe, but have you seen any other kinds of people in the world who are more ugly? Mr Universe seems to be the ugliest. I don't think any woman can fall in love with a Mr Universe. He looks so animalistic – all muscles and no man, just a kind of mechanism. Just see his muscles moving: just a kind of mechanism, a machine, but no soul. The Indian statue of Buddha is the yogic statue. When they made Buddha's statue in China, they made it with a big belly.

When one laughs and when one breathes naturally, the belly becomes slowly bigger, because then one breathes from the belly and not from the chest – the breath goes the whole way down. If Zen were to make a religion out of Christianity, Jesus would be on the cross, but with laughter – such laughter that it would resound down the centuries. But that may not have been a successful religion, because how would it suit the people who know only crying and weeping? He would look completely eccentric, outlandish. To be on the cross and sad looks perfectly right, because everybody is on a certain cross and sad. And you must have been taught from your very childhood that the world is a wrong place. How can you be happy in this place? We are suffering a kind of punishment. God ordered Adam and Eve to leave Paradise because they disobeyed, and humanity is under that curse. How can you be happy? To be a Christian and happy will be a contradiction in terms.

So, you must have been taught that the world is a miserable place: misery is perfectly right in it, in tune with it, and everybody is miserable – it will be very hard and cruel on your part to be happy and joyous. That's why even when there are moments to enjoy people feel guilty and they hold back.

Larson took Charlotte for a drive way out in the country and parked the car in a desolate stretch. "If you try to molest me," said Charlotte, "I'll scream."

"What good would that do?" asked Larson. "There's not a soul around for miles."

"I know" said Charlotte, "but I want to satisfy my conscience before I start having a good time."

People even make love with sad faces as if they are on the cross – doing a duty – and even if they want to enjoy, they hide it. They feel guilty.

If people really make love with joy they will scream, they will shout, they will cry, they will weep, they will laugh. One never knows what kind of emotions will surface, so it is better to keep yourself in control; otherwise you will look so foolish. And then what will the neighbors think? And modern walls are so thin that you even have to make love in a yoga posture – *shavasana,* the dead-body posture – and be finished with it as soon as possible, don't let it become orgasmic. "What are you doing? And Jesus suffered for you on the cross! And you are shouting with joy? Think of Jesus, poor Jesus and of what he will think of you! And think of God – who is a kind of peeping Tom who always looks through keyholes – what will he think?"

If you think of all the gods and then the angels and the christs and the saints and they are all watching and you making love…and with such relish! You will suffer in hell! It is better to keep control, it is good to feel guilty. That's why after making love people feel a kind of sadness, a kind of frustration, as if they have done something criminal. Again they enjoyed themselves and that is not right.

Just see: whenever you are feeling miserable, something feels good. It will look like a contradiction, but it is like this: whenever you are miserable you feel blissful and whenever you are blissful you feel miserable.

You say, "Please explain about bliss and misery, for whenever I encounter love or beauty I only feel tremendous pain but not bliss, and I don't understand this."

You will not be able to understand this at all because your whole understanding has been poisoned. You will have to drop the whole mind. There is no need to understand. You have to go into it with innocence, not with understanding, because that understanding is again a kind of calculation; that understanding is again the knowledge that has been given by the society. And that knowledge is creating the whole trouble! You have to become a child again, innocent.

But you want to understand. Forget all about understanding. Understanding is again calculation, cunningness.

I have heard:

An elderly couple went to a doctor. The man said, "We want to know if we are making love properly. Will you look at us?"

"Go ahead," said the doctor. They made love.

"You are making love perfectly," the doctor said. "That will be ten dollars." They came back six weeks in a row and did the same thing. On the seventh visit the doctor said, "What are you coming here like this for? I told you you are making love properly."

"She can't come to my house," said the man, "and I can't go to her house. A motel costs twenty dollars. You charge us ten dollars and we get eight dollars back from Medicare."

Don't be calculating, cunning with life. Now what kind of love will this be? Business and business and business... Knowledge is needed for business, innocence is needed for life. Knowledge is a must in the marketplace, but not needed at all when you are moving into the mysteries; you cannot know, you can only be. You drop this mind, you drop all this conditioning and start moving. When you feel joyous, *feel* joyous, help yourself to feel joyous: dance, sing.

The old habits will pull you back; don't listen to them. You will have to get rid of the old habits slowly, slowly. It will be a kind of struggle, because no habit leaves you easily. But these habits are against you and against God, because anything that is against joy is against God. If God can be defined by any word, that word is *bliss* and nothing else.

Whenever you feel something beautiful and the pain arises in you, that pain is not in your being, that pain is in your mind: your being is trying to go into the beautiful, but your mind is pulling you back. Whenever you feel love arising, bliss arising, and pain also, choose the bliss. Neglect the pain, ignore it. Ignoring it, it will die. If you go on paying attention to it you will feed it. Attention is food. Never pay attention to anything that is wrong; otherwise you are helping it to be there, you are giving it more and more strength. Ignore it – there is nothing better than ignoring it. Yes, let it be there. Just say, "Okay, you be there. You are just a hangover from my past. You be there. I am going ahead, l am not going to listen to you."

Listen to blissful provocations and always go with them, and you are in the right direction – you are moving towards God. Never listen to anything that gives you guilt, pain, misery – you are moving away from God. Whenever you are miserable, you are in hell – farthest away from God – and whenever you are utterly joyous, you are in God, you are in heaven.

You say, "Please explain about bliss and misery..."

Misery is unnatural, bliss is your nature. Misery is taught by others, bliss is given by God. Misery is a conditioning, bliss is your inner soul, your essence. Misery is personality, just the structure around you; bliss is your freedom, it is unstructured.

"Please explain about bliss and misery, for whenever I encounter love or beauty I only feel tremendous pain but not bliss, and I don't understand this."

Don't try to understand this at all. Just leave the pain there, accept it for a few days. And go into love – go into love madly – and go into beauty. Dance around a tree, and you will feel something of the shape of the tree has started reaching you. Dance under the stars. In the beginning you may feel that your legs are not moving and *you* have to move, because you have been forced to live without dance for so long, your legs have forgotten the language of dance. But soon they will learn because it is a natural language.

Each child knows how to dance, each child knows how to be joyous. You will have to learn it again, but because it is natural, it comes fast. Just a few efforts and suddenly one day, you are out of the trap. Your crutches have to be thrown away. Even if sometimes you fall it is perfectly good, but you have to stand on your own feet. The crutches of the society, of the organized religion, of the priests, have to be thrown. Even if for a few days you will feel impoverished – it is natural to feel impoverished for a few days – you have to accept it. But if you go on moving towards the natural, you will find Tao in your life. Tao is a natural flowering. Follow nature.

Nobody wants to be miserable and everybody is. They are not following nature. They do not want to be anything other than blissful and nobody is blissful. Listen to the desire: the deepest desire indicates the right path. Your longing is for bliss, for beauty, for something that will overwhelm you, for something that will take you to the other shore, for something which will be so tremendous and incredible that the past and the future will be washed away and you will just be in the here and now.

But don't try to understand. If you start trying to understand you will become a victim of psychoanalysis, and analysis is a process *ad infinitum*. You can go on analyzing and analyzing and it is never finished. There is not a single person in the world who is totally psychoanalyzed. There can never be.

This is where I differ from a psychoanalyst. Don't go into analysis. Put the whole mind aside. Jump out of it! There is no need to understand. All that is needed is to live, authentically live. All that is needed is to be.

Enough for today.

CHAPTER 3

The Atomic Moment

Master Lu-tsu said:
Only the primal spirit and the true nature overcome time and space.

The primal spirit is beyond the polar differences. Here is the place whence heaven and Earth derive their being. When students understand how to grasp the primal spirit they overcome the polar opposites of light and darkness and tarry no longer in the three worlds. But only he who has envisioned human nature's original face is able to do this.

When men are set free from the womb, the primal spirit dwells in the square inch, but the conscious spirit dwells below in the heart. This heart is dependent on the outside world. If a man does not eat for one day even, it feels extremely uncomfortable. If it hears something terrifying it throbs; if it hears something enraging it stops; if it is faced with death it becomes sad; if it sees something beautiful it is dazzled. But the heavenly heart in the head, when would it have moved in the least? Dost thou ask: "Can the heavenly heart not move?" Then I answer: "How could the true thought in the square inch move!"

The lower heart moves like a strong, powerful commander who despises the heavenly ruler because of his weakness, and has usurped

the leadership in affairs of state. But when the primal castle can be
fortified and defended, then it is as if a strong and wise ruler sat
upon the throne. The eyes start the light circulating like two ministers
at the right and left who support the ruler with all their might. When
rule in the center is thus in order, all those rebellious heroes will
present themselves with lances reversed, ready to take orders.

The way to the Elixir of Life knows these three as supreme magic –
seed-water, spirit-fire and thought-earth. What is seed-water?
It is the true, one energy, eros. Spirit-fire is the light, logos.
Thought-earth is intuition.

One day, a king called his clever jester and gave him a staff in front of all the court saying, "Take this staff as a wand of office and keep it till you find a greater fool than yourself. If you find one, give this wand to him."

Some time later, the king was sick and lay dying. He wanted to see his jester, of whose truthfulness he was sure. When the jester came the king said to him, "I have called you to tell you that I am going on a long journey."

"Where are you going?" asked the jester.

"To a faraway country – to another world."

"My master, have you made provision for your journey and your stay there?"

"None whatever, my little fool."

"Have you any friends to welcome you there?"

"No one!" replied the king.

Then the jester shook his head sadly and put the staff into the king's hand and said, "Take this staff, your majesty. This belongs to you, for you are going to another world without preparation. Surely this wand belongs to you and to nobody else."

Life is an occasion to prepare for death and the beyond. If you don't prepare for death and for the beyond you are a fool – you are missing a great opportunity. Life is only an opportunity.

This life that you know is not real life. It is only an opportunity to attain real life. The real life is just hidden somewhere in this life, but it has to be provoked, it has to be awakened. It is fast asleep. It is not yet aware of itself. And if your real life is not aware of itself, your whole so-called life will be nothing but a long dream. And it cannot be sweet either – it will be a nightmare.

To live without being rooted in the real life is to live like a tree without being rooted in the soil. That's why there is no beauty, that's why there is no grace. That's why you don't see the splendor of man that the buddhas talk about.

Jesus goes on saying again and again, "The Kingdom of God is within you." But you don't seem to be like an emperor. Jesus says to his disciples, "Look at the lilies in the field. How beautiful they are! Even Solomon, the great king, was not so beautiful, attired in all his grandeur, as these poor lily flowers." Why are the lilies so beautiful and man so ugly? Why is only man ugly? Have you ever seen an ugly parrot, or an ugly peacock, or an ugly lion, or an ugly deer? Ugliness seems to be something human. A peacock is a peacock and a deer is a deer, but a man is not necessarily a man.

A man is man only when he is a Buddha or a Christ or a Krishna – when he has become aware of his total being – otherwise you live groping in the dark. You live in the dark caves of the unconscious. You only appear to be conscious. Your consciousness is very fragile. It is very momentary, it is a very thin surface. It is not even skin-deep – just a little scratch and you lose your consciousness.

Somebody insults you: just a word or just a glance, and all your consciousness is gone and you are rage, anger, violence, aggression. In a moment your humanity disappears – you are again wild, again an animal – and man can fall below the animals, because when he falls there is nothing to stop him. Man can rise above the angels, but it rarely happens because to rise above the angels is an uphill task, arduous; one has to work for it. It needs hard work, it needs guts, courage, to explore the unknown.

Millions of people are born and die, but they never live. Their life is only apparent because they remain rooted in unconsciousness. And whatsoever you do on the surface may not be true about you at all; in fact, exactly the opposite is the case. That's why Sigmund Freud has to go into your dreams to see your reality. Just see the irony of it: your reality has to be searched for in your dreams, not in your reality. You cannot be believed – what you say about yourself. Your dreams have to be asked, because you have become so false and you are wearing so many masks that it is almost impossible to penetrate to your original face.

But it is very difficult to know your original face, even from dreams and dream analysis. Who is going to do the analysis? Freud is as unconscious as you are. One unconscious person is trying to interpret the dreams of another unconscious person. His interpretations are bound to be very limited; his interpretations will reflect more about him than about you. That's why if you go to a Freudian analyst with the same dream, you will get a different interpretation than you will get if you go to a Jungian analyst or to an Adlerian analyst – and now there are many. And you will be puzzled: a single dream has different interpretations. They are not saying anything about you, they are saying something about themselves. The Jungian is saying, "I am a Jungian. This is my interpretation." Your dreams cannot reveal your truth. If your conscious activities cannot reveal you, how can your sleep activities or your unconscious reveal you? But still, Freud is on the right track. One has to go a little deeper.

One has to go beyond the dreams to a state of mind where no thought, no dream, no desire exists; when all thinking... And dreaming is a kind of thinking, a primitive kind of thinking – thinking through pictures – but it is still thinking. When you have gone beyond thinking, and if you can still remain alert, aware, as if one is fast asleep but still alert – deep down at the very core of one's being a lamp goes on burning, a small candle of light – then you will see your original face. And to see your original face is to be back in the Garden of Eden. Then you drop all your clothes.

Your personality consists only of clothes and clothes and clothes – clothes upon clothes. Remember two words which will be very important to understand this strange but immensely valuable book, *The Secret of the Golden Flower*: one word is *essence*, the other word is *personality*. Personality comes from a root, *persona* which means a mask. In ancient days, the actors in Greek dramas used to wear masks. Persona means a mask; personality comes from persona. The actors used to wear one mask, you are wearing many, because for different situations you need different masks. When you are talking to your boss you need one kind of mask and when you are talking to your servant, of course, you need another kind of mask. How can you use the same mask?

Have you ever watched? When you are talking to your boss, you are all smiles; your every breath says, "Yes, sir." Even though you are offended, angry, you are ready to kiss his feet. And when you are talking to your servant, have you seen the arrogance on your face? You have never smiled. How can you smile talking to your servant? It is impossible. You have to dehumanize him. How can you smile and relate to him as a human being? You have to possess him as a thing: he is a slave. You have to behave in a different way than you behave with your boss. There, *you* are a servant; he remains arrogant, he remains bossy. When you are talking to a friend you have a different mask to use. When you are talking to a stranger, of course, a different mask is needed. You have to use many masks and you have many faces, and you go on changing them as circumstances change. Your personality consists only of false faces.

And what is essence? Essence is your original face without any masks. Essence is that which you brought into the world when you were born. Essence is that which was with you in the womb. Essence is that which has been given to you by God – or whatsoever you call the totality, the whole, existence. Essence is a gift from existence to you.

Personality is a gift of the society, parents, school, college, culture, civilization. Personality is not you, it is pseudo – and we continue to polish this personality, and we have completely forgotten the essence. And unless you remember the essence, you will have lived in vain, because real life consists of essence. A real life is the life of essence. You can call it soul, or God within you, or whatsoever you will. But remember the distinction: you are not your clothes – not even your psychological clothes.

I must remind you of Moses. When he came face to face with God, when he saw God on the mountains as fire arising out of a green bush – and the bush was not burning, the bush was as fresh, as green as ever – he was puzzled. He could not believe his eyes. It was impossible…such fire! The bush was aflame and yet the bush was not burning. And then he heard from the bush a voice coming to him, "Moses, put off your shoes, because you are on holy ground."

This is one of the most beautiful of Jewish parables: God is the fire, your personality is just the bush; and God is a cool fire – it will not burn your personality, the personality can remain green. God gives you so much freedom that if you want to be false, it is allowed, it is okay with him. If you want to be pseudo, it is also allowed. Freedom means that you can be right or you can be wrong – this is up to you. Your essence is always there, the flame is always there, and your personality is also always there.

The personality is false, and naturally one will think, "Why doesn't the fire within you burn it?" The fire is cool, the fire cannot burn it. If you have decided to have this personality, the fire allows it: you can remain green in your personality, the personality can go on gathering more and more foliage. You can become more and more false, you can become utterly false, you can be lost in the falsehood of the personality and God is not going to interfere.

Remember this: God never interferes, freedom is total. That is the dignity of man, the glory of man, and the agony too. If you were not given freedom you would not be false. No other animal is false, no animal has personality. And I am not counting pet animals: because they live with you, they are destroyed – they start having personalities. Your dogs forget their essence. The dog may be angry but goes on wagging his tail – this is personality. He knows who is the boss and he knows how to buttress the ego of the boss, he has become diplomatic. He is as much a politician as the people who live in New Delhi: he goes on wagging his tail.

Have you seen the dog puzzled sometimes? A stranger comes in and the dog does not know how to behave – what face to show to the stranger. Feeling ambiguous, he barks – maybe that is the right thing to do – and still he goes on wagging his tail. He is watching for the right hints from the boss – whether the person who has entered the house is a friend or a foe. If he is a foe he will stop wagging his tail, if he is a friend he will stop barking at him. He is waiting for a hint, a signal – how the master behaves. He has become a shadow of the master. He is no longer a real dog.

To live with human beings is contagious – they destroy. You even destroy animals if they live with you, you don't allow them their natural essence. You civilize them just as you have become civilized. You don't allow nature to have its own way, you don't allow Tao to have its own flow.

Essence is that which you bring into the world, the personality is that which the world imposes upon the essence. The world is very afraid of the essence because the essence is always rebellious. The essence is always individualistic, and the world does not need any individuals. It needs sheep, it does not need rebellious people. It does not need people like Buddha, Krishna, Lao Tzu – no, these people are dangerous. It wants people who are obedient – obedient to the status quo, obedient to the vested interests, obedient to the organized church, obedient to the state and the stupid politicians.

Society requires obedience, and society requires efficiency. The more mechanical you are, the more efficient you are. When you are more alive, you cannot be so efficient. A machine is more efficient than man. The society's effort is to reduce every man into a machine. And how to reduce a man into a machine? Make him more and more unconscious, make him more and more robot-like, let his essence completely disappear from his consciousness, let him become perfectly pseudo. Let him be a husband, let her be a wife, a servant, a boss, this and that, but never let him be his essential self. Don't allow that, because that essential self is not obedient to anybody except to God. It has no other commitment, its sole commitment is to the source. It knows no other masters.

That type of being will be very inconvenient to this so-called society, because this society is not created to fulfill the needs of human beings. It is created to exploit human beings. It is not according to you and for your growth. It has no intention to help you to grow, and it has every intention not to allow you to grow because the more you grow the more independent you become, the less you grow the more dependent you remain. And a dependent person is reliable because a dependent person is always afraid. A dependent person always needs somebody to lean on – always needs somebody to lean on. He is childish and he leans on the parents, he leans on the priests, he leans on the politicians. He cannot stand on his own feet. The society goes on covering you with many many clothes – not only physical but psychological too.

The society is very much afraid of physical nakedness, because physical nakedness is the beginning of psychological nakedness. The society goes into a panic seeing a naked man because this is the beginning: if he is naked physically, he has taken the first step. Now who is going to prevent him from becoming psychologically naked?

And the voice that called forth from the burning bush to Moses said, "Put off your shoes." It is a very symbolic thing. "Put off all your clothes," it says. "Put off your shoes." Shoes cover your feet. Shoes cover you. "Be naked on the ground. Be without shoes." The shoe represents personality, and nakedness represents essence. "You are on holy ground, put off your shoes."

The moment you encounter your essence – the burning bush within you – you will have to take off your shoes, you will have to take off all your clothes, you will have to take off all that is hiding your essence. That is revolution, *metanoia*. That is the turning point in a life: the society disappears and you become an individual – and only individuals can relate with God. But a great and visible consciousness will be needed to realise this.

Gurdjieff once, in 1933, treated the American novelist Fritz Peters to a demonstration of this at the former's New York apartment in the Henry Hudson Hotel where a meeting was to be held.

Peters was a young disciple of Gurdjieff, and Gurdjieff was one of the greatest masters the world has ever known – and not a conventional master at all, because no master can be conventional. Conventionality is the quality of the priest, not of the master. The master is always revolutionary. And this is a beautiful experiment. Listen attentively:

When Peters arrived he was asked to wash dishes and prepare vegetables for some very important people who were coming to dinner. Gurdjieff said he needed Peters to give him an English lesson consisting of words for all those parts and functions of the body "that were not in the dictionary." By the time Gurdjieff had mastered the four-letter words and obscene phrases the guests started arriving, who turned out to be some fifteen well-dressed, well-mannered New Yorkers, of which a number were reporters or journalists.

After staging a late and obsequious entry, Gurdjieff humbly began responding at table to the guests' blasé questions on his work and reasons for visiting America. Then, with a wink to his English teacher, he suddenly changed tone and explained that the sad degeneration of humankind and its transformation into a substance only describable by a four-letter expletive was particularly striking in their country; hence his coming to observe this phenomenon in the raw. The cause behind this distressing state of affairs, he continued, lay in the fact that people – especially Americans – never followed the dictates of intelligence or propriety, but only that of their genital organs. Then singling out one particularly handsome woman, Gurdjieff complimented her on her attire and makeup. He then confided with everyone in the room that in all honesty, between them, the real explanation behind her adornment was an irresistible sexual urge she felt for some particular person – graphically spelled out by Gurdjieff with his newly acquired vocabulary. Before the guests could react, he launched into a discourse on his own sexual prowess, followed by intimate and detailed descriptions of the sexual mores of various races and nations.

By the time dinner was over and the guests well plied with good old Armagnac as always, they lost their inhibitions and joined in an exchange of obscenities which soon became more than verbal. Gurdjieff retired with the lady he had insulted, and the others, by now conditioned to believe that an orgy was in the tenor of the evening, began entangling physically in different rooms of the apartment in various stages of undress.

Just when the carousal was at a climax, Gurdjieff briskly disengaged himself and thundered forth orders for the revels to cease. He proclaimed that the lesson had been accomplished, that the guests had already amply verified through their comportment the soundness of the observations he made earlier in the evening – that thanks to him they were now partly conscious of their true condition and that he would gladly accept checks and cash in payment for this important lesson. Peters noted – without surprise, knowing Gurdjieff – that the total came to several thousand dollars.

When everyone had left, Gurdjieff went into the kitchen to help Peters with the dishes, asking at the same time how he had enjoyed the evening. "I was disgusted," came the reply. Gurdjieff laughed and scrutinized his companion with a piercing look. "It is a fine feeling you have – this disgust. But now it is necessary to ask yourself one question: with who are you disgusted?"

This is the real situation. What you show on the surface is one thing. Those guests were annoyed, angered by the observation of George Gurdjieff that humanity has become very degraded, that what you do on the surface is one thing, what you mean deep inside is another. You may give explanations and you may rationalize, but your rationalizations are just rationalizations and nothing else. Deep down something else goes on working in the unconscious. You are not even aware of it.

Psychologists say that when a woman is raped, in the majority of cases the woman wanted to be raped – she had the desire. She was inviting it, she was using certain gestures; the way she walked, the way she dressed, the way she talked were all gestures inviting rape – and then one day it happens. And then she looks surprised, angry, violent, goes to the police, fights in the court. If she had looked deep down in her own mind she would have been surprised: it was her own effort, her own desire which had been fulfilled.

There are people who go on living in this double way, not even aware what their real motives are inside. Watch, and that watching will make you very, very alert. Just watch. What is your real motive? Don't try to convince yourself that this is not so. Just become a mirror and see your behavior. Just become a silent watcher of your behavior – always alert as to why you are doing a certain thing, from where it is coming – and then you will see you have a dual being. One is the personality which says one thing and the other is your reality which goes on doing just the opposite. And somehow they both have to manage with each other, hence the conflict, the friction, and the wastage of energy.

And it happens almost in all cases that you have one desire inside and just the opposite on the outside. And why the opposite? – because through the opposite you are repressing that desire. The person who feels inferior deep inside pretends to be very superior on the outside. Only inferior people want to be superior. Those who are really superior don't care a bit. All people who suffer from inferiority complexes become politicians, because that is the only way to prove that they are very superior. The person who has the look on his face of holier-than-thou knows that deep inside just the opposite is the case: he is suffering from guilt, he is suffering deep down from unworthiness – he knows that he is unholy. Now the only way to hide it from the world is to have a mask of holiness.

Your so-called saints are not a bit different from the sinners. The only difference is that sinners are honest and your saints are not honest. Out of one hundred saints, if you can find even one saint who is really a saint, that will be more than enough, more than one can expect; ninety-nine are just pretending. And I am not saying that they are pretending only to you. The pretension can go so deep that not only are they deceiving others, they start deceiving themselves. In fact, to deceive yourself, first you have to deceive others, only then can you believe in it. When others start believing that you are a saint, only then can you believe it.

The real saint is not concerned with others at all. He knows who he is. Even if the whole world says that he is not a saint, that doesn't matter. His understanding is inner, his encounter is directly with himself, his experience is immediate and existential. He knows his essence. And to know one's essence is the first step to knowing God, to becoming immortal, to going beyond death.

Henri Bergson spoke at the beginning of this century. He said, "The addition to the body brought by technology calls for a corresponding addition to the soul."

The modern man looks more soulless than in any other age, and the reason is: science and technology have added much to the body. The body has become stronger, lives longer. The brain has become stronger, has become more knowledgeable. Compared to the body and the brain – and the brain is part of the body – the soul has remained very, very poor. It is almost neglected, ignored. Nobody cares about it.

Who thinks about one's own essence? Going to the church or to the temple is not going to help. You will have to go within yourself: you will have to take off your shoes, you will have to go into your naked essence. Only then will you be able to reconnect yourself with the cosmos. It is from there that you can be bridged again with reality.

Now the sutras:

> Master Lu-tsu said:
> Only the primal spirit and the true nature overcome time and space.

What I have been telling you about essence, Master Lu-tsu calls "the primal spirit." The primal spirit is your essential soul, that which you have brought from God – untaught, unconditioned, as you were in your mother's womb. How did you exist in your mother's womb? Nothing was taught to you, you had no mind, you existed in a state of no-mind, hence the blissfulness of it.

Psychologists say that because of the experience of the mother's womb, those nine months, man has been searching for God – because of that nine months' experience the memory haunts him. Those nine months were the most beautiful that you have known. Maybe you have forgotten consciously, but deep down in the very cells of your body, in the very fibers of your being, those days are still pulsating, those days are still carried by your existence. They may not be conscious in your mind, but they are there. Just as when in the night you fall into deep sleep, you don't know where you go and what happens to you, but in the morning you feel the relaxation, the freshness, the joy. Life has again happened to you, all the dust that you had gathered has disappeared. You are again fresh, you are rejuvenated, your body carries the feeling. Your body is calm and quiet and remembers something. The remembrance is not in the brain – you don't know what happened exactly, where you had gone.

Only a buddha knows where he goes in his deep sleep, because even in his deep sleep he remains alert. You are not alert even when you are aware – the so-called awareness, you are not alert when you are in that so-called wakeful state. Your eyes are open, but your mind goes on weaving and spinning a thousand and one thoughts. The inner talk continues, the inner noise continues. You see and yet you don't see and you hear and yet you don't hear, because deep inside there is a wall of thoughts, dreams – continuously floating in the sky of your consciousness. You are not alert even when you are awake. The buddha is alert even when he is fast asleep. Only he knows where he goes.

Where does he go? He goes to the essence, to the source, to the primal spirit. And even if for a few moments at night you fall into the primal source, you are rejuvenated. The man who cannot fall into deep sleep is really in hell. He goes to bed tired, exhausted, bored with life, and gets up in the morning even more tired, more bored, more exhausted. His life is hell.

In deep sleep you simply slip back into the primal source of your being. That primal source is always there; you have not lost it, you have only forgotten it. And that primal source is beyond all dualities: it is neither light nor darkness, it is transcendental; it is neither life nor death as you know them, it is transcendental; it is neither man nor woman as you know them, it is transcendental. It is beyond all kinds of dualities. It is God.

Only the primal spirit and the true nature overcome time and space.

When you are in the primal spirit you are in your true nature. When you are in your personality you are untrue, you are just a plastic phenomenon. Watch, and you will be surprised how many things are plastic in you. You smile when there is no smile in the heart, then it is plastic. You sympathize when there is no sympathy in you – it is plastic. You show joy when there is no joy in you – it is plastic. You can even cry and weep without your heart feeling anything, then those tears are plastic. Just watch how many things are plastic in you. And remember, whatsoever is plastic is not you. God has not made you a plastic thing; God has given you eternal life. But that eternal life you can find only when you put off your shoes, put off your personality.

Drop all personas, all masks. Let all masks disappear. It will be painful because you have become identified with those masks; you think they are your faces. It is going to be a very painful process of death. And not only once – you will have to die many times – because each time a face falls you will find a death has happened. But again new life will be released in you, fresher, deeper, more vibrant. When all the faces disappear and the essence is left alone, you have transcended all duality, even the duality of time and space.

When you enter deep meditation, when you enter your essential being, there is no space and no time – you cannot say where you are. All "wheres" disappear, you cannot pinpoint the place. Either you are nowhere or you are everywhere. These are the only two possibilities. Both mean the same.

A few people have chosen to say one is everywhere. Vedanta has chosen to say that in deep meditation one is everywhere: *Aham Brahmasmi*, "I am God." "God" means one who is everywhere, who permeates the whole existence – you become space itself. And "I am always, I am eternal" – it means you permeate time. This is one way of expressing it, the positive way. Buddhism has chosen the other, the negative way.

Buddha says: "In deep meditation you are nowhere."

All space has disappeared. And there is no time, you are in a timeless state. And when there is no time and no space, how can you exist? Man exists only at the crossing point of time and space. One line of time and another line of space cross, and at that crossing the ego arises. Take away these two lines and the point of the ego disappears. It was only a crossing of two lines. It was a fallacious idea.

So Buddha says: "There is nobody."

In deep meditation, time disappears, space disappears, and you disappear – all disappears. There is only nothingness, *shunya*, zero. This is the negative way of saying the same thing.

Either you can say, "I am God," if you choose the positive expression – which has its own dangers, its own beauties too; or you can choose the negative expression, *anatta* – no-self, nothingness – nirvana. It has its own beauties and its dangers too. The very idea of nothingness puts people off – that is the danger. Who wants to be nothing?

In his forty years of ministry, again and again Buddha is asked, "Why should one try to be nothing? That would be a death, ultimate death."

And Buddha says, "Yes, it is an ultimate death. But it is beautiful."

And the questioners ask, "But to whom is it beautiful? – because there is nobody."

And Buddha says, "There is only beauty, beatitude – nobody to experience it."

Naturally the human mind says, "But then what is the point? If I am not there, and it is very beautiful, so let it be beautiful. But I am not there, so whether it is beautiful or not makes no difference to me. Why should I lose myself? It is better to be in a world which is not so beautiful but where at least I am."

The goal of nothingness puts people off. That's why Buddhism disappeared from India and it learned a lesson: in China it dropped the negative language, in Tibet it dropped the negative language. Indian Buddhism, the original Buddhism, was absolutely negative. Under the influence of Buddha thousands were transformed, but you cannot find a man like Buddha every day.

The impact of Buddha was such that people were even ready to die and become nothing. That was because of Buddha; otherwise there is no enchantment, no charm in being nothing. But Buddha's magnetism was such, his charisma was such, that thousands of people were ready to become nothing: "If Buddha says it, it must be right." His word was so important, his eyes were a witness to it: "He has disappeared, so let us also disappear. And if he says so then we can trust."

But once Buddha disappeared from the earth, Buddhist priests could not convince people; they had to disappear from India completely. Then they learned a lesson: outside India, Buddhism started using positive language, started using all that Buddha had denied. It survived, but it did not really survive as Buddhism. It survived as Vedanta, it survived as a positive language, and Buddha's greatest contribution was the negative expression.

The beauty of the negative expression is that it never allows your ego any satisfaction, any gratification. That is the danger of the positive language. If you say, *Aham Brahmasmi* – "I am God," *Ana'l haq* – "I am truth," the danger is that truth may become secondary and the "I" may become primary. Truth may become your shadow; the emphasis may start concentrating on the word "I": "I am God." If the emphasis remains on God and the "I" remains just a shadow to God, it is perfectly good. But that is very difficult. The "I" is very cunning, the ego's ways are very subtle. It will use the opportunity, it will jump upon the idea.

It will say, "Right, I am God and nobody else is. I am truth and everybody else is a lie." But then the whole point is missed.

But one thing is certain: time and space disappear. Either you have to declare, "I am all" – the whole space, the whole time – "I am everywhere and everywhen," or you have to use the Buddhist expression, "I am not. Time is not. Space is not. There is only an absolute silent nothing – from eternity to eternity, a silence, not even a ripple." But both statements indicate the same thing. Expressions are different, fingers are different, but they point to the same moon. That moon is your essence.

> *Master Lu-tsu said:*
> *Only the primal spirit and the true nature overcome time and space.*

And unless you overcome time and space you will not overcome death. Death exists in time, and death exists in space. Unless you overcome time and space you will not overcome mind and body.

Try to understand: body corresponds to space and mind corresponds to time. Mind is a time phenomenon and body is a space phenomenon. Body exists *somewhere* and mind exists *somewhen*. Think of mind without time and you will not be able to think of it; mind is either past, present or future, either memory or imagination, or the present facticity. Mind exists in three tenses.

You are listening to me attentively, alert, your mind is in the present. If you are here thinking of other things – you have read something in the Bible and it corresponds with me or does not correspond with me – you have gone into your imagination or into your memory. You cannot think of mind if time disappears; time is synonymous with mind.

Man is a miniature cosmos, a miniature universe. All that exists outside on a greater scale exists on a small scale in man. If you can understand man you will have understood the whole universe: as above, so below. Man is the atomic constituent of this whole universe. If one atom is understood you have understood all matter. If one man is understood, if you can decipher your own mystery, you have deciphered all the mysteries that are possible – in the past, present, future – all.

And these two things have to be remembered: body is space, mind is time. When you meditate you disappear from the body, you don't know who you are. Man, woman, ugly, beautiful, black, white – you simply don't know who you are. When you go in, the body is left far behind. A moment comes when you cannot even locate your body and you cannot even feel its presence. You are no more attached to the form; you have become formless. And the same happens with the mind: you don't know where your mind is, where that mind has gone. All that noise, that traffic noise that was constantly inside becomes distant, distant, distant, and disappears. Suddenly a great silence explodes in you. In this state of no space and no time, you come to know your essence. And to know one's essence is to have the first glimpse of Tao.

The primal spirit is beyond the polar differences.

All the polar differences disappear. Man-woman, summer-winter, hot-cold, love-hate, positive-negative, time-space, life-death – all polar opposites disappear.

The primal spirit is beyond the polar differences.

And that's why I insist again and again that you don't get attached to any polarity. You have been taught to become attached to some polarity. Your so-called religions have been teaching you: either be worldly, or renounce and go to the monasteries. I say remain in the world and don't be of it; otherwise you will become attached to a polarity. If you go to the monastery you will be afraid of the marketplace. What kind of attainment is this? If there is fear there is no attainment.

And I know people who have lived in the Himalayas – then they become afraid. Then they don't want to come to the world because whatsoever they have been experiencing in the Himalayas disappears when they come to the marketplace. If it disappears in the marketplace it is no attainment. It may have been just the silence of the Himalayas that you mistook for your silence. It was borrowed. Certainly, the Himalayas are silent, and if you live in that silence, slowly, slowly that silence starts permeating you. But it is not your music, it is borrowed; go away from the Himalayas and it will disappear. This is creating a fallacy. This is enjoying a reflected glory, this is not your own glory.

Live in the marketplace and create a Himalaya in the heart, become silent in the noise. Remain a householder and yet be a sannyasin. That's why I emphasize so much that I don't want my sannyasins to renounce. Nothing has to be renounced. The way of renunciation is the way of the escapist, and the way of renunciation will make you attached to a polar phenomenon. That will not give you freedom. Freedom is in transcendence, and transcendence comes only when you live in the polar opposites simultaneously, together.

So be in the world, but don't let the world be in you. Love, and yet don't be lost in it. Relate, and yet be alone, utterly alone. Know perfectly well that all relationship is a game: play the game and play it as beautifully as possible and as skillfully as possible. A game is after all a game and has to be played beautifully. And follow all the rules of the game, because a game cannot exist without rules. But remember always that it is just a game. Don't become attached to it, don't become serious in it. Always allow the sense of humor to remain alive in you: remain sincere but non-serious. And then, slowly, slowly you will see that the polarities are disappearing. Who is worldly and who is otherworldly? You are both or neither.

> *The primal spirit is beyond the polar differences. Here is the place*
> *whence heaven and Earth derive their being. When students*
> *understand how to grasp the primal spirit they overcome the polar*
> *opposites of light and darkness and tarry no longer in the three worlds.*

The world of heaven, the world of Earth and the world of hell – the three worlds – they all disappear for the person who knows how to transcend polarities.

I told you just a few moments ago that past, present, future – these are the three worlds. Past is hell because it is dead, it is ghostly: ghosts following you. Present is the earth: the facticity, the fact, that which is right now and here. And future is heaven: hopes, aspirations, desires, longings.

These are the three worlds, and you have to move in these three worlds constantly; you are shuttled back and forth. From the past you jump to the future, from the future you jump to the past, and this goes on. And the present is so minute that you are not very aware of it: it is sandwiched between the past and the future, and they are vast. The present is an atomic moment – so small that you don't see it. The moment you become aware of it, it is already past.

To be present to the present one needs to be very attentive, utterly attentive. And that's why to be present to the present becomes the door to going beyond time. You cannot go from the past, because the past is so vast – infinite; you can go on and on, you will not find the end of it. That's why I say psychoanalysis will not help. It goes into the past and it goes on unraveling the past, digging up the past. You can go on... Psychoanalysis continues for years: three years, seven years, then too it is not complete. One simply becomes bored with the psychoanalyst and then changes the psychoanalyst and goes to somebody else and starts from *ABC* again.

And one thing I would like to say to you: Sooner or later psychoanalysis is bound to discover that this life is not the end of the past. You can go on moving backwards, and you can come to what Janov calls "the primal scream." Primal scream is the ultimate of psychoanalysis: the first scream of the child when he started breathing – through it he started breathing – the first scream. But once you have reached there you will be surprised: that is not the beginning either. Then you have to move into the womb.

In the East we have tried it. We have a very, very deep-rooted method called *prati prasav* – going back, going back. Mahavira used it, Buddha used it – they went through the womb. And then again you have to go through death, because before the womb you died, and then the whole life again…layer upon layer. It is through deep psychoanalysis that the East became aware of the phenomenon of many lives. Christianity, Judaism, Islam are not aware of it. They never tried so hard. They have never tried psychoanalysis.

Freud is the first Jew to have tried it, and of course, Christians and Jews and all the so-called religious people were against him. The fear is that if psychoanalysis goes deeper, sooner or later the Hindu idea of rebirth will be proved right. That is the fear. If you go on digging you will find layer upon layer – where will you end? Thousands of lives you have lived as man and we have tried to penetrate all those; but then too there is no end. One day, suddenly you see that before this life you were not a man, you were an elephant or a tiger or a dog, and then you start moving into animal lives. And after millions of lives, you will suddenly one day discover that before that you were a bush or a tree, and then a rock.

In India we say you have passed millions of lives. Where can it lead? The analysis of the past cannot lead anywhere. It can drive you crazy, but it leads nowhere. And so is the case with the future. Where to stop? How far is far enough? Where to make a point that "Now we will not look ahead"? In the East we have tried that too, because we have worked tremendously on the concept of time. And both are unending: memory is unending, imagination is unending. Between the two is the present moment, very tiny, so tiny that you cannot become aware of it if you are not absolutely alert – it goes so fast, it is so fleeting.

But if you become aware of the present, then a door opens, the door to eternity. It is from there that mind moves into no-mind. It is from there that personality moves beyond personality into essence.

You know perfectly well Jesus was crucified. There were two thieves who were crucified with him: one was on his left side, the other was on his right side. You may not have ever thought of it as a tremendously significant symbol that Jesus represents the present moment. One thief is the past, the other thief is the future, and Jesus represents the present moment – closest to God, closest to essence. One thief mocked Jesus – the past always mocks you; he condemned Jesus – the past always condemns you. The other thief asked Jesus about the future, "What will happen after death? Will I be able to see you in heaven?" One is past, the other is future, and Jesus is just sandwiched between these two thieves.

And why call them thieves? Past is a thief, future is a thief, because they go on stealing your present. They *are* thieves. To me this is a parable. I don't know whether any Christian will agree with me or not, but that is not my business at all; I don't care whether anybody agrees with me or not.

Jesus is present, here and now, closest to the essence, just ready to die and disappear from the body and the mind. He hesitates a little bit – everybody hesitates. When you come to the present and you will see eternity facing you – no past, no future, but eternity – a totally different dimension. Past, present, future are horizontal; eternity is vertical. Again, to me the cross is the symbol of these two lines crossing.

A cross is made of two lines – one horizontal, the other vertical. This is a representation of time and eternity. Everybody hesitates when facing eternity, nowhereness, nothingness or all-ness. It is so much, one is going to disappear into it like a drop. And the ocean is so big, one will not be found again. Even a dewdrop falling into the ocean from a grass leaf hesitates.

Jesus hesitated, and I love this man because he hesitated. His hesitation shows that he was human. His hesitation shows that he belonged to us – he was son of man. He cried to God, "Have you forsaken me? What are you doing to me? Have you abandoned me? Are you no more with me? I am disappearing and I don't see your hands protecting me". The dewdrop is falling in the ocean – "Where are you? I am falling into a deep nothingness. Death has arrived, and I had always hoped that in death you would be there waiting and you would embrace me, you would take me in your fold, you would be warm and loving. But where are you? Have you forsaken me? Have you abandoned me? I don't see you anywhere."

In fact, there is no God to be seen. God is not a person, God is a positive name for this absolute nothingness.

But Jesus has lived with the Jewish idea of God as a person, hence this turmoil in his mind, the fear in his mind. He can't see. He was waiting to see the beloved, the father. He used to call the father *Abba* – he was waiting to find his father. But there seems to be nobody. The world is finished and beyond is nothing but a yawning nothingness, an abyss with no bottom.

It is very human – the life of Jesus is very human – and that is the beauty of it, that's why it has impressed so many people. His very humanity is touching. But then he saw the point: he must have looked deep into the eternity, the nothingness, he must have seen the point that "God cannot have a human face, this is his face," that "God cannot have human hands," that "This nothingness is ready to embrace me, to take me deep into its heart." And then he said to God, "Thy kingdom come. Thy will be done. So, be it so, let it be so. So you are nothingness: I am ready, I trust you. I will trust even your nothingness."

Every Christian, every Mohammedan, every Hindu, every Jew – whosoever has lived with the idea of God's personality will have to face this, will have to go through this anxiety period, this anguish. That is the beauty of the Buddhist idea and the Taoist idea that God is nothingness, another name for nothingness. One who has lived with that idea of nothingness from the very beginning will not hesitate, he will simply disappear into it.

> The primal spirit is beyond the polar differences. Here is the place
> whence heaven and Earth derive their being. When students
> understand how to grasp the primal spirit they overcome the polar
> opposites of light and darkness and tarry no longer in the three
> worlds. But only he who has envisioned human nature's original face
> is able to do this.

Unless you have been able to see your own inner nothingness you will not be able to do it. First meditate and go into your inner nothingness, then you will be able to enter into the nothingness of existence itself.

> When men are set free from the womb, the primal spirit dwells in the
> square inch…

This is a Taoist map – don't get puzzled. There are different maps of human consciousness. Different maps use different symbols. This is a Taoist map.

Taoists say that after a child is born from the womb, the primal spirit starts dwelling in the third eye. Between the two eyes, between the two exists the third, exactly in the middle. What the yoga map calls *agya chakra*, the third-eye center, that's what Taoists call the dwelling place of the primal spirit.

...the primal spirit dwells in the square inch but the conscious spirit dwells below in the heart.

"*But the conscious spirit dwells...in the heart,*" the ordinary physical heart.

This heart is dependent on the outside world. If a man does not eat for one day even, it feels extremely uncomfortable. If it hears something terrifying it throbs; if it hears something enraging it stops; if it is faced with death it becomes sad; if it sees something beautiful it is dazzled. But the heavenly heart in the head...

...that is, in the third-eye center.

...when would it have moved in the least? Dost thou ask: "Can the heavenly heart not move?" Then I answer: How could the true thought in the square inch move!

This physical heart is constantly dependent on the outside world, it is affected by the outside world. It is part of the outside world inside you. This is not the true heart. Taoists say the true heart is in the third eye; it moves not, it is unmoving, it is always the same. The physical heart is always in chaos, and the spiritual heart in the third eye is always in order. It is order itself. That's why Hindus have called it agya chakra – the center from which orders arise, discipline arises. If something comes from the third eye it is immediately followed; the whole body follows it, the whole being follows it. It is the center from which commandments are issued. But it is fast asleep. You live from the physical heart. You have not known your spiritual heart yet.

The lower heart moves like a strong, powerful commander who despises the heavenly ruler because of his weakness...

But the physical heart thinks that the spiritual heart is weak because it moves not. And because it moves not you remain unaware of it. You only become aware of things when they move. If something remains absolutely unmoving you become oblivious to it. And the lower heart thinks itself very strong and thinks the heavenly heart, the spiritual heart, as being weak, almost dead, because it moves not.

...and has usurped the leadership in affairs of state.

And because of this, the lower heart has become the master of you.

> *But when the primal castle can be fortified and defended, then*
> *it is as if a strong and wise ruler sat upon the throne.*

But if you start becoming more and more alert and more and more conscious, you will find that you have fortified the primal castle in the third eye. Whenever you become aware you will be surprised: you start functioning from the third eye. Just become a little bit aware and you will see a little strain on the third eye. Whenever you become alert, the strain is more on the third eye. Something starts throbbing in the third eye, something starts pulsating in the third eye.

Once awareness has made the third eye function, once awareness has moved in the third eye and the third eye starts functioning, becomes alive.... That's why Hindus call it a chakra. "Chakra" means a wheel. The wheel needs energy; once the energy comes in, the wheel starts moving. By "movement" I mean that it starts functioning. Then a great revolution happens in your being: immediately the lower heart bows down to the higher heart. When the higher comes, the lower always bows down. It rules only when the higher is not present. And that is the difference between a real religion and an unreal religion.

The unreal religion says to you, "Try to control yourself. Control your senses. Discipline your body." The real religion says, "Just go into the third eye center and let the spiritual heart function, and all will be controlled, and all will be disciplined. Let the master arrive and everything will be settled immediately."

> *The eyes start the light circulating like two ministers at the right*
> *and left who support the ruler with all their might. When rule in*
> *the center is thus in order, all those rebellious heroes will present*
> *themselves with lances reversed, ready to take orders.*

Just let the master come in, and there is no need to make any effort to create an order in your life, there is no need to cultivate character. That's why I say don't be worried about character. Simply put all your energy into being more conscious. Consciousness is followed by character as you are followed by your shadow. If you try to cultivate a character, your character will be false, pseudo, and you will become a hypocrite. And this is not the way to reach to the ultimate.

The way to the Elixir of Life knows these three as supreme magic...

This is the supreme magic. Why call it magic? – because once the higher heart has started functioning, it is as if a magical miracle happens.... Your senses were never in order, your mind was always confused. You were always hesitating: to do this or to do that, to be or not to be? You were in constant tension: where to go, what to choose? Suddenly, as if somebody has performed a miracle: all confusion disappears, clarity arises, life becomes transparent – you simply do that which has to be done. In fact, once the heavenly heart has started functioning, all that you do is good; you cannot do wrong – it is impossible.

The way to the Elixir of Life knows as supreme magic...

And there are three constituents of this supreme magic:

...seed-water, spirit-fire, and thought-earth...

These are Taoist symbols.

...these three. What is seed-water? It is the true, one energy, eros.
Spirit-fire is the light, logos. Thought-earth is intuition.

You will have to understand these three. Seed-water is eros – the energy that you know now as sexual energy, the energy of passion. Right now it creates only troubles for you and nothing else. Right now it pretends to be your friend but proves to be your foe. The more you follow it, the more it takes you into miseries. That's why it is said that love is blind.

Mulla Nasruddin was saying to me, "Love is blind and marriage is an eye-opener."

Love is blind because you don't have eyes yet, and a great energy that could have become a great blessing to you becomes only misery. Eros is your energy.

And Freud is right to seek and search for everything in your eros, in your sexual energy. But he is wrong because he does not know that this ordinary state of sexual energy is not its natural state, it is a perverted state. In its natural state, sexual energy rises higher and higher, it takes you upwards not downwards. In its natural state, sexual energy becomes the golden flower within you. In the so-called ordinary, perverted state it simply takes you into new prisons, because it moves outward and downward. It dissipates you. It only brings your death closer and closer. If the same energy starts moving upwards, it brings a new life, life in abundance. It becomes "the Elixir of Life."

Just as the mud can become a lotus – the mud contains the lotus, the seed of it – so your sexual energy contains the seed of the golden flower. But the energy has to move upwards, you cannot move it upwards. There are people who try to make it move upwards; they become sexual perverts and nothing else. You cannot do it directly, but you can do it indirectly. Once your third eye, your spiritual heart, starts functioning, energy starts moving on its own accord. You have created the third eye and the energy is attracted as if towards a magnet.

Right now your energy moves outwards because you have magnets outside, far greater than you have inside. You see a beautiful woman and the energy starts moving outwards; the woman functions as a magnet. When your third eye functions you have such a strong magnet that nobody can pull you outward. It is just a question of having a bigger magnet inside than the one which exists outside. Then the energy moves upwards, inwards.

If you go outwards you will move into the world of duality. If you go inwards you will move into the world of non-duality; you will become non-polar.

This is exactly the foundation of what I call metapsychology, or the psychology of the buddhas. This is pure religion – not the religion of the rituals, but pure religion: nothing to do with Christianity and Hinduism but something to do with your energy source.

The second is spirit-fire. It is light, logos; it is conscious mind. Eros moving upwards takes you beyond conscious and unconscious mind. Logos is conscious mind. It is psychology, it is science.

Thought-earth is darkness, unconsciousness, intuition. It is parapsychology, art. It is intuition, darkness. Women live in thought-earth, in the intuitive vision. Women live as unconscious, illogical beings. Men live in spirit-fire, logos, logic, conscious mind. Artists are feminine, scientists are masculine, and the seed-water – eros, the one energy – is non-dual. It takes you beyond art and beyond science, it takes you beyond the conscious and the unconscious, it takes you beyond man and beyond woman. It takes you into the non-dual, the transcendental.

But the secret of the magic is to let your heavenly heart, which exists between your two eyes, function. Later on we will go into the methodology of it – how to help it function.

Enough for today.

CHAPTER 4

I Mean Business Here

The first question:

> *Osho,*
> *The river ultimately reaches the sea. The body goes and there remains*
> *only existence, the infinite. What then is this urge and the purpose of*
> *getting there now? Isn't it pushing the river?*

The problem is that man is not a river, man is very much frozen. There is no flow in man's being. Man is like ice, not like water.

If man is a river, there is no need to push it, it will reach ultimately to the ocean – it has already reached. In that very flow it has become part of the ocean: to be flowing is to be oceanic. But man is not flowing, hence the urge. The ice wants to melt, hence the effort. Once the ice has melted, then there is no need to push anything, then everything happens of its own accord.

Man has become a rock. And the reason why man has become a nonflowing rock is the mind. The body is perfectly flowing, so is the soul, but between the two, the link – the mind – is frozen ice. Once the mind goes deeper into meditation it starts melting. That's what meditation is all about: an effort to melt the mind.

You say, "The river ultimately reaches the sea." That's true, but first become a river. You say, "The body goes and there remains only existence, the infinite." True. But between the body and the soul there is a mind clinging to you, or you clinging to it. The body goes, but you don't become the infinite because you are not only surrounded by a body – that is your physical limitation; there is a psychological limitation inside it. Through the death of the body, mind will not die, it will take rebirth. It will move into another womb because it will carry so many desires which are to be fulfilled. It will again seek another womb, another body with which to fulfil those desires. That is the very foundation of the theory of reincarnation.

Mind desires, and if desires are there, then opportunities will arise in which those desires will be fulfilled. God cooperates with you. If you have desires like a dog, you will become a dog, you will have the body of a dog. Your mind creates the blueprint, and then the body follows. The body is a projection of the mind, not vice versa. Unless mind disappears completely, you will be born again and again. Once the mind is gone, then it is perfectly true: the body disappears and you are the infinite. In fact, if the mind is not there, you are the infinite – without the disappearance of the body, without the death of the body. There is no need to wait for that.

Buddha is infinite even when he is in the body because he knows he is not the body. Buddha is infinite when he leaves the body. There is no difference for him: living in the body or leaving the body is the same. You live in a house, but you don't think that you are the house. Exactly like that, an awakened consciousness lives in the body, uses the body – just as you use a car. You sit in the car, you drive the car, you know that you are not the car – you can get out of it at any moment. You need not wait for an accident to happen when the car is destroyed to feel that you are not the car. And if you don't know it when the car is there and you are in it, how are you going to know it when the car is not there? The death of the body alone will not show you that you are infinite. Either you are infinitely in the here and now, or you will never be. Infinity is your nature.

The real problem is not the body. The body is not the culprit as the so-called religions have been telling you – "The body is the culprit!" The body is not the culprit at all. The body is utterly innocent and beautiful. The culprit is the mind, the mind is the devil. You will have to dissolve the mind, hence the urge, and the purpose of all the methodologies that have developed down the ages: Tao, Yoga, Tantra, Zen, Hassidism.

Become a river and then nothing is needed. That's what *The Secret of the Golden Flower* says: Achieve inaction through action, achieve effortlessness through effort. But first comes the effort, the action – it will melt you – and then the river starts flowing. In that very flow it has reached the ocean.

The second question:

Osho,
I find it almost impossible to surrender to the male ego. Instead

I become competitive, resistant or frightened. Can you say
something about this?

The ego is neither male nor female. The ego is simply the ego. The one who becomes resistant to the male ego is the female ego.

You are aware of the male ego; you are not aware of your own ego. Who is resistant to surrender? Become more aware of your own ego and then things will be easier. Everybody is aware of the ego of the other, but nothing can be done about the ego of the other. All that can be done is only with yourself.

You say, "I find it almost impossible to surrender to the male ego." Who is this who finds it almost impossible? Find out! And then you will be surprised: ego is ego, it is neither male nor female. Don't divide it. Egos have no sex, no gender; it is the same disease. If a woman has cancer, it is cancer; if a man has cancer, it is cancer. It is not male and female. Exactly like that is the ego: the cancer of the mind.

And who is telling you to surrender to the male ego? Surrender is *never* to the other. When two persons fall in love, both surrender to love, nobody surrenders to the other. If there is an effort from the other that you should surrender to him, avoid him – this is not love. Love never demands surrender. Surrender happens naturally in love. There is no demand for it.

If the man demands surrender from your side, he does not love you. Don't get entangled into such an unloving affair. He hates you, otherwise why should he demand surrender? He wants to possess you, he wants to reduce you to a thing. He wants to use you, exploit you. He thinks of you only as a body, as a mechanism. He does not respect you as a person, as a presence. This is humiliating, this is not love. Avoid it.

But surrender happens when there is love. And nobody demands, and nobody surrenders to the other – neither the man to the woman, nor the woman to the man. They both surrender to the god of love. They both surrender to this new opening in their being. And when both surrender to love there is beauty and there is freedom. You are not reduced to being a slave. In fact, only in love do you attain dignity, only in love do you attain to your grandeur, only in love is your splendor released. This is the indication of real love: that you become more than you were before, not less, and you are freer than you ever were.

Love gives freedom. That is the very taste of love. If it is missing, if it is anti-freedom, then avoid it as one avoids the plague. Don't get into it: it is something else masquerading as love. But when love is there you will find surrender has already happened, it is simultaneous. The moment you feel love for somebody, the surrender has happened. That is what love is: not surrender – let me repeat again – to the other, but surrender to an unknown force that has taken possession of the two of you. But that is totally different from you and totally different from the other. You both have bowed down to an unknown energy. You become two pillars separate from each other, still supporting the same roof: you support something that is beyond you, above you, transcends you, but you remain separate.

Love makes you more of an individual. It does not efface your individuality. It gives you individuality, it gives you uniqueness. Love is very respectful.

You say, "I find it almost impossible to surrender to the male ego. Instead I become competitive, resistant or frightened."

These are the ways of the ego. The other may have the ego, may not have the ego – I don't know about the other, who is that other? – but one thing is certain: you have a very subtle ego. That ego becomes competitive. Ego is competitive, intrinsically competitive. The ego becomes resistant or frightened, and in the fear, in the resistance, in the struggle, in the competitiveness, love is destroyed.

One thing is certain: you have to become aware of your subtle egoistic approach towards life. Drop it. At least from your side let it disappear. And then you will be surprised: maybe the other was not demanding any surrender; it was just your ego that projected it on the other. If it is so, now you can surrender to love. If it is not so and the other is still demanding…. And you will be able to know rightly only when there is no resistance in you, when there is no fear in you, no competition in you. Then you will have clarity, you will have a transparency, you will be able to see through and through, and immediately you will know whether the other is demanding a surrender to him, or the demand is coming from something which is beyond you both. If it is from beyond you both, surrender. If it is coming from the other, avoid it – that other person is mad. He needs all compassion, pity him, but don't fall in love, because to fall in love with an egomaniac is dangerous: he will destroy you.

This much you owe to yourself.

The third question:

Osho,
You spoke of the silence one finds in the Himalayas – that it is of
the Himalayas, borrowed, and will leave when one returns to the
marketplace. Is this true of the silence I am finding in your presence?
Is it borrowed? Will it disappear when I leave from here?

This place is a marketplace. Can you find any other place which is more like the market? I could have made the ashram somewhere in the Himalayas. I love the Himalayas! For me it is a great sacrifice not to be in the Himalayas. But for a certain purpose I have not made my ashram in the Himalayas: I want to remain part of the marketplace.

And this ashram is run almost as part of the marketplace. That's why Indians are very much annoyed – they cannot understand. They have known ashrams for centuries, but this ashram is beyond their comprehension. They cannot think that you have to pay to listen to a religious discourse. They have always listened free of charge – not only free of charge, but after the discourse the ashram distributes *prasad* too. Many go to listen to the discourses not because of the discourses but for the *prasad*. Here you have to pay. What am I doing?

I want it to be absolutely a part of the marketplace because I want my sannyasins not to move into the monasteries. They have to remain in the world, their meditation should grow in the world, their meditation should not become escapist. So whatsoever peace you are finding here you will be able to retain it anywhere you go. There will be no problem, not at all. I have been managing in such a way that all that can disturb you anywhere else is present here, so you need not be afraid.

Meditators have always been afraid of a few things. For example, they have been afraid of women. Can you find anywhere in India more beautiful women than here? More alive? Living here, being here, you will become completely oblivious of the fact of who is a man and who is a woman. How long can you go on persisting in making the distinction?

The future belongs neither to man nor to woman. The future will be a kind of androgyny. The distinction between man and woman is going to disappear more and more.

In the past the distinction was very much created, culture-oriented. A girl had to be brought up in a different way than a boy – in an utterly different way. I am not saying that there is no difference. There is a difference between man and woman but that difference is only biological. But the society creates a psychological difference: "These things are allowed for boys only, because 'boys are boys' and these things are not allowed for girls." A psychological difference is created from the very beginning. The difference that you see between men and women in the world is ninety-nine percent created, nurtured; it is not natural. There is a one percent difference that is biological – that doesn't matter. Living here you live in such a togetherness that you will become oblivious of the fact of who is a man and who is a woman.

In the old days, with the old-style sannyas, people had to go away from women to the caves, to the monasteries. There are Christian monasteries where no woman has ever entered, has ever been allowed to enter. On Mount Athos there is a monastery – for twelve hundred years not a single woman has been allowed to enter. And what to say of a woman? – not even a girl of the age of six months, not even a six-month-old girl has been allowed. Just see the fear! And what kind of people must be living there if they cannot even allow a six-month-old girl? Maniacs called monks – or monkeys – but not men. They must be mad. And it is in the monasteries that all kinds of monstrosities have arisen.

Homosexuality was first born in the monasteries; it is a religious phenomenon. It was bound to be so. If you force men to live together in a place where no woman is ever allowed, sooner or later homosexuality will come. Masturbation is a monastic practice, it came out of monasteries. All kinds of perversions are bound to be there.

There are monasteries for women too – only women are allowed, no men ever – and their whole fantasy world consists of men. They cannot get magazines like *Playboy,* but who needs them when you have enough time to fantasize? Their fantasy is so pornographic that magazines like *Playboy* are nothing. Their fantasies are more psychedelic.

These people who have lived in such a monastery, if they are allowed to come back to the world, naturally, their meditation, their prayer, their religion, all will be disturbed.

Monks have been very afraid of money. Naturally, if they come into the world, money has to be tackled. You cannot live in the world without money. And monks have been so afraid that they will not even touch money. See the fear, the obsession.

Acharya Vinoba Bhave, the chief disciple of Mahatma Gandhi, does not touch money. But what kind of obsession is this? Touching a ten-rupee note, how can it harm you? And if it can harm you, what kind of spirituality is this? Such an impotent spirituality. Not only is he unable to touch it, but if you bring money in front of him he closes his eyes – he cannot even look. His guru, Mahatma Gandhi, used to keep three monkeys – somebody had given him a present. Knowing him, the present was exactly the right present. One monkey is sitting with both his hands over his eyes, not looking: "Don't look at many things in life because it is dangerous." Another monkey is sitting with his hands over his ears: "Don't listen to many things because it is dangerous." And the third monkey is sitting with his hands over his mouth: "Don't say many things because it is dangerous." And the monk has to do all three things together. That's why I say a monk is a monkey three times over.

Such a person – who cannot open his eyes, cannot open his ears, cannot open his mouth – if he comes into the world, will naturally be in difficulties. He will find that all is disturbed, all is destroyed. And in India the calamity is that these monkeys have become the leaders of this country – perverted people, suffering from abnormalities, not natural, not flowing, not in Tao.

My whole effort here is to create a miniature world where money is absolutely accepted; where women and men live together in joy, in celebration, without fear; where all that goes on in the world also continues, and alongside the meditation grows. It becomes stronger and stronger because all the challenges are there.

You can go anywhere you like: nobody can take your peace away. Your silence is yours! It is not because of me. You have earned it, you have gained it.

And a related question:

> *So what! What do you mean "society with its rules"? What about*
> *this place?*

> *Bullshit, Osho, bullshit. It's all bullshit!*

The question is from Sucheta. I have not been hard on her yet, hence the question. But from now onwards she will know: I have been really nice to her, and I am rarely nice to people.

This place has more rules than any other place. Those rules are a device – to create a certain situation in you, a challenge.

The question has arisen in her mind because she wants to work with children, and I have said no. I have told her to work somewhere else.

If I go with your likes and dislikes, your choices, I am "Osho." In this question she has not written "Osho"; otherwise she always writes "Beloved Osho," "Beloved Master." The question directly starts: "So what!"

I cannot leave you to yourself, otherwise I will not be of any help. Just because Sucheta wants to work with children I cannot allow her, because I have to take care of children too – I cannot spoil their life. Sucheta, you are spoiled by your parents, by your family, by your society; I cannot send you to the children. You are not yet capable of that. Just because *you* choose…. Anybody can choose anything, but here things have to go according to me, not according to you. Remember it! If you cannot be patient enough, then this is not the place for you, then you can leave. Guards are at every gate to prevent people from coming in, but I have not put any guards there to prevent people from going out. You can leave immediately.

If you have to be here, you have to be according to me, only then can I be of any help. I know what is needed. It is not always that which you like which is your need. Your like comes out of your mind, and your mind has to be destroyed. I cannot listen to your likes and dislikes. All these rules are made by me. The moment you become a sannyasin, you give this much authority to me: that I will decide a few things for you. And if you want to become an ashramite, then you have to give one hundred percent authority to me – that is the meaning of becoming an inmate of the ashram. She wanted to be in the ashram and I have put her outside because she is not yet capable of it. Just listen to the question and you will see. You will have to earn it; and this is not the way to earn it, remember.

It is very easy to lose this opportunity that is available to you. Your ego can become a problem, can create problems for you. Either you have to listen to *your* ego or you have to listen to me. You will have to change your whole pattern of thinking, you will have to change your very language of life; otherwise you will misunderstand.

These rules are for a certain purpose.

Madhuri was living in Lao Tzu House and suddenly I sent her to live in Jesus House. She cried, but accepted it. And she has come closer to me – closer than she ever was – in that very acceptance. More love will be showering on her from my side. You can live physically very close to me, that is one thing. She could have resisted, she could have written me an angry letter, but she has not done anything. She has not even uttered a single angry word. She cried, she was sad – and that is natural – but no anger. To live with me in the same house and then to be sent to live in another house is hard, I know. But she survived the shock and something immensely valuable has happened through it. Only later on will she understand that this was a blessing. It takes time for you to understand things. But I live in a totally different reality, and I decide from there. And I know you live in a different reality – misinterpretations are bound to be there from your side – but try to understand me. Even if you cannot understand sometimes, silently, patiently do what I say.

It happened....

The teacher asked the student, "Do you like Kipling?"
The student said, "I don't know. I have never kipled."

Marriage counselor to wife, "Do you usually wake up grumpy in the morning?"
Wife, "No, he gets up before I do."

"How did you get on with your date last night?" one hippie was asked by an elderly neighbor.

"Just great," was the reply. "I finally persuaded her to say yes."

"Oh, congratulations! When is the wedding to be?"

"Wedding? What wedding?"

To a hippie it is a different world. Yes does not mean marriage.

"Vicar, you told me I must have Faith, Hope and Charity."

"That's right."

"Well, when I tried, they called the police."

And the last:

"Are you sure that it was a marriage license you gave me last month?"

"Yes, sir. What's the matter?"

"I thought there might be some mistake, seeing that I have lived a dog's life ever since."

Sucheta, if you want to be here, you will have to learn my language, my way of seeing things, and you have to come with me; otherwise this is not the place for you. Don't waste your time here. Then it is better to leave this place soon – the sooner the better – because if you don't go with me, one day or other you will have to leave. And then you will feel very miserable because all those days that you stayed here will look like a wastage. If you want to be with me, then be with me totally, as totally as possible, then only something can happen. This happening is difficult because from your side there are so many hindrances.

The fifth question:

> Osho,
> I found the comments on rape in yesterday's discourse very offensive,
> namely, that women who are raped "wanted it." This has been
> proven to be absolutely incorrect.

Then why have you not signed the question? First: I had not said that all the women who are raped were desiring it, I said "in the majority of cases." Remember it; it makes a lot of difference. And it is only an example. There are thousands of car accidents and I say again, the majority of people who go through a car accident wanted it, were accident-prone, were hoping somehow that something would happen, were desiring it deep down, were suicidal.

The mind that you know is not all; below it there is a greater unconscious mind. In that unconscious mind you harbor many things of which you are not aware. There may be a person who is suicidal but not courageous enough to commit suicide. He will seek ways and means to commit suicide in a vicarious way: a car accident – he will not be responsible at all, nobody will say that he committed suicide. Nobody will say later on that he was a coward, that he could not face life. It is easier to have a car accident than to commit suicide.

And as far as rape is concerned, just look into your unconscious, look into your dreams. It is very rare to find a woman who has not dreamed of being raped. There is a certain attraction in it. What is the attraction? The attraction is that you are so irresistible that a person is ready to commit rape, you are so irresistible that a person is ready to go to jail for ten years, or if it is a Mohammedan country, is ready to die. If a rape is committed in a Mohammedan country and the person is caught, death is the penalty. And you will be surprised: more rapes are committed in Mohammedan countries than anywhere else.

Maybe the person who commits the rape wants to commit suicide. And this is a beautiful way to commit suicide. Can you find a better way of committing suicide? – a brave way too. And dying for love…so poetic, so romantic.

There is some violence involved in sex. Even in ordinary sex when no rape is committed, something of rape is involved. The woman always says no. Why? – because if she says yes too easily, then there is no longer that feeling, "I am needed, utterly needed." She goes on saying no and goes on meaning yes. She goes on saying no, she is provoking the man: she wants the man to be after her, she wants the man to force her. The very effort to force her, the very effort to drag her into lovemaking makes her feel good: she is "needed." This is a poor state of mind, but it is how people are.

So first I said "in the majority of cases." There are accidents also. You may not be thinking of rape at all, and a madman comes and rapes you. I am not excluding those cases, that's why I didn't say "a hundred percent." In the majority of cases, whatsoever happens to you – rape, murder, disease – is somehow, somewhere, desired by you. But I am not saying in all cases.

Now psychologists are aware that when people are prone to certain diseases... For example, nearabout the age of forty-two people have heart attacks. Why near the age of forty-two? – because that is the time when people start succeeding or have succeeded. They have the money they always wanted and now they don't know what to do: success is there and they are shocked by success. They have always lived in the hope that they will have this much money, this woman, this house, this car – and they have it. Now what? Suddenly the heart stops beating. Now what? All direction seems to be lost. If they don't have a heart attack they will be very miserable. The heart attack relieves them. Now they can say to the world, "I have to rest. The doctors have suggested rest. I cannot do any hard work."

They cannot rest without an excuse; a heart attack becomes the excuse. If they simply rest, people will say, "What are you doing? At the prime of your life, on the last rung of your success, what are you doing? You can have more money. This is the time, because when you have money more money comes. When you have success, more success comes. What are you doing relaxing, retiring?" And they will not have any excuse. A heart attack is a beautiful excuse. Nobody will say they have escaped from the world. Nobody will throw the responsibility on them. What can they do? The whole responsibility goes to the heart attack. People are not conscious of all that goes on deep inside them.

You say, "I found the comments on rape in yesterday's discourse very offensive..." But why are they so offensive – and only to one person? Nobody else has written, nobody else has felt any offense. If you are a lady – and I hope that you are a lady, because if you are a gentleman then things will be more complicated, so I trust that you are a lady – why are you feeling so offended? You must be carrying the desire inside you, hence the offense; otherwise there is no offense.

I am a madman, I go on saying things. Why should you be offended? I am not a scientist, I am not a psychologist, I am nobody – I just like gossiping. I am not a consistent man, I go on contradicting myself. You can just wait for a few days and I will contradict myself. I will say, "Never has it happened! Whenever a woman is raped she is not responsible. It is the male ego, male violence." Just wait! You have to be patient with me – I contradict myself!

But why are you offended? I must have touched a sore spot in you, something like a wound must be there. Deep down somewhere in the unconscious you want to be raped? That's why there is so much anger, so much offense. And you are afraid too – naturally – that's why you have not signed the question.

Always remember to sign it. And if you are very much afraid, you can write somebody else's name – but sign it! Then you can enjoy, and the other will be beaten. No need to be worried about it.

And you say, "This has been proven to be absolutely incorrect." Do you know that nothing is ever proven absolutely? Nothing! Man has not proved anything absolutely. There is no possibility of proving anything absolutely: new discoveries, new facts, new data, and changes have to be made. Even scientific discoveries are not absolute, so how can psychological discoveries be absolute? Psychology is not yet a science, it is still fictitious. At most you can call it, if you like the word *scientific*, you can call it science fiction. But it has nothing to do with science yet. It is struggling to be scientific, but I don't think that it ever will be, because man's mind is like mercury – you cannot make a science out of it.

And man's mind is not a single phenomenon. There are as many minds as there are people. All that psychology can hope for is to think about the average mind. But you never come across "the average," you always come across the unique. No scientific explanation is possible about the unique mind.

Psychology is not yet a science, and even science cannot claim absoluteness. What Newton did is no longer right. It looked so absolute in those days – it is no longer right. Do you think what Einstein has done will remain right for long? It cannot, it is not in the very nature of things. Life is such a mystery that the more you know about it, the more you will have to create new hypotheses – to include the new facts.

Have you known man and woman totally? Have you fathomed the feminine mind totally, so that you know absolutely that this is incorrect? Nothing is absolutely correct, nothing is absolutely incorrect. All are guesses – all are guesses. One may be a little more close to the truth, another may not be so close. But what I said has not to be taken as a general statement. It has to be taken as an object for meditation. You just meditate over it.

I am not concerned about general truths. I am talking to disciples! You have to look into yourself. If you are a woman disciple just look into yourself. Is there not somewhere a lurking desire to be raped? And if it is there, it is better to know about it, it is better to bring it to the conscious completely, because once something becomes conscious, it disappears. It can exist only in the unconscious. In the unconscious it is dangerous. If you bring it to the conscious, it evaporates. It is like pulling a tree out of the earth: bringing its roots to the light, then the tree dies. And that's exactly what happens: anything that goes on lurking in the unconscious, in the dark chamber of your soul – which is nine times bigger than your conscious mind – bring it into the conscious mind, bring it into sunlight, and if it comes there, it withers away.

What I am saying here is meant for you to meditate on. If you felt offended, then this is very good for you to meditate over: go into it, search into yourself, and don't conclude from the very beginning. Don't say, "This is wrong and has been proved absolutely wrong." First meditate, and don't try to prove it wrong or right. Just go with an open mind into your own being and search for it. And you will be surprised that the desire is lurking there. It has a kind of charm in it.

One woman went to the priest to confess. She confessed that she had been raped. And she confessed that she had come to the priest because she enjoyed it. That's why she was feeling guilty: if she had not enjoyed it, there would be no question of coming to confess.

Then she came next time and again confessed. And then she came again.

And when she came for the fourth time, the priest said, "But this is too much! Are you being raped every week?"

She said, "No, this is the same rape."

"But then why do you go on coming?"

She said, "I enjoy telling it. It feels so good."

Just go into yourself and you will find all kinds of desires lurking in you. You will find something of the sadist: that you want to torture others. You will find something of the masochist: that you want to torture yourself. You will find all kinds of things in you because man is vast and the unconscious is not an ordered place – it is chaos, it is a madhouse. But we go on repressing all that. We are so afraid to see. That's why you felt so offended. I must have touched the right spot in you, hence the offense. It is not a question of whether it is proved right or wrong. And I am not interested in that at all.

My interest is in making you more and more meditative, more and more aware of your intrinsic, innermost desires, longings, perversions, obsessions. If they can be brought to light, they will disappear. And if the unconscious can be emptied completely, you will become a buddha.

So don't simply go on arguing with me, because that is a waste of time and energy. Go in. If you cannot find any desire like that in you, so far so good. If you find it, that too is very good – you can bring it into the light and it will disappear.

The sixth question:

Osho,
I am getting old and losing all interest in women.
What should I do?

Sir, go on losing your interest! That's perfectly good, nothing is wrong in it. And be perfectly assured that no woman is going to miss you. On the contrary, they will all be very happy.

But in the West particularly, since Freud opened the Pandora's box the idea has arisen that you have to remain sexual to the very end, because sex is synonymous with life. So even if you are seventy or eighty you have to remain interested in sex. If you lose interest in sex that means you are losing interest in life, that means you are no more needed, that means you are useless now. You can drop dead or go to parliament, but you are useless.

This idea that sex and life are synonymous is utterly baseless. Sex and life are synonymous at a certain stage. In childhood they are not synonymous, in youth they are synonymous, in old age they are again not synonymous. There are phases. The child is not interested, the young man is interested – and his only interest is in sex.

But in the West there is an effort going on to remain young, you should not get old. People go on befooling themselves in many ways that they are still young. New panaceas have been found again and again – new kinds of elixirs that will keep you young forever – and people are so foolish that they are always ready to accept any nonsense to remain young. Old age is thought to be a kind of disease. To be old means you are ill – in the West. That is not right.

Old age has its own beauties, its own treasures, just as youth has its own beauties and treasures. And certainly the treasures that an old man comes upon are far more valuable than the treasures of youth, because the old man has lived his youth. He has known all that, he has seen that, he has gone through it. He has lived the illusion and he has known the disillusionment of it all. Now he is wiser than he ever was; he is becoming innocent again. When sex disappears you attain to a kind of innocence: you become a child again – and a mature child.

In the East we have a totally different vision of life. In the East we have respected the old men, not the young, because the old are at the peak – life's journey reaching its goal. In the West the old are just something to be discarded, the old are just to be thrown on some junkyard. You make houses for the old where you go on piling them up, or in the hospitals. Nobody wants anything to do with old people – as if they are meaningless, worthless. And they have lived their whole life, and they have learned many secrets of life – they can be great teachers, only they can be teachers.

In the East this has been the traditional way, that the old person should become the teacher of the young, because he has lived, grown, understood. He can give you a better direction, with more maturity, with more clarity. Old age is the age to prepare for death. And that is the greatest preparation because you will be going on the longest journey – into the unknown. If you remain interested in sex, it will keep you diverted from death. That's what is happening in the West.

In the West people have not accepted death yet as part of life. Death is a taboo, just as sex was a taboo just a hundred years ago. Nobody talked about sex a hundred years ago. It was impossible to talk about it or to write about it. It was such a taboo that in the Victorian age ladies used to cover the legs of their chairs too – because they are legs, and legs should not be shown.

Freud introduced a great revolution. The world is waiting for another Freud to destroy the greater taboo of death. He destroyed the taboo of sex, and the world is far better because of it. Freud is one of the greatest benefactors. Another Freud is needed to destroy another taboo – which is greater.

Death has to be accepted. With the acceptance of death you start accepting old age. And in acceptance there is relaxation. And once you are no more interested in sex, your whole attention can be focused on death. Remember, sex and death are polar opposites; if you remain interested in sex, when will you prepare for death? Your attention will remain focused on sex and you will die without any preparation.

Meditation is a preparation for death. Now prepare for death – meditate. You are no more interested in women – good. Now become interested in your own self. The woman is outside you; that is the interest in the other. Or if you are a woman, then the man is outside you, and that is her interest in the other. Now become interested in yourself: now go on the discovery of the self, now go on an inward journey that will prepare you for the what is to come.

You ask, "I am getting old and losing all interest in women. What should I do?" Lose interest. Allow it to happen. Don't try to create it unnecessarily. If it is going on its own, it is beautiful.

I have heard…

Max, aged seventy-six, upon returning to his apartment late one night, was startled to find a girl of about eighteen ransacking the place.

"Young woman, you are a thief!" he said. "I'm going to call the police."

"Mister," she pleaded, "if I'm arrested again, I'll be sent away for years. Please don't call the police."

"I'm sorry, but I have to do it." Max replied.

"Look," she cried, "I'll do anything. I'll give you my body."

"Okay," said the senior citizen, "take off your clothes and get in bed."

The girl did and Max quickly followed. He tried and tried and tried for about twenty minutes. Exhausted and in defeat, he finally gave up.

"It's no use," sighed Max. "I just can't make it. I'll have to call the police."

And you ask me what to do: "What should I do?" Do you want to call the police? Enough is enough. Now let that nonsense go, let that obsession go. Now turn your energy towards death: now look into death face to face, now encounter death. And to encounter death is the greatest experience in life. And if you can encounter death, you will come to know that you are deathless. To face death is the only way to know that you are deathless, that only the body dies and you never die. And once you have known it, you are ready, ready for the journey, and when death comes you will go laughing and dancing and singing into it.

And a man who can go laughing, dancing and singing into death – prayerfully, meditatively – comes to know the greatest orgasm that is in the world. Sexual orgasm is nothing, because in sexual orgasm only a small, minute part of your life energy leaves your body and you feel a great relaxation. In death your whole life energy leaves the body. No sexual orgasm can be compared with that cosmic orgasm, that total orgasm that death brings to you.

Don't miss death. Death is going to give you the greatest gift in life, the parting gift. But only a few people come to it because nobody is ready for it. Death takes you unawares. And you are so frightened, and you are so concerned with sex that you cling to life.

Do you know that it almost always happens…? In the East it has been one of the secrets to know about a man. When a man dies, if he is clinging too much to life and is still interested in sex, he will die with an erection. That shows that the poor fellow died without any readiness – even in death he was full of sex fantasies. It happens almost always – unless you have become a great meditator it is going to happen to you too – that while dying you will fantasize about sex: you will be making love, at least in your imagination. This is no way to die. This is very insulting to death, and insulting to God, and very insulting to yourself.

Let sex disappear – it is time. Relax into nonsexuality. Nonsexuality will make you centered. Stop chasing women and start chasing yourself; you cannot do both. And get ready: death may knock you down any moment. One never knows when it is coming: prepare, allow yourself to enjoy meditation as much as possible. Transform your sexual energy into meditative energy. It is the same energy, just the direction changes: it no longer flows downward and outward, it starts flowing inward and upward. And this same energy opens the bud of the golden flower in you. This is the whole secret.

Now you have come naturally to the right point, and you are asking me, "What should I do?" You are asking for some recipes to again create the disappearing sexuality. You are asking for some props, you are asking for some help, so that you can go on playing the same foolish game – even in your old age.

It is good when you are young because then you are foolish. It is very rare to become alert and aware and meditative when you are young. If you can become, you have a rare genius. But if you cannot become meditative even in old age, then you are just stupid, utterly stupid. It is good to fool around when you are young. That foolishness is part of growth, it helps you. The woman or the man outside becomes the mirror; they reflect you, they help you to see who you are. Love is very revealing. But finally one has to come to see oneself within, not in a mirror. Even the mirror has to be dropped. One has to be alone. And the purity of aloneness is infinite. And the bliss of aloneness is eternal.

Now the moment has come. Just let this interest in women go and suddenly you will find another interest arising in you – it is almost simultaneous – the interest in meditation. And then you can have the last gift that life can give to you: a meditative death – a death in *satori*, in *samadhi*, in ecstasy – and you will know the total orgasmic experience. That experience is enough; then you will never be coming back into life, into the body, into this prison.

In the East this has been our goal – how not to be born again – because this whole process of being born and dying again and again is a boring process. It is utterly futile. In the final analysis it is just a dream, and not even a nice dream but a nightmare.

My suggestion to you is: you have lived your life, you have seen the pleasures of the body, you have looked into relationships and you have learned whatsoever was to be learned from them, now it is time to turn inwards.

The last question:

Osho,
What is philosophy?

I don't know, and I don't think that anybody else knows either. Philosophy is a useless passion. I am using Jean-Paul Sartre's words. He says, "Man is a useless passion," I say man is not a useless passion – but philosophy is.

You ask me, "What is philosophy?" Nobody has ever defined it, it has remained vague. Not that definitions have not been given to it – millions of definitions have been given – but *the* definition is still missing. Each philosopher gives a definition and others contradict it. It is a game: enjoying the gymnastics of logic. It is logic-chopping. It is like chess – a very intellectual game, very absorbing, but there is no conclusion in it. It is inconclusive. The game continues from generation to generation. Slowly slowly out of this game two things have arisen: one is science, the other is religion.

Science is objective, religion is subjective. Science is experimental, religion is experiential. Philosophy is neither; it is just hanging in a limbo between the two. And slowly, slowly it is disappearing because that which is objective is being taken by science every day, and that which is subjective has already been taken by religion. Nothing is left for philosophy. So now modern philosophy only goes on thinking about language – language analysis.

Philosophers are asking the most absurd questions because they have lost all the meaningful questions; either those questions have been covered by science or by religion. Philosophy is becoming more and more empty. They cannot find even their own questions now, so either they take questions from science and they think about them, or they take questions from religion and they think about them. Their questions are borrowed. Philosophy is a dying phenomenon. It will not be a surprise that one day you suddenly come to know that philosophy has died. It is on its deathbed. You can go to any university and you can see: philosophy on its deathbed.

But why have you asked the question? That is more relevant, more important to think about. I am not teaching philosophy here. What I am saying has nothing to do with philosophy. It is absolutely experimental and experiential. My effort is to create a scientific religion – the psychology of the buddhas. So I am giving you experiments and I am giving you possibilities to experience something that you have not experienced yet. This is a lab, a workshop. We are bent upon doing something – I mean business here! Philosophy is not the concern at all.

I am very anti-philosophic and I avoid philosophy because it is playing with shadows, thoughts, speculation. And you can go on playing infinitely, *ad infinitum, ad nauseam*; there is no end to it. One word creates another word, one theory creates another theory, and you can go on and on and on. In five thousand years much philosophy has existed in the world, and to no purpose at all. But there are people who have the philosophic attitude. And if you are one of them, please drop it; otherwise you and your energy will be lost in a desert.

I will tell you about the four stages of philosophy in four stories. The first stage of philosophy, the first story:

One of my favorite stories is that of a boy and girl in New England where sleigh riding is popular during the cold winters. While riding one Sunday afternoon, bundled up in their blankets, the girl snuggled up to the boy and said, "Johnny, I'm cold."

Johnny looked over to her and said, "I'm cold, too, Jane. Why not tuck in the blankets?"

So Jane pulled the blankets closer, but pretty soon she moved even closer to Johnny and said, "My hands are still cold."

He didn't pay much attention to her and soon she nudged him with her elbow and said, "Johnny, did you hear me? My hands are cold…and besides, nobody loves me."

This time he looked over to her and said, "Jane, remember that God loves you, and you can always sit on your hands to keep them warm."

This is the first stage of being philosophic. The second stage, the second story:

A study group of philosophers had been meeting for years to study the Talmud. One member of the group had a pernicious habit of sipping a little brandy during the meeting. One night he drank just a little more than usual and became quite tipsy. His companions decided to teach him a lesson. While he was in his drunken stupor, they carried him off to the cemetery and laid him prone among the tombstones.

After a while the philosopher woke up. He looked about, frightened and aghast. Then he started to reason, "Am I alive? Or am I dead? If I'm alive, what could I be doing here in the graveyard on top of the graves? And if I'm dead, then why do I feel that I must go to the bathroom immediately?"

This is the second stage of philosophy. And the third stage, the third story:

Professor Steinberg had been having his lunch in the same Lower East Side restaurant for twenty years. Every day he left his office at noon, went to the restaurant and ordered a bowl of chicken soup – never a change.

But one day the professor called the waiter back after receiving his soup.

"Yes, professor?" inquired the waiter.

"Waiter, please taste the soup."

"What do you mean, taste the soup? For twenty years you've been eating the same chicken soup here, every day, yes? Has it ever been any different?"

The professor ignored the waiter's comments. "Please, taste this soup," he repeated.

"Professor, what's the matter with you? I know what the chicken soup tastes like."

"Taste the soup," the professor demanded.

"All right, all right, I'll taste. Where's the spoon?"

"Aha!" cried the professor.

This is the third stage. And the fourth stage, the fourth story:

A woman went to a philosophic psychologist for treatment of her delusion that she was covered with feathers. After a few sessions the philosopher said to her, "I feel that we have come to the root of this problem through our discussions and analysis, and it is now behind us. What do you think, Mrs Smith?"

"Oh," said Mrs Smith, "I think we have had some wonderful sessions and I do feel that the problem has been taken care of. But," she added, "the only thing that bothers me now is what I'm going to do with these feathers."

She raised her hand to her shoulders and began to brush, and the psychologist, the philosopher, suddenly jumped back.

"Now hold on just a minute, Mrs Smith. Don't brush those feathers on to me."

This is the fourth stage: slowly slowly, philosophy becomes a kind of madness, it leads you into neurosis because philosophy is a mind phenomenon. Science has taken the body, religion has taken the soul, only the mind is left for philosophy. And mind is potential madness. If you go on too much into the mind, you will be moving slowly slowly towards madness. It is very rare to find a philosopher who is sane. And vice versa is also true: it is very rare to find a madman who is not a philosopher.

I am not teaching philosophy here because I am teaching no-mind. And if you become a no-mind all philosophy disappears: Christian, Hindu, Mohammedan, Buddhist – all philosophies disappear; Hegelian, Kantian, Russellian – all philosophies disappear. If the mind disappears, where can the philosophy exist?

Where can it grow? Mind is the breeding ground of philosophy.

Let the mind disappear. And the beauty is, when there is no mind and nobody to philosophize and nothing to philosophize about, one comes to know. Philosophy is the blind man's effort. It is said: Philosophy is a blind man in a dark room on a dark night, searching for a black cat which is not there....

Enough for today.

CHAPTER 5
To Be One Again

In the body is the anima. The anima is feminine, yin; it is the substance of consciousness.

But, besides this, there is the animus in which the spirit shelters. The animus lives in the eyes: it sees, it dreams. But whoever is in a dark and withdrawn mood, and chained to his bodily form, is fettered by the anima. Therefore the concentration of the animus is brought about by the circulation of the light, and in this way the spirit is maintained, the anima subjugated. The method used by the ancients for escaping from the world consisted in melting out completely the slag of darkness in order to return to the purely creative. This is nothing more than a reduction of the anima and a completion of the animus. And the circulation of the light is the magical means of reducing the dark, and gaining mastery over the anima. If this method is followed, plenty of seed-water will be present of itself; the spirit-fire will be ignited, and the thought-earth will solidify and crystallize. And thus the holy fruit matures.

The one nature, when it descends into the house of the Creative, divides into animus and anima. The animus is the heavenly heart. It is of the nature of light; it is the power of lightness and purity. It is that which we have received from the great emptiness, that which is identical in form with the primordial beginning. The anima partakes

of the nature of the dark. It is the energy of the heavy and the turbid;
it is bound to the bodily fleshly heart. The animus loves life. The
anima seeks death. All sensuous desires and impulses of anger are
effects of the anima. But the pupil understands how to distill the dark
anima completely so that it transforms itself into pure light.

Once the Empress Wu asked the Master Fa-tsang if he could possibly give her a practical and simple demonstration of the principle of cosmic interrelatedness, of the relationship of the one and many, of God and his creatures, and of the creatures one to another.

Fa-tsang went to work and appointed one of the palace rooms so that eight large mirrors stood at the eight points of the compass. Then he placed two more mirrors, one on the ceiling and one on the floor. A candle was suspended from the ceiling in the center of the room.

When the empress entered, Fa-tsang lit the candle. The empress cried, "How marvelous. How beautiful."

Fa-tsang pointed at the reflection of the flame in each one of the ten mirrors and said, "See, Your Majesty, this demonstrates the relationship of the one and the many, of God to each one of his creatures."

The Empress said, "Yes, indeed, Master. And what is the relationship of each creature to the others?"

Fa-tsang answered, "Just watch, Your Majesty, how each mirror not only reflects the one flame in the center, each mirror also reflects the reflections of the flame in all the other mirrors, until an infinite number of flames fills them all. All these reflections are mutually identical; in a sense they are interchangeable, in another sense each one exists individually. This shows the true relationship of each being to its neighbor, to all that is. Of course, I must point out, your majesty," Fa-tsang went on, "that this is only a rough approximate and static parable of the real state of affairs in the universe, for the universe is limitless and in it all is in perpetual multidimensional motion." Then the master covered one of the infinite number of reflections of the flame and showed how each apparently insignificant interference affects the whole organism of our world. Kegon expresses this relationship by following the simple formula: *One in all, all in one, one in one, all in all.*

Then Fa-tsang, in order to conclude his command performance, held up a small crystal ball and said, "Now watch, Your Majesty, how all these large mirrors and all the myriad forms they reflect are mirrored in this little sphere.

See, how in the ultimate reality, the infinitely small contains the infinitely large and the infinitely large the infinitely small, without obstruction. Oh, if only I could demonstrate to you the unimpeded mutual interpenetration of time and eternity, of past, present and future. But alas, this is a dynamic process that must be grasped on a different level..."

Man is not an island; nothing is. All is interrelated, all is interdependent. Independence – the very word – is false; so is dependence. The reality is interdependence – meaning that all things are dependent on each other.

Everything is so deeply connected with everything else that nothing can exist apart. If you can understand a small roseflower in its totality, root and all, you will have understood the whole cosmos, because the whole cosmos is involved in that small roseflower. In the smallest leaf of grass all is contained. But remember, as Fa-tsang said to the empress: All illustrations, all descriptions are static, and existence is a dynamic flux. It is a river. Each thing goes on moving into each other thing. It is impossible to draw lines where one thing ends and another begins; there are no demarcating lines – there cannot be. So all distinctions are only for practical purposes, they have no existential value.

This is the first thing to be understood. This is very fundamental to the Taoist alchemy. Once this is understood, then the whole alchemy of Taoism becomes comprehensible. Then the lower can be transformed into the higher, because the lower contains the higher already. The baser metal can be transformed into gold because nothing is separate. The baser contains the gold already: as above, so below; as below, so above.

The very idea that all is interconnected makes transformation possible. Where things are not interconnected there is no possibility of any transformation. If the world consists of the philosopher Liebnitz's monads – windowless, separate, atomic individuals, not connecting with each other at all because they are windowless – then there is no possibility of any transformation.

Transformation is conceivable only because you are me, I am you; we interpenetrate. Can you think of yourself as separate even for a single moment? You cannot even imagine yourself as separate. The flower cannot be separated from the tree; the moment it is separated it dies. The tree cannot be separated from the earth, the earth cannot be separated from the sun, the sun cannot be separated from other stars, and so on and so forth. You separate the leaf and the leaf dies. You separate the flower, the flower dies. You separate the tree from the earth, the tree dies. You separate the earth from the sun and the earth dies.

Death means separation; life means no separation. Hence the ego is bound to die because that is your idea of separation. To think of oneself in terms of ego is the only cause of death – because the ego is already dead. You can go on flogging the dead horse, but for how long? It is going to die. It is already dead, that's why it is going to die. That which is alive in you cannot die – life is eternal. But life is not yours, you cannot possess it. Life belongs to all. Life has a vastness, infinity. Death is tiny, death is individual; life is universal. So when you live you are part of the universe, and when you die you die only because you think you are separate. The more you feel part of the whole, the more life you will have.

Jesus says, "Come to me and I will give you life abundant." What is the secret of life abundant? The secret is: die as the ego, disappear as a separate entity, and the whole universe and all that it contains is yours. Stop possessing and all is yours. Possess, and you are tiny and limited, and you are going to die. The secret of becoming more alive consists of a single phenomenon of dropping the idea of separation. And whenever it happens, you feel life becoming aflame in you. Even if it happens in small measures…

If you fall in love with somebody, life is aflame in you. And it is not that much has happened – just two persons are feeling one. Learn the lesson from love: just two persons feeling one, and what joy and what ecstasy! Think, if you fall in love with the whole then how much ecstasy and how much joy is going to happen. That is life abundant, life infinite.

Separate yourself… There are a few people who live so egoistically that they cannot love; they are the most miserable people in the world. My definition of hell is: to live in separation. To live in non-separation is heaven, to disappear completely, utterly into the whole is *moksha,* nirvana – it is ultimate freedom.

The second thing that we must all understand: that life is polar. That is also very fundamental to the Taoist approach. But the polarity is not that of opposition. The polarity means that the opposites are complementary to each other, they support each other. Life cannot exist without death, hence death is not the enemy. How can death be the enemy of life if life cannot exist without it? It has to be the friend: it prepares the fundamental ground for life, it helps life, it provokes life, it challenges life.

Just think: if your body were going to live for eternity, you would not live at all, because you would have an infinity to postpone everything. "Why love today if there is tomorrow? And if tomorrow is infinite, then why bother? Why dance today? We will see tomorrow." Just imagine: if your bodily life were going to be eternal, your postponement would become eternal.

You cannot postpone because you are not certain whether there is going to be any tomorrow or not. Nobody knows whether the next breath will come in or not, hence only foolish people postpone. The wise man lives, and the wise man lives in the here and now. He cannot afford postponement because he knows, "Only this moment is mine, only this very moment is mine. The next moment may be, may not be. How can I postpone? How can I say 'tomorrow'?"

The foolish man postpones until tomorrow, the wise man lives now. The wise man knows no other time than now and no other space than here, and the foolish man goes into things which could have been postponed for eternity – he lives them right now. If he is angry, he lives it right now. If he is loving, he says, "We will see tomorrow." All that is stupid he goes on living, and all that is luminous he goes on postponing. The wise man also postpones, but he only postpones stupid things.

Gurdjieff used to say to his disciples, "When my grandfather died I was only nine years old. He called me close to his death-bed and whispered in my ear." He had tremendous love for this small boy. He must have seen the potential of the boy. He whispered in the ears of the boy, "I have nothing to give to you except a simple piece of advice, and I don't know whether you will be able to understand it right now or not. But remember it! Someday you may become capable enough, mature enough to understand it. Just remember it. And it is simple advice: If you want to do anything wrong, postpone it for twenty-four hours and if you want to do something right, never postpone it even for a single moment. If you want to be angry, violent, aggressive, postpone it for twenty-four hours. If you want to be loving, sharing, do not postpone it even for a single moment. Just live it right now, immediately!"

And Gurdjieff used to say to his disciples, "That simple advice transformed my whole life."

How can you be angry if you can postpone it for twenty-four hours? It is impossible. To be so calm and quiet as to postpone it for twenty-four hours is enough guarantee that you are not going to be angry. And who can be angry if he can postpone it for twenty-four hours? Twenty-four hours of contemplation and the whole absurdity will be plain to you, and the whole thing will look ridiculous. And Gurdjieff was really transformed by this simple message. Sometimes very simple messages can transform you…but you have to live them.

Life exists because there is death. Death gives intensity to life, death challenges life. It provokes you to live and to live to the maximum, at the optimum, because who knows? – there may be no tomorrow. Death is always provoking you, goading you to live, and to live totally. Then death is not against life but its friend.

So is the case with all the polarities: the negative and the positive, love and hate, beauty and ugliness, day and night, summer and winter, and so is the case with man and woman. Man cannot be without the woman, and the woman cannot be without the man. They are part of one dialectical process. Between these two poles there is both attraction and repulsion, because attraction and repulsion cannot be separated. Hence you feel attracted towards the woman or towards the man and repulsed at the same time. A part of you wants to be with the woman, a part of you wants to be alone. You are always hesitating.

If you are with the woman or with the man, you start longing for the freedom – to be on your own, to be alone. Suddenly you become very interested in being alone and free, and you don't know where this desire to be free is coming from. The woman or the man, the other, is provoking it. The moment you have left the other, this desire, this longing, this great longing to be alone will disappear. And then you are surprised, really surprised: when you are alone you simply feel lonely. You don't feel that joy that you had contemplated, you don't see any freedom; you simply see loneliness surrounding you, and your whole existence becomes cold, frozen, dark. Again the desire arises to be with the other. Now you hanker for love, for togetherness.

This is the problem between man and woman: they are attracted and repulsed together, simultaneously. They want to come to be together and they want to be separate and alone, on their own. Hence the constant conflict between man and woman.

Marriage is a love-hate affair, an attraction-repulsion affair. If the marriage lasts long it only can last if there are mini-divorces happening every day – only then can it last long. If the man and the woman have decided not to fight, then it is a plastic marriage. They will be together, they will manage to be together, but they will never be together in reality; they will never know those moments of unity. They are only pretending. They are being polite, but not true, not authentic.

Marriage is a kind of intimate enmity. It is an intimate enmity, it is a friendly fight, it is a war. Yes, between two wars there are peaceful moments too, and they are beautiful because of the two wars.

Couples go on fighting – that's how they keep the flame of love alive. Once they fight, they go away from each other. When they are far away from each other in their psychologies, they start hankering for the other, they start missing the other. Then they start seeking and groping for the other. Then they come close, and very close...because they have tasted something of loneliness. Now they want to be very close. Once they have tasted of closeness they want to be separate again.

So don't be worried about it. It is a fundamental phenomenon. You cannot escape it. The only way to escape is to have a pretend marriage, which is not a true marriage: remain polite to each other. It is a kind of contract that, "I need you and you need me," that, "I will scratch your back and you scratch my back" – that's all – "because I need you and you need me. You are my security, I will be your security." It is a legal contract, but not marriage.

This is the second fundamental to be understood before you can move on and enter into the sutras.

And the third and the most important thing: the third fundamental is that no man is only man and no woman is only woman. Man is both, woman is both – both are both. Man contains a woman within him, and so is the case with a woman: the woman contains a man within her. So it is not only a question of the outside man or outside woman; it is also an inner phenomenon because the outer and the inner correspond. Just as I said, "as below, so above," I can say, "as outer, so inner."

Your inner reality is also the same as your outer reality: they correspond, they balance. Now more complexity arises because each man has a woman within him, and he has to come to terms with her. It is not just a question of having a woman outside that you love; otherwise things would have been less complicated.

Whenever two persons are in love, there are really four persons. In each bed there are four persons – you can understand the complexity. Whenever two persons make love, there are four persons making love – it is always group sex! – because the man has a woman inside him and the woman has a man inside her. And it is bound to be so because each is born out of the marriage of a man and a woman. Something of the father will be in you – fifty percent, something of the mother will be in you – fifty percent. To each person the father contributes and the mother contributes. You may be biologically a man – that simply shows that physically you have the mechanism of the man – but deep in your psyche you are neither man nor woman, you are both. That's why I say if we have to use one word for both, man and woman...

Up to now we have been using "man" – that means it contains both. This is only because man has been very dominant in the past. But in the future the pendulum may swing to the other pole and that will be far more true, because the word *man* does not contain "woman," but the word *woman* contains "man." It will be better to use "woman" as a general word for both. And so is the case with "he" and "she." "She" contains "he," but "he" does not contain "she." It will be better to use "she" for both and "woman" for both. It will be better to use "she" for God than "he."

Both contain each other. Because of this there is a possibility of homosexuality – because of this fundamental duality inside. You may be a man on the outside, and you may become attuned to your inner woman inside. There is no problem in it. Your spirit remains free. Inside it can either become identified with the inner man or it can become identified with the inner woman. If you are physically a man and you become identified with the woman inside, homosexuality will be the consequence. It can happen in many ways, it can happen for many reasons. So homosexuality is possible because of this inner duality.

And now science is even capable of changing your physical sex. That too is possible, because the Taoist finding has been found to be scientifically true, too. Now just by changing the hormones and your chemistry a little bit, the man can become a woman and the woman can become a man – even physiologically. That simply shows that naturally you are both. Even the difference in the body is only of emphasis.

And sometimes it happens of its own accord too. It has been found that a woman becomes a man or a man becomes a woman. The difference must not have been much – perhaps only very, very slight: fifty-one percent man, forty-nine percent woman; the balance is just a little more on the side of being a man. It can change in the course of life. New hormones, new food, new climate, new atmosphere, new emotions, illnesses, or anything can change the balance, and the man can become a woman or the woman can become a man. And now science knows that it can be done very easily.

There is every possibility that in future people will change their sex more often, because if you can live both the polarities in one life, then why not? If you can enjoy both visions, then why not? You will have more freedom. You have lived as a man for thirty-five years, and enough is enough. And you would like to see how it is from the other side, because there is no other way to know how it is from the other side than to be on that side.

My own observation of thousands of people has been this: that if a person is a man in this life, in the next life he is born as a woman and vice versa. And the reason is simple: he becomes tired of being a man or becomes tired of being a woman, and starts hankering deep down for the other pole. And naturally, in the next life, because of this great desire to be the other, he is born as the other.

These are the three fundamentals. First: everything is interdependent. Second: life is polar and the polarities are not opposites but complementaries. And third: that each is double inside, no one is single.

In India we have the concept of *ardhanarishwar*. That corresponds to the Taoist approach. Shiva has been sculpted, painted as both – half man, half woman. Half of his body is that of a man and half of his body is that of a woman. When for the first time those statues were discovered by the West, the West laughed – it looked so absurd. What is the point of it? Now they have understood what the point of it is. It is one of the most fundamental things of life. So are you, just like Shiva: half-half.

These sutras are concerned with this inner polarity, and unless you transcend this inner polarity you will not attain to the one, you will remain two. Meditation is a way to transcend this polarity within you. Meditation takes you away from all dualisms and enables you to realise your inner focus.

In ordinary life you remain dual and in the space of twenty-four hours you change many times from one pole to the other. Watch. You may be a man, but sometimes you are very feminine, very vulnerable. You may be a woman, but there are moments in the daytime you are very masculine. When the woman is masculine she becomes very, very aggressive – more aggressive than any man can ever be, because her aggressiveness is very fresh, unused, just like unused land is very fertile. And so is the case with man. If a man is tender, he is very tender – more than the woman – because that is unused soil. That part of his being has not been used; it is fresh, very alive. So this strange phenomenon is observed again and again if you become a little watchful.

Woman is generally loving; man is not generally loving. Woman is only sometimes quarrelsome, but when she is, then she really is. Man is only loving at certain moments, but when he is, he really is. Those are the unused parts of their being. When they are used they have a freshness.

This inner polarity keeps you in a kind of anguish, conflict; without it you cannot exist. The one remains invisible – that's why God is invisible. To become visible the one has to become two. You have to write with white chalk on a blackboard, only then can those words be seen.

To exist, one needs contrast. That is why in the daytime you cannot see stars, in the nighttime you can: the darkness of the night becomes the background. The stars are there as much as in the night – they don't go anywhere, they can't go anywhere. They are where they are. They don't start coming in the night, they don't start hiding somewhere in the day – they are where they are – but in the day the contrast is missing. You cannot see them, they are invisible.

God is invisible. If he wants to become visible he will have to become man and woman, he will have to become two. He will have to become matter and spirit, he will have to become body and soul, he will have to become this and that. Only the two are visible. The world consists of the two, the world is dual. And the moment you can manage to make this duality disappear in oneness, you will become invisible. That is the meaning of the Taoist saying, which seems very mysterious, that the man of Tao becomes invisible. It has great significance, but it is a metaphor. It does not mean that you cannot see Lao Tzu or you cannot see me. You are seeing me already, but still you are not seeing *me*. That part has become invisible. The polarity has disappeared inside, the duality is no more there. Only the dual can be seen, the non-dual becomes unseen.

God has to become two, only then the game, the play, is possible. Ancient Indian scriptures say, "He felt very lonely." "He" means God. He felt very lonely, he longed for the other, that's why he became two. He became man and woman, cow and bull, and so on and so forth. The whole existence is sexual; by "sexual" I mean dual. The whole existence is sexual. Sooner or later science is going to discover that there are planets which are male and there are planets which are female. It has to be so. Ancient astrology says so, and I perfectly agree with it: Everything is dual. That's why the sun is represented as being male and the moon as being female. It is not poetry, it is fact. Science may not yet have discovered it, but it has to be so. If everything is dual, then there cannot be any exceptions.

Your attraction for the woman or for the man keeps you in manifestation. Now you will be able to understand why the great mystics down the ages have been teaching you how to go beyond sex – because unless you go beyond sex you will not go into God, unless you go beyond sex you will never go beyond the two; you will remain tethered to the duality of the world. The "world" means God manifest, and "God" means the world disappearing into unmanifestation again. That too is a duality: manifestation, nonmanifestation.

In Christian theology things are not so deep, they are very superficial. In Christian theology you have only creation. What about de-creation? How can there be creation without de-creation? In the Eastern theology they are both together: *srushti* means creation, *pralaya* means de-creation. There is a moment when God becomes manifest, and then there is a moment when God becomes unmanifest again – all disappears into nothingness, zero follows. Just like you, as I told you in the beginning: you are with your beloved, you become tired, you want to meditate, you want to go to the Himalayas; God also becomes tired of the world – naturally so – then he wants to go into retirement, then he disappears into oneness. Dissolution follows, all disappears. But again, how long can you sit in a Himalayan cave? Even God becomes tired of it. He starts seeking and searching and creating the other again.

And it happens exactly so in each individual soul: you live life, then you become tired, then you want to go beyond life; you have lived your body and you are tired, now you want to go beyond the body. And then you can understand my insistence, why I say don't be afraid of the world and don't escape from the world, because the world is the very place where renunciation happens; it is a polarity. That's why I don't say escape from the woman or the man. If you escape you may remain interested.

Don't escape. Live it through and through. Indulge in the world, and the very indulgence will become renunciation. Out of that very indulgence you will start feeling that now it is time to disappear into absolute aloneness. And if you are really tired, only then can you go into that absolute aloneness.

People are bound to misunderstand me. In India I am one of the most misunderstood men. They think I am teaching people indulgence – I am teaching renunciation. They think I am teaching a worldly kind of sannyas. They don't understand. I am teaching real sannyas, because real sannyas arises only out of worldly experience. Real sannyas is not possible in a cave in the Himalayas. It will be unreal, imposed, and deep down you will remain worldly and you will continue to hanker and dream of the world.

Live in the world. Really live in it so you get tired, wearied, finished with it – so much so that one day suddenly it loses all meaning for you, and the renunciation has happened. To me, the real renunciation happens in the marketplace, and only in the marketplace.

Now the sutras.

> In the body is the anima. The anima is feminine, yin; it is the
> substance of consciousness.

In each being there is anima. "Anima" means the feminine principle, the passive principle, the inactive principle, the woman, "...yin; it is the substance of consciousness". It is not consciousness itself but the substance – without it consciousness cannot exist. It is the very matter. It is the house in which consciousness lives – without it consciousness cannot live. The woman…and remember by "woman" I don't mean just woman, I mean the woman principle. And that you have to remember continuously, otherwise you will start feeling that these Taoist people seem to be against woman. They are not. They are not saying anything against or for; they are simply describing. And they are not saying anything for man or for woman; they are talking about the principles of womanhood and manhood.

> In the body is the anima. The anima is feminine yin; it is the
> substance of consciousness.

That's why, because of the feminine principle, women remain too much attached to their bodies. Man is not so attached to his body, really he is careless about the body. If there is no woman around, the man becomes dirty, dusty, the room becomes unclean as if he is not aware of all this. You can see whenever you enter a room whether the man lives alone or if there is a woman in the house. It is so simple. You can see whether the man is a bachelor or not just by seeing his room. The books have collected dust for months. He is not careful about the body, the material part of himself. But the woman is very careful, immensely careful, hence she stands so long before the mirror.

One day Mulla Nasruddin was catching flies. He caught a few flies and he told his wife, "I have found two female flies and two male flies."
The woman said, "This is surprising. How did you discover the sex of the flies?"
He said, "Two were sitting on the mirror and two were reading the newspaper!"

It is very simple. The woman is immensely tethered to the body, to the substance, to the house. If man had been left alone, at the most there would have been tents but not houses. It is woman who has created the whole of civilization, because without houses there would be no civilization, remember. Without houses there would be no cities, and civilization grows in cities. The very word civilization comes from citizens – the people who live in the cities. Woman has created the whole civilization. Man would have remained a vagabond, a wanderer, a traveler, a hunter: he would have rushed from one place to another. You can see it in many ways. There are many manifestations of it. The West is more male-oriented, hence you see so many Western tourists moving around the world. You don't see so many Eastern tourists. The East is very feminine.

The woman remains attached to property: the house, the car, the land, her ornaments, her clothes. This is because of the principle inside: she is the substance of consciousness. And remember, without a woman the spirit cannot soar high. Great poetry is born through man, but the cause is always the woman.

You don't come across great women poets. I have looked into the poetry that women write. They try hard, but nothing much happens. Madhuri writes great poetry, but it is not really poetry. Woman cannot write poetry. She can inspire poetry – that is true. No great poetry arrives in the world without a woman somewhere in the background. She inspires. Her presence, her love, her caring creates it. She need not write it, the man will write it. But she is the inspiration, the cause – a very subtle cause. No women are great painters; not that they don't paint. Particularly in the modern age, they do everything that man has always been doing…there is great competition. They think they have to do all the things that man has been doing. They think it is because of these things that man has become important. The logic is fallacious. They will only become merely imitation men; they will lose their own soul and in the end they will always remain secondhand. In the world of men, to compete with men, they will remain secondary. They will never be primary. That is not the way to compete.

If you become like a man, you will never be as competent as a man – how can you be? His male principle is behind him. You will become ugly, you will become rough, you will lose all softness. That's why the "Lib Movement" has been one of the most disastrous things that has happened to women. And the reason is not that their ideology is wrong, its implementation is wrong.

Woman *is* equal to man, but she is not the same as man…and she should not be. She should follow her own nature, she should listen to her own soul. She has a different vibe, she has a different function to fulfill in the world, a different destiny. If she follows man and imitates, she is lost. And the more she is lost, the more she will become uprooted from her being. The more she becomes false, plastic, synthetic, the more desperate she will be. That's why the "Lib" women are very angry, constantly in a rage. The rage is that they are feeling frustrated. They are not as they want to be, they cannot be – it is against nature. There is no need either.

> *In the body is the anima. The anima is feminine, yin; it is the*
> *substance of consciousness.*

Meditate over the words "substance of consciousness," the very foundation of consciousness. It is not consciousness itself but the house where consciousness lives.

But, besides this, there is the animus in which the spirit shelters.

Animus is the male principle, yang.

The animus lives in the eyes: it sees, it dreams.

The feminine principle lives in the body, it is very material. That's why women are always materialistic. Their considerations are very practical, they are very pragmatic.

Mulla Nasruddin was saying to me one day that he never quarrels with his wife.

I asked him, "How do you manage it? Surely it is almost impossible, or next to impossible to be able to get through the day in total agreement."

He said, "We have managed it perfectly well for many years. On the first night we decided a single principle and we have followed it. And the principle is: she decides about the small things and I decide about the big things."

I asked, "What do you mean by small things and big things?"

He said, "For example, what car to purchase, what house to live in, what school the children have to be sent to, what food has to be eaten, what clothes have to be purchased – all these small things she decides."

And I said, "What do you decide?"

He said, "Whether God exists or not, whether there is a hell and heaven or not. All the great problems – that is for me. And the principle has worked out perfectly well. She never interferes in the great things, I never interfere in the small things. I am master of my own world, she is master of her own world. We never have the cause to overlap."

The feminine principle is rooted in matter, rooted in the body. But man dreams.

Man is a dreamer. The male principle is the principle of dreaming. No woman can understand why people are so interested in going to the moon. It looks so foolish. For what? What are you going to get there – some shopping? Better to go to M.G. Road than to go to the moon. What will you be doing there? For what? And risking your life? No woman can understand why man wants to climb Everest. What are you going to get there? It looks so ridiculous. And all women deep inside know that all men are childish: "Let them play, let them go and do their things." She knows perfectly well that they are interested in foolish things. The football match, cricket – all nonsense, it makes no sense. You throw the ball on that side and they throw the ball to your side, and this goes on and on…What is the point of it?

The woman is practical, down-to-earth. She is earthly. The male principle is like the sky and the female principle is like the earth. Man dreams, plans, desires, longs for unknown things. Man is an adventurer, ready to risk his life for any dream that takes possession of him.

The woman lives in the ears and the man lives in the eyes, hence the desire in women to gossip. Such immense joy in gossiping… Just look at two women gossiping – they look as if they are in such ecstasy.

I have heard…

Once there was a competition in China – a competition to decide who was the greatest liar in the country – and many people came and told many lies. But the man who won the prize was the man who said, "I saw two women in a park sitting silently on one bench for half an hour."

He won the first prize. It is impossible!

Because of the woman, the fall, the original sin happened. The snake must have tried on Adam first. But Adam is not the ears, he is the eyes; he must have seen the tricky snake, and he must have said, "Keep to yourself. Don't bother me. I have my own dreams." But the snake persuaded Eve. He must have gossiped with her. This was gossip that "What are you doing? Here is the tree of knowledge and God has deceived you. If you eat the fruit of this tree you will become as immortal as God. If you eat the fruit of this tree you will know all that God knows. You will be omniscient, omnipotent, omnipresent."

The woman naturally became curious – such a practical thing. The snake persuaded her. The snake is the first salesman. Salesmen don't go to men; they only knock on the door when the man has gone to the office. The woman has to be persuaded. Only the woman has ears.

The ears are the passive part of your being, the receptive part. Something can enter through the ears. The eyes are the aggressive part. You cannot be aggressive with the ears, remember. But with the eyes you can be aggressive. You can look in such a way at a person as if your eyes were daggers. You can offend people with your eyes or you can love people with your eyes. You can reach people with your eyes or you can become unreachable. Somebody can look into your eyes so vacantly that he becomes unreachable. Somebody can look into you so absently that he is unreachable. Or somebody can look with such desire, such passion, such longing, such caring, that his eyes almost start caressing your body. The eyes are the aggressive parts; they can project, they can reach.

In India, the person who stares at women offensively is called *luchcha*. And you will be surprised: the word *luchcha* comes from *lochan*. *Lochan* means eyes. He is raping with his eyes; his eyes can almost become his genital organs. Eyes are dangerous.

Ears are very innocent. They only take in. They are feminine.

> *The animus lives in the eyes: it sees, it dreams. But whoever is in*
> *a dark and withdrawn mood, and chained to his bodily form, is*
> *fettered by the anima.*

But whenever you are in a withdrawn mood, in a mood of passivity, then you are chained to the body and you are chained by the anima. It does not matter whether you are man or woman. If a woman is using her eyes and is trying to see rather than trying to listen, she becomes animus. If a man is trying to listen, he becomes anima. A disciple becomes anima – has to become – because a disciple needs to become all ears and nothing else.

The master is all eyes, and the disciple is all ears. The master has to see and has to see the deepest in you, he has to penetrate your very core. And the disciple has to listen, to be attentive, to be available – to be allowing the master to reach the very innermost core of his being.

The disciple becomes feminine. That's why women are the best disciples in the world. Man finds a little difficulty in becoming a disciple. Even if he becomes, he becomes a disciple reluctantly. He resists, he fights, he doubts, he creates many, many ways to somehow escape. If he cannot, then helplessly he relaxes – but helplessly. The woman jumps joyously. The greatest disciples have been women, and the proportion has always remained the same. If there are five disciples one will be a man, four will be women; that has been the proportion. It was so with Mahavira, it was so with Buddha, it is so with me. It has always been so.

Man thinks women are starry-eyed, hypnotically available, suggestible. These are a man's condemnations. He thinks that he himself cannot be hypnotized. Women are very, very ready to be hypnotized, he thinks. In a way he is right and in a way he is wrong too. If the woman comes to the snake she will be converted by the snake. If the woman comes to a buddha she will be converted by a buddha. Yes, she is suggestible, it all depends to whom she comes. If a man listens to the snake, he will not be converted; he will be saved from the snake. But if he comes to listen to Buddha, he will not be converted there either. Now he has missed his salvation.

> *Therefore the concentration of the animus is brought about by the*
> *circulation of the light, and in this way the spirit is maintained, the*
> *anima subjugated.*

The light has to circulate in the eyes. The eyes are the most lighted part of your being. Taoists say your eyes are parallel to the sun. If you don't have eyes you cannot see light, and only the similar can see the similar. Your eyes are condensed light, that's why you can see light through the eyes. Your ears are condensed sound, that's why you can hear through the ears.

The anima in everybody, whether man or woman, has to be subjugated. Why? – because it is the form, it is the body, it is matter. The spirit has to be the master, the spirit has to rise above the body. The spirit has to make the body follow it, not vice versa. So whether one is a man or a woman doesn't matter; the anima inside has to be made a follower of the animus because only the animus can search and seek. And if the woman is following on behind, the animus can then go perfectly, deep into reality.

If the poet knows that the woman is behind him, supporting him, his poetry can soar very high. If the man knows that the woman is always with him, he has great strength, he can go on any adventure; the moment he feels that the woman is not with him, his energy is cut off. Now he has only dreams, but they are impotent – they have no more energy, they cannot be realized.

The realizing factor is the woman, the dreaming factor is the man. In the search for God or truth, the man has to lead and the woman has to follow. Inside you the animus has to become the master and the anima has to become the disciple – and remember again, irrespective of whether you are man or woman.

> *The method used by the ancients for escaping from the world*
> *consisted in melting out completely the slag of darkness in order to*
> *return to the purely creative.*

Woman is stagnant, man is dynamic. That's why you see women looking so restful and men looking so restless. Even when you were a child, just a small child, a baby, the difference was there. The boy baby is very restless, is trying to grab this, to grab that, trying to reach somewhere; he is a nuisance. And the girl baby is never a nuisance; she sits silently hugging her doll. She is also a doll, a tremendous restfulness. The principle of rest is woman and the principle of restlessness is man, hence the roundness and the beauty of woman and the constant feverish state of man.

But to grow you will need the restless principle in you, because growth means change. The woman is basically orthodox, the man is basically unconventional. The woman always supports the status quo and the man is always ready to go for any stupid revolution. Anything changing and he is for it. Whether it is changing for good or bad, that is not such an important thing: change is good. The woman is always for the old, the established – whether it is good or bad is not the question: because it has always been so, so it has to be so.

Growth needs the principle of stasis in you to melt. The woman in you is frozen; it has to be melted so you can become a river. But the river also needs the support of the banks – which are static. If the river has no banks it will never reach the ocean. And if the river is frozen it will never reach the ocean. So the river has to melt, become water, and still has to take the support of the banks, which are static. The perfect man is one who has used his dynamism as the river and who has used his stasis as the banks. This is the perfect balance. Then you have used your animus to grow and you have used your anima to make your growth an established fact, not just a momentary phenomenon.

This is nothing more than a reduction of the anima and a completion of the animus.

But ordinarily, men, women – everybody has become static. Even men are so orthodox. Christians, Hindus, Mohammedans, Jainas – even men are so orthodox. They have fallen victim to their anima, their animus has been subjugated. It has to be released.

That's my whole effort here: to release your animus from the grip of the anima. Once the animus is released from the grip of your anima, then we can use the anima too, but not before. Hence my insistence on dynamic methods of meditation. Only once in a while do I suggest that people go to Zazen, Vipassana – only when I see that their animus is flowing, now they can use their anima. Vipassana, Zazen are anima methods, feminine methods. Sufi Dancing, Dynamic Meditation, Nataraj, they are animus methods. First you have to become a river, only then can your banks be used as supports.

*And the circulation of the light is the magical means of reducing
the dark, and gaining mastery over the anima. If this method
is followed, plenty of seed-water will be present of itself; the
spirit-fire will be ignited, and the thought-earth will solidify and
crystallize. And thus the holy fruit matures.*

The holy fruit is neither male nor female. The holy fruit matures only in
wholeness, when your anima and animus are supporting each other like the two
wings of a bird. Then eros is released, logos is released, intuition is released.
Then you start flying into the sky and yet you remain rooted in the earth.

A tree, to go high in the sky, will need deep roots in the earth. The earth is
anima, the sky is animus. And the higher the tree goes into the sky, the deeper it
has to go into the earth – in the same proportion.

*The one nature, when it descends into the house of the Creative,
divides into animus and anima.*

God is one, but when he becomes creative, he divides himself into two: animus
and anima. Without it there is no possibility of manifestation, without it there
will be no dialectic. God divides himself into thesis and antithesis, because only
through thesis and antithesis the challenge, the conflict, the struggle. And through
the struggle, the friction, energy is created. It is just like when you strike two stones
and fire comes up. It is just like when you clap two hands and sound is created.

Zen masters say, "Find the sound of one hand clapping." What do they
mean? They mean go beyond the two so you can find the One. But that One
is the unmanifest God, that One is the very source from which we have come.
And we can reach the source only when our two-ness has disappeared. Now
this two-ness has to be used in such a way that the thesis and antithesis become
synthesis. That is the whole art of life and that's what I am teaching you.

My sannyasin has to be a synthesis of man and woman, of day and night, of
world and renunciation, of matter and spirit, of earth and sky.

*The animus is in the heavenly heart. It is of the nature of light;
it is the power of lightness and purity. It is that which we have
received from the great emptiness, the great sky, that which is
identical in form with the primordial beginning. The anima
partakes of the nature of the dark.*

Hence the mystery of the woman. No man has ever been able to unravel the mystery. Only if one has gone beyond both, only if one has become a buddha can one know the mystery of both man and woman. Otherwise no man has ever been able to plumb the depths of a woman; the woman remains mysterious, dark, a dark night – you cannot see clearly, you can grope at the most. You can never be logically clear about the woman. She never follows logic. Her path is very zig-zag: she jumps to conclusions directly without ever going through the process. The man goes step by step, through the process; he is methodical.

The woman is a poet in the sense that she is intuitive. She may not create poetry – she is a poet without creating any poetry. Her life is her poetry, and it is as dark as poetry – mysterious, vague, ambiguous. Nothing is clear, nothing can ever be clear: the woman cannot be demystified, she remains always a question mark.

Man is clear, like light. Hence man looks shallow, woman looks deep. Hence man seems to be completely on the surface: you can know about him. If you know about him you can predict him, but you can never predict a woman. She remains unpredictable, hence the darkness. These are metaphors.

It is the energy of the heavy and the turbid...

And the woman, the principle of the feminine, keeps you tethered to the earth; it is gravitation.

...it is bound to the bodily fleshly heart. The animus loves life. The anima seeks death.

The woman is more like death. Don't feel offended, this is just a description. If the words *anima* and *animus*, *man* and *woman* create some trouble in you, you can replace them with X and Y. But that is what *The Secret of the Golden Flower* is doing. These are just metaphors. To make them anthropomorphic helps them to be understood more clearly.

Man is interested in life, woman is interested in security. Man is interested in love, woman is interested in safety. Man is interested in adventure, woman is interested in comfort, convenience. Woman is death. By "death" there is no condemnation meant or supposed, just that the quality of death is security. You are secure only when you are dead: then nothing can happen to you anymore.

But man wants to seek and search, to risk. That's why the husband goes on looking for other women and the woman goes on watching the husband.

She cannot conceive why he is still interested in other women – "I am here!" But the male principle is always interested in something new, in the sensational, the new thrill. And sometimes it happens that his own wife may be a beauty and he may start fooling around with an ugly woman. Nobody can see the point of it – what is happening. "You have such a beautiful woman, and what are you doing?"

But you don't understand the male principle. The male principle is basically polygamous and the feminine principle is monogamous. She wants to settle. She is more interested in marriage than in love. She is interested in love only to get married, and man gets married only because he is interested in love.

There is an ancient saying that the world would be immensely joyful if every man remained unmarried and every woman was married. But how can it be done? It is impossible.

> *The animus loves life. The anima seeks death. All sensuous desires*
> *and impulses of anger are effects of the anima. But the pupil*
> *understands how to distill the dark anima completely so that it*
> *transforms itself into pure light.*

But the alchemy consists in understanding these two principles in each of you – man or woman – and in transforming the anima, the dark part in you, into the light part; in helping the dark part to move, in helping the dark part help the light part and not to fight with it.

If your anima can help your animus that is real marriage, the inner marriage. Then you start becoming integrated, then your light is no more shallow – it has the depth of darkness; and your darkness is no more dark – it has the light of lightness. Then anima and animus melt into each other. And when they melt utterly, the world has disappeared, you are again one. And to be one is to know God, to remain two is to remain in the world. And the secret, the experiment, has to happen within you; it has nothing to do with the outside world.

Inside you these two principles are constantly in fight. Call them life-death, darkness-light, man-woman, X-Y – whatsoever you will – but these two principles are there, continuously in fight. And that is your anguish, your misery, your hell.

Let them become friends. Let your energy circulate in them, not against each other. Let them come closer to each other. Let there be an inner orgasm, an inner intercourse between the woman and the man. That's what in Tantra is called *yuganaddha,* the meeting of the man and woman within you. That is real Tantra. The meeting of the man and woman on the outside is just an introduction.

Sudha leads the Tantra Group. That is just an introduction. The real Tantra has yet to begin. She is just preparing you. The real Tantra group will soon start when I see that now you are ready to go in and meet *there* with your inner woman and inner man. When I see your outer interest is no longer so strong as to keep you out, is no longer so binding on you – the chain is broken – then the real Tantra group will start. I am waiting for the new commune to happen, because the new Tantra group will need a totally different kind of climate, a totally different kind of atmosphere.

This is the greatest experiment that a man can go through. And this experiment releases in you cosmic ecstasy, total orgasm.

Enough for today.

CHAPTER 6

Born with Joy

The first question:

Osho,
Why is it so difficult to enjoy?

It is difficult to enjoy because you will have to disappear. Joy is possible if you are not. You and joy cannot coexist: when joy is there you are absent, when you are there joy is absent. They are like light and darkness – they can't exist together in the same place.

Hence to enjoy is difficult – it is not easy – because to die is difficult, to die is not easy. And only those who know how to die moment-to-moment know how to enjoy. The more capable you are of dying, the deeper your joy will be: intense will be the flame of it and great will be the flowering of it.

It is also difficult to enjoy, because you have so many investments in remaining miserable. Unless you see it, you can go on trying to enjoy, but you will never enjoy. Those investments in misery have to be dropped. And from childhood everybody learns that misery pays. If you are miserable the parents are more loving. If you are ill the parents are more caring. If you are happy, healthy, nobody cares – you don't get attention. And attention is food for the ego; without the attention the ego cannot live – it is its very breath. Just as the body needs oxygen, the ego needs attention.

Whenever you are healthy, happy, the parents don't pay any attention to you; there is no need. But when you are ill, miserable, crying, weeping, the whole family becomes attentive to your needs, as if you have created a kind of emergency. They drop all their work: the mother runs from the kitchen, the father drops his newspaper, and everybody is focused on you. It gives you great ego-fulfillment. And slowly, slowly you learn the way of the ego: remain miserable and people will pay attention to you, remain miserable and they will sympathize with you. And whenever you are enjoying, nobody sympathizes with you. That's why people pay so much respect to ascetic people. Somebody is fasting and people say, "Look, what a great saint!" He is simply being miserable. If you are feasting, nobody is going to sympathize with you, but fast, and people sympathize.

If you are in love with a woman, who is going to sympathize with you? On the contrary, people will be jealous. You are a competitor. They wanted the same woman themselves. You are an enemy. Renounce sex, become celibate, move to a cave, and people will come from faraway places to pay their respects – "Here is a great ascetic" – and you are simply being miserable…but misery pays. Misery can make you a mahatma.

That has been the whole history of humanity: misery has always paid, you have respected miserable people. And if the misery is self-inflicted, of course, you gain more respect; it is voluntary. Mahatma Gandhi became such a great name in the world because he was voluntarily miserable, inflicting misery upon himself. How can you not be attentive to him? If he had been enjoying and living a total life, a whole and healthy life, you would have been jealous, you would have been antagonistic.

See these tricks and strategies of the mind and you will be able to drop them. Don't ask for attention, otherwise you will remain miserable. Attention can only be given when you are miserable; that is part of a natural mechanism.

It happens in your body too: if you have a headache, your attention moves to the head – you forget the whole body. If you have a pain in the leg, then the whole attention moves towards the leg – you forget the whole body. Then the leg becomes very important. It is good that legs and heads and hands are not politicians, otherwise they would constantly be in pain, they would remain constantly in pain. It is good that they don't have any egos. If the leg had some kind of ego, then the leg would continuously create trouble, because only when there is trouble do you pay attention: you massage the leg, you take care of it.

This is the inner mechanism too: attention goes to the part which is in pain. And this is the mechanism of the family, of the society, of the world at large. Once you have learned the trick it becomes unconscious, it becomes autonomous; you simply go on using the trick. The husband comes home and the wife immediately starts being miserable. This I have watched.

I used to stay with many families when I was traveling around this country. The wife is laughing and is happy, and suddenly the husband comes – and I am watching – and her face changes. Not that she is doing it, no; it is not needed to be done anymore, it is automatic: seeing the husband coming, seeing the key move in the hole, suddenly an automatic change happens in her. Her face becomes miserable because the husband will only pay attention to her if she is in misery, otherwise not.

This mechanism has to be made conscious. Watch out for it otherwise it will destroy all possibilities of joy in life – it has destroyed. Millions of people live in misery and hell because they hanker for attention. It is stupid to hanker for attention; it does not give you anything. It only strengthens the ego – which is not you. It is not your essence; it is only your personality, your pseudo self. It goes on nourishing the pseudo self and the essential self goes on starving.

The essential self need not have any attention. The essential self can live without any attention because it is not dependent on anybody else. And the essential self is capable of rejoicing in its aloneness. It does not even need the other, so what to say about attention? It does not even need the other. Its bliss is inner. It does not come from the outside, it does not depend on any condition. It is unconditional. It is a spontaneous, inner, intrinsic phenomenon.

Watch and see how you are profiting from misery, and then you will know why you are finding it so difficult to enjoy. Stop these investments in misery, and the joy will begin to flow again.

We are born with joy. Joy is our very being. It does not need anything to be joyous. One can simply be joyous sitting by oneself. Joy is natural, misery is unnatural. But misery is profitable and joy is purposeless – it will not bring you any profit.

So one has to decide. If you want to be joyous, you have to be a nobody – this is the decision. If you want to be joyous, you will have to be a nobody because you will not get any attention. On the contrary, people will feel jealous, people will be antagonistic to you. People will not like you. People will like you only if you are in misery, then they will sympathize. In sympathy your ego is fulfilled and their ego is fulfilled. Whenever they sympathize with somebody, they are higher and you are lower. They have the upper hand. They are enjoying the trip of sympathy. Sympathy is violent. They are seeing the fact that you are miserable and they are not. They are in a position to sympathize and you are in a position to be sympathized with. Their ego is fulfilled and your ego is fulfilled because "Look," you say to yourself, "how important you are: everybody is sympathizing with you." So ego is fulfilled from both sides. It is profitable, nobody is in a loss.

When you are joyous, rejoicing, dancing, singing, just being happy for no reason at all, your ego will disappear because it will not get attention. And others will not feel good because you are not giving them an opportunity to fulfill their egos.

That's the reason why people were against Jesus and against Buddha, and why they are against me. They would like me also to be an ascetic, they would like me also to be fasting, living under a tree like a beggar, then they would be very happy. They would come in thousands, they would worship me. But if I live in my own way – and my way is the way of the feast, my way is the way of festivity – then they are shocked. They are perfectly happy if somebody leaves the palace and becomes a beggar. They are perfectly happy – they love the man. But if a beggar moves into the palace, they will all be against him. They will not like the idea at all.

Just watch: you also do such things. If a man is lying on a bed of thorns, immediately you prostrate yourself as if he is doing something great, as if he is bringing some bliss to humanity. He is just being a masochist, but you love, you respect him. Your respect seems to be morbid, your respect seems to be ill, sick, and because of your respect he is lying there on the thorns. He wants your attention and this is the most simple way to get your attention and your respect. His ego is fulfilled. He is ready to lie down on those thorns and suffer.

This thing is happening on a smaller scale or a bigger scale everywhere. Beware of it – it is a very ancient trap – and then you can enjoy, then there is nothing else but to enjoy. If you are ready to become a nobody, if you are not in need of others' attention, there is no problem at all. You can enjoy…in small things you can enjoy. Very small things can give you the greatest joy possible.

Just see Jesus with his friends, eating, drinking… People could not tolerate it. They would have loved him if he had been an ascetic, but he was not.

One day he came into a town and Mary Magdalene came to see this man for the very first time. And she fell in love with this man. This man was worth loving. How can you avoid it? How can you manage not to fall in love with such a man? She brought very precious perfume and poured it on Jesus' feet, and washed Jesus' feet with that precious perfume. And she was crying with joy. And Judas said to Jesus, "This is wrong. You should have prevented the woman. The perfume was very precious. It could have been sold. It could have fed a few poor people in the town."

Now with whom are you going to agree – with Judas or with Jesus? If you are honest you will agree with Judas. If you are honest with yourself, you will agree with Judas. He seems to be the beginning of socialism, communism, Gandhism. He seems to be very logically right. He was the most intellectual disciple of Jesus, the *only* educated disciple of Jesus, and his logic is flawless.

But what did Jesus say? Jesus said something absurd. He said, "You can feed the poor when I am gone. The poor will always be there, you need not worry. But while I am here, rejoice."

Do you agree with Jesus? If you agree, you can be joyous. If you don't agree, you are going to remain miserable. "But look," your head will say, "Judas seems to be right." Jesus seems to be utterly absurd. What is he saying? "The poor will always be there, but right now you are with the bridegroom: enjoy, celebrate." This is celebration.

Now if the people were against Jesus, it seems to be absolutely fitting with our so-called intellect. Jesus says, "I cannot prevent the woman because she is in such joy. I cannot destroy her joy. Look at her tears, look at her being. She is in such a festive mood. This is just symbolic. This pouring of the precious perfume on my feet is just symbolic that she is utterly happy. She is celebrating. I cannot stop anybody from celebrating." Then, if you agree with Jesus, you can be joyous.

So it depends on you, whether you agree with Judas or you agree with Jesus.

The second question:

> Osho,
> You had no master. No buddha has had a master. Sometimes I think
> that choosing a master means to prevent one's own enlightenment.
> I mean the need of one's own way, the impossibility of guidance.
> Please tell me what you mean.

Andreas, I never asked anybody any such question. To ask the question is to search for guidance, is to seek for guidance. A question is always a need for an answer from somebody else. If you have questions to ask, you will have to choose a master.

A master is one who is ready to answer you. A disciple is one who is not only asking from curiosity but is ready to stake his whole being on his questioning, is ready to transform his life according to the answer given. If you really ask the question you have already become a disciple. That is the meaning of being a disciple: to ask.

Jesus says, "Ask and it shall be given to you. Knock and the door shall be opened unto you. Seek and ye shall find."

"Ask and it shall be given unto you…" Asking is the beginning of disciplehood. And unless you are a disciple, the master will not take much note of you, because many come just as curiosity seekers – out of curiosity but not really ready to inquire. Inquiry needs commitment, inquiry needs involvement, inquiry is risky, dangerous. It is not only intellectual, it is existential. So if you really want to ask, remember – let me make you alert – you are already becoming a disciple. And if you think that to choose a master is to prevent one's enlightenment, please don't ask questions.

And I was surprised, because Andreas has asked at least seven questions today. The largest number of questions is from him.

Secondly, you say, "You had no master." That is true, I had no master. That does not mean that I was not a disciple. I accepted the whole existence as my master. It needs more courage to accept the whole existence as your master. If you cannot accept even a single man as your master, how can you accept the whole existence as your master – the trees and rocks and the rivers and the clouds? If you cannot love a single human being, how can you love the whole? It is true I had no master, but that does not mean that I was not a disciple. My disciplehood was a greater involvement than your disciplehood is. I trusted the clouds – which is very difficult. I trusted the trees – which is almost impossible. I trusted existence as such. If that is possible then you need not have any master in particular, because then everything is your master.

When a great Sufi mystic, Hassan, was dying, somebody asked, "Hassan, who was your Master?"

He said, "Now it is too late to ask. Time is short, I am dying."

But the inquirer asked, "You can simply say the name. You are still alive, you are still breathing and talking, you can simply tell me the name."

He said, "It will be difficult because I had thousands of masters. If I just relate their names it will take months and years. It is too late. But three masters I will certainly tell you about.

"One was a thief. Once I got lost in the desert and when I reached the village it was very late. Half the night was already gone; shops were closed, caravansaries were closed. There was not a single human being on the roads. I searched for somebody to inquire of. I found one man who was trying to make a hole in the wall of a house. I asked him where I could stay, and he said, 'I am a thief, and you look like a Sufi mystic to me.'" His robe, his aura…. "And the thief said, 'Right now it will be very difficult to find any place to stay, but you can come to my home. You can stay with me – if you can stay with a thief.'"

Hassan said, "I hesitated a little bit. Then I suddenly remembered: if the thief is not afraid of a Sufi, then why should the Sufi be afraid of a thief? In fact, he should be afraid of me. So I said, 'Yes, I will come.' And I went, and I stayed with the thief. And the man was so lovely, so beautiful, I stayed for one month. And each night he would say to me, 'Now I am going to my work. You rest, you pray, you do your work.' And when he would come back I would ask, 'Could you get anything?' He said, 'Not tonight. But tomorrow I will try again.' And he was never in a state of hopelessness.

"For one month continuously he came empty-handed, but he always appeared to be happy. And he said, 'I will try tomorrow. God willing, tomorrow it is going to happen. And you could also pray for me. At least you can say to God: Help this poor man.'"

And then Hassan said, "When I was meditating and meditating for years on end and nothing was happening, and many times the moment came when I was so desperate, so hopeless that I thought to stop all this nonsense. There is no God and all prayer is just madness, all meditation is false – and suddenly I would remember the thief who would say every night, 'God willing, tomorrow it is going to happen.'

"So I tried one day more. If the thief was so hopeful, with such hope and trust, I should try at least one day more. And many times it happened, but the thief and the memory of him helped me to wait one day more. And one day it happened – it did happen! I bowed down. I was thousands of miles away from the thief and his house, but I bowed down in his direction. He was my first master.

"And my second master was a dog. I was thirsty and I was going towards the river, and a dog came, he was also thirsty. He looked into the river, he saw another dog there – his own image – and became afraid. He barked and the other dog barked too. But his thirst was so much that he would hesitate. He would go back and come again and look into the water and find the dog there. But the thirst was so much that he suddenly jumped into the water and the image disappeared. He drank the water, he swam in the water – it was a hot summer. And I was watching. I knew that a message had come to me from God: one has to jump in spite of all fears.

"When I was on the verge of jumping into the unknown, the same fear was there. I would go to the very edge, hesitate, and come back. And I would remember the dog – if the dog could manage, why can't I? And then one day I jumped into the unknown: I disappeared and only the unknown was left behind. The dog was my second master.

"And the third master was a small child. I entered into a town and a small child was bringing a candle, a lit candle, hiding it in his hands and going to the mosque to put the candle there. Just jokingly I asked the boy, 'Have you lit the candle yourself?' He said, 'Yes, sir.' And I asked jokingly, 'Can you tell me from where the light came? There was a moment when the candle was unlit, then there was a moment when the candle was lit, can you show me the source from which the light came? And you have lit it, so you must have seen the light coming – from where?' And the boy laughed and blew out the candle and said, 'Now you have seen the light going, where has it gone? You tell me!' And my ego was shattered, and my whole knowledge was shattered. And that moment I felt my own stupidity. Since then I dropped all knowledgeability."

Hassan talked about three masters. And he said, "There have been many, and no time is left for me to talk about them all."

Yes, this is true, I had no master, because I had millions of masters. I have learned from every possible source. If you can be that kind of disciple you need not have a master. But remember, it is not that you do not have a master. Either you choose one or you choose all, but in any case you have to be a disciple. To be a disciple is a must on the path.

What does it mean to be a disciple? It means to be able to learn, to be available to learn, to be vulnerable to existence. What actually happens when you choose a master? You start learning how to learn. And with one master, slowly slowly you get in tune, and slowly slowly you see the point that in the same way you can get in tune with the whole existence.

The master is just a miniature of the whole. Coming closer to the master you start becoming aware of the beatitude, of the closeness – of love, of intimacy, of involvement, of commitment. And slowly slowly you see the point that if just being so close to one single person can be such a tremendous joy, how much more it will be when you are close to the whole. The master is just the beginning, the master is not the end. And the true master is only a door – through him you pass and go beyond. The true master helps you to go beyond…

You say, "You had no master. No buddha has had a master. Sometimes I think that choosing a master means to prevent one's own enlightenment."

Enlightenment is simply enlightenment; it is neither mine nor yours. The ego is separate, the essence is not separate. To think in terms of your own enlightenment is to be caught in the net, in the trap of the ego again. You miss the whole point. If you think of your own enlightenment just as you think of your own car, your own house, your own wife, you are starting to think of enlightenment also as something that you will possess. You will not be there to possess it. You will be possessed by it.

And to surrender to a master simply means an experiment in being possessed by somebody: you drop yourself and the other enters you and fills you. You learn surrender. It is just the *ABC* of surrender. But you cannot learn the *XYZ* if you have not even learned the *ABC* of it. When you go to learn how to swim you don't go directly to the ocean, you don't go to deep waters; you learn in shallow water near the bank or you learn in a swimming pool.

The master is like a swimming pool where you can learn how to swim. Once you have learned, all the oceans are yours, then you can go anywhere. Then this whole existence belongs to you. But you are no more there. In fact, it will be better to say you belong to the whole existence – not that you possess enlightenment, enlightenment possesses you.

"Sometimes I think that choosing a master means to prevent one's own enlightenment."

You don't have a master yet, then who has prevented you from becoming enlightened? Why are you not enlightened yet? If choosing a master prevents enlightenment, then those who don't have masters must be enlightened. Choosing the master does not prevent enlightenment. Getting caught by the master, getting caught into the master prevents enlightenment – and these are two different things. That is why Buddha says, "If you meet me on the way, kill me immediately." And I say to you too: If you see me on the way, kill me immediately.

The master is a ladder: you have to use it and you have to go beyond it. The master is a boat: you have to use it, and when you have reached the other shore you have to leave the boat. You need not carry it on your head. If you carry it on your head you are stupid and you have not reached anywhere – you must be dreaming…because such stupid people never reach to the other shore.

Choosing the master does not prevent enlightenment, but a moment comes when you have to go beyond the master, don't cling – clinging to the master will prevent you. But if there is a real master he will not allow you to cling to him. That is the definition of a real master: he teaches you to get involved, he teaches you to become committed, and one day he teaches you to become uncommitted again, to become uninvolved again. Then the master is perfect.

The ordinary so-called masters just teach you one thing: how to become attached to them and then to remain attached to them. That's the definition of a pseudo master. Avoid the pseudo masters.

But to find a true master is not going to prevent your enlightenment. You will not become enlightened without him. It is a paradoxical phenomenon: you have to choose the master and you have to go beyond the master. If you understand this paradox, my answer will be clear to you.

The third question:

Osho,
I want to conquer the kingdom of God. How can I do this?

God cannot be conquered. The very idea is foolish. You have to be conquered by God, you have to allow God to conquer you. On the contrary you are saying, "I want to conquer the kingdom of God." This is the male ego, the aggressive mind: it always thinks in terms of conquering – conquer nature, conquer God, conquer love. And you have destroyed everything that you have conquered. You have destroyed the beauty of nature, the ecology, the inner harmony of nature by your conquering it.

Even a man like the British philosopher Bertrand Russell writes about "the conquest of nature." But this is how the Western mind has been thinking continuously – in terms of conquering. Either conquer this world or conquer that world, but you remain an Alexander.

This is not the way to approach love, this is not the way to pray. The very word *conquering* is ugly. Surrendering, letting God conquer you, allowing him to enter you... Don't prevent him. You need not go in search of him, you need not become a soldier to conquer. That's the difference between a soldier and a sannyasin: the soldier wants to conquer, the sannyasin wants to be conquered.

There was a loud hammering on the door of heaven. St. Peter appeared and said, "I say, that's a tremendous racket. Who is making all the fuss?"

The shabby man standing there said, "I'm Paddy McGinnis and I'm strong with the IRA these thirty years."

St. Peter said, "I'm sorry, Mr McGinnis, but we have no record of you. You can't come in."

"And who is saying anything about coming in?" said Paddy. "I'm here a tellin' you, you've got fifteen minutes to evacuate the place!"

This is the meaning of conquering God and the kingdom of God. Drop this whole mind. This mind won't allow you. This mind is irreverent. This mind is incapable of knowing what worship is. Be a little more aware about what you are asking. Do you want to possess God in your hands? Do you want God to be in your bank balance? God is not a treasure to be put in the bank, and God is not a thing that you can hold in your fist. God is not a thing, God is not a property.

Remember not to use the words that you use in your ordinary ego trips; these words will mislead you. These words show your ambition. These words are political. These words are not religious. A religious person surrenders, he prays, he waits, he opens up his being, he trusts. He says to God, "Thy kingdom come. Thy will be done." He prays, "Let me be destroyed utterly, completely, so there is no hindrance left. Let me be absolutely empty so you can come and fill me totally."

The fourth question:

> *Osho,*
> *My orthodox Christian parents think that you are a dangerous*
> *sophist, and some wicked force is working through you to destroy*
> *religion. Why do they think like that?*

It is nothing new; it has always been so. It has nothing to do with Christians – this is so with Hindus, this is so with Buddhists, and this has always been so. They were thinking in the same way about Christ too. These are all the same people. They were thinking in the same way about Buddha too, and these are the same people. Man is a very strange animal. The most strange thing about man is that he never learns; he goes on doing the same thing again and again.

Why did they crucify Jesus? What was wrong with this man? They thought him wicked, they thought him a representative of evil, a personification of the Devil. They were angry. And of course, the people who were interested in Jesus were younger people, because only young people can be interested in the new. The older generation has too much of an investment with the established, is too involved with the status quo. Do you think Jesus' followers were old people? He himself was young and the people that surrounded him were young people. Parents were angry, very angry. Rabbis were angry, priests were angry, because he was bringing a revolution. If Jesus is right, then the whole established religion is wrong. If Jesus is right, then what about the priests? Jesus and the priests can't both be right – either Jesus or the priests. The priests became organized against this man. They had to kill him. And the older generation was with them, naturally.

The mind always feels comfortable with the old because it is familiar, one is accustomed to it. The new always feels dangerous, one feels suspicious of it. And religion is always new. True religion is always new, true religion is always rebellious. Whenever there is a man like Jesus or Buddha, there is bound to be great trouble. But Jesus is crucified, and then slowly slowly Jesus' life becomes the foundation of a new, established religion. Once Christianity becomes an established religion, supported by the state and supported by the elders and Christianity itself has its own priesthood, then there is no problem. Then if a man like me comes, problems arise.

You say, "My orthodox Christian parents think that you are a dangerous sophist, and some wicked force is working through you to destroy religion."

In a way they are true. What they call religion is not religion, and I am certainly in favor of destroying it. What I call religion they cannot understand; it is impossible for them to conceive. They have become too stereotyped in their thinking, their minds are too conditioned, fixed. They are no longer fluid, flexible; they are rigid. The older a person becomes, the more rigid he becomes.

Let me tell you a few things that were said about Christians in the early days of Christianity, then you will understand what your parents say about me.

Tacitus says, "There is a group, hated for their abominations, called Christians."

And Suetonius says, "The Christians are a class of men given to a new and wicked superstition."

And Celcius says, "They worship, to an extravagant degree, this man who appeared recently. They are like frogs holding a symposium round a swamp, debating which of them is the most sinful."

And Lucian says, "The poor wretches have convinced themselves that they are going to be immortal and live for all time by worshipping that crucified sophist and living under his laws.... They receive their doctrines by tradition, without any definite evidence."

And Pliny the Younger says, "It is their habit, on a fixed day, to assemble before daylight and recite by turns a form of words to Christ as a god. The contagion of this perverse and extravagant superstition has penetrated not only the cities but the villages and the country too. Yet it seems possible to stop it and set it right."

These things were not said about me, these things were said about Christ.

And similar things have been said about Buddha.

Hindus have created a beautiful story about Buddha. They say that he was an incarnation of God. They had to say it. Hindus are more polite and, of course, more cunning, more sophisticated, and they know how to play with words. Buddha was an incarnation of God, they say, but not a good incarnation. But how can an incarnation of God be bad? They have a beautiful story to illustrate it.

They say when God created the world he created hell and heaven and Earth, the three worlds. Then millions of years passed and nobody went to hell; it remained empty. And the Devil was very angry, and also his disciples, and they were waiting and waiting and nobody would come. And every arrangement was ready: the fire was burning, and nobody was coming. Finally they had to go to God, and the Devil said, "This is nonsense. Why did you create hell if nobody is going to come there? And what are we doing there? – just waiting and waiting. And how long do we have to wait? Not even a single soul has entered, the whole thing is pointless. Either send a few people so we become occupied…. And we have rehearsed and we have trained ourselves and made ourselves so skillful that we are hankering…we have to do something. You are driving us mad. Either send a few people there or drop the whole project."

God said, "You wait. Soon I will have to come to the earth. I will be born as Gautama the Buddha and I will mislead people and misguide people. Then they will start falling into hell automatically."

Then God came as Gautama the Buddha and he misguided people, because hell needs people. And since Buddha misguided people, hell has been overcrowded.

Now see the beauty of the story and the cunningness of it. Buddha is accepted as an incarnation of God, but it is just to send people to hell – so beware of Buddha, don't follow him; otherwise you will go to hell. Buddha was here to help the Devil, to give him some occupation. Since then hell has been overcrowded; there is no space, people have to wait for years outside the gate.

This has always been so and this is going to remain being so: religion, whenever it comes fresh from the beyond, is very shattering to tradition, and the traditional people become afraid – not that they are worried about religion being destroyed. They are not religious at all, otherwise they would not be afraid of it; their religion is only a social formality. They talk about God because it is convenient to talk about God. They go to the church too, because it makes things easier. The church functions as a lubricant. It is a Sunday religion. It is good; it keeps you in good company and everybody knows that you are religious. That helps in many ways.

The church is no more than a Rotary Club or a Lions Club. If you are a Rotarian, it helps you; people know that you must be good if you belong to the Rotary Club. And in the Rotary Club you become acquainted with all the topmost people of the town: friendship arises, it helps in your business, in your day-to-day life. The church is nothing but a kind of religious club: it is convenient. Nobody is sincerely there. People are just showing respect to Christ, paying service – but that service is lip service. They don't bother a bit about Christ, Christianity and all his teachings.

Who bothers about Christ's teachings? Who follows them? If you had followed Christ the world would have been totally different: there would not have been any wars. And half of the world is Christian. If Christians really follow Jesus.... Jesus says, "Love your enemies," and Christians go on bombing the enemy. It is Christians who bombed Japan, who used the first atomic bomb. Now think of Jesus watching from his place – what will be happening to him? Christians dropping atom bombs? And he has said to these people, "Love your enemy as yourself."

Who has followed Jesus? There is no question of following. People just go to the church. It is a good feeling – to go to the church, to remain religious.

I have heard....

The airplane was going through some especially turbulent weather, but the pilot knew he had everything under control. He tried to calm the passengers with soothing words spoken over the loudspeaker system. He also asked the stewardesses to reassure the people that everything would be all right.

One very religious little old lady, however, would not be comforted. The stewardess told her how capable the pilot was and how reliable the plane's technology was, but the woman was still sure she'd never see the ground again.

At a loss, the stewardess finally called on the highest court of appeal, "Just trust in providence," she said soothingly.

The little old lady's eyes opened even wider, "Is it as bad as that?" she asked.

A religious old lady.... But to really think of God means that death is certain – "Is it as bad as that?"

People have double faces. Their original face is not even known to themselves. People have split personalities. Your parents will be thinking they are Christian and religious; they are neither Christian nor religious. If they are really religious they will understand me, because whatsoever I am saying is the same – exactly the same, precisely the same. My language may be different from Jesus' – it has to be, twenty centuries have passed – but what I am doing is exactly the same work, the continuity of the same work. But I can understand their problem too: they are losing their hold on you and they are afraid.

Just the other night I was reading an article. In Germany, parents have formed a certain society to prevent young people from going into new religions, particularly Eastern mystic experiences; in America they are creating a lot of trouble for the young people.

You will be surprised that parents are hiring kidnappers. Young people are being kidnapped by their own parents, and then they are being given to psychologists. Certain psychologists are trying to deprogram them, they are called deprogrammers. They think the young people have been conditioned.

For example, if you really become too involved with me, and your parents become very afraid, and you don't want to go back to your country, you can be kidnapped. Your own parents can do it, "For your own sake," because you have fallen in the trap of a devil, of some evil force. And it looks to them… "What are you doing with orange clothes and a beard and long hair and the *mala*? And who is this man…very evil-looking? And what is wrong with wearing a cross, having a picture of Jesus? What are you doing there?" And if they come and see the dynamic meditation, kundalini, they will go crazy. They will become very concerned.

Yes, you can be kidnapped, and then you can be forced into what they call deprogramming to decondition you. They think you have been hypnotized, so you have to be dehypnotized. So they will teach you Christianity and the Christian catechism again. And they will force you day in, day out, for months, so that you can again become a Christian, and you can again say, "Yes, I believe in God and the Son and the Holy Ghost," and then they are at ease. When you believe in the Holy Ghost, then all is okay. And when you start reading the Bible again, all is okay: now you have come back, you have become religious. When you start making atom bombs again, you are really Christian, Catholic. If you go to the army and they cut your long hair and make you a soldier, then you are a perfect Christian, a Catholic. When you start a cut-throat competition in the world for money, for power, for prestige, when you start destroying others so that you can reach higher and higher for worldly possessions, you are perfect, you are a religious person.

Even politicians are thought to be religious persons because they go to the church, they listen to the sermon of the priest. Politicians are "religious," and my sannyasins are "not religious"!

You will have to understand it. You will have to be very very patient with your parents. You will have to be very kind too. They need compassion. They are encaged in a certain ideology and they cannot look outside it. They are incapable of feeling anything new, of being anything new. They are incapable of understanding; they have become too rigid, their whole ideology has become a settled phenomenon, and they are afraid. If they see you happy, they can only think you have gone mad, because they have lived an unhappy life and a very religious life.

And they know religious people are unhappy people – sad, with long faces. They cannot believe that you can be religious and dancing, and you can be religious and laughing, and you can be religious and yet happy. Then what about all their saints? Were they fools? They lived with long faces the whole of their lives, they carried their life as a burden, as if a mountain were being carried on their head, and you are so light-footed, so weightless, with no burden, with no seriousness around you. You are such a joy, how can they believe you are religious? The only thing possible is that you have been hypnotized. How can you be so happy in such an unhappy world? It is not possible. You must be living in a kind of illusion. Hence they say, "This man is an evil force, he has hypnotized you. The laughter that you are going through is false, the joy that you are experiencing is false." Their misery is right and true, and your joy is false. When they will be able to make you miserable again they will be at ease: their son has come back home, or their daughter has come back home.

You will have to be understanding. They cannot understand me, they cannot understand you, but they are your parents and you owe something to them. Be loving to them. Don't be antagonistic. Don't resent them. Don't start arguing and fighting with them because that will make them more convinced that they are right and you are wrong. Be more loving. Nobody has loved them; they have lived in a false world where all is pretension. Nobody has loved them. If you love them, it will be more convincing than logic.

Listen to them. Don't start arguing. Listen patiently. Nobody has ever listened to them. That's why psychoanalysis has become so important in the world. Psychoanalysis is nothing but just finding a patient listener, the psychoanalyst, to whom you can talk to your heart's content and say whatsoever you want – sense, nonsense, whatsoever you want.

People are feeling suffocated, boiling, within. They want to say something but nobody is there to hear, the world has turned deaf. The man cannot talk to his woman, because the moment you talk conflict starts. You say something, she understands something else. The woman cannot talk to the man because talking is always risky. It is better to keep quiet and to remain silent. At least it gives you a feeling of peace, that all is quiet. Say a single word and the argument and anger starts. Sooner or later people learn that it is better to remain silent, and not to say anything at all.

Nobody has listened to them. Just see the misery of the fact that they have to go and find a person to listen... But they have to pay for it, and the costs are really very high. Psychoanalysis is one of the highly paying professions. It is a Jewish concern and Jews know how to do business. Freud founded the greatest empire and his followers are just looting, just enjoying. And what are they doing? They simply listen; no other help is needed. If you listen to the person for months together, years together, he loses steam. And once he has thrown his steam out he feels calm and quiet, and he thinks this is because of psychoanalysis. It is not because of psychoanalysis.

In older societies, more primitive societies, this is not needed because people are very willing to listen. Go to an Indian village – people are very willing to listen. They have enough time to listen, nobody is in a hurry. People are sitting and talking and listening to each other. You cannot convince Indian villagers that there is any need for psychoanalysis, they are psychoanalyzing each other already; they need not pay for it.

But in a highly sophisticated, cultured, civilized society, people are in such a hurry that nobody is available to talk to anybody else. Parents never see their children, or even if they see them, then just polite words, "Hello, how are you?" and they are gone. Or a pat on the head which is almost mechanical, or a hug which is false, or even a kiss which is just an empty gesture. But nobody talks, nobody faces the other. There is no friendship, no love. Parents live in one world, the children live in another.

Parents are so suffocated by their own misery, helplessness, turmoil, that they have to drown themselves in alcohol. Children are getting drowned in drugs. And the strange thing is that the people who drown themselves in alcohol are very much against drugs. And they are doing the same thing; it is not different. It is the same thing: somehow to drown oneself, to forget all about oneself and the world and the problems. Even children have so many problems because we teach them competition, ambition. We send them to the school and the competition starts. "You have to be first. You have to bring an *A* grade." Now you have made them anxious. They are continuously in turmoil, anxiety: whether they will be able to make it or not.

Small children are having ulcers, young people are having heart attacks, young people are going mad, committing suicide – this has not happened ever before. Or if you don't want to commit suicide, you don't want to go mad, you don't want to have ulcers, cancer, heart attacks, then drown yourself in drugs. But then the state is against you, then the society is against you, and you feel guilty. You are doing something that is illegal, you are a criminal; they will throw you into jail, away from society.

The only possibility of getting out of this whole nonsense is to find a new space in your being through prayer, through meditation; to find your original source of life and energy. And that's what you are doing here with me. If you really go into meditation you will not need alcohol, you will not need drugs. If you really go into meditation, your life will be a life of love, of sharing, of joy – noncompetitive, nonambitious. You will not become a politician, you will live as a nobody. You will not suffer from an inferiority complex because you will not compare yourself with anybody else. And you will live in great gratitude because your life will have joy. You will not be attached to misery because you will not have any investment in misery. If you don't have any ego, you need not have any investment in misery. Then you can feast and your life can be a festival. That's what I am teaching here.

And to me this is religion: to make life a feast, a festival; to transform energy in such a way that you become a celebration.

But your parents will find it difficult. Help them to understand. Be loving. Listen patiently to their arguments, and don't argue; rather, love. Just show by your being, by your integrity, by your patience, by your caring about them that you are moving on the right path. It is up to you: if you can prove by your love that you are moving on the right path, only then will they think that the man you are with is not evil. If you argue and fight and become antagonistic – which seems to be very natural because they will be antagonistic and in a fighting mood, and the natural reaction is to be the same, tit for tat – if you do that, then you will be proving that your master is evil and you will be proving that you have moved on a wrong path.

What I am proved to be in the world, depends on you.

The last question:

Osho,
Can't sex be transcended without going into it?

Then what is the need to transcend it? The need of transcendence arises only because you are in it. You are born in it and you are born out of it: you are a sexual phenomenon.

Except for Jesus, nobody has been born of a virgin. And Christians insist too much on the theory that Mary was a virgin, so that they can condemn sex. If Jesus is also born of sex, then it will be difficult to condemn sex. In fact, Jesus was born out of sex as much as anybody else.

The body *has* to be constituted of male and female energy, otherwise the body cannot be constituted. To say that Mary was a virgin is to say that you have electricity in your house with only one pole: positive, or negative. That will be just as nonsensical. Electricity needs to have both poles, positive and negative. Without those two poles electricity cannot exist, cannot come into existence – not even in Jesus' house; the electricity will need two poles. The electricity does not care who you are – even in my house it needs two poles.

You can ask Haridas. He tries, the whole day he tries, continuously working to make electricity pure. But up to now he has not succeeded. But later on you can write stories about me that, "In Osho's house the electricity had only one pole." These stories are always created later on and this is because you have to prove that your master was exceptional.

Jainas say that Mahavira never perspired. Now what kind of foolishness is that? He missed the joy of perspiring in the sun. And he lived naked and moved naked; in fact, he must have perspired more than anybody else. If you say I don't perspire it may be right because I live in an air-conditioned room, but Mahavira, moving naked, never perspired? Something seems to be suspicious, fishy; he must have been stinking. To hide the fact, you have to cover it and say that he never perspired, so the whole root is cut. He never defecated, never urinated. How can you think of Mahavira pissing? That does not look right at all.

These stories are created. These stories simply prove that the followers are stupid. They don't say anything about Mahavira or Christ or Mohammed; they simply prove that the followers that came in their wake are neurotic. Jesus was born out of two sexes just as everybody else is. You come out of sex, each cell of your body is a sexual cell. Each cell of your body has two poles: the feminine and the masculine, yin and yang.

You ask me, "Can't sex be transcended without going into it?" The only possibility is not to be born. Once you are born you are already a sexual being. Whether you make love to a woman or man doesn't matter. You can be a celibate, but to be a celibate does not mean to go beyond sexuality. Sexuality has already penetrated. The moment you were in the womb of your mother you became a sexual being. There is no way to avoid it. So all that you can do is repress it. You will become unnatural and your whole life will be a perverted life. Repression is possible, but transcendence is not possible in the way you are asking about.

I have heard....

Ellen and Dolph had been married thirty years and never missed a night of connubial bliss. One day Ellen visited her doctor and was told that she must have complete rest and quiet for six months or she would not live.

Ellen and Dolph decided they should stay completely apart during this period. She moved into an upstairs bedroom and he remained downstairs.

After three months of complete abstinence and solitude, his will-power collapsed and Dolph started for her bedroom. As he started to climb the stairs, he saw her coming down.

"Dear," she said, "I was just coming down to die."

"I'm glad, honey," he said, "because I was just going up to kill you."

Don't be mad, let things be simple. There is no need to kill or die. Repression will make things very complicated in your life; you will become split, schizophrenic – just celibate on the surface and deep down just the opposite of it.

Transcendence means the disappearance of the need for the other, the disappearance of the desire to get lost into a woman or into a man. And this is possible only if you have understood – and understanding comes only through experience. So I don't say drop out of your relationships; rather, become more meditative in your relationships.

Making love, let it be a meditation too. And you will be surprised: if while making love you also move in a meditative state you will have great insights into what is happening, and the whole urge called sex will become conscious. And once it has become conscious it can disappear. And it disappears on its own; you need not cultivate, you need not practice anything for it. When it goes on its own it is beautiful. Yes, sex disappears – one transcends it – but not by fighting it. This is true, and because of this truth much misunderstanding has happened in the world.

Sex disappeared in Buddha's life, sex disappeared in Christ's life. People have seen sex disappearing, and people have seen that when sex disappears there is great splendor: something of the sky dances on the earth, the beyond reaches to the earth, the mundane becomes suffused with the sacred. And because people have seen these things, great desire has arisen in them too to transcend sex. But then the whole thing goes wrong: they start fighting with it.

It is a secret science, and if you don't move rightly, everything will go wrong.

A man is told by a friend that he should pick a wife who is "an economist in the kitchen, a lady in the parlor, and a prostitute in bed."

They meet sometime after the wedding and the friend asks if he is satisfied with his choice.

"Well," says the newlywed, "I did what you said, but I guess I made a mistake somewhere. The woman I married turned out to be a prostitute in the parlor, a lady in the kitchen, and an economist in bed!"

Just a little mismanagement, just a thing here and a thing there misplaced and everything goes wrong.

Transcendence is never through repression; transcendence is through understanding, transcendence is through awareness.

The other night I was giving sannyas to a psychoanalyst – a beautiful man. I have given him the name *Anand Veetkam*. It means bliss beyond sex. And to him I said that if you become meditative while making love, you will come to know a few immensely significant things. The first and the most significant thing is that when you are going into a deep orgasm – when the climax is happening – there is great joy because in that moment sex disappears. Sex brings you to the orgasmic state, and once its purpose is fulfilled, sex disappears. In the orgasmic state there is no sexuality left in you: you are simply throbbing and there is no desire, you are utterly in the here and now; there is no future, no fantasy, no imagination, nothing. And when the orgasm happens, the man is alone – the woman may be there but he is not aware of the woman. And the woman is alone – the man is there but she is not aware of the man.

Orgasm is individual: it is happening inside the man, it is happening inside the woman. The other has triggered it, but then the function of the other is finished; you are no more interested in the other. In deep orgasm you are simply inside yourself, there is no sex in it; hence the bliss. And after a good orgasm, for hours you will feel very very blissful, and for hours you will not think of sex again – the desire has left you. What has happened? If you are feeling blissful, the desire cannot be there. If the desire is there, bliss cannot be there. Desire and bliss are never together.

And if you meditate deeply while making love, you will become aware that time disappears; at the peak there is no time, suddenly you are in the here and now. Only then do you know the meaning of here and now, otherwise you are in the past or in the future. And when time disappears, mind disappears, because mind is another aspect of time, another name for time. Mind is past plus future. When there is no time there is no mind. Just think: no mind, no time, no sexual desire – and there is great bliss.

But people miss it because they are not alert about it. People go into lovemaking unconsciously, mechanically. Go consciously, mindfully, remembering what is happening, watching, remaining a witness, and that will release understanding in you, that will release awareness in you. And awareness is transcendence, awareness is freedom.

Enough for today.

CHAPTER 7

Turning the Key

Master Lu-tsu said:
When the light is made to move in a circle, all the energies of heaven
and Earth, of the light and the dark, are crystallized. When one
begins to apply this magic it is as if, in the middle of being, there
were nonbeing. When in the course of time the work is completed,
and beyond the body there is a body, it is as if, in the middle of
nonbeing, there were being. Only after concentrated work of a
hundred days will the light be genuine, then only will it become
spirit-fire. After a hundred days there develops by itself in the midst
of the light a point of the true light-pole. Then suddenly there
develops the seed-pearl. It is as if a man and woman embraced and
a conception took place. Then one must be quite still and wait. In
the midst of the primal transformation, the radiance of the light is
the determining thing. In the physical world it is the sun; in man,
the eye. This energy is directed outward – flows downward.
Therefore the Way of the Golden Flower depends wholly on the
backward-flowing method.

The circulation of the light is not only a fantasy.

By concentrating the thoughts, one can fly; by concentrating the
desires, one falls. When a pupil takes little care of his thoughts and
much care of his desires, he gets into the path of submersion. Only

through contemplation and quietness does true intuition arise: for
that the backward-flowing method is necessary.

A great master was asked what is the Buddha? "Mind is the Buddha," he answered. When after many years he was asked the same question again by the same disciple, he said, "No Buddha, no mind."

"Then why did you say before, 'Mind is the Buddha'?"

"To stop the baby crying! Once the baby stops crying, I say, 'No mind, no Buddha'!"

Philosophy is just a toy – a toy to stop the baby crying – and so is theology. Religion really consists of experience, experimentation; it has nothing to do with speculation. In its essential nature it is the science of the inner; it is as scientific as any other science. The difference between religion and science is not of their methodology but only of their object.

Science looks at the objective world where our energy is flowing, where our light is flowing. Religion searches into the subjective where our light is not flowing but can be turned to flow. Hence science is easier than religion. Never for a single moment think that religion is simpler than science. It is a higher science, how can it be simpler than science? It is a superior science.

First the light has to flow inwards, then it falls on your being, then your being is revealed and you can enter into your being. And to enter into one's own being is to enter into the kingdom of God. There, you are not and God is: you exist only in the shadow. When the light flows outward you exist only in the shadow. You exist because you remain unaware of your real self. Your real self is the supreme self. Your real self is a "Self" with a capital *S*. It has nothing to do with you, it is the self of all. But for that, a great transformation has to take place.

Nature has prepared you for the outward flow. Nature's function is finished. With man, nature has reached to its climax; now nothing else is going to happen naturally unless man makes a decision to go further than nature. Nature has brought you to the point from where you are capable of standing on your own. Man is no longer a child, man has become adult. Now nature will no longer parent you; there is no need.

Natural evolution has stopped at man. This is a fact. Even scientists are becoming more and more aware of it: that for thousands of years nothing has happened to man, man has remained the same – as if nature's work is done. Now man has to take the course of further growth into his own hands. That's what religion is.

Religion means man starts standing on his own feet, becomes responsible for his own being, starts looking and searching and inquiring into what is the case – who am I? And this should not only be curiosity.

Philosophy is out of curiosity. Religion is a very sincere, authentic search; it is inquiry. And there is a great difference between curiosity and inquiry. Curiosity is childish, just a little itching in the head; you would like to scratch and then you feel satisfied. Philosophy is that scratching; religion is a life-and-death matter. In philosophy you never become involved, you remain aloof. You play with the toys, but it is not a question of life and death. You accumulate knowledge, but you never practice it.

I have heard....

Once upon a time there lived an eminent Confucian scholar. He was a gentleman of nearly eighty and was said to have no equal in the breadth of his learning and understanding.

Then a rumor arose that far away a new doctrine had sprung up that was even deeper than his knowledge. The old gentleman found this intolerable and decided that the issue had to be settled one way or the other.

In spite of his age he set out on the long journey. After months of hardship on the road, he arrived at his destination, introduced himself and told his host about the purpose of his visit.

His host, who was a master of the new Zen school, merely quoted, "To avoid doing evil, to do as much good as possible, this is the teaching of all the buddhas."

On hearing this, the Confucian gentleman flared up, "I have come here in spite of the dangers and hazards of such a long and rough journey and in spite of my advanced age, and you just quote a little jingle that every three-year-old child knows by heart! Are you mocking me?"

But the Zen master replied, "I am not mocking you, sir. Please consider that though it is true that every three-year-old child knows this verse, yet even a man of eighty fails to live up to it!"

Religion is not a question of knowing but of living up to it. Religion is life, and unless you live it, you will not know anything about what it is. And to live religion one has to drop all philosophizing and one has to start experimenting. One has to become a lab. The scientist's lab is outside; the religious person's lab is his own being – his own body, his own soul, his own mind. The scientist has to concentrate on the object on which he is experimenting: his work has to be done with open eyes. The work of religion has to be done with closed eyes: he has to concentrate upon himself.

And the complexity is great because in the world of religion the experimenter and the experimented upon are the same – hence the complexity, hence the strangeness, hence the incomprehensibility, hence the illogicalness. The knower and the known are the same in the world of religion. In the world of science the knower is separate. The known is separate – things are clear-cut, demarcated. But in religion everything merges, melts into everything else – even the knower cannot remain separate! Religion does not give you knowledge separate from the knower. It gives you experience, not separate from the knower, but as the very essence of the knower.

To be a religious seeker one has to drop all philosophizing, one has to drop all a priori knowledge, because all a priori knowledge is a hindrance. It stops your inquiry, inquiry becomes dishonest – from the very beginning it becomes poisoned. How can you inquire if you have already concluded? To be a Christian and to be religious is impossible, or to be a Hindu and to be religious is impossible. How can you be religious if you are a Hindu? Being a Hindu means that you have already concluded, you have decided what truth is. Now what is the point of inquiry? What are you going to inquire into? All that you will be doing is finding support, arguments for what you have already concluded. And your conclusion may be wrong – nobody knows – because your conclusion is not yours, it has been handed to you by the society.

Society is very interested in giving you conclusions. The society is not interested in giving you consciousness so that you can conclude on your own. Before you become conscious, before any inquiry starts, the society stuffs you with all kinds of conclusions – to *stop* the inquiry – because the inquirer is dangerous to society. The non-inquirer is convenient, the non-inquirer is obedient. He simply takes the orders, the commands, and follows them. He is conformist, he is conventional. Once you have stuffed somebody's mind a bit with a belief, you have drugged him; belief is a drug. He starts believing, he goes on believing…slowly slowly he starts thinking that his belief is his experience.

Belief is a system of hypnosis. You go on suggesting to the child, "You are a Hindu, you are a Hindu," you take him to the temple, you lead him through religious, so-called religious rituals, ceremonies, and by and by he becomes conditioned to the idea that he is a Hindu, and that all that is Hindu is right and all that is non-Hindu is wrong.

And the same is being done in every kind of society – you have drugged the child, his very source of consciousness has been poisoned. And if you believe something, it starts appearing to be true. If you start believing something, you will find all kinds of supports for it, all kinds of arguments to help it – your ego becomes involved. It is not only a question of truth, deep down it is a question of, "Who is right, me or you? How can I be wrong – I have to be right." So you choose all that supports you. And life is so complex, you can find all kinds of things in life – whatsoever you choose, whatsoever you decide. If you are a pessimist, you will find all kinds of arguments in life which support pessimism. If you are an optimist, there are all kinds of arguments available to you.

Life is dual, life is paradoxical, life is multidimensional. Hence so many kinds of philosophies, "isms," theologies exist in the world. And every theology lives confined by its own conclusions and feels perfectly right.

It is only in this age that the believers are finding a little difficulty – and this is a great blessing – because they have become aware of other believers too. Now the Hindu is not so complacent, he cannot be; he knows that there are Christians. And the Christian cannot go on believing that he has the sole copyright for truth, because he knows that there is the Mohammedan and there is the Taoist and there is the Buddhist, and who knows?

This age is very confused – it has never been so before. But remember, this confusion is a great blessing; something is on the way, something tremendously important is going to happen. This chaos in the mind is the beginning of a new dawn. In the future people will not be Mohammedans and Hindus and Buddhists. People will be inquirers. Belief is disappearing and the darkness of belief is disappearing. Nobody in the future is going to believe. People will inquire, and when they find the answer, they will trust. Belief is borrowed, trust is one's own experience.

What I am teaching you here is that kind of religion which is going to happen more and more in the future. I am bringing the future to you in the present: I am making you pure inquirers with no belief system, ready to go into experimentation but with no conclusion, open to whatsoever the truth may be, ready to accept it – but only ready to accept the truth.

The man who believes is a closed man: his windows and doors are closed, he lives in a kind of prison. He has to live in a kind of prison; if he opens the windows and doors and the sun comes in and the wind comes in and the rain comes in, it is possible that his belief systems may be disturbed. If the truth enters from every side, it will be impossible for him to protect his belief. He has to hide from truth, he has to live in an enclosed world, windowless, so nothing can disturb him, so he can go on believing, undisturbed. This is good for the society, but very hazardous for the health of the individual.

Society has been giving you toys to play with – just as you give toys to the children so that when they become involved in playing they don't disturb you. The parents are at ease, the father can read his newspaper, the mother can work in the kitchen – the child is involved in the toys.

In India, in the villages, this has been the usual practice: poor women who have to go to work in the fields have to take their small children with them. If the children are big enough they can play on their own, but if they are very small and they cannot play on their own, they are a constant distraction for the mother. They will cry, they are hungry or they have wet the place or they are cold, and the mother has to come and care for them continuously, and this is distracting to the work and the boss won't allow it. So it has been the usual practice to give a little opium to the child. Then the child is fast asleep in the blissful slumber that the opium has given to him, dreaming beautiful dreams, and the mother can remain undistracted in her work. This is good for the work, this is good for the mother, this is good for the landlord, but this is very hazardous and dangerous for the health of the child – for his future also this is poisonous. But this is what has been happening.

Society gives you beliefs so that you need not experiment, so that you need not be distracted into the inquiry, because the inquiry will take so much of your energy that you will not be able to be a good clerk or a good stationmaster or a good collector or a good policeman. You will be distracted by your inquiry; you will become more interested in the inner and your interest in the outer will start disappearing.

Society wants you to live an extrovert life, society wants you to be efficient in the world, to be more productive in the world – whether the production is good or bad is not the point. If you work in a factory where bombs are created you have to be efficient and productive. If you work in the army you have to be efficient and always obedient. Wherever you are, whether the work is good or bad is not the question: whatsoever the society has decided you have to follow, you have to fall in line.

If you become an inquirer, then there is danger: you will become more and more of an introvert, your priorities will change, your values will be different. You may not care much about money, you may not care much about power, you may not remain ambitious, you may not be possessive anymore, your interest in property may disappear. You will start searching for inner riches, the inner kingdom of God. But then you will become less and less efficient for the society, and the society cannot afford it – although it will be a better world, where more people are introverted and are doing their own thing rather than being pulled and pushed by others to do their things. It will be a better world where people are more meditative. Then politicians will not be able to create as much mischief as they have been creating in the past. Wars will disappear automatically if people are more introverted. But then it is uncertain who will care to fight and who will care to kill and murder?

And violence is being painted in such ways so that it appears beautiful. Murder in the name of "nation," murder in the name of Islam, murder in the name of Christianity – and then murder becomes beautiful. Murder is murder; whether you murder for Christianity or the Church or the country or the nation doesn't matter. These are just excuses to conduct murder, excuses to be destructive, excuses to be mad.

After every ten years a great world war breaks out upon the world, because in each ten-year period people gather so much pus in their beings that it has to be poured out. They gather so much poison in their beings that they cannot contain it anymore – a madness, a global madness, explodes.

If people are more introverted, wars will disappear, politics will disappear. If people are more introverted, of course they will not be so efficient, but there is no need – they will be happier. They may not be so continuously occupied, madly occupied in things, but they will be happier, more joyous, celebrate more. They will create enough of what is needed, they will not waste energy and be concerned with the unnecessary.

But we have become too concerned with the unnecessary, which is not needed at all – we can afford to be without it. But yet we cannot, because our training has made it in such a way that we have to go on rushing and running. We don't know any other way to be.

Society drugs you with beliefs and kills your inquiry from the very beginning. Religion means reviving your inquiry, religion means taking you back to your original source.

And remember, it is not curiosity; it is a very sincere search. To live without knowing oneself is almost synonymous with being dead. How can one really live without knowing who one is? What will life mean if you don't know yourself? What will you do with yourself if you don't know who you are? How will you decide what is going to be your destiny? Yes, there will be much noise, but there will be no music. There will be much calculation, but there will be no celebration. And there will be much running and rushing hither and thither but no arrival. Between birth and death you will live in a kind of constant tension but you will not know the beauty, the benediction of life and existence, because you could not even know the beauty and benediction of your inner being – which is the closest thing to know, the first thing to know.

The first step towards life is that of self-knowledge. It cannot be just curiosity. There are many people who inquire out of curiosity, but curiosity can never be life-transforming; again it is just an itch which can be satisfied very easily.

Once upon a time there was an innkeeper who, strange to say, was unable to make ends meet. Nothing that he tried was of any effect. He tried to put his house under an entirely new management, but that was in vain. So in despair he consulted a wise woman.

"It is quite simple," she said, as she pocketed her fee. "You must change the name of your inn."

"But it has been 'The Golden Lion' for centuries," he replied.

"You must change the name," she said. "You must call it 'The Eight Bells' and you must have a row of seven bells as the sign."

"Seven?" he said. "But that's absurd! What will that do?"

"Go home and see," said the wise woman.

So he went home and did as she told him. And straightaway every wayfarer who was passing paused to count the bells and then hurried into the inn to point out the mistake, each apparently believing himself to be the only one who had noticed it and all wishing to refresh themselves for their trouble.

And the innkeeper waxed fat and made his fortune.

This is how people are. The name of the inn is "The Eight Bells" and the symbol has only seven bells – enough to make people curious, enough to keep them occupied. But this kind of curiosity is not going to lead you anywhere.

People ask about God, people ask about truth, but you can see from their eyes, by the way they have asked, that they don't mean business. Just as people talk about the weather, people talk about God too – it is polite conversation. Nobody seems to be involved, nobody seems to be in a passionate search. And unless your search is of great passion, of tremendous commitment, of utter involvement, you will not be able to know the secrets of your being, because much work will have to be done. The curious person cannot do that much work.

Curiosity is not enough to take you far away; its energy is very small, very tiny. Only a sincere passion to know can take you through all the trouble that will be needed. It is an uphill task.

So the first thing to understand in *The Secret of the Golden Flower* is: not to be philosophic, not to be drugged by society, not to believe and not to disbelieve either. Remember, whenever I say, "Don't believe," I am not saying that you should disbelieve – disbelief is another kind of belief, a negative kind. When I say, "Don't believe," I am saying both belief and disbelief have to be dropped. You have to be simply open, with no conclusion. You have to be simply aware of your ignorance, with no knowledge hiding your ignorance. You have to be innocent, innocently ignorant. You have to say, "I don't know."

All right approaches begin with this: "I don't know." If you "know" anything already without knowing, if you are knowledgeable, then that very belief will hinder, that very belief will create experiences which are not true. And when you are drugged by a belief – and belief is like LSD or marijuana or hashish – when you are drugged by a belief, it creates its own projected world, it gives your imagination free play. And when your imagination starts playing around you, you are no longer part of reality – you have created a separate private world – you are an idiot.

That is the meaning of the word *idiot*: one who lives in a private world, who has his own reality, who has completely broken away from the real, whose imagination has become so real to him that reality has simply disappeared from his vision. And that's what happens when you take LSD or marijuana or other kinds of drugs: it creates a small fantasy world in you, very colorful – at least it looks colorful when you are lost in the drug – and when you are in the drug, all that you experience appears to be ultimate truth.

Every day somebody or other comes to me and he says, "It is through drugs that I became aware how beautiful the world is." What you became aware of is only your dream world; the drugs simply take away your critical faculty. Drugs just drug your reason and then your dream world opens all its doors and flows in all directions. And when there is no critical faculty functioning, when there is no reason functioning and the imagination has full play and absolute autonomous power, it feels as if it is the ultimate truth – but it is not. This vision has absolutely nothing to do with truth.

Truth is available only to those who are completely undrugged – not only chemically, but religiously too. Those who are *completely* undrugged, only they have the capacity to know the truth.

I have heard....

Under the influence of nitrous oxide, the great psychologist, William James, came to an ultimate "truth." He was one of the first experimenters – and in those days there were no drugged-up people around.

Under the influence of nitrous oxide, he felt that he had stumbled upon the ultimate truth. He was a great psychologist, and a great philosopher too, but he did one thing that very few people do: he immediately wrote it in his notebook. He still had that much sense to know that something of immense value had arisen in his consciousness and it had to be written down immediately. Who knows? – once he was out of the drug experience he might forget it. So he wrote it down and he waited for the moment when the drug and its impact disappear so that he could read what ultimate truth he had come upon. He was thinking that he had become a Buddha or a Christ, seen God or seen something which the seers of the Upanishads saw, or Lao Tzu, or Zarathustra, or Mohammed – but something of that importance.

But he was very puzzled and surprised when he came back to his senses and looked at his notebook. What he had written was this:

"Hogamous, Higamous,
Man is polygamous.
Higamous, Hogamous,
Woman is monogamous."

This was the ultimate truth that he had stumbled upon.

Any absurd thing can look ultimate when you are not in your senses, when the reason is not functioning, when the critical faculty has completely gone to sleep – any stupid thing. But in that moment it is not stupid, in that moment it looks like the ultimate truth.

Aldous Huxley says that when he first took LSD, he was sitting in a very ordinary room and just in front of him was a very ordinary chair. Once LSD started working into his system, into his chemistry, the chair started looking so beautiful that he could not believe his eyes: he had never seen anything so beautiful in his life. It was luminous, light was flowing from the chair in all directions – multicolored, psychedelic. The chair is the same chair – your imagination is creating the whole game, LSD has driven you mad. It has taken away all possibility of being critical.

That's why I say belief is against doubt, but trust is not against doubt. Trust grows through doubt, belief grows by repressing doubt. That's why belief is a kind of drug. That's exactly what the drug does: it represses your doubting faculty, which only keeps you alert – not to become an idiot, not to fall victim of your own imagination. And that's what religions have been doing down the ages. They say, "Don't doubt. Doubt, and you will fall in hell. Believe! If doubt comes, repress it, throw it away. Just go on believing. And believing," they say, "is seeing. If you believe, you will see."

Trust is a totally different phenomenon. It comes out of an undrugged consciousness, an open consciousness – neither believing nor disbelieving, with no conclusions tethered to it – just free, innocent.

Doubt remains useful. Until you arrive at truth doubt helps. Doubt is a friend of trust. The very process of doubt helps you not to become a victim of your imagination; otherwise, imagination has been playing havoc.

For example, if you are a born Hindu and you have been reading about kundalini, then your imagination can create the whole experience: any day, down from the spine, the snake will start uncoiling, and with a great hushing sound it will rush towards the seventh chakra. And the experience will look so real that you cannot doubt it, if you have ever believed in it. But Jesus never came across kundalini, Mohammed never knew anything about it...even Buddha, who was born a Hindu. But because he was a man of sincere inquiry and had dropped all kinds of beliefs he never came across kundalini. Mahavira never knew anything about it, Zarathustra has not talked about it. So what happened? Did they miss? It is a belief: if you believe in seven chakras, those seven chakras will become facts in your life. If you believe in anything you will start seeing it.

Gopi Krishna, who has become a propounder of kundalini energy in the modern age, says he was working for thirteen years, sitting and waiting for the kundalini to arise. Thirteen years is a long time. If for thirteen years you can believe in kundalini and you can wait and you can go on looking deep down into the spine, it is not a miracle if it happens.

Then one day it happened: the serpent uncoiled himself, rushed with great energy, penetrated the brain with a sound, the roaring sound of a waterfall – and since then Gopi Krishna thinks that his genius has been released. He thinks that if your kundalini rises you will become a genius. But I don't see what his genius has done. Yes, he writes some stupid poetry, very ordinary, fourth-rate. If that is genius then it will be good if people keep their kundalini deep down, repressed. If everybody becomes a fourth-rate poet, that will not be a good situation. What kind of genius is released?

These are not the ways, these are just imaginings. And if you believe in a certain thing, you will start seeing it – that is the danger. Don't start with belief. That is the vision of Tao: inquire, experiment, and wait for the conclusion to come on its own.

The sutras.

> *Master Lu-tsu said:*
> *When the light is made to move in a circle, all the energies of heaven*
> *and Earth, of the light and the dark, are crystallized.*

Your consciousness is flowing outward – this is a fact, there is nothing to believe in it: when you look at an object your consciousness flows towards the object.

For example, you are looking at me: then you forget yourself, you become focused on me; then your energy flows towards me, then your eyes are arrowed towards me – this is extroversion. You see a flower and you are enchanted, and you become focused on the flower; you become oblivious of yourself, you are only attentive to the beauty of the flower. This we know – every moment it is happening. A beautiful woman passes by and suddenly your energy starts following her.

We know this outward flow of light – this is only half of the story – but each time the light flows out, you fall into the background, you become oblivious of yourself. The light has to flow back so that you are both the subject and the object at the same time, simultaneously, so that you see yourself. Then self-knowledge is released. Ordinarily, we live only in this half way – half-alive, half-dead, that's the situation – and slowly slowly, light goes on flowing outward and never returns. You become more and more empty inside, hollow. You become a black hole.

This is exactly what happens on a greater scale in the universe. Now physicists have discovered black holes. Taoists discovered black holes long before, but they were not concerned about the black holes there in the faraway space, they were concerned about the black holes inside you. A black hole is a state when all your energy is spent, exhausted and you have become empty, and you have forgotten completely how to go on nourishing this source of energy. Scientists say that sooner or later this sun will become a black hole, because continuous energy is being released but nothing is returning to it. It is an immense source of energy. For millions of years it has been giving light to the solar system. For millions of years trees are growing, flowers are flowering, man is living, animals are moving, birds are flying, because of the sun's energy. But the sun is becoming spent. Slowly slowly, one day, it will collapse; there will be no more energy left. Suddenly all light will disappear, the last rays will disappear from it. Then it will be a black hole.

And that's how many people live their lives: they become black holes

– because of this constant extroversion. You see this, you see that, you are continually seeing without ever returning the energy to the seer. In the day you see the world, in the night you see dreams, but you go on remaining constantly attached to objects. This is dissipating energy. By the time a man is thirty he is almost finished; then he is a black hole.

People die nearabout thirty, although they are buried nearabout seventy – that is another matter – but they die nearabout thirty. And I see a grain of truth in the hippie idea that don't believe a man above thirty. There is a grain of truth in it, because it is very rare to find a man beyond thirty who is alive. People become black holes – spent, utterly exhausted. They go on dragging somehow, they live without being alive, as if just the momentum of the past helps them to remain alive.

It happens: if you love bicycling, you have to pedal the bicycle. But sometimes you can just stop pedaling and out of the momentum created by the past pedaling the bicycle goes on for a while without pedaling. And if it is a downward slope, it can go far. And after thirty or thirty-five it is a downward slope. Thirty-five is the peak; if seventy is the average age of dying, then thirty-five is the peak. After thirty-five you are on a downward slope: you can go on rolling down without any energy.

The Taoist experience is that this energy that you spend in your extroversion can be made more and more crystallized rather than spent. If you learn the secret science of turning it backwards, it is possible. That is the whole science of all methods of concentration.

Just standing before a mirror someday, try one small experiment. You are looking at the mirror, your own face in the mirror, your own eyes in the mirror – this is extroversion. You are looking into the mirrored face – your own face, of course, but it is an object outside you. Then, for a moment, reverse the whole process. Start feeling that you are being looked at by the reflection in the mirror – not that you are looking at the reflection but the reflection is looking at you – and you will be in a very strange space. Just try it for a few minutes and you will be very alive, and something of immense power will start entering you. You may even become frightened because you have never known it, you have never seen the complete circle of energy.

And this seems to me, although it is not mentioned in Taoist scriptures, but this seems to me the most simple experiment anybody can do, and very easily. Just standing before the mirror in your bathroom, first look into the reflection: you are looking and the reflection is the object. Then change the whole situation, reverse the process. Start feeling that you are the reflection and the reflection is looking at you, and immediately you will see a change happening – a great energy moving towards you. In the beginning it may be frightening because you have never done it and you have never known it. It will look crazy, you may feel shaken, a trembling may arise in you, or you may feel disorientated, because your whole orientation up to now has been extroversion. Introversion has to be learned slowly slowly. But the circle is complete. And if you do it for a few days you will be surprised: how much more alive you feel the whole day – just a few minutes standing before the mirror and letting the energy come back to you, so the circle is complete. And whenever the circle is complete there is a great silence. The incomplete circle creates restlessness, when the circle is complete it creates rest, it makes you centered, and to be centered is to be powerful. The power is yours. And this is just an experiment; then you can try it in many ways.

Looking at the roseflower, first look at the roseflower for a few moments, a few minutes, and then start the reverse process: the roseflower is looking at you. And you will be surprised how much energy the roseflower can give to you. And the same can be done with trees and the stars and with people. And the best way is to do it with the woman or man you love. Just look into each other's eyes. First begin looking at the other and then start feeling the other returning the energy to you; the gift is coming back. You will feel replenished, you will feel showered, bathed, basked in a new kind of energy. You will come out of it rejuvenated, vitalized.

> Master Lu-tsu said:
> When the light is made to move in a circle...

This is what they mean by moving light in a circle. Your light is moving in an arc: it simply goes out and never comes back. You become a black hole sooner or later. If the circle is complete you will become a white hole. Now, after black holes, physics is discovering white holes too. A white hole is very pregnant with energy, just the opposite of the black hole.

> When the light is made to move in a circle, all the energies of
> heaven and Earth...

Heaven and Earth mean inner and outer, above and below, God and the world, the invisible and the visible, the unknowable and the knowable. Heaven represents God and Earth represents the manifested world. They become one when the circle is complete. Then you are not only dust unto dust; something of the sky has penetrated you. Then you are no longer just earthly, no more just a human being – you have become divine.

Remember the root of the word *human*: it comes from *humus*. *Humus* means the earth. Man is made of the earth, that's why man is called human. Man is dust, hence he is called human. When the dust starts becoming luminous with the divine, then you know the splendor of life. And that is possible if the energy comes back. And it can be brought back, from everywhere; there is no problem in it, you just have to practice the secret. And once you have got the knack of it, you will find it, from everywhere.

Looking at a green tree you can be so alive – as if the whole sap of the tree has flown towards you, the whole juice of the tree has gone into your being. Looking at the moon and you will be surprised: there is no need to get drunk with any alcohol or any other drug, with the moon you can become a drunkard. The moon can return so much energy if you know how to take it back.

In India, in the ancient Rig Veda, there is talk of *soma*. Scientists think that soma is something like LSD. Scientists think it must have been a kind of mushroom that has disappeared from the Himalayas because of the change in the climate or something. Or maybe it has not disappeared, maybe people have just forgotten about it. It may be still growing somewhere in the deep valleys of the Himalayas and we have simply forgotten what it is. Maybe the ancient seers knowingly helped humanity to forget about it; it may have proved too dangerous.

Aldous Huxley says that soma was the ultimate drug, and in the future when we will have discovered the ultimate LSD we will again call it soma. But you will be surprised to know that in Sanskrit soma is another name for moon. Hence, Monday in Hindi is called *somwar*, the day of the moon. Soma is another name for the moon; it is not a mushroom, it is not some kind of LSD, it is not a drug. It is a secret science of getting in communion with the moon. And just as the ocean is affected by the moon, if you can get the energy back from the moon, you will be surprised: great juice, great nectar, showers on you – you can be drunk without getting drunk on any drug.

The moon can affect you to the very core of your being, and it will make you cool and calm because the moon is the feminine energy. Just as when you embrace a woman that you love and suddenly you feel great calm and quietude arising in you, exactly the same happens on a greater scale when energy returns to you from the moon.

The moon is the feminine principle, just as the sun is the masculine principle.

The moon is yin, the sun is yang. The moon can mother you. There is no need to go in search to the Himalayan valleys for some mushroom; that mushroom is always there in the sky – it is the moon. You have to learn the secret of how to get energy back from the moon. There have been secret methods to get energy from the moon and from the sun too.

Sun worship was born out of a certain technique; great temples of the sun arose. The sun temple of Konarak was just an expression of gratitude to the sun. It was not just worship, it was a science – how to get yang energy in you. It is particularly good for women to get sun energy in them so that their hidden, dormant yang becomes active and it is good for men to get moon energy so that their dormant feminine principle becomes alive, moving again. It is good for a woman to be a sun worshipper and good for a man to be a moon worshipper. But the worship has not to be just a ritual, it has to be this method.

> *When the light is made to move in a circle, all the energies of heaven*
> *and Earth, of the light and the dark, are crystallized.*

Light and dark symbolize man-woman, light-heavy, grace-gravitation, life-death, movement-rest. All these things are represented by light and dark.

In short, if the energy can move in a circle, slowly slowly you will not know who you are – whether a man or a woman. Extroversion is the principle of yang, introversion is the principle of yin. Man is naturally extrovert, woman is naturally introvert. Even while making love, man keeps his eyes open – he wants to see, he is a voyeur; hence the possibility of pornography. No woman is interested in pornography; no woman sees any point in it. Even while making love to her beloved, she closes her eyes. She is an introvert, her energy moves inwardly.

But the energy has to become a circle, otherwise one remains a man, one remains a woman, and both are half – two halves of the same whole – hence the attraction and the need for the other. The day you are able to circulate your energy in a circle you will not need another woman, you will not need another man, because your own man, your own woman will meet and merge into each other. You will be whole, and to be whole is to be holy.

This is Tao and this is Tantra too: to be whole is to be holy.

> *When the light is made to move in a circle, all the energies of heaven*
> *and Earth, of the light and the dark, are crystallized.*

This is what Carl Gustav Jung called "individuation," crystallization. This is what George Gurdjieff used to call "the birth of the self" or "the soul."

Ordinarily you are just fragments, ordinarily you are a crowd, you have many selves. You don't have a single "I," you have many "I's", small "I's," and all struggling and competing with each other to dominate. This is the misery of man: that he is many. How can you be at ease if you are many? One part says, "Do this," another part says, "No," and a third part says, "Do something else."

Whichever you follow you will repent, because the other parts which were not willing to go will create trouble. They will go on insisting that you are on the wrong path, that the other alternative would have been far better: "If you had followed me, you would have arrived by now. And look, you didn't listen to me." But if you had listened to that part, then the other parts would have taken revenge.

Man is never contented – cannot be – because he is many. If you become one, contentment follows of its own accord. If you are many, discontent is natural. You live in constant conflict. If you are one, conflict disappears; you have come home. This is what Taoists call crystallization, and the method to achieve it is to make the light move in a circle so your yin and yang are no longer separate.

The light has to move just exactly as your breathing moves: in and out, out and in, you exhale, you inhale. Just think of a person who only exhales: he will not be able to live, his body will die. Or think of the person who only inhales: he will also die. And that's exactly what has happened to your soul: your soul is dead, because either you exhale light or you inhale light. You have not yet learned that exhalation and inhalation have to become a circle, one process. Exhale deeply and inhale deeply.

Just as breath is necessary for the life of the body, consciousness is necessary for the soul. So consciousness should not be left as a half, the circle should be completed. The woman has to learn how to be a man too, and the man has to learn how to be a woman too. And when the man and the woman have come to an equal balance, when they are utterly balanced, that is crystallization, individuation – the soul is born.

> When one begins to apply this magic...

And, yes, it is magic, because its effects are really unbelievable.

> When one begins to apply this magic it is as if, in the middle of
> being, there were nonbeing.

This is what I meant by "black hole."

> *When one begins to apply this magic it is as if, in the middle of*
> *being, there were nonbeing.*

As if you are surrounded by being, but you are an island of nonbeing, of nothingness – a black hole. The trees are alive, the stars are alive, the birds are alive, the earth is alive, the sun and the moon are alive, everything is alive, and you...just a dead black hole. In this vast ocean of being you are a nonbeing. This is the situation when you begin.

> *When in the course of time the work is completed, and beyond*
> *the body there is a body, it is as if, in the middle of nonbeing,*
> *there were being.*

Then everything changes; then you become a being, a white hole. You become so integrated, so crystallized, that compared to you, all the suns and the moons and the trees and the birds and the animals look like nonbeing.

Just think of a buddha: he has being – the whole existence feels pale compared to him. He has life – life eternal, life abundant. The whole existence is poor, he is rich. He is an emperor, the whole existence is beggarly.

> *When in the course of time the work is completed, and beyond the*
> *body there is a body...*

When this circle of light becomes stabilized in you, crystallized in you, you will start feeling another body within the body. This body is made of dust, that body is made of God, of divinity. This body has form, that body has no form. This body is gross, that body is subtle. This body will have to die, that body knows no death. This body is part of time, that body is part of eternity.

When this second body is born – and it can be born only when you have learned how to inhale and exhale light... Just as you are inhaling and exhaling breath, when you have learned how to inhale and exhale light – the second body, the body of light... This is the body of darkness, this is the body which is part of the earth, part of gravitation. It is heavy, it is pulled downward. The other body is pulled upwards, it is part of grace, it is light – light in both senses of the word: it is illumined and it is weightless – you can fly.

That's what Zen people call "flying without wings." Then the whole sky and the infinity of it is available to you.

> ...as if, in the middle of nonbeing there were being. Only after
> concentrated work of a hundred days will the light be genuine.

In the beginning the light will look almost like imagination – in the beginning it has to be imagination. Only after a time, a hundred days, the

> ...concentrated work of a hundred days...

It depends on how concentrated your work is; a hundred days is not a fixed time. If your work is totally concentrated, then a hundred days; otherwise it will take a hundred years or a hundred lives – one knows not. It depends on the intensity. If your being is totally involved in it, committed to it, you are bent upon it, you are ready to risk all for it, then in one hundred days the light will become genuine. In the beginning it will be imagination.

Imagination is not wrong; imagination is wrong only when it takes you against reality, when it becomes a barrier. Imagination is not wrong when it cooperates with reality. Then it is a great blessing. In the beginning you will feel it as imaginary – just looking in the mirror you will feel, "This is all imagination, that the reflection is looking at me." It is imagination in the beginning, but soon you will realize that it was not imagination – you were just turning the key in the lock of reality – it starts happening.

In the beginning, if you touch a tree with great love, you know the tree cannot respond – and if you feel some response from the tree, you will think it is imagination. It is not – the tree responds – but it will take a little time for you to recognize the truth of it. When you are loving, the tree responds with love – love is always responded to with love. And if love is not responded to with love, then know well your love is not love, that's all; then something else is masquerading as love.

> ...then only will it become spirit-fire.

After a hundred days' concentrated effort it will become spirit-fire.

> After a hundred days there develops by itself in the midst of the light
> a point of the true light-pole.

First it is a diffused light, you just feel it very slightly there; sometimes it is there and sometimes it is not there, it is very dim and very fragile. But slowly slowly it becomes very centered, it becomes a light-pole.

Then suddenly there develops the seed-pearl.

Then, just at the very center of the light-pole, the seed-pearl.

It is as if a man and woman embraced and a conception took place.

And it is exactly so: the inner man and the inner woman have embraced. It is a kind of inner intercourse. It is real Tantra: your feminine part and your masculine part are making love to each other, are joined together, and then there is no need for them to separate.

With the outer woman you will have to separate, otherwise it will become very ugly. With the outer woman you will have to separate, otherwise it will become repulsive. With the outer man you will have to separate – it can only be momentary, only for a moment can you have the glimpse of unity – but with the inner there is no need to separate.

A buddha lives in a constant orgasmic state: the inner woman and the inner man go on making love. You must have seen the *shivalinga* in Hindu temples; that is a symbol. Just below that *linga* is the *yoni,* the feminine part; it is a symbol of the inner man and woman meeting. It is not just phallic as Freudians will interpret it. It is symbolic. It symbolizes the inner polarity.

And once this meeting has happened, you are born anew. When Jesus says to Nicodemus, "Unless you are born again…" this is what he means. I don't know what Christians say and I don't care either, but this is what he means. "Unless you are born again…" This is the birth he means. And this is what Hindus call *dwija,* twice-born: you have given birth to yourself. If the outer man meets with the outer woman you create a child, you reproduce. If the inner man meets the inner woman you again create a child, but you are the parent and you are the child. A new life begins in you – the life of a buddha, the life of enlightenment, the life of deathlessness.

Then one must be quite still and wait.

When this conception has been felt inside, when you feel that the inner man has penetrated the inner woman and the woman is pregnant, then nothing is left but to wait – just as the woman waits for nine months. With great joy, with great prayer, with great hope, she waits. Nothing else has to be done, no need to do anything – the doing part is finished.

The male part is action. To make light circulate is the male part. Once the conception has taken place and the inner woman is pregnant, then the male part need not work, it has to rest. Now things will grow on their own.

Meditation is the first part. Now there is only prayer left. Hence I say to you that without meditation you will never know what prayer is. Prayer is the highest form of meditation. Prayer is like fragrance, meditation is like the flower. One has to go through meditation.

People ask me why, if their path is that of prayer, are they supposed to do so many meditations here in my ashram. Prayer will come; you have to pave the way for it to come. You have to go through all kinds of meditations – these are cleansing processes. This is the male part of you that has to be satisfied, and then the female part will take possession. You will be pregnant! And to be pregnant is to be prayerful, because then nothing is left to be done. Effort is finished and now you are effortless. This is what Taoists call "inaction through action."

You have been doing many experiments on moving the light in a circle, you have succeeded – after a long concentrated effort something has crystallized in you, the man and woman are no more separate, they have become one, the child is there – now except for waiting, nothing is needed. Wait with hope, wait with trust. And this is what prayer is.

> In the midst of the primal transformation, the radiance of the light is
> the determining thing.

And what will make you alert that the pregnancy has happened? You will start seeing an inner radiance. Whenever you close your eyes you will not see darkness but radiance. And not only will you see it; those who love you, they will start seeing an aura around you.

> In the midst of the primal transformation, the radiance of the light is
> the determining thing.

How do you know that a woman is pregnant? Have you not seen a certain aura around a pregnant woman? Have you not seen some light coming out of her eyes, her face, her very being? It is exactly the same, but on a much higher plane: when you are pregnant with God within you, you will see radiance. Whenever you close your eyes you will be all light inside – a sourceless light, coming from nowhere, very cool light, moonlight, but immensely enchanting, magical – and others who love you and are very close to you will also start feeling it.

That's why we draw an aura around the pictures of saints: it is not available to everybody. If you had seen Christ you would not have seen his aura...but his disciples saw it. Certainly the people who crucified him didn't see that aura. They could not see; they were blind, they were closed. The aura was seen around Buddha...by the disciples.

These secrets are available only to lovers. They are such intimate secrets that they are not available to all and sundry, to any Tom, Dick and Harry. They are only available to those who are intimate, those who come close, close, closer and closer, and those who are open, vulnerable.

> In the midst of the primal transformation, the radiance of the
> light is the determining thing. In the physical world it is the sun;
> in man, the eye.

And when the inner radiance starts growing in you, the eyes become aflame, they look drunk. There is a dance in the eyes – a subtle light, a totally different quality comes to the eyes. Now the eyes not only see things, but they share too. Tao cannot be divided but it can be shared, and the sharing of Tao is through the eyes.

When I initiate you into sannyas, I ask you to look at me. I want to look into your eyes, I want my eyes to dig deep into your eyes, to have a contact there, because behind your two eyes is hidden the third eye. If the third eye is contacted – and if you are open it happens within a split second – time is not needed. If the third eye is contacted, I know a disciple has come. If it is not contacted, then I only hope that you will become a disciple someday. In that hope I give you sannyas. But that is a hope; it may be fulfilled, it may not be fulfilled – it will depend on a thousand and one things. But when I see a disciple, when the third eye immediately starts responding to me, then you have come to the place you have been seeking and searching for. Now there will be no need to go anywhere, now you will not need any master, any teaching – you have come home.

> This energy is directed outward – flows downward.

Ordinarily, the energy that is coming from the eyes flows outward. "Outward" and "downward" are synonymous.

*Therefore the Way of the Golden Flower depends wholly on the
backward-flowing method.*

Ordinarily the energy is going outward and downward. You have to bring it
backward, inward – and "inward" is synonymous with "upward." Once it starts
coming back to you and you become a circle of energy, you will be surprised – a
new dimension has opened up: you start moving upwards, your life is no longer
horizontal. It has taken a new route – the vertical.

God exists on the vertical route. You will not come across him in the world
– not that he is not in the world, but unless you are moving vertically, you will
not come across him. Just as a blind man cannot see light, the horizontal man
cannot see God.

Many come to me and say, "If you show us God, we will believe." But how
can I show you God? How can I show a blind man light unless he is prepared to
go through the treatment so that his eyes open? I will have to turn you from your
horizontal way of life into a vertical way of life. That's what sannyas is all about:
a vertical way of being. And once the light starts moving upwards, the golden
flower opens up.

These are symbols; there is no flower inside you. "Flower" simply represents
flowering, "golden" simply represents its lightfulness, its radiance.

The circulation of the light is not only a fantasy.

Remember: the circulation of the light is not only a fantasy. In the beginning
it may appear so – you will have to be patient – soon it becomes a fact. It is a
fact, it is a fact from the very beginning, but just because you have never been in
contact with it, in the beginning it looks like a fantasy.

*By concentrating the thoughts, one can fly; by concentrating the
desires, one falls.*

Desire is the Taoist name for energy moving downward, outward, and
"thought" is the Taoist symbol for energy moving inward. So don't misunderstand.
By "thought," Taoists don't mean your so-called thoughts; by "thought" they
mean thought-energy purified of desire. If it is purified of desire and all desire has
disappeared, then there is no need to go out, because you go out only because
you are desirous of something. You desire a house, you desire money, you desire

power, you desire a man, a woman, this and that – then you go out. If there is no desire, thought need not go out; it starts turning inwards – the one-hundred-and-eighty-degree turn happens.

Desireless thought is inward-moving, desireful thought is outward-moving. Hence the insistence of all the buddhas on desirelessness.

> *When a pupil takes little care of his thoughts and much care of his*
> *desires, he gets into the path of submersion.*

When a disciple takes little care of his thought and too much care of his desires, he is drowned in the world.

> *Only through contemplation and quietness does true intuition arise:*
> *for that the backward-flowing method is necessary.*

Thought has to be purified of desire. Once thought is purified of desire it is no-thought. Mind without desires is a no-mind. It is what Patanjali calls *samadhi,* Zen people call satori, Taoists call crystallization: the balance of the outward and the inward. And no energy is lost; it goes into the world and comes back like a bird flying in the morning into the sky, and by the evening it comes back to the nest.

Let your energy come back to the nest again and again. Don't let it go forever without turning it back to you. And you will become a reservoir, and you will become tremendously powerful inwardly. Only in that power does intuition start functioning. In that power spirit-fire is born. In that power the true light-pole arises. In that power suddenly there develops the seed-pearl.

> *It is as if a man and woman embraced and a conception took place.*
> *Then one must be quite still and wait.*

Meditation is complete and prayer begins. To bring meditation to prayer is the whole work of Tao.

Enough for today.

CHAPTER 8
Real is for Always

The first question:

Osho,
Would you talk about the relationship between disillusionment and
celebration? I'm feeling a strange mixture of the two – a dying and
a coming to life at the same time.

Venu Gopal, mind lives in illusions. And to live in illusions is to be miserable, because they cannot be fulfilled. You can go on hoping but you will always be moving into a mirage. The moment you reach the place you were hoping for, the mirage will disappear, you will be in despair. Out of your despair you will again hope.

Hope is just an effort to keep oneself alive somehow. You will again create illusion. This is how the whole game goes on: you are in despair, out of despair you create an illusion; out of illusion more despair is created, and out of more despair, more illusions. One goes on from despair to illusion, from illusion to despair. No energy is left to celebrate. You are in a constant tension between despair and hope. Your life becomes nothing but a tension between that which is and that which should be. You cannot feel being, you remain engrossed in becoming; becoming is misery, being is celebration.

Celebration is not because some desire is fulfilled – because no desire is ever fulfilled. Desire as such cannot be fulfilled. Desire is only a way to avoid the present moment. Desire creates the future and takes you far away. Desire is a drug; it keeps you stoned, it does not allow you to see the reality – that which is here and now.

Celebration means dropping this whole trip of becoming – just being here. When becoming disappears, all the smoke of becoming disappears, there is the flame of being, and that very flame is celebration.

Celebration is without any cause. Celebration is simply because we are. We are made out of the stuff called celebration. That's our natural state – to celebrate – as natural as it is for the trees to bloom, for birds to sing, for rivers to flow to the ocean. Celebration is a natural state. It has nothing to do with your desires and their fulfillment, with your hopes and their fulfillment; it is already the case. But to see the celebration that is already happening at the deepest core of your being you will have to drop becoming, you will have to understand the futility of becoming and realise that you are as you are.

So something tremendously beautiful is happening, Gopal. Allow it. Yes, it is exactly so: when you are utterly disillusioned and you don't create any more illusions – that is what I mean by utterly disillusioned… Disillusionment comes many times in everybody's life, but out of disillusion you again create new illusions. You cannot live without illusions; it has become a habit, a habit of many lives. You cannot live in the reality as it is, you want it to be something else – you are always wanting it to be something else – and reality has no obligation to anybody to change itself. And it is good that it doesn't bother about your desires, otherwise there will be chaos because there are so many people desiring, projecting.

Reality remains as it is, utterly unaffected by what you desire. It never takes any notice of your desires. But once you are absolutely disillusioned – and by "absolute disillusionment" I mean you no longer create any more illusions, you simply remain with it – even if it is despair, you remain with it, you remain in it, you accept it. The moment you accept despair, it starts disappearing, because it can exist only as a shadow of hope; it cannot exist on its own. You cannot just be in despair without any illusion, that is impossible – it is as impossible as if there were just a shadow walking on the road. If you walk there will be a shadow, but the shadow cannot walk alone. Despair is a shadow of illusion. If you are utterly disillusioned, despair starts disappearing, and a new being, a fresh being, a resurrection, a celebration arises in you.

Aniruddha has written a question saying that when he came here he was thinking about me as vast, special and extraordinary. Now he says, "Living here with you for so many days, you now appear to me as ordinary, just as any other man. So what is the fuss all about?"

I have no obligation to fulfill your demands. I am just as I am, utterly ordinary. Reality is ordinary. The rose is a rose is a rose, the rock is a rock, the river is a river. Reality is absolutely ordinary, utterly ordinary. I am an ordinary man. Then what is the difference between you and me? The difference is: I celebrate my ordinariness, you don't celebrate it. That is where the difference is. I welcome it, I am utterly blissful with it; you are not. I am a being, you are a becoming. There is the difference. Not that I am special and you are ordinary – that is utter nonsense. If I am special then everybody is special, if you are ordinary then I am ordinary. We belong to the same reality. I am utterly ordinary, but the difference is that I am celebrating it: I have no grudge, I have no complaint, I am not trying to become somebody that I am not. I have accepted myself in absoluteness – not even a single thing do I want to change. In this relaxation, in this acceptance, celebration has started happening to me.

Now Aniruddha says he is in a difficulty. He created his difficulty himself. I have never told anybody that I am special. That was your idea, your projection. And in fact, why was Aniruddha thinking that I am special? Deep down *he* wants to be special. Deep down he wants to be special, that's why he stayed here, seeing that "Here is a special man, so there must be some secrets to being special. Learn from this man so you can also become special, so you are no longer ordinary."

People have such condemnation for the ordinary. I have tremendous respect for it because the ordinary is the real. God is the *most* ordinary thing in existence – has to be. How can he be special? – compared to what, compared to whom? He alone is, he cannot be special. He can only be ordinary, as ordinary as the rose and the peacock and the eagle, and the river and the rock and the cloud.

But Aniruddha must have had a desire deep down to become special. People search for masters in order to become special. People search for masters out of their ego desires. The very search is an ego trip. Then naturally, one day you will be disillusioned. That was your illusion; I have nothing to do with it. If you project something on me, how am I supposed to be responsible for it? You project; sooner or later your projection will fall down. In fact, I will help in every way so that it is broken, shattered, so that you can see me as I am, so that one day you can see yourself too as you are.

My whole teaching is drop all these stupid efforts to become special, extraordinary. Just enjoy reality as it is – wherever you are, whosoever you are. Celebrate it. This I call prayer, this I call being religious: celebrating one's being. It is a gift from God. Just to be is more than you can ask for. Just to be is the greatest miracle. What more of a miracle can happen?

Venu Gopal, something tremendously beautiful is on the way. Don't create any more illusions again. The mind will try. Don't listen to the mind. Remain disillusioned. It will be a kind of dying, because you have lived up to now through illusions. That has been your nourishment. You will feel like dying. But die – and with this death a new life will arise in you, you will be resurrected. Let this be a death – and a total death. Don't die in a lukewarm way; die totally, wholly. Allow this death to happen, and the next moment, out of this death, some new life arises that you have not seen and that has been always within you – but you were not available to see it.

And to Aniruddha also I would like to say: It is very good, Aniruddha. Now you are seeing my reality. I am an ordinary man and I am here to make you ordinary also. I am here to help you come out of your ego trips. I am here to help you to celebrate this immense ordinariness. Only then are you grateful to God.

What are you trying to do – trying to become somebody else, trying to decorate yourself? But all those decorations will be falsifications. You can never be anybody else, you can only be yourself. There is no way for the roseflower to become a lotus. There is no way for the lotus to become a roseflower. You can only be yourself. If you allow it there will be celebration, because there will be no possibility of misery, and the energy that becomes misery becomes celebration. If you don't allow it to move into becoming misery, what else will you do? It is the same energy that cries in you – it can become laughter. It is the same energy that becomes hate in you, sour, bitter – it becomes love. It can become destruction – it becomes creation. The energy is not different. When you are engaged in an ego trip of becoming somebody special, then your whole life will be a long tragedy.

What is the difference between Alexander and Buddha? Alexander wants to be special, wants to possess the whole world, wants to be unique. And Buddha? – Buddha simply wants to be himself. There is no need to go anywhere, there is no need to become at all. No future is needed, no time is required: Buddha can be *this* very moment what he wants to be because he already *is* that. But for Alexander even millions of lives will not be enough, his journey will remain incomplete. He will never be able to bring it to a conclusion. It is a vicious circle: he will be frustrated again and again, and out of frustration he will create bigger illusions, stronger illusions. He will need bigger illusions and stronger illusions.

It is like a drug, I say again. If you take a drug, any drug, sooner or later you become accustomed to it. Then you need more quantities of it, stronger doses of it, and so on and so forth. Small illusions won't do; once you have become accustomed to them, you will need greater illusions. This is how people become mad. A madman is one whose illusions have gone completely contrary to reality. Now he lives only in his illusions – there are not even intervals when he sees reality as it is, not even moments of truth. He simply lives in his illusions – he is a madman. And what others are may be a lesser madness, but the madness is there. The difference is only of degree, quantity, but not of quality. Unless you are ready to relax into your being as you are, you are not sane.

I am ordinary, and I say to you Buddha is ordinary. And I say to you all the buddhas have always been ordinary. That is their specialness, because in this world nobody wants to be ordinary. That is their extraordinariness, because they are people who have chosen to be ordinary. That is their humbleness. Jesus says, "Blessed are the meek for theirs is the kingdom of God." By "meek" he means exactly this: to be just what God has meant you to be; not to aspire to anything at all, to live in a relaxed state.

It is good, Aniruddha, that your illusion is broken. Thank me for it, feel grateful for it, that I have not supported your illusion at all. If you carried it for so many months it was just your work. I was not a support to it.

But his question shows that now he thinks I am ordinary so the problem is arising for him again. Then what is he doing here? Then he should go again to somebody else who is extraordinary. Now will be the decisive moment for him. If seeing that I am ordinary he understands the beauty of being ordinary, celebration will start. If he is feeling frustrated – as if I had deceived him, as if I had been pretending to be extraordinary and now he has found that I am not – then he will have new illusions. He will project his desires onto somebody else. He will find another screen and again he will be frustrated. And he will need bigger and bigger doses, and sooner or later he will be a victim of somebody who is there to exploit people, who is there to pretend, according to your illusions.

That's why I am so much against Satya Sai Baba: he is trying to help your projections. That is my criticism of his effort. He tries to go with your projections. He is not an independent man, he depends on you. You project and he will try to fulfill your projections – at least he will pretend that you are in the close vicinity of a special man who can do miracles, who can make things appear from nowhere.

Now Aniruddha can become a victim of a man like Satya Sai Baba because then he will think this is special; no ordinary man can do it. That's true, but ordinary magicians are doing it. But these tricks are very dangerous. They are very subtle in their exploitation. Aniruddha can easily become a victim of any charlatan, of any deceiver. Now will be the decisive moment for him. He will have to decide either to live with this man who is ordinary and drop all desire for extraordinariness and all projections and to become ordinary himself and let celebration happen, or he will have to project his illusions somewhere else.

And then you can go on and on. That's how you have been going on for centuries. For so many lives you have been going on and on: you simply change your screen, but you don't drop your projection; you carry your projector and your whole film of hopes, dreams, desires. You just become frustrated with the screen – "This screen is not right" – so you find another screen. When are you going to drop the projector and the film? When are you going to burn the whole ego trip? In that very moment death has happened, and resurrection.

Venu Gopal, you say, "I'm feeling a strange mixture of the two – a dying and a coming to life at the same time." That's how it will happen in the beginning: you will die a little bit and you will be born a little bit. Learn a lesson from it: die totally so that you can be born totally. And then you know: each moment one has to die so that each moment one becomes again fresh, young – is born. This can happen each moment, and a true life consists of death-resurrection, death-resurrection. Each moment it happens. Each moment one has to die to the past, only then does the present become available – and there is celebration, and there is great joy, and there is great flowering.

The golden flower blooms if you are ready to die to the past, if you are utterly in the present. And you can be utterly in the present only if you have no desire to be anywhere else in the future, if you have no desire to be somebody else. *This* I call enlightenment.

The second question:

Osho,
Why is love so essential for spiritual growth?

Love and awareness is the highest form of polarity – just like man-woman, life-death, darkness-light, summer-winter, outer-inner, yin-yang, the body and the soul, the creation and the creator. Love and awareness is the highest form of polarity – the last polarity – from where transcendence happens.

Love needs two. It is a relationship; it is outgoing, it is energy moving outwards. There is an object: the beloved. The object becomes more important than yourself. Your joy is in the object. If your beloved is happy, you are happy; you become part of the object. There is a kind of dependence, and the other is needed. Without the other you will feel lonely.

Awareness is just being with yourself in utter aloneness, just being alert. It is not a relationship, the other is not needed at all. It is not outgoing, it is ingoing.

Love is the movement of the light out of your being. Awareness is the reverse movement: the backward movement of the light to the source again, returning to the source. This is what Jesus calls repentance – not in the sense of repentance, but in the sense of returning to the source. Patanjali calls it *pratyahara*, coming back home; Mahavira calls it *pratikraman*, coming back to oneself – the circle is complete. *The Secret of the Golden Flower* is based, totally based, on this backward movement of your energy. But the backward movement is possible only if you have moved forward. You have to go into love, you have to relate in order to come to yourself. It looks paradoxical.

The child has to get lost into the world to become a child again. The innocence has to go into all the turmoil of cunningness and calculation to become really innocent again. A child is innocent, but his innocence is that of ignorance. A saint is also innocent, but his innocence is not of ignorance but of experience, of ripeness, of maturity. He is again innocent, but that "again" has great importance – he cannot be distracted from his innocence anymore. The child is bound to get distracted: every Adam has to leave the Garden of Eden, the world of innocence. Every Adam has to go into the world, into the mud of it, because only there will you mature, will you ripen. Only there will you learn, only there will you see in contrast the beauty of innocence, will you understand the splendor of innocence. The day you have learned the beauty of innocence, you have become aware of it, you will have come back home.

The Adam cannot become Christ if he does not leave paradise; he will remain a child. Adam means outward movement, Christ means inward movement. Adam means love, Christ means awareness. The circle is complete. The difference between Adam and Christ is only that of direction. Adam is going extrovertedly, and the same person, when he turns back and becomes introverted, is Christ. Adam is the potential Christ, Christ is the actualized Adam.

Love is very essential. You have to lose yourself to gain yourself. Love is the only possibility of losing yourself totally. When you are lost totally, then you will be able to remember what you have done.

It is like a fish which has always lived in the ocean: it will never become aware of the ocean and the benediction of it; it has to be caught in a net, a fisherman has to come to take it out, throw it on the shore. Only on the shore, in the hot sun, will it remember for the first time. Although it lived for years in the ocean it was oblivious, completely oblivious of the ocean. Now the thirst, the heat, makes it mindful of the ocean. A great longing arises to go back to the ocean. It makes every effort to jump back into the ocean.

That is the state of a seeker: thirsty to go back into the original source. And if this fish can enter the ocean again…can't you imagine the celebration! And the fish has lived in the ocean forever but there was no celebration. Now there is the possibility of celebration; now it will feel so delighted, so blessed.

Love is a must for spiritual growth. And moreover, love functions as a mirror. It is very difficult to know yourself unless you have looked at your face in the eyes of someone who loves you. Just as you have to look into the mirror to see your physical face, you have to look in the mirror of love to see your spiritual face. Love is a spiritual mirror: it nourishes you, it integrates you, it makes you ready for the inner journey, it reminds you of your original face.

In moments of deep love there are glimpses of the original face, although those glimpses are coming as reflections. Just as on a full moon night you see the moon reflected in the lake, in the silent lake, so love functions as a lake. The moon reflected in the lake is the beginning of the search for the real moon. If you have never seen the moon reflected in the lake you may never search for the real moon. You will go again and again into the lake to search for the moon because in the beginning you will think, "This is where the real moon is, somewhere deep down at the bottom of the lake." You will dive again and again and you will come up empty-handed; you will not find the moon there.

Then one day it will dawn on you that maybe this moon is just a reflection. That is a great insight. Then you can look upwards. Then where is the moon if this is a reflection? If it is a reflection you have to look in the opposite direction. The reflection was there, deep in the lake – the real must be somewhere above the lake. For the first time you look upwards and the journey has started.

Love gives you glimpses of meditation, reflections of the moon in the lake – although they are reflections, not true. So love can never satisfy you. In fact, love will make you more and more dissatisfied, discontented. Love will make you more and more aware of what is possible, but it will not deliver the goods. It will frustrate you, and only in deep frustration, the possibility of turning back to your own being. Only lovers know the joy of meditation. Those who have never loved and have never been frustrated in love, those who have never dived into the lake of love in search of the moon and are never frustrated, will never look up to the real moon in the sky; they will never become aware of it.

The person who loves is bound to become religious sooner or later. But the person who does not love – the politician, for example, who cannot love any person, only power – will never become religious. Or the person who is obsessed with money, who loves only money, who knows only one love, love of money, will never become religious. It will be very difficult for him for so many reasons. Money can be possessed; you can have money and you can possess it. It is easy to possess money, it is difficult to possess a beloved – impossible, in fact. You will try to possess, but how can you possess a living person? The living person will resist in every way, will fight to the last. Nobody wants to lose their freedom.

Love is not as valuable as freedom is. Love is a great value, but not higher than freedom. So one would like to be loving, but one would not like to be imprisoned by love. Hence, sooner or later you become frustrated: you try to possess, and the more you try to possess, the more love becomes impossible and the more the other starts going away from you. The less you possess, the closer you feel to the other. If you don't possess at all, if there is freedom flowing between the lovers, there is great love.

Firstly, the effort to possess a person is bound to fail; in that frustration you will be thrown back on yourself. Secondly, if you have learned not to possess the person, if you have learned that freedom is a higher value than love, a far more superior value than love, then sooner or later you will see: freedom will bring you to yourself, freedom will become your awareness, meditation.

Freedom is another aspect of meditation. Either start with freedom and you will become aware, or start with awareness and you will become free. They go together. Love is a kind of subtle bondage – they go together – but it is an essential experience, very essential for maturity.

There is a beautiful definition of realness through love, in Margery Williams' beautiful book *The Velveteen Rabbit*.

"What is real?" asked the Rabbit one day. "Does it mean having that buzz inside of you and a stick-out handle?"

"Real isn't how you were made," said the Skin Horse. "It's a thing that happens to you. When a child loves you for a long time, not just to play with, but *really* loves you, then you become real."

"Does it hurt?" asked the Rabbit.

"Sometimes," said the Skin Horse, for he was always truthful. "When you are real, you don't mind being hurt."

"Does it happen all at once like being wound up," he asked, "or bit by bit?"

"It doesn't happen all at once." said the Skin Horse. "You become. It takes a long time. That's why it doesn't often happen to people who break easily or have sharp edges or who have to be carefully kept. Generally, by the time you are real, most of your hair has been loved off, and your eyes drop out and you get loose in the joints and very shabby. But these things don't matter at all, because once you are real, you can't be ugly, except to people who don't understand... Once you are real, you can't become unreal again. It lasts for always."

Love makes you real; otherwise you remain just a fantasy, a dream, with no substance in it. Love gives you substance, love gives you integrity, love makes you centered. But it is only half of the journey; the other half has to be completed in meditation, in awareness. But love prepares you for the other half. Love is the beginning half and awareness is the ending half. Between these two you attain God. Between love and awareness, between these two banks, the river of being flows.

Don't avoid love. Go through it, with all its pains. Yes, it hurts, but if you are in love it doesn't matter. In fact, all those hurts strengthen you. Sometimes it really hurts badly, terribly, but all those wounds are necessary to provoke you, to challenge you, to make you less sleepy. All those dangerous situations are necessary to make you alert. Love prepares the ground, and in the soil of love the seed of meditation can grow – and only in the soil of love.

So those who escape from the world out of fear will never attain meditation. They can sit in the Himalayan caves for an entire life together, they will not attain to meditation. It is not possible – they have not earned it. First it has to be earned in the world; first they have to prepare the soil. And it is only love that prepares the soil.

Hence my insistence for my sannyasins not to renounce the world. Be in it, take its challenges, accept its dangers, its hurts, wounds. Go through it, don't avoid it. Don't try to find a short-cut because there is none. It is a struggle, it is arduous, it is an uphill task, but that is how one reaches the peak.

And the joy will be more, far more, than if you are dropped on the peak by a helicopter, because you will reach there ungrown; you will not be able to enjoy it. Just think of the difference... You try hard to reach Everest – it is so dangerous, every possibility of dying on the way, every possibility of never reaching to the peak – hazardous, dangerous, death waiting for you at each step; so many traps and so many possibilities of being defeated rather than being successful – out of one hundred possibilities there is only one possibility that you may reach. But the closer you come to the peak, the higher the joy rises in you, your spirit soars high. You earn it, it is not free, and the more you have paid for it, the more you will enjoy it. Then think: you can be dropped from a helicopter on the top. You will stand on the top and you will just look silly, stupid

– what are you doing here? Within five minutes you will be finished. You will say, "So I have seen it! There is nothing much here!"

The journey creates the goal. The goal is not sitting there at the end of the journey, the journey creates it at each step. The journey is the goal. The journey and the goal are not separate, they are not two things. The end and the means are not two things. The end is spread over all the way; all the means contain the end in them.

So never miss any opportunity of living, of being alive, of being responsible, of being committed, of getting involved. Don't be a coward. Face life, encounter it, and then slowly slowly something inside you will crystallize.

Yes, it takes time. The Skin Horse is right: "Generally, by the time you are real, most of your hair has been loved off, and your eyes drop out and you get loose in the joints and very shabby. But these things don't matter at all, because once you are real, you can't be ugly, except to people who don't understand... And once you are real, you can't become unreal again. It lasts for always."

It is forever, but one has to earn it. Let me repeat it: in life you cannot get anything free, and if you do get it, it is useless. You have to pay for it, and the more you pay for it the more you will get out of it. If you can risk your whole life in love, great will be your attainment: love will send you back to yourself, it will give you a few reflections of meditation. The first glimpses of meditation happen in love, and then a great desire arises in you to attain to those glimpses – as states so that you can live in those states forever. Love gives you the taste of meditation.

A loving, orgasmic experience is the first experience of samadhi, of ecstasy. It will make you more thirsty. Now you will know what is possible and now you cannot be satisfied with the mundane. The sacred has penetrated you, the sacred has reached your heart. God has touched your heart, you have felt that touch. Now you would like to live in that moment forever, you would like that moment to become your whole life. It becomes. And unless it becomes, man remains discontented.

Love on the one hand will give you great joy, and on the other hand will give you a thirst for eternal joy.

The third question:

Osho,
Why do you live like a king?

Why not? I am an old Jew! You know Jews? – if you ask them a question, they answer it with another question.

There is a famous story about a king. He had many Jews in his court because they were rich people, but he was very annoyed by their habit. Whenever he asked anything, they would answer it with another question. He became so tired, so irritated that he asked his Grand Vizier, "What to do about these people? They cannot be thrown out of the court, but they annoy me very much. Whenever I ask something they always answer with another question."

The Vizier said, "It will be good if we ask the rabbi. Call the rabbi. He is a wise old man; he will help us and he will be able to explain to us too what is the cause of this Jewish habit."

So the rabbi was called and the king asked the rabbi, "Why do you Jews always answer a question with another question?"

And the rabbi said, "Why not?"

You ask me, "Why do you live like a king?"

There are four possibilities after you become enlightened. The first possibility Janak and Marcus Aurelius followed: they were born as kings, after they became enlightened they remained kings.

The second possibility Jesus and Kabir followed: they were born as beggars, after they became enlightened they remained beggars.

The third possibility was followed by Mahavira and the Buddha: they were born as kings, when they became enlightened they still remained beggars.

Then, I thought, for a change.... I was born as a beggar, I decided to live as a king. That is the fourth possibility and there is no other, so I am finishing the last. Somebody had to do it, otherwise history remains incomplete.

One Zen master was dying. Just before he breathed his last he opened his eyes and asked his disciples, "Please help me to find an alternative way to die."

They asked, "What kind of question is this?"

He said, "Should I die lying down or sitting or standing? Have you ever heard of anybody dying sitting?"

They said, "Yes, we have heard that many people, particularly Buddhist monks – they sit in a *siddhasan,* in the full lotus posture, and die. We have heard of many dying in a sitting posture."

"Have you ever heard," the master asked, "of anybody dying standing?"

They said, "It is very rare, but we have heard one story that once a master died standing."

Then he said, "Then no other alternative is left. I will die standing on my head."

And he died – standing on his head. Somebody has to fulfill it. All alternatives have to be tried.

The fourth question:

Osho,
My question concerns the quantum leap. How to jump, where to jump, and who or what is doing the jumping?

The meaning of the quantum leap is that you find nobody there inside you who can jump, you find no place where you can jump and you find no means to jump. That is the meaning of a quantum leap. The quantum leap is not a leap, it is a disappearance. The quantum leap is utter discontinuity with the past. If it is continuous it is just a leap, not quantum. That is the meaning of the word *quantum*.

You have been somebody up to now; if you do something, then you will remain continuous with the past because the doer will be the past. If you ask how to take the quantum leap, who will use the methodology? The old, the past, the mind, the accumulated mind will use the methodology. But how will you become new? It is the old trying to become new. You may have new clothes, a new face, new varnish, but you will remain the same; you continue. A quantum leap is a moment of understanding that the past is no more there, that it is just a memory, just a figment of imagination now; it has no reality. If the past is no more there, who are you? – because you consist only of your past.

Krishnamurti says, "The process of thought creates the thinker." And he is right – it is not vice versa. Ordinarily you think, "I am a thinker, hence the process of thought." It is not so. There is no thinker in you but only a process of thought. And when you think about the whole process of thought and you take it together, the thinker is born.

The thinker is not there. Let your thoughts disappear, and as your thoughts disappear, the thinker will disappear. If there is no thought, there is no thinker inside of you. So "thinker" is nothing but another name for the whole thought continuum. If you can understand this – that the past is just nothing but thoughts – suddenly a great emptiness will arise in you, a great abyss. You are nothing and nobody is there inside of you. This is what Buddha calls *anatta,* no-self, no ego. In that moment when you cannot find yourself, the quantum leap has happened.

The Emperor Wu of China asked Bodhidharma, "My mind remains very tense, in anxiety. I am always feeling restless, uneasy. I never find any peace of mind. Help me, sir."

Bodhidharma looked into his eyes. And that was not an ordinary look – Bodhidharma was a very ferocious master. The king was a very brave man, had fought in many battles and won, but he started trembling when Bodhidharma looked into his eyes.

And he said, "Okay, you come tomorrow, early in the morning at four o'clock, and bring your mind to me and I will put it at ease forever."

When the king was going down the steps, Bodhidharma shouted again, "Listen, don't forget to bring your mind! Come at four o'clock and bring your mind. And I am going to put it at ease forever!"

The king was a little puzzled. "What does he mean, 'Bring the mind, don't forget'? Can I come without the mind too? I and my mind are the same. This man looks mad! And the way he looked at me...those ferocious eyes.... And he looks murderous too! And going alone, early in the morning at four o'clock when it is dark, to this madman...and one never knows what he will do, how he will treat me."

But he could not sleep. Many times he decided not to go, but there was a great attraction too, something like a great magnetic pull. The man was ferocious, but there was great love in his eyes too. Both were there – his eyes were like swords and also like lotuses. He could not resist. He said, "I have to take this risk." And at four o'clock he had to go.

Bodhidharma was waiting with his big staff. He told the king, "Sit in front of me. And where is your mind? I have told you to bring it with you!"

And the king said, "What nonsense are you talking about? If I am here, my mind is also here. My mind is something that exists inside of me. How can I forget it? How can I 'bring' it?"

Bodhidharma said, "So one thing is certain: that mind is inside. So close your eyes and go inside and try to find it. And whenever you catch it, just tell me and I will put it at rest forever. But first the mind has to be caught, only then will I be able to treat it."

The king closed his eyes. The whole thing was stupid, but there was nowhere to go now – it had to be done. He closed his eyes. And the master was sitting there with his staff – and he might beat or he might hit, so it was no ordinary situation. He could not go to sleep. He had not slept the whole night – he had been thinking of whether to come or not to come.... And the presence of the master and the silence of the forest and the darkness of the night and the whole weird situation: that this man could even cut his head…he became very alert! The danger was such that he became very attentive. For the first time in his life he looked inside himself.

But the book of *The Secret of the Golden Flower* says, he turned his light inwards for the first time: he looked inside, he searched inside – he really searched, sincerely he searched – and the more he searched, the more aware he became that there is no mind. There is nobody inside – it is an empty house – we had only believed in it. We have accepted others' belief about the soul, the self, the ego. We never looked at it, we never checked it. And the more he found that there is nobody to be found, the more happy, joyous he became. His face relaxed, a great grace surrounded him. Hours passed, but for him there was no question of time at all. He was sitting and sitting, and enjoying this blissfulness that he was tasting for the first time in his life. Something immensely delightful was descending in him.

Then the sun started rising, and with the first rays of the sun Bodhidharma said to him, "Sir, it is time enough. Now open your eyes. Have you found yourself inside or not?"

And the king opened his eyes, looked at the master, saw the beauty that the ferociousness was out of compassion, saw the love, bowed down, touched the feet of the master and said, "You have put it at rest forever. It is not there. Now I know that I was creating an unnecessary fuss about somebody who doesn't exist at all."

This is the quantum leap. Searching inside you find you are not; then there is no question of "how" and no question of "where." It has already happened.

I would like to tell you: just for a few hours every day, close your eyes – become as alert as Emperor Wu became; remember me just in front of you with a sword in my hand, ready to cut you at any moment if you fall asleep – and go in. And one day, the quantum leap. You will know only when it has happened. You don't do it, it is nothing of your doing; it is a happening. You can't do it because *you* are the hindrance – how can you do it? There is nowhere to jump, nobody to jump, no method to jump. When all these three things have been realized, it has happened. Then one lives as an emptiness, utterly empty and yet utterly full.

The fifth question:

Osho,
I desire to become a sannyasin, but at the very idea a great fear grips
my heart. It is so new. And moreover, I had not come here to become
a disciple, I had just come to see a friend who is a sannyasin.

But you are caught, you are trapped! Now it will be very difficult to escape. It is always difficult to choose the new, but only those who choose the new, live. To choose the old is to choose death, not life. To choose the familiar is to remain in the prison of the familiar. To choose the known is to avoid really the unknown that is knocking on the door. To choose the known is to reject God, because God is always unknown – not only unknown, but unknowable.

God is always fresh, as fresh as the dewdrops. God is always utterly new, unfamiliar, unmapped, unscheduled, uncalculated. God comes only as the unknown. And if you become afraid, if you shrink back, then you have to live in your so-called dark hole.

What is your past that you cling to? What is there to cling to, except that it is familiar? But it is all misery, it is all tragedy. But people even cling to miseries if they are familiar – they look friendly. Even if health is knocking on your door, you don't listen to the knock; you cling to your tuberculosis, to your cancer, because they are familiar, you have lived with them so long, it looks almost like a betrayal to leave them and become healthy.

That is why people are clinging to miseries. Even when opportunities arise for them, when miseries can be dropped and the celebration can start, they continue to cling to the misery. They persist in it, insist on it. Even if it drops they catch hold of it again. If one misery disappears, they create a similar misery, immediately. They don't even give a little interval for joy to enter in their being.

But remember, only those who choose the new, live. Life means readiness to go into the uncalculated, unscheduled. Life means to be ready always to listen to the challenge that comes from the unknown source. It is dangerous, but to live is dangerous. The most secure and safe place in the world is the grave – there, nothing ever happens.

In a small village where Mulla Nasruddin lives, the municipal committee was thinking of creating a wall around the graveyard. Mulla Nasruddin was also a member of the committee. He stood up, and he said, "There is no need."

The whole committee looked puzzled, because everybody was in favor of making a wall around the graveyard. People don't want to see graves and people don't want to see death. People don't want to become aware that death is. That's why graveyards are made outside the town, far away. When you have to go there, only then do you go there, otherwise it is better to avoid.

The village had grown bigger and the graveyard that used to be outside the town was no longer outside the town – the town had grown and spread. So the whole committee was agreeing, but Mulla said, "There is no need."

And the president asked, "Why do you say that there is no need?"

He said, "For two reasons. One: those who are outside – they don't want to go in so they don't need any wall to prevent them. And two: those who are inside – they cannot come out. So what is the point of making a wall? The wall is needed only to prevent either those who are in from coming out or to prevent those who are out from coming in. Those who are out, they don't want to go in; they go in only in utter helplessness. When they have to go, when they have to be carried by four persons, then they go. And once they are in they cannot come out – nobody has ever heard of anybody coming out. It is pointless."

The grave is the most safe and secure place in the world, because nothing new will ever happen there. Remember it: don't become a grave.

Sannyas is new for you, and you did not come here to become a sannyasin. Do you think all those who are sannyasins here came to become sannyasins? They have been caught unawares! Before they could escape I caught hold of their hearts. You are also caught now. If you escape, you escape at your own risk. You will repent forever and you will feel sorry forever, because there was an opportunity of being transformed, an opportunity to learn the ways of let-go, an opportunity of falling into your own being, resting into your own being, an opportunity to bloom. But you became afraid because it is new.

Meditate on these lines of Robert Frost:

Two roads diverged in a yellow wood,
And sorry I could not travel both,
And be one traveler, long I stood
And looked down one as far as I could
To where it bent in the undergrowth;

Then took the other, as just as fair,
And having perhaps the better claim,
And because it was grassy and wanted wear;
Though as for that, the passing there
Had worn them really about the same,

And both that morning equally lay
In leaves no step had trodden black.
Oh, I kept the first for another day!
Yet knowing how way leads on to way,
I doubted if I should ever come back.
I shall be telling this with a sigh
Somewhere ages and ages hence:
Two roads diverged in a wood, and I –
I took the one less traveled by,
And that has made all the difference.

Always choose the new, the "less traveled by". Always choose the unknown, the less traveled by, "And that has made all the difference."

Life grows only by choosing challenges. Life grows only by going into the storms. Life grows only by risking, gambling.

Sannyas needs courage. The old sannyas was not so dangerous. People think my sannyas is easier than the old, ancient idea of sannyas. They are utterly wrong. The old sannyas was very simple because it expected – not only expected but demanded – that you renounce the world. It was simple. You went into a monastery, you lived there – undisturbed, undistracted by the world. Meditation became your whole life with no distractions. It was a monotonous life. The words *monastery* and *monotony* come from the same root, so does the word *monk*. Life was settled, monotonous, repetitive, the same, and the world was left far behind. It was easy.

My sannyas is far more complex. You have to live in the marketplace and yet live as if you were living in a monastery. You have to accept all the distractions of life and yet remain undistracted. You have to be in the world and not be of it.

I have thrown a great challenge to you. The old concept of sannyas was not challenging enough. It was very appealing to the cowards, to the escapists – those who were weary of life, those who were tired of life, those who were incapable of life, those who were feeling incompetent, inferior somehow.

It became very attractive to the inferior, the untalented, the unintelligent.

If you go to the Himalayas or into a monastery and look at the monks, you will be surprised. One thing you are bound to find: their faces show no signs of intelligence, their eyes don't shine with any light from the beyond. They look dull, insipid, stupid, unintelligent, incompetent. They have escaped from life.

It is life that gives you sharpness, otherwise your sword will never be sharp. It is the struggle in life that provokes all the springs of your talents to come to the surface. You have to be intelligent to survive. In the monastery you are protected by the monastery, by the sect, by the church. You need not make any effort to survive. Food is given, clothes are given, and you just have to do some prayer, some chanting, and you have to repeat, parrot-like, the words of others. Naturally, if one becomes unintelligent there is no wonder in it. It will be a wonder if somebody becomes intelligent there, because all the opportunities for intelligence have been prevented – because they are the same opportunities which are opportunities for distraction too.

Distraction is an opportunity. You can be distracted – that is for you to decide – or you can remain undistracted, then it will give you centering, crystallization.

My sannyas is the most complicated phenomenon that has ever happened on the earth because I don't say to you leave the world. I say live in it, indulge in it, love it, enjoy it, go as deeply as possible so your intelligence is sharpened, your life provoked, your dormant sources of energies become dynamic, flowing. And yet, keep yourself centered in your being – a watcher on the hills. Remain an actor and let the life be just a drama where you are fulfilling a certain role. But don't get identified with the role. Remember continuously that this is a role. That you are a carpenter or a doctor or an engineer or a teacher, husband, wife, mother, father, son – that these are all roles, and the earth is a great stage and a great drama is on. God is the author of it and the director of it, and you are just actors, participating. When the curtain falls, your roles will disappear. You will again be just a pure being, you will not be the role that you had played.

The world has to be transformed into an opportunity to remember yourself, for self-remembering. Hence sannyas is arduous. And I know that everybody hesitates before they take the jump. But if the desire has arisen, if the longing is there, don't kill it, because that will be suicidal. Experiment with it, explore this new dimension. You have lived one way – what is the point of going on repeating it again and again? Live this new style too. Who knows? – you may come across God on this way. Who knows? – fulfillment may await you on this path.

The last question:

Osho,
Why do I love, then hate and then show indifference to the same
person again after these mixed feelings?

You don't know yet what love is. You don't know yet that many other things masquerade as love, play tricks on you. Yes, sometimes even hate can have the mask of love, sometimes sheer sexuality pretends to be love. And this must be so.

You say, "Why do I love, then hate, and then show indifference to the same person?"

You have not loved yet; it is just a sexual appetite in you. And I call it appetite knowingly. When you are hungry you are interested in food. The aroma coming from Vrindavan canteen attracts you, everything else becomes unimportant. You find yourself moving towards Vrindavan. Once you have eaten, all interest in food disappears, and if you have eaten too much, you even become repelled by food. If you have eaten too much, more than was needed, you feel nauseous – a sickness arising in you. And when you are satiated with food, you can pass by Vrindavan – you don't smell the aromas, you can go on thinking a thousand and one thoughts and you can remain indifferent to food.

Your love is nothing but sexual appetite. That's why first you feel attracted, "in great love." That attraction you call love. Just as people say they love ice cream, that's the way you love people. But how long can you love ice cream? You can eat, but how much?

Once I stayed with a family in Bombay. The people are beautiful people, but they have a strange idea of how to serve a guest. Because I was staying there, they invited many people – they gave a feast – and then the four brothers started forcing each guest to eat more and more. They actually started physically forcing food into people's mouths, and people were saying, "No!" looking very aghast and puzzled, "What is happening?" And there were four persons on each guest!

I asked, "What is the matter? What are you doing? If they don't want to eat, leave them to themselves!"

They said, "But this is our tradition. In our family, unless the guest starts fighting, we have to…otherwise we have not been real hosts."

And this was their idea of being a real host: unless the guest starts fighting… And that actually happened. When the guest…how long can you suffer? There is a limit! The body is not infinite and the stomach has a limit. And the guests started shouting. And they were very happy because they had been good hosts.

First, you *think* you are in love, but that is not love – just a physical appetite, a bodily phenomenon, a chemical phenomenon – nothing to do with love.

Love is a very different thing. It has not necessarily anything to do with sex. Sex may be a part of it, may not be a part of it. You can be in love with a person without any sexual relationship. That's what we call friendship. It has disappeared from the world. Now friendship has almost disappeared from the world because we know only one kind of love, which is sexual. A non-sexual love has become non-existent. In fact, *that* is love. Friendship is a deeper love than sexual relationship because friendship gives and asks nothing in return.

Sexual relationship is mutual exploitation: you are exploiting the other's body and he or she is exploiting your body – both are using each other. But just to say it is pure sex looks ugly so we call it love. It will be very good if you call it simple sex – it will be true, sincere – and there will be no problem arising, because then you will know it is appetite. You are fulfilled one moment and then, if the other goes on demanding and you go on playing the game, there will be hate because you will be repulsed. And sooner or later you will become indifferent, because you have explored the other's body and he has explored your body – now there is no more to it, the territories are known. Now there is no more intrigue, no more mystery to go into. You are finished: indifference arises.

What you call love is just sex. Call it sex, don't call it love. And it will be good to call it sex because then you know it is sex – there is no need to pretend. If you don't pretend, it will not turn into hate. If you pretend that it is love and it is not, sooner or later you will see it is turning into hate. If you don't pretend, if you call it simply sex, you will be grateful to the other, you will not hate the other. And it will never become indifference, you will always feel thankful.

But calling it by a big name, "love," creates the whole trouble. Then the problem arises – why does it turn into hate? Love never turns into hate. Love goes on becoming more and more love. Love ultimately becomes prayer, and God.

But this is not love. The first thing, my suggestion is: call it simple, pure sex. And there is nothing wrong in pure, simple sex; it is natural. There is no need to hide it behind the beautiful word *love*, there is no need to create a cloud of romance around it. Be simple, be true, sincere. If this is done, half the work is done. Then one day you will be able to see the difference. One day you will fall in love and you will see there is not physiological, chemical attraction only, but something higher – two vibes falling in tune, two beings feeling harmonious.

My own words are: if two bodies are feeling attracted to each other, it is sex; if two minds are feeling attracted to each other, it is love; if two souls are feeling attracted to each other, it is prayer. And prayer is the highest form. Sex is the lowest form. Don't think of the lower as the higher, otherwise you remain misguided.

A man and woman had been going together for some time and finally she agreed to go to bed with him. While going to his apartment, they passed some swanky shops. The woman admired some expensive Italian shoes.

"Don't worry, baby, I'll get them for you," he said. Then she saw a real Parisian dress.

"Don't worry, baby, I'll get that for you, too." Finally, a mink coat caught her eye. "Don't worry, baby, I'll get that coat for you."

They finally got to the apartment, made love, and in leaving, again passed the shops.

"There is the coat you are going to buy me," she said.

"Come on away from there," he snapped.

"Oh, and there is the dress."

"Come on away from there," was again the reply. Finally she saw the shoes and pointed them out. Again he responded, "Come on away from there."

She began to cry and sobbed, "I don't understand. Before we made love, you promised me all those things. Now, just two hours later, you are breaking your promises."

"Baby, it's like this. When I am hard I am soft, but when I am soft I am hard."

Enough for today.

CHAPTER 9

Riding on a Miracle

Master Lu-tsu said:
Release is in the eye…
The seed-blossoms of the human body must be concentrated
upward in the empty space.

Immortality is contained in this and also the overcoming of the
world.

The light is not in the body alone, nor is it only outside the body.
Mountains and rivers and the great Earth are lit by sun and
moon; all that is this light. Therefore, it is not only within the
body. Understanding and clarity, perception and enlightenment,
and all movements of the spirit are likewise this light; therefore, it
is not just something out-side the body. The light-flower of heaven
and Earth fills all the thousand spaces. But also the light-flower of
the individual body passes through heaven and covers the earth.
Therefore, as soon as the light is circulating, heaven and Earth,
mountains and rivers, all are circulating with it at the same time.
To concentrate the seed-flower of the human body above in the
eyes, that is the great key of the human body. Children, take heed!
If for a day you do not practice meditation, this light streams
out, who knows whither? If you only meditate for a quarter of an
hour, by it you can do away with the ten thousand aeons and a

thousand births. All methods end in quietness. This marvelous
magic cannot be fathomed.

But when the practice is started, one must press on from the
obvious to the profound, from the coarse to the fine. Everything
depends on there being no interruption. The beginning and the
end of the practice must be one. In between there are cooler and
warmer moments, that goes without saying. But the goal must be
to reach the vastness of heaven and the depths of the sea, so that
all methods seem quite easy and taken for granted. Only then have
we mastered it.

An old fable has it that when God was creating the world he was approached by four questioning angels. "How are you doing it?" the first one asked. The second queried, "Why?" The third one said, "May I have it when you finish?" The fourth one said, "Can I help?"

The first one was the question of the scientist, the second, the philosopher's, the third, the politician's, and the fourth was the question of the religious one.

The scientific inquiry into existence is that of detached observation. The scientist has to be objective. To be objective he has to remain uninvolved; he cannot participate, because the moment he becomes a participant he becomes involved. Hence the scientist can only know the outer circumference of life and existence. The innermost core will remain unavailable to science; its very methodology prohibits it.

The philosopher only speculates, he never experiments. He goes on asking *ad infinitum*, "Why?" And the question is such that whatsoever the answer, it can be asked again – "Why?" There is no possibility of any conclusion through philosophy. Philosophy remains in a state of non-conclusion. It is a futile activity, it leads to nowhere.

The politician simply wants to possess the world, to own it. He is the most dangerous of all because he is the most violent. His interest in life is not in life itself but in his own power. He is power-hungry, power-mad; he is a maniac, he is destructive. The moment you possess something alive you kill it, because the moment something becomes a property it is no longer alive. Possess a tree and it is no longer alive. Possess a woman or a man and you have killed them. Possess anything and death is the outcome, because only death can be possessed.

Life is freedom. It remains basically free. You cannot possess it, you cannot put it into the bank, you cannot draw a line around it. You cannot say, "This is mine"; to say so is disrespectful, to say so is egoistic, to say so is mad.

Life possesses us. How can we possess it? We have to be possessed by life more and more. The whole gestalt has to change: from being possessive one has to become capable of being possessed by the whole.

The politician never comes to know the truth of life.

The religious person participates. He dances with life, he sings with existence, he helps life, he is surrendered to existence and he is not detached and aloof. He does not really ask any question, he is not after knowledge; his whole effort is how to be in harmony with existence, how to be totally one with it. Hence the Eastern word for the ultimate experience: *samadhi*.

It comes from two words. *Sam* – sam means together with. The same root "sam" has moved into English too; it is in "sympathy," it is in "symphony." A little bit changed it is in "synthesis," "synchronicity." Sam means together with. *Adhi* means the lord, God. Samadhi means union with God, to be one with God. And that is exactly the meaning of the English word *religion*. It means to become one with existence; not to be divided, not to remain separate but to become one. And only in this oneness does one come to know, see, experience and be.

Religion is also a great experiment – the greatest, in fact – but with a difference. Science experiments with the object, religion experiments with the subject itself. Its whole concern is: Who am I?

One should begin from the beginning. Unless I know myself, I am not going to know anything else. If deep down I remain ignorant, then my whole knowledge is just garbage. It is based on ignorance, it is rooted in ignorance. First the light has to happen inside me and then it can spread, then it can go to the very boundaries of existence – if there are any boundaries. But first this has to happen within me. The first flame has to come from my subjectivity. When *my* center is full of light, then only will whatsoever is known really be known. Unless you know yourself, unless the knower is there, how can you know anything else? If you yourself are in deep darkness, all the lights that you have created outside are deceptions, illusions.

The religious quest is the greatest quest in existence. A few things have to be understood about this quest.

The first thing: religion cannot creep; it has to dance or die. And that's what is not happening in the world – religion is not dancing, hence it has died. Religion is creeping and crawling; it has forgotten how to fly. Religion has become dogma.

Dogma is death, it is a corpse. To be flowing and alive and flying, religion has to exist as an experience not as a theory, not as theology but as meditation – not as a philosophy about God but as a personal experience of God. And know perfectly well: to know about God is not to know God. You can go on knowing about and about, but you will never know God. To know about is to go round and round without penetrating the very center of it.

Religion cannot creep, and religion is creeping. Christianity, Hinduism, Islam – they are all creeping. They have all become apologetic. They are all afraid of the scientific growth in the world. They have been fighting against science. They tried all that they could do to prevent scientific growth, but they failed. Now they try to get all the support from science – whatsoever they can manage – but they know perfectly well that they have become secondary. They can exist only if science supports them. They can exist only if scientific argument becomes a prop. This is creeping: religion is no more on its own ground, on its own feet; it needs support from science. It is living a borrowed existence, a borrowed life. Its time is gone.

Why has it happened? Once a religion becomes dogma and is no more experience, it dies automatically. And a dead body cannot stand on its own, it needs support. All the churches and the temples are supported, they are not standing on their own.

When there is a buddha he stands on his own. When there is a christ he stands on his own. Then religion dances and sings a song. Then it is alive, it blooms – there are a thousand and one flowers, and great, beautiful fragrance is released for all to enjoy.

My effort here is to make religion dance again. There is no need for any support, because religion in itself is the greatest authentic experience: others should look towards religion for support, not religion towards others. If religion starts dancing, starts becoming alive, science will need its support, because science itself is losing ground. It is becoming uglier and uglier every day. It is becoming more and more life-negative every day. It is becoming more and more political every day. All that science discovers is possessed by the politician. And all that science discovers serves death; it is no more serving life. Ninety percent of scientific effort goes on war. Science is losing face. Unless religion starts dancing, even science will no longer have any future. Science will need some release of energy from religion to support it. And if religion can be alive again and science becomes a part, a shadow of religion, then only can it be free of the politician and his madness; otherwise it seems impossible.

Man is coming closer and closer to the ultimate destruction of life on the earth. Only a release of religious energy can save him, can save humanity. What we are doing here may look like a very small experiment but its potential is infinite. The future of humanity depends on only one thing: if religion can again lead man, if religion can again become the central influence on man, if religion can again become humanity's dream.

And remember, it is a very difficult dream – almost impossible. To dream to be with God, to dream to be in God, is bound to be something like an impossible dream. Man has lost courage. His dreams are tiny now, his dreams are very mundane; he no longer dreams of the transcendental. And remember, if you stop dreaming about the transcendental, you will live a meaningless life.

Meaning arises only in contact with the transcendental. Meaning arises only when you are part of a greater whole, when you are part of something higher than you, something bigger than you. When man tries to surpass himself, then there is religion. And that's what I call the dance of religion: man trying to transcend himself. No other animal can do it, no other animal is capable of it: only man has the potential and the possibility to surpass himself. A few men have surpassed themselves; a few men have reached to the other shore.

And when I am talking to you, I am talking from the other shore. Hence I am not saying it from borrowed knowledge, I am saying it from my own experience. I know the impossible can become possible. It has become possible in me, it can become possible in you. Once your inner being becomes full of light, once you know no darkness within yourself, then you are religious.

Dream the impossible dream. It may look almost absurd in the beginning – it does look – but if it is strong enough, it transforms your reality. I have heard....

Three trees once grew on a hillside, and as they swayed in the breeze they would dream what they would like to be.

"I should like to be cut down one day," said the first tree, "and turned into a baby's cradle."

"I should like to be cut down one day," said the second, "and become a great ship sailing the seas, carrying treasure and precious stones."

And the third said, "I should like to stand on a hilltop and point people to heaven."

One day the woodcutters came along and cut down the first tree. "Let's make it into a cattle stall," they said.

"But I don't wish to be a cattle stall," cried the tree. "I want to be a baby's cradle." But they turned it into a cattle stall, and when the child Jesus was born they laid him gently in the cattle stall for there was nowhere else to put him. And the tree said, "Why this is far far more wonderful than ever I dreamed."

The woodcutters said of the second tree, "Let's make this tree into a fishing boat."

But the tree said, "No! I don't wish to be a fishing boat; I want to be a great ship carrying treasure and precious stones." But they turned the tree into a fishing boat and put it on an island lake, and a fisherman called Simon Peter bought the boat, and Jesus sailed in the boat and taught the people from it. And the tree said, "Why, this is far far more wonderful than ever I dreamed."

And of the third tree they said, "Let's make it into a cross." But the tree said, "I don't want to be a cross – a thing of shame on which men die. I want to stand on a hilltop and point people to heaven." But they turned the tree into a cross and Jesus was nailed to that cross. And all down the years men have looked to that cross and it has pointed them to God.

Even if trees can dream something, they become it, so what to say about man?

Man has the greatest potential on the earth, in existence. If you are lacking something, it means you are lacking a great dream of surpassing yourself. You have become satisfied with the mundane. You have started creeping on the earth, crawling on the earth. You don't look upwards. There is a great beyond calling you forth. There is a great beyond challenging you. And only that man is truly a man who accepts the challenge of the beyond. All others are only men in name, in form, but not really men.

Be a man: accept the challenge of the unknown, of the beyond. Let it become a great dream in your being. That which you appear to be is only a seed and the seed has to fall into the soil and must then die, and then this has to become a tree and has to bloom.

If you cut the seed, you will not find flowers there. That's where science is missing the whole point – it goes on cutting the seed. It says, "You say this seed will bring great flowering? We will cut, dissect the seed and see." And they cut and dissect the seed – and they have the methodology to dissect the seed – but no flower is found, so they say there is no flower. That's how they have come to the conclusion that there is no God in existence, that there is no soul, that there is no beyond, that life is just an accident and there is no destiny to life.

There is a famous saying of the Zen master, Ikkyu.

"If you break open the cherry tree, where are the blossoms? But in springtime, how they bloom!"

Wait for the springtime. If you want to see, then wait for the springtime; and then you will find a Buddha not a man, and you will find a Jesus not a man, and you will find a Krishna not a man. Then you will find the flower and the seed is no more found there; the seed has disappeared, its function fulfilled. It was protecting something of immense value; it was carrying a blueprint, now it is no more needed: the soil has been found, the spring has arrived, and the seed was courageous enough to die.

Man's ego is nothing but a seed. It is very protective. People ask me, "If ego is such a barrier towards God, then why in the first place does ego exist? If mind is such a barrier to God, then why does mind exist at all?" It exists to protect you, just as the hard shell of the seed exists to protect the potential. The potential is very soft; it will be destroyed if the hard shell is not around it. The hard shell is not the enemy. The hard shell will be the enemy only if the spring has come and the soil has been found, and the seed rejects death. If the hard shell says, "Now, I will go on protecting you, even against the spring. I will protect you against this soil," then there is going to be trouble. That's where the problem arises.

The ego in itself is not a problem. The child needs it, otherwise the child will be very unprotected. He will not know how to survive in this world of struggle. He will not know how to protect himself against so many hazards. He is so soft, tender, he will die before he becomes a buddha. The ego helps him. The ego is a kind of armor, and so is the mind – it protects him.

It is not your enemy. It is the enemy only when the moment has come and you are ready to move into meditation: you have found a master, you have found a method and you are ready, but the mind says, "No, I cannot die. Just think of all the blessings that I have showered upon you. Just think of all the benefits that I have given you. Just think of all that I have done for you and feel grateful! And don't try to destroy me." Then the problem arises: then the protector becomes destructive. Then you have to fight against your own mind, you have to fight against your own ego, you have to fight against your own armor, because the armor is no more needed. You have to release your inner potential – the spring has come. So when spring has come, only then is it a problem; otherwise it is not a problem, it is a help. When its time is gone, it has to go.

Dream of the impossible: dream of surpassing yourself, dream of nirvana, dream of *moksha,* dream of the kingdom of God. Only then will you start working and moving towards it, and only then with that dream, will your feet have the quality of dance. Without the dream you will become dull. That's why people are dragging. How can they dance? For what? Just to go every day to the office and work, and come back home and quarrel with the wife and listen to all the complaints of the children? And next day the same rut starts again – year in, year out. What is there to dance about? In fact, it is a miracle how man goes on living, and does not commit suicide. What does he live for?

There is nothing that is awaiting him, there is nothing that he can look up to. There is no star in the night; it is all darkness. It is a miracle how man goes on living, how he manages. The people who commit suicide seem to be more logical. The people who go on living seem to be very illogical. Miserable, bored, dragging – but they go on living. But it shows something. It shows one thing, that your innermost being knows that the possibility is there: any day you may become alert about the potential, about the possible, any day the dream will possess you – and then there will be meaning and there will be dance.

"Religion is art," said William Blake. "Religion is art, not money." This is a very very pregnant statement. And only a man like William Blake could have made it. He is a mystic poet.

What is art? "Art is a way," he says, "of doing something" – painting, poetry, dancing, sculpture, music, pottery, weaving. "Art is a way of doing something" – he does not say anything about creating oneself. But that is exactly what religion is. It is not painting, it is not poetry, it is not sculpture, it is not music, it is something on the same lines, but beyond – creating oneself. Religion is a way of doing something – living, loving, seeing, being.

All art is "making." It is helping God to create. That's why I call the man who said to God, "Can I help?", the religious man. If you want to know the creator you will have to become a creator in some measure on your own. Poetry may not be religion proper, but it points in the right direction. When a poet is really in a creative state he knows something of religion – a faraway distant music – because when he is in a creative state, he is no more himself. He participates – although in a very small measure, but he participates in God: just a drop of divinity enters into him. That's why great poets have always said, "When we write poetry, we are not the creators of it. We become possessed. Some unknown energy enters, sings, dances in us. We don't know what it is." When a painter is lost into his painting, he is utterly lost into his painting, his ego disappears. Maybe only for moments, but in those egoless moments God paints through him.

If you participate in God, God participates in you. Art is an unconscious form of religion. Religion is conscious art. Art is as if you are religious in a dream, but it is pointing in the right direction. The artist is the nearest to the religious. But it is not understood that way. You don't think of a poet as religious or a painter as religious; on the contrary, if somebody fasts, tortures his body, makes his being ugly, you start thinking that *he* is religious. He is simply being violent with himself. He is just suicidal, he is neurotic, and you think he is religious.

Neurotics become mahatmas: they are respected and worshipped as saints; they are not religious at all. The difference between a so-called saint and a murderer is not much. The murderer murders somebody else, and your so-called saint murders himself. But both do the same thing: both are violent, both are destructive. And whenever you are destructive you are farthest from God, because God is creativity. To me, aesthetics is the closest neighbor of religiousness, not ethics.

Lenin is reported to have said, "Ethics will be the aesthetics of the future." I say no, just the contrary: aesthetics will be the ethics of the future. Beauty is going to be the truth of the future, because beauty can be created. And a beautiful person who loves beauty, who lives beauty, who creates beauty is moral – and with no effort. His morality is not a cultivated morality; it is just his aesthetic sense that makes him moral. He cannot kill because he cannot think of killing as being beautiful. He cannot cheat, he cannot be dishonest, because all these things make him feel ugly. His criterion is beauty. And I agree with William Blake that religion is art.

All art is making. All making necessitates a kind of faith. You see what is not there and work in such a way that what was invisible, intangible, inaudible is given shape in time and space. What is produced will be apparent to the senses – a painting, a poem, or a garden. Art is not to be confused, however, with the object it produces. It is a beautiful distinction to be remembered. It will help you immensely to understand religion.

Art is not a painting or a piece of sculpture. What art dealers buy and sell are works of art, not art itself. Works of art are a form of property. Just as art is not the same thing as works of art, so religion is not to be confused with the objects and effects it produces – such as dogmas, doctrines, Bibles, Korans, Gitas, churches, temples, cathedrals. These are *works* of art. You can call them works of the art of religion, but religion should not be confused with them.

A church is a church. It may be beautiful, but it is not religion in itself. It is a by-product, a spin off. A Koran is a beautiful poem – but as a work of art, a spin off. Something happened in Mohammed's heart – that was religion, but that remains invisible. Because something stirred in his soul, he started singing, he went into a mad expression. That's exactly what he thought when for the first time alone on the mountains he started feeling the presence of God. He became so frightened, so afraid, he thought he had either gone mad or become a poet.

He rushed home. He was in a feverish state, trembling. His wife thought he had suddenly got a high fever. She asked, "What has happened to you?" And he said, "Either I have gone mad or I have become a poet. Something tremendously great is happening and I don't know what it is or from where it is coming. And I am so unworthy of it...I cannot believe my own eyes, and I cannot believe my own heart – what I am feeling. It is so immensely beautiful, so great, so vast, I am incapable of conceiving it." That was religion.

After a few days of fever Mohammed cooled down and settled into his new state, his ecstasy, his samadhi. And then the flow started: the beautiful Koran was born. But the Koran is a by-product, so is the Gita, so is the Dhammapada. Remember always that no scripture contains religion – cannot contain it. All scriptures are by-products of religion – shadows, footprints, left on the banks of time. But footprints are footprints.

When Buddha walks on a sea beach, naturally, he will leave footprints, but those footprints are not Buddha himself. Those footprints are beautiful because they belong to Buddha – bow down to them – but don't forget: they are just by-products, and you have to be a buddha, not just the worshipper of a footprint.

Works of art are a form of property, that's why you can sell them, purchase them; but you cannot sell art and you cannot purchase art. If you ask Pablo Picasso to sell you his art, it will be impossible. You may be ready to pay any fantastic price for it, but he cannot sell it. He can sell his paintings, but he cannot sell his art. There is no way of selling it because it is not a thing. It remains always invisible. Only effects become visible.

God remains invisible, only in the world does he become visible. You are invisible, only the body is visible. That's why Blake says religion is not money. He is right. He means religion is not property. Religion is not like that, religion is like love – you cannot buy it, sell it, or keep it in a bank. You cannot possess it; on the contrary, it possesses you.

The work of art can be possessed; it is property, it is dead. You can learn the Koran and the Gita and the Bible, but you cannot learn religion. You have to live it – there is no way of learning it. You have to be possessed by God, you have to become available to God. You have to open up your being. You have to withdraw, you have to become empty so that God can enter and possess you totally. In that very possession, you have transcended humanity. You are no more a human being, you are a god – a christ, a buddha.

These sutras are the secrets to help you release this buddhahood that you are carrying as a blueprint, that you are carrying in a seed form; they will show you how to help it bloom, how to help it become a great tree with great foliage and many flowers.

The sutras.

> Master Lu-tsu said:
> Release is in the eye...

This potential that I have been talking to you about, this buddhahood, this Christ-consciousness or Krishna-consciousness, or whatever you wish to call it, is in the third eye. Just between your two physical eyes there is an empty space, and that empty space is the seed of your being a god. Unless that third eye starts functioning, your potential will not be released.

Hence,

> Master Lu-tsu said:
> Release is in the eye...

Release means nirvana, moksha, deliverance, freedom. Release means enlightenment. If your third eye can start functioning – which is currently dormant, nonfunctioning as your energy has not reached up to it... It is a perfect mechanism – but without any energy reaching it. Your energy is flowing downward into your sexuality, into your greed, into your anger, into your worldly affairs – your energy is moving downwards and outwards. You don't have enough energy to bring to the third-eye center. Unless you have an abundance of energy, it will not reach the third eye.

You have to become a reservoir of energy. And when you become a reservoir and energy is not wasted, its level starts going higher and higher every day – one day it reaches the third eye. And the moment the energy touches the third eye, immediately, instantly, it starts functioning. And then you know, and then you see for the first time. Then you have the vision of life – what it is. And only through the third eye will you be able to know God, reality, that which is.

Through the two physical eyes you know the world. And because the eyes are two, your world is divided – it is dual. Your two eyes make the world divided. The world in itself is not divided, but your way of seeing it divides it. It is like a ray passing through a prism. The ray is one; the moment it passes through a prism, it becomes seven, it is broken up into seven colors. That is how the rainbow is created: sunrays passing through drops of water hanging in the clouds. Those hanging drops function as prisms, and the sunrays passing through them are immediately split into seven colors.

Your energy moves through your two eyes and the whole world becomes dual. Then you see day and night as opposite, life and death as opposite, love and hate as opposite, matter and consciousness as opposite. Your two eyes make all things dual and polar, and because of these two eyes you cannot see the oneness of existence. Unless your two eyes become one eye, you will never know the indivisible, the universal.

The book, *The Secret of the Golden Flower*, says: energy going outwards becomes dual; if you bring it backwards it becomes again one – it loses duality, it becomes non-dual. When energy moves back from the two eyes, it starts falling into the original source.

If you mix the seven colors of the rainbow into one, it becomes white, it becomes one color. The method is the same. Energy moving outwards passes through two eyes and the whole existence becomes dual. Energy moving backwards passes through two eyes and moves into one eye, the third eye – which is just exactly in between the two – and suddenly all is one. This is samadhi: you are one with God.

> *Release is in the eye…*
> *The seed-blossoms of the human body must be concentrated*
> *upward in the empty space.*

Right now it is an empty space. But once energy starts moving inwards, it becomes full of light.

> *Immortality is contained in this and also the overcoming of the*
> *world.*

And the moment you have reached the one point in your being – Jesus says, "When your two eyes become one, you have entered the kingdom of God." – you know immortality, because now you know life and death are not opposite but two wings of the same bird. Death does not destroy life but helps it to renew itself again. Death is not the enemy but the friend. It simply helps life to change its garments because they have become rotten; they have been used and they cannot be used anymore. It simply helps you to change the house, it does not end you. It only gives you a new beginning, a fresh lease of energy.

Then darkness and light are not two. Then opposites disappear and they become complementaries. Then the whole existence becomes a dance between the masculine energy and the feminine energy – then it is an orgasmic dance. Then both are one – meeting, melting into each other – the conflict disappears. And when you see the whole existence without any conflict, certainly, great joy arises – there is no death. Death one sees only from the outside. You see somebody else dying, you have never seen yourself dying. Nobody has ever seen himself dying.

When Socrates was given poison, he was very enchanted. His disciples were crying and weeping, and he said, "Don't weep. Soon I will be gone, and then you can weep to your heart's content. Right now, see this great experiment that is happening to me. I am very intrigued by the idea of death – whether I am really going to die or not. Don't miss this opportunity! Just sit around me and watch."

A master teaches through his life and also teaches through his death. A master uses every opportunity – even his own death he will use to teach his disciples.

Because he shouted and was very angry and said, "Stop crying and weeping and come close! Don't miss this opportunity!" the disciples looked. And Socrates said, "Wait. The poison was given to me. Now I will tell you what is happening to me inside, so you can become aware of something that you cannot see." And then he said, "Up to my knees, my legs are dead. But as far as I am concerned, I am intact and I am as whole as before."

Then he said, "My whole legs have gone dead – below the waist I cannot feel anything." He asked a disciple to touch his feet, to pinch them, but he could not feel anything. He said, "I cannot feel them, so half of my body is dead, but I am as whole as ever. My inner feeling is not that I am half-dead and half-alive, I am as alive as ever! Half of the body is gone, but my being is untouched by it."

And slowly slowly his hands became dead, and his chest started sinking. And then he said, the last words he said, "My tongue will not be able to say any more words. It is getting numb. But the last thing that I want to tell you is this: that although almost ninety percent of my body is dead, I am a hundred percent alive. If it is an indication of something, it shows that even when the body is one hundred percent dead, I will be alive, because I have seen ninety percent of my body go, but I am as whole as before. So ten percent more will go…. You cannot see what is happening to me inside, but I can see it."

Socrates is not an ordinary philosopher as other Greek philosophers are. Even his own disciples, Plato, Aristotle… Aristotle, in fact, is not a disciple but an enemy. He does not understand Socrates at all, and what he proposes is absolutely against Socrates.

Socrates is a mystic. His philosophy is just a method of inquiry – and a very penetrating inquiry. He will not leave even death; he inquired into death. To the very last moment he was true to his method of inquiry.

Death one sees only from the outside – you see other people dying – but to be alive is different: you can see it from the inside. To be alive is to feel pain and pleasure, to love and to fear. To be alive is to be able to create; to think of something which is not and make it happen. That's why the creative person only knows the highest form of life because when you create you are at the optimum of your energy. When you create you are part of God. How one can do it is a mystery. How one can exist is a mystery. Every effect must have a cause. That is what we call the law of causation – that is what we are taught – but I can see no cause for the effect which I am.

I wake up riding on a miracle. My reason serves me well, but with the mystery of my being, it fails. My reason itself is a tool of this mystery, it cannot know it.

You have to look within. First, to see what life is, you have to feel it from the interior. And the best way to feel your life is to be creative, because then you are at your maximum. Ordinarily, people live at their minimum, and whatsoever people go on doing can be done at the minimum because those are just habits, those are just routine things your body has learned. They have been transferred from your consciousness to the robot part of your body which goes on functioning on its own. For example, once you learn driving: when first you learn you are very alive, very alert, because there is danger. You have to be alert – you don't know what is going to happen. You have to keep aware of so many things. The steering wheel, the road, the clutch, the gears, the accelerator, the brakes – so many things to be aware and alert about – and the traffic, and the people passing by, and the cars passing by. But once you have learned, your knowledge is transferred to the robot part of your body. Then you need not bother; you can talk to your friend, you can sing a song, you can smoke, you can listen to the radio, and your body goes on doing. You need not be alert – only in exceptional situations. If some accident is going to happen, for a moment you will wake up because the danger is so great and the danger is so unknown that the robot part cannot face it; it has not happened before, it is new.

Ordinary life becomes a mechanical routine, and you start living at the minimum. You never flare up to your maximum. In creativity you flare up. And that is going to be one of my messages to my sannyasins: be creative, because to be creative is worship, to be creative is prayer, to be creative is meditation, and to be creative is to be close to God. There is no need to go to the Kaaba, because

God is here as much as in the Kaaba. There is no need to go to the Himalayas, because God is everywhere, equally available – but available only to those who live at their maximum, whose life flame is not a dull flame, who pour their whole energy into it. And that happens only through creativity.

So, to me, the definition of a sannyasin is not the definition of the old kind of saints, sitting dull and dead. The definition of a sannyasin is to be creative. Dance, sing, create music, paint, sculpt, or whatsoever you feel like doing. Find out what is your innermost joy – and do it! And doing means bring it from the invisible to the visible, doing means make the dream exist on the earth. Let the dream become actual, transform the potential into the actual, and that is the greatest joy there is. The real bliss is attained only when you are able to bring something from the unknown to the known, when you make, create, when you are able to transform a dream into reality, when you have helped existence. When in a certain way, in your own way, you have made the world a little more beautiful, when you have enhanced its joy, then you are a sannyasin.

And to know this way, your inner life, will help you to know that you are deathless, because once you know who you are in your uttermost capacity, when your inner torch is burning from both the ends together, at the optimum, then you will know there is no death. And at the optimum your third-eye center starts functioning – and only at the optimum. So don't live life as a drag. Don't live it as if it is a burden, a duty to be fulfilled. Make it a dance, let it be a celebration.

> *Immortality is contained in this and also the overcoming*
> *of the world.*

If you can allow your energy, your flame of life, to reach to the third eye, you will see there is no death, and you will suddenly see that you are no more attached to the world.

Now, the difference has to be remembered. The old sannyas, the so-called, old religious way of life, has been teaching people to renounce the world. I don't teach renunciation, I teach: bring your life energy to the optimum, and once you have seen the truth in your being, the world carries no meaning anymore. The higher has happened, the lower becomes insignificant. You need not renounce it; it has already dropped. You need not escape anywhere. You can live in the world, but you have overcome it. And remember, escaping and overcoming are two totally different things. The real sannyasin has to overcome the world, not renounce it.

The light is not in the body alone, nor is it only outside the body.

And once you have seen the light inside, then you will become aware that it is not only inside, it is also on the outside. It is not confined to you. Remember, darkness is individual, light is universal. Death is individual, life is universal. Misery is individual, bliss is universal. For misery to exist you have to exist as separate, and for bliss to come into existence you have to become part of the whole, in harmony with the whole.

> *The light is not in the body alone, nor is it only outside the body.*
> *Mountains and rivers and the great Earth are lit by sun and moon;*
> *all that is this light.*

Once you have seen it on the inside you will recognize it everywhere: in the moon, in the sun… All light is the same – inner and outer make no difference.

> *Therefore it is not only within the body. Understanding and clarity,*
> *perception and enlightenment, and all movements of the spirit are*
> *likewise this light…*

It is the same light that you see in the moon, and that you see inside yourself in the third eye. Once you have seen that it is the same light, the inner and the outer are no longer distinct. The inner is the outer, the outer is the inner. That's why the Zen masters say that *samsara* is nirvana; the world – the *very* world – is enlightenment. This very body the Buddha, this very Earth the paradise. That's why when Buddha became enlightened, he said, "It is incredible, it is unbelievable that the moment I became enlightened, the whole existence became enlightened with me."

Down the centuries Buddhist meditators have been meditating over it, "What does he mean? What does he want to say – 'The moment I became enlightened the whole existence became enlightened'? But how can it be? – because there are still so many unenlightened people. What can he mean?" The meditator himself thinks, "I am as yet unenlightened, so how has the whole existence become enlightened?" It has become enlightened for the Buddha because he has seen that the distinction between the inner and the outer was nothing but the ego – the small thin curtain of the ego. Once that curtain has fallen there is nothing inner, nothing outer.

So Buddha cannot say, "I have become enlightened." He says, "The whole has become enlightened." All the trees, and all the rivers, and all the mountains, and all the people, and all the animals, and all the planets – all have become enlightened, because now he has no separate identity. He does not mean that you have become enlightened; he is simply saying, "I cannot say that I have become enlightened. I was in bondage, that much I can say. I was ignorant, that much I can say. I was in misery, that much I can say. But now, I am no more."

Existence is blissful. Existence is full of light. And the inner and the outer light are the same – there is nothing inner, there is nothing outer, all distinctions disappear. When the light enters into the third eye – the one eye, the single eye – all distinctions disappear: the rainbow again becomes a single ray of white light.

Just the other day there was a question, "Osho, why do you tell us to wear orange and you wear white?"

It is just symbolic, just to tell you that you have to come to the point where colors disappear and the single white ray remains, without any distinctions.

> *Understanding and clarity, perception and enlightenment, and*
> *all movements of the spirit are likewise this light; therefore it is*
> *not just something outside the body.*

It is neither outside nor inside; it is everywhere – inside too, outside too. And it is the same light – the same light that you see shining on the greenery and the flower, and dancing on the lotus. It is the same light that becomes clarity inside – enlightenment, perception, understanding.

And remember, the master says understanding, not knowledge. The master says clarity, not answers. One simply becomes so clear that the questions disappear, not that you attain to some answers; only you are so clear that the confusion is no more there, that's all. It is absence of questions not presence of answers, hence it is called understanding, not knowledge.

Just the other day, Aniruddha also asked, "What is the difference between our knowledge and your knowledge? I don't see any difference," he says.

The difference is not in knowledge. He must have been thinking that I know more than he knows. Just the contrary is the case: I don't know more than you know; in fact, you know and I have no knowledge. I am only clear – a clarity, an understanding – not knowledge. Here are many people who know more than me – and that is their problem – and they will have to drop that knowledge.

I don't know a thing, but there is only clarity…

When you ask me a question, it is not that I have an answer for it, but I just focus my clarity on it, try to understand, and whatsoever response comes out of the clarity I give to you. It is not knowledge. It is just a capacity to see.

Knowledge makes people blind. Their eyes become so full of knowledge they cannot see. Even before you have asked the question they have the ready-made answer there. They are ready to answer it. They don't listen to your question, they don't listen to the questioner, they don't listen to his being. They don't look into him to see what he means; they have a ready-made answer. They are in a hurry to answer you – and they must prove the answer with arguments and scriptures, and they must give all kinds of support to it.

I have only a kind of understanding, a vision, a capacity to see. That's why the master says:

Understanding and clarity, perception and enlightenment...

It is not knowledge, it is just an utterly cloudless sky within.

The light-flower of heaven and Earth fills all the thousand spaces.
But also the light-flower of the individual body passes through heaven
and covers the earth.

It is a light-flower, this whole existence. This is the experience of the mystics...that existence is made of nothing else but light – it is all light, light is the basic constituent of existence. And modern physics agrees with it. They call it electricity. "Light" is much too poetic a word for them, they have to drag it down to earth – it becomes "electricity." But what they are saying is exactly the same.

Matter has disappeared from modern physics, matter is no more. At the deepest core of matter is nothing but electricity, electrons, electrical particles dancing, energy particles dancing, with no matter in them, no weight. This has been experienced by mystics down the centuries, unexceptionally; whether the mystic was born in India or in China or in Tibet makes no difference. This has been the most fundamental experience of all the mystics: that the existence is made of light and nothing else.

The Secret of the Golden Flower says, "This light, this flower of light, these petals of light fill all the spaces outside and also inside."

Therefore, as soon as the light is circulating, heaven and Earth,
mountains and rivers, are all circulating with it at the same time.

The same thing that Buddha said is said in different words. The moment you see light circulating in you, you will be able to see the dawn of light all over. Stars moving, and mountains and rivers – all will be nothing but streams of light, a tremendous dance of light energy.

> *To concentrate the seed-flower of the human body above in the*
> *eyes, that is the great key of the human body. Children. take heed!*
> *If for a day you do not practice meditation, this light streams*
> *out, who knows whither? If you only meditate for a quarter of an*
> *hour, by it you can do away with the ten thousand aeons and a*
> *thousand births. All methods end in quietness. This marvelous magic*
> *cannot be fathomed.*

The Master Lu-tsu says only fifteen minutes in twenty-four hours will do. If you can sit silently for fifteen minutes, concentrated in the third eye, that will be enough to change your future. You will not need to be born into the body again, you will not need to be thrown into the world again. You have learned the lesson, you have become worthy of moving without the body and its limitations. Your soul will be free, unentangled, without any bondage, and then there will be no death, no birth. You will be an eternal flowering of light in this infinite existence.

Only fifteen minutes? Yes, only fifteen minutes can do the miracle. But people are not even ready to give fifteen minutes…to quietness, to silence.

I have heard…

When Ignatius Loyola heard the news that an unfriendly man had been elected pope, he was asked what he would do if the new head of the church should order the Society of Jesus dissolved, the work in which Loyola had invested his whole life. He replied, "Fifteen minutes in prayer and all will be the same."

An immensely significant reply.

An unfriendly pope had come into power and there was every possibility that Loyola's whole work would be dissolved. He had created a small society of mystics. The work was esoteric, and Christianity has always been against esoteric work, has always been afraid of the mystics because these are the dangerous people: they bring truth to the world. And once they bring truth to the world, people are no longer interested in rituals, impotent rituals. Who cares about the church then?

So Christianity has consistently been destroying all mystic schools so that nobody can go outside the church, so that nobody can have any other door to reach God, so that everybody has to come to the priest. Whenever the desire to seek and search for God arises, no alternatives are to be left. Because of this stupid idea, Christianity destroyed religion in the whole world, because there are different types of people and they need different types of schools and they need different types of techniques. And those who are really sincere in their search have to find esoteric groups. They cannot become part of the formal religion – that is not enough for them; it is very lukewarm, it is very superficial.

In the West, real religion had to go underground because of the Church. People have to create many false facades to hide behind. Alchemy was one; the real work was something else, but the alchemist was trying to create the idea that he was working to transform baser metal into gold. This was allowed. The Church was very happy: if you are trying to turn baser metal into gold, it is perfectly okay. If you succeed, the church will have more gold, that's all; there was no fear about it. But this was just a facade, it was not real alchemy, it was just on the outside. Behind the curtain the real work was totally different: it was transforming the lower being into the higher being. It was exactly the secret of the golden flower: how to transform your sexuality, the baser metal, into spirituality, the gold.

But unnecessary trouble had to be taken: they had to make arrangements on the outside such that the society remained convinced that their work was something to do with gold. And everybody is interested in gold. The church is very interested in gold, not in God.

Loyola was a great mystic – he had created the Society of Jesus – and a very antagonistic pope was in power. Somebody said to him, "What will you do? What will happen now? The Society can be dissolved by the order of the pope."

Loyola said, "Fifteen minutes in prayer and all will be the same. It will take me just fifteen minutes to go deep into meditation, that's all, because whenever I am there, nothing matters. Nothing matters at all."

Master Lu-tsu says: Just fifteen minutes…

> …*by it you can do away with the ten thousand aeons and a*
> *thousand births. All methods end in quietness.*

Remember it. Whatsoever the method, the goal is the same: quietness, utter silence inside, thoughtlessness, only consciousness without any content.

This marvelous magic cannot be fathomed.

It is an unfathomable depth. When thoughts disappear and you are simply silent, then the silence is a bottomless abyss; it cannot be fathomed. The Pacific Ocean can be fathomed – it has a five-mile depth; but the Pacific Ocean inside you cannot be fathomed – it is infinite. You can go on digging and digging and diving deeper and deeper: you will not come to fathom it, you will not come to the bottom of it at all.

Only thoughts can be measured, thoughtlessness is immeasurable. Hence, thoughtlessness is another name for God. But remember, thoughtlessness should not be a kind of sleep, because that is very ordinary, it happens every day. Deep in sleep, when dreams disappear, you fall into that abyss, that's why deep sleep is so rejuvenating, so refreshing. In the morning you feel alive again, new, reborn. But that is unconscious. Patanjali has said deep sleep and samadhi are very similar, with only one difference: in sleep you are unconscious, in samadhi you are conscious. But you go to the same space, the same unfathomable, magical space within you, where there is no thought, no desire, no vibration in your mind – all is quiet. All methods lead to it. Yoga, Tantra, Tao, Hassidism, Sufism, all methods lead to it. From different angles, for different people they have been created.

> But when the practice is started, one must press on from the obvious
> to the profound, from the coarse to the fine.

In the beginning great effort is needed. One must press on from the obvious to the profound. What is obvious? – the obvious is your continuous process of thought. And what is profound? – just a state of no-thought. What is gross? – *all* contents of the mind are gross. And what is subtle? – a state of no-content is subtle. One must go pressing on. In the beginning, great effort will be needed. In the beginning, you have to be utterly committed to the work, only then the blissful moment arises, when meditation becomes effortless.

First, meditation has to be masculine energy. Only then, in the end, can it become feminine energy. Hence my insistence for dynamic methods in the beginning. Bring all your effort to the maximum, put all that you have at stake, don't hold anything back, and then one day, you will be able to relax without effort: you will be able, just by closing your eyes, to reach the third eye.

> …when the practice is started, one must press on from the
> obvious to the profound, from the coarse to the fine. Everything
> depends on there being no interruption.

And make it a regular phenomenon.

> *The beginning and the end of the practice must be one. In between there are cooler and warmer moments, that goes without saying. But the goal must be to reach the vastness of heaven and the depths of the sea, so that all methods seem quite easy and taken for granted. Only then have we mastered it.*

The real mastery is when no effort is needed, when all efforts can be dropped. The real mastery is when meditation is no longer a thing to do but has become your very state. You live in it, you walk in it, you sit in it: sitting in Zen, walking in Zen. You eat in it, you sleep in it, you *are* it– that moment also comes. But in the beginning one has to go with all one's energy.

Remember, just as water evaporates at a hundred degree' heat – not at ninety-nine, not at ninety-nine point nine, but exactly at a hundred degrees – so whenever you put your total energy, one hundred degrees at stake, immediately the baser metal turns into gold: immediately the sexual energy has penetrated into the spiritual world, immediately the energy that was going out has taken a one-hundred-and-eighty-degree turn, and the two eyes become one eye. And then all, inner and outer, is enlightened.

Jesus has said, "Cleave the wood and you will find me. Strike the stone and I am there."

This is the ultimate state: when you cleave the wood and you find God, and you strike the stone and you find God. Then you walk on God, in God, as God; then you breathe God, then you eat God, you drink God – because all is God.

This ultimate experience is what Master Lu-tsu says is released. And it is in the third eye.

Enough for today.

CHAPTER 10
The Zorba-Buddha Synthesis

The first question:

Osho,
All my life I have said yes and now that I am here with you and the
yes seems really right, there comes only no. What is this no?

It is very natural. If all your life you have been saying yes, it must have been false, it must have been pseudo. You must have forced yourself to say "yes", you must have repressed your "no" continuously. And I teach relaxation, and I teach expression, so the repressed no is coming up, surfacing. You allow it. Please don't repress it anymore. If you repress it here, then where are you going to express it? Once it is expressed, you will be free of it, and then the real yes will come.

The yes that you have known up to now was not real. You have been cultivating this yes. It was just on the surface. Deep down the no has always existed in you. But this is how we are brought up, this is how we are conditioned. This is how people have become utterly false, hypocrites – split: their face says one thing, their being is saying just the opposite. This is how the whole of humanity has been turned into a kind of schizophrenia.

My approach is that yes and no are both absolutely necessary, part of inner rhythm. The man who cannot say no cannot say yes either; and if he says yes, his yes will be impotent. Only the man who can say "no" vitally can say "yes" vitally.

They depend on each other – just as life and death depend on each other, just as darkness and light depend on each other, just as love and hate depend on each other. This is the intrinsic polarity of life.

In a better world, with more freedom, with more understanding, a child will not be taught to say yes when he feels like saying no. He will be taught courage. Whenever he feels like saying no, he *has* to say no, and then his yes will have meaning.

A child will not be taught religion, because religion is yes-saying. He will not be forced to become a theist – Hindu, Christian, Mohammedan. He will be encouraged by the parents, by the school, by the university, to be honest, to be sincere, and to wait for the real yes to come on its own.

The world has become so false – can't you see? From where is this falsity arising? Millions of people go to the churches, temples, mosques, *gurdwaras,* and not a single person is religious. What kind of neurosis is this? They go just as a formality, they go because they have been taught to go, they go because they have become addicted to the habit of going. It is just a habit. If they don't go they feel guilty, if they don't go they feel as if they are betraying their parents, their society. If they go there is no joy in it, they simply drag themselves into it. They simply wait there until the ritual ends, the prayer ends, so that they can escape out of the temple, out of the church. It is a bogus kind of religion. And the reason is that they have never been allowed to say no.

No has to come first, only then can yes come. To really be a theist, first one has to go through the process of atheism. To really be a believer in God, first one has to go through the dark night of doubt – only then the dawn. There is no other alternative.

It is good, that the no is arising. You are being true for the first time in your life – let it happen – and the yes will follow just as day follows night.

But this mischief has been done to you – and in the name of great things: God, prayer, country, love, religion, church, Jesus, Buddha, Krishna. In the name of these great things much mischief has been done to you, you have been manipulated. And what is the outcome? You have become a plastic phenomenon, you don't have that sincerity which can make a person really religious.

My own observation is this: that a person who has not said no to God will never be able to say yes, or if he says it, his yes will be pointless.

The so-called religion is what Gregory Bateson calls "the double bind;" one is ordered to do two things which are mutually exclusive: to be sincere and to believe. How can you be sincere if you are told to believe? To believe means to be insincere. To believe means to believe in something that you don't know, to which your whole heart says, "No, I don't know. How can I believe?" Belief is insincerity, and you have been told to be sincere *and* to believe – this creates a double bind in you.

Your religion, so-called religion, is based on insincerity and hypocrisy. How can it be religious? – when the very beginning is poisoned, the very source has gone sour, embittered. No child should be taught religion. Every child should be taught inquiry, doubt, logic and reason.

And why are you so afraid of logic, doubt and reason? Because if a child really goes deep into doubt, he will find the futility of it on his own. And out of that finding trust arises, and then that trust has beauty, grandeur.

If a child reasons to the very end, he will come to the point where he will be able to see that when reasoning finally comes to an end, existence continues on and on. Existence is something beyond reasoning. But it is important to let every child feel it in his own guts!

A religion, to be true, has to be a religion of the guts, not of belief. Let the child think as much as he can, to his full capacity. Let him burn with doubt, logic, reasoning, to the maximum, and he will see the limitations of the intellect. It is bound to happen. And when the limitations of the intellect have been seen, experienced by yourself, you start moving into the beyond; you start surpassing the mind.

Belief is of the mind. This so-called yes-saying is of the mind. I teach you another kind of yes which is not afraid of no, another kind of trust which is not afraid of skepticism; which on the contrary, uses skepticism as a jumping board, which uses doubt as a process of cleansing.

Truth is to be trusted – to trust is an act of faith; but any statement of truth is to be tested too – to test it is an act of doubt. Faith and doubt both serve truth – this is what I teach you. Faith and doubt are two wings of the bird called trust; if you cut off one wing, the bird cannot fly. Yes and no are two wings, they work together; use them, and use them in their totality. Never be insincere, not even in the name of God.

Sincerity is far more valuable than any dogma, than any Christianity, Hinduism, Islam. Sincerity is the foundation. But to be sincere means you have to give expression to all that is within you. Sometimes it is yes and sometimes it is no, and you have to accept both.

So, it is something beautiful that is happening, don't be worried. I am not trying to force any yes on you. I am simply helping you to go through the whole process of both yes and no, so that one day you become aware that they are not enemies – not opposites, but complementaries.

Man is a question mark...and it is a blessing – celebrate it. It is a blessing because only man is a question mark; no dog is, no tree is. The rose bush is beautiful but not as beautiful as man, and the moon is beautiful but not as beautiful as man – because they are all unconscious. Only man is consciously on a quest. And how can you be on a quest if you don't have a question mark in your being?

God sends you with a question mark in your being. Celebrate it – it is a great responsibility, a great heritage. Ask questions, inquire, doubt. And don't be worried, because I know that if you doubt long enough you will arrive at trust. And that arrival is incredible, because then you have arrived on your own, it is your own experience. It is no longer belief, it is knowing.

Sri Aurobindo was asked by a philosopher, "Do you believe in God?" and he said, "No." The philosopher was for a moment shocked. He had come a long way, believing that this man had come to know God, and this man says, "I don't believe in God." For a moment he could not gather courage to ask anything else. Shocked, he was dumb.

Then he said, "But I thought that you had seen God."

Sri Aurobindo laughed and said, "Yes, I have seen, that's why I say I don't believe. Belief is out of ignorance. I know! I don't believe."

And remember it: you have to know, you are not here to believe. My help is available for you to *know*. Belief is a trick of the mind: without knowing, it gives you the feeling that you have known. Man is a question mark – and it is a blessing. Celebrate it, dance it, rejoice in it, because without that question mark there could be no faith, or doubt – nothing but dead certainty. That's where animals live: in dead certainty. And that's why your priests and your politicians want you to live in this dead certainty.

Life hesitates. Life is uncertain. Life is insecure. That's why it is life: because it moves and changes constantly.

Socrates is reported to have said, "I would not like to become a contented pig. Rather than being a contented pig, I would like to remain a discontented Socrates."

Meditate over it – a statement of immense value. The pig is contented and absolutely certain. That's why people who are stubborn and think themselves as being absolutely certain are called piggish. Poor Morarji Desai is called piggish.

People who are stubborn are bound to be stupid. A man who is alive moves into uncertainties, moves into the unknown. He cannot live in a dead certainty.

Certainty simply means you have not doubted. There is another kind of knowing which comes out of doubting, which comes out of growth. And when that kind of knowing comes, again you are not certain. But now the uncertainty has a totally different flavor. If you had asked Buddha about God, he would have kept quiet. That's where he is far superior to Sri Aurobindo. He would have kept absolutely silent, he would not have said yes or no. Why? – because he says, "The ultimate is so tremendously vast that to say yes will be wrong, to say no will be wrong, because our words are so small they cannot contain the ultimate. The ultimate can only be conveyed through silence."

A Zen master was asked, "Can you say something about God?" He remained utterly silent; he listened to the question with open eyes and then he closed his eyes. A few moments went by. For the questioner those few moments seemed very long. He was waiting and becoming restless, and the master had moved into some other space. There was great ecstasy on his face but no answer.

That ecstasy was the answer. There was utter silence in his being, and the silence was vibrant all around him. You could have almost touched it, it...it was so solid. But the restless questioner was not aware of it at all; he was too concerned with his question and he was waiting for the answer.

He shook the master and said, "What are you doing? I have asked a question and you closed your eyes and you are sitting in silence. Answer it!"

And the master says, "But that's what I was doing. This is my answer."

Certainly this is far superior to Sri Aurobindo's answer.

But the man, the questioner, was not satisfied. He wanted something conveyed verbally. He insisted and he would not leave the master. So the master said, "Okay."

They were sitting on a river bank. The master wrote in the sand with his finger: meditation.

Now, the question is about God and the answer is about meditation – it is utterly irrelevant. And the questioner was right to say, "Are you joking or something? I am asking about God and you write on the sand: meditation."

And the master said, "That's all that I can say, or that I am allowed to say. You ask about the goal, I talk about the way, because the goal is incomprehensible – so mysterious, nothing can be said about it: I can simply sit in silence. If you have eyes to see, see! If you have ears to hear, hear! Hear my silence and the song that my silence is and the music that arises in it. If you cannot hear it, that simply shows you need meditation. So meditate."

The man said, "Just this much – one word, *meditation*? Won't you elaborate on it a little?"

He wrote again in bigger letters: meditation. That was his elaboration.

The man was puzzled and he said, "But you are simply repeating. Just writing it in bigger letters won't help."

So he wrote again in even bigger letters: meditation. He said, "Nothing more can be said about it. You will have to do it. You will have to be it."

There is a kind of uncertainty when you don't know, because how can you be certain when you don't know? And there is a kind of uncertainty when you do know, because how can you be certain about the ultimate? It is so vast – to be certain about it will make it small, to be certain about it will show that it is in your grasp, that it is in your fist. And God cannot be possessed; on the contrary, you have to be possessed by God.

Accept your no, accept your yes, and don't think that they are opposites; they are not. Just as there can be no courage without danger, so there can be no faith without uncertainty, or without doubt. Risk comes as part of the game that we are born to play. We must learn to lean on possibilities – not on certainties but on possibilities.

I can only say to you: God is possible. I can only say to you: yes is possible. Lean on the possibilities, don't ask for certainties. Because you ask for certainties, you create authorities; out of your need to be certain you become victims of people who are stubborn, ignorant, but certain. Only parrots can be certain because they have ready-made answers. Pundits can be certain because pundits are nothing but parrots.

A real man of knowledge will help you to be silent: will help you to go through yes and through no, through faith and through doubt, through warmer moments and through cooler moments; will help you to go through days and nights, peaks and valleys, and will not teach any dogma, but will only teach you courage, adventure, quest.

Listening to your question, I remembered two stories.

There was a boy, about five or six years old, who had acquired the habit of using swear words in his ordinary conversation. His parents tried their best to break him of this habit, and in final desperation hit upon a plan which they thought would work. They called their son into a family consultation and laid out the facts before him, saying, "Now, son, we just can't have a little boy in our home who continues to use this kind of language. So we have decided that if you cannot break yourself of the habit, something drastic must be done. We are giving you fair warning that the very next time we hear a swear word in your conversation, you are simply going to have to pack your bag and move out of this house. We can't put up with that language any longer. Do you understand?"

He did not say anything, although he did nod his head. But the habit, it seemed, was too great for him to break all at once, and they soon heard him interspersing his favorite swear words in conversation.

His mother said, "Son, we have given you fair warning and now you are going to move out. Go pack your bag."

The boy went to his bedroom, reluctantly, packed his suitcase, said goodbye to his mother and left. He did not know what in the world he was going to do, so he sat on the front steps trying to collect his thoughts. As he waited there a neighbor came by, looked at him and asked, "Is your mother home, dear?"

He looked at her with a sour face, and said, "How the hell should I know? I don't live here anymore."

You cannot force, you cannot repress, you cannot order these things. These things need understanding. And parents are doing it all the time, just saying, "Don't do this, do that" – just giving commandments, never giving understanding, insight. Children need insight, not commandments. They need your love, they need your help to understand things. They don't want to imitate you. In fact, they should not be forced to imitate you, because if you force them to imitate you, you will be destroying their very soul. Give your love and give them freedom, and help them to become aware, help them to be more meditative.

But that is not being done. We simply force. Forcing a thing seems to be a very short-cut procedure. Who bothers? Because you don't love enough, that's why you don't bother. Who bothers to give an insight to a child? It is very simple: "Just go and do this because I say so, because I am your father and I know more because I am older than you." The child may be forced to do a certain thing because he is helpless, but deep down he will carry the wound. And, you must have been carrying many wounds deep down.

My love to you, my help to you is bringing your wounds to the surface. It is good, because once the wounds come to the surface, in the sunlight they can be healed – there is no other way to heal them. You are coming to health: don't be afraid, let all those no's come up; they will be released and you will be free of them.

A little girl had disobeyed her parents and they decided she should be punished. They took her upstairs to the bedroom, put her in the clothes- closet, closed the door and said, "Now dear, you just take time to think it over and see if you can't make up your mind to be more loving toward your parents and not disobey them."

After a few minutes the parents' consciences began to bother them and they went up, knocked on the door and said, "Dear, how are you?"

"Oh, I am fine."

"What are you doing?" asked her mother.

"Well," she replied, "I spit on your dress, I spit on your coat, I spit on your shoes, and I am just sitting here waiting for more spit."

The second question:

> Osho,
> Please say something about this news item: The Indian Express of
> 18th August reports that the Osho film won't reflect the real image
> of India. The Union Information Minister, L.K. Advani said in the
> Parliament, "Foreign television and film units have been refused
> permission to document the activities of the Osho Ashram, as it is felt
> that a film on the activities of the Ashram would not reflect favorably
> on India's image abroad."

This is really surprising from a politician, because the politicians are the people who destroy the images of countries. The politicians are the people who are the most corrupt – from the peon to the prime minister. Their corruption is not going to help the image of the country in the world. They should think about it. Their continuous quarreling for stupid reasons destroys the image of a country – and you cannot find more quarrelsome politicians than in India. And the quarrels have no ideological basis at all; the quarrels are simply quarrels which are personal – their own personal greed.

The Indian politicians seem to be the most greedy – greedy for power, hungry for power – continuously fighting with each other. Their whole time is wasted in quarreling. The country is going to the dogs, and sitting in New Delhi, all that they do is fight with each other – how to topple the other. Everyone wants to become the prime minister. And once you become the prime minister, all that you do is protect your prime ministership. The whole time spent working to become the prime minister is wasted – almost your whole life.

Morarji Desai's whole life was wasted in becoming the prime minister. Now at the age of eighty-three, he has arrived. Now the whole time is wasted: how to remain in the seat till you die? And once you are in the seat you don't want to die. You can do anything. He drinks his own urine; he thinks he is going to become immortal through it.

Now is this urine-drinking prime minister helping the Indian image abroad? They should think about it. They should not be worried about me and my people. But politicians are the lowest as far as intelligence is concerned. They are the most inferior people in the world.

I have heard…

A politician went to the psychoanalyst and he said, "I suffer from an inferiority complex."

The psychoanalyst worked upon the politician – many sessions of analysis – and then finally he said to him, "You need not worry."

The politician said, "I need not worry? So there is no problem?"

And the psychoanalyst said, "Yes, there is no problem, because you simply *are* inferior. You need not suffer from any inferiority complex. It is simply so."

Once I was staying in a circuit house with a politician. In the morning we were sitting on the lawn. He was reading the newspaper. That's all they read – that is their Koran, Bible, Gita. Suddenly he looked up at me and said, "I'll never be able to understand how people always seem to die in alphabetical order."

And another time, I was traveling in a train and unfortunately, in the same compartment was a politician. I say unfortunately because they stink. Nothing stinks like politics. It is the dirtiest thing in the world.

He started talking to me, and I asked him if he had heard the latest joke about politicians.

"I am warning you," he said, "I am a politician myself."

"That's all right," I told him, "I will tell it very very slowly."

I am not part of any tradition, that's what is creating trouble for the Indian politicians. I don't belong to the past, I belong to the future. They cannot understand me – it is impossible for them. If I had belonged to the past, there would have been no difficulty. But I don't belong to the past. A really religious person never belongs to the past. Buddha never belonged to the past, that's why

Hindus were angry. Jesus never belonged to the past, that's why Jews were angry. Jesus, Buddha, Krishna – they all are pointing to the future, not to the past.

Do not embrace the past or you will have missed the whole point. Tradition is not religion. Religion is always a surpassing, a transcending, a going beyond.

If I had been a Hindu there would have been no difficulty. I am not. If I had been a Mohammedan there would have been no difficulty. I am not. I am neither a Buddhist nor a Jaina. And they are very confused: they cannot categorize me, they cannot pigeonhole me. No religious person can ever be pigeonholed, because religion basically is freedom – freedom from the past, freedom to be in the here and now, and freedom to be available to the future.

What I am trying to bring to you is something of the future: people will be able to understand it only after hundreds of years, and then these same politicians will pay respect, as they pay respect to Jesus. And these are the people who crucified him, and these are the people who stoned Buddha and Mahavira, and these are the people who poisoned Socrates. These are the same people – beware of them!

They are always against the future. Why are they against the future? – because their vested interest is always rooted in the past. They can manipulate the past, they cannot manipulate the future. They can exploit the past, they cannot exploit the future. They can exploit irreligious people, they cannot exploit religious people. They can exploit the pseudo-religious very easily, there is no problem in it, because a pseudo-religious person is almost a shadow, not a reality. And the pseudo-religious person is always ready to be manipulated, to be transformed into a slave.

I am creating rebellious people here, rebellious in a multi-dimensional way. The politicians are bound to be afraid. And they will find excuses.

Now he says, "The Osho film won't reflect the real image of India..."

I would like to say to him: Do you understand the meaning of the real? The real means that which is happening – and this ashram is happening, I am happening. Any image of India that does not include me will be unreal – only because it will not include something which *is* happening. What do you mean by "real image"?

A real image means that which is existential, that which is happening. You may not like me, you may not like my people, but you cannot say that I don't reflect the real image of India. You may be against me, but still I am part of this country. I am here and I am going to be here! And my people are going to increase. This is part of reality. This may be just a seed now, but soon it will become a great tree. How can you deny its reality?

We have two million sannyasins all over the world. Nobody else can claim that. And we have almost a million lay followers, lay disciples. It is part of reality now. Three thousand sannyasins are almost always present here. Every year nearabout 25,000 people visit from all over the world, from all the countries. No other place can claim this. How can you say this is not real?

I think, Mr Advani, you will have to learn language a little bit more. Real is that which is happening. It may not be according to you – right, that is another point – but it is real. And I would like to tell you also that it is not something which is alien to the spirit of India; what is happening is this phenomenon which is really the very soul of India. It happened in Buddha's time, it happened in Mahavira's time, it happened in Krishna's time. It has happened again and again. The *real* India – if you really want to say what the real India is – consists not of politicians but of the mystics. The politicians come and go; the mystics remain.

Do you remember any politician's name of the time of Buddha? Where are they? And they must have been as noisy as Mr Advani. In their own time they must have been very noisy, must have created much fuss. Do you remember the politicians who crucified Jesus? And if you remember the name of Pontius Pilate, you remember it only because he crucified Jesus; otherwise who would have remembered? There have been thousands of governor-generals in the world.

A politician said to the dying Socrates, "We are sorry that you had to be sentenced to death."

Socrates opened his eyes and said, "Don't be worried. You cannot kill me, I will live. And remember, your name will be remembered only because of me."

And that is so.

The real India is a quest of the innermost soul of man – not the geography, not the political history, but the inner journey. The journey of meditation is the real India. Mahavira represents it, Buddha represents it, Krishna and Christ and Nanak – they represent the real India. And I have the heritage of all of them – and much more.

But it has been always so. If Mr Advani were Minister of Broadcasting in Mahavira's time, he would have stopped the BBC from filming Mahavira because Mahavira used to live naked. Or, if he had been a minister in Lalla's time... Lalla was a mystic woman; she lived naked. Certainly he would have prevented any television unit, any film unit from approaching these people – for the same reason: that they don't represent, they don't reflect, the real image of India.

Mr Advani reflects the real image of India? You will be gone soon, down the drain. I predict: by the next election you will be heard of no more – you and your whole company will just go down the drain, because the country has seen that you have deceived and cheated it. In the name of democracy all kinds of wrong people have become powerful in India. And they have not done a single thing since they have been in power, except quarreling.

I must remind you of the three monkeys of Mahatma Gandhi. You must have heard of them – those three monkeys are very famous. He had always a statue of them. Somebody from Japan or from China had presented him three monkeys. One monkey keeps his hands on his eyes, representing that you should not see that which is wrong. Another monkey keeps his hands on his ears, symbolizing that you should not hear that which is not worth hearing. And the third monkey keeps his hands on his mouth: you should not say what is not worth saying.

These three monkeys have come to rule. Now they are called the *trimurti* – the three monkeys are Mahatma Gandhi's. The chief monkey keeps his hands on his ears; he will not listen. The whole country is shouting, "We are dying. We are starving. The population is growing." But he will not listen. His name is Mahatma Morarji Desai. He will not listen. The whole country is crying, "Your son is a criminal, his activities should be investigated – he is accumulating money by illegal means." But he will not listen. He is the chief monkey of Mahatma Gandhi: he keeps his ears shut and goes on smiling; drinks his own urine and keeps himself healthy. That's all that he is doing.

The other monkey keeps his eyes shut, because he represents the untouchables, the down-trodden, the lowest of the low – and they are being burned alive. They are being killed, butchered, murdered, raped. And never before has it happened like this: all over the country their lives are in danger. And the man who represents them, Jagjivan Ram, simply keeps his eyes closed because if he opens his eyes and sees what is happening he will not be able to say that he is their representative there.

But the third monkey who was supposed to keep quiet and not say anything has betrayed the others and has said something – Charan Singh – and because of his saying something he has been thrown out of the trinity. But he is trying to get back in again, and the other two monkeys are trying to keep him out because he started saying things that he should not say. And why did he start saying things? – because he is getting old. Heart attacks are happening to him, and he seems to have no chance of becoming the prime minister of India. He has to speak: time is running out – he has to struggle, he cannot keep quiet anymore.

These monkeyish people in New Delhi, is it that they think that *they* represent the real India? In reality they simply represent the neurotic part of India, they represent the people who suffer from inferiority complexes. That's what the great psychologist Adler says: a man goes into politics only if he suffers from an inferiority complex. He wants to prove to himself that he is somebody. He has to prove it, otherwise there is great anguish in his belief that "I am inferior." Untalented people, unintelligent people go into politics. Those who are talented become artists, painters, poets, philosophers, mystics, dancers. They have a thousand and one other beautiful things to do, not politics. Only the third rate, the most unintelligent part of a country, moves into politics. Those who cannot do anything else, at least they can go into politics. The politicians are almost hidden criminals; the same quality of people become criminals. If they cannot reach to power, they become destructive. And what wrong is happening here that they are afraid should not be known in the world at large?

One thing: a great synthesis is happening here – something that has never happened before, of which they are afraid – and which *needs* to happen. It is a *must* for humanity's survival. I am trying to create a great synthesis: the synthesis between Zorba the Greek and Gautama the Buddha, the synthesis between materialism and spiritualism. I am trying to create a spiritual materialism. These two things have always remained separate, antagonistic to each other. And because of their antagonism man has remained schizophrenic because man is both, body and soul. Man is not only soul, man is not only body. To insist that man is only body is materialism; to insist that man is only soul is spiritualism. Both are half, and both are wrong because they are half. And both are unsatisfactory, they have proved unsatisfactory.

Man has to be accepted in his totality. As far as the body is concerned, a man has to be Zorba the Greek, and as far as the soul is concerned, a man has to be Gautama the Buddha. If body and soul can exist together, why cannot Buddha and Zorba exist together in a single man? That will be the highest synthesis.

The West has remained materialistic. It suffers from materialism. It has all the benefits of materialism: great technology, beautiful houses, better medical facilities, longer life, more beautiful bodies, more healthy bodies. It has all the benefits of materialism – it is rich, affluent – but it suffers because it has lost its soul, the inner world is empty, hollow. The West has all that is needed on the outside, but in managing the outside it has leaned too much towards materialism and forgotten its own inner world. The master is lost, the soul is lost; the kingdom is there but the king is dead. Hence the Western anguish, hence the Western search for the king, hence the inquiry into meditation, because meditation is the only way to seek and search for the inner king. Where has he gone? Where is the inner light?

The East has remained spiritual. It has all the beauties of spirituality: calmness, quietness, relaxedness, lovingness, compassion. It has a certain quality – a flavor of the inner – but the body is sick and there is great poverty and starvation all around, and the outer world is ugly. It has suffered much too. And both are tense, because unless you are whole you will be tense.

Can't you see that the East is no more interested in meditation? That's why you don't see many Indians here. The East is no more interested in meditation, it is no more interested in Buddha; its interest has shifted, and it is natural. It wants to know more about physics, chemistry, engineering, medical science. The Eastern talent goes to the West – to Oxford, to Cambridge, to Harvard, to Princeton – to learn what has happened in the West. The Eastern talent has only one desire: how to go to the West and learn something of modern science. The Eastern talented person cannot believe: Why are you Westerners coming to the East? You have Oxford and you have Harvard, why are you coming here? We are trying to get there and you are coming here. It looks so absurd.

But the West has to come to the East; Harvard and Oxford have proved lacking. They have given much, but they have not given inner richness. The West is affluent, and because the West is affluent, the West has become more aware – in contrast to its affluence – of the inner poverty, the inner black hole. The outside is so full of light that the inner black hole, in contrast, has become very clear. The search has started: the West is moving towards the East, the East is moving towards the West.

The Eastern intellectual becomes a communist and the Western intellectual becomes a meditator. This can go on and this can lead again to another kind of shift and misery. The West can become the East and the East can become the West and the problem will remain the same. My effort here is a great experiment in bringing the East and West together.

Kipling has said: East and West shall never meet. I would like to tell Kipling – he must be somewhere in his grave, because he is a Christian and he will not leave the grave before the last judgment day – "Sir, East and West *are* meeting; they have already met, they are meeting here in this place," which Mr Advani says does not represent the real image of India.

It represents the East, but it represents more than the East: it represents East plus West, it represents the whole of humanity – it is an experiment in universal brotherhood. You will find Christians, Jews, Mohammedans, Parsees, Jainas, Buddhists, Hindus – all kinds of people – here. They have all dropped their identities, they have fallen into a universal brotherhood...and you say this does not represent the real image of India?

And remember also: India is not a small country, it is a vast continent; it is not one tradition, it is many traditions. But the people who are in power now are basically Hindu chauvinists. A very wrong kind of person has come to power. Their whole idea is of a very narrow Hinduism – so narrow that it does not even contain the whole current of Hinduism. Hence it is very much afraid.

If these people are allowed to have their say, sooner or later they will bulldoze Khajuraho, Konarak, because they will say they don't represent the real image of India.

Why are they so much against me? – because here Yoga is happening, Sufism is happening, Zen is happening, Tao is happening, Tantra also – and Tantra is creating trouble. These people in New Delhi are utterly sexually frustrated, repressed people.

Khajuraho is being born again here. To whom does Khajuraho belong? I have not made that temple. I would suggest to Mr Advani: Destroy Khajuraho, because the people from the BBC may come and film it. It is a beautiful temple, one of the most beautiful on the earth – because there is nothing more beautiful than love, there is nothing more graceful than a couple who are in deep love, in a deep loving embrace. There is nothing more divine than that. Something of God descends when a couple is in deep love, in an orgasmic ecstasy. Khajuraho represents that. Konarak represents that. And there are thousands of Tantra scriptures. Please destroy them before anybody comes to know about them. Destroy Vatsyayana's *Kama Sutra*.

Why are you so afraid of me and my people? They are not doing any harm to anybody. They are not training for any war, they are preparing for a more loving life. Yes, alongside with Yoga, Tao, Zen, Tantra is also a part. And because a few newspapers – and they also belong to the same repressed sexual mind – print some nude pictures about the ashram.... That is all they have against me.

That nudity in itself is part of a long Indian tradition. Jaina *digambara munis* are nude – prevent them, they are still nude. Thousands of Hindu sannyasins live in nudity – prevent them. Destroy all the temples of the Jainas, because Mahavira and the other twenty-three *tirthankaras* have their nude statues there. And destroy all the Hindu temples of Shiva, because the *shiva-linga* is nothing but a phallic symbol. Then only can you say...

First, destroy all these things, then only can you say that Osho and his ashram don't reflect the real image of India. Otherwise, India is a vast continent; thousands of years have passed and many traditions have lived together. Tantra has existed side by side with Yoga.

Yoga is repressive, Tantra is expressive. Yoga is afraid of sex, Tantra rejoices in sex. Yoga says, "Avoid sex if you want to go to God," and Tantra says, "*Use* sex if you want to go to God." And my own observation is that Tantra is far more profound than Yoga, because sex is the energy given to you by God; repressing it will be very disrespectful to God. Use it. And it is the creative energy in you: it creates the child, it brings new life. It has some other aspects also, hidden aspects: if you use it meditatively, if you use it as prayer, it can create you anew, it can give you a rebirth. You will become a *dwija*, a twice-born.

Sex energy has two poles to it. One is if it moves downwards, it reproduces children; a tremendous miracle, the birth of a child. If it moves upwards, it creates *you*: a new integrity, a new individuation, a new center of being is born. Tantra is one of the greatest sciences ever born for the transformation of man. And this place is not an ordinary ashram, just as Indians have become accustomed to ashrams – dull, dead. This place is an alchemical academy. We are doing great experiments in expanding the human consciousness and we are now using all kinds of techniques available to humanity, both Eastern and Western. They are very much afraid of this.

He says, "The Osho film won't reflect the real image of India...it is felt that a film on the activities of the ashram would not reflect favorably on India's image abroad."

But just by preventing the BBC, the Spanish TV unit, the Australian TV unit, the German TV unit, and journalists from reaching here, do you think you will be able to prevent me from reaching people? If Jesus could reach without the BBC, do you think you will be able to prevent me from reaching people? If Buddha could reach without any modern media available to him, do you think you will be able to prevent me?

It cannot be prevented. Truth can never be prevented. If there is some truth in me, it has to reach people. It will reach, and people will reach me. No government can prevent me from reaching people. Yes, you can prevent newspapers, you can prevent television stations, you can prevent radio. Who cares?

I will reach through my people to millions of people. If there is truth, people will come from all over the world, seeking and searching. If they are thirsty, they are bound to seek and search, because I have something here which can quench their thirst.

And without ever coming here – Mr Advani has never come here, no other minister has ever come here – saying such silly things is not right.

And, sir, I would suggest to you…your government is very skillful in creating commissions. That's all that you have done within this year and a half that you have been in power. All that you have done is to create commissions. Why don't you create a commission to visit the ashram, to see what is happening here? Just remember one thing: be careful, because people who come here get caught. And be careful also whom you send. All the information that you have about the ashram you depend on getting from your police departments. How can they understand? What can they understand? All the information that you have you depend on getting from your government machinery. What can they understand?

So don't appoint a commission with some senile, retired judge – that won't help. Remember that what is happening here is something so scientific that only people who know something about modern developments in humanistic psychology, who know something about encounter therapy, gestalt, psychodrama, primal therapy, who know something about psychoanalysis, psychosynthesis, who know something about est, Arica, who know something about Vipassana, Zazen, Sufi whirling – only they will be able to understand what is happening here.

This place has great intellect, great intelligence, great talent. We have hundreds of DLitt, PhD, DPhil graduates, and thousands who have an MA, MSc and other qualifications. No other Indian university can claim as much talent as we have here. Even PhD graduates are cleaning toilets!

So send some educated people, not your MPs – they won't understand a thing – and then decide. You are also invited, Mr Advani.

And what kind of democracy is this? You came to power in the name of democracy. Even Indira did not dare to interfere with my work. And you are democrats? – nothing but Hindu chauvinists!

India is a vast continent. Do you think Charvaka and his materialism is not Indian? Do you think Buddha, who denies God, who denies the soul, who denies the world, who is a nihilist – an utter nihilist, a nihilist par excellence – was he not a Hindu? Do you think Tilopa and Saraha were not Indians, great *tantrikas*?

Who do you think is Indian? Just Mahatma Gandhi and Mahatma Morarji Desai – these two persons are Indian? Then you don't even know much about Mahatma Gandhi. The whole of his life he repressed sex and he found in his old age that he had been on a wrong path. And then he started – he *had* to start – Tantra experiments. What about that? In his last years of life he was sleeping with a naked young girl. His whole life of repression had failed because even when he was seventy he was suffering from wet dreams and sexual fantasies. Then, as an ultimate resort, as an ultimate shelter, he started looking into Tantra. He died a tantrika. What about that? And you call him the Father of the Nation? Stop calling him Father of the Nation; he does not represent the real image of India. What do you think about him – at the age of seventy, sleeping with a young girl, an eighteen-year-old girl, naked? And you call him Father of the Nation?

And one thing more. These are the people, Mr Advani and company, who created the climate in which this man, Mahatma Gandhi, was murdered – these Hindu chauvinists. But what kind of hypocrisy is this? Now they pay tribute and call him Father of the Nation – and these are the murderers! They created the climate in the country to murder that man and now they worship him. In his name now they are in power.

India has many currents. And it is beautiful. It is not a monolith, that's why it is beautiful. It is a rainbow, it has all the colors: Buddhists have a different ideology, Jainas have a totally different ideology, and Hindus have many ideologies. Hinduism is not a narrow religion. In Hinduism there is nothing like a pope or a church; it is not an organized religion at all. And that is the beauty of it: it allows all kinds of people to have all kinds of ways; it says all ways lead to God. It is the most tolerant religion in the world. But the Hindu chauvinist cannot tolerate; he starts trying to make Hinduism also as narrow as he is narrow. These are the ideas in their minds. These ideas are creating trouble for them.

All kinds of people come to me. You will find scientists here, you will find psychologists here – in hundreds. You will find psychotherapists here, you will find poets, painters, artists, musicians, actors. You will find all kinds of talented people here – except the politicians.

Why is the politician so afraid to come here? There is a reason: the politician is the least religious person in the world, the most anti-religious person in the world. Politics and religion are polar opposites. Politics is ambition, religion is non-ambition. Politics is an ego trip, religion is the dissolution of the ego. Politics is struggle, a cut-throat competition; it is violent – basically, essentially. Religion is love – no competition, no comparison. Hence you will not find politicians here.

And because I call a spade a spade, they are afraid of me, they can't come face to face with me. Mr Advani, I invite you and your colleagues to come here and encounter me, encounter my people. It will give you some insight into what is happening here.

It is one of the greatest experiments ever done: how to expand human consciousness *without* drugs. And, let me tell you, politics is a drug. Politicians are alcoholics. Politics is a kind of neurosis. You can go to the parliament and sitting there for one day just watch and you will see: you will not see such madness even in a madhouse. And these people are going to decide who represents India?

India is vast, let me say it again: nobody can represent the whole of India – nobody has that authority to represent the whole of India. It is not a tiny, small place; not one tradition, not one religion, not one language either. And these Hindu chauvinists are trying to force one language on the country. Behind Hindi there is nothing but Hindu chauvinism. They are trying to force one language, Hindi, on the whole country – which is nonsense; it cannot be done, it should not be done. And remember, my own mother tongue is Hindi, and I love it. It is a beautiful language. But that is another matter. This country has many beautiful languages. No language should be forced on the country; that will be violent, undemocratic. But that's what they are trying to do – directly, indirectly. And let me warn the country: if these people persist in trying to force Hindi on the whole of the country, that will be the reason one day or other that India becomes split. South India is bound to go on its own way against the North, because the North is becoming too Hindu chauvinistic.

If this country is going to be destroyed one day, the reason will be these people who are in power today. India cannot have one language. And if it can have one language, that language has to be neutral; either it will be English or Esperanto, but not Hindi, not Gujarati, not Marathi, not Bengali, not Tamil. It will have to be a neutral language. English is neutral; it is nobody's mother tongue in India. And English is international too, so it is perfectly good. I support a two-language formula: English as the national language, because it is also international and the second language, the mother tongue. Each child should be taught two languages. Forget all about Hindi, and forget all about creating one monolith in this country of variety, of multiplicity.

And they are trying to do the same thing with religion too, in the same way. They want to force me not to do what I am doing here because my approach is non-political. I have no vested interest in anything – in any language, in any province, in any religion, in any tradition. My approach is that the whole past is ours – and not only the Indian past, the whole past of humanity is ours. That's why I have chosen to speak on Chinese masters, Japanese masters, Greek masters, Hebrew masters. I am going to speak on *all* the masters of the world so that listening to all these different songs, you can become universal.

They are afraid of all this. They would like me only to talk on the Bhagavad Gita. The Bhagavad Gita is beautiful and I have talked on it, but I am not going to talk *only* on this. I don't belong to any tradition, to any past. I claim the whole past as mine, and the whole future too.

It happens sometimes that a politician wants to come, but then he sends "feelers," he sends people, and those people come and they want me to invite the politician. Why should I invite? All the people come here; whosoever wants to come here can come here. We are not here to pay special respect to anybody – to politicians…certainly not. They send messages to me that "X is ready to come to inaugurate the ashram," that "Y is ready to lay the foundation for the new commune."

I will not allow any politician to lay the foundation of my commune; it will be sacrilegious. I will not allow any politician to come and inaugurate my ashram. Politicians – what have they to do with religion? What do they know about religion? They have the dirtiest vibe possible.

But there were good days also in the past, and great people also. Listen to this anecdote.

The Emperor came to visit the Zen Master Joshu, who was meditating in his room.

"Tell him to come in and make his bows," the master said to his horrified attendant. The Emperor entered and made his obeisance.

When Joshu was later asked about his rude behavior, he explained, "You just don't understand. If a visitor of low class comes, I go to the temple gate to greet him. For a middle class guest I get up from my seat. A great emperor cannot be treated like that."

The Emperor, of course, had been delighted with his reception.

But those were great days: an emperor was delighted! But these poor politicians, they send messages that they should be received at the gate, garlanded, they should be treated as VVIPs. What nonsense! If I even allow you entry, that is enough respect for you. If Sant does not prevent you at the gate, you should feel fortunate enough.

In the new commune, I am going to put a board on the gate: Politicians and dogs are not allowed.

Enough for today.

CHAPTER 11
The Whole and
Holy Circle

Master Lu-tsu said:
Nothing is possible without contemplation. Perceiving brings one
to the goal.

What has to be reversed by reflection is the self-conscious heart,
which has to direct itself towards that point where the formative
spirit is not yet manifest. Within our six-foot body we must strive for
the form which existed before the laying down of heaven and Earth. If
today people sit and meditate only one or two hours, looking only at
their egos, and call this reflection, how can anything come out of it?

One should look at the tip of one's nose. But this does not mean
that one should fasten one's thoughts to the tip of the nose. Neither
that, while the eyes are looking at the tip of the nose, the thoughts
should be concentrated on the yellow middle. Wherever the eye looks,
the heart is directed also. How can it be directed at the same time
upward and downward? All that means confusing the finger with
which one points to the moon with the moon itself.

What then is really meant by this? The expression "tip of the nose" is
cleverly chosen. The nose must serve the eyes as a guideline. If one is

not guided by the nose, either one opens wide the eyes and looks into the distance, so that the nose is not seen, or the lids shut too much, so that the eyes close, and again the nose is not seen. But when the eyes are opened too wide, one makes the mistake of directing them outward, whereby one is easily distracted. If they are closed too much, one makes the mistake of letting them turn inward, whereby one easily sinks into a dreamy reverie. Only when the eyelids are lowered properly halfway is the tip of the nose seen in just the right way. Therefore, it is taken as a guideline. The main thing is to lower the eyelids in the right way, and then to allow the light to stream in of itself; without effort, wanting the light to stream in concentratedly. Looking at the tip of the nose serves only as the beginning of the inner concentration, so that the eyes are brought into the right direction for looking, and then are held to as guideline: after that, one can let it be. This is the way a mason hangs up a plumb line. As soon as he has hung it up, he guides his work by it without continually bothering himself to look at the plumb line.

One looks with both eyes at the tip of the nose, sits upright and in a comfortable position, and holds the heart to the center in the midst of conditions. It does not necessarily mean the middle of the head. It is only a matter of fixing one's thinking on the point which lies exactly between the two eyes. Then all is well. The light is something extremely mobile. When one fixes a thought on the midpoint between the two eyes, the light streams in of its own accord. It is not necessary to direct the attention especially to the central castle. In these few words the most important thing is contained.

"The center in the midst of conditions" is a very subtle expression. The center is omnipresent; everything is contained in it; it is connected with the release of the whole process of creation.

Fixating contemplation is indispensable; it ensures the making fast of the enlightenment. Only one must not stay sitting rigidly if worldly thoughts come up, but one must examine where the thought is, where it began, and where it fades out. Nothing is gained by pushing reflection further. One must be content to see where the

thought arose, and not seek beyond the point of origin; for to find the
heart-consciousness, to get behind consciousness with consciousness
– that cannot be done. Together we want to bring the states of the
heart to rest, that is true contemplation. What contradicts it is false
contemplation. That leads to no goal. When the flight of the thoughts
keeps extending further, one should stop and begin contemplating.
Let one contemplate and then start fixating again. That is the double
method of making fast the enlightenment. It means the circulation
of the light. The circulation is fixation. The light is contemplation.
Fixation without contemplation is circulation without light.
Contemplation without fixation is light without circulation!
Take note of that!

A blind man visited his friends. It was dark when he left, and they gave him a lantern to help him on his journey through the night.

"Thank you, but I don't need it. Light or dark, it is all the same to me."

"Yes, but carry it anyway so people won't bump into you."

Off he went, and soon someone collided with him and shouted, "Why don't you look where you're going?"

"Why don't you see my lantern!"

"Sorry, brother," said the other, "your candle went out."

The scriptures in the hands of people who don't know what meditation is, are just like a lantern in the hands of a blind man – utterly useless – and the blind man cannot know whether the lantern is still lit or not. He will simply be carrying an unnecessary weight – in fact, not helpful at all; on the contrary, it can be a hindrance. If the blind man had been moving without the lantern he would have been more careful, more cautious. Because of the lantern in his hand, he must have been walking as if he had eyes, he must have put all caution aside.

That's what has happened to humanity at large: people have the Bible, the Koran, the Gita – these are lamps of immense beauty and light, but your eyes are blind. And the Gita is five thousand years old – the light went out long long ago. When Krishna died the light went out. So is the case with the Bible and the Koran and all the other holy scriptures of the world: when the master dies, the light goes out and people cannot become blind.

But people go on carrying the scriptures, believing the scriptures, hoping that their life will remain full of light because they are carrying a message from a great master. That message is nothing more than words; it is an unnecessary burden. If all the scriptures of the world disappear, man may become more cautious, may become more alert, may start looking for the source of light on his own. Because there will be nothing to lean on, he will have to learn to stand on his own feet.

Lung-t'an was once visited by Te-shan, who, seeking further and further elucidation, remained until it grew late. Lung-t'an finally said, "The night deepens. Why don't you retire?"

Te-shan, taking his leave, raised the bamboo blind and went out. Seeing the intense darkness without, he returned and said, "It is dark outside."

Lung-t'an then lit a lantern and offered it to Te-shan. Just as Te-shan was about to take it, Lung-t'an abruptly blew it out. With this, Te-shan suddenly attained awakening, whereupon he bowed.

Lung-t'an said, "What kind of truth did you see?"

Te-shan said, "Never after today shall I doubt the utterances of all the old masters under heaven."

The next day Lung-t'an went before the disciples and said, "Within this group there is a man whose canine teeth are like sword trees, whose mouth resembles a bloody plate, and who won't turn his head even when given a blow with a stick. One day he will establish my way on the top of a solitary mountain peak."

Te-shan then took out his sutra commentaries and in front of the meditation hall, raised a torch and said, "Endless deep analysis is like placing a single hair in the emptiness of space; worldly power is like throwing one drop of water into an immense gorge."

So saying, he took his commentaries and burned them.

Now, if you don't have eyes even light is useless; a lantern in your hands is nothing, utterly nothing. But if you have eyes, even the blowing out of a candle can become an experience of enlightenment. The question is of eyes.

This man Lung-t'an was visited by Te-shan. Lung-t'an is the Master, Te-shan is his disciple. Seeing the darkness outside, the disciple said to the master, "It is too dark."

The master lit a candle and gave it to the disciple, and as he was going to take it, he blew it out. Suddenly, all became dark again, more dark than it was before. And this abrupt blowing out of the candle must have been a shock – unexpected. For a moment the disciple must have fallen into the interval between two thoughts. For a moment thinking disappeared and there was contemplation.

For a moment there was utter silence. In that silence he could see the point.

The next day he burned all his scriptures. Now they were no longer needed; now he knew the truth through his own experience.

A little bit of experience is more valuable than mountains of knowledge. Just two small eyes are more valuable than the sun and the moon and all the stars. The whole point is that religion is an experience. It is not speculation, it is not continuous analysis – it is insight.

Now the sutras. These sutras are of immense value because they give you the technique in the simplest terms possible. And the method is really simple – unless you are determined to make it complex.

The mind always turns simple things into complexities – beware of that – because the mind cannot exist with the simple; it is not needed. If things are really simple, what is the need of the mind? The mind is needed only when things are complex. Then you have to depend on the mind because then the mind will find the way out of the riddle. But if there is no riddle, the mind is utterly useless; you can discard it. So the investment of the mind is in complexity. Remember it.

These sutras are very simple. Truth is always simple, utterly simple.

> *Master Lu-tsu said:*
> *Nothing is possible without contemplation.*

What is contemplation? – a moment of no-thought.

The English word *contemplation* does not give the right idea of *dhyana*. In English there is no word which can translate the word *dhyana*.

There are three words available. One is *concentration*, which is very far-off, because concentration means effort, tension – a forced state, not a flowing spontaneous state – and dhyana is a flowing spontaneity. There is no strain in it, so the word *concentration* cannot be its translation.

Then the other word is *contemplation*. But in English, contemplation gives the idea of thinking. When you say somebody is contemplating, you mean thinking about something.

Or the third word is *meditation*. But that too means thinking: to meditate upon something. Of these three words no word carries the meaning of dhyana. Dhyana means a state of no-thought, a state of silence, a state of being conscious but without any content. The mirror is there but reflecting nothing, nothing whatsoever. Just like the mirror, the consciousness is there, but nothing is occupying it. That unoccupied awareness is dhyana.

Taoists use the word *contemplation* to translate it. It is only because some word has to be used. So remember the meaning – it is not the meaning in the dictionaries. If you look into the dictionaries you will have a totally false idea of contemplation. In fact that is what *The Secret of the Golden Flower* calls "false contemplation." False contemplation means thinking about something. It may be God – that's what Christians mean by contemplation: thinking about God, thinking about holy things, transcendental things. But things are things; whether they are holy or unholy makes no difference. And thinking is thinking; whether you think about sex or *samadhi* makes no difference.

A state of no-thought, an interval…and it is always happening, but you are not alert about it, otherwise there is no problem in it. One thought comes, then another comes, and between these two thoughts there is always a small gap. And that gap is the door to the divine, that gap is contemplation. If you look into that gap deeply, it starts becoming bigger and bigger.

The mind is like a road full of traffic: one car passes by, then another car passes by, and you become so concerned with the cars that you don't see the gap that is always there between two cars. Otherwise they would collide. They don't collide; something is there between them that keeps them separate. Your thoughts don't collide, they don't run over each other, into each other. They don't even overlap in any way. Each thought has its own boundary, each thought is definable. But the procession of thoughts is so fast, so speedy, that you cannot see the gap unless you are really waiting for it, searching for it.

Contemplation means changing the gestalt. Ordinarily we look at thoughts: one thought, another thought, another thought. When you change the gestalt you look: one interval, another interval, another interval. Your emphasis is no longer on the thoughts but on the interval.

For example, you are sitting here. I can look at you in two ways: either one person, another person, another person – my emphasis is on persons, I can count how many people there are – or I can forget about the persons and I can count the gaps between the persons, how many gaps are there. This is the change of gestalt. If you count the gaps you will be surprised: persons become vague, you don't see them clearly because you are looking into the gaps, you are counting the gaps.

Someday, standing by the side of the road, just count how many gaps pass by and you will be surprised that you don't see the color of the cars, you don't see the make of the cars, you don't see the drivers and the passengers in the cars, but you do see gaps. One gap gone, another gap gone – you go on counting the gaps. Your gestalt is different.

Contemplation is the change of gestalt: not jumping from one thought to another thought, but jumping from one gap to another gap. Slowly slowly you become very very aware of the gaps. And that is one of the greatest secrets of life, because it is through those gaps that you will fall into your own being, into your own center.

Master Lu-tsu said:
Nothing is possible without contemplation. Perceiving brings one to the goal.

Perceiving, just perceiving…what in India we call *darshan*. Seeing brings one to the goal, not going anywhere. You need not go anywhere – just *seeing*! Once you start looking into the intervals, into the gaps, you will be able to see who you are. And you are the goal, you are the source and the goal, both – the beginning and the end, the alpha and the omega. You contain all that you have ever longed for, you have all that you have ever desired. You need not be a beggar. If you choose to look into the gaps you will be an emperor, if you continue to look into the thoughts you will remain a beggar.

Perceiving brings one to the goal.

Not even a single step has to be taken beyond yourself because God is already within you, God is already the case. It is your innermost core. God is not there above, somewhere in the sky; God is within you, somewhere where thoughts no more disturb you, where silence prevails, where utter unoccupied consciousness is present, reflecting nothing.

Then you experience your own taste for the first time, then you are full of the fragrance of your own being: the golden flower blooms.

What has to be reversed by reflection is the self-conscious heart, which has to direct itself towards that point where the formative spirit is not yet manifest.

The thought is the manifest, the no-thought is the unmanifest. If your gestalt consists only of thoughts you will not know anything more than the ego. The ego is called "the self-conscious heart." You remain nothing but a bundle of thoughts. That bundle of thoughts gives you a consciousness of the self, "I am."

Descartes, the father of modern Western philosophy, says, "I think, therefore I am." His own meaning is very different because he is not a meditator, but the statement is beautiful; in a totally different context it is beautiful. I give it a different meaning. Yes, I am – only if I think. If thinking disappears, the I also disappears. "I think, therefore I am" – this I-amness, this self-conscious heart is nothing but a continuum of thoughts. It is not really an entity, it is a false entity, an illusion. It is just like taking a torch in your hand and if you start revolving the torch in your hand you will see a fire circle which is not there. But the torch is moving so fast that it creates an illusory circle of fire, it creates the illusion of a fire circle. It is not there. Thoughts are moving so fast that they create the idea of I.

Lu-tsu says one has to move from the self-conscious heart to the unself-conscious heart: one has to move from ego to egolessness, one has to move from self to no-self. The self is the manifest part – tiny, very small, gross. The unself is the unmanifest part – infinite, eternal. The self is a temporal phenomenon, born one day, will have to die one day. The unself, what Buddha calls *anatta*, no-self, is part of eternity – never born and never going to die – it abides forever.

> Within our six-foot body we must strive for the form which existed
> before the laying down of heaven and Earth.

And within your six-foot body you have that original quality still alive, vibrating – that original quality that was there before heaven and Earth were made. Zen people call it "the original face": when nothing was born– not even Earth, not heaven – all was unmanifest; when all was silence, no sound was born; when there was no form and all was formless, all was in seed.

You have that original silence in you. Hindus call it *anahat nad*. Buddhists have a special expression for it, "The sound of one hand clapping." It is within you, it is your reality. To taste it is to become immortal, to taste it is to be golden. Then dust is transformed into the divine.

The goal of all alchemy is to transform the lower metal into gold.

> If today people sit and meditate only one or two hours, looking only
> at their egos, and call this reflection, how can anything come out of it?

One can sit in meditation and can only look at one's ego. That's what people call contemplation: they look into their thoughts, they don't change the gestalt. All that happens to them is: ordinarily they are occupied with so many things they cannot look into their thoughts; when they sit specially for meditation they forget the world, for the moment, and the thoughts become more clear-cut, they are more alert of their thoughts.

This is the state of a philosopher, this is how philosophers have been thinking, speculating, philosophizing. This is not true contemplation. And this will never take you beyond the ego, beyond death, beyond time. And that is where one's goal lies.

Let me repeat: if you want to meditate you will have to change the gestalt. Just closing your eyes and looking into the ego won't help.

The great English philosopher, David Hume, wrote, "Listening to and reading again and again the great maxim and the advice of all the great masters, 'Know thyself, meditate,' I also tried to meditate. I found nothing inside except thoughts, memories, imagination, dreams. But I have found nothing else."

He is right because he does not know what meditation is. He is a philosopher, and one of the most talented philosophers of the world – very very logical, consistent – but just a philosopher, not a meditator. He must have tried if he says so, and he must have come across many thoughts wandering around inside. And then he said, "But I don't see any self, I don't see any silence, I don't see any God. It is all futile."

He missed because he was not aware that first you have to change the gestalt. You have not to look at the thoughts, you have to look in the gaps, for the gaps; you have to search for the gaps and you have to jump into the gaps. If he had jumped into the gaps he would have seen thoughts disappear, dreams disappear, memories disappear – all is left behind. Slowly slowly it becomes a very very distant noise, and then a moment comes: it simply disappears and you have gone beyond, you have reached the further shore.

One should look at the tip of one's nose.

Now the practical point of the whole sutra – very simple, but try to understand it correctly, because mind wants to distort even simple things. Mind is a distorting mechanism.

One should look at the tip of one's nose.

Why? – because this helps, it brings you in line with the third eye. When both your eyes are fixed on the tip of the nose it does many things. The basic is that your third eye is exactly in line with the tip of the nose – just a few inches above, but in the same line. And once you are in the line of the third eye, the attraction of the third eye, the pull, the magnetism of the third eye is so great that if you have fallen in line with it you will be pulled even against yourself. You just have to be exactly in line with it so that the attraction, the gravitation of the third eye starts functioning. Once you are exactly in line with it there will be no need to make any effort. Suddenly you will find, the gestalt has changed, because the two eyes create the duality of the world and thought, and the single eye between the two eyes creates the gaps. This is a simple method of changing the gestalt.

> One should look at the tip of one's nose. But this does not mean that
> one should fasten one's thoughts to the tip of the nose.

That's how the mind can distort it. The mind can say, "Okay, now look at the tip of the nose. Think of the tip of the nose, concentrate on it." If you concentrate too much on the tip of the nose you will miss the point, because you have to be there at the tip of the nose but very relaxed so that the third eye can pull you. If you are too concentrated on the tip of the nose – rooted, focused, fixed there – your third eye will not be able to pull you in, because your third eye has never functioned before. Its pull cannot be very great in the beginning. Slowly slowly it grows more and more. Once it starts functioning and the dust that has gathered around it disappears with use and the mechanism is humming well, then even if you are fixed on the tip of the nose you will be pulled in...but not in the beginning. You have to be very very light, not a burden, without any stress and strain. You have to be simply there, present, in a kind of let-go.

> Neither that, while the eyes are looking at the tip of the nose, the
> thoughts should be concentrated on the yellow middle.

So don't concentrate on the tip of the nose or – the second trick the mind can play... The master is simply trying to make you alert of all the possibilities, of all the games that the mind is capable of. First it will say, "Okay, so the master says, 'Concentrate on the tip of the nose.'" He is not saying, "Concentrate on the tip of the nose," he is simply saying, "Look. Just a very light, effortless look." Or the mind can say, "Okay, if you are just looking at the tip of the nose, then concentrate on the third eye."

Mind is always in favor of concentration because mind feeds on concentration, lives on concentration. Hence in your schools, colleges, universities, concentration is taught not meditation, because they are all factories for creating the mind, they manufacture the mind.

> *Wherever the eye looks, the heart is directed also. How can it be directed at the same time upward and downward?*

And then the mind can say, "Look, this is impossible, the demand is illogical. How can you look in two directions simultaneously, at the tip of the nose and at the third eye? It is not possible, it cannot be done. Don't be foolish!"

Now the third game of the mind – of condemning something as illogical. First it creates a bogus idea and then it starts destroying it. And when it destroys, it has great joy – a very masochistic, sadistic joy. It says, "Look, this is what he means. Absurdity! First look at the tip of the nose and then look at the third eye – how can you do both, look upward and downward? It is impossible."

> *All that means confusing the finger with which one points to the moon with the moon itself.*

> *What then is really meant by this? The expression "tip of the nose" is cleverly chosen. The nose must serve the eyes as a guideline.*

That's all – just as a guideline: so you are in the field, in the force field of the third eye, so that you are very close to the magnetic energy of the third eye. It can't work in any other way. You have just to be present in the magnetic force, in the field of it, and then it takes you in. You need not go in, you need not make any effort to go in; it happens of its own accord.

> *If one is not guided by the nose, either one opens wide the eyes and looks into the distance, so that the nose is not seen, or the lids shut too much, so that the eyes close, and again the nose is not seen. But when the eyes are opened too wide, one makes the mistake of directing them outward, whereby one is easily distracted.*

And another function of looking very lightly at the tip of the nose is this: that it doesn't allow you to open your eyes wide. If you open your eyes wide the whole world becomes available, and there are a thousand and one distractions. A beautiful woman passes by and you start following – at least in the mind.

Or somebody is fighting; you are not concerned, but you start thinking, "What is going to happen?" Or somebody is crying and you become curious – and a thousand and one things are continuously moving around you. If the eyes are wide open, you become masculine energy, yang.

If the eyes are completely closed you fall into a kind of reverie, you start dreaming; you become feminine energy, yin. To avoid both just look at the tip of the nose – a simple device, but the result is almost magical.

And this is not only so with the Taoists; Buddhists know it, Hindus know it. Down the ages all the meditators have somehow stumbled upon the fact that if your eyes are just half open, in a very miraculous way you escape two pitfalls. One is being distracted by the outside world; another is being distracted by the inside dream world; you remain exactly on the boundary of the inner and the outer. And that's the point: to be on the boundary of the inner and the outer means you are neither male nor female in that moment; your vision is free of duality, your vision has transcended the division in you. Only when you are beyond the division in you do you fall into the line of the magnetic field of the third eye.

> If they are closed too much, one makes the mistake of letting them turn inward, whereby one easily sinks into a dreamy reverie. Only when the eyelids are lowered properly halfway is the tip of the nose seen in just the right way. Therefore it is taken as a guideline. The main thing is to lower the eyelids in the right way, and then to allow the light to stream in of itself...

That is very important to remember: you are not to pull the light in, you are not to force the light in. If the window is open, the light comes, on its own accord; if the door is open, the light floods in. You need not bring it in, you need not push it in, you need not drag it in. And how can you drag light in? How can you push light in? All that is needed is that you should be open and vulnerable to it.

And that's exactly what happens when you are looking at the tip of the nose: just looking without any concentration, just looking without any heaviness in it, without any strain in it, suddenly the window of the third eye opens and the light starts streaming in. The light that has always been going outwards starts coming inwards too, and the circle is complete. And this full circle makes a man perfect. And this circle makes a man utterly restful, relaxed – he is content.

This circle makes a man whole and holy – he is no more divided. Otherwise everybody is schizophrenic, more or less. Only this man who has been able to create the circle of light and the circulation of the light, is beyond schizophrenia, is really healthy, is really non-neurotic. Otherwise the difference between people is not much. The neurotic and the so-called non-neurotic differ only in degree. In fact, the patient and the psychoanalyst are not different kinds of people, they are the same – one neurotic trying to help another neurotic. And sometimes it happens: the one who is helping may be more neurotic than the one he is trying to help.

More psychoanalysts go mad than any other profession in the world. More psychoanalysts commit suicide than any other profession in the world. Why? In a way it seems reasonable, logical: continuously dealing with neurosis, all kinds of madnesses – when they themselves are not completely whole either – naturally, they are going to be affected. They are feeding themselves with these neuroses. When a psychoanalyst is listening to the patient and all his nonsense and rubbish, unconsciously he is collecting it in himself. The patient is dumping all his nonsense on the psychoanalyst. In fact, he pays for that. Slowly, slowly the psychoanalyst has so much neurosis dumped in him that it is going to explode. It is natural.

If I were going to decide about who should be the psychoanalyst, then this process of making light circulate would be the basic requirement, the fundamental requirement for a psychoanalyst: unless a person is capable of circulating his light, he will not be allowed to treat anybody. And if a person is capable of circulating the light in himself he will never be affected by any kind of neurosis; he can listen, he can help, he will remain untouched. His circulation of light will keep him clean, purified. He will be a holy person. That is the difference between a guru and a psychoanalyst.

Only a guru can really be a psychoanalyst, only a guru can really be a therapist. Only a person who has come to his wholeness can be of real help to others who are on the way, struggling, stumbling in the dark. Otherwise the blind man is leading another blind man – both are going to fall in some well.

This book, *The Secret of the Golden Flower, must* become the most fundamental practice in the future for anybody who wants to become a psychotherapist. You will be surprised: the man, Wilhelm, who translated this book into Western languages for the first time was himself a great psychologist; that's how he became interested in this book. But after he translated it, he went mad; he became very disturbed. His whole psychoanalytic training and this book created such a contradiction in him, created such a riddle in him, that he became more divided. The translation of this book drowned him in a kind of madness. He became so disoriented because his whole training, his whole understanding, was disturbed.

Remember it. The secret is not very difficult. That is the difficulty of it: it is so simple that you only have to be on guard so that your mind does not make it difficult, does not give it twists and turns and contortions and distortions.

> *Therefore it is taken as a guideline. The main thing is to lower*
> *the eyelids in the right way, and then to allow the light to*
> *stream in of itself; without effort, wanting the light to stream in*
> *concentratedly.*

There is no need to bring the light in concentratedly, it comes of its own accord. And when it comes of its own accord it is beautiful. If you start trying to bring it in you will be a failure, your effort is doomed to fail. And the more you fail the harder you will try, and the more you try the more your failure will be guaranteed. Don't try to bring it in. Just leave yourself in the right situation where it becomes available.

For example, if the moon is there in the night, just come to the window and stand at the window, and the moon starts showering its nectar on you. You need not do anything else. Just be in a place where the moon is already streaming; just make yourself available in the right field and things start happening – things which have immense value.

> *Looking at the tip of the nose serves only as the beginning of the*
> *inner concentration, so that the eyes are brought into the right*
> *direction for looking, and then are held to the guideline: after that,*
> *one can let it be. This is the way a mason hangs up a plumb line.*
> *As soon as he has hung it up, he guides his work by it without*
> *continually bothering himself to look at the plumb line.*

> *One looks with both eyes at the tip of the nose…*

Remember, you have to look with both eyes at the tip of the nose so that at the tip of the nose both of your eyes lose their duality, so that on the tip of the nose, the light that is streaming out from your eyes becomes one, falls on a single point. Where your two eyes meet, that is the place from where the window opens. And then all is well. Then let it be. Then you simply enjoy, then you simply celebrate, delight, rejoice. Then nothing has to be done.

One looks with both eyes at the tip of the nose, sits upright...

It is helpful to sit upright. When your spine is straight, the energy from your sex center also becomes available to the third eye – just simple devices, nothing complex about them. Just that when your two eyes meet at the tip of the nose, you are available to the third eye; make your sex energy also available to the third eye, then the effect will be double. The effect will be forceful, because your sex center has all the energy that you have. When the spine is erect, straight, the sex center is also available to the third eye. It is better to attack the third eye from both dimensions, to try to penetrate the third eye from both directions.

One...sits upright and in a comfortable position...

The master is making things very clear: upright, certainly, but don't make it uncomfortable, otherwise again you will be distracted by your discomfort. That is the meaning of a yoga posture. The Sanskrit word *asana* means a comfortable posture. Comfort is the basic quality of it. If it is not comfortable then your mind will be distracted by the discomfort. It has to be comfortable.

If you cannot sit on the floor like the Eastern people can – because they have been sitting for centuries... If a Western seeker cannot sit on the floor straight, comfortably, and has to force himself and it becomes uncomfortable and painful, then it is better to sit straight on a chair. But let the back of the chair be straight.

You must have seen pictures and statues of ancient Egyptian kings and queens: their chairs have very straight backs. Then sit like that. That also is a yoga posture. Those ancient Egyptians knew the secrets.

Anyway, two things: your spine should be straight and your posture should be comfortable. If both are not possible...sometimes it is so, both are not possible – if you make your spine straight it becomes uncomfortable, if you become comfortable the spine is no longer straight – then choose comfort. It will not be as good but the next best thing is to choose comfort. Then forget about the spine and its straightness, because if the mind is distracted, nothing is going to happen. If it is possible to have both then it is very beautiful.

One...sits upright and in a comfortable position, and holds the heart
to the center in the midst of conditions.

And don't escape from the world. Live in the world, in the conditions of it. The noise of the traffic is there, and the airplane passes by, and the trains are shuttling and all kinds of things are there – all these situations, the world – but you sit silently *in* the world. Because escaping to a Himalayan cave is always dangerous – dangerous for the single reason that the silence of the Himalayas is contagious and you will feel that you have become silent. And the coolness of the air is contagious, and you will think that you have cooled down. It will be borrowed, and whenever you come back to the marketplace all will be gone. And then you will know that all those years in the Himalayas were a wastage, a sheer wastage: you were simply befooling yourself.

It is better to be in the world and attain to centering, because then it cannot be taken away from you. So wherever you are, you have to become centered in those conditions.

It does not necessarily mean the middle of the head.

And by centering it is not meant that you have to be centered in the middle of the head.

It is only a matter of fixing one's thinking on the point which lies
exactly between the two eyes.

And remember, not concentrating but just remaining alert, just a slight alertness: look at the tip of the nose and remain slightly alert to the third eye. In fact, the moment you look at the tip of the nose you will become alert to the third eye, because that is the other pole of the nose. One pole is the tip, the outer pole – one end; the other end of the nose is joined with the third eye. The moment you become aware of the tip you will suddenly become aware of the other end too. But just remain aware, effortlessly aware.

It is only a matter of fixing one's thinking on the point which lies
exactly between the two eyes. Then all is well.

A tremendous statement:

Then all is well.

You have started arriving home. You are on the threshold of a revolution.

The light is something extremely mobile.

Light is always moving, light is movement. And light is the greatest movement in the world. In a single second, the speed of light is one hundred and eighty-six thousand miles. Nothing moves at a greater speed than light. Light is pure speed, it is another name for speed. Light is never dormant, it is always dynamic, it is always moving, always flowing.

The light is something extremely mobile. When one fixes a
thought on the midpoint between the two eyes, the light streams
in of its own accord.

You need not be worried: just open the window and wait. Light is such a moving phenomenon that if the window is open it is going to move in. In fact, it has been knocking on the window for many many lives, but the window has not opened, so it cannot force it open. It is just like in the morning the sun has risen and you are fast asleep, and the rays come on the window and they knock on the window – but their knock is silent, they don't make any noise, and they wait there. The moment you wake up and you open the window, the light streams in. And with light comes life, and with light comes delight.

When one fixes a thought on the midpoint between the two eyes,
the light streams in of its own accord.

Remember the words

...of its own accord.

You are not a doer, you are just in a kind of let-go: you are surrendered to light.

It is not necessary to direct the attention especially to the central
castle. In these few words the most important thing is contained.

The very secret of transforming your whole being, the very secret of the kingdom of God, the very secret of nirvana...

"The center in the midst of conditions" is a very subtle expression.
The center is omnipresent; everything is contained in it; it is
connected with the release of the whole process of creation.

And when you have reached to the third-eye point and you are centered there and the light is flooding in, you have reached to the point from where the whole creation has arisen – you have reached the formless, the unmanifest – call it God if you will. This is the point, this is the space, from where all has arisen, this is the very seed of the whole existence. It is omnipotent, it is omnipresent, it is eternal.

Now you will not know any death. Now you will not know any identity with any kind of body – young, old, beautiful, ugly. Now you will not know any kind of disease – not that diseases will not happen to the body, but they will not happen to you anymore because you are no more identified.

Ramana Maharshi died of cancer. The body was in great agony but he was smiling. The doctors were puzzled, they could not believe it. It was not believable. The body was in such agony and he was in such great ecstasy. How was it possible? And they asked again and again, "How is it possible?" And he would say again and again, "There is nothing strange about it. I am not the body. So whatsoever is happening in the body, it is just as you are witnessing my body, I am also witnessing my body. You are not feeling any pain so why should I? You are a witness, I am a witness. The body is just an object – an object in the middle of both of us. You are seeing from the outside that it is in agony, I am seeing from the inside that it is in agony. If you are not affected just by seeing it, why should I be?"

In fact, the doctors were affected. They were feeling very sympathetic. They were sad, they were feeling helpless; they would have liked to save this…one of the most beautiful men that has ever walked on Earth, but they could not. They were crying, but Ramana was not affected at all.

There is a transcendence point within you from where suddenly you become disconnected from all that is manifest and you become connected with the unmanifest. To be connected with the unmanifest is to be free – free from all misery, all limitation, all bondage.

Fixating contemplation is indispensable…

And this is something which you *cannot* avoid – it is indispensable. If you want to reach a state of beatitude you will have to go through this fixating – this process of contemplation, meditation, or dhyana.

*...it ensures the making fast of the enlightenment. Only one must
not stay sitting rigidly if worldly thoughts come up...*

Now the second, very important advice from the Master:

*...one must not stay sitting rigidly if worldly thoughts come up, but
one must examine where the thought is, where it began, and where it
fades out.*

This is not going to happen in the first try. You will be looking at the
tip of the nose and thoughts will come. They have been coming for so
many lives, they cannot leave you alone so easily. They have become part of
you, they have become almost built-in. You are living almost a programmed life.

Have you ever watched what you go on doing? Then tomorrow morning do
one thing: the moment you wake up in the morning, simply watch what you
do – how you get out of bed, how you move, what thoughts you have in the
mind.... Just watch. And for one week, watch: you will be surprised – you do
exactly the same thing every morning – the same gestures, the same face, and
almost the same thoughts. You have become a programmed phenomenon, and
you have been doing this your whole life – maybe for many lives, who knows?

When you become angry, watch – it is always the same process. You move
through the same spaces. When you are happy, watch; when you fall in love,
watch; and when you fall out of love, watch. It is almost the same process. And
you go on doing the same stupid things again and again, and you go on making
the same stupid statements again and again. You are not living a conscious
life. Ninety-nine percent of you is programmed – programmed by others,
programmed by society or programmed by yourself, but it is programmed.

So it is not so easy, when you sit for the first time, looking at the tip of the
nose, thoughts will say, "Now we should not go to this man. Look at the poor
fellow – how deeply he is meditating! And he is looking at the tip of the nose....
This is not the time to go to him." They will not bother. They will go on rushing.
They will not be prevented by your looking at the tip of the nose. They may
come even more forcibly, seeing that "This man is trying to get out of our grip."

This happens: when people sit silently in meditation more thoughts come
than they do ordinarily, than they usually come – unusual explosions. Millions
of thoughts rush in, because they have some investment in you – and you are
trying to get out of their power? They will give you a hard time.

So thoughts are bound to come. What are you going to do with thoughts? You cannot just go on sitting visibly there, you will have to do something. Fighting is not going to help because if you start fighting you will forget to look at the tip of the nose, the awareness of the third eye, the circulation of the light; you will forget all and you will be lost in the jungle of thoughts. If you start chasing thoughts you are lost, if you follow them you are lost, if you fight them you are lost. Then what is to be done?

And this is the secret. Buddha has also used the same secret. In fact, the secrets are almost the same because man is the same – the lock is the same, the key has to be the same. This is the secret: Buddha calls it *sammasati,* right remembrance. Just remember: this thought has come, see where it is – with no antagonism, with no justification, with no condemnation. Just be objective as a scientist is objective. See where it is, from where it is coming from, where it is going? See the coming of it, see the staying of it, see the going of it. And thoughts are very mobile; they don't stay long. You have simply to watch the arising of the thought, the staying of the thought, and the going of the thought. Don't try to fight, don't try to follow – just be a silent observer – and you will be surprised: the more observation becomes settled, less and less thoughts come. When observation is perfect, thoughts disappear, there is only a gap left, an interval left.

But remember one more point: the mind can again play a trick.

Nothing is gained by pushing reflection further.

But don't try to push the reflection further.

That's what Freudian psychoanalysis does, the free association of thoughts: one thought comes, and then you wait for another thought, and then another, and the whole chain…. That's what all kinds of psychoanalysis do: you start moving backwards into the past but one thought is connected with another, and so on and so forth, *ad infinitum.* There is no end to it. If you go into it you will be moving into an eternal journey – that will be a sheer wastage. Mind can do that, so beware of it.

> *Nothing is gained by pushing reflection further. One must be content to see where the thought arose, and not seek beyond the point of origin; for to find the heart-consciousness, to get behind consciousness with consciousness itself – that cannot be done.*

You cannot go with consciousness beyond consciousness, so don't try the futile, the unnecessary; otherwise one thing will lead you to another and so on and so forth, and you will completely forget what you were trying to do there. The tip of the nose will disappear, the third eye will be forgotten, the circulation of the light will be miles away from you.

So only this much – the single thought. Don't go into the chain. The single thought arises: watch where it is, where it is coming from and when it disappears, watch – it has disappeared. Take note.

Buddhists say when a thought arises say, "Thought, thought," so that you become alert. Just as when a thief comes into the house you say, "Thief! Thief!" and everybody becomes alert, simply say, "Thought, thought," and you will become alert, watchful. A thief has entered: now watch what the thief is doing.

The moment you become aware, the thought will stop; it will look at you and be a little surprised because you have never done this before. It will feel a little unwelcome. "And what has happened to this man? He has always been such a good host, and now he says, 'Thief! Thief! Thought, thought.' What has happened to this man?" The thought will be puzzled, will not be able to comprehend what is happening. "Is this man going mad, saying 'Thought, thought' and looking at the tip of the nose?"

The very awareness will stop the movement of the thought for a time. It will be stuck there. And go on watching. Don't condemn, don't throw it out, don't fight, because either condemnation or justification, both will make you identified with the thought. Simply be there, alert, looking at the thought. Then it starts disappearing. Just as it came, it disappears. It came out of imagination, it disappears into imagination. Once it disappears, you come back to contemplation. You need not go to the very origin of it because there is none; then you will have to go to the very origin of existence.

That's why psychoanalysis has no end, it is never finished. There is not a single person in the world who is totally psychoanalyzed. Nobody can be totally psychoanalyzed. One year, two years, three years, four, five, six, seven – you can find people who have been going into psychoanalysis for seven years. Then what do you think – do they stop because the psychoanalysis is complete? No. They are bored with the psychoanalyst, the psychoanalyst is bored with them. And everything has to be finished somewhere. One has to put a full point. How long can one go on?

But no psychoanalysis is ever complete – it cannot be. It is an infinite onion: you can go on peeling it and peeling it and peeling it, and you will never come to the end of it. But it helps. It makes you more adjusted to yourself and to society. It does not transform you, it makes you normally abnormal, that's all. It helps you to be adjusted to the neurotic society in which you are. It makes you not a transformed, luminous being, but an ordinary person who is accepting of all that life brings, good and bad, and who starts dragging himself as everybody else is dragging. It teaches you a kind of sad acceptance of life. It is not true acceptance either, because true acceptance always brings celebration.

Sigmund Freud has said that man cannot be happy, at most he can be comfortable. Life can be made more comfortable, that's all, but happiness is impossible.

It is not impossible. It is impossible through psychoanalysis. Because there have been happy people, we have seen them. A Buddha, a Lao Tzu, a Krishna – we have seen these dancing people. Freud is not happy – that is true – and he cannot be happy. Unless he drops psychoanalysis and moves into some meditative process, he will not be happy. It will take a few more lives for him to learn meditation.

In fact, he was very afraid of meditation. And not just Sigmund Freud, but even a man like Carl Gustav Jung was afraid. Carl Gustav Jung has written a commentary on this book, *The Secret of the Golden Flower;* but it is only intellectual. It has no existential value. He had no experience of meditation himself – how can it have any existential value? And he was a very egoistic person, and the egoistic person finds it very difficult to enter into meditation because on the very door, you have to drop your ego.

Jung came to India while Ramana Maharshi was alive, and many people suggested to him, "Since you have come to India and you are so interested in the inner mysteries of life, why don't you go to Ramana? You write commentaries on *The Secret of the Golden Flower* and here is a golden flower in full bloom – why don't you go to Ramana?" But he never went. He traveled in India, met many people, but never went to see Ramana. Why? What was the fear? He was afraid to encounter this man, afraid to face this mirror.

Have you ever looked at Jung's picture? Even in the picture the ego is so apparent. Freud doesn't seem as egoistic as Jung. Maybe it was his ego that took him away from his master, Sigmund Freud – that made him betray Freud. Just look at his picture, his eyes: very cunning, calculating, as if ready to jump on anybody; tremendously egoistic, but very clever, intelligent, intellectually skillful.

Remember, psychoanalysis or analytical psychology or other brands of the same game cannot lead you to happiness. They can lead you only to a lukewarm life of adjustment. They cannot help you to become aflame with celebration; this is beyond their capacity. And the reason? The reason is that they go on analyzing the thought. Analysis is not needed.

Hence *The Secret...* says:

> *Together we want to bring the states of the heart to rest, that is true contemplation.*

We want to bring the whole being into a kind of absolute rest. Analysis is not going to help, because analysis will create a turmoil, a restlessness.

> *What contradicts it is false contemplation.*

Analysis is a false contemplation.

> *That leads to no goal. When the flight of the thoughts keeps extending further, one should stop and begin contemplating.*

So these two things have to be remembered, these are two wings. One, when there is an interval, no thought is coming: contemplate. When a thought comes then just look at these three things: where the thought is, where it has come from, where it is going. For a moment stop looking into the gap, look at the thought, watch the thought, say goodbye to it; when it leaves, again immediately move back to contemplation.

Again, just as an example: if you are looking at the gaps between the cars passing on the roads, when the car comes what will you do? You will have to watch the car too, but you don't become concerned about the car. You don't become concerned about the make, the vintage, the year, the color, the driver, the passenger. You don't become concerned about all that analysis – you simply take note of the car: the car has come, the car is there in front of you, the car has gone, and again you become interested in the gap. Your whole interest is in the gap. But the car comes, so for a moment you have to pay attention to it. Then it is gone, you again start falling into rest, into contemplation, into the interval.

> *When the flight of the thoughts keeps extending further, one should stop and begin contemplating. Let one contemplate and then start fixating again.*

So whenever the thought comes, fixate. Whenever the thought goes, contemplate.

> *That is the double method of making fast the enlightenment. It*
> *means the circulation of the light. The circulation is fixation. The*
> *light is contemplation.*

Whenever you contemplate you will see light flooding in, and whenever you fixate you will create the circulation, you will make the circulation possible. Both are needed.

> *The light is contemplation. Fixation without contemplation is*
> *circulation without light.*

That's what has happened. That calamity has happened to *hatha* yoga: they fixate, they concentrate, but they have forgotten light. They have completely forgotten about the guest, they only go on preparing the house. They have become so engrossed in preparing the house that they have forgotten the purpose for which they are preparing the house, for whom. The hatha yogi continuously prepares his body, purifies his body, does yoga postures, breathing exercises, and goes on doing, ad nauseam. He has completely forgotten what he is doing it for. And the light is standing there but he won't allow it, because the light can come in only when he is completely in a let-go.

> *Fixation without contemplation is circulation without light.*

This is the calamity that happens to the so-called yogis. The other kind of calamity happens to psychoanalysts, philosophers.

> *Contemplation without fixation is light without circulation!*

They think about the light, but they have not made the preparation for it to flood in; they only *think* of light. They think of the guest: they imagine a thousand and one things about the guest, but their house is not ready. Both miss.
The Master says:

> *Take note of that!*

Otherwise you can also miss. Prepare and then wait. Get ready. Looking at the tip of the nose, alert to the third eye, an erect spine, a comfortable posture

– that's all that you have to do – more than that is not needed. There is no need to go on for years doing yoga postures, year in, year out. That is stupid. And that's why you will find the so-called yogis looking so stupid, unintelligent. Maybe their bodies are strong and they will live long, but what is the point of it?

Without light, life is going to remain unintelligent and dark. Whether you live long or short makes no difference. The real point is to live in light even for a single moment, and then it is enough – that single moment is eternity.

And there are philosophers who go on thinking about the light – what it is, how to define it, and which definition is the best and they constantly create many theories, dogmas, great systems of thought – but they are not ready for it…and the light is just waiting at the door.

Take note of that!

Don't fall into either of these two fallacies. If you can remain alert, it is a very simple process and immensely transforming. In a single moment, a man who understands rightly can enter into a separate kind of reality.

God is not far away, God is within you.

Enough for today.

CHAPTER 12
To Create a Balance

The first question:

Osho,
Is it fair to put politicians with the dogs?

I am sorry, I apologize – because dogs are so innocent. It is not fair at all.

The second question:

Osho,
What is neurosis and what is the cure for it?

Neurosis has never been so epidemic in the past as it is now. It is almost becoming a normal state of human mind. It has to be understood.

The past was spiritually more healthy, and the reason was that mind was not fed so many things simultaneously – the mind was not overloaded. The modern mind is overloaded, and that which remains unassimilated creates neurosis. It is as if you go on eating and stuffing your body: that which is not digested by the body will prove to be poisonous. And what you eat is less important than what you hear and see. From your eyes, from your ears, from all your senses, you go on receiving a thousand and one things each moment, and there is no extra assimilation time, as if one were constantly sitting at the dining table, eating, eating – twenty-four hours a day. This is the situation of the modern mind: it is overloaded, so many things are burdening it; it is not any surprise that it breaks down. There is a limit to every mechanism. And mind is one of the most subtle and delicate of mechanisms.

A really healthy person is one who takes fifty percent of his time to assimilate his experiences. Fifty percent action, fifty percent inaction – that is the right balance. Fifty percent thinking, fifty percent meditation – that is the cure. Meditation is nothing but a time when you can relax utterly into yourself, when you close all your doors, all your senses, to the outside stimulus. You disappear from the world. You forget the world, as if it exists no more – no newspapers, no radio, no television, no people. You are alone in your innermost being, relaxed, at home.

In these moments, all that has become accumulated is assimilated: that which is of worth is assimilated, that which is worthless is thrown out. Meditation functions like a double-edged sword: on the one hand it assimilates all that is nourishing, and it rejects and throws out all that is junk. But meditation has disappeared from the world.

In the old days, people were naturally meditative. Life was uncomplicated and people had enough time just to sit and do nothing, or look at the stars or watch the trees or listen to the birds. People had intervals of deep passivity. In those moments you become more and more healthy and whole.

Neurosis means you are carrying such a load in the mind that you are dying under it. You cannot move – there is no question of your consciousness flying. You cannot even creep – the burden is too much…and the burden goes on increasing every moment. One cracks up. It is very natural.

A few things to be understood. Neurosis is the mouse endlessly trying the dead end, not learning. Yes, not learning is neurosis – that is the first definition. You go on trying the dead end. You have been angry – how many times have you been angry? And how many times have you repented being angry? Still, let there be a stimulus and your reaction will again be the same – you have not learned a thing. You have been greedy and greed has created more and more misery. You know it – greed has never given anybody blissfulness – but you are still greedy, you still go on being greedy. You don't learn. Nonlearning creates neurosis, is neurosis.

Learning means assimilation. You try one thing and then you find that it doesn't work: you drop it, you move in another direction, you try another alternative. This is wise, this is intelligent. Just knocking your head against a wall where you know perfectly well there is no door is neurosis.

People are getting more and more neurotic because they go on trying the dead end, they go on trying that which doesn't work. The man who is capable of learning never becomes neurotic – cannot become. He immediately sees the point that this is a wall. He drops the whole idea. He starts moving into other dimensions – there are other alternatives available. He has learned something.

It is said of Edison that he was trying one experiment in which he failed seven hundred times. His colleagues became desperate. Three years were wasted and he went on trying new alternatives again and again. And every morning he came with great enthusiasm – the same enthusiasm that he had come with on the first day – and three years were wasted.

One day his colleagues gathered together and they said to him, "We don't see the point. We have failed seven hundred times. It is time to drop the experimentation."

Edison is reported to have said, "What are you saying – failed? We have learned that seven hundred alternatives were wrong alternatives. It has been a great experience! Today we are not going to try the same experiment, I have found another one. We are coming closer to the truth. How many false alternatives can there be? – there must be a limit. If there are one thousand false alternatives, then seven hundred have already been dropped and only three hundred are left, and then we will be reaching the right point."

This is learning: trying one experiment, seeing that it doesn't work; trying an alternative, seeing that it doesn't work, the wise man drops it. The fool clings to it. The fool calls it consistency. The fool says, "I did it yesterday and I am going to do it today too. And I will do it tomorrow too." He is stubborn, pig-headed. He says, "How can I leave it? I have invested so much in it, I cannot change it." Then he goes on insisting on it and his whole life is wasted. And as death comes closer, he is desperate, he is hopeless. He knows perfectly well deep down in his guts that he is going to fail. He has failed so many times and he is still trying the same thing without learning anything at all. *This* creates neurosis.

The man who is capable of learning will never become neurotic. A disciple will never become neurotic. A disciple means one who is capable of learning. Never become knowledgeable; always be in the process of learning. Knowledgeability drives people neurotic. It is not just accidental that professors, philosophers, psychiatrists, scholars, easily go mad: they have learned and they have reached the conclusion that there is no more to learn. The moment you decide that there is no more to learn, you have stopped growing. To stop growing is neurosis – that is the second definition.

The world was very different in the past, obviously. About six weeks' worth of sensory stimuli six hundred years ago is what we now get in a day. Six weeks' worth of stimulation, information, we are getting in a single day – about forty times the pressure to learn and adapt. Modern man has to be capable of learning more than man has ever been before, because there is more to learn now. Modern man has to become capable of adapting to new situations every day because the world is changing so fast. It is a great challenge.

A great challenge, if accepted, will help tremendously in the expansion of consciousness. Either modern man is going to be utterly neurotic or modern man is going to be transformed by the very pressure. It depends on how you take it. One thing is certain: there is no way of going back. The sensory stimuli will go on increasing more and more. You will be getting more and more information and life will be changing, with faster and faster rhythms, and you will have to be capable to learn, to adapt, to new things.

In the past man lived in an almost static world. Everything was static: you would leave the world exactly as your father had left it to you. You would not have changed anything at all. Nothing was changed. There was no question of learning too much, a little bit of learning was enough. And then you had spaces in your mind, empty spaces, which helped people to remain sane. Now there is no more empty space...unless you create it deliberately.

Meditation is needed more today than ever before. Meditation is needed so much that it is almost a question of life and death. In the past it was a luxury; few people – a Buddha, a Mahavira, a Krishna – were interested in it. Other people were naturally silent, naturally happy, sane. There was no need for them to think of meditation; in an unconscious way they were meditating. Life was moving so silently, moving so slowly, that even the most stupid people were capable of adapting to it. Now the change is so tremendously fast, with such speed that even the most intelligent people feel incapable of adapting to it. Every day life is different, and you have to learn again – you have to learn and learn again and again. You can never stop learning now; it has to be a life-long process. To the very point of death you will have to remain a learner, only then can you remain sane, can you avoid neurosis. And the pressure is great – forty times greater. How to relax this pressure? You will have to go deliberately into meditative moments.

If a person is not meditating at least one hour a day, then neurosis will not be accidental; he will create it himself. For one hour he should disappear from the world into his own being. For one hour he should be so alone that nothing penetrates him – no memory, no thought, no imagination; for one hour no content in his consciousness, and that will rejuvenate him and that will refresh him. That will release new sources of energy in him and he will be back in the world, younger, fresher, more able to learn, with more wonder in his eyes, with more awe in his heart – again a child.

This pressure to learn and the old habit of not learning is driving people crazy. The modern mind is really super-loaded and no time is given to digest it and assimilate it into one's own being. That is where meditation comes in and becomes more significant than ever: without a time given for the mind to rest in meditation, we repress all of the messages that are pouring in continuously. We refuse to learn. We say we do not have time. Then the messages begin to accumulate.

If you don't have time enough to listen to the messages that your mind is receiving continuously, they start accumulating just like files accumulating on your table – piles of letters accumulating on your table because you have not time enough to read and answer them. Exactly like that your mind becomes cluttered: so many files waiting to be looked into, so many letters to be read, to be answered, so many challenges to be taken, to be faced.

I have heard…

Mulla Nasruddin was saying one day, "If something wrong happens today, I will not have time for at least three months to look into it. So many wrong things have already happened which are waiting there. If something wrong happens today," he said, "I will not have time to look into it for three months at least."

A queue – you can see that queue inside yourself – and the queue goes on growing. And the bigger the queue, the less and less space you have; the bigger the queue, the more and more noise inside, because everything that you have accumulated demands your attention.

This usually starts at about the age of five, when real learning virtually stops, and lasts until death. In the old days it was okay. Five or seven years were enough to learn all that you would need in your life – that would do: seven years' learning would do for seventy years of life. But now that is not possible. You cannot stop learning because new things are always happening and you cannot face those new things with old ideas. You cannot depend on your parents and their knowledge, you cannot even depend on your teachers in the school and the university, because what they are talking about is already out of date. Much more has happened; much water has gone down the Ganges.

This was my experience: when I was a student I was surprised at my professors' knowledge because it was thirty years old. It was when they were young that they had gathered it from their teachers. Since then they had not looked at what has happened. That knowledge was absolutely useless.

I was constantly in conflict with my professors. I was thrown out of many colleges, expelled, because the professors said that they could not cope with me. And I was not creating any trouble. I was simply making them aware that what they were saying was out of date. But that hurts the ego. They had learned it in their own university days and they were thinking that the world had stopped then and there.

Now students cannot depend on teachers and children cannot depend on their parents, hence a great rebellion is on the way all over the world. It has nothing to do with anything else. Students cannot respect their teachers anymore. Unless those teachers continuously learn, they cannot be respected. For what? – there is no reason. And children cannot respect their parents because the approach of their parents looks very primitive. Small children are becoming aware that what their parents say is out of date. Parents will have to continuously learn if they want to help their children to grow, and teachers will have to continuously learn. Now no one can stop learning. And this speed is going to grow continuously.

Firstly: learning has not to be stopped, otherwise you will go neurotic, because to stop learning means you are accumulating information which you have not assimilated, digested, which has not become your blood and your bones and your marrow. It will hang around you with a great insistence, to be taken in.

Secondly: you will need time to relax – this pressure is too much. You will need some time to disappear from this pressure. Sleep cannot help you anymore because sleep itself is becoming overburdened. Your day is so overloaded that when you go to sleep only the body falls limp on the bed, but the mind continues to sort things out. That's what you call dreaming: it is nothing but a desperate effort of the mind to sort things out…because you won't give any time to it.

You have to relax consciously into meditation. A few minutes of deep meditation will keep you non-neurotic. In meditation the mind unclutters: experiences are digested and the overload disappears, leaving the mind fresh and young and clear and clean.

In the past, the input volume was one-tenth of one's time and the meditative time was nine-tenths. Now just the reverse is the case: nine-tenths input volume time and one-tenth meditative time. Very rarely do you relax, very rarely do you just sit silently, doing nothing. Even that one-tenth time of unconscious meditation is disappearing. Once that happens, man will be utterly mad. And that is happening.

What do I mean by unconscious meditative time? You simply go into the garden, you play around with your children – that is unconscious meditative time. Or you swim in the swimming pool – that is unconscious meditative time. Or you mow your lawn, or you listen to the birds – that is unconscious meditative time. That too is disappearing because whenever people have time, they are sitting before their TVs, glued to their seats.

Now, tremendously dangerous information is being put into your mind by the TV; you will not be able to digest it. Or you are reading newspapers – all kinds of nonsense is being fed to you. Whenever you have time you put the radio or the TV on. Or someday you are feeling very good and you want to relax and you go to the movies. What kind of relaxation is this? The movie will not allow you relaxation because continuously information is thrown into you.

Relaxation means no information is thrown into you. Listening to a cuckoo will do, because no information is fed to you. Listening to music will do, because no information is thrown into you. Music has no language; it is pure sound. It does not give any message; it simply delights you. Dancing will be good, music will be good, working in the garden will be good, playing with children will be good, or just sitting doing nothing will be good. This is the cure. And if you do it consciously, the impact will be greater. Create a balance.

Neurosis is an unbalanced state of mind: too much activity and no inactivity at all, too much masculine and no feminine at all, too much yang and too little of yin. And you have to be fifty-fifty, you have to keep a deep balance. A symmetry is needed inside you. You have to be an *ardhanarishwar* – half man, half woman – then you will never turn neurotic.

And that is the whole process of the book, *The Secret of the Golden Flower*: it will make you disappear as man, as woman; it will make you one whole, one unity; it will give you individuation.

The individual is neither male nor female, it is simple unity. Strive to achieve it between time spent doing, versus time spent not doing. This is wholeness, this is what Buddha called his middle way, *majjhim nikai*. Just be exactly in the middle. And remember, you can become unbalanced to the other extreme too: you can become too inactive. That will be dangerous also. That has its own pitfalls and dangers. If you become too inactive, your life loses dance, your life loses joy, you start becoming dead.

So I am not saying become inactive, I am saying let there be a balance between action and inaction. Let them balance each other and you be just in the middle. Let them be two wings of your being. No wing should be bigger than the other.

In the West, action has become too big, inaction has disappeared. In the East, inaction became too big and action disappeared. The West knows affluence, richness on the outside and poverty inside; the East knows richness, affluence inside and poverty on the outside. Both are in misery because both have chosen extremes.

My approach is neither Eastern nor Western, my approach is neither male nor female, my approach is neither of action nor inaction. My approach is that of utter balance, symmetry in you. Hence I say to my sannyasins: Don't leave the world; be in the world and yet be not of it. This is what Taoists call *wu wei wu*, action through inaction. The meeting of yin and yang, anima and animus – it brings enlightenment. Imbalance is neurosis, balance is enlightenment.

The third question:

Osho,
Are all women really soft, feminine and loving?

I have not said that – that all women are really soft, feminine and loving. Neither are all men aggressive, violent, ambitious, hard, because deep down in you the consciousness is neither. The anima and the animus, the male and the female exist in your body chemistry. You can be a man physically, but you may have chosen, deep inside, the feminine part. A woman may be a woman physically but she may have chosen the masculine part. Both parts are available. Then the body remains feminine but the woman will become masculine. That is what is happening to women connected with the Women's Liberation movement: they are dropping their feminineness, they are becoming as aggressive as man. They are trying to compete with all kinds of foolishnesses that man has: they want to have all those foolishnesses themselves, too. They cannot be left behind.

The idea of being equal is creating a foolish idea of being similar. To be equal does not mean to be similar. Equality is a totally different dimension. Similarity is different.

Yes, a woman can choose her masculine part too much – can become identified with it – then her softness will disappear. A man can choose his feminineness, then his hardness will disappear. The body will remain sexually male or female, but the quality surrounding the body, the vibe, will have to be that which you have chosen inside. A man can choose to be a woman inside, a woman can choose to be a man inside. And it is not a choice that you make once and forever, you can change it every moment. There are moments when a woman is very soft and there are moments when she can be very hard, very cruel. There are moments when a man is very hard, aggressive, but there are moments when he can be very soft. Even a Genghis Khan is very soft to his children. To his wife he is very soft.

I have heard…

The plain and strongly built daughter of a Field Marshal was engaged to be married to a young officer on her father's staff. "Couldn't you do something for Frank now that he has asked me to marry him?" she asked her father one day.

"There's not much I can do really," replied the Field Marshal, "except get him a medal for gallantry."

Or, listen to this…

He was undersized, meek, diffident and subdued, and he had applied for a job as a nightwatchman.

"Yes," said the manager, dubiously, "but the fact is we want someone who is restless and uneasy, especially at night – someone who thinks the worst of everybody, someone who sleeps with one eye open. The kind of person in short, who when roused, is the devil himself."

"Alright," said the meek lad as he walked away, "I'll send my wife."

It depends on what you choose inside you. It is a choice. The body is not your choice, but the vibe that will surround your body is a choice. And if you consciously choose, you will have great freedom in your being, because you will know who you are and what you are doing with your body.

The body has tremendous potential – much can happen through it – but people take it for granted. It is as if a beautiful guitar has been given to you as a present and you just keep it, not knowing the potential of it. You can play on the guitar, you can learn to play on the guitar and great music will be born. And then it depends on you what kind of music it will be. You can create a music which is sad and you can create a music which is celebrating, you can create music which is violent and you can create a music which is soothing, loving, silent – there are many different kinds of music.

Classical music has a different quality: it soothes, it brings you to a silence, rest. Modern pop music makes you restless, sexual; it drives you into a kind of frenzy.

The instruments are the same, so is the body. A really wise person chooses to play the kind of music he wants to play on the body. You can make your body like a Buddha or you can become a Mohammad Ali. It depends on you. Look at Buddha's body: how soft – although he is a man, how feminine – although he is a man. He has chosen grace.

It depends on you. It is your choice. You are not confined by your chemistry. You can be confined only if you remain unconscious in your chemistry, otherwise your chemistry has infinite potential: it can be put to a thousand and one uses. And to learn how to use one's body, how to behave with one's body, how to relate with one's body, is a great art. Millions of people just take their body for granted; they never search for its possibilities. Their body remains a seed, it never becomes a golden flower.

The fourth question:

> Osho,
> Your discourse on politics, and the poison it is, was extraordinary!
> I have lived in many communities, all sincere and well-meaning,
> yet everywhere I was appalled at the unconscious political
> ambition and intrigues which are underlying and dormant but
> come up in spite of the good intentions.
>
> How are you handling it here? Are you allowing it free play so that
> people can work it out of their systems or are you nipping it in the
> bud and weeding out those that show the slightest tendencies?
>
> My humble experience is that some people can never, never get
> anything going without politics – without getting themselves
> higher and higher in the power game. They are all over – perhaps
> even here – spreading their poison.

I don't believe in repressing anything, not even the poisonous politics, because repressed it remains in your system – sooner or later it will take you over. And the longer it has been repressed, the more dangerous it becomes, because the deeper it goes into your unconscious, the deeper it goes into your very source of being. And if you are poisoned at your very source, at the very center, then it becomes really difficult to uproot it.

My approach about everything is to bring it to the surface. So I never nip anything in the bud, I help it to become a flower. And after the flowering, the flower starts withering of its own accord. That's the natural way.

So in *my* commune, nothing is prevented. Ambitions are allowed, accepted, as a part of human beings – their ignorance, their unawareness. But I make my people aware that these are games, so play them but play consciously, become more and more alert, and never let them become serious. If the games don't become serious, there is no need to be afraid of them. The problem is, when a game becomes so serious then you forget completely that it is a game.

That's where the politician is lost: he thinks he is doing something very serious. He is doing something very silly, but he thinks he is doing something very serious. All that is needed is to make him aware that this is a game; if you want to play it, play, but don't become so serious about it. Keep a little bit of humor. A sense of humor is one of the greatest keys to transform human personalities.

Yes, you are right – here also! – because these people come from the world and they bring all kinds of infections from the world. They are not coming here fresh, they have been already conditioned. Ambition has already been put into them. Their parents, society, church, school, college, university – everywhere they have been poisoned, they bring all that poison here. You cannot nip it in the bud; otherwise they will become split and hypocritical. Then on the surface they will show humility, humbleness, and deep down they will think, "There is nobody more humble than me" – and politics has come in. Deep down they will think, "I am the greatest egoless person in the world" – but the greatest. Now a new kind of ambition has entered. It is the same ambition, now the direction is new. And it is more subtle and of course, more dangerous too. And because it is "pious" now, it is in the name of religion. So even the poison no longer looks like poison, it is labeled nectar. It is religious poison, pious poison.

It is more difficult to get rid of the pious poison, so I don't repress anything and I don't help any kind of repression. I help people to bring whatsoever they have in them to the surface. I help them to be aware of it, to watch it, to see the foolishness of it, to see the stupidity of it – *not* because I say it is stupid, because if *I* say something and you only believe, you will repress. I help you – my function here is to help you become aware on your own. The day you see the stupidity of it, it will drop of its own accord.

So I have created all kinds of games here. Yes, there is a hierarchy too, so people who want to play, they can play the game of hierarchy. But sooner or later – because the whole effort is to make them conscious – they become aware that this is a game. And the moment *they* see it is a game, they are out of it. Seeing something as a game makes you laugh at it – a hearty laugh at your own self. And when a man can laugh at his own stupidities he is becoming wise. Laughter has to come out of awareness.

Ambitious people also laugh. Just the other day I was reading that when Jimmy Carter came to power he was laughing so beautifully that you could have counted his teeth. And some people have counted – eleven teeth were showing. Now only seven are showing. Now the smile is disappearing because his prestige is falling every day: people's expectations are not fulfilled, what he has promised he cannot deliver. Only seven! Soon you will see five, three, two. By the time he goes, the smile will have disappeared completely. You will not see a single tooth. This is not real laughter. Even this laughter is political, managed, practiced, cultivated.

There is a different kind of laughter that comes to you when you see all kinds of foolishnesses that you have been in – and how seriously – when you see the whole ridiculousness of your life pattern, your whole gestalt and its stupidity. But not because I say or Buddha says or Master Lu-tsu says…. It is not a question of belief, it is not a question of somebody else's knowledge and you borrow it – borrowed knowledge never helps. It has to arise in you.

My effort here is to make you aware of all that is hidden in you. All that you have been doing unconsciously has to be done consciously, that's all. And sometimes miracles happen.

Once a professor came to me. His problem…and it was really a problem, because to be a professor and have such a problem is really difficult. His problem was that he walked like a woman. So whenever he passed by, students would come and laugh and giggle and he felt really bad – what to do about it? And he had been to the doctors and the psychoanalysts and they could not help. They said, "What can we do?" From his very childhood he had been walking that way. And he tried not to walk like that, and the more he tried, the more he failed.

There is a certain law – hypnotists call it the law of reverse effect: you try hard to do something and just the opposite happens.

So he was trying hard. His whole effort, his whole mind was concerned with not walking like a woman, but he was walking like a woman more and more. I told him, "Just do one thing – because it is a miracle that you can walk like a woman, it is really a miracle."

He said, "What are you saying?"

I said, "It is a miracle! A woman can walk that way because of a different musculature. Because of the womb she walks in a certain way; no man can walk like that. You are unique!"

He said, "What are you saying? And everybody is laughing at me."

I said, "You are really unique. You have done something miraculous. It is magical. You forget all about it. My suggestion is that you start walking consciously like a woman, make it a point to walk like a woman."

He said, "What are you suggesting? I have tried my whole life not to walk like a woman, then I walk like a woman too. And if I start walking like a woman, what will happen?"

I said, "You just try in front of me." And at least twenty, thirty people were sitting there.

He said, "Here?"

I said "Here. You try."

He tried and he failed! He could not walk...he could not walk like a woman. And he looked very surprised. He said, "What happened?"

I said, "You have to understand the law of reverse effect. Now go to the university, anywhere, and consciously try to walk like a woman – because it is very difficult to walk like a woman unless you are a woman."

And since then he has not walked like a woman. He became conscious of it. It was an unconscious mechanism. Unconsciousness was the root cause of it. Just become conscious, and it disappears.

Man's problems are rooted in the unconscious. And what do you go on doing? You go on repressing those problems into the unconscious. Where else will you repress them? There is nowhere else to repress them. Whenever you repress something, you repress it into the unconscious; that's how the unconscious is created.

I don't have an unconscious because I never repress anything. The unconscious is created by repressions. The child does not have an unconscious – by and by he will have. And the old man has more of the unconscious than the conscious because he has been repressing his whole life. The unconscious functions like a basement: whatsoever is useless, you throw into the basement, it accumulates there – it becomes a junkyard! That is what your unconscious is. And from the unconscious, things arise and take possession of you.

All the ghosts that take possession of you come from the unconscious not from the graveyards. Your unconscious is the graveyard where those ghosts are born. And whenever they can find an opportunity, an occasion to sneak up and possess you, they will possess you – and they possess with revenge, with a vengeance. Now, to repress it is to help the unconscious more. That is the law of reverse effect. Your unconscious will become more and more powerful. You are feeding it and nourishing it.

My whole approach is that consciousness is liberation, awareness is the solution. Just become more conscious of whatsoever you are doing.

Once it happened...

A thief came to a great master, Nagarjuna. He had come for a certain reason. Nagarjuna used to live naked – one of the great Indian mystics and one of the greatest alchemists. He would have been the right person to comment on *The Secret of the Golden Flower*. C.G. Jung was not the right person to comment on it.

He came into a great capital. The queen was a follower of Nagarjuna. She came with a golden begging bowl and told Nagarjuna, "Give your wooden begging bowl to me. I will keep it as a treasure. And I have brought this golden begging bowl for you."

She was afraid that maybe Nagarjuna would say, "I don't touch gold, I am an ascetic."

But Nagarjuna was an enlightened person. He said, "Okay." So he took the golden begging bowl studded with valuable diamonds.

A thief saw Nagarjuna moving with the golden begging bowl, naked, and all those diamonds shining in the sun. He said, "Look! How long can this man have this? Somebody is going to take it from him. Why not me? This naked man cannot keep it long. From where did he get it?"

So the thief followed Nagarjuna. Nagarjuna was staying outside the capital in the ruins of an old temple where there were no doors, not even windows – nothing – just walls all falling down, just a small shelter. A little bit of roof was still safe. The thief said, "How will he protect his valuable thing? In the night at least he will go to sleep."

So he waited outside by the side of the wall near a window. Nagarjuna wanted to have a little sleep in the afternoon – that was his habit. Seeing the thief following him, he knew that he was not following Nagarjuna, he was following the golden bowl – so why force him to wait there? Anyway he was going to take it. "When I fall asleep," thought Nagarjuna, "he will take it, so why unnecessarily force him to wait?" He threw the begging bowl out of the window.

The thief could not believe what was happening. But this man looked really charismatic – naked, so beautiful, so divine-looking, with such a precious thing with him, and he has thrown it! Now the thief could not leave: he was so attracted by the person, so enchanted, almost hypnotized. He looked in through the window and said, "Sir, can I come in and have a little chit-chat with you?"

Nagarjuna said, "That's why I have thrown the bowl outside – so that you could come in! You would have come in when I had gone to sleep but that would have been meaningless. Come in!"

The thief came in and he said, "Looking at you, seeing that you can throw such a valuable thing away so easily – and I know why you have thrown it, you have thrown it away for me – a great desire has arisen in me: Will there be a time, ever, when I will also be so detached, so aloof, so free of possessions as you are?"

Nagarjuna said, "The time has come. Accidentally you are already caught. I will give you the secret of how to become transcendental to the world, how to go beyond, how not to possess."

The man said, "But let me first tell you that I am a thief. And I have gone to many saints before, but they all say – because I am a well-known thief – they all say, 'First you stop stealing, only then can you meditate.' So let me tell you first. You may not know."

Nagarjuna said, "Then it simply shows that you have never been to a saint up to now. They must have been ex-thieves, otherwise who cares who you are? And why make a condition that first you have to stop stealing? I will give you the meditation – it is very simple. You go on stealing, just do one thing: do it consciously, do it with full awareness. When you are going to steal, move fully aware, alert to what you are doing, and after fifteen days you report to me."

But by the seventh day the thief was back and he said, "You deceived me. For seven days continuously I have not been able to steal. And it was not that I was prevented; I reach the places where great treasures are available, but I cannot do it. If I become aware, I start laughing at my foolishness. What am I doing – stealing things which will be taken away from me? Sooner or later I will have to die. The whole thing looks so childish. If I become aware, I cannot steal; if I steal, I lose my awareness. Both cannot go together."

Nagarjuna said, "Then you decide. Whichever you choose, you can choose. You can drop awareness and steal, or if you want to have awareness, then drop stealing."

And the man said, "I have tasted awareness. It is impossible to drop it. I will drop stealing because awareness is far more valuable, far more significant. I have only tasted a little bit of it, but it gives such joy. And I have been stealing my whole life and I have accumulated many valuable things in my house, but they have never given me any joy. They only give me more and more fear."

Awareness is the only secret key: it transforms. It doesn't matter what your illness is, awareness is the only medicine: it cures all illnesses. If you are politically minded – and everybody is… In some way or other everybody is trying to be higher than the other, everybody is trying to be more powerful than the other. Even in relationships politics continue. The husband tries to be more powerful than the wife, the wife tries to be more powerful than the husband, hence the constant conflict, even between parents and children. Everywhere there is conflict. It is all politics, different faces of politics.

So when you come to me I cannot expect you to come without politics – that is impossible. If you are without politics, you will not need to come; wherever you are, God will come to you. When you come here I accept all your human weaknesses. I have no condemnation. I don't tell you to repress; I don't want to make you feel guilty about anything. If you want to play the game of politics you are allowed to play it, with only one condition: become more and more alert while playing it, have a sense of humor, and then all is well. Sooner or later it will wither away of its own accord.

And so is the case with sensuality, sexuality, so is the case with possessiveness – so is the case with everything that man suffers from.

The fifth question:

> Osho,
> This morning in the lecture, I went so deep that I was sure the body
> was going to die right then and there. I became very afraid and
> struggled back to the surface. Now I am afraid it will happen again.
> What to do?

Saguna, you are a fool. You should have allowed it to happen. You missed a great opportunity. If again at any time you start feeling that you are dying in my presence, die immediately! That means your ego was on the verge of disappearing and something tremendously valuable was about to happen. You missed it.

But it happens the first time to everybody: one shrinks back in fear, escapes back into his ego, clings, holds. Where can you find a better place to die? If you can die in my presence you will attain to life, eternal life, life abundant. If you can die in *satsang*, in the presence of the master, you will be resurrected.

But that courage has to be there. Gather your courage, and next time it starts happening, let it happen.

The sixth question:

Osho,
Is psychoanalysis really that useless?

No, not always. Sometimes it helps too. Meditate on this story.

Felix Simons was a nice guy but a social flop. Although he was thirty-five, he had never conquered his childhood habit of bed-wetting. Finally, one of his friends told him, "Look, Felix, you might as well know the truth. We're all very fond of you, but nobody can stand to come into your house because it smells, and you're driving your wife up the wall. Why don't you see a psychiatrist about your problem? Enuresis is not too uncommon and it can be cured. Get it over with once and for all!"

Felix was convinced that he must do something to change this. After six months of treatment, he ran into the same friend.

"Well, Felix, did you take my advice?"

"Yes," answered Felix, "I've been seeing a psychiatrist three times a week for six months now."

"Well, have you had any results?"

"Oh," beamed Felix, "great results!"

"You don't wet your bed anymore?"

"I still do, but now I'm proud of it!"

Psychoanalysis helps only in this way: it makes you proud of things you have been guilty about. Religion has created guilt in people. Psychoanalysis has moved to the other extreme: psychoanalysis is a reaction to religious guilt. This has to be understood.

Religion has done a great wrong to humanity. It has wounded the human heart by creating guilt. It lives on guilt. The whole religious world – Hindu, Christian, Mohammedan, these are only different names for the same trick: how to create guilt in people. Once you have created guilt in people they are caught in your net, you can exploit them. Guilt is the spider's net: make people feel guilty and they are in your power. Then you can manipulate them, you can force them to surrender, you can force them to do things for you – for the church, for the priest. They are guilty, they are afraid, they are going to suffer – they want to find a way out.

First create guilt, then they are bound to come to you, because they will have to find a way out of guilt. Then tell them to pray, then tell them to do some ritual, some mantra. But first the guilt has to be created.

I have heard…

Two persons were doing great business. They were partners. The business was simple. One would enter a town in the night and throw coal tar on people's windows, and after two, three days, the other would come to clean. And he would make it known in the town that he knew how to clean coal tar from the windows. By the time he had cleaned the windows, the other would have prepared another town for him. Then he would go to the other town. They were doing really great business. They were partners.

Religion depends on creating guilt: first throw coal tar on people's hearts and then tell them how to cleanse it…and then they have to pay for it.

Psychoanalysis is a reaction. I don't call it a revolution but only a reaction. It reacted against this whole business and it started doing the opposite: it makes you proud of your things. It says, "This is perfectly normal. If you are wetting your bed this is perfectly normal. There is nothing wrong in it. You should be really proud of it." It gives support to you as you are.

Religion condemns you as you are. Psychoanalysis convinces you that this is the only way you can be and you are perfectly right. You are okay – that is the message of psychoanalysis. Both are wrong. Neither do you need to feel guilty nor do you need to feel perfectly okay. If you feel guilty you will become a victim to the church, to the priest, and they will exploit you. If you start feeling you are perfectly okay, you become dormant, your growth stops.

You have to know one thing: that life means evolution, growth, life means going higher and higher – to new plenitudes, to new planes of being. There is no need to feel guilty for what you are, but there is every need to have a tremendous longing to rise higher, because you are a seed, a potential – and you can become God. If you accept yourself as you are and you settle with it, you will remain a seed – you will never become a tree and you will never be able to have a dialogue with the stars. You will not be able to play with the wind and the rain and the sun. You will remain shrunk into a seed. But there is no need to feel guilty! A seed is a seed

– there is no need to feel guilty – but the seed has to become a tree. There is really a great need to inquire into one's potential. Never feel guilty, never feel proud. Just feel tremendously happy that a great opportunity has been given to you to grow.

And this whole life is a challenge to growth. That is true religion and that is true psychology too – because a true religion cannot be anything other than a true psychology. I call that psychology "the psychology of the buddhas." It does not make you feel guilty – it accepts you, it loves you – but it doesn't make you feel proud to be as you are. It gives you a great challenge to be more than you are. It gives you a divine discontent. It makes you aflame with a desire to go higher and higher – not higher than others, but higher than yourself. Tomorrow should not be just a repetition of today – that is the meaning of divine discontent. Today should not be just a repetition of yesterday, otherwise you have not lived. Today must bring some new gifts to you, some new flowers, some new rays. Some new windows *must* open today.

To feel guilty means to remain possessed by the past, to feel proud means to remain wherever you are, whatsoever you are. To have a divine discontent means to grow, to search, to seek, to explore. And life is nothing but an adventure, a constant adventure into the unknown. So I don't want you to feel guilty and I don't want you to feel proud. When you drop both, real life begins.

And the last question:

Osho,
Why is communication so difficult?

It is not only difficult, it is impossible. It is really a miracle if sometimes it happens, because two persons are two persons – their past experiences are different, their gestalt is different, their knowledge is different, their personalities are different. They are two worlds. They speak different languages; it may be in the same language, but they speak different languages. They give different meaning to words, different nuances, different shades and different colors.

When you are looking at a roseflower and if there are five persons looking at the roseflower, don't think for a single moment that you are looking at the same roseflower – you cannot! Only five buddhas standing beside the flower will be able to look at the same roseflower – you cannot – because five buddhas means five zeros, five no-minds. Only two no-minds can commune because there is nothing to hinder now, nothing to interpret – it is direct.

But when five minds are standing by the side of the roseflower they only believe that they are looking at the same roseflower, because they have different ideas of the rose, different experiences of the rose, different past impacts of the rose. All that is there in their eyes, layer upon layer; this rose is so far away, so distant.

For example, one may have loved a woman who was obsessed by roses, but she betrayed him. Now the rose will only remind him of that betrayal and the woman. That is not the others' experience. Another may have seen a dead man garlanded with a rose garland. The rose will remind him of death – he may feel a little fear. The third may have his own experience about the rose. It will depend. And that's how it is with each experience.

Only two no-minds can communicate; even without words, then communication happens. It is a communion. But minds are bound to clash, conflict.

I will tell you a few stories.

The first story:
Seated in an elegantly appointed restaurant, Chico Marx was studying the oversized menu when the head waiter approached his table. The waiter folded his hands in front of him and with proper Continental demeanor inquired, "And what is your pleasure, Monsieur?"

"Girls," Chico replied. "What's yours?"

The second story:
The young husband and his bride flew to Miami for their honeymoon and for days neither hide nor hair was seen of them. On the morning of the sixth day, they entered the dining room for breakfast. As the waiter approached them for their order, the bride turned to her husband and said coyly, "You know what I'd like, honey, don't you?"

"Yes, I know," he replied wearily, "but we have got to eat sometime too!"

And the third story:
The boss had been after his secretary for almost a year. He had been suggesting all kinds of things to her. On this particular evening he was unusually persistent.

"Oh, come on!" he said. "Let's go out and have supper, then go to the theater, then to a nightclub and then we will go up to my apartment."

The blond clipped back, "I would like you to comprehend that I am adamant and didactic in my refusal of your salacious, mendacious and denigrating proposition."

The boss said, "I don't get it."

The secretary answered, "That's just what I have been trying to tell you."

Language is the problem – different experiences, different minds, different pasts, different patterns, different habits, different personalities.

You ask me why it is difficult to communicate. It is not only difficult, it is almost impossible. If once in a while it happens, feel tremendously fortunate. Yes, once in a while it happens. When you are deeply in love with somebody, it happens. Then language is not needed. Then your very presence, your very vibe communicates. Then, for a moment, in deep love, you slip out of your minds. In deep love, for a moment you become buddhas, you become no-minds.

So only in rare moments of love communication happens, otherwise it is always a quarrel, a subtle conflict. You say one thing, the other understands something else. The other says something, you understand something else. If you really want to communicate, become more and more loving – because love is needed, not language. Language is a barrier, love is a bridge. If you really want to communicate, start slipping out of your mind. Become more and more zeros, no-minds, and suddenly you will see miracles happening. It is happening here.

The new people who come here are not in tune with me for a few days: I say something, they understand something else. But as they become more and more open to my love, communication starts happening. To those who have really lived long with me and have become intimate, to those with whom the barrier of language has disappeared, just a look in their eyes or just a touch by my hand and there is communication – not only communication, but communion. That's why just recently I have started a new way of communing with my sannyasins: just to touch them, just to let them feel my energy.

The more you become intimate with me, the less and less words will be needed – because you will start hearing *me*! Then there will be no need of words. I will continue to speak for the new people, I will continue to speak for those who will be coming – more and more will be coming, thousands are on the way – but those who have been here with me long enough or deep enough.... And depth can happen even in a single moment. It is not only a question of time, it is a question of intensity.

Sometimes it happens that when a person comes to me for the first time, the first moment of contact and he becomes intimate as if he has been with me for many lives. And not only do I feel that, he also immediately feels that he has come home, that this is the place he has been searching for his whole life, or for many lives. Then communication immediately happens. Then there is no conflict.

In fact, the moment there is communion and there is no conflict is the moment of your real initiation. Then what I say is secondary. What I am becomes primary. Then you relate to me directly. Then you are not distracted by my words – because I am not a consistent man. I contradict myself, and I contradict myself deliberately to help you to get rid of your expectation of consistency, to help you to get rid of language. Listening to me contradicting myself again and again, slowly slowly you will see that words are only games; you will not be serious about words. The day *that* awakening has happened in you, you relate to me directly. Then there is no medium needed, then you are bridged.

I am in love, I am love. The moment you are in love and you become love, communion happens. Communion is a function of love, not of language. In fact, language functions as a hindrance, not as a help.

Remember it: to be with me is to be with an emptiness, a nobody. I have nothing to offer to you, I have nothing to teach you, I have no philosophy. I am, but I have no philosophy. I am, but I have nothing to offer. I am, but I have nothing to teach. And you have to learn to be with this I-amness…and then you will know what communion is.

Communion is a phenomenon of love, a flowering of love. It has nothing to do with language, with words – not at all. It is silence.

Enough for today.

CHAPTER 13

A Listening Heart

Master Lu-tsu said:
The decision must be carried out with a collected heart and not
seeking success; success will then come of itself. In the first period of
release there are chiefly two mistakes: indolence and distraction. But
that can be remedied; the heart must not enter into the breathing
too completely. Breathing comes from the heart. What comes out of
the heart is breath. As soon as the heart stirs there develops breath-
energy. Breath-energy is originally transformed activity of the heart.
When our ideas go very fast they imperceptibly pass into fantasies
which are always accompanied by the drawing of a breath, because
this inner and outer breathing hangs together like tone and echo.
Daily we draw innumerable breaths and have an equal number of
fantasies. And thus the clarity of the spirit ebbs away as wood dries
out and ashes die.

So, then, should a man have no imaginings in his mind? One cannot
be without imaginings. Should one not breathe? One cannot be
without breathing. The best way is to make a medicine of the illness.
Since heart and breath are mutually dependent, the circulation of
the light must be united with the rhythm of breathing. For this, light
of the ear is above all necessary. There is a light of the eye and a
light of the ear. The light of the eye is the united light of the sun and
moon outside. The light of the ear is the united seed of sun and moon

within. The seed is thus the light in crystallized form. Both have the same origin and are different only in name. Therefore, understanding (ear) and clarity (eye) are one and the same effective light.

In sitting down after lowering the lids, one uses the eyes to establish a plumb-line and then shifts the light downward. But if the transposition downward is not successful, then the heart is directed towards listening to the breathing. One should not be able to hear with the ear the outgoing and intaking of the breath. What one hears is that it has no tone. As soon as it has tone, the breathing is rough and superficial, and does not penetrate into the open. Then the heart must be made quite light and insignificant. The more it is released, the less it becomes; the less it is, the quieter. All at once it becomes so quiet that it stops. Then the true breathing is manifested and the form of the heart comes to consciousness. If the heart is light, the breathing is light, for every movement of the heart affects breath-energy. If breathing is light, the heart is light, for every movement of the breath-energy affects the heart. In order to steady the heart, one begins by taking care of the breath-energy. The heart cannot be influenced directly. Therefore the breath-energy is used as a handle, and this is what is called maintenance of the concentrated breath-energy.

Children, do you not understand the nature of movement? Movement can be produced by outside means. It is only another name for mastery. One can make the heart move merely by running. Should one not also be able to bring it to rest by concentrated quietness? The great holy ones who knew how the heart and breath-energy mutually influence one another have thought out an easier procedure in order to help posterity.

"The hen can hatch her eggs because her heart is always listening." That is an important magic spell. The hen can hatch the eggs because of the energy of heat. But the energy of the heat can only warm the shells; it cannot penetrate into the interior. Therefore she conducts this energy inward with her heart. This she does with her hearing. In this way she concentrates her whole heart. When the heart penetrates, the energy penetrates, and the chick receives the

energy of the heat and begins to live. Therefore a hen, even when at
times she leaves her eggs, always has the attitude of listening with
bent ear. Thus the concentration of the spirit is not interrupted.
Because the concentration of the spirit suffers no interruption, neither
does the energy of heat suffer interruption day or night, and the spirit
awakens to life. The awakening of the spirit is accomplished because
the heart has first died. When a man can let his heart die, then the
primal spirit wakes to life. To kill the heart does not mean to let it dry
and wither away, but it means that it has to become undivided and
gathered into one.

A story…

The ancient Zen master, Dogo, had a disciple called Soshin. When Soshin became a novice under Dogo he doubtless expected that the master would instruct him in Zen the way a schoolmaster instructs his pupils. But Dogo said nothing special to him, and indeed, appeared to have no intention of conveying anything unusual to the disciple. Finally Soshin could stand it no longer and reproached his master for not having shown him anything of Zen. "But I have been giving you lessons in Zen ever since you arrived," said Dogo.

"Oh?" said Soshin, "When could that possibly have been?"

"When you bring me my morning tea," said Dogo, "I accept it. When you serve me a meal, I eat it. When you bow to me, I acknowledge it. How else do you expect to learn Zen?"

Tao can be shared but cannot be divided. Tao can be shown but cannot be said.

The master lives in Tao. The disciple has to imbibe the spirit of it. It is not a teaching, it cannot be a teaching – all teachings are superficial. It has to be deeper than a teaching. It has to be an energy transfer. It has to be heart to heart, soul to soul, body to body. It cannot be verbal. And the disciple has to see, watch, observe, feel, love the energy that is manifesting in the master. Slowly slowly, by and by, just sitting by the side of the master, the disciple learns many secrets, although they are never taught.

One of the greatest secrets is that sitting by the master's side, the disciple starts breathing in the same way the master breathes. There arises a synchronicity, and in that synchronicity the two meet. It happens to lovers too. If you are in deep love with someone, sitting side by side, sitting together with your beloved, you will be surprised if you observe, that suddenly, for no reason at all, not cultivated by you, you are breathing in the same way. When the beloved exhales, you exhale; when the beloved inhales, you inhale. And suddenly you are connected, linked together.

Breath is of immense importance. That's how the mother is connected with the child. And sometimes even, the distance may be of a thousand miles between the child and the mother, but the mother's heart is immediately affected if the child is in danger. Their breathing is so connected – they breathe alike. And there is an obvious reason for it. The child in the mother's womb was breathing through the mother for nine months. He had no breath of his own. It was his mother's breath, and he was simply following the mother's breathing. The mother was breathing for him, on his behalf; for nine months they lived in a deep synchronicity. Even after the child is born it continues. If there is real love, it can continue for the whole of their lives.

Now there have been scientific proofs for it too. In America, in Russia, and in other countries also, many experiments have been done lately with birds, with animals. The child is taken far away and then killed, and they watch the mother with all the sophisticated instruments available. The moment the child is killed – it may be a thousand miles away – immediately the mother's breath changes – immediately, in the exact moment. Her breath becomes shaken, a trembling arises in her. She feels panic, pain – for no reason, for no apparent reason: something intuitive, something without any medium between the two. They are not visibly connected by anything, but there are some invisible threads too.

The disciple has to learn not what the master is teaching but how the master is being. That's what Dogo means when he says, "But I have been giving you lessons in Zen ever since you arrived. When you bring me my morning tea, I accept it. Have you not watched it – the way I accept it? Have you not fallen in deep harmony with me when I accept the tea from you? When you serve me a meal, I eat it. When you bow to me, I acknowledge it. How else do you expect to learn Zen?"

The master is saying: Watch my gestures – the way I walk, the way I sit, the way I breathe, the way I simply sit with you, the way I look at you, the way I respond in a thousand and one small ways. Don't wait for a doctrine; the master's presence is the only doctrine there is. The real teaching is not a teaching at all, it is a transfer – a transfer beyond words and beyond scriptures. And the transfer happens through the harmony of the breath.

I would also like to say to you that I have also nothing to offer to you as a teaching, as a doctrine, as a philosophy, as a religion. I have nothing to teach at all. I have much to share, but nothing to teach – or, *only nothing* to teach! But to feel that *nothing* that I would like to be transferred to you, you will have to fall in rhythm with me. And small things disturb, very small things. And you have to become aware slowly slowly what the disturbances are.

In evening *darshan* sometimes I call a few sannyasins to help me transfer energy to somebody. I have been calling Pradeepa many times, but each time I call her, afterwards I feel nauseous. I was puzzled. What is happening? She is such a beautiful woman, with great love for me. That's why I call her to help me. But it has been happening each time. Just the last time I felt it so much that I had to look into it, into the whole matter of it. Then I saw the point. She must be eating non-vegetarian food – meat, eggs and other things. That is making her breath ugly, that is making her whole inner harmony disturbed. That's why she cannot fall in tune with me. And if she cannot fall in tune, it creates a disturbance. She loves me but her love is still unconscious. If she becomes a little more conscious she will see it; she will see that to be with me you will have to change many things in you.

To be with me and to move deeper with me, to have a heart-to-heart contact, you will have to drop the unnecessary luggage that you carry. Now there is no need to be a non-vegetarian – it is not for a meditator; otherwise you are creating unnecessary hindrances. It will disturb your softness, it will create a kind of cruelty in you. You may not be aware of it because you are not aware at all, but when you come to me I am just a mirror.

Now Pradeepa must be creating a great nauseousness in her own being. She may have become accustomed to it, so she is not aware. But again and again I was feeling nauseous, because when you relate to me with energy it is not one-way: my energy moves into you, your energy moves into me. It can't be one-way. A circle is created, circulation starts happening. This is just an example. And this is not only for Pradeepa, it is for you all.

If you want to be more and more deeply in tune with me, if you want to share the Tao that has happened to me, you will have to be more conscious, more alert to what you are doing, what you are eating, what you are reading, what you are listening to, where you are going, with whom you are mixing. It has to be a total effort. It has to be a twenty-four-hour awareness, because small things gather together and their impact is great.

If you have been angry with somebody and you have been fighting with somebody and then you come to see me, naturally you will be far away from me. That's why Jesus says if you go to the temple to pray and you remember that you have hurt somebody, insulted somebody, that you are angry at somebody or if you have angered somebody, first go and ask to be forgiven, only then come to pray; otherwise you will not be able to relate with God. First go and apologize. First clear things.

It happened...

When Michelangelo was working in the Sistine Chapel, he was making a painting of Jesus. The painting was almost complete – just the last finishing touches – but he was finding those last finishing touches very difficult. Jesus was not coming out Jesus-like; something was missing in Jesus' face – that softness, that feminineness was not there, that love quality was not there. He tried and tried for days, and then he remembered that he had quarreled with a friend and he was carrying it in himself. And then he remembered the saying of Jesus, that if you go to pray and you are not feeling good about a friend or a brother, then first go and ask forgiveness.

He rushed out of the chapel, went to the friend, asked his forgiveness and told the whole story. "For days together I have been working, but I cannot bring out Jesus' face as it should be. Something angry remains in it" – because something was angry inside him. And if there is anger and a hurt feeling – and you are going to paint, your hands will paint – your painting will represent you, your painting will basically reflect you. And the day he asked forgiveness and was forgiven, he came into a totally different mood. And just a few minutes' work and the painting was complete. And it is one of the most beautiful paintings of Jesus. Just a few strokes and the painting came alive and Jesus surfaced, because now Michelangelo's heart was in tune.

Tao can be shared. But then you have to learn the ways of how to share it with the master, and you have to be very watchful about many things. It is simple in a way and yet very complex too – simple, because if you are really open and in harmony, it can happen in a single split moment; complex, because you will have to change your very small habits of which you are not aware at all. You will have to change your total life.

That's why I say I have nothing to offer to you as a teaching; I have some energy to impart to you as a provocation. I am not giving you a system of philosophy, a theology; I am giving you myself. It is a challenge. My effort here is to wake you up. You will have to be open, rhythmic, and you will have to watch small things in your life. And the breath is the most important. You will have to learn how to breathe in *satsang*, how to breathe in the company of a master, how to breathe when you are in love.

The breathing continuously changes with your emotions. When you are angry, your breathing is unrhythmic, asymmetrical. When you are in sexual lust, your breathing is almost insane. When you are calm and quiet, joyful, your breathing has a musical quality to it – your breathing is almost a song. When you are feeling at home in existence, when you have no desires and are feeling contented, suddenly breathing almost stops. When you are in a state of awe, of wonder, breathing stops for a moment. And those are the greatest moments of life, because only in those moments when breathing almost stops are you in utter tune with existence: you are in God and God is in you.

Your experience of breathing has to be more and more profound, scrutinized, observed, watched, analyzed. See how your breathing changes with your emotions, and vice versa, how your emotions change with your breathing. For example, when you are afraid, watch the change in your breath, and then one day try to change the breath to the same pattern as when you were afraid. And you will be surprised that if you change your breath to exactly what it was when you were afraid, and fear will arise in you – immediately. Watch your breathing when you are deeply in love with somebody; holding his hand, hugging your beloved, watch your breathing. And then one day, just sitting silently under a tree, watch yourself again breathing in the same way. Make the pattern, fall into the same gestalt again – breathe in the same way as if you were hugging your beloved, and you will be surprised: the whole existence becomes your beloved, again there is great love arising in you. They go together. Hence in Yoga, in Tantra, in Tao – in all these three great systems of human consciousness and the science of expansion of human consciousness – breathing is one of the key phenomena. They have all worked on breathing.

Buddha's whole meditation system depends on a certain quality of breath. He says, "Simply watch your breath, without changing it, without in any way changing it. Simply watch." But you will be surprised: the moment you watch, it changes – you cannot help it. Buddha says, "Don't change your breath, simply watch it." But the moment you watch, it changes, because watchfulness has its own rhythm. That's why Buddha says, "You need not change it. You simply watch." Watchfulness will bring its own kind of breathing – it comes by itself. And slowly slowly you will be surprised: the more watchful you become, the less you breathe; the breath becomes longer, deeper.

For example, if in one minute you were breathing sixteen breaths, now you may breathe six, or four, or three. As you become watchful, the breath goes deeper, becomes longer, and you are taking less and less breaths in the same time period. Then you can do it from the other side too. Breathe slowly, quietly, deep long breaths, and suddenly you will see watchfulness arising in you, as if each emotion has a polarity in your breathing system: it can be triggered by your breathing.

But the best way is to watch when you are in love. When you are sitting by the side of your friend, watch your breath, because that loving rhythm of breath is most important. It will transform your whole being.

Love is where you feel most sharply the absurdity, the falsity of your position as a separated being. Yet by this very separation, this absurdity, you are able to express what you could not express in any other way. By your very otherness you are able to celebrate identity. Hence, the paradox of love: you are two and yet you feel one; you are one, yet you know you are two. Oneness in twoness: that is the paradox of love – and that has to be the paradox of prayer too, and meditation too. Ultimately you have to feel as one with existence as you feel with your beloved, with your lover, with your friend, with your mother, with your child, in some rare, valuable moments. By your very otherness you are able to celebrate identity.

The Vedas say: *Tattvamasi*, I am that. This is the greatest statement of love: I am that or Thou art that. There is a clear-cut awareness of separation, and yet a deep unity too. The wave is separate from the ocean and yet not separate from the ocean.

Watch your loving moments more and more. Be alert. See how your breathing changes, see how your body vibrates. Just hugging your woman or your man, make it an experiment, and you will be surprised: one day, just hugging, melting into each other, sit at least for one hour, and you will be surprised – it will be one of the most psychedelic experiences. For one hour, doing nothing, just hugging each other, falling into each other, merging, melting into each other, slowly slowly the breathing will become one. You will breathe as if you are two bodies but one heart. You will breathe together. And when you breathe together – not by any effort of your own, but just because you are feeling so much love that the breathing follows – those will be the greatest moments, the most precious, not of this world, but of the beyond, the far out. And in those moments you will have the first glimpse of meditative energy. In those moments grammar gives up, language expires.

In the attempt to say it, language expires, and by its very death does point at last to what it cannot say. And that has to be, on a profounder level, the relationship with the master. Then only can Tao jump as a flame, from the master to the disciple. You will have to learn the art of breathing.

The sutras.

> *Master Lu-tsu said:*
> *The decision must be carried out with a collected heart and not*
> *seeking success; success will then come of itself.*

A tremendously significant statement, a key statement:

> *The decision must be carried out with a collected heart...*

The first thing: a man is born only when he becomes decisive; with decision is the birth of man. Those who live in indecisiveness are not really men yet. And millions live in indecisiveness, they cannot decide about anything. They always lean upon others, somebody else should decide for them. Hence people hang around authorities.

Authoritativeness continues in the world for the single reason that millions of people cannot decide for themselves. They have always to be given an order. Once the order is given, they follow it. But this is slavery, this is how they are preventing the birth of their own souls. Decision should arise in your being, because with decisiveness integrity arises. Remember to make a few decisions; decisions will make you individual.

What is indecisiveness? It means you are a crowd; many voices in you are contradicting each other and you cannot decide whether to go this way or that. Even in small things people are indecisive: whether to go to see this movie or that and they are indecisive. Indecisiveness has become almost their very style of life. To purchase this or to purchase that? Just watch people when they go shopping, see their indecisiveness. Just sit in any shop and just watch people coming and going – customers – and you will be surprised: people don't know how to decide. And those who don't know how to decide will remain vague, cloudy, confused. With decision comes clarity. And if the decision is far-reaching, if the decision has something to do with your foundations, certainly, one is born.

Now there are many people who come to me and they say, "We cannot decide whether to take the jump into sannyas or not." They want me to tell them to take the jump. But then they miss the whole point. If I say to you, "Take the jump and become a sannyasin," you have missed an opportunity, a great opportunity, of taking a decision – again you have leaned on somebody else – and that is not the way a soul grows. And this is a profound decision, of immense significance, because it is going to change your whole lifestyle, it is going to give you a new vision. You will be moving in a new direction, you will not be the same again. Such far-reaching decisions one should be capable of taking on one's own. One should risk. Only with risk, with courage, is one born.

And whenever you take a decision, remember, if you take it then follow it, otherwise don't take a decision, because then it is more dangerous – more dangerous than being indecisive. To take a decision and not to follow it will make you very very impotent. Then it would have been better not to have decided. There are people who decide and then never follow their decisions. Slowly slowly they lose all trust and confidence in their being. Slowly slowly they know perfectly well that whatsoever they decide they are not going to do. They become split, they become deceptive – to themselves. When they are taking a decision, even in that moment they know that they are not going to follow it because they know their past and their past experiences. Whenever they did decide, they never followed it.

And then very small decisions can be very destructive. Just a small decision – "I will not smoke from today" – just a very ordinary decision, nothing much is involved in it…. Whether you smoke or not doesn't matter: the existence continues. In twenty years' time you may have tuberculosis, but that can be cured, or you may die two or three years earlier. So what? – you never really lived.

Just the other day I was looking at a cartoon.

A man is asking a woman, "Do you believe in life after death?" And the woman says, "This is it!"

There is no need to believe in it, this is it. You are living such a dead life, what more can there be after death? It will be just the same. This is what it is!

But a small decision, a very trivial decision not to smoke, and then not to follow it is very dangerous. You will lose self-confidence, you will lose trust in your own being. You will become distrustful. It is better not to take such decisions – go on smoking. And if you decide, then you are committed. Then whatsoever happens you have to do it. And if you can do it, you will find a clarity arising in you, a cloud disappearing, something settling, centering, in you. A decision is tremendously significant and meaningful.

The decision must be carried out with a collected heart…

That's what Lu-tsu means: if you do decide, then let your whole heart be in it, then make it certain that you are not going back. That's what I mean when I say again and again to my sannyasins, "Break the bridges." Because you are not going back – why keep the bridge? Throw the ladder, drown the boat, because you are not going back to the old shore again. If you keep the boat safe, harbored, that means you are still wavering, you are still thinking, "Maybe someday I have to go back."

Just a few months ago, Anup went to the USA, and I told him when he was going, "Break the bridges completely now." And he said, "Yes, Osho".

And now he comes, and I ask him, "What happened? What about the bridges?" He says, "I could not do that."

What does that mean? He will be here only half-heartedly. He has kept the door open to go back, he has kept every security there, safe. And the problem is if he is not totally here, he will not grow. And this is the vicious circle: if he does not grow, after a few months he will think, "It is good that I had not broken the bridges. Had I listened to Osho and broken the bridges, now I would have been in trouble. Nothing is happening to me here. It is good that I have saved everything there, and I can fly back home any moment." And he will think he has been doing the most clever, intelligent thing.

But in the first place, because he has kept the bridges safe and the doors open to escape back, he will be here only in a lukewarm way, in an indecisive way, in an uncertain way – wavering. And with the wavering you will not be with me. You can be with me only if you have taken a decision with a collected heart. And then growth is possible! Growth is possible only then.

So see the point: if you are totally here with me, growth is possible and there will be no need to go back and there will be no need to have bridges. But if you are not totally here with me, then the bridges will be needed. And you will feel very intelligent – that it was good that you didn't listen to me. "Now look, nothing is happening here, and I have to go back. Had I broken all the bridges then where would I have ended?" This is how the logical mind functions: it creates its own suicidal situations.

> *The decision must be carried out with a collected heart and not seeking success; success will then come of itself.*

And the most important thing is, if you are seeking success you are already divided. Then your heart is not in the work, your heart is already in the result.

If you are divided, you will not succeed. Success happens only to undivided hearts who are not worried about the consequence, the result, who are enjoying tremendously the journey itself and are not concerned about the goal. Only those arrive who are not concerned with the goal at all – because their mind is so undivided each moment of the journey, each step of the journey becomes a goal. Wherever they are, there is the goal. Success comes to those people on the spiritual path who are not concerned about success at all.

If you are concerned about success, success is not going to come to you, because your mind will be somewhere in the future and you will not be working in the present – and success can only come if the work is totally done in the present. This moment is going to give birth to the next moment. If this moment has been totally lived, the next moment is bound to be of a deeper totality, of a higher quality of totality. But people go on remaining divided. These problems you have to think about, because these are everybody's problems.

Just a few days ago, Ashoka wrote me a letter saying that he is here but he still keeps Satya Sai Baba's picture in his room. Now that is his room – he can keep anybody's picture in it. It is not only a question of the room... Now he will be in trouble. I told him, "You go to Satya Sai Baba, and there please don't keep my picture in your room, otherwise there also you will fail. Either be here or be there, but anywhere be with a collected heart, an integrated heart. It is better to be with Satya Sai Baba than to be with me if you are here only half-heartedly." But I understand his problem: I know he will keep my picture there too, so his failure is destined.

One has to choose, one has to decide. On each step in life's journey there are alternative paths, and one has to choose. And you cannot have all the paths and you cannot walk on all the paths. And I am not saying what is right and wrong. I am saying: whatsoever you choose totally is right for you. Sometimes it has happened that a disciple has become enlightened even with an unenlightened master if his total surrender was there. And thousands of times it happens that you may be with a perfect master and nothing happens.

It is more a question of your totality than of the perfection of the master. Even with a wrong person you can be transformed. Not that the wrong person can transform you, but if your *total* decision is there, your total decision transforms you. That is far more important, otherwise you can be with a buddha and nothing will happen if you are half-half, if you are divided. Any kind of division – in the future, in the present, with the goal and the journey, this way or that, this master or that – any kind of division is dangerous. Then your energy will be wasted and you will throw the responsibility on others.

For example, if nothing happens to Ashoka here – and nothing is going to happen in this way – then naturally, he will come to the conclusion that he has been in a wrong place. He will not see the point that he has been a divided person, he will only see that he has been in a wrong place, that "This place was not for me." But wherever you are, if you are divided, this is going to happen again and again.

Gather courage. I know the mind wants to be clever. The mind says, "Why not keep both? Who knows? Keep both alternatives open. If this does not work, then that may work." But this is not how life functions. You want to have the cake and eat it too. It is impossible.

Lu-tsu says, *...and not seeking success,* because even that will become a division. Be utterly here and now, with no division: *...success will then come of itself.* And when success comes of itself, it has tremendous beauty. You need not drag it, it opens like a flower; you need not open the flower forcibly. And if you open the flower forcibly you will have killed it. That will not be right. And you will have opened it before its right time, and there may be no fragrance, because the flower has to wait for the right moment to gather fragrance, to create fragrance. And when the fragrance is ready, only then it opens on its own accord, because now it has something to share with the existence.

One should enjoy the moment. One should be totally in the moment and forget all. And then one day, suddenly success has come. One day, suddenly the golden flower has opened and you are transported into a separate reality.

In the first period of release there are chiefly two mistakes: indolence and distraction.

These two mistakes have to be understood: one is the mistake of the feminine mind, the other is the mistake of the masculine mind. The feminine mind can create indolence, laziness, because it is passive. And the masculine mind can create distraction because it is too active. It wants to do this and that – and that too. It wants to rush everywhere, in all directions. The feminine mind is passive; it wants to wait, to let things happen. But that too can be a danger if it becomes lethargy, if it becomes laziness, if it becomes a kind of death.

Remember, passivity can be either positive or negative, just as activity can be either positive or negative. The positive passivity means to be alert, awake, yet waiting. The negative passivity means to be asleep, snoring, and calling it waiting.

Your lover is coming, any moment he will knock at the door – now you can wait in two ways. The positive waiting will be that the door is open, your eyes are fixed on the gate, your ears are alert. Any sound – the sound of footsteps, a knock on the door, even if a dead leaf flutters in the wind – you will rush to the door. Somebody passes by on the road and you rush to the door – maybe he has come. This is positive waiting. It is beautiful.

But if you lock the door and you put the light out, and as you go to sleep, you say, "When he comes he will knock and then I will see him," and you start snoring, this is the negative kind of passivity, this is indolence. It is perfectly good to wait for God, but your passivity should be alive, vibrant.

And the second is distraction: that is the quality of the male mind. The male mind is continuously distracted. That's why the feminine mind is monogamous and the masculine mind is polygamous, continuously distracted – any woman that passes by and he becomes attracted. He forgets completely that he is already married. He forgets completely the woman to whom he has said, "You are my life and I will live only for you. You are my joy. My love is forever." In a single moment he forgets all that nonsense. He is distracted very easily.

The male mind is too active. Activity is good if it is positive. Positive activity means concentrated activity, undistracted activity – digging a well on one spot continuously. Negative activity means digging a well here for a few moments, then in some other place, then in some other place-destroying the whole ground and nowhere reaching to the water source. That's what happens to the masculine mind: he loves this woman and that woman and never reaches the reality of love. It remains just a superficial phenomenon. It never becomes intimacy, it never takes depth. It never becomes a real involvement in each other's being – superficial contact, body-to-body, at the most, sexual. It never reaches the heart, and certainly never the soul, because to reach the heart, to reach the soul, time will be needed. One will have to wait and dig deep.

These are the two chief possible mistakes. Beware of them. Don't become too active and don't become too lazy – remain in the middle. Inactively active, actively inactive, remain in the middle. Your action should have the quality of waiting, and your waiting should have the quality of action. And then success is absolutely certain, you need not think about it – it comes of its own accord. But these mistakes can be remedied.

> But that can be remedied; the heart must not enter into the breathing too completely.

Master Lu-tsu is giving you one of the most important secrets

> ...the heart must not enter into the breathing too completely.

You should learn to breathe very silently, as if there were no hurry to breathe, as if you were indifferent to it, aloof, far away, distant. If you can be aloof, far away and distant to your breathing, you will be able to attain to the middle. In that moment you will be neither masculine nor feminine, you will be both and neither. You will be transcendental. And then both mistakes will disappear.

Breathing comes from the heart. What comes out of the heart is breath. As soon as the heart stirs, there develops breath-energy. Breath-energy is originally transformed activity of the heart.

When you are distracted, watch: your breathing will be distracted too. When you are not distracted, when you are sitting silently with no distraction, your breathing will be cool, silent, rhythmic; it will have the quality of a subtle music. And that quality is the exact middle because you are not doing anything, yet you are not fast asleep; you are neither active nor inactive – you are balanced. And in that moment of balance you are closest to reality, to God, to heaven.

When our ideas go very fast they imperceptibly pass into fantasies which are always accompanied by the drawing of a breath, because this inner and outer breathing hangs together like tone and echo. Daily we draw innumerable breaths and have an equal number of fantasies. And thus the clarity of the spirit ebbs away as wood dries out and ashes die.

Remember, your each breath is not just a breath, it is a thought too, an emotion too, a feeling too, a fantasy too. But this will be understood only if you watch your breathing for a few days. When you are making love, watch your breathing. You will be surprised: your breathing is chaotic because sexual energy is very rough, it is raw energy. Sexual fantasies are rough and raw, animalistic. There is nothing special about sexuality – every animal has it. When you are sexually aroused, you are just behaving like any other animal in the world. And I am not saying that there is anything wrong in being an animal. All that I am saying is just a fact, stating a fact. So whenever you are in sexual love, watch your breath: it loses all balance.

Hence, in Tantra, lovemaking is allowed only when you have learned how to make love and yet keep your breath cool, rhythmic. Then a totally different quality comes to your lovemaking: it becomes prayerful. Then it is sacred. Now for the outsider there will be no difference because he will see you are making love to a woman or making love to a man, and it will be the same for the outsider. But for the insider, for those who know, there will be great difference. In the old Tantra schools where all these secrets were developed, experimented upon, observed, this was one of the central focuses of their experimentation: if a man can make love without his breath being at all affected by it, then it is no longer sex – then it is sacred – and then it will take you to great depths of your own being. It will open doors and mysteries of life. Your breath is not just breath, because breath is your life; it contains all that life contains.

> *So, then, should a man have no imaginings in his mind? One cannot be without imaginings. Should one not breathe? One cannot be without breathing. The best way is to make a medicine of the illness.*

This is the Tantra approach and this is the approach of Tao too:

> *...to make a medicine of the illness.*

And this is something special to Tao and Tantra. Yoga says: Avoid sex, bypass it – it is dangerous. But Tao and Tantra both say: Don't avoid it. Transform its energy and then the illness itself can become the medicine. And you can ask scientists, they are doing exactly that, particularly in allopathy: injections are prepared out of the illness itself, to be injected, and they become medicinal. What allopathy has discovered recently is a very ancient discovery for Tantra and Tao.

Anything that is God-given must have some tremendous purpose behind it. Don't avoid it. Avoiding it, you will remain poor. Don't escape from it, because then something will remain unlived in you. That's why the so-called yogi is continuously tortured by sexual fantasies. He cannot sleep well – it is impossible – because whatsoever he has been denying in the day comes with a vengeance in the night. Whatsoever he has repressed in the unconscious, when he goes to sleep and the controls are withdrawn, surfaces again: it becomes dreams. The yogi, the so-called yogi, is continuously afraid. He is afraid of seeing a woman, he is afraid of touching a woman. He is afraid. And what kind of freedom is this? This fear can't bring freedom.

Tao and Tantra have a totally different approach. They say: Whatsoever is God-given, transform it – it is raw material – something of a great treasure must be hidden in it.

Sexual energy can be transformed if you can change your breathing system. Anger can be transformed if you can change your breathing system. Just watch how you breathe when you are angry. And the next time you feel angry, don't breathe the same way that you have always breathed whenever you are angry. And you will be surprised: you cannot be angry either. If you don't breathe in a certain way, anger is not supported, anger disappears. Instead of anger, compassion arises. And so disappears sex, and instead of sex, love arises. Love is absolutely human. Sex is not just human, it is animal too. But no animal knows about love.

Sex is animal, love is human, prayer is divine. Sex has to be transformed into love, and love has to be transformed into prayer.

In sex, the breathing goes chaotic. That's why I have chosen chaotic meditation for certain purposes: it is cathartic – chaotic meditation, this familiar chaotic breathing hits all your repressed anger, sex, greed, jealousies, hatred, and brings them out on the surface. It is a great cleansing process. In sex the breathing is chaotic. In love, the breathing is musical. In prayer, it almost stops.

Since heart and breath are mutually dependent, the circulation of the light must be united with the rhythm of breathing.

When you breathe out, let the light go out of your eyes. When you breathe in, let the light go back inside. Make a connection between your breathing and your light circulation. This way you will give some work to your breathing so it need not have any other imagination. This is an imagination – you have given something. That's why Lu-tsu says: Man "cannot be without imaginings"– not in the beginning at least. It is only at the highest peak that imagination can be dropped. But we can use it, we can make a stepping-stone of it.

Imagine: when your breath is going out your light is going out, when you breathe in your light goes in. Try it in a simple way: just when you breathe out, feel all the light that was in being thrown out, and when you breathe in feel all the light of the existence entering you. And soon the imagination will become joined together with your breathing, will be welded with breathing – so you have used imagination. And then slowly slowly, let your breathing become calmer and quieter.

There is no need to practice any particular rhythm as they do in yoga, in *pranayama,* because each person has to find his own way. The body is different, the mind is different – your breathing cannot be alike. You will have to find your own way. Slowly slowly, one thing has to be kept in mind: that it has to be made calm and quiet and musical.

For this, light of the ear is above all necessary.

And then Lu-tsu introduces another thing. He says: Just as light enters from the eyes – comes in, goes out, it also enters from the ear – comes in and goes out. You will be surprised, because from the ear we don't see any light coming in and going out. But then ask modern physics. They say that sound is nothing but electricity, a function of electricity. Sound is electricity. That's what in the ancient language Lu-tsu is calling light. Sound goes in and comes out from the ear.

The ear is the feminine part of your body just as the eye is the masculine part of your body. Just as the eye is extrovert, the ear is introvert. Hence, there are two kinds of meditations in the world: either meditations concerned with eye-energy or meditations concerned with ear-energy.

The meditations concerned with ear-energy are feminine meditations, passive – you have just to listen, not doing anything. Listening to the birds, the wind passing through the pine trees, or to some music, or to the noise of the traffic – just listening, doing nothing – and great silence comes in, and great peace starts falling and showering on you. From the ear it is easier than from the eye. It is easier through the ear because the ear is passive, non-aggressive: it cannot do anything to existence, it can only let it happen. The ear is a door: it allows.

> *There is a light of the eye and a light of the ear. The light of the eye is the united light of the sun and moon outside.*

It is extrovert.

> *The light of the ear is the united seed of sun and moon within.*

It is introvert.

> *The seed is thus the light in crystallized form. Both have the same origin and are different only in name.*

Light and sound are only different in name.

There are stories in India – and possibly true stories – sooner or later science is going to prove them right. There are stories in India that there is a certain kind of melody that can create fire. You can put an unlit candle before the musician, and if he plays a certain melody, a certain *raga,* suddenly the candle becomes lit.

Now it looks impossible, it looks just like a story – maybe a myth or maybe a metaphor. But if sound is electricity, then vibrations falling into a certain pattern can create it. Now experiments are on the way. And my feeling is, sooner or later it will be possible scientifically, to do it again.

It is a well-known fact that whenever an army passes over a bridge they are told to break their rhythm. Ordinarily they walk in a certain rhythm: left, right, left, right, left, right. Many times it has been observed that when the army is passing in a certain rhythm, the bridge collapses. So now it is a well-known fact that passing over a bridge the army has to drop its right-left, right-left rhythm; that certain vibe is dangerous to the bridge.

In Canada they were experimenting with plants and their relationship with music. A small experiment, but immensely significant. They planted a few seasonal flowers, the same seasonal flowers in two places, at the same time, with the same manure, the same gardener looking after them – everything exactly the same for both plots. But to one plot a recording of Ravi Shankar's sitar was made available – continuously played – and to the other plot, pop music. And it was a very revealing phenomenon. In the plot where pop music was fed, all the plants started moving away from the mechanism. They started leaning away from the mechanism, as if wanting to escape, not wanting to hear it – tired of it. And their flowers were smaller and they took a longer time to grow – almost double the time of the other plot. In the other plot where Ravi Shankar's sitar was played, the plants started leaning towards the mechanism; they all covered the mechanism – embracing it, hugging it. And the growth was double, and the flowers were bigger, and they came sooner than expected. Even plants feel the difference of sound waves.

These airplanes passing by are driving humanity crazy. And the noise is growing so much every day that if man can survive it, it will be a miracle.

Both have the same origin and are different only in name.

In fact, everything is the same. It is all made of the stuff called light, fire, electricity – or whatsoever name you choose. Only the forms are different.

Therefore, understanding (ear) and clarity (eye) are one and the same effective light.

Understanding comes through the ear and clarity comes through the eye. Clarity is masculine, understanding is feminine. Hence, I say always that a woman finds it easier to become a disciple, a woman finds it easier to surrender, finds it easier to understand, than a man. The man asks for logical clarity, logical conviction. The woman asks for something else: the rhythmic conviction. The woman listens intuitively, she feels the vibe of the person who is saying it. She is not very concerned about what is being said but *who* is saying it, *how* it is being said, *from where* it is arising. She goes deeper, she catches hold of the very spirit. Man remains concerned with the letter. And because of the printing presses and the scriptures becoming available to everybody in the form of books, a great change has happened.

Originally all the teachings were available only from the mouth of the master. They were transmitted orally, so the receiving center was the ear. Now books are available. When Krishna talked to Arjuna, Arjuna listened to it: he functioned from the ear. Great understanding happened – he was transformed. But Arjuna functioned as the feminine.

Now you read the Gita. Reading means: through the eye. And the eye is not bothered about understanding; the eye wants logical clarity. It is a totally different approach. All the religions of the world, for centuries insisted that their scriptures should not be written. And there was a reason for it because once they are written their whole quality changes. Once they are written, the eye becomes important, and the ear is no more important.

Listening to me is one thing, reading is totally another. When you read, you function as male mind. When you listen, you function as female mind.

> *In sitting down, after lowering the lids, one uses the eyes to*
> *establish a plumb-line and then shifts the light downward.*
> *But if the transposition downward is not successful, then the heart*
> *is directed towards listening to the breathing. One should not be*
> *able to hear with the ear the outgoing and intaking of the breath.*
> *What one hears is that it has no tone. As soon as it has tone, the*
> *breathing is rough and superficial, and does not penetrate into*
> *the open. Then the heart must be made quite light and*
> *insignificant. The more it is released, the less it becomes;*
> *the less it is, the quieter.*

So listen to your breathing. If you can listen to it that means it is rough. If it has a tone, that means it is rough; when you can only feel it and you cannot hear it, then it is still and quiet. And that is the right way to be in tune with existence, to be in tune with yourself, to be in tune with reality. And the more quiet it is the deeper you are. When it stops sometimes, it stops! It is happening to many sannyasins here: they come and report to me because they become very frightened – when the breathing stops they think they are going to die!

Just the other day there was Saguna's question: that he started feeling as if he were going to die. He became frightened. Do not become frightened. If breathing stops, allow it, enjoy it – you are not going to die! In that very stopping of the breath you will know the true form of reality, you will know life eternal, you will know something that knows no death.

> All at once it becomes so quiet that it stops. Then the true
> breathing is manifested and the form of the heart comes
> to consciousness.

If you can allow…. That's why I told Saguna, "Saguna, you fool, you missed! Don't miss it again when it happens."

If the breathing stops …*then the true breathing is manifested,* true life is manifested – life that does not depend on breathing, life that is eternal, life that is not part of the body, life that will be there even after the body has fallen into dust and disappeared. And in that moment consciousness is attained, one becomes a Buddha. Buddha means: utterly conscious, awakened.

> If the heart is light, the breathing is light, for every movement of
> the heart affects breath-energy. If breathing is light, the heart is
> light, for every movement of the breath-energy affects the heart. In
> order to steady the heart, one begins by taking care of the breath-
> energy. The heart cannot be influenced directly. Therefore the
> breath-energy is used as a handle, and this is what is called the
> maintenance of the concentrated breath-energy.

> Children, do you not understand the nature of movement?
> Movement can be produced by outside means. It is only another
> name for mastery. One can make the heart move merely by
> running. Should one not also be able to bring it to rest by
> concentrated quietness? The great holy ones who knew how the
> heart and breath-energy mutually influence one another have
> thought out an easier procedure in order to help posterity.

You know it: if you run, the breath becomes very chaotic, it starts moving faster and faster. Hence the yoga postures, the full lotus posture-sitting erect, utterly silent, as if you have become a marble statue, with no movement – is just the opposite of running. It is just an outside device to help your breathing become quiet. If your breathing can become fast by running, it certainly will become quiet by sitting utterly as a Buddha statue. Sitting like a statue, with no movement in the body, certainly breathing becomes slower and slower and slower...and stops – in the beginning it is only for a few moments. Don't be afraid that you are having a heart attack or anything. It is not a heart attack, it is a God-attack.

> *"The hen can hatch her eggs because her heart is always listening."*
> *That is an important magic spell. The hen can hatch the eggs*
> *because of the energy of heat. But the energy of the heat can only*
> *warm the shells; it cannot penetrate into the interior. Therefore she*
> *conducts this energy inward with her heart. This she does with her*
> *hearing. In this way she concentrates her whole heart. When the*
> *heart penetrates, the energy penetrates, and the chick receives the*
> *energy of the heat and begins to live. Therefore a hen, even when at*
> *times she leaves her eggs, always has the attitude of listening with*
> *bent ear. Thus the concentration of the spirit is not interrupted.*

This is not only so with a hen. This is so with every woman – every mother, even the human mother. There may be a thunderstorm and she will not hear it and she will not be awakened from her sleep. But let her child just start crying or just start moving and she will be awakened immediately, as if her ears are continuously focused on the child. The train will pass by and she will not be awakened, the airplane will pass and she will not be awakened. But let the child show a slight restlessness and she is immediately alert: her whole ears are listening to the child, she is connected heart-to-heart with the child from the ears. She is constantly listening, as if she could hear the very heartbeat of the child.

And this is the way for all meditators: to be connected with the ear, so deeply that you can hear your breathing, your heartbeat. In the beginning you will be able to hear it because it is chaotic. But if you go on listening, listening, listening, just the very effort to listen makes it quieter. And when your listening is profound – you have become skillful, and you know how to be aware – all tone, all sound disappears. And there are moments when breathing stops. And those are the great moments of ecstasy, insight, satori, samadhi.

Because the concentration of the spirit suffers no interruption,
neither does the energy of heat suffer interruption day or night, and
the spirit awakens to life. The awakening of the spirit is accomplished
because the heart has first died.

That's why I said: if suddenly in meditation you feel your heart is dying, don't think it is a heart attack. When the breathing stops you will feel as if the heart is dying – it is not dying. It is giving birth to your real heart.

When a man can let his heart die, then the primal spirit wakes to
life. To kill the heart does not mean to let it dry and wither away, but
it means that it has become undivided and gathered into one.

This is the secret of the golden flower: if the heart can die the flower will bloom, die as you are so you can be reborn. Jesus says, "Unless a man is born again, he will not enter into my kingdom of God."

Enough for today.

CHAPTER 14

The New Man

The first question:

Osho,
What according to you is the most significant thing that is happening
today in the world?

A New Man is emerging. The image of the New Man is not yet clear, but the horizon is becoming red and the sun will soon be there. The morning mist is there and the image of the New Man is vague, but still, a few things are very crystal clear about the New Man.

And this is of tremendous importance because since the monkeys became man, man has remained the same. A great revolution is on the way. It will be far more deep-going than the revolution that happened when monkeys started walking on the earth and became human beings. That change created mind, that change brought psychology in. Now another far more significant change is going to happen that will bring the soul in, and man will not only be a psychological being but a spiritual being too.

You are living in one of the most alive times ever. The New Man, in fragments, has already arrived, but only in fragments. And the New Man has been arriving for centuries, but only here and there. That's how things happen: when the spring comes it starts with one flower. But when the one flower is there, then one can be certain the spring is not far away – it has come. The first flower has heralded its coming. Zarathustra, Krishna, Lao Tzu, Buddha, Jesus – these were the first flowers. Now, on a greater scale, the New Man is going to be born.

This new consciousness is the most important thing that is happening today, according to me. I would like to tell you something about this new consciousness – its orientations, and its characteristics – because you are to help it to come out of the womb, because you *have* to be it. The New Man cannot come from nowhere, it has to come through you. The New Man can only be born through your womb: you have to become the womb.

Sannyas is an experimentation: to clean the ground so that new seeds can fall in. If you understand the meaning of the New Man, you will be able to understand the significance of sannyas too. And it is because sannyas is concerned with the New Man that the old orthodoxies of all kinds are going to be against me and against sannyas – because this is their end. If sannyas succeed, if the New Man succeeds, the old will have to go. The old can live only if the New Man is prevented from coming.

It cannot be prevented now, because it is not only a question of the New Man's coming into existence. It is a question of the survival of the whole earth – of consciousness itself, of life itself. It is a question of life and death. The Old Man has come to utter destructiveness. The Old Man has reached the end of its tether. Now there is no life possible with the old concept of man, but only death. The Old Man is preparing for a global suicide. The Old Man is piling up atom bombs, hydrogen bombs, in order to commit a collective suicide. This is a very unconscious desire: rather than allowing the New Man to be, the Old Man would like to destroy the whole thing.

You have to understand, you have to protect the new, because the new carries the whole future with it. And man has come to a stage where a great quantum leap is possible.

The Old Man was otherworldly, the Old Man was against *this* world. The Old Man was always looking to the heavens. The Old Man was more concerned with life *after* death than life before death. The New Man's concern will be life before death. The New Man's concern will be *this* life, because if this life is taken care of, the other will follow on its own accord. One need not worry about it, one need not think about it.

The Old Man was too concerned with God. That concern was out of fear. The New Man will not be concerned with God, but will live and love *this* world, and out of that love will experience the existence of God. The Old Man was speculative, the New Man is going to be existential.

The Old Man can be defined in the Upanishadic statement: *neti neti,* not this, not this. The Old Man was negative – life-negative, life-denying. The New

Man will be life-affirming: *iti iti*, this and this. The Old Man's concern was *that,* the New Man's concern will be *this,* because out of *this, that* is born, and if you become too concerned with *that,* you miss both.

Tomorrow is in the womb of today: take care of today and you have taken care of tomorrow. There is no need to be in any way worried about tomorrow. And if you become too worried about tomorrow you have missed today! And tomorrow will come as today – it always comes as today. And if you have learned this suicidal habit of missing today, you will miss tomorrow also. You will go on missing.

The Old Man was continuously missing, was miserable, sad. And because he was sad he was against the world, he blamed the world, he blamed *samsara.* He said, "It is because of the world that I am in misery." It is not so. The world is immensely beautiful – it is all beauty, bliss and benediction. There is nothing wrong with the world. Something was wrong with the old mind. The old mind was either past-oriented or future-oriented – which are not really different orientations. The old mind was concerned with that which is not.

The New Man will be utterly in tune with that which is, because that is God, that is reality: *iti iti*, this is it. This moment has to be lived in its totality. This moment has to be lived in its spontaneity, with no a priori ideas. The Old Man was carrying ready-made answers. He was stuffed with philosophy, religion and all kinds of nonsense.

The New Man is going to live life without any a priori conclusion about it. Without any conclusion, one has to face existence and then one knows what it is. If you have already concluded, your conclusion will become a barrier, it will not allow you inquiry. Your conclusion will become a blindfold, it will not allow you to see the truth. Your investment will be in the conclusion, you will distort reality to fit your conclusion. That's what has been done up to now.

The New Man will not be Hindu, will not be Mohammedan, will not be Christian, will not be communist. The New Man will not know all these "isms." The New Man will be simply an opening, a window to reality. He will allow reality as it is. He will not project his own mind upon it, he will not use reality as a screen. His eyes will be available, they will not be full of ideas.

The New Man will not live out of belief, he will simply live. And remember, those who can simply live without belief, only come to know what truth is. The believer or the disbeliever never come to know what truth is – their beliefs are too heavy on their minds, they are surrounded too much by their belief systems. The New Man will not know any belief system. He will watch, he will observe, he will see, he will live, and he will allow all kinds of experiences. He will be available, he will be multidimensional. He will not carry scriptures in his head, he will carry only alertness, awareness. He will be meditative.

The Old Man lived out of fear – even his God was nothing but a creation out of fear. His temples, mosques, *gurdwaras,* churches – they were all out of fear. He was trembling, he was afraid. The New Man will live out of love, not out of fear, because fear serves death, love serves life. And if you live out of fear you will never know what life is, you will only know death, again and again.

And remember, the person who lives out of fear creates all kinds of situations in which he has to feel more and more fear. Your fear creates situations, just as your love creates situations: if you love you will find so many occasions to be loving, if you are afraid you will find so many occasions to be afraid. Love is going to be the taste of the new consciousness.

Because fear was the taste of the old consciousness it created wars. In three thousand years man has fought five thousand wars – as if we have not been doing anything else – continuous fighting somewhere or other. This is a very mad state of affairs, humanity's past is insane.

The New Man will become discontinuous with this insane past. He will believe in love, not in war. He will believe in life, not in death. He will be creative, not destructive. His science, his art – all will serve creativity. He will not create bombs. He will not be political, because politics is out of hatred. Politics is rooted in fear, hate, destructiveness. The New Man will not be political, the New Man will not be national. The New Man will be global. He will not have any political ambition, because it is stupid to have political ambition. The New Man is going to be very intelligent. The first signs of that intelligence are rising on the horizon. Those who have eyes, they can see it: the children are rebelling.

It is a great moment of rejoicing that the young people all over the world are rebelling against all kinds of orthodoxies – whether the orthodoxy is that of church or state doesn't matter. They are not ready to obey – not that they have determined to disobey, they are not determined to disobey either. They will meditate, and if they feel like obeying they will obey, if they feel like disobeying they will disobey. They have no fixed ideology. "My country right or wrong" – such stupid statements they cannot make. Sometimes it is wrong, sometimes it is right. When it is right, the New Man will support it, when it is wrong whether it is one's own country or not doesn't matter. It may be one's own family – one's own father, mother – but if it is wrong, it is wrong.

The New Man will live not out of prejudices but out of spontaneous responsibility. The Old Man was a slave, the New Man will be free. The New Man will have freedom at the very core of his being.

The Old Man was very serious, the Old Man was a workaholic. The New Man will be playful – *homo ludens*. He will believe in enjoying life. He will drop words like *duty*, *sacrifice*. He will not sacrifice for anything. He will not be a victim to any altar – that of the state or of the religion, of the priest or of the politician. He will not allow anybody to exploit his life that "Go and die because your country is at war." His commitment is towards life, his commitment is not towards anything else. He wants to live in joy, he wants to rejoice in all the gifts of God, he wants to celebrate. Alleluia will be his only mantra.

Jesus says, "Rejoice, rejoice. I say unto you rejoice."

Man has not rejoiced yet. Man has lived under a great burden of seriousness. Work for the country, work for the family, work for the wife, work for the children, work for your father and mother – just go on working and working and then one day die and disappear into the grave. And then others will work and it goes on and on. Nobody seems to have any time to enjoy life.

And I am not saying that the New Man will not work. He will work, but that will not be his addiction, he will not be a workaholic. It will not be a drug to him. He will work because he needs a few things, but he will not continuously work for more and more. He will not be accumulative. He will not believe in having a big bank balance, and he will not believe in being on a very high post. Rather, he would like to sing a song, play on the flute, on the guitar, dance. He would not like to become famous. He would like to live, authentically live. He will be ready to be a nobody.

And that is already happening. The first rays are already available. It is still hidden in the morning mist, but if you search you will find: the new children, the new generation, are a totally different kind of generation. Hence the generation gap, it is very real. It has never been so – never before has there been any generation gap. This is the first time in the whole of human history that there is a gap. The children are speaking a different language from their parents. The parents cannot understand because the parents want them to succeed. And the children say, "But what is the point of success if you cannot sing a song and you cannot dance, and you cannot enjoy and you cannot love, what is the point of being successful? Why? What is going to happen through success? Even if the whole world knows my name, what is that going to give me?"

The old generation believes in money. And you will be surprised, that the belief in money is so deep that even those who renounce money, they also believe in money; otherwise there is no need to renounce it. And those who praise renunciation, they also believe in money: the more money you renounce, the greater you are. So the measurement is through money, money remains the criterion. In the world if you have more money you are great. And even in the world of the monks: "How much have you renounced?" If you have renounced more money, then you are more important. Money remains important even there.

The new generation is not going to be money-manic. And remember, I am not saying it is going to be against money – it will *use* money. In the past money has used man, in the past man has lived in such an unconscious way that he thought he possessed things, but things possessed him. The New Man will be able to use: the New Man will use money, will use technology, but the New Man will remain the master. He is not going to become a victim, an instrument. This, according to me, is the greatest thing that is happening. A few characteristics....

The new consciousness is going to be counter to all orthodoxies – any kind of orthodoxy, Catholic or communist, Hindu or Jaina. Any kind of orthodoxy is a kind of paralysis of the mind – it paralyzes, you stop living. It becomes a rigidity around you. You become a fanatic, you become stubborn, you become rock-like. You don't behave like a liquid human being, you start behaving like a mule. That's why for Morarji Desai I have another name: Mulishjibhai Desai. One starts behaving in a mulish way – stubborn, dead set, no possibility of changing, no flexibility, no fluidity. But in the past that has been praised very much: people call it consistency, certainty. It is not. It is neither consistency nor certainty. It is simply deadness.

An alive person has to remain flowing. He has to respond to the changing situations – and situations are continuously changing. How can you remain fixed in your attitudes when life itself is not fixed? When life is a river how can you remain stubborn? And if you remain stubborn you lose contact with life, you are already in your grave.

The new consciousness will be non-orthodox, non-fanatic. It will be fluid. It will not react, it will respond. And the difference between these two words is great.

Reaction is always rigid: you have a fixed idea, you react out of it; before the question is raised, the answer is ready. Response is totally different: you listen to the question, you absorb the question, you see the situation, you feel the situation, you live the situation and out of that very living, your response arises. A responsible man cannot be stubborn, cannot be certain, cannot be rigid. He will have to live moment to moment. He cannot decide beforehand. He will have to decide every day, each moment. And because he has to move continuously with life, its changing challenges, he cannot be consistent in the old sense. His consistency will be only one: that he will always be in tune with life. That will be his consistency, not that he has a certain idea and he remains consistent with that idea, and goes on sacrificing life for it.

There was a case against Mulla Nasrudin in the court and the magistrate asked him, "Mulla, how old are you?"

He said, "Forty."

The magistrate said, "But this is strange. You surprise me, because five years ago you were in court and that time also you said forty."

Mulla said, "Yes, I am a consistent man. Once I have said something, you can believe me. I will never say anything else."

This is one type of consistency.

The new man will find it ridiculous. But the Old Man has been this way, consistent: in his character, in his statements, in his hypocrisy. The Old Man used to decide once and for all.

Psychologists say that almost fifty percent of your life is decided by the time you are seven years old – fifty percent! – and then you remain consistent with it. And life goes on changing – no wonder that you are left behind, that you start dragging, that you lose joy, that you lose the quality of dance. How can you dance? – you are so far behind life, you are dead wood, you don't grow. An alive tree grows, changes; as the season changes, the tree changes. An alive person continuously grows. To the very moment of death he goes on growing.

Psychologists say the average mental age of man is thirteen. This is the situation, this is how the Old Man has lived up to now. A thirteen-year mental age means at the age of thirteen people have stopped growing. Yes, they go on growing old, but they don't grow up. Growing old is one thing, but growing up is totally different. Growing old is a physiological phenomenon, whilst growing up means wisdom. Only those who go on flowing with life grow up.

The New Man will not be obedient to silly ideas that have been given from the past – and they may not have been stupid when they were born, they may have been relevant in those circumstances. But as circumstances change, things become stupid. If you carry them, if you go on persisting in your old fixed routines, you start behaving in an absurd way.

Now, look: some religion is five thousand years old – that means five thousand years ago its rituals were born and since then they have remained fixed. How dangerous it is, how crippling! How can man be alive if these five-thousand-year-old rituals surround his soul?

The New Man will be creative. Each moment he will find his religion, each moment he will find his philosophy, and everything will remain growing. He will not be obedient to the past, he cannot be. To be obedient to the past is to be obedient to death because the past is dead. He will be obedient to the present, and in being obedient to the present, he will be rebellious against the past.

To be rebellious is going to be one of his most prominent characteristics. And because he will be rebellious he will not fit in a dead society, he will not fit in a dead church, he will not fit in a dead army. He will not fit anywhere where obedience is a basic requirement. The New Man is bound to create a new society around himself.

First consciousness becomes new, then the society becomes new. There is going to be a long period in which the old will resist the new, will fight with the new, will try to destroy the new. But the old cannot succeed. Time, time spirit, will not be in its favor – the old has to die. Just as the old body dies and makes space for some new child, so old societies, old orthodoxies, have to die. They have already lived overtime, they have lived too long.

The new consciousness will not be moralistic, will not be puritan – not that it will not have any morality. But it will have a different kind of morality – a morality that arises out of one's own feeling for life, one's sensitivity, one's own experiences – not a morality learned from others, borrowed. The New Man will not be a man of character in the old sense, because all character is binding. It creates an armor around you. The New Man will be characterless in the sense that he will not have any armor, and in the sense that he will not have a prison cell around him. He will give a new definition to character. He will not be a hypocrite.

The old puritanism, the old moralistic attitudes have created hypocrisy in the world. They have made man schizophrenic: on the surface one thing, deep within something else, almost the opposite. The Old Man lived a double life. The New Man is going to live in a unitary way. He will live a single life. Whatsoever is inside him will also be his outside. He will be authentic. Remember this word *authenticity* – that is going to be the New Man's religion. That is going to be the New Man's truth, his temple, his God: authenticity. And with authenticity, neurosis disappears. The Old Man was neurotic because he was constantly in conflict: he wanted to do one thing and he was always doing something else, because something else was required. He was taught to do something against himself, he was repressive. His own authenticity was repressed, and on top of it, a bogus character was imposed.

We have praised these phony people too long. Now the time has come: their phoniness should be exposed. We have praised these mahatmas and saints so long. Now we have to see their neurosis: they were all psychologically ill, they were pathological.

A healthy person is a whole person. His inside, his outside are the same. If he loves he loves passionately, if he is angry he is angry passionately. His anger has truth in it as much as his love has truth in it. The Old Man boils within and smiles on the outside. He lives without passion, without energy. He lives without any flame. His whole life is an exercise in phoniness, and naturally he suffers. A long futile story is all that his life is: "...a tale told by an idiot, full of sound and fury, signifying nothing."

The New Man will not be a tale told by an idiot but will be a poetry sung out of wholeness, will be a dance of immense joy for God's gift of life and being – for the flowers and the trees and the birds and the sun and the sand and the sea. The New Man will not look somewhere faraway for God. He will look here, close-by. Now will be his only time, here will be his only space.

The New Man will be earthly, and by "earthly" I don't mean materialistic. The New Man will be a realist, he will love this earth. Because we have not loved this earth and our so-called religions have been teaching us to hate this earth, we have destroyed it. It is a beautiful planet, one of the most beautiful, because it is one of the most alive. This planet has to be loved, this planet has to be rejoiced – it is a gift. This body has so many mysteries in it that even a Buddha is possible only because of this body. This body becomes the temple of the greatest possibility: buddhahood, nirvana. This body has to be loved, this earth has to be loved.

The New Man will find his religion in nature – not in dead stone statues, but in living dancing trees in the wind. He will find his religion surfing on the sea, climbing on the virgin mountain. He will find his prayer with the snow, with the moon, with the stars. He will be in dialogue with existence as it is. He will not live with abstract ideas. He will live with realities. His commitment will be with nature, and through that commitment he will come to know super-nature. God is hidden here in this earth, in this very body: this very body the buddha, this very Earth the paradise.

The New Man will read the scripture of nature. This will be his Veda, his Koran, his Bible. Here he will find sermons in the stones. He will try to decipher the mysteries of life, but he will not try to demystify life. He will try to love those mysteries, to enter in those mysteries. He will be a poet, he will not be a philosopher. He will be an artist, he will not be a theologian. His science will also have a different tone. His science will be that of Tao – not an effort to conquer nature, because that effort is just foolish. How can you conquer nature? – you are part of nature. His science will be of understanding nature, not of conquering nature. He will not rape nature, he will love and persuade nature to reveal its secrets.

The New Man will not be ambitious, will not be political. Politics has no future. Politics has existed because of the neurosis of humankind. Once the neurosis disappears, politics will disappear.

Ambition simply means you are missing something and you are consoling yourself that in the future, you will get it. Ambition is a consolation: today it is all misery, tomorrow there will be joy. Looking at tomorrow you become capable of tolerating today and its misery. Today is always hell, tomorrow is heaven: you keep on looking at heaven, you keep on hoping. But that hope is not going to be fulfilled ever because tomorrow never comes.

Ambition means you are incapable of transforming your today into a beatitude, you are impotent. Only impotent people are ambitious: they seek money, they seek power. Only impotent people seek power and money. The potential person lives. If money comes his way, he lives with money too, but he does not seek it, he is not after it. He is not afraid of it either.

The old man was either after money or afraid of money, either after power or afraid of power, but in both ways his whole focus was on power and money. He was ambitious. The Old Man is pitiable: he was ambitious because he was unable to live, unable to love. The New Man will be able to live and able to love. And his here and now is going to be so beautiful, why should he be worried about tomorrow? His concern will not be having more, his concern will be being more – another very important distinction to be remembered. Having more is just a substitute for being more. You may have more money – you think you are more, you have more power – you think you are more. Deep down you remain the same beggar. Alexander the Great dies as empty-handed as any beggar.

Being more is a totally different dimension. Being more means getting in touch with your reality, getting in tune with your being, and helping yourself to fall in harmony with the universe. The more you are in tune with existence, the more you are. If the harmony is total, you are a god. That's why we call Buddha a god, Mahavira a god: utter total harmony with existence, no conflict at all. They have dissolved themselves into the whole, they have become the whole, just as a dewdrop disappears into the ocean and becomes the ocean. They have died in their egos, now they live as existence itself.

The New Man will have no use for sham, facade or pretense. He will be true, because only through truth is liberation. All lies create bondages. Tell a single lie and you will have to tell a thousand and one to defend it, ad nauseam you will have to tell lies. Then there is no end to it: a single lie sooner or later will spread all over your being – it is like cancer.

Be truthful and you need not hide. You can be open. Be truthful – you need not protect yourself against existence. You can be vulnerable. In that vulnerability existence penetrates you, God reaches to your heart.

Tell a lie and you are afraid. You will be afraid of God too, you will be afraid of facing him, you will be afraid of facing yourself. You will be continuously escaping – from yourself, from others, from God. You will be constantly hiding behind your pretensions, hypocrisy will become your lifestyle, and that's where hell exists. Hypocrisy creates hell. Authenticity is the only joy – the only joy, I say. And if you are not authentic you will never be joyous.

The new consciousness will not put up with double-talk. The new consciousness will hate this kind of thing with a passion. This hatred for phoniness is the deepest mark of the New Man. The New Man will be opposed to structured, inflexible and infallible systems, because life is a beautiful flow. It is not structured, it is freedom. It is not a prison, it is a temple. He would like organizations to be fluid, changing, adapting and human. Our states are inhuman, our armies are inhuman, our churches are inhuman. They dehumanize man, they reduce man into a thing because they don't respect man's freedom. The New Man will respect *his* freedom and respect the freedom of others too.

The Old Man is constantly interfering, poking his nose into everybody's affairs, trying to manipulate, criticizing, condemning, rewarding, punishing. The Old Man is continuously concerned with others: "What are you doing?" I was staying in Bombay once. A Parsi woman came to me because just the day before I had criticized Satya Sai Baba and had called him a phony guru. The Parsi woman came to see me and she said, "I have come to tell you a few more things." She was thinking that I would be very happy because she had brought some information against Satya Sai Baba. She said, "He is a homosexual. And I know it from reliable sources."

I said, "But why should you be concerned? Homosexual or heterosexual – that is his business. It is his life. Who are you? Why should you be bothered about it?"

She was very shocked when I said that. She had come feeling that I would be very grateful to her because she was giving me such great information. Why should you be concerned? Can't you leave people to their own life? I criticize only when the other's life is concerned; otherwise there is no question. What Satya Sai Baba is doing with his sexuality is his business, it is nobody else's business. But the Old Man was constantly poking his nose into everybody's affairs.

Here it happens every day: the old kind of people come and they are very much in agony because some man is holding some woman's hand. Why? But he is not holding your hand. And if those two persons have decided to hold hands, they have absolute freedom to do that. And if they are enjoying, who are you to interfere? If the man is holding some woman's hand against her will, then maybe your help is needed, but if they both are willing then you should not be concerned at all.

But this is the old consciousness. It was always trying to find ways and means to manipulate others, to be dominant over others. The new consciousness will leave everyone to his own life. Unless somebody is harming others, he should not be prevented. Unless somebody is a danger to others, he should not be prevented. Unless somebody is interfering in somebody else's freedom, he should not be interfered with.

The old world remained without individuality – it hated individuality! It liked only sheep, crowds – people behaving in the same way and everybody following the same routine and the same structure. The New Man will allow all kinds of possibilities. The New Man will love liquid structures. He will be human, he will respect human beings. His respect will be almost religious.

The New Man will have to find new forms of community, of closeness, of intimacy, of shared purpose, because the old society is not going to disappear immediately – it will linger. It will give all kinds of fight to the new society – as it always happens. It has so many vested interests, it cannot go easily. It will go only when it becomes impossible for it to remain in existence.

Before it goes the New Man will have to create new kinds of communes, new kinds of families, new communities of closeness, intimacy, shared purpose. That's why I am trying to create a small commune where you can be totally yourself – away from the structured and the rotten world – and you can be given absolute freedom. It will be an experimentation, because on those lines, the future is going to move. It will be a small experiment but of immense significance.

The new consciousness will not have anything to do with institutions like marriage. The New Man will have a natural distrust of marriage *as* an institution. A man-woman relationship has deep value for him only when it is a mutually enhancing, growing, flowing relationship. He will have little regard for marriage as a ceremony or for vows of permanence...which prove to be highly impermanent. He loves the moment and lives it in its totality. Marriage has no future. Love has a future.

In the past, love was not a reality, marriage was a reality. In the future, love is going to be the reality and marriage is going to become more and more unreal. In the past people were married to each other, hence by and by they started liking and loving. In the future people will love and like each other, only then will they live together. In the past to live together came first, and naturally when you live together a liking arises, a dependence arises. It was a need phenomenon; the husband needed the wife, the wife needed the husband, and then the children needed the parents to be together. It was more or less an economic phenomenon, but it was not out of love.

The future will know a different kind of relationship which is based purely on love and remains in existence only while love remains. And there is no hankering for its permanence, because in life nothing is permanent; only plastic flowers are permanent. Real roses are born in the morning and are gone by the evening. And that is their beauty: they are beautiful when they come, they are beautiful when their petals start withering away. Their life is beautiful, their birth is beautiful, their death is beautiful, because there is aliveness. A plastic flower is never born, never lives, never dies.

Marriage has been a plastic flower in the past. The new consciousness can have no respect for marriage. It will have to create a new kind of intimacy – friendship – and it will have to learn to live with the impermanent phenomenon of love and of everything.

It needs guts to live with the impermanence of life because each time something changes you have to change yourself again. One wants to remain fixed – it seems safer, secure. That's how the Old Man has lived: the Old Man was not adventurous, his whole concern was security.

The New Man will have the spirit of adventure. His concern will not be security, his concern will be ecstasy. He will not believe, because belief is a search for security – he will explore. He may not have neat answers to every question, but he will accept every challenge to inquiry, to exploration. He will go as far as life can take him. He will try to reach to the stars. But he will remain open. He will not start with a belief, with a conclusion, he will start only with a quest, a question.

To start with a belief is not to start at all. To start with a belief is just playing a game with yourself. You have already believed – how can you explore? To explore one has to be agnostic, and that is going to be the religion of the future:

agnosticism. One will be capable and courageous enough to say, "I don't know, but I am interested in knowing. And I am ready to go into any dimension, into any adventure."

The New Man will be ready to risk. The Old Man was very businesslike, never ready to risk: risk was anathema, security was his goal. But with security you start dying. It is only in adventure, continuous adventure, that life grows to higher and higher plenitudes, that it reaches to the Himalayan peaks.

The new person will be a spontaneous person – unpredictable, willing to risk newness, often willing to risk saying or doing the wild, the far-out thing. He will believe that everything is possible and anything can be tried. He will not cling to the known, he will always remain available to the unknown, even to the unknowable. And he will not sacrifice for any future because he will not be an idealist. He will not sacrifice for any abstract ideas, ideals, ideologies. He has a trust in his own experience and a profound distrust of all external authority.

The New Man will trust only his own experience. Unless he knows, he will not trust it. No external authority can help the New Man. Nobody can say, "I say so, so you have to believe, because we have always believed so you have to believe, because our forefathers believed so you have to believe, because it is written in the Vedas and the Bible, you have to believe." The New Man is not going to have anything to do with such nonsense. The New Man will believe only if *he* knows. This is real trust: trust in one's own possibilities, potential. The New Man will respect himself. To believe in external authorities is disrespectful towards one's own being.

And, finally, the New Man will like to be close to elemental nature: to the sea, the sun, the snow, flowers, animals, birds, to life, growth, death.

This, according to me, is the most important phenomenon that is happening today: a New Man is coming into existence, the first rays are already on the horizon. Prepare yourself to receive the New Man, get ready – become a host to the guest who is going, just any moment, to knock on your doors. And that's what sannyas is all about: a preparation – getting ready to receive the New Man. It is going to be a great adventure to receive the New Man, it is going to be risky too, because the old will not like it.

Now you can understand why the orthodox mind is against me: I am preparing their graveyard and I am preparing for something new – I am preparing a garden for the new. You are to open your hearts for the new, uproot all the weeds of the old, drop all the conditionings that the old has given to you so you can receive the new. And remember, the days of the messiahs are over. Don't wait for Christ's coming again, and don't wait for Buddha's coming again. Nobody comes again, not at least Buddha and Christ. Those who come again are the people who live without learning anything from life. Buddha has learned the lesson – he will not be coming again. Christ has learned the lesson – he will not be coming again. Don't wait for any messiah to come but wait for a *new* consciousness, not for a messiah to deliver you. That is what the Old Man used to believe: somebody will come. Hindus think Krishna will come: "When things are really dark and difficult and dismal, Krishna will come and deliver us." All nonsense! All holy cowdung!

A new consciousness is going to deliver you, not some person – Buddha, Krishna, Christ. They had been here and they could not deliver. No single person can do it – it is impossible. A new consciousness can only deliver man from his bondage. And the new consciousness can come only through you: you have to become the womb, you have to accept it, receive it, prepare yourself for it.

Sannyas is nothing but getting ready for something immensely valuable, so that when the gift comes you are not fast asleep, so when the new consciousness knocks on your door you are ready to embrace it.

The second question:

> Osho,
> Oh that I could have died of the shame that you've been nauseated
> by me…. Thank you for such a drastic reason to give up non-
> vegetarian habits. It hasn't arisen out of my own awareness yet,
> and I suspect this was my conditioning. My childhood was ruled
> by Jewish dietary laws and rituals – there were so many foods
> forbidden by my father, forbidden by his fathers for the so-called
> "chosen people."
>
> Maybe an external, non-existential morality imposed on my early
> years blunted my sensitivity? But now it hurts so much to have
> nauseated you. This decision and a small light fill me.

Pradeepa, it is not that *you* nauseated me, something in you… And of course, you are unconscious, that is why I have been so drastic and hard on you: so that you can become conscious of it. Just a habit… And when a person is born in a non-vegetarian family it is natural to learn the ways of the family, just as vegetarians learn the ways of a vegetarian family. Both are unconscious.

And I don't give any value to the unconscious vegetarian – he is not superior to the unconscious non-vegetarian – because both are unconscious. Only consciousness has value. If you are consciously vegetarian then there is some value in it, otherwise there is no value.

In India there are so many vegetarians – unconscious – just because by accident in their childhood, they were taught vegetarianism – they have learned it. You have learned in the same way, non-vegetarian habits. You are both alike. There is no difference – not at all – not even the difference of an inch. Unconsciousness is unconsciousness. What you do out of unconsciousness is a robot-like phenomenon.

I had to hit so hard on Pradeepa's head so that she becomes a little more alert. I hit you only because I love you. And remember, the more you will become meditative, the more your non-vegetarian habits will be more nauseating. When a person comes, new to me – who has not meditated, who has no intimacy with me, no love for me, who is not close to me – his vibe is not nauseating to me. Why? – because his whole vibe is the same. But when a person starts meditating, starts becoming more and more silent – as is happening to Pradeepa, her energy is moving in beautiful dimensions – now a disparity will be felt.

It is just like on white cloth, a little dirt will show; on black cloth it won't show. When your whole being is unconscious and there is no silence and all is noise, you can be non-vegetarian – it will not make much difference, it will not show. There is no contrast to show it. You can even be a cannibal and it will not show. But when you start getting clean – some space inside becomes fresh, young, natural, some part of you becomes clear, is purified – then the dirt shows. Then even small things will show.

Pradeepa, you should be happy that I could see it so clearly that something inside you, just out of old habit, is poisoning your whole being. If it is dropped you will have a great leap, your growth will be immensely enhanced.

And I am here only to facilitate your growth. And I will do everything that I can do: if a shock is needed I will shock you, if you need hammering on the head I will hammer you. Whatsoever is needed has to be done – nothing has to be left undone, all possible methods have to be tried – because your entanglements with the past are deep, there are many many sources and they all have to be cut.

Slowly slowly you will arise out of your past completely free. That shock can become a transformation in you. And I hope that it has already changed you. And I hope, next time you come to me, that vibe will have disappeared.

But you will have to remain conscious, alert – old habits die hard, they persist. And remember, you cannot deceive me. Your mind can say, "If once in a while you eat non-vegetarian food how is Osho going to know?" It is not so. If you do something, your whole vibe will express it: your guilt will show it, your shame will show it, your face will show it. You will not be flowing when you will be close to me. You will be afraid, you will be caught again.

And remember, I am not against non-vegetarian foods for any other reasons. If a man is not meditating, if a man is not trying to grow inwards, if a man is not in the search of God, then it is perfectly okay – he can eat whatsoever he wants to eat. The higher you are trying to reach, more and more unnecessary luggage will have to be dropped, only then you can fly. These are unnecessary luggages, they can be dropped.

But remember, it is not that *you* have nauseated me, just an unconscious habit in you that has nauseated me. And you are not your habit – the habit can be dropped – and you will come closer to me and you will be able to receive more of my love. And you don't know how much I have to give to you; you only know that much that you receive. And you receive only that much that you *can* receive.

Become more and more capable of receiving more and more – there is no end to it. This place can become your absolute fulfillment.

The third question:

Osho,
I want to say many things to you. Should I write them to you or not?

Meditate on this small story.

"Have you heard, O Socrates…"
"Just a moment, friend," said the sage. "Have you sifted what you are going to tell me through the three sieves?"
"The three sieves?"
"Yes, my friend. Let us see whether what you mean to tell me will stand the test. The first of the sieves is that of truth: have you made sure that all you are going to tell me is true?"
"Well, no. I just heard others say it."
"I see. Insofar as it is not even true, we can scarcely bother with it, unless it happens to be something good. Will it stand the test of the sieve of goodness?"

"Oh no, indeed, on the contrary…"

"Hmm, 'I'm not sure he said it, and what he is supposed to have said serves no good'? Perhaps somehow it is necessary that I know this in order to prevent harm to others?"

"Well, no. If you look at it in that way…"

"Very well then," said Socrates, "since what you have come to tell me about the case is neither true nor good nor needful, let us forget all about it. There are so many worthwhile things in life, that we can't afford to bother with what is so worthless as to be neither good nor true nor needful."

Meditate on this statement of Socrates…and you will know: what to write to me, what not to write to me, what to ask, what not to ask.

There are a few people who go on writing letters every day. It is not a problem to me – just Arup is troubled. She has to read hundreds of letters, sometimes late in the night… Look, she is fast asleep. She has to sleep sometime! Late in the night she has to go on reading those letters and summarizing them – don't torture her!

Unless it is really important, something valuable, something which will help you or somebody else, don't write. If you feel it is of some importance then certainly you can write. And then too, make it as short as possible, make it telegraphic. There is no need to write long long letters. A few people are very much into writing letters – ten pages, twelve pages. Just write a few sentences, just say exactly what you want to say. And before you write anything, ponder over this statement of Socrates – it will help you: let them pass through the three sieves.

The last question:

> *Osho,*
> *Why don't you say exactly what your philosophy is?*

And what am I doing every day? Morning and evening I am continuously doing that. But maybe you have some ideas already fixed in your mind and you would like my philosophy to fit and adjust with those ideas – and it is not going to fit. Hence you feel puzzled, confused.

I am not here really, trying to give you a set doctrine. I am trying to *provoke* something in you. It is not a question of giving you an exact statement, of what my philosophy is. Rather, I am a challenge to provoke you: into thinking, into meditating. Something is lying dormant in you and it has to be provoked – I am hammering it. It is not that I have to give you a philosophy and you have to believe in it – then the whole point will be missed.

I am not a philosopher and I am not trying to give you a dogma in which you have to believe. In fact, I am just doing the opposite: I am destroying all dogmas and all philosophies – this is my philosophy! I am trying to create a vacuum in you, because when the vacuum is there the dormant energy in you will immediately start rising – it needs some space to rise. But you must be having some ideas. People come to me....

There was one Christian missionary who said, "It will be very good if you write a small book, a catechism, just as we Christians have done – just a few statements of all that you want to teach."

I cannot give you a catechism because I have none. I respond to your potential, to your possibilities – this way and that I provoke you. And I will go on provoking...unless you are awakened!

But if you have a Christian-missionary type mind, you will be waiting: that I will deliver to you a few fixed statements, so that you can believe in them for ever and ever. I cannot do that to you, because that is harmful, that is poisoning you. And if that mind is there, you will not be able to understand what I am doing here. It is a totally different kind of work...

A famous film star announced that she was about to get married for the sixth time. "Oh," said Mulla Nasruddin. "Against whom?"

People have their own understandings. Now Mulla's experience of marriage is such that he can ask only one thing: "Against whom?"

I said to Mulla Nasruddin one day, "I hear your daughter has got married. I am sure you found it hard to part with her."
"Hard?" he said. "It was almost impossible."

People have their own deep-rooted ideas: they listen from those conclusions. He was trying to get rid of her, he was trying hard to get rid of her – he was very worried. So when I said, "I am sure you found it hard to part with her," this was his reaction: "Hard?" he said. "It was almost impossible."

One day I asked Mulla Nasruddin, "Hi, Mulla! How is your wife?"

He looked at me and said, "Compared to what?"

You must be listening with your mind all intact: you will have to put it aside. Then you will see that it is not a verbal transmission that I am making here, it is an energy transmission – I am trying to contact *you* – your mind is in between. I am trying in every way to destroy your mind, I am taking away all your knowledge – making it look ridiculous, absurd.

First you start feeling confused because you were so certain, and when I go on hitting hard on your knowledge, you start feeling confused. And then problems arise: you were thinking that you would become clear and now you are becoming confused. In the beginning it is going to happen: certainty destroyed, you become confused. But only when you are confused can you drop all your knowledge, not before it. When the confusion becomes too much, maddening, one day you simply drop it – it is no more possible to carry it any longer. And then you will understand what I am doing here to you.

I am not giving you any philosophy. I am provoking your understanding. It is not a verbal doctrine. It is a heart-to-heart communion, a soul-to-soul communion – I am trying to connect with you. And in that connection, a spark from my being will jump into your being, and your inner will be lit – just a small spark is needed and there will be great light in you – and that light will give you eyes to see, ears to hear, heart to feel. That light will make you alive, that light will bloom in you as a Golden Flower.

Enough for today.

CHAPTER 15

Beyond Indolence and Distraction

Master Lu-tsu said:
The two mistakes of indolence and distraction must be combated
by quiet work that is carried on daily without interruption;
then success will certainly be achieved. If one is not seated in
meditation, one will often be distracted without noticing it. To
become conscious of the distraction is the mechanism by which to
do away with distraction. Indolence of which man is conscious,
and indolence of which man is unconscious, are a thousand miles
apart. Unconscious indolence is real indolence; conscious indolence
is not complete indolence, because there is still some clarity in it.
Distraction comes from letting the mind wander about; indolence
comes from the mind's not yet being pure. Distraction is much
easier to correct than indolence. It is as in sickness: if one feels
pains and irritations, one can help them with remedies, but
indolence is like a disease that is attended by lack of realization.
Distraction can be counteracted, confusion can be straightened
out, but indolence and lethargy are heavy and dark. Distraction
and confusion at least have a place, but in indolence and lethargy
the anima alone is active. In distraction the animus is still present,
but in indolence pure darkness rules. If one becomes sleepy during
meditation, that is an effect of indolence. Only breathing serves

to overcome indolence. Although the breath that flows in and out through the nose is not the true breath, the flowing in and out of the true breath takes place in connection with it.

While sitting, one must therefore always keep the heart quiet and the energy concentrated. How can the heart be made quiet? By the breath. Only the heart must be conscious of the flowing in and out of the breath; it must not be heard with the ears. If it is not heard, then the breathing is light; if light, it is pure. If it can be heard, then the breath-energy is rough; if rough, then it is troubled; if it is troubled, then indolence and lethargy develop and one wants to sleep. That is self-evident.

How to use the heart correctly during breathing must be understood. It is a use without use. One should only let the light fall quite gently on the hearing. This sentence contains a secret meaning. What does it mean to let the light fall? It is the spontaneous radiation of the light of the eyes. The eye looks inward only and not outward. To sense brightness without looking outward means to look inward; it has nothing to do with an actual looking within. What does hearing mean? It is the spontaneous hearing of the light of the ear. The ear listens inwardly only and does not listen to what is outside. To sense brightness without listening to what is outside is to listen inwardly; it has nothing to do with actually listening to what is within. In this sort of hearing, one hears only that there is no sound; in this kind of seeing, one sees only that no shape is there. If the eye is not looking outward and the ear is not harkening outward, they close themselves and are inclined to sink inward. Only when one looks and harkens inward does the organ not go outward nor sink inward. In this way indolence and lethargy are done away with. That is the union of the seed and the light of the sun and the moon.

If, as a result of indolence, one becomes sleepy, one should stand up and walk about. When the mind has become clear one should sit down again. In the course of time there will be success without one's becoming indolent and falling asleep.

One hot afternoon an owl was sitting in a tree and a swan flew up and sat there too.

"Phew, it is hot, Brother Owl," he said. "The sun is bright and I am all hot and sweaty."

"What?" said the owl. "What? What are you talking about? Sun? Hot? When darkness gathers it gets hot. What is this sun you are talking about? Are you mad or something? What are you trying to tell me? There is no such thing as the sun. There has never been. What is this light that gets hot? We have never heard about it. It gets hot when darkness gathers. Are you trying to make a fool of me? And I'm not alone in saying so. All our scriptures also say so."

The swan was flabbergasted with all this. "How can I explain it to this blind old owl?" he thought.

"Look, brother, I can see with my eyes – it is the middle of the day and the sun is shining brightly and it is very hot. You are saying that it is dark? How can I explain it to you?"

"Let us go then," said the owl. "There is a big tree over there where there are lots of owls and great scholars too. We will ask them about it – and they know all about the scriptures, and a few of them are very learned. Come on. We will see if you are making a fool of me."

They flew over and there were many many blind owls there. "This swan has turned up," the owl said, "and he says that it is the middle of the day and the sun is beating down and that there is light everywhere and that's why it is hot. What do you people say?"

"What is all this?" they cried. "Our fathers and their fathers and their fathers, in fact the whole of our community has never seen a sun, so there is no such thing as a sun. How can it be there? He is having you on. Don't listen to him. He is either mad or a very fraudulent fellow. He is trying to corrupt our religion. We have always lived in darkness and we have always worshipped darkness. It is the very foundation of our way of life. He will destroy our way of life. That is the sort of person he is. If you want, we will take a majority vote on it."

One owl got up and said, "What is the truth? Does darkness exist or does light?"

"Darkness, and darkness alone," they all cried in unison.

"Why then has it got so hot?"

"Because it is so dark," they cried. "Heat is a function of darkness."

"Don't let him stay here," they all cried again. "He will spoil our religion, our tradition, our very cherished past. Drive him away immediately. He is either totally blind or utterly mad."

This small parable contains a few truths of immense value.

First: truth cannot be transferred – there is no way to transfer it – my truth is my truth. I can talk about it to you, but talking about it is not transferring it to you, listening to it is not understanding it. You will have to open your own eyes.

The function of a real master is not to say to you that God exists but to help you to open your eyes, to open your windows of the soul so that you can see, so that you can realize the meaning of the word *God* in your own bones, in your own blood, in your very marrow. I cannot see for you through my eyes and I cannot walk for you with my legs and I cannot fly for you with my wings. You will have to live your life and you will have to die your death.

This is one of the most fundamental things to be remembered; otherwise one becomes burdened with borrowed knowledge which is not knowledge at all but a pseudo coin. It looks like knowledge, hence it can deceive you.

And that's what has happened to humanity: humanity is living under the curse of borrowed knowledge. People go on reciting the Bible, the Koran, the Gita like parrots – blind old owls reciting the Koran, the Gita, the Bible. But this is not their own experience; their own experience is just the opposite. Their own experience simply denies the truth of the Gita and the Bible and the Vedas and the Dhammapada. Their own experience simply says that "Buddha is mad," that "Jesus is deceiving us," that "Socrates may be very clever, but beware of him, don't listen to him. He will destroy our religion."

Man has created a religion with his blind eyes – not one, many religions – because blind eyes cannot see the one, blind eyes can only believe in the many. Hence there are so many religions – nearabout three hundred religions on this small earth – and each religion proclaiming that, "My truth is the only truth," that, "My God is the only God," that, "All other Gods are false," that, "All other truths are fabrications," that, "All other paths only lead into wastelands – only my path is the path to paradise."

These three hundred religions are continuously fighting with each other. None of them is aware, none of them has seen, none of them has looked into reality face to face – they have believed. These religions are not religions but traditions – they have heard. They have heard down the ages and they have believed, because to believe is cheap, to explore is risky; to repeat like a parrot is comfortable, to go into the adventure of discovery is to risk your life. It is dangerous. Exploration is dangerous; belief – convenient, consoling, you need not go anywhere. It is given to you ready-made, but it is secondhand.

And miserable is the man who lives with a secondhand God, because God can only be firsthand. The experience has to be authentically yours. Nobody else's experience can become a foundation of a true life. Buddha may have seen, but to become a Buddhist is not going to help. Buddha was not a Buddhist – certainly not. Jesus may have looked, encountered, realized, but to become a Christian is utter stupidity. Unless you become a Christ you will never know God.

The really religious person avoids traditions, the really religious person avoids secondhand gods, avoids beliefs, keeps himself open, available for the truth to happen. Certainly he works – only he works. The believer never works upon himself; there is no need for the believer to work upon himself. The explorer, the inquirer, the seeker of truth works hard upon himself because there are many things which have to be dropped, many impurities which have to be dropped, many hindrances and blocks which have to be dissolved. The eyes have to be opened and the ears have to be unplugged and the heart has to be made to feel.

One has to fall in rhythm with the existence. When you are utterly in rhythm with existence your eyes are open, and then for the first time, you see. And that seeing is transformation, that seeing changes you, root and all. That seeing becomes a new vision, a new life, a new gestalt. You are no more confined then by your body, no more confined by your mind, no more confined by anything whatsoever. You are unconfined, infinite, eternal. And to feel this eternity flowing in you is to know God, to see this infinity extending into the eternal past and into the eternal future is to see God. To feel godliness inside your own being is to know God. This can't be secondhand.

When I see a Christian or a Hindu or a Jaina or a Mohammedan, I see secondhand people. You would not like to purchase secondhand shoes from the market and you would not like to purchase secondhand clothes that have been used by others from the market. But for your soul you purchase secondhand beliefs, secondhand shoes, secondhand clothes – dirty, ugly, used, rotten – and you think you are beautifying your life? You are insulting your very soul, you are dehumanizing yourself. To become a Christian or to become a Buddhist is to dehumanize yourself. The search has to be alone, the search has to be authentically individual.

Truth cannot be decided by the vote of the majority because truth is utterly individual and private. It is not an objective phenomenon. You can see my body – it is an objective phenomenon: whether my body exists or not can be decided easily by others. But whether I am enlightened or not cannot be decided by anybody else – certainly not by any majority vote.

A buddha is a buddha not because people have voted for him and given their majority vote that he is a buddha. He is a buddha by his own sheer declaration. Except himself there is no witness – it is utterly private. It is so interior that nobody else can penetrate it.

Truth cannot be decided by a majority vote. But that's how people decide. That's why religions are so interested in increasing their population, because if they have more people, certainly they have more truth. Christians can claim more truth than Jainas because they have a big crowd behind them. If there is a voting, then Christians will win and Jainas will be defeated. But it is not a question of voting. Even if a thousand owls vote that it is dark and there is no sun and light has never existed, even then, the lie remains a lie. A single swan is enough to declare that it is day.

Truth is not a question of democratic decision, it has nothing to do with the crowd. Catholics are against birth control, Mohammedans are against birth control, for the simple reason, for a political reason; the reason is that if birth control is allowed their population will start decreasing. That is their only strength. They want to increase their population so one day they can prove: "Look, if we have so many people on our side, it must be that truth is on our side."

I would like to remind you of a famous statement of George Bernard Shaw. Somebody was arguing with him and the man said, "But so many people believe in what I am saying. How can so many people be wrong?"

And Bernard Shaw retorted, "If so many people believe in it then it must be wrong, because how can so many people be right?"

See the point of it: how can so many people be in the right? The crowd is blind, the crowd is not enlightened. Truth has always been in the minority. When Buddha arises he is alone, when Jesus walks in Jerusalem he is alone, when Socrates fights he is alone. Of course, a few seekers gather together around Socrates, a school arises, but that school is a minority. And to be with Socrates needs courage, needs guts, because he is not there to console you. He will take all your consolations away, he will shatter all your illusions, because that is the only way to bring you to truth. He will force you to open your eyes, he will not sing a lullaby to help you to go to sleep. He will shout from the house tops to wake you up, he will shock you, he will hit you.

Just the other day Pradeepa came to see me. She was crying – naturally. I had shocked her tremendously. She would not have ever dreamt that one day, out of nowhere, I would just hit her exactly on the head with a hammer. And she was also disturbed because she has been a cause to create nausea in me – she feels for me, she loves me, as you all love me. She was crying for all these reasons.

But I have to tell you, and to her particularly, that you should feel grateful whenever I hit you hard, because I will hit you hard *only* when you are worthy of it; I will not hit just anybody. I will hit only when somebody is really growing. The more you will be growing the more demands will be made on you.

I have not told everybody to drop non-vegetarian food, but I have told Pradeepa, in a very shocking way, to drop it. Her consciousness is growing, now this is a hindrance. People who are not soaring high, they can carry as much of a burden as they like. But those who are starting, soaring high, they have to drop all unnecessary luggage. The more pure your energy becomes, the more you will have to be careful about it, because something precious can be lost! And it is very difficult to create that precious energy, it is very easy to lose it. Those who don't have anything to lose, they need not worry. They can go on doing all kinds of stupid things, their whole being is in tune with those stupidities.

This has to be remembered by you all: that as you will be growing I will be making more and more demands on you.

There is a beautiful story...

India has known a great painter, one of the greatest of all – Nandalal Bose, a genius. He was a disciple of another genius, Avanindranath Tagore. Avanindranath Tagore was an uncle of Rabindranath Tagore. Rabindranath and Avanindranath were sitting together one day, sipping tea early in the morning, chit-chatting, and Nandalal came with a painting of Krishna. Rabindranath has written in his memoirs: "I have never seen such a beautiful painting of Krishna – so alive that it looked as if he is just going to come out of the painting any moment, that any moment his flute will start singing a song. I was dazed."

Avanindranath looked at the painting, and threw the painting out of his house and told Nandalal, "Is this the way one paints Krishna? Even poor painters in Bengal do far better."

Rabindranath was very shocked. Rabindranath knew his uncle's paintings too, because he also had been painting Krishna his whole life, and he was absolutely certain that no painting of his uncle's could be compared with Nandalal's painting. Nandalal's painting was far superior. But he kept quiet. It was not right for him to interfere between the master and the disciple. Nandalal touched the feet of Avanindranath, went out, and for three years disappeared.

Rabindranath many times asked Avanindranath, "What have you done to this poor man? – and his painting was superb."

And Avanindranath will cry and he will say, "You are right. His painting is superb. I have never been able to do such a beautiful thing." And when Nandalal left, Avanindranath took the painting inside and had it always, in his room.

"Then why," Rabindranath asked, "did you behave in such a rude way?"

And Avanindranath said, "But I expect much more from him. It is not a question that he has done a beautiful painting – this is just the beginning. He has much more potential – I am going to make many more demands on him."

And for three years Nandalal went around the villages of Bengal because the master had said, "Even the village painters do far better paintings of Krishna." So he learned from village painters – ordinary, poor painters. For three years he moved around in Bengal – the whole province. And then one day he appeared, touched the feet of the master and said, "You were right. I have learned a lot. You did well to throw my painting out."

Avanindranath hugged him and said, "I was waiting. I was getting old, and I was getting frightened whether you would be coming back or not. I am happy. Your painting was beautiful, but I see much more potential in you."

Whenever I will see much more potential in you I will hit you hard, because that is the only reason you are here with me and I am here with you. I have to provoke you, to your very depths, so that all that is dormant in you can start rising, can start soaring high. And you don't know your potential...I know. So whenever I make demands, feel grateful!

You will be surprised to know that in Zen monasteries whenever the master hits somebody's head with his staff, the person who is hit bows down seven times and touches the master's feet to thank him. And disciples wait for that moment when they will be hit, for that blissful moment to come when the master will take so much trouble as to hit their head with his staff. They dream about it, they pray, they hope that someday that blissful moment will come.

Remember, this is an alchemical academy. You are not here just to be entertained but to be transformed. And transformation is painful, because much that is old has to be dropped. And that old stuff is not like clothes you can easily drop – it has become your skin: your skin is peeled, it hurts. But this is the only way to bring you to your senses, this is the only way to destroy your shock absorbers, this is the only way to destroy your armor, that surrounds you and keeps you in bondage. Slowly slowly your own energy will start rising, your eyes will open, your ears will be able to hear. Then God is firsthand. And always keep in mind that only a firsthand experience of God is a true experience. It is not decided by the majority, it is not decided by tradition, it is not decided by anything except by your own energy encounter with God.

It was perfectly alright for the owls to think that the swan is mad. That's how people have always been thinking – Buddha is mad, Mohammed is mad, Zarathustra is mad – because how can they believe what they cannot see?

It was perfectly alright for the owls to throw the swan out, to drive him away. They became afraid, shaken: if this swan is allowed to live in the tree he is going to disrupt their tradition, he is going to destroy their way of life. They have always lived in darkness and they have always believed in darkness. Darkness is their God, all their rituals have arisen out of darkness. Their priests praise darkness, their learned people write great treatises on darkness. Their whole philosophy is centered on the basic theme of darkness. In their philosophy there is no place for sun and light and day. Now this mad swan comes up and is trying to infiltrate, smuggle some alien ideas into their world: their whole structure will collapse.

That's why Jesus is crucified. That's why people are so much against me. I am trying to give you a new gestalt, a new pattern, a new way of life, a new approach to reality. I am trying to open a new door to existence. Naturally, those who have very much invested in the old patterns of life will be angry, will be madly angry. They would like to drive me out of their world – that's exactly what they are trying to do. It is all natural, it is all simple; once you understand, you start laughing about it.

How do you go on believing in God? Why? How do you manage to believe in the soul, and why? The same reason: "Our fathers and their fathers and their fathers, in fact the whole of our community has never seen a sun, so there is no such thing as a sun. He is having you on. Don't listen to him. He will corrupt our religion." You have heard your father say to you, "God is, and God is a Christian," or "God is a Hindu," and they had heard it from their fathers and so on and so forth – rumors, gossip. Neither your father has known nor you have known. Gather courage to drop all that which is not *your* knowledge.

This is the first requirement for being a sannyasin, and this is the first requirement for going into the inquiry of truth scientifically: drop all prejudices, drop all a priori conceptions; start from the beginning, from the very beginning, from *ABC*, as if you are Adam and Eve – that there has been no tradition before you, that there has been no scripture before you.

D.H. Lawrence once said – and I perfectly agree with him – "If all the scriptures of the world are destroyed, man may become religious."

If whole traditions are simply dissolved, then only is there some hope, otherwise who bothers to inquire? When the tradition can supply you so easily and you have not to pay anything at all, why bother? Others have known, you can simply believe. But to know is one thing, to believe is just the opposite.

To believe means to go on living in darkness. To know means to be transformed, transmuted, transplanted into another vision – luminous, eternal.

These sutras are not to be believed, they have to be experimented upon. These sutras are simple clues on how to work it out within your own being. Unless you work on them you will go on missing the point. You have to start looking at your own body as a great spiritual lab and you have to look upon your life as a great adventure into reality. And you have to be very alert, watchful, to see what is happening – within and without.

These sutras are keys. If you really try to work upon your being you will be surprised: that you are emperors – having great treasures, inexhaustible treasures in your being – and yet behaving like beggars.

> Master Lu-tsu said:
> The two mistakes of indolence and distraction must be combated by
> quiet work that is carried on daily without interruption; then success
> will certainly be achieved.

Success is a by-product; one need not think about it. And if you think about it, you will not get it – that is a condition. Don't think about success because if you start thinking about success you become divided. Then you are not totally in the work; your real mind is in the future: How to succeed? You have already started dreaming how you will be when you have succeeded, how you will be when you have become a buddha – what beauties, what benedictions, what blessings will be yours! Your mind has started playing the game of greed, ambition, ego. Never think of success; success is a natural by-product. If you work really sincerely upon yourself, success will follow you just as your shadow follows you. Success has not to be the goal. That's why Lu-tsu says, "Work quietly, silently, untroubled by any idea of success or failure."

And remember, if you think too much of success you will be thinking constantly of failure too. They come together, they come in one package. Success and failure cannot be divided from each other. If you think of success, somewhere deep down there will be a fear also. Who knows whether you are going to make it or not? You may fail. Success takes you into the future, gives you a greed game, an ego projection, ambition; and the fear also gives you a shaking, a trembling – you may fail. The possibility of failure makes you waver, and with this wavering, with this greed, with this ambition, your work will not be quiet. Your work will become a turmoil; you will be working here and looking there, you will be walking on this road and looking somewhere far away in the sky.

I have heard about a Greek astrologer who was studying stars, and one night, a very starry night, he fell into a well, because he was watching the stars and moving and he was so concerned with the stars that he forgot where he was – he moved closer and closer to a well and fell into it.

Some woman, an old woman who used to live nearby, rushed up. Hearing the sound, she looked inside the well, brought a rope, and pulled the great astrologer out. The astrologer was very thankful. He said to the old woman, "You don't know me but I am the royal astrologer, specially appointed by the king. My fee is very large – only very rich people can afford to inquire about their future. But you have saved my life. You can come to me tomorrow and I will show you: I will read your hand, I will look into your birth-chart and I will interpret your stars, and your whole future will be plainly clear to you."

The old woman started laughing. She said, "Forget all about it. You cannot see even one step ahead that there is a well, how can you predict my future? All bullshit!"

Don't look too much ahead, otherwise you will miss the immediate step. Success comes, Lu-tsu says, of its own accord. Leave it to itself. This existence is a very rewarding existence, nothing goes unrewarded.

That is the whole Indian philosophy of karma: nothing goes unrewarded or unpunished. If you do something wrong, punishment follows like a shadow; if you do something right, rewards are on the way. You need not bother about them, you need not think at all, not even an iota of your consciousness need be involved with them, they come – their coming is automatic.

When you move on the road do you look again and again for your shadow – whether it is following you or not? And if somebody looks back again and again to see whether the shadow is following or not, you will think that he is mad. The shadow follows; it is inevitable. So if your work is in the right direction, with the right effort, with the totality of your being, the reward follows automatically.

And what is the work? The first thing:

The two mistakes of indolence and distraction must be combated...

Indolence means laziness, lethargy; it is because of the feminine part in you. The feminine part *is* lazy, lethargic, because it is passive. And the other is distraction; it is because of the masculine part in you. The masculine part is always restless, active: it wants to do a thousand and one things simultaneously.

A character of Camus' says, "I want all the women of the world. I cannot be satisfied by one or by a few or even by many. I want all the women of the world." This is the extreme male attitude. The woman is satisfied by one, the man is not even satisfied by many. Contentment is natural to the woman, discontent is natural to the man.

Both have positive and negative polarities. If the woman allows her passivity to become negative, it will create lethargy. That's why women have not created much in the world, or very little – you don't find great women painters and poets and scientists. And it is not only because man has not allowed them. Even if freedom comes – which is coming – and the woman is liberated, this lethargy is part of her being. She is not much interested in doing, her interest is more in being. And this interest can be a great blessing too, or a curse; it depends. If this restfulness becomes meditative, if this restfulness really becomes contentment with existence, harmony with existence, it will be a blessing. But usually, out of a hundred, in ninety-nine percent of cases it becomes lethargy. We don't know how to use our blessings. Then blessings become bitter and prove curses.

And the male mind is restless. There also a blessing is possible: he can be very creative. But it has not been so. Rather than being creative he has become destructive; the blessing has turned into a curse. Man's restlessness has made him very anxious, full of anxiety, tension. His whole mind is constantly boiling, he is always on the verge of madness. Somehow he goes on managing to contain himself, but deep inside him there is a crowd ready to burst forth. Any small excuse, and the man can go mad. Because of this restlessness man has lost his beauty, his grace.

The woman is graceful, beautiful. Just watch a woman: the way she walks, the way she sits – there is elegance. Her being has a subtle silence, a restfulness you can feel in her vibe. In a house where there is no woman you will see chaos. You can immediately know whether the house is lived in by a bachelor: you will see chaos, all the things are topsy-turvy, nothing is in its right place. You can immediately know whether a woman is part of the house or not because everything is in harmony, in its place. There is a grace, a kind of exquisite climate, a very subtle climate of love, of culture, a musical quality to the house. When man lives alone there is a neurotic quality to the house.

Both of these are beautiful if used rightly. Then the feminine part gives you grace and the male part gives you creativity. And when grace and creativity meet, you are whole. But that rarely happens – in a Buddha, in a Meera, in a Teresa, in a Jesus, in a Magdalene – very rarely. Ordinarily, just the opposite happens: the wrong sides meet. Man's restlessness, neurosis, and woman's lethargy – these two things meet, and then you see the ugliest phenomenon possible.

Let me remind you again: when I am talking about man and woman I am not using biological terminology. Each man has a woman within as well as a man within, and each woman has a man within as a woman within. Man is not just man and woman is not just woman. They are both. Both are both Their being is bisexual. Maybe one is predominant, that's why one is man: the male part is predominant – the animus is in the conscious and the anima is deep in the unconscious – then you are a man. Or if you are a woman that means that the anima is in the conscious, the feminine part is predominant, and the male part, the animus, is in the unconscious. But both are always present together. Just as electricity cannot be without two poles, positive and negative, no being can be without two poles. Man and woman, yin and yang, positive and negative, Shiva and Shakti – you can find your own names for them.

These two mistakes have to be combated. Quiet work is needed to be…

> …*carried on daily without interruption; then success will certainly*
> *be achieved.*

And what is that quiet work? This is the quiet work:

> *If one is not seated in meditation, one will often be distracted without*
> *noticing it.*

And you must have observed – thousands have reported it to me because thousands have been meditating around me and it is an accepted experience of all meditators – that when a person starts meditating, he suddenly becomes aware of a strange phenomenon: his mind has never before been so restless as it becomes when he meditates. That is very puzzling in the beginning because one hopes that through meditation the mind will become quiet. And this is just the opposite that is happening: the mind becomes more restless, you see more thoughts coming than in your ordinary day-to-day life. Working in your shop, in the office, in the factory, thoughts don't bother you so much. But when you sit in a temple or in a mosque or a church to meditate for a few minutes, suddenly a great crowd of thoughts comes, surrounds you, starts pulling you to this side and to that. A maddening experience, and puzzling, because the meditator was hoping to become quiet and silent – and this is just the reverse that is happening.

Why does it happen? The reason is this: you have always been with all these thoughts; even when you are occupied in your shop, in your factory, in your office, these thoughts have always been there. But you were so occupied that you didn't notice them, that's all. What is new is not the crowd of thoughts. Thoughts don't know where you are sitting – in a church, in a temple, in a meditation hall, they don't know. All that is happening is that when you are sitting in meditation you are not occupied with anything on the outside, so your whole mind becomes aware of all that is always clamoring within you.

It is not because of meditation that more thoughts are coming to you, through meditation you become aware of their presence – they have always been there, you just notice them more.

> *If one is not seated in meditation, one will often be distracted without noticing it. To become conscious of the distraction is the mechanism by which to do away with distraction.*

Hence it is insisted that: sit in meditation at least one or two hours every day so that you become unoccupied, completely unoccupied with the outer engagements, and your full observation is focused on your inner world. In the beginning you will see you have opened a Pandora's box, in the beginning you will see you have entered into a madhouse, and you will want to escape and become engaged again. Avoid that temptation. To avoid this temptation is a must, otherwise you will never be able to meditate.

Many tricks have been found to avoid the inner turmoil. Transcendental Meditation is a technique, *not* of meditation, but of avoiding facing your inner reality. A mantra is given to you and you are told to repeat the mantra. That helps – not to meditate but to remain occupied. You go on repeating, "Ram-Ram-Ram" or "Coca-Cola, Coca-Cola, Coca-Cola." You go on repeating something – any word will do, your own name will do, any absurd sound will do. You go on repeating. By repeating it you are occupied, and through that occupation you are avoiding your inner turmoil. This is not different. You were occupied in your office, you were occupied within the movie, you were occupied listening to the radio, you were occupied reading the newspaper; now you are occupied with this mantra. This is neither meditation nor transcendental.

Real meditation means: don't avoid the inner madhouse; enter into it, face it, encounter it, be watchful, because it is through watchfulness that you will overcome it. It is because of avoiding it that it has been growing on and on. You have avoided enough! Now there is no need to take the help of a mantra. No help is needed – just sit silently. Zen is the purest of meditations: just sit silently, doing nothing.

The most difficult meditation is sitting silently, doing nothing. People ask me, "Please give us some support. If you give us some mantra it will be helpful, because just sitting silently doing nothing is very difficult, most arduous." A thousand and one things arise. The body starts driving you crazy, the head starts itching, suddenly you feel ants are crawling upon your body, and when you look there is no ant – just the body playing tricks. The body is trying to give you some support to be engaged. The body wants to change the posture, the legs go to sleep – the body is simply making things available to you so that you can become occupied.

Avoid all occupation. For a few moments just be unoccupied and just see whatsoever is happening inside here and now, and you will be surprised. You will be surprised because one day, just by looking and looking and looking, thoughts start disappearing: "Sitting quietly, doing nothing, spring comes and the grass grows by itself."

This is the purest form of meditation, *this* is transcendental meditation. But nobody can call it transcendental meditation because Maharishi Mahesh Yogi has made it a trademark. Transcendental meditation is now a trademark! Nobody has ever done business in such a way. You can be sued in a court if you call your meditation, "transcendental meditation." It is patented. Look at the whole ridiculousness of it: meditation has become a thing, like a commodity, a product to be sold in the marketplace.

This has been happening again and again: the so-called Indian gurus who go to America, they never succeed in changing anybody but America succeeds in changing them. They all become businessmen, they all start learning American ways. They never change anybody, they cannot. If they were able to change anybody they would not have gone anywhere; those who want to be changed would have come to them. There was no need for them to go anywhere: when somebody is thirsty he starts searching for water. The well need not go to the thirsty, the well never goes – the thirsty come to the well. And if you see a well on wheels, beware!

> *To become conscious of the distraction is the mechanism by which to do away with distraction.*

A tremendously pregnant sentence. The only way to get rid of distraction is to become aware of it, to watch it, to silently be aware of it, to see what mind is doing with you – continuously distracting you. Just watch it. Many times you will forget, because mind is cunning, very clever, very diplomatic, knows all the strategies of the politicians. Mind is essentially a politician: it will try all its magic charms on you.

Whatsoever you have been repressing it will bring. If you have been repressing sex, when you start meditating, immediately you will see *apsaras* descending from heaven. The mind says, "Look! What are you doing, wasting your time? Beautiful women are being sent by the god Indra, and what are you doing?" And if you have been repressing sex then your mind will use sex as a bait for you. If you have been repressing ambition, your mind will start imagining that you have become the president or the prime minister and you will start falling into that trap. If your mind has been deprived of food and you have been fasting, the mind will create such beautiful, delicious dishes for you: the aroma, the smell of the food and you are distracted.

Hence one of my insistencies for my sannyasins is: don't repress, otherwise you will never be able to meditate. If you repress, then in meditation you will have to encounter your repression. And whatsoever you have repressed becomes powerful, immensely powerful; it takes roots in your unconscious.

Do you think the old stories of Indian seers – old people they were, all old and almost dead, shrunken, just bones, skeletons, because they were fasting and living in forests, and suddenly, one day they see that Urvasi, the most beautiful dance-girl of the god Indra is dancing around them…. What would Urvasi see in these skeletons? How does she become interested in these skeletons, and for what? The stories say that the god Indra sends them to tempt. That is all nonsense! There is no god Indra and there is nobody functioning as a tempter. There is no devil, no Satan; the only devil is your repressed mind. These are the people who have been repressing their sexuality, and they have repressed so much that when they relax in meditation all that repression starts surfacing: it takes beautiful forms.

Repress anything and you will see. Just do a three-day fast and you will come to know what I am telling you. Just a three-day fast and all your dreams will become full of food. And there is every possibility that one day in your sleep you will simply start moving, sleepwalking, towards the fridge. Your whole mind will become food-obsessed. Hence I say, don't repress.

All the therapies available in this ashram are just to help you to vomit the repressions that the society has forced on you. Once those repressions are vomited, thrown out of your system, once those toxins are taken out of your system, meditation becomes such an easy, simple thing – just like a feather falling slowly towards the earth or a dead leaf falling from the tree, slowly slowly.... Meditation is a very simple phenomenon, it *has* to be, because it is your spontaneity; you are going towards your nature. Movement towards nature has to be easy, movement away from nature has to be difficult. Meditation is not difficult, but between your mind and your being, there are a thousand and one repressions which distract you.

Lu-tsu is right: just watch those distractions, be alert. If you are distracted and you forget meditation, don't be worried. The moment you remember that you have been distracted, again go back, again cool down, again make the heart quiet, again start breathing silently. Don't feel guilty that you have been distracted because that will be another distraction. That's why I say mind is cunning. First it distracts you, and then one moment you see...what are you doing? You were meditating, and you have gone to Vrindavan and you are eating and...what are you doing? You drag yourself. Now you start feeling guilty. This is not good. Now feeling guilty is another distraction, now guilt makes you feel miserable – misery is another distraction. One distraction leads into another.

Don't feel guilty, don't feel angry. The moment you find yourself caught red-handed, simply go back – with no complaint. It is natural. For millions of lives you have been repressing, it is but natural that the mind distracts. Take it for granted and move back, bring yourself again to your center, again and again and again. And slowly slowly the time at the center will become greater and greater, and distractions will be fewer and fewer. And one day, suddenly it happens: you are at the center and there is no distraction.

This is success. And why is this called success? – because this is the point where you know that you are a god, that you have never been anybody else, that you had fallen in a dream and dreamt that you had become a beggar.

Indolence of which man is conscious, and indolence of which man is

unconscious, are a thousand miles apart. Unconscious indolence is
real indolence; conscious indolence is not complete indolence, because
there is still some clarity in it.

If you are lazy, be consciously lazy. Know that you are lazy. Watch your laziness. Just as you watch distraction, watch your laziness. At least watching is not lazy, watching is not laziness, so something is there which is not lazy. Being attentive of your inattention, one thing in you is still attentive, so you are not completely inattentive. And all hope hangs around that small spot of no laziness, of no distraction. That small spot is like a seed. It looks small but if time and patience is given to it, it will become a big tree with great foliage. And one day the Golden Flower will arrive.

Distraction comes from letting the mind wander about; indolence
comes from the mind's not yet being pure. Distraction is much easier
to correct than indolence. It is as in sickness: if one feels pains and
irritations, one can help them with remedies, but indolence is like a
disease that is attended by lack of realization.

Distraction is easier to tackle because distraction is outward. Indolence is more difficult because it is inward. Distraction is male, indolence is female. Distraction, by its very activity, creates tensions which become unbearable, and you can become aware of it easily. But indolence is very silent, dark; it makes no noise, it is simply there. It is very difficult to become aware of it. First one has to become aware of distractions. When all distractions disappear, then one becomes aware of indolence. Then the whole energy is available to look inward, then you see it there, like a rock holding you – inactive, uncreative. Then watch it.

And remember, watching is the only key. Observation is meditation – there is nothing more to meditation. It is another name for being aware. And the miracle is that when you become aware of something, utterly aware, it disappears. It remains only if you are unaware. Your unawareness is a food for distraction, for indolence. Your awareness means they are no more being fed, they start starving; sooner or later they wither away of their own accord.

Distraction can be counteracted, confusion can be straightened
out, but indolence and lethargy are heavy and dark. Distraction
and confusion at least have a place, but in indolence and lethargy

the anima alone is active. In distraction the animus is still present,
but in indolence pure darkness rules. If one becomes sleepy during
meditation, that is an effect of indolence. Only breathing serves
to overcome indolence. Although the breath that flows in and out
through the nose is not the true breath, the flowing in and out of the
true breath takes place in connection with it.

If you feel very sleepy while meditating, then start watching your breath and sleep will disappear. That's why many Buddhist monks who do *vipassana* start suffering from insomnia. I have come across many people who were suffering from insomnia because they were practicing vipassana and they were not aware of it: if you watch your breath, it destroys your sleep.

So to my sannyasins I say: never practice vipassana for more than two or three hours a day, and those three hours should be between sunrise and sunset, never after sunset. If you practice vipassana in the night you will disturb your sleep, and to disturb sleep is to disturb your whole body mechanism.

One monk from Ceylon was brought to me. For three years he had not been able to sleep. A sincere monk…that was his problem. Thinking that vipassana was so great, he was practicing it day in, day out. Even when he was in bed feeling that no sleep was coming, he would practice vipassana. Now if you practice vipassana in bed, it is impossible for sleep to come: sleep never comes to a person who is becoming very alert of the breath. You can try it – if you need insomnia you can try it. To watch the breath is the best way to destroy sleepiness in you, because breath is life and sleep is death; they are antagonistic to each other.

The child starts his life by breathing. The first act of life is breath, and the last act of life will be letting the breath out and never breathing again. The first act is inhalation and the last act is exhalation. When there is no breathing we say this man is dead.

Remember it: sleep needs that you forget all about your breath. Sleep is a small death, a tiny death – and a beautiful death, because it gives you rest, relaxation, and tomorrow morning you will come out of the death chamber fresh, younger, rejuvenated.

Watch your breath when you feel sleepy in meditation. And never do such meditations in the night.

And the second thing of great importance which the sutra says is: this breath that we take in and out is not true breath, this is just the vehicle of the true breath. What is true breath? In India we call it *prana*. This breath is just the horse; the rider is invisible. This breath is just the horse of the rider called "prana," vitality, or what Henri Bergson used to call "élan vital." It is invisible.

When you take breath in you are not only taking air in, you are taking life in. Without air life will disappear. Life exists through air; it is the invisible part of air. Breath is like the flower and life is like the fragrance that surrounds it. When you breathe there is a double process going on. Hence yoga became very much interested in *pranayama*. Pranayama means expansion of breath. The deeper your breath goes, the more deeply you become alive; the better your breath, the longer you will be able to live. Yoga became very interested in the secret. The elixir is in the system of breathing. One can live very long. Yogis have lived the longest.

I am not telling you to live long because you can live a long but stupid life. Length is not the question at all; intensity, depth, is the question. I am not interested in long life. What is the point? If you are stupid it is better to die sooner.

Genghis Khan once asked a great wise man, "What do you say – should one live long? Should one do something to live long? Is life a blessing or not?"

The wise man said, "Sir, it depends. For example, if *you* live long that will be very bad. If you die soon that will be a great blessing. If you sleep twenty-four hours a day that will be really great, because there will be less trouble in the world."

It depends. But yoga became very interested in long life as if that in itself were a goal. And that's where yoga got lost: it became more and more physiological – its concern became focused on something unimportant.

But the secret is there – it is in the breath. Breath is a vehicle of two energies: one is the visible air, the tangible air that contains oxygen; and somewhere around the oxygen is élan vital, prana, that makes you more and more deeply alive, aflame with life. So whenever you feel sleepy, just watch your breath and sleep will disappear. And because of breath more life will enter in you; your indolence will disappear.

> While sitting, one must therefore always keep the heart quiet and the energy concentrated. How can the heart be made quiet? By the breath.

Again, …*By the breath*. Breath has functioned as one of the greatest of techniques.

> Only the heart must be conscious of the flowing in and out of the breath…

Just watch the breath coming in, the breath going out. In that very watchfulness your sleep will disappear, your indolence will disappear, and you will feel centered.

Breath can be watched at two points: either at the tip of the nose where the air touches on first entering your body, or at the last center, at the navel center, where the breath goes and makes your belly move up and down. These are the two centers which you can watch.

Just the other day somebody asked, "Osho, watching the tip of the nose is good, but what about Jewish noses?" In fact, only Jews have noses, others only believe they have. If you have a Jewish nose then watch the tip of the nose where the air enters in. A Jewish nose is immensely helpful in such meditations. Feel happy that you have a Jewish nose. And at least fifty percent of people here have Jewish noses because fifty percent of people here are Jews.

Reading the question I was really surprised because then I became very concerned about Master Lu-tsu and his Chinese people to whom he was giving these methods. They don't have any noses at all! It must have been really difficult for them to watch the tip of the nose. What tip?

> *Only the heart must be conscious of the flowing in and out of the breath; it must not be heard with the ears. If it is not heard, then the breathing is light; if light, it is pure. If it can be heard, then the breath-energy is rough; if rough, then it is troubled; if it is troubled, then indolence and lethargy develop and one wants to sleep. That is self-evident.*

> *How to use the heart correctly during breathing must be understood. It is a use without use.*

Effort without effort, practicing without practicing, a pathless path, a gateless gate – these are the expressions of Tao and Zen. You have to do something without effort, without strain.

So the Master says:

> *It is a use without use. One should only let the light fall quite gently on the hearing.*

You are to be in a let-go.

That is the difference between yoga and Tao: yoga is the path of will and Tao is the path of surrender. Yoga says breathe in this way, take this much breath deep inside, hold it there for this long, then exhale deeply, then hold it out for that long – make a certain pattern through will; Tao says let it happen.

One should only let the light fall quite gently on the hearing.

Just as you are listening to me, my words are falling on your ears: you need not jump upon them, you need not drag them in – there is no need. You simply remain attentive, silent, available, open.

> *This sentence contains a secret meaning. What does it*
> *mean to let the light fall? It is the spontaneous radiation*
> *of the light of the eyes. The eye looks inward only and not*
> *outward. To sense brightness without looking outward*
> *means to look inward...*

Whenever you are in a kind of let-go you will feel a great light inside you.

That happens automatically in a let-go. When you are surrendered to existence you will feel very very bright inside – a great light inside and a great delight outside. It happens naturally. And when you feel that brightness inside this is what is meant by looking in.

> *To sense brightness without looking outward means to look*
> *inward; it has nothing to do with an actual looking within. What*
> *does hearing mean? It is the spontaneous hearing of the light of*
> *the ear. The ear listens inwardly only and does not listen to what*
> *is outside. To sense brightness without listening to what is outside*
> *is to listen inwardly...*

When you start feeling a light behind your eyes and within your ears, deep inside you, a source of your own, then you are settled, centered, then the heart is quiet. And then you are in the world and yet beyond it. This is transcendence.

> *...it has nothing to do with actually listening to what is within. In*
> *this sort of hearing, one hears only that there is no sound; in this*
> *kind of seeing, one sees only that no shape is there.*

You will not see any shape, you will not hear any sound within; you will see only a silent light – a soundless sound, a formless light. Hence God is defined as soundless sound, formless form.

> *If the eye is not looking outward and the ear is not harkening*
> *outward, they close themselves and are inclined to sink inward.*
> *Only when one looks and harkens inward does the organ not go*
> *outward nor sink inward. In this way indolence and lethargy are*
> *done away with. That is the union of the seed and the light of the*
> *sun and moon.*

If your hearing is inward, your seeing is inward – and that means you are feeling light without form, sound without sound, a silent music inside – your inner man and inner woman have met. This is the union, the total orgasm, *unio mystica*.

> *If, as a result of indolence, one becomes sleepy, one should stand up*
> *and walk about. When the mind has become clear one should sit*
> *down again. In the course of time there will be success without one's*
> *becoming indolent and falling asleep.*

These sutras have to be practiced: without practice make efforts to enter into the secrets of these sutras, without strain learn to surrender and be in a let-go.
Enough for today.

CHAPTER 16
In the Lake of the Void

The first question:

Osho,
Would you please comment further on the differences between C. G.
Jung's "process of individuation" and the essence of The Secret of the
Golden Flower?

Habib, Carl Gustav Jung was groping in the right direction but he had not yet arrived. It was not his own experience, it was a philosophy. He was thinking about individuation, he was going into the idea of individuation, deeper and deeper. But it was not his own meditation, it was not his own existential experience.

The Secret of the Golden Flower is an alchemical process. These are the words of those who have known.

Jung was not an individual in the sense of individuation; he was yet divided: he had the conscious mind and the unconscious mind and the collective unconscious mind. He was not one, he himself was a multiplicity. He was a crowd as everybody else is. He had all the fears, all the greeds, all the ambitions that any normal human being is expected to have. He was not a buddha, he was not enlightened. He had not known his own inner being which is timeless.

In the moment of inner illumination, all differences and distinctions disappear. There is only pure consciousness – neither conscious nor unconscious nor collective unconscious. The same was happening with Sri Aurobindo in India. He was also talking about conscious mind and the superconscious mind.

In the moment of illumination mind disappears. Mind means division. Whether you divide it into conscious and unconscious or you divide it into conscious and superconscious does not make a difference: mind means division. Individuality means undividedness. That is the meaning of the word *individual*: indivisible. Mind is bound to be a crowd. Mind cannot be one – by its very nature it has to be many. And when the mind disappears, the one is found. Then you have come home. That is individuation.

But still I say Jung was groping in the right direction – but still groping in the dark. He has not yet arrived at the door, he had dreamt about the door.

There are parallels in human history. For example, Democritus, the Greek thinker, had stumbled upon the idea of the atom without any experimentation. There was no possibility to experiment in his days, no modern sophisticated techniques were available. He could not have divided the atom, he could not have come to the atomic structure of matter, but he speculated. He must have been a great thinker – but only a thinker. He stumbled upon the idea of atomism.

Then there is Albert Einstein and modern physics. Both talk about the atomic structure but the difference is tremendous: Democritus only talks, modern physics knows.

In the East also there has been talk about atomism. Kanad, one of the great thinkers of India, has talked about atomism – and in a very subtle, refined way – but it is all talk. In fact, because he talked so much about atoms – his whole philosophy is based on the hypothesis of atoms – that his name became Kanad. *Kan* means atom, *Kanad* means one who continuously talks about atoms. But still, it was philosophy. He had no real experimentation, it was not based on any scientific exploration – he must have been a great thinker, almost three thousand years before Albert Einstein – but he stumbled, and I say stumbled, upon the truth of atomism. But it was an unproved hypothesis. And there are many other parallels like that.

The same is the case with Carl Gustav Jung and the process we are talking about: the process given by *The Secret of the Golden Flower*.

The book of *The Secret of the Golden Flower* is an alchemical treatise – it knows – and if you follow the method you will come to know. It is absolutely certain. And when I am saying this, I am saying because I know – because I have gone through the process. Yes, the golden flower blooms in you: you come to a point when the many disappear, the multitude disappears, the fragments of the mind disappear and you are left all alone. That is the meaning of the word *alone*: all alone, all one. If you think about it, the thinking is bound to take you to a certain line. If you think about it, then you will ask how to come to the one, how to make these fragments of the mind join together, how to glue them together. But that will not be real unity. Glued or unglued, they remain separate. A crowd can be transformed into an army: that means now it is glued together, it is no more a mob. But the many are still many, maybe in a certain discipline, as if there is a pile of flowers and you make a garland out of those flowers: a thread runs through all the flowers and gives them a certain kind of unity.

That's what Jung was trying to do. How to bring these fragments together, how to glue them together, that is his whole process of individuation.

The real experience of individuation is totally different: you don't glue these fragments, you simply let them disappear, you drop them. And then, when all the fragments of the mind have disappeared – receded farther and farther away from you – suddenly you find the one. In the absence of the mind it is found – not by joining the mind together in a certain discipline, not by putting mind together into a certain kind of union. Union is not unity. Union is only an imposed order on a chaos.

This can be done, and then you will have a false kind of individuation. You will feel better than before, because now you will not be a crowd, a mob, many noises will not be there. They would have fallen in a certain kind of harmony, a certain adjustment would have arisen in you. Your conscious mind will be friendly with the unconscious, not antagonistic. Your unconscious will be friendly with the collective unconscious, not antagonistic. There will be a thread running through the flowers: you will be more like a garland than like a pile. But still, individuation in the sense I am talking about here has not happened.

Individuation is not the unity of mind but the disappearance of the mind. When you are utterly empty of the mind, you are one. To be a no-mind is the process of real individuation.

Jung was groping in the dark, coming very very close – just as Democritus was coming closer to the atomic structures of matter – but he was as far away from real individuation as Democritus was far away from real modern physics. Modern physics is not a speculation, it is a proved phenomenon.

For the book of The Secret of the Golden Flower, individuation is not speculation – it is experience. Before one can know the one, the many have to be said goodbye to: one has to be capable of becoming utterly empty. Individuation is the flowering of inner emptiness – yes, exactly that: the golden flower blooms in you when you are utterly empty. It is a flower in the void; in the lake of the void the golden lotus blooms. So the process is totally different. What Jung is doing is trying to put all the pieces together – as if a mirror had fallen and now you are trying to put it together, gluing it together. You can glue it together, but you will never find the same mirror again. A broken mirror is a broken mirror.

In the East the work has moved from a totally different dimension: we have to let this mind go, each part of the mind has to be dropped slowly slowly. In deep awareness, meditativeness, thoughts disappear, mind sooner or later becomes contentless. And when the mind is contentless, it is no-mind, because mind as such is nothing but the whole process of thought. When you are without thought, not even a single thought stirring in your being, then there is no-mind. You can call it individuation, you can call it *samadhi*, you can call it nirvana or what you will.

But beware: people like Jung can be very alluring, because they talk in terms which are really beautiful. They talk about individuation and you may start thinking that the individuation of Jung is the same. It is not the same, it can't be the same – he never meditated himself.

He was really afraid of meditation. He was basically afraid of the East. And when his friend, Richard Wilhelm, who had translated the *I Ching* into German and who was also the translator of *The Secret of the Golden Flower*, went mad, he became even more afraid. Then he started saying that the methods of the East are not useful for the West, they are dangerous. Then he started saying that the Eastern methods should not be used in the West because the West has followed a totally different line of evolution. Yoga, Tantra, Tao, Zen, Sufism – no Eastern methods should be tried by the Western mind – then he started saying that. He was really afraid. And he was not aware of what he was talking about – he had never tried these methods.

Wilhelm went mad, not because he tried these methods; he became mad because he was trying to make a synthesis of the Western psychology with the Eastern psychology. That thing can drive you mad. He was not practicing, he was not a practicing meditator. He was philosophizing.

In philosophy, East and West cannot meet – it is impossible. In philosophy you cannot make death and life meet, in philosophy you cannot make positive and negative meet. But in actuality they meet: in actuality, the positive never exists without the negative, in actuality death is nothing but the culmination of life, in actuality silence and sound are two aspects of the same phenomenon. In reality, man and woman are together, one, but in philosophy you cannot make them meet, because philosophy is a process of the mind. Mind divides, mind cannot unite; only in a state of no-mind, in existential experience, they meet.

It happened…

A Sufi mystic, Baba Farid, was given a present from a king. The present was a beautiful pair of scissors, golden, studded with diamonds. The king had loved them very much – some other king had given them to him as a present.

When he came to see Farid he thought, "This will be a beautiful present." So he brought those scissors.

Farid looked at them, gave them back to the king and said, "What will we do with them here? – because a pair of scissors cuts, separates and divides. They will not be of any use to me. Rather than a pair of scissors, give me a needle, which joins and which puts things together. A needle will be more representative of me than a scissors."

The mind is a pair of scissors: it goes on cutting. It is like a rat, a mouse, which goes on gnawing.

You will be surprised to know that one of the mythological figures in India is Ganesh, the god with the head of an elephant. He is the god of logic. He rides on the back of a rat; the rat is his vehicle. Logic is rat-like: it gnaws. It is a pair of scissors.

Mind always makes things divided. Mind is a kind of prism: pass the white ray of light through it and immediately it is divided into seven colors; pass anything through the mind and it becomes dual. Life and death are not life-and-death. The reality is lifedeath. It should be one word, not two, not even a hyphen in between. Lifedeath is one phenomenon, lovehate is one phenomenon, darknesslight is one phenomenon, negativepositive is one phenomenon. But pass this one phenomenon through the mind and the one is divided immediately in two. Lifedeath becomes life and death – not only divided but death becomes antagonistic to life – they are enemies. Now you can go on trying to make these two meet, and they will never meet.

Kipling is right – that "East is East and West is West and the twain shall never meet." Logically it is true. How can the East meet the West? How can the West meet the East? But existentially it is utter nonsense; they are meeting everywhere. For example, you are sitting here in Pune: is it East or is it West? If you are comparing it with London it is East, but if you are comparing it with Tokyo it is West. What exactly is it, East or West? On each point East and West are meeting, and Kipling says, "The twain shall never meet." The twain are meeting everywhere. No single point is such where East and West are not meeting and no single man is such where East and West are not meeting – it cannot be otherwise. They have to meet, it is one reality: East, West – one sky.

But mind divides. And if you are trying to put things together through the same mind, you will go crazy. That's what happened to Richard Wilhelm – a beautiful man, a genius in his own right, but just intellectual. And when he went mad, Jung was naturally afraid: it was Wilhelm who had introduced Jung to these secret books of the East, the *I Ching* and *The Secret of the Golden Flower*. He had persuaded Jung to write a commentary on this book. He became really afraid of the East. He talked about these things but he never tried in any way to practice them. And he has prescribed to the Western man that the West has to evolve its own yoga, its own methods of meditation, it should not follow the Eastern methods. It is as stupid as some Eastern chauvinist saying that the East should evolve its own science, its own physics, its own chemistry. It should not follow the West because these methods have been developed in the West. They cannot be followed because "East is East and West is West."

Do you think that the East has to evolve its own chemistry? What difference will there be? Has the East to evolve its own physics? What difference will there be? Will water evaporate in a different way in the East than it evaporates in the West? Nothing will be different. And if it is so with outer matter, it is so with the inner consciousness too.

All the differences are superficial. All the differences are in your conditionings, not in your being. Your essential being is the same; whether you have the skin of a white man or a black man does not matter. The difference between them is only of a little bit of color. In the old days they used to say: the difference is only of a little pigment – four annas' worth. The white man has a little less pigment than the black man. Remember, the black man is richer – four annas richer in color in the body. Sooner or later we will be able to invent injections so that the white man can become black and the black can become white. Just an injection and in the morning you are a perfect negro! The difference is not much – it is only superficial, just on the surface. And so too is the difference in the mind.

A Hindu has a different mind – certainly – than a Mohammedan or a Jew, but the mind is nothing but that which has been taught to you. When the child is born he is neither Jew nor Hindu nor Christian. He is simply pure essence. If the child is born out of Jewish parents and is brought up by Hindu parents, he will have a Hindu mind, not a Jewish mind; he will never become aware, that he was a Jew, his blood will not show it. Blood doesn't show at all, who is who. You cannot go and be tested by the doctor, through your blood, to show whether you are a Hindu or a Mohammedan. Your bones will not show... So the difference is only in that which is taught to you, imposed upon you.

The difference is only of clothing, dresses, and nothing else; behind the dresses, the same naked humanness. So what nonsense is Jung talking about, that the West has to develop its own alchemy, its own Tantra, its own Tao? But he was afraid: this is his way of avoiding, to face his own fear.

The West has not to evolve anything just because it is the West. Yes, every age has to evolve its own methods, but that is a different matter. It has nothing to do with East and West. I am evolving new methods because many things have changed. In these twenty-five centuries since Buddha much has changed. Buddha was working on a differently conditioned consciousness.

Much has changed – man has become more mature: doubts more, is more skeptical – "yes" has become more difficult to say – would like to explore, but without any belief, cannot trust easily, distrust has become very deep-rooted, is no more innocent, knowledge has corrupted him. These changes have happened. According to these changes, a few changes have to be made in the devices. But it has nothing to do with East and West. And particularly in the modern age to talk of East and West is sheer crap.

The globe is one. For the first time this beautiful phenomenon has happened in the world: we are global, we are universal. Nations are just hangovers, just hangovers from the past – old habits that die hard. And because old habits die hard, man is suffering unnecessarily.

Now science and technology have made it possible that no human being should remain in a kind of semi-starvation. But the old boundaries of the nations are preventing this. If people are poor in the world it is not because now, methods are not available to help them, but because of the nations and the states and the political boundaries. Man is capable enough now to make this whole earth a paradise, but politicians won't allow this. The one thing that the new generation has to do sooner or later – and the sooner the better – is to dissolve nations. We need one world, and that one world will be the answer for many questions and many problems.

Poverty can disappear immediately – if the world is taken as a whole and if all that man has invented, discovered, is used. Otherwise poverty cannot disappear, it is going to persist. Illness can disappear from the world, man can become healthier and healthier. All the means are available, just the old rotten mind goes on clinging.

My own suggestion is for a world government. No national government is needed anymore, all national governments are outdated. But politicians won't allow it to happen. Why? – because if it happens then they all disappear. Where will Morarji-bhai Desai be? Where will all these so many prime ministers and presidents be? All these people will become insignificant. Then they cannot make much fuss and they cannot create much noise on the stage. They will be forgotten. They are really useless, they have to be put in the museums. They are no longer needed.

The world needs one government. The world needs all nations to disappear, only then will wars disappear, otherwise stupid wars, just for small pieces of land which belong to nobody or belong to all. Wars can disappear only if nations disappear: they are by-products of nations. But politicians don't like that, their whole importance will be gone. In fact, politicians like more and more nations.

India was one nation but Indian politicians decided to have two, India and Pakistan, so there can be double prime ministers, presidents, ministers, and all kinds of buffoons. But then Pakistan was divided in two again because if Pakistan was one, then the Bengalis were suffering: they were not prime ministers and they were not presidents. They had to separate from Pakistan. Now India has become three countries, and if it goes on, India will become many countries.

Now, deep down, South India wants to separate from North India over the question of language. Now they say that they are a different race – Dravidians, and the North is a different race – Aryans. "Our blood is separate, our ideal is separate, our language is separate." So the idea of separating from the North is getting more and more powerful because then they will have their own prime minister. Up to now all the prime ministers have been from the North.

They make the president from the South just to console them, because the president in India is a nonentity. He is like the Queen of England: he is a nominal head of the country, without any power. Just to console the South, all the presidents are from the South. And the prime minister is the powerful man, the whole power is his; he is from the North. Now the South is suffering, the South politicians particularly, are suffering very much. Sooner or later the South would like to separate.

The world goes on dividing into small parts. If all the politicians are allowed, then each village will be a nation because then each village will have its own politicians, its own parliament, president, prime minister, ministers – if it is allowed. But why is it not allowed? It is not allowed, again for a political reason: because if South India goes separate, then half of Morarji Desai's power is gone. So those who are in power resist: they would not like the country to be divided. And those who are not in power, they try to divide the country. This goes on.

The world simply needs to decide one day to drop all this nonsense and to become one. No passports should be needed, no visas should be needed. We need a world citizenship. We need freedom to move. Why so much distrust? Why so much antagonism, against each other? This earth is our planet, we should be able to move freely. This world is not yet a free world because of the hangovers of the past. They can be dropped. And with the dropping of them, the world can become as rich as you would like, as healthy as you would like, poverty can disappear.

Poverty cannot disappear by Mahatma Gandhi's traveling in a third-class compartment. These are just strategies, political strategies. How can poverty disappear by Mahatma Gandhi's traveling in a third-class compartment? In fact, he is crowding the third-class compartment which is already crowded! If he had moved in an air-conditioned compartment, at least one person less would have been in the crowd. And these things don't help. But poor people like these things.

They think their poverty is something very special: "Look, even Mahatma Gandhi moves in a third-class compartment. Look at Mahatma Gandhi, he lives like a poor man."

So poverty has something spiritual in it. Poverty has been worshipped, that's why the world remains poor. And wherever poverty is worshipped, those people are going to remain poor.

In India poverty is worshipped – as if there is something spiritual in it. It is pathological. Nothing is spiritual in it. To be poor simply means: you are stupid, you cannot manage. To be poor means only: that you are too attached to old forms which are no longer useful in the world. To be poor simply means: you are not inventive, not creative. To be poor simply means that you are not intelligent. It is nothing spiritual; it simply shows lack of energy, lack of intelligence.

Poverty should be condemned. Poverty should not be worshipped. We have to change the whole consciousness of man about these things, then they can disperse very easily. Technologically we are able to live in a very affluent world, but psychologically we are not capable of living in an affluent world.

It happens that a person becomes rich but still goes on living the life of a poor man – and people appreciate it very much. They say, "Look, he has so many riches, so rich, and still: look at the simplicity of the man." It is the sheer foolishness of the man! Why should he not live the riches that he has attained through great labor and effort? He is just a miser. He does not know how to live richly. He hides his impotence to live richly behind a beautiful facade: that he is "simple." We have to change these ideals.

Poverty is ugly, as ugly as illness. But it is going to remain there if nations remain, it is going to remain there if politicians remain. It is going to remain there if the world remains divided. Wars will continue. We can go on talking about peace but we will go on preparing for war, because peace is just talk. The hangover of the past is big. What is the hangover? Three thousand years of continuous quarreling and fighting and murdering and killing – that is our past.

We have to disconnect ourselves from the past. The Western man has to disconnect himself from the Western past, the Eastern man has to disconnect himself from the Eastern past, the Hindu from the Hindu past and the Christian from the Christian past. And the methodology of disconnecting oneself from one's past is going to be the same – it cannot be Eastern, it cannot be Western. The methodology to disconnect oneself from all past hangovers is going to be the same.

But Jung was very much afraid. He was afraid to move into silence, he was afraid to move into his own inner being, because that inner being is first experienced as utter emptiness. But he will not say that he is afraid; he will say he has to devise Western methods.

There are no Eastern methods, no Western methods; methods are methods. And when you are trying to go beyond mind, it is the same method: awareness. What will you do in the West, what can you do except be aware? To be aware, alert, to be in the moment, spontaneous and total, wherever you are, will help you to get rid of the whole past – political, social, religious. And once you are disconnected from the past, your mind disappears because your mind is nothing but the past hanging around you. Mind is memory, memory is past, and when there is no mind you are utterly here, brilliantly here and now. In that luminous state of being here and now is individuation, in the sense of the book of *The Secret of the Golden Flower*. But Jung was thinking in the right direction – only thinking.

Habib himself is a Jungian analyst, hence the question. It may be very hard for him to understand what I am saying. He has asked another question too. He says, "Osho, when you mention Freud, Jung and Adler in one line, it hurts. It appears as if you are mentioning Buddha, Christ and Nixon together."

It will be hard for you, Habib. But the truth is: that Freud is a genius, Jung and Adler are just pygmies – just pygmies – they don't reach to his height. Freud is a pioneer. He has contributed something of immense value to humanity. Freud is the source, the very tree. Jung and Adler are just branches. Freud can be there without Jung and Adler – he will not miss anything – but Jung and Adler cannot even exist without him. You cannot conceive of it. Can you conceive of Jung and Adler if there had been no Freud? It is impossible, even to conceive of it – they are *his* children. Even if they have disobeyed him, even if they have rebelled against him, it makes no difference: you can fight with your father, you can go against him, but still he is your father. You can fight with him, you can murder him, but still he is your father. You cannot kill the relationship. You can kill the father, but you cannot kill his fatherhood. That is absolutely determined. Now there is no way to undo it.

Freud is the father, Jung and Adler are just rebellious children – small branches which are trying to go away, as far away from the father tree. But they cannot go very far because deep down they still get the shape from the same tree, deep down they are still joined. They are reactions against Freud. And the reason is not that they have been able to develop something very new – nothing of the sort. Jung is to Freud exactly what Judas is to Christ.

It always happens: the closest disciple can betray the master very easily. Judas was the closest disciple of Jesus, the most intelligent, educated disciple – more intelligent, more educated than anybody else. In fact, he was more educated than Jesus himself – the most sophisticated one. And of course, he was hoping that he will be the second: after Jesus is gone, he will be the leader. He was next to Jesus, and naturally a deep jealousy and ego started arising in him. Was that why he can't be the first? How long will he have to wait? Especially when he knows more and he is more articulate than Jesus; Jesus was uneducated. Naturally, he must have started thinking in these terms, and the conflict arose. He must have been very egoistic.

And this is not that it has happened only once, it has happened many times. With Mahavira it happened: his own son-in-law betrayed him – was his disciple and then left with five hundred other disciples. Buddha's own cousin-brother, Devadatta, betrayed him – tried to murder Buddha, poison him. Why? – because Devadatta was always thinking that he is as good as Buddha, "So why is Buddha respected so much, and why not me? We have grown up together, we have been educated by the same teachers, we are both from the same family, the same royal family – why has he become the enlightened one and I am still a disciple?" He wanted to declare himself also an enlightened one. It was ambition, it was jealousy, it was ego. And the same was the case with Jung and Adler and a few others.

Freud is a revolution, Freud is a milestone in the history of human consciousness, a great transforming force – not himself enlightened like Buddha or Mahavira or Jesus, but a great revolutionary as far as thinking is concerned and he has opened a door which makes many things possible. Without Freud it would not have been possible for Tantra to be understood by the West. Without Freud the Western man would have lived with Victorian puritanism, with Victorian pseudoness, hypocrisy. Freud opened the doors: to be more real, to be more authentic, to be more honest and true. Jung and Adler are just offshoots.

Jung was second to Freud. Freud himself had chosen him as his successor – that's why I say he was almost like a Judas. But Freud missed, in the very choice he missed. He himself was not enlightened. He must have chosen the most egoistic because the most egoistic is the most active. Jung was the most egoistic. You can look at the old pictures of him with Freud and with the other disciples: Jung seems to be the most egoistic – even in pictures he cannot hide it – it is impossible to hide. It is written all over his face.

Freud must have chosen him because he was articulate, talented, active – tremendously active – was capable to philosophize, speculate, argue. But all those qualities were such that sooner or later Jung became aware that he can become a master in his own right, he can start a new school of psychology in his own right – why should he bother to play second fiddle? He can be the one, the first, the foremost. He started his own school.

His school is just a reaction – reaction to Freud – and his understanding never went very deep. Although he was groping in the right direction, but, I repeat: it was groping, he was not conscious of it. He was just moving as far away from Freud as possible.

Freud had a very scientific attitude, Jung started moving into the world of art – just to be away from Freud. By accident he started moving in the right direction. Freud was very mathematical, Jung started becoming poetic. Freud was very factual, Jung started becoming more and more mythological. This was because of reaction: he has to prove himself separate, utterly separate from Freud, he had to drop all kind of links with Freud, he had to become his polar opposite – unknowingly, unconsciously. But in a way, it was good. It was good in the sense that he stumbled upon a few facts which Freud would never have stumbled upon on his own – because he was down-to-earth, practical, pragmatic, scientific, a realist, and there are many things which cannot be contained by facts.

There are millions of things which cannot be reduced to facts. And the higher you go, the deeper you go, the more difficult it becomes to talk the language of science or to use the language of science. One has to have more poetic freedom; one needs poetry, one needs fiction to express. Mythology becomes the only means to express certain heights and depths.

But Habib must be feeling hurt. He has been a Jungian analyst and now he has fallen into my hands. And I am going to beat him as hard as possible… because I have to create something totally new out of him: not an analyst but an individual. I have to give him individuation and for that he will have to suffer much too, he will have to pass through many fires. This also is a fire. And once I see your attachments I start attacking them. His attachment is with Jung. Now, because of your attachment, Habib, even Jung has to suffer.

The second question:

Osho,
Why do you use parables?

A parable is a way of saying things which cannot be said. A parable is a finger pointing to the moon: forget the finger and look at the moon. Don't catch hold of the finger, don't start biting the finger. The parable has to be understood and forgotten.

And that is the beauty of a parable, a story: when it is told, you listen attentively because a story always creates curiosity – what is going to happen? You become attentive, you become all ears, you become feminine. You become very intrigued, you start expecting – what is going to happen? The parable creates suspense. It brings a climax and then suddenly, the conclusion. And when after the climax the conclusion happens, you are so hot that the conclusion sinks deep into your heart.

To say something about truth is not an easy matter. One has to devise parables, poetries, different methods and means so that the listener can be aroused into a kind of passion, can become vibrant, available, can wait for what is going to happen.

And it is not that only I am using parables; that has been always so. Buddha used them, Chuang Tzu used them, Jesus used them – all the great teachers of the world have been using the parable as a methodology. And it has served its purpose down the ages, and it is still tremendously meaningful – and it is going to remain meaningful.

A parable is not just a story; it is not to entertain you but to enlighten you. That is the difference between an ordinary story and a parable: a parable has a message in it, a coded message in it; you will have to decode it. Sometimes it will take you your whole life to decode the message, but in its very decoding you would be transformed.

A parable is not an ordinary story, just to entertain you for the moment; its significance is eternal, its significance is not momentary. In fact it is more significant than your so-called facts, because facts have a limited impact. A fact is an event: it happens and then it disappears. And after it has disappeared, there is no way to be certain about it – no way at all.

You cannot be certain whether Jesus existed or not, whether Jesus is a historical person or not – you cannot be absolutely certain. At most you can feel the probability, that he may have been. But the doubt persists: he may not have been – who knows? Because except for his four disciples, nobody mentions him, nobody at all.

Now these four disciples may have been just inventions of a novelist – the whole story is so dramatic. It has all that a dramatic story needs, all that a modern film is based on: a prostitute falling in love with Jesus, a carpenter's son declaring himself the son of God, a young man doing miracles – opening eyes of blind people, giving limbs to those who had none, helping people to be healthy and whole, who had suffered their whole life – not only that, but calling forth Lazarus out of his grave. What more suspense, what more do you need to make a story dramatic? And then being caught, then all the political intrigue, then the efforts to kill him, and then one day he is crucified. And the story does not end there: then after three days he is resurrected. Now no detective novel has so much in it.

Resurrection... Then he is seen again by the disciples. He again meets his disciples and they cannot even recognize him. And then this son of a carpenter – uneducated, unsophisticated – becomes the founder of the greatest religion in the world, also becomes the founder of the greatest religious empire in the world, defeats all other prophets and all other messengers of God. Now what credentials did he have? Buddha is the son of a king, but this carpenter's son has defeated Buddha as far as the number of followers is concerned. Socrates has not a single follower in the world today and he was such a sophisticated man – so intelligent, so utterly intelligent – and he has the same story. He was poisoned and killed, yet he could not gather any followers. What happened? How did it happen? And was this man Jesus really there, a historical figure? – because no history books carry his name, no monuments are there. He may have been just a fictitious story.

Historical events cannot be proved once they have happened – cannot be proved totally, absolutely. At the most they remain more or less probable. But a parable has eternal reality about it. It does not claim any historicity, it simply claims a message. It has nothing to do with events that happen in time. A parable is something that happens in timelessness, it remains relevant.

Whether Jesus existed or not is not the point, but the stories that he has told are, whether he told them or they are some fictitious invention of some novel writer, it doesn't matter. But those parables have eternal messages in them, something so eternal that time cannot make them irrelevant, no passage of time can make them irrelevant.

The truth of a parable is timeless. The truth of history is
the truth about particular events in the present or the past.
Once past, there is no way to prove, beyond all doubt, that
they actually happened; all that can be established is only a
probability. The only truth which we can trust is the truth which
is in the present tense. Only the truth of a parable, because it is
beyond all time, can speak to us forever in the present tense.
A parable remains always in the present tense; it is never past.

A parable is always present; if you are ready to understand it, it is ready to deliver all its treasure to you. And it does not depend on arbitrary conditions of history.

Parable and history may coincide: a story which is
historically true may also present us with the truth of
parable. The Jesus or the Buddha story may be historically
accurate, but even if it is, it is by the truth of the parable not
by the truth of history that we are healed.

It does not matter whether Jesus existed or not, whether Buddha was ever born on the earth or not, that doesn't matter. Just the parable, the possibility, that a buddha is possible is enough to stir our hearts in a new longing, is enough to make us feel thirsty for the divine. It is enough – the very possibility of the parable is enough – to make us look upwards towards heaven, to send us into an exploration; not to be contented with the limitations that we have created around ourselves. It provokes us into adventure.

A man is drowning, a rope comes spinning down.
He clutches it and he is saved. Who wove the rope?
This parable.... Some say Buddha, some say Jesus, some
say Mohammed, but to the drowning man the important
question is: "Will it bear my weight or not?" Who wove
the rope is a question about history: you may get it all
wrong and still be saved.

That is the beauty of a parable: Buddha may not have ever existed, but if you understand the parable you will be saved.

What is a parable? For example:

Buddha is going to participate in a youth festival in his beautiful golden chariot. Suddenly he sees an old man for the first time in his life, because this is the parable: that when Buddha was born, great astrologers came to his father to depict the future, to predict the potential of the child.

All the astrologers said, "Either he will become a world ruler, a *chakra-vartin* who will rule all the six continents, or he will become a sannyasin who will renounce the whole world. These are the two possibilities."

All the astrologers except one raised two fingers to the king and said, "One possibility: he will become the greatest ruler in the world, never known before, never heard of before – such will be his power. And the second possibility: that he may renounce the whole thing completely and move into a forest, become a sannyasin and meditate, and attain to buddhahood."

Out of all the astrologers there was one astrologer, the youngest, who raised only one finger. The king said, "All have raised two fingers, and you are raising one?"

He said, "Because he is going to become a buddha. There is no other possibility."

But he was the youngest astrologer and the king was not puzzled by him and not worried – how much can he know? And the old people, all were saying, "Two are the possibilities."

So he asked the old people, "What should I do so he never renounces the kingdom?"

And they suggested, "Make beautiful palaces for him, separate palaces for separate seasons. In India there are four seasons, so four palaces, with beautiful gardens, acres and acres of flowers. Make it almost like a paradise.

"And make it a point that no old man ever enters into his gardens, no ill person ever comes across him, he never sees a sannyasin, the ochre-robed, he never comes across the phenomenon of death – these four things are prohibited. Even if leaves are falling they should be removed before he sees the old dying leaf. Flowers should be removed from his garden before he becomes aware that flowers fade and die.

"And he should be surrounded by beautiful, the most beautiful women of the kingdom. And he should be kept continuously entertained. Remember, then only can he be saved from the desire of enlightenment: keep him continuously entertained, exhausted, tired. By the morning, he gets up and he should see beautiful women dancing around him to the very last moment when he falls asleep. He should fall asleep with the tunes of music and dance."

And this is how it was managed.

Now whether it is history or not is not the point; this is how we are all managing in some way or other – this is a parable: this is how all parents are afraid – maybe not so much as Buddha's father because that is the extreme point. To make the parable absolutely clear it has to be stretched to its logical end, that's all. But all fathers, all mothers are afraid: you should not become a drop-out, you should not renounce.

Now one woman from America has written to Morarji Desai that her daughter is caught by an Indian master, hypnotized – "Save my daughter! Send her back to me." The papers have not said who this man is who has hypnotized her. More is the possibility it must be me and the daughter must be here. Where else?

Now parents are making associations, societies, forming groups – protecting their children from getting into any Eastern trips. They are more afraid of meditation than drugs. In America there exists an organization of the parents to kidnap their children if they become meditators. And then those children have to be given to deprogrammers, psychoanalysts to peform a mindwash.

This is illegal. And one psychoanalyst has been sent to jail in California for deprogramming, because he was too enthusiastic. First parents were giving him the authority to kidnap their children, then he started on his own. Not even a parent has that authority. Once the child is of age no parent has the authority to kidnap the child. But maybe they can manage: they have lobbies in the parliament, they can manage because the judge is also a parent, a father, and the police and the lawyers and all are parents. They can manage, they can enforce it.

But the psychoanalyst, on his own, became a missionary; started kidnapping, had an organization of kidnappers and started mindwashing programs. He called them "de-programming" – so that a person becomes anti-meditation, anti-East, and falls back into the old fold. If he is a Catholic, becomes a Catholic, goes to the church; if he is a Protestant, becomes a Protestant, reads the Bible. These people are afraid – not only now, they have always been afraid. Buddha's story is just a logical extreme. Parents are afraid their children may renounce the world, that is the eternal truth in it.

But the parable goes on:

Whenever Buddha moved into the capital town, roads were cleaned, all old people were removed, sannyasins were barred. When his chariot will pass, he will never come across anything ugly, ill, old, dead. But that day something happened.

The parable says that the gods in heaven became very worried. They wondered, "Is Buddha going to remain in this stupid kind of continuous entertainment? Will he never become enlightened?"

Roads were cleaned, traffic was managed and controlled, but those gods managed: one god appeared as an old man, another god appeared as a sannyasin, another as a very ill, coughing, almost-dying person, and another as a dead man being carried by other people to the cemetery.

The parable is beautiful – gods became worried. It has a significant message. This existence wants you to become enlightened – that is the meaning of it – existence becomes worried, existence cares, existence wants you to become free of all bondage, free of all darkness. Existence wants to help you. And when it sees that you are going and going and going and wasting your life, it creates situations in which you can be provoked. That is the meaning of the parable.

There are no gods in heaven and no gods will come and walk like old men, but the parable is a way of saying certain hidden truths. The hidden truth is: that the existence cares for you, that you have been sent into this existence to learn something – don't get lost.

Now this is an eternal message. It doesn't matter whether Buddha was born or not, whether he is an historical person or not, all that matters is that existence cares for you. If it cared for Buddha, it cares for you too, it will create occasions for you. And if you are a little bit alert you will be able to catch hold of those occasions, and those occasions will prove a transforming situation, an awakening.

Buddha saw the old man and asked his charioteer, "What happened to this man?"

Naturally, because he had never seen an old man. You would not have asked because you see it every day. It was so strange: he was married, he had a son, and he had never seen an old man. Suddenly he was shocked at seeing the old man. And the charioteer was going to lie because he knew Buddha's father.

But, the story says, one god entered into the charioteer's body and told the truth. He said, "Everybody has to become old."

And Buddha asked, "Am I also going to become old? And my beloved, my wife, Yashodhara too? And my little child, Rahul, who was just born a few days before, he too?"

And the god forced the charioteer to say, "Yes, everybody is going to become old."

And then the dead man was seen. "And what has happened to him?" Buddha asked.

And the god, through the charioteer said, "Everybody has to come to this state – illness, old age, then death."

"Am I also going to die? And what about my beautiful woman, Yashodhara, and my child, Rahul, who was born just a few days before?"

And the god said, "All are going to die without any exception."

And then Buddha saw the ochre-robed sannyasin. And he has said, "Why is he wearing ochre, orange?"

And the god said, "This man has also seen illness, old age, death happening; now he is trying to find the source of immortality. He has become aware that this life is contaminated with death. He has seen the fact that this body is going to disappear – sooner or later, dust unto dust. So he is trying to seek and search for something which is undying. He has become a meditator. He has renounced entertainment. He is in search of enlightenment."

And Buddha said, "Then wait. There is no need to go to the youth festival anymore, because if youth is just a momentary phenomenon, I am already old. And if life is going to disappear into dust, I have died."

See the insight of the parable:

Buddha says, "If it is going to happen, what does it matter whether it is going to happen tomorrow or after seven years or seventy years? If it is going to happen, it has already happened. Turn back! I am no longer interested in any festival. All festivals are finished for me. I have to seek what you call enlightenment. Before this body disappears, I have to use this body as a stepping-stone towards something that is undying. I have to search for nectar."

And he turned back. The same night he left his palace and escaped into the deep forest to meditate.

Now this is a parable. Whether it happened or not, I am not concerned at all. How does it matter whether it coincides with history or not? That's why many times people who are too obsessed with history become angry with me – because I have no commitment to history at all. I take all poetic freedom.

My commitment is to parables, not to history. If I see that the parable can become more beautiful, then I play with the parable; I don't bother whether it is written so or not. Who cares? My whole commitment is to the poetry and the parable and the hidden message in it. And whether it happened or not, it can save you still.

"Who made the rope – Jesus, Buddha, Mohammed?" What is the point when you are drowning ? The point is: whether this rope can bear your weight.

Try it – and you may get it all wrong and still be saved. The rope may have been made by Buddha and you may think it has been made by Jesus – it doesn't matter, you can still be saved. The Bible may have been written by a ghostwriter – it doesn't matter, it has the message – and whosoever the writer was, he must have been enlightened otherwise he could not have written such a beautiful parable. *He* was Jesus. Whosoever has created the story of Buddha, *he* was Buddha. Whether the story existed or not doesn't matter. Hence I use so many parables.

The parable embodies the hope, the danger and the
possibility held out by Lao Tzu or Zarathustra. If all the
Bibles were destroyed, if the name of Jesus were forgotten,
it would not matter anymore so long as the fire kindled the
hope, the beauty – the possibility still went on burning.

If it is proved, absolutely proved, that Buddha never happened, Jesus was never born, Mohammed never walked on the earth, Mahavira is a myth, Lao Tzu is an invention of some fictitious writers – if the hope continues and if man continues to hope to surpass himself, if the fire continues to burn, if the longing remains to seek and search the truth, that's enough: you can forget all about the Bibles and the Korans. If the longing continues, the Koran is going to be born in you. If the longing is intense enough, you will see one day, Buddha arising out of you, you will see Jesus being born in you.

The last question:

Osho,
You say that one has to pay for everything in life. Is not there any
exception?

Listen to this anecdote…

An American in Paris asked a taxi driver to give him the address of a good brothel. He went there alone, selected his partner and ordered dinner. Later that evening, after satisfying his every whim, the thoroughly-drained gentleman went downstairs and asked the Madame for his bill.

"There is no charge, Monsieur," said the lady of the house. Astonished, but not disposed to argue the matter, the gentleman departed. The next night he returned to the brothel and repeated his performance of the previous night. Upon leaving this time however, he was shocked to learn that his bill was eight hundred francs.

"Impossible!" the American shrieked. "I was here yesterday evening and I got everything and you didn't charge me a sou."

"Ah," said the Madame, "but last night you were on television."

Yes, sometimes you may get something for free, but be aware: you may be on television.

In fact there is nothing in life that you can get without paying for it – and you only get as much as you are ready to pay for. When you are ready to pay with your life, you get eternal life in return. Nothing is free, nothing can be free.

Enough for today.

CHAPTER 17
A Little Bit of Sky

Master Lu-Tsu said:

Your work will gradually become concentrated and mature, but before you reach the condition in which you sit like a withered tree before a cliff, there are still many possibilities of error which I would like to bring to your special attention. These conditions are recognized only when they have been personally experienced. First I would like to speak of the mistakes and then of the confirmatory signs.

When one begins to carry out one's decision, care must be taken so that everything can proceed in a comfortable, relaxed manner. Too much must not be demanded of the heart. One must be careful that, quite automatically, heart and energy are coordinated. Only then can a state of quietness be attained. During this quiet state the right conditions and the right space must be provided. One must not sit down (to meditate) in the midst of frivolous affairs. That is to say, the mind must be free of vain preoccupations. All entanglements must be put aside; one must be detached and independent. Nor must the thoughts be concentrated upon the right procedure. This danger arises if too much trouble is taken. I do not mean that no trouble is to be taken, but the correct way lies in keeping equal distance between being and not being. If one can attain purposelessness through purpose, then the thing has been grasped. Now one can let oneself go, detached and without

confusion, in an independent way. Furthermore, one must not fall
victim to the ensnaring world. The ensnaring world is where the
five kinds of dark demons disport themselves. This is the case, for
example, when, after fixation, one has chiefly thoughts of dry wood
and dead ashes, and few thoughts of the bright spring on the great
Earth. In this way one sinks into the world of the dark. The energy
is cold there, breathing is rough, and many images of coldness and
decay present themselves. If one tarries there long, one enters the
world of plants and stones.

Nor must a man be led astray by the ten thousand ensnarements.
This happens if, after the quiet state has begun, one after another
all sorts of ties suddenly appear. One wants to break through them
and cannot; one follows them, and feels as if relieved by this. This
means the master has become the servant. If a man tarries in this
stage long he enters the world of illusory desires.

At best, one finds oneself in heaven, at the worst, among the fox-
spirits. Such a fox-spirit, it is true, may be able to roam in the
famous mountains enjoying the wind and the moon, the flowers
and fruits, and taking his pleasure in the coral trees and jeweled
grass. But after having done this, his reward is over and he is born
again into the world of turmoil.

Once some hunters went deep into a dark forest and found a hut in which
a hermit was praying before a wooden cross. His face shone with happiness.

"Good afternoon, Brother. May God give us a good afternoon. You look very
happy indeed. Why so?"

"I am always happy."

"You are happy living in this lonely hut doing penance? We have everything
and are not happy. Where did you find happiness?"

"I found it here in this cave. Look through that hole and you will catch a
glimpse of my happiness." And he showed them a small window.

"You have deceived us, for all we can see is some branches of a tree."

"Take another look."

"All we see are some branches and a little bit of sky."

"That," said the hermit, "is the reason for my happiness – just a little bit of heaven."

Bliss is man's intrinsic nature. It has not to be attained, it has only to be rediscovered. We already have it. We are it. Searching for it somewhere else is a sure way to miss it. Stop searching and look within and the greatest surprise of your life is awaiting you there, because whatsoever you have been seeking down the ages, through so many lives, is already the case. You need not be a beggar, you are a born emperor. But the Kingdom of God is within you and your eyes go on searching without, hence you go on missing it. It is behind the eyes, not in front of the eyes.

The Kingdom of God is not an object, it is your subjectivity. It is not to be sought because it is the very nature of the seeker. And then, even in the darkest forest, utterly alone in a cave, one can be happy. Otherwise even palaces only create misery.

There are all kinds of miseries in the world: the poor suffer one kind of misery, the rich suffer another kind of misery, but there is no difference as far as misery is concerned. And sometimes it happens that the rich suffer more, because he can afford more. He has more possibilities, more alternatives open for him. The poor cannot purchase much misery, but the rich can purchase. Hence the richest people feel the most miserable in the world. The richest people become the poorest in this sense. In fact, when you become rich, for the first time you feel the poverty of life. When you are poor you can hope that someday you will be rich, and there will be joy and there will be celebration; but when you have attained to the riches of the outside, suddenly the hope disappears and great hopelessness settles in. You are surrounded by a despair: now there is no hope and no future, now the last hope has disappeared.

You had lived with the idea that "One day I will be rich and then everything will be all right." Now you are rich and nothing has changed; the inner misery continues as ever. In fact, because of the outer riches, in contrast to the outer riches, you can see your inner poverty more clearly, more accurately, more penetratingly. The outer richness only provides a background for feeling the inner poverty: outer possessions make you aware of the inner emptiness. Hence, it is not surprising that rich countries become religious.

India was religious when India was rich. In the days of Buddha, Mahavira, India was affluent; because of that affluence India was aware of the inner poverty. And when you become aware of inner poverty, then you start searching inwards. When you become aware that no outer thing can fulfill the inner longing – that all that is outer remains out, you cannot take it in – when this becomes an absolute certainty then you start a new search, a new adventure. That adventure is religion.

India cannot be religious today. India is one of the poorest countries in the world – how can it be religious? It cannot afford to be religious. Religion is the highest kind of luxury, the ultimate in luxury. It is the ultimate music, ultimate poetry, ultimate dance. It is the ultimate drunkenness with existence itself. Hungry and starved, you cannot search for it. When a man is hungry he needs bread, he does not need meditation. When a man is ill he needs medicine, not meditation. Only a healthy person can become aware that something is missing which can be fulfilled by meditation – and by nothing else.

People ask me why there are not many Indians here listening to me. It is not surprising. They are not interested in meditation. Their interest is in material things, their whole obsession is with matter. Of course they talk about spirituality but that is mere talk, a hangover from the past. It gives them a good feeling: at least they are spiritual; if they are missing in material things they can brag about their spirituality. But to me, spiritualism is a higher stage than materialism; materialism functions as a stepping-stone.

Only a rich country starts feeling spiritual poverty. And if you have started feeling spiritual poverty then there are only two possibilities: either you commit suicide or you go through an inner transformation. Meditation is the method of inner transformation. When suicide and meditation remain the only two alternatives and nothing else is left – either destroy yourself because your whole life is meaningless, or transform yourself into a new plane of being – one has to choose between suicide and meditation. The rich countries of the world have always been in this dilemma of choosing between suicide and meditation.

Rich countries suffer more from suicide, from madness, than poor countries. A poor person has no time to think about suicide; he's so preoccupied with life. A poor person has no time to think of transforming his energies; he's so occupied with how to feed his children, how to have a shelter. He's not interested at all in anything else higher than the body, deeper than the body – and it is natural, I am not condemning it. It is absolutely natural, it is how it should be. That's why poor countries of the world are leaning more and more towards communism, and the capitalist countries of the world are leaning more and more towards spiritualism.

Marx's prediction has failed. Marx has said that rich countries will become communist. It has proved nonsense: only poor countries have become communist. Russia was one of the most poverty-stricken countries, so was China, and so is India. India can be a victim of communism any day: it is preparing, it is on the way. America has not turned communist.

Marx predicted that rich countries would become communist. I predict that rich countries always become religious, poor countries become communist. And once, through communism, a country becomes rich, it will start searching and seeking for religion. That's what is happening deep down in the Russian soul now: now Russia has come to a point where it can again think of God and meditation, prayer.

You will be surprised to know that in Russia people meet in secrecy to pray, because prayer is not allowed by the government any more. To be religious is to be a criminal. Here, there are temples and nobody goes; and churches are there and people have to be persuaded somehow to go to the churches, at least on Sunday. People have to be bribed to go to the temples, to the churches, to the mosques, to the *gurdwaras*. Can you conceive of a country where people meet in secrecy, in their basements, to pray – silently, so that nobody can hear? Deep in the Russian soul, religion is surfacing again. It *has* to surface: now Russia is rich enough to think of higher things.

In my vision of life, materialism and spiritualism are not contraries; materialism paves the way for religion. Hence I am utterly materialistic and utterly spiritualistic. That is one of the most fundamental teachings that I am delivering to you: never create an antagonism between the body and the soul, between the world and God. Never create any antagonism between materialism and spiritualism – they go together, just as body and soul. Remain materialistic and use your materialism as a stepping-stone towards spirituality.

That creates much confusion in people's minds because they have always been thinking that poverty is something spiritual. That is utter nonsense. Poverty is the most unspiritual thing in the world. A poor man cannot be spiritual. He can try, but his spirituality will remain superficial. He has not yet been disillusioned by riches – how can he be spiritual? A great disillusionment is needed – a great disillusionment with the outer world – then you turn in. The turning in comes only at a certain point when you are utterly disillusioned with the outside – when you have seen the world, you have lived the world, you have experienced – and you have come to know that there is nothing in it: all soap bubbles, momentary experiences. They promise much but they deliver nothing, and in the end only emptiness is left in your hands.

The outer world can only give you death and nothing else. Life has to be searched for within. The sources of life are *in* you.

The tree is in the seed. If you cut the seed open you will not find the tree – true – because that is not the way to find it. You will have to let the seed grow, then the blueprint that is hidden in the seed comes out. When a child is conceived in a mother's womb he is just a seed, but he has all the blueprint, all the possibilities. What kind of body he will have, what kind of face, what color of eyes and hair, what height, how long he will live, healthy or unhealthy, man or woman, black or white – all is contained in the seed. Life grows out of that seed.

Meditation is turning back towards the innermost core from where all has arisen – the body has arisen, the desires have arisen, the thoughts have arisen, the mind has arisen. *You* have to go back to the source. Religion is a return to the source – and to know the source is to know God, to know the source is to know the goal, because they are both one. To come back to your innermost core from where you had started means you have come to the ultimate where you wanted to reach – the circle is full. There is a moment where the alpha becomes the omega, and then there is fulfillment. When the circle is complete there is fulfillment.

And that is the whole teaching of *The Secret of the Golden Flower,* of Master Lu-Tsu. He's trying to make the path clear to you: how the circle can be complete, how the light can circulate, how you can move inwards – how you can also have a little bit of sky, a little bit of heaven – and then you can be happy anywhere. Even in hell you will be happy.

Right now, as you are, you would be unhappy anywhere, even in heaven. You will find ways and means of being unhappy there too, because you will carry all your jealousies, all your anger, all your greed, all your possessiveness, you will carry all your rage, all your sexuality, all your repressions – you will carry this whole luggage. The moment you reach heaven, you will create hell around yourself there too, because you will be carrying the seeds of hell.

It is said that if you are pure, if you are silent, you reach heaven. The truth is just the opposite: if you are pure, if you are silent, heaven reaches you. One never goes anywhere, one is always here, but once the inside becomes full of light the whole world outside is transformed. Buddha moves in the same world in which you move, Buddha passes through the same streets as you pass, but Buddha lives in a totally different world – Buddha lives in paradise and you live in hell. You may be sitting by the side of a buddha, you may be holding his hand or touching his feet – so close yet so far away, so distant, worlds apart. What is the secret of being in heaven, of being in utter bliss, of being in benediction, of being in that splendor called God? These are the secrets:

Master Lu-Tsu said:
Your work will gradually become concentrated and mature.

The path of Tao is not that of sudden enlightenment. It is not like Zen. Zen is sudden enlightenment, Tao is a gradual growth. Tao does not believe in sudden, abrupt changes. Tao believes in keeping pace with existence, allowing things to happen on their own, not forcing your way in any way, not pushing the river in any way. And Tao says: There is no need to be in a hurry because eternity is available to you. Sow the seeds in time and wait, and the spring comes as it has always been coming. And when the spring comes there will be flowers. But wait, don't be in a hurry. Don't start pulling the tree upwards so that it can grow fast. Don't be in that kind of mind which asks that everything be like instant coffee. Learn to wait, because nature is very very slow-moving. Because of that slow movement there is grace in nature.

Nature is very feminine, it moves like a woman. It does not run, it is not in a hurry, there is no haste. It goes very slowly, a silent music. There is great patience in nature, and Tao believes in the way of nature. "Tao" exactly means nature, so Tao is never in a hurry; this has to be understood. Tao's fundamental teaching is: learn to be patient. If you can wait infinitely, it may even happen instantly. But you should not ask that it should happen instantly: if you ask, it may never happen. Your very asking will become a hindrance, your very desire will create a distance between you and nature. Remain in tune with nature, let nature take its own course. And whenever it comes it is good, and whenever it comes it is fast, *whenever* it comes. Even if it takes ages to come, then too it is not late – it is never late. It always comes in the right moment.

Tao believes that everything happens when it is needed: when the disciple is ready the master appears, when the disciple is ultimately ready God appears. Your worthiness, your emptiness, your receptivity, your passivity makes it possible; not your hurry, not your haste, not your aggressive attitude. Remember, truth cannot be conquered. One has to surrender to truth, one has to be conquered by truth.

But our whole education in all the countries down the ages has been of aggressiveness, of ambition. We make people very speedy. We make them very much afraid. We tell them, "Time is money and very precious, and once gone it is gone forever, so make haste. Be in a hurry."

This has been driving people mad. They hurry from one point to another point, they never enjoy any place. They rush around the world from one intercontinental hotel to another intercontinental hotel – and they are all alike. Whether you are in Tokyo or in Bombay or in New York or in Paris makes no difference. Those intercontinental hotels are all alike, and people go on rushing from one intercontinental hotel to another thinking that they are traveling around the world. They could have stayed in one intercontinental hotel and there would have been no need to go anywhere else – it is all alike – and they think they are reaching somewhere. Speed is driving people neurotic.

Tao is the way of nature, as the trees grow and rivers move, and the birds, and the children – exactly in the same way one has to grow into God.

Your work will gradually become concentrated and mature.

Don't be in a hurry and don't become desperate. If you fail today, don't feel hopeless. Because if you fail today it is only natural. And if you go on failing for a few days it is natural.

People are so afraid of failing that just because of the fear of failing they never try. There are many people who will not fall in love because they are afraid – who knows? They may be rejected – so they have decided to remain unloving, so nobody ever rejects them. People are so afraid of failing that they never try anything new – who knows? If they fail, then what?

And naturally, to move into the inner world you will have to fail many times, because you have never moved there. All your skill and efficiency is of the outer movement, of extroversion. You don't know how to move in. People listen to the words "move in, go in," but it doesn't make much sense to them. All that they know is how to go out, all that they know is how to go to the other. They don't know any way to come to themselves. It is bound to happen, because of your past habits, that you will fail many times. Don't become hopeless. Maturity comes slowly. It comes sure and certain, but it takes time.

And remember, to each different person it will go at a different pace, so don't compare. Don't start thinking, "Somebody is becoming so silent and so joyful and I have not yet become. What is happening to me?" Don't compare with anybody, because each has lived in a different way in his past lives. Even in this life people have lived differently. For example, a poet may find it easier to go in than a scientist; their trainings are different. The whole scientific training is to be objective, to be concerned with the object, to watch the object, to forget subjectivity. The scientist, to be a scientist, has to withdraw himself completely from his experiment. He has not to be involved in the experiment, there should be no emotional involvement. He should be there completely detached, like a computer. He should not be human at all; then only is he a real scientist, and then only will he succeed in science. Now this is a totally different skill.

A poet gets involved. When he watches a flower he starts dancing around it; he participates, he's not just a detached observer. A dancer may find it even more easy because a dancer and his dance are so one, and the dance is so inner that the dancer can move into his inner space very easily. Hence, in the old, mysterious mystery schools of the world, dance was one of the secret methods. Dance evolved in the mystery schools and temples. Dance is one of the most religious phenomena. But it has lost its meaning so completely that it has almost fallen to the opposite polarity; it has become a sexual phenomenon. Dance has lost the spiritual dimension. But remember, whatsoever is spiritual can become sexual – if it falls; and whatsoever is sexual can also become spiritual – if it rises. Spirituality and sexuality are intertwined. A musician will find it easier than a mathematician to move into meditation. You have different skills, different minds, different conditionings.

For example, a Christian may find it more difficult to meditate than a Buddhist, because with twenty-five centuries of constant meditation, Buddhism has created a certain quality in its followers. So when a Buddhist comes to me he can fall into meditation very easily. When a Christian comes, meditation is very alien, because Christianity has completely forgotten about meditation; it knows only about prayer.

Prayer is a totally different phenomenon. In prayer the other is needed, it can never be independent. Prayer is more like love, prayer is a dialogue; meditation is not a dialogue, it is not like love. It is *exactly* the opposite of love. In meditation you are left all alone, nowhere to go, nobody to relate to, no dialogue because there is no other. You are simply yourself, utterly yourself. This is a totally different approach.

So it will depend on your skills, your mind, your conditioning, your education, the religion you have been brought up in, the books that you have been reading, the people you have been living with, and the vibe that you have created in yourself. It will depend on a thousand and one things – on how much you can take – but it comes sure and certain. All that is needed is patience, silent work, patient work, and concentration happens and maturity arrives. In fact a mature person and a concentrated person are only two aspects of the same phenomenon. That's why children cannot be in concentration: they are constantly moving, they cannot be at one point, fixed – everything attracts them. A car has passed by, a bird calls, somebody starts laughing, the neighbor has put the radio on, a butterfly moves – everything, the whole world is attractive. They simply jump from one thing to another thing – they cannot concentrate. They cannot live with one thing so utterly and so totally that all else disappears, becomes nonexistential.

With maturity, concentration arises. Maturity and concentration are two names for the same thing. But the first thing to remember is that it comes gradually; don't compare, don't be in a hurry.

> *But before you reach the condition in which you sit like a withered*
> *tree before a cliff, there are still many possibilities of error, which I*
> *would like to bring to your special attention.*

Master Lu-Tsu says: Before the condition arises in you in which you sit *like a withered tree before a cliff*... This is a Taoist expression of tremendous beauty and significance. It means alive and yet dead, dead and yet *utterly* alive. It means living in the world with great joy and celebration but not being part of the world, being in the world but not allowing the world to be in you – *like a withered tree before a cliff* – living like a dead man.

Alexander wanted to take a sannyasin from India to his own country because his master, the great philosopher, Aristotle, had asked him, "When you come back from India, bring a sannyasin" – because India's greatest contribution to the world is the way, the lifestyle of a sannyasin. Aristotle was very interested. He wanted to see what kind of a man a sannyasin was, because it had happened only in India. This is its special contribution to world culture and humanity, a totally different way of living in the world: living in the world and yet not being of the world, remaining unattached and aloof; like a lotus flower in the pond, living in water and yet untouched by the water. When dewdrops gather on the lotus petals they look beautiful in the morning sun, like pearls, but yet they are not touching the flower at all and the flower is not touching them. So close and yet so far away...

"What kind of a man is a sannyasin?" – Aristotle was philosophically interested. He was not the man to become a sannyasin, but he had asked Alexander to bring a sannyasin: "You will be bringing many things. For me, remember to bring a sannyasin." When Alexander was leaving the country he remembered. He had looted much, then he suddenly remembered, "What about a sannyasin?" He inquired at his last station in India. He inquired about a sannyasin and the people said, "Yes, we have a beautiful sannyasin, but it is almost impossible to take him."

Alexander said, "Leave it to me. Don't be worried. You don't know me. If I order the Himalayas to come with me they will have to come with me, so what about a sannyasin? Where is he? You just give me the address" – and the address was given.

The sannyasin was a naked fakir living by the side of the river. Four strong men were sent with naked swords to bring the sannyasin to Alexander. The sannyasin, seeing those four strong men with naked swords, started laughing.

They said, "You don't understand – this is an order from the great Alexander, that you have to be brought to his court. He is waiting for you."

And the sannyasin said, "I have stopped coming and going long ago. If he wants to see me I can oblige him; he can come. But I have stopped coming and going. That coming and going disappeared with my mind. Now there is nobody to come and nobody to go. I exist no more!"

Of course, those Greeks could not have understood. The Greeks are the polar opposite of the Hindus. The Hindus are basically illogical, and the Greeks are basically logical. The Hindus are poetic, intuitive; the Greeks are intellectuals.

Those four soldiers said to him, "What nonsense are you talking to others? We can drag you!"

The sannyasin said, "You can drag my body but not me. You can put my body in a prison, but not me. My freedom will remain intact. I am a lotus flower, the water cannot touch me."

Now this was utter nonsense to those Greeks. They said, "You wait. Let us inform Alexander, lest we do something wrong." Alexander was informed of those beautiful sentences of the sannyasin, and given the report that "He is a beautiful man, sitting naked in the sun on the riverbank. He looks like a great emperor, and there is nothing around him. He possesses nothing, not even a begging bowl. But the grandeur, the grace! You look into his eyes and it seems as if he is the emperor of the whole world. And he laughed at our foolishness – that we had come with naked swords, and he was not afraid at all. And he said, 'You can kill my body but you cannot kill me.'"

Alexander became intrigued. He went to see this naked sannyasin. He was impressed, greatly impressed, and he said, "You will have to come with me. This is my order!"

But the sannyasin said, "The day I became a sannyasin I stopped receiving any orders from anybody. I am a free man, I am not a slave. Nobody can order me. You can kill me but you cannot order me."

Alexander was angry. He took his sword out and he said, "I will immediately cut off your head!"

And the sannyasin started laughing again. And he said, "You can cut it off, because in fact I have cut it off long ago myself. I am a dead man."

Now this is the meaning of real sannyas: a dead man.

And the man said, "How can you kill a dead man? It would be utter foolishness. How can you kill a dead man? A dead man is dead, he cannot die anymore – all is already finished. You came a little late: I exist no more. Yes, you can cut off the head – you will see the head falling on the sands, I will also watch the head falling on the sands. I am a watcher, a witness."

This is the meaning of *a withered tree before a cliff*. Alexander was the cliff, and the sannyasin was the withered tree. What can the cliff do to the withered tree? The withered tree is already dead, gone. The cliff cannot destroy the withered tree. The withered tree will not be afraid of the cliff.

There are still many possibilities before this can happen to you:

> *...many possibilities of error, which I would like to bring to your*
> *special attention. These conditions are recognized only when they*
> *have been personally experienced.*

Remember all these things that Master Lu-Tsu is saying to you in his immensely valuable message – this is one of the greatest treatises for the seeker. He's saying these things because he has experienced these things on his own journey, he has come across these errors and he would like to enlighten his disciples so that they need not be hindered by these errors, so that they need not be distracted by these errors.

Those who have never meditated will not understand what these errors are. When they have been personally experienced, only then does one understand them. But those who are on the Way, they have to be prepared, they have to be told what the pitfalls on the Way are. The Way is not just simple: many other paths fork out of it at many places and you can take a path which will be a dead-end. But you will come to know that it was a dead-end after many many years, or maybe after many lives. And all the effort and the journey will have been wasted and you will have to come back again to the point from where you lost the main road. And there are no milestones, no fixed map is available, cannot be made, because God goes on changing. His existence is a constant change. Except for change, everything goes on changing, so no fixed map is possible. Only hints can be given; these are hints. If you understand the hints you will be able to follow the right path, and whenever there is a possibility of going into errors your understanding will help you.

> *First I would like to speak of the mistakes and then of the confirmatory signs.*

Lu-Tsu says: First I will talk about the mistakes that are possible and then I will tell you what the confirmatory signs are which make it certain that you are on the right path.

> *When one begins to carry out one's decision, care must be taken so that everything can proceed in a comfortable, relaxed manner.*

This is the first thing to be understood. Once you take the decision to follow the inward path, once you take the decision to be a sannyasin, to be a meditator, once you take the decision that now the inner has called you and you are going to seek and search on the quest of "Who am I?", then the first thing to be remembered is: don't move in a tense way, move in a very relaxed manner. Make sure that your inner journey is comfortable. Now this is of immense importance.

Ordinarily, this first error happens to everybody: people start making their inner journey unnecessarily complicated, uncomfortable. It happens for a certain reason. People are angry at others in their ordinary life. In their ordinary life they are violent with others. In their ordinary extrovert journey they are sadists: they enjoy torturing others, they enjoy defeating others, they enjoy competing with others, conquering others. Their whole joy is in how to make others feel inferior to themselves. This is what your extrovert journey is. This is what politics is. This is the political mind, constantly trying to become superior to the other. Legally, illegally, but there is constant effort to defeat the other, whatsoever the cost. Even if the other has to be destroyed, then the other has to be destroyed. But one has to win: one has to be the prime minister, one has to be the president, one has to be this and that – at any cost! And all are enemies because all are competitors. Remember this: your whole education prepares you, makes you ready to fight. It does not prepare you for friendship and love, it prepares you for conflict, enmity, war.

Whenever there is competition there is bound to be enmity. How can you be friendly with people with whom you are competing, who are dangerous to you and to whom you are dangerous? Either they will win and you will be defeated, or you will win and they have to be defeated. So all your so-called friendship is just a facade, a formality. It is a kind of lubricant that makes life move smoothly. But deep down there is nobody who is a friend. Even friends are not friends because they are comparing with each other, fighting with each other. This world has been turned into a war-camp by the education of ambition, politics.

When a man turns inwards the problem arises: what will he do with his anger, enmity, aggression, violence? Now that he is alone, he will start torturing himself, he will be angry with himself – that's what your so-called mahatmas are. Why do they torture themselves? Why do they fast? Why do they lie down on a bed of thorns? When there is a beautiful shady tree, why do they stand in the hot sun? When it is hot, why do they sit by the side of fire? When it is cold, why do they stand naked in the rivers or in the snow? These are inverted politicians. First they were fighting with others, now there is nobody left – they are fighting with themselves. They are schizophrenic, they have divided themselves. It is a civil war now; they are fighting with the body.

The body is a victim of your so-called mahatmas. The body is innocent, it has not done a single wrong thing to you. But your so-called religions go on teaching you that the body is the enemy, torture it.

The extrovert journey was the journey of sadism. The introvert journey becomes the journey of masochism – you start torturing yourself. And there is a certain glee, a perverted joy in torturing oneself. If you go into history you will be surprised, you will not believe what man has been doing to himself. People have been wounding their bodies and keeping those wounds unhealed – because the body is the enemy.

There have been Christian sects, Hindu sects, Jaina sects and many others, who have become very very cunning, clever, efficient in torturing their bodies. They have developed great methods of how to torture the body. There was a Christian sect which was not only in favor of fasting, but of beating one's body, flogging one's body, and the greatest saint was the one who was most wounded by his own beating. People would come and count their wounds. Now what kind of people were these who were counting their wounds? They must have also been enjoying – a perverted joy.

In India there are Jaina *munis* who go on torturing their bodies. The Digambara Jaina monks pull out their hair every year, and a great gathering happens when they pull out their hair. It is painful, and the people are joyous: "Great austerity is being done." The man is simply a perverted psychopath. He needs electro-shocks – nothing less will do.

There is a certain kind of madness in which people start pulling their hair – and you know if you are a husband, your wife sometimes tries it, when she is in a rage, mad. Women try it more because they have been taught not to hit their husbands. Then what to do? They want to hit but the husband cannot be hit because the scriptures say your husband is your god, and she knows it is all bullshit but the scriptures are the scriptures. She knows the husband perfectly well – that if he is a god, then who will the devil be? But it is not to be said; she has to touch his feet. When she writes love letters to the husband she has to sign "your slave," and she knows who the slave is! Everybody knows in fact, but it is a formality.

And if she hits the husband guilt arises, that she has done something irreligious, something like a sin, so she cannot hit the husband. But she wants to hit! Now what to do? Either she breaks plates – and that is costly, and she herself suffers that way, that is not of any use – or the easiest way, the cheapest way, economical, is to beat oneself, pull one's hair, throw oneself against the wall, hit the head against the wall. This is the cheapest. She wanted to hit the husband's head but she could not do it, it is not allowed; it is immoral. Who has taught her this idea? – the husband…the husbands and their priests and their politicians.

If you go into a madhouse you will find many people pulling their hair. There is a certain kind of madness in which people pull their hair.

Now a Jaina monk pulling his hair is really pathological, but people gather together to celebrate the occasion – "Something great is happening! Look! What a great saint!" And because I call these people pathological, they are against me. That's simple, very simple; they have to be against me.

In Christian sects…in Russia there was a sect whose members used to cut their genital organs, and great gatherings would collect. There were certain days when people would do that. It was a frenzy. One person would cut his genital organs and throw them, and there was blood flowing all over the place. Then a frenzy would take over other people who had only come just to see: then somebody else would jump in and he would do it. And by the time the festival was over there would be a pile of genital organs. And these were great saints.

Now women were at a loss: they would start cutting their breasts, because how could they be defeated? They started cutting their breasts. All kinds of stupidities became possible because of a simple error, and the error is: in life you try to make life difficult for others; when you start turning in, there is a possibility that the old mind will try to make your life difficult.

Remember, the inner seeker has to be comfortable, because only in a comfortable situation, in a relaxed state can something happen. When you are tense, uncomfortable, nothing is possible. When you are tense, uncomfortable, your mind is worried, you are not in a still space. When you are hungry how can you be in a still space? And people have been teaching fasting, and they say fasting will help you to meditate. Once in a while fasting may help you to have better health – it will take a few pounds away from your body, unnecessary pounds – but fasting cannot help meditation. When you are fasting you will constantly think of food.

I have heard...

A married couple went to the parish priest for marital counseling. In the course of the conversation which was serious at first, the priest commented on the number of good-looking girls in the parish.

"Father," said the husband, "you surprise me."

"Why?" he asked, "just because I am on a diet does not mean I can't look at the menu."

Those people who are repressing their sex will be constantly looking at the menu, and those people who are repressing their hunger will be constantly thinking of food. It's natural! How can you meditate? When you are fasting, menus upon menus will float in your mind, will come from everywhere – beautiful dishes. With all the smell of food, and the aroma, for the first time you will start feeling that your nose is alive, and for the first time you will feel that your tongue is alive.

It is good to fast once in a while so that you can gather interest in food again, but it is not good for meditation. It is good to make your body a little more sensitive, so you can taste again. Fast should be in the service of feast! It is good once in a while not to eat so that the appetite comes back. Healthwise it is good, but meditation has nothing to do with it. It will be more difficult to meditate when you are hungry than when you are fully satisfied. Yes, eating too much will again create trouble, because when you have eaten too much you will feel sleepy. When you have not eaten at all you will feel hungry.

To be in the middle is the right way: the Golden Mean.

Eat so that you don't feel hungry, but don't eat too much so that you feel overloaded, sleepy – and meditation will be easier. The Golden Mean has to be followed in all ways, in all kinds of situations.

Be comfortable, be relaxed. There is no need to torture yourself, there is no need to create unnecessary troubles. Drop that mind of anger, violence, aggression, and then only can you move inwards – because only in a relaxed consciousness does one start floating inside, deeper and deeper. In utter relaxation one reaches to one's innermost core.

> *When one begins to carry out one's decision, care must be taken so*
> *that everything can proceed in a comfortable, relaxed manner. Too*
> *much must not be demanded of the heart.*

And don't demand too much, because if you demand too much you will become tense, anxiety will arise. In fact, don't demand at all. Just wait. Just put the seed in the heart and start working – wait for the spring.

> *Too much must not be demanded of the heart.*

And people start demanding too much: they want immediate *satoris,* *samadhis,* they want immediate nirvana.

Sometimes it happens – foolish people come to me and they say, "We have been meditating for seven days and nothing has happened yet." Seven days? And for seventy million lives they have been doing everything against meditation! And in seven days – as if they have obliged God, or me – they come with a complaint: "Nothing has happened. Seven days have passed, only three days are left of the camp," and they are not yet enlightened!

Don't demand too much, don't be too greedy. Be a little more understanding. Everything takes time.

> *One must be careful that quite automatically heart and energy are*
> *coordinated.*

Remember that you need not be worried about the result. It is always according to your need and according to your worth: whatsoever you are ready for is going to happen. If it is not happening that simply shows you are not ready for it. Get ready. Demanding it will not help. Just remember that you are not yet worthy. So cleanse your heart more, concentrate more, meditate more, become more silent, be relaxed. Become more and more attuned with the inner, and wait, because when the heart and energy are coordinated, the result automatically follows. If you have sown the seeds you need not dig the ground every day and look at the seeds to see what is happening; otherwise you will destroy the seeds. Nothing will ever happen.

You just wait. For months nothing happens – and you have to water and you have to put manure and you have to go on caring and nothing happens for months. Then one day suddenly, one early morning, the miracle: the seeds have sprouted. Just two small leaves have come out, the miracle has happened – that which was invisible has become visible. This is the greatest miracle in the world: a seed becoming a sprout. Now dance!

But it always happens in its own time.

> *Only then can a state of quietness be attained. During this quiet state, the right conditions and the right space must be provided.*

Naturally, if you are preparing a rose garden you have to change the whole soil. Stones have to be removed, old roots have to be removed, weeds have to be removed. You have to create a right condition and a right space, protected. You have to make a fence around it. When you are going to cultivate roses all these preparations will be needed. Meditation is a rose – the greatest rose, the rose of human consciousness. That's why this book is called *The Secret of the Golden Flower*...a golden rose.

What are the right conditions? And what is the right space?

> *One must not sit down (to meditate) in the midst of frivolous affairs.*

You should find a place which enhances meditation. For example, sitting under a tree will help, rather than going and sitting in front of a movie house or going to the railway station and sitting on the platform; going to nature, to the mountains, to the trees, to the rivers where Tao is still flowing, vibrating, pulsating, streaming all around. Trees are in constant meditation, silent – unconscious is that meditation, and I'm not suggesting you become a tree. You have to become a buddha! But Buddha has one thing in common with the tree: he's as green as a tree, as full of juice as a tree, as celebrating as a tree, of course with a difference – he is conscious and the tree is unconscious. The tree is unconsciously in Tao, a buddha is consciously in Tao. And that is a great difference, the difference between the Earth and the sky.

But if you sit by the side of a tree, surrounded by beautiful birds singing, or a peacock dancing, or just a river flowing and the sound of the running water, or by the side of a waterfall and the great music of it... Find a place where nature has not yet been disturbed, polluted. If you cannot find such a place then just close your doors and sit in your own room. If it is possible, have a special room for meditation in your house; just a small corner will do, but especially for meditation. Why especially? – because every kind of act creates its own vibration. If you simply meditate in that place, that place becomes meditative. Every day you meditate it absorbs your vibrations when you are in meditation. Next day when you come, those vibrations start falling back on you: they help, they reciprocate, they respond.

That's the idea behind temples and churches and mosques; the idea is beautiful. The idea is that it may not be possible for everybody to have a special room for prayer or meditation, but we can have a special place for the whole village – a temple surrounded by trees, on the bank of a river, where crowds don't gather, where mundane affairs are not done. When one wants to meditate one can go to the temple. And everybody knows that he is in the temple, he is not to be disturbed.

A sacred place is nothing but a right space for meditation and right conditions. If you are feeling very angry, that is not the time to meditate: it will be going against the flow. If you are feeling very greedy this is not the time to meditate, you will not find it easy. But there are moments when you are easily available to meditation. The sun is rising and you have seen the sun rising, and suddenly all is silent within you, you are not yet part of the marketplace – this is the moment to meditate. You have been feeling good, healthy, you have not been fighting with anybody today – this is the time to meditate. A friend has come to visit and you are full of love – this is the time to meditate. You are with your woman and you both are feeling tremendously happy – sit together and meditate, and you will find the greatest joy of your life happening if you can meditate with your beloved.

Find the right conditions, and they are always available. There is not a single man who cannot find right conditions. In twenty-four hours many moments come which can be transformed into meditation very easily, because in those moments you are naturally going inwards. The night is full of stars: lie down on the ground, look at the stars, feel in tune, and then meditate. Sometimes it is good to go for a holiday into the mountains – but don't take your radio with you, otherwise you are taking the whole nonsense with you. And when you go to the mountains don't give your address and your phone number to anybody, otherwise there is no need to go anywhere. When you go to the mountains forget all about the world for a few days. That is the meaning of a holiday: it has to be holy, only then is it a holiday. If it is not holy, if it is not in tune with the sacred, it is not a holiday; people carry their world with them.

Once I went to the Himalayas with a few friends, and then I had to ask them to leave me because they had brought their transistor sets and their newspapers and magazines, and the novels that they were reading, and they were constantly talking – talking about things that they had always been talking about. So I told them, "Why have you come to the Himalayas? You were saying these things at your home perfectly well, and again you are talking the same things, the same gossiping, the same rumors."

And whenever they would go with me to some beautiful spot they would take their cameras, they would take pictures. I told them, "*You* have come here to see. You have not brought your camera to see the Himalayas!"

But they said, "We shall make beautiful albums, and later on we will see what beautiful places we had visited." And right there they were not there, they were just clicking their cameras. This stupidity has to be left behind.

It is good once in a while to go to the mountains. And I am not saying to start living there – that is not good – because then you become addicted to the mountains and you become afraid of coming back to the world. The holiday has to be just a holiday. Then come back into the world and bring all the peace and the silence and the experience of the sacred with you. Bring it with you, make an effort so that it remains with you in the marketplace.

These suggestions are for the beginners. When a person has really become a meditator, he can meditate sitting before a cinema, he can meditate on the railway platform.

For fifteen years I was continuously traveling around the country, continuously traveling – day in, day out, day in, day out, year in, year out – always on the train, on the plane, in the car. That makes no difference. Once you have become really *rooted* in your being, nothing makes a difference. But this is not for the beginner. When the tree has become rooted, let winds come and let rains come and let clouds thunder; it is all good, it gives integrity to the tree. But when the tree is small, tender, then even a small child is dangerous enough or just a cow passing by – such a holy animal – but that is enough to destroy it.

When you are beginning, remember, Lu-Tsu's suggestions are of immense importance.

> *That is to say, the mind must be free of vain preoccupations.*
> *All entanglements must be put aside. One must be detached*
> *and independent.*

When you are trying to meditate, put the phone off the hook, disengage yourself. Put a notice on the door that for one hour nobody should knock, that you are meditating. And when you move into the meditation room take off your shoes, because you are walking on sacred ground. And not only take your shoes off, but everything that you are preoccupied with. Consciously leave everything with the shoes: go inside unoccupied. One can take one hour out of twenty-four hours. Give twenty-three hours for your occupations, desires, thoughts, ambitions, projections; take one hour out of all this. And in the end you will find that only that one hour has been the real hour of your life; those twenty-three hours have been a sheer wastage. Only that one hour has been saved and all else has gone down the drain.

Nor must the thoughts be concentrated upon the right procedure.

And the second thing to be remembered: don't become too preoccupied with the right procedure, otherwise that becomes a preoccupation – that one should sit in a certain posture. If you can sit, good, but if it becomes an unnecessary preoccupation, drop it. For example, if you cannot sit in a full lotus posture – which is difficult for people who have been sitting for their whole lives on chairs; it is difficult because their musculature has developed in a certain way – then your legs will not feel good. They will go to sleep or they will start creating trouble for you, they will constantly hanker for attention. So there is no need to force a lotus posture. A lotus posture, if easy, is good. Otherwise any posture is a lotus posture.

If you cannot sit on the ground, if it is difficult, sit on a chair. Meditation is not afraid of chairs. It can happen anywhere.

Just the other day Renu had asked one question: "Can enlightenment happen on a rocking horse?" It can happen. It can even happen to the rocking horse! You need not be worried about it. So, Lu-Tsu says:

Nor must the thoughts be concentrated upon the right procedure.

Just take a little care, that's all, but don't become too worried about it – whether the spine is absolutely erect or not, whether your head is in line with the spine or not, whether your eyes are exactly as Lu-Tsu wants them. Now you have a different kind of eyes than Lu-Tsu; you know the Chinese and their eyes. In fact they always seem to look at the tip of the nose, their eyes are only half-open. When I give sannyas to a Chinese, then I have much difficulty looking into their eyes.

You have different kinds of eyes. Everybody has different kinds of eyes and different kinds of noses, so don't become too occupied with these minor things. They are just indications: understand them, absorb them, and then go on your way. Find out your own way. The basic note to be remembered is: you have to be comfortable and relaxed.

> *This danger arises if too much trouble is taken. I do not mean that*
> *no trouble is to be taken, but the correct way lies in keeping equal*
> *distance between being and not being.*

One has to be exactly in the middle. People either become too active or become too inactive. If they become too active, anxiety is created – a kind of rush, hurry, speed, restlessness; if they become too inactive, sleep, a lethargy, indolence. Be in the middle. This being in the middle is a criterion to be used always. Don't eat too much, don't starve too much. Don't sleep too much, don't sleep less than needed. Remember always to be in the middle: excess is prohibited, all kinds of extremes have to be dropped, because only in the middle is there a relaxed state of mind.

> *If one can attain purposelessness through purpose, then the thing*
> *has been grasped.*

If one can attain this kind of balance, between effort and effortlessness, between purpose and purposelessness, between being and no-being, between mind and no-mind, between action and no-action...

> *If one can attain purposelessness through purpose – effortlessness*
> *through effort, inactivity through action – then the thing has been*
> *grasped. Now one can let oneself go, detached and without confusion,*
> *in an independent way.*

This is the basic: then one can allow oneself to flow with the flow of things, *one can let oneself go.*

> *Furthermore, one must not fall victim to the ensnaring world.*
> *The ensnaring world is where the five kinds of dark demons*
> *disport themselves. This is the case, for example, when after fixation*

one has chiefly thoughts of dry wood and dead ashes
and few thoughts of the bright spring on the great Earth.

Remember, the greatest problem for a religious person is not to be too serious, the greatest problem for the religious person is not to be sad, the greatest problem for the religious person is not to be negative, because ordinarily that happens. Religious persons become very sad, very serious, very life-negative: they forget all about spring. They only think of *dry wood and dead ashes.* They have lost balance. A few thoughts of the bright spring on the great Earth have to be remembered.

The really religious person is one who knows the sense of humor. The really religious person is sincere but never serious, utterly devoted to his work but never with that attitude of "holier-than-thou," *never;* never feeling any superiority because of it, but humble. The really religious person is one who can dance with the wind and the rains, who can smile and giggle with children, who can feel at ease with all kinds of situations in life. That is freedom, that is freedom from the ego. Ego makes one serious.

In this way one sinks into the world of the dark.

If you become too serious you will sink into the world of the dark, into the negative world.

The energy is cold there, breathing is rough, and many images
of coldness and decay present themselves.

Remember, you are not to become cold. You will find your so-called saints very cold: they have misunderstood the whole point. Become cool, but never become cold – and there is a lot of difference between the two, and a very deep paradox is there. I call it "cool": compared to the heated state of passion, it is cool; it is warm compared to the coldness of death. It is warm compared to the coldness of death and it is cool compared to the passionate lust for life. It is warm and cool both. A really religious person is cool because he has no lust, and he is warm because he is not sad, he is not serious.

If one tarries there long, one enters the world of plants
and stones.

And if you become too cold, sooner or later you will become a rock: you will become unconscious, you will fall from humanity. Many of your saints, in my observation, are people who have fallen from humanity. They have not become superhuman, they have become subhuman. They belong to the worlds of rocks and stones.

> Nor must a man be led astray by the ten thousand ensnarements.
> This happens if after the quiet state has begun, one after another
> all sorts of ties suddenly appear. One wants to break through and
> cannot. One follows them and feels as if relieved by this.

This is where psychoanalysis has gone wrong. Psychoanalysis has become the method of free association of thoughts. You can go on and on: one thought leads to another, *ad infinitum*. One should remain detached from the procession of thoughts. They will come, they will surround you from everywhere, they will be like clouds – even the little bit of sky will be lost. And when there are too many thoughts, the natural instinct is to fight with them, because you have read that meditation means thoughtlessness. But by fighting one never becomes thoughtless. If you fight, you will be defeated. The very fight becomes the cause of your defeat. You cannot fight with shadows, otherwise you will be defeated. Try fighting with your own shadow and you will be defeated – not that the shadow is very powerful, but because the shadow is not. And fighting with something which is not, how can you win? Thoughts are shadows, don't fight with them.

And if you don't fight then the other alternative opens up – that's what psychoanalysis has chosen: then move with them, then let them move wherever they move – free association of thoughts. Then one thought is tied with another and with another and with another, and it goes on and on *ad infinitum, ad nauseam*. This will feel like a kind of relaxation. That's why out of psychoanalysis people feel helped, saved. They are not saved, they are not helped; just the fight disappears. Because you fight you become tense. When you don't fight the tension disappears – and that disappearance of the tension gives you the feeling as if you are saved.

Mulla Nasruddin uses very tight shoes, two sizes less than he needs. The whole day he complains, and the whole day he is angry with the shoes.

I asked him one day, "Why don't you change these shoes? Why do you go on complaining? Who is forcing you to wear these shoes? You can purchase another pair."

He said, "That I cannot do! Never!"

I said, "Why?"

"Because," he said, "this is my only solace. When after the whole day's struggle with the shoes I come home and throw these shoes away and lie down on my bed, it feels so good!"

It will feel good. When you fight with your thoughts and you cannot win, then you drop fighting and you allow the thoughts to move and you start moving with them, it feels good. That's what the whole secret of psychoanalysis is. Psychoanalysis does not help at all: it simply makes you feel good because it helps you to stop fighting.

Lu-Tsu says, "Both are not right. There is no need to fight, there is no need to allow the thoughts and become a follower of them. You remain a watcher, a witness."

This means the master has become the servant.

If you follow the thoughts, the master has become the servant.

If a man tarries in this stage long, he enters the world of illusory desires.

The master has to be claimed back. You have to be the master, not the servant. And what is mastery? – to be a witness is to be a master. Just watch those thoughts; utterly calm and quiet, watch. Let them come, let them go, let them arise, let them disappear: you simply take note – the thought is arising, the thought is there, the thought is gone. And soon you will come to a point where they arise less and less and less, and then one day, the gap…all thoughts have disappeared. In that gap, the first experience of God.

> *At best one finds oneself in heaven, at the worst, among the fox-spirits. Such a fox-spirit, it is true, may be able to roam in the famous mountains, enjoying the wind and the moon, the flowers and fruits, and taking his pleasure in coral trees and jeweled grass. But after having done this, his reward is over and he is born again into the world of turmoil.*

If you succeed in meditation you are born in heaven, in eternal bliss. If you don't succeed, if you go astray… That going astray in Taoism is called:

At worst, one is born among the fox-spirits.

A fox-spirit is the spirit of a poet. The fox-spirit is the spirit of imagination. Even if you fail in your meditations something will be gained. This will be your gain: you will enjoy the trees more and the flowers more, and the world and the beauty more. But sooner or later the energy that had been created by meditation will disappear and you will have to fall back again to the old turmoil.

Remember, if you succeed in meditation the joy is eternally yours. But even if you fail you will find a few moments of beautiful joy and poetry. Those who fail in meditation become poets, those who succeed become seers. Seers are poets of the eternal, poets are the poets of the momentary.

That's why sometimes it happens: a little bit of meditation and you feel so good that you stop meditating – you think all is attained. Trees are greener, roses are rosier, love is going beautifully, things have started happening – why bother? But soon the energy that had been created will disappear: you have become a fox-spirit. That's what is happening through drugs all over the world: drugs only create fox-spirits. But meditation, if not completed, can also do the same.

Once the decision has been taken, then it is a commitment: you *have* to go to the very end of it. It is a challenge. Accept this challenge and go for this most beautiful journey of your inner search. And never stop in the middle anywhere unless you have arrived, unless you have arrived to the center of the cyclone.

Enough for today.

CHAPTER 18
Love is the Only Friend

The first question:

Osho,
While in therapy myself, I spent much time praying. Over the years I
felt better. I never knew whether it was the therapy or the prayer. As a
therapist I want to urge others to pray but feel embarrassed.

Love is therapy, and there is no other therapy in the world except love. It is always love that heals, because love makes you whole, love makes you feel welcome in the world, love makes you a part of existence. It destroys alienation. Then you are no more an outsider here, but utterly needed. Love makes you feel needed, and to be needed is the greatest need. Nothing else can fulfill that great need. Unless you feel that you are contributing something to existence, unless you feel that without you the existence would be a little less, that you would be missed, that you are irreplaceable, you will not feel healthy and whole.

And prayer is the highest form of love. If love is the flower, then prayer is the fragrance. Love is visible, prayer is invisible. Love is between one person and another person, prayer is between one impersonal presence and the impersonal presence of the whole. Love is limited, prayer is unlimited. If you can pray, no other therapy is needed.

Therapies are needed in the world because prayer has disappeared. Man was never in need of therapy when prayer was alive, flowing, when people were dancing in great gratitude, singing songs in praise of God, were ecstatic just for being, for being here, were grateful just for life. When tears were flowing from their eyes – of love, of joy – and when there were songs in their hearts, there was no need for therapy. Therapy is a modern need, a poor substitute for prayer.

Psychoanalysis is a poor substitute for religion, very poor. But when you cannot get the best, then you settle for second-best or the third-best, or whatsoever is available. Because temples have become rotten, churches have become political, religion has been contaminated by the priests, man is left alone – uncared for, with nobody to support him. The very ground on which he has been standing for centuries has disappeared. He is falling in an abyss, feeling uprooted. Psychoanalysis comes as a substitute: it gives you a little bit of rooting, it gives you a little bit of ground to hold onto. But it is nothing compared to prayer. Because the psychoanalyst himself is in need, he himself is as ill as the patient, there is not much difference between the psychoanalyst and the patient. If there is any difference, that difference is of knowledge – and that makes no difference at all. It is not a difference of being. If there is any difference it is quantitative, it is not that of quality, and quantity does not make much difference. The psychoanalyst and his patient are both in the same boat.

In the old days there was a different kind of person moving in the world, the religious person – the Buddha, the Christ. His very presence was healing. Because he was healed and whole, his wholeness was contagious. Just as diseases are contagious, so is health. Just as illnesses can be caught from others, so can you catch something of the healing energy from the other. But for that, the psychoanalyst will not be of much help. He may help a little bit to solve your problems, intellectually. He may find out the causes of your problems – and when you know the cause you feel a little better, you are not in ignorance. But just by knowing the cause nothing is helped. You are suffering: the psychoanalyst will show that you are suffering because of your mother, because of your upbringing, because of your childhood. It makes you feel a little good: so it is not you who is the cause, it is the mother, or there is always something else you can put the blame on. Psychoanalysis shifts the responsibility, makes you feel a little weightless, unburdened, but the problem is not solved. Just by knowing the cause, the cause does not disappear.

Religion has a totally different orientation: it does not shift the blame on others. In fact, it makes you feel responsible for the first time in your life. Hence psychoanalysis is a kind of bribery. It is a kind of lubricant, it is a kind of help in your ego, strengthening your ego, throwing the blame on others. It is a very dangerous game because once you start throwing the blame on others you will never be transformed, because you will never feel responsible. This is one of the greatest calamities that has happened to this age.

Marx says that it is the society that is responsible for all the ills that you are suffering. You are not responsible: it is the class-divided society, it is the economic structure. Freud says it is not the economic structure but the conditioning that has been given to you by the parents, by the society, by education, by the priest, by the church. It is the conditioning, that's why you are suffering. You are not responsible.

This is the old game. In the past it was called "the game of fate": fate is responsible, you are not responsible. This is the same game played with new names and new labels, but the trick is that you are not responsible. Of course, one feels a little bit happier, but nothing changes. Sooner or later that happiness disappears because the cause remains where it was, the wound remains: how does it matter who has wounded you? Just by knowing that your mother has wounded you or your father or the society or the church, how does it matter? The wound is there, full of pus, growing, becoming bigger every day. You can feel a little bit good for the moment, unburdened: so you are not responsible, you are just a victim. You can sympathize with yourself, you can feel pity for yourself and you can feel anger for others, for those who have created the wound. But this is not a way of transformation. The wound is there and the wound will continue to grow, the wound does not bother about what you think about it. Your thinking makes no difference to the wound.

Religion is a totally different approach: it makes you feel responsible. It is against your ego. It says, "It is you! It is your responsibility to have chosen a certain pattern of life. All patterns were available, no pattern has been imposed on you."

Buddha was born in the same society in which others suffered, suffered hell, and he attained here-and-now, the ultimate state of bliss. So society cannot be responsible. Christ was born in the same society in which Judas was born, in which everybody else was born, but he turned to God.

Religion makes you feel responsible *and* free. Freedom and responsibility are two aspects of the same coin. If you are not ready to feel responsible, you will never be free. You will remain in bondage, in the bondage of others.

Psychoanalysis makes you feel in bondage. It can't really help. Prayer makes you free. Prayer means religion. Prayer means: you are responsible, you have chosen a certain way of life. Now there is no need to make much fuss about it. If you don't like it, drop it! It is up to you, it is *absolutely* up to you. And you can drop it in a single moment of awareness. That's what *satori* is, *samadhi* is: dropping the whole nonsense, in a single moment of understanding, seeing the point that, "I am carrying it and if I don't want, there is no need to carry it. Nobody can force it on me – no fate, no society, no church."

It can be dropped because your inner essence remains free of your personality. Personality is just like clothing: you can drop it, you can be naked any moment. Your essence can be naked any moment. And when the essence is naked, you are healed – because the essence knows no illness. The essence is always in the state of health, in the state of wholeness.

Prayer is the ultimate way of dropping all personalities – Christian, Hindu, Jaina, Buddhist, Indian, German, English. Prayer is the way to put aside the whole paraphernalia of personality and just to be, pure, innocent. In that purity and innocence one starts bowing down. You may not believe in God, there is no need to believe in God; a believer is not a religious person either. But when you are utterly nude in your essence, when you have dropped all clothing – you have dropped all that has been given to you, you have disconnected yourself from the learned, from all that you have learned, the taught, the cultivated – suddenly you are in your pristine clarity, as you were before your birth. Your original face is there. It is as fresh as dewdrops in the early morning, as shiny as the stars in the night, with all the grandeur of the flowers and the trees, and with all the simplicity and innocence of children, animals, birds.

In that moment you feel so joyous, out of joy you bow down – not to a God. Remember, there is no need to believe in a God. You simply bow down out of gratitude, there is no object in your bowing. You simply bow down because to see such infinite joy showering on you for no reason at all – and you are not worthy, you don't deserve it, you have never earned it – how can you remain without giving a heartful thank-you to existence? Your head bows down, you surrender. You lie down on the earth in utter silence, your heart throbbing, pulsating with ecstasy. Your breathing has a different rhythm to it, a different melody to it. Your whole energy is dancing, streaming. You have fallen in harmony with existence. This is what I call prayer, not that which is going on in the churches and the temples. That is parrot-like, it is formal. It has nothing to do with real prayer. And this prayer heals, this prayer is real therapy.

You are right. This question arising in you is of tremendous significance: whether you have been healed by therapy or by prayer? You have been healed by prayer. Therapy has not helped anybody. At the most, therapy can make you adjusted to the society. Prayer helps you to fall in tune with existence itself.

Society is man-made, its values are man-made, hence they are different everywhere. In India there are different values, in the West there are different values. Something that is perfectly okay in the West is absolutely wrong in the East, and vice versa. These values are man-created.

You live in a society, you have to adjust to the society. Psychotherapy is in the service of the society you live in. When you start going out of the society, you start becoming a little rebellious: the society pounces on you and declares you ill. This is an ancient trick, one of the most dangerous tricks that the society has played on you. Whenever you are not falling in line with the society, the society starts condemning you. In the past it used to call you "sinners," and then it prepared hells for you. Now, that language is out of date: it calls you "sick," "mentally sick," "a mental case." That is a new condemnation.

In Soviet Russia, whenever somebody differs from communism, has his own ideas about life, existence, society, he is immediately declared a psychopath, a mental case. Once he is declared a mental case, now society is able to manipulate him. You can give him electric shocks, insulin shocks, drugs, you can force him to live in a mental asylum. And all that he has done is: he has done a little bit of thinking. His sin is that he was not obedient to the established order of the society; he was disobedient. Unless the society forces him back, gives him a mind-wash, forces him to fall in line, he will be kept in a hospital and will be treated as an ill man. This is very humiliating, degrading, dehumanizing, but that's what has been done all over the world, more or less: whenever a person is different from you, wants to live a different life, wants to be free from the bondage you have created in the name of the society, you declare him mad.

Jesus was declared neurotic, Mansoor was declared mad, Socrates was declared dangerous to the youth of the society: "Kill them now!" Now the society can kill them without any prick of conscience. In fact, the society is doing the right thing: first condemn somebody, put a label on him. If you kill somebody without putting a label on him, you will feel guilty; to avoid guilt declare him mad and then it is so easy to kill, so easy to destroy. Now we have the technology too, to destroy the mind, to give the mind a complete brainwash, and to force the man to say yes to the established order, whatsoever it is: communist, capitalist, fascist.

Therapy, the so-called therapy, is in the service of the established society. It is in the service of death, of the past. Prayer serves nobody. Prayer is freedom. Prayer is a way to commune with the whole, and to commune with the whole is to be holy.

You say, "While in therapy myself, I spent much time praying. Over the years I felt better. I never knew whether it was the therapy or the prayer."

It was *certainly* prayer.

"As a therapist I want to urge others to pray but feel embarrassed."

I can understand. Prayer has become a dirty word. To talk about prayer is embarrassing, to talk about God is embarrassing: people think that you are a little bit eccentric, crazy or something. But don't be afraid. Drop this embarrassment, gather courage. Talk about prayer – not only talk about prayer, fall into prayer when the patient is with you. Let the patient feel the climate of prayer.

Once Jesus' disciples asked him, "What is prayer?" He simply knelt down, started praying, with tears coming from his eyes. His eyes raised towards heaven, and he started talking to his father – which is just a symbol. He started calling, "Abba." He created the climate: that is the only way to show what prayer is. There is no other way.

If somebody asks, "What is love?", be loving: hug him, hold his hand, let your love flow towards him. That is the only way to say what love is. This is the only way to define the indefinable.

Fall in prayer while you are helping your patient. Just kneel down. The first time the patient may feel strange, a little weird – "What is happening?" – because he has come with a certain idea that he would have to lie down on the Freudian couch and he would talk all kinds of nonsense, and the psychoanalyst would listen very attentively, as if he is delivering a gospel or a revelation. He has come with certain expectations; he will not be able to believe what is happening.

But if prayer is there it is bound to have effects: it is such a potential force. Whenever there is one person praying, he creates a vibe of prayer around himself. And patients particularly are very sensitive people – that's why they have become patients. Remember it! They are more intelligent than the common lot, hence they are ill! The common lot is so insensitive, so dull, so thick-skinned, it goes on carrying all kinds of nonsenses without being disturbed by them. It goes on living this so-called, meaningless life without ever becoming aware of its meaninglessness, its utter stupidity and absurdity. Remember always that the patient is a person who is more sensitive than the common lot, more alert, has more heart to feel. Hence he finds it difficult to adjust to the society.

The society exists for the lowest because it exists for the mass, the mob, the crowd. The society is a herd-phenomenon. Whenever there is somebody who is a little more intelligent, has a slightly higher IQ, has some more potential for love and for poetry, he will feel a little maladjusted, he will not feel at home. Seeing the beggar on the street he will suffer, seeing all kinds of exploitations going on he will suffer; seeing the state of humanity and its degradation he will suffer – and all this will become too much. He will start cracking underneath this burden.

Remember that the patient is more intelligent, more sensitive, more vulnerable – hence he is a patient. If you create the climate of prayer around him, maybe the first time he will think you are strange, but don't be worried. Everybody knows that psychoanalysts are a little weird.

I have heard...

"I got insomnia real bad," complained a psychotherapist to his physician.

"Insomnia," said the doctor, "is insomnia. How bad can it be? What do you mean, 'real bad insomnia'?"

"Well," said the psychotherapist. "I got it real bad. I can't even sleep when it is time to get up!"

Or this story:

A young doctor who was studying to be a psychoanalyst approached his professor and asked for a special appointment. When they were alone in the professor's office, the young man revealed that he had had a considerable amount of trouble with some of his patients. It seemed that in response to his questions, these patients offered replies which he could not quite understand.

"Well," said the older man, "suppose you ask me some of these questions."

"Why, certainly," agreed the young doctor. "The first one is, what is it that wears a skirt and from whose lips comes pleasure?"

"Why," said the professor, "that's easy. It's a Scotsman blowing a bagpipe."

"Right," said the young doctor. "Now the second question. What is it that has smooth curves and at unexpected moments becomes uncontrollable?"

The older doctor thought for a moment, and then said, "Aha! I don't think that's too difficult to answer. It's a major league baseball pitcher."

"Right," said the young man. "Now, Professor, would you mind telling me what you think about two arms slipped around your shoulders?"

"A football tackle," replied the professor.

"Right again," said the young doctor. "But you would be surprised at the silly answers I keep getting."

So, don't be worried. You can pray, you can go into prayer. The first time, maybe the patient will think you a little eccentric. And in orange, and with the *mala*, you are eccentric! Don't be worried! You are allowed to do anything once you are a sannyasin: this is a certificate.

But if you can create a climate of prayer, soon you will find the patient participating with you. He may feel, for the first time, something of the unknown and the beyond. And if he can again feel something of the unknown, his life will start having meaning, significance. If he can have a little contact with the transcendental, just a little contact, his life will never be the same again. Just a little opening into the beyond, a little window, and the light coming in and the sky and the clouds and the stars – just a little window and you have transformed his whole being.

Use your therapy too, but the real help will come from prayer. Use therapy as a stepping-stone to prayer.

The second question:

> *Osho,*
> *I am in love, and I feel like a moth dying into a candle flame. Am I*
> *meant somehow to extricate myself and be aware and alone, or to die*
> *into the flame. In joy, in agony, it goes on and on...*

Die! because to die in love is to be reborn. It is not death, it is the beginning of true life. To die without love is death. To live without love is death. To be in love is to know something of God, because as Jesus says, "God is love." I have even improved upon it; I say: Love is God.

Die, die. Utterly. Abandon yourself. Be lost.

There is no need to protect yourself against love, because love is not the enemy. Love is the only friend. Don't protect yourself. Don't hide from love. Don't be afraid of love. When love calls, go with it. Wherever it leads, go with it, go in trust.

Yes, there will be moments of agony, because they are always there when there are moments of ecstasy. They come together. It is one package, just like day and night, summer and winter, they come together. But when there is ecstasy of love, one is ready to pay – whatsoever agony it brings, one is happy to pay.

And remember, nothing is free. We have to pay for everything. The more you can pay, the more you will get. If you want to move to the higher peaks of the Himalayas, you take the risk of falling into the valleys. Those who cannot take the risk of falling into the deep abysses surrounding Himalayan peaks will never know the joy of rising higher and higher. Love is the highest peak of consciousness, the Everest of consciousness, and sometimes one slips and falls.

And naturally, when you are moving on a height, you fall very deep, it hurts. When you know light and you fall into deep darkness, it hurts. But once you have known those peaks, you are ready to go into any valleys for those peaks. A single moment of ecstasy is enough: one can suffer for it in hell for eternity, then too it is worth having.

Meditate on these words of Kahlil Gibran:

When love beckons to you, follow him,
though his ways are hard and steep.
And when his wings enfold you yield to him,
though the sword hidden among his pinions
may wound you.
And when he speaks to you believe in him,
though his voice may shatter your dreams
as the north wind lays waste the garden.

But if in your fear
you would seek only love's peace and love's pleasure,
then it is better for you that you cover your nakedness
and pass out of love's threshing-floor,
into the seasonless world where you shall laugh,
but not all of your laughter,
and weep,
but not all of your tears.

Love gives naught but itself and takes naught
but from itself.
Love possesses not nor would it be possessed:
for love is sufficient unto love.

When love beckons to you, follow him – follow to the very end, follow to the point where you disappear completely. Become a moth. Yes, love is a flame and the lover is a moth. Learn much from the moth, it has the secret: it knows how to die. And to know how to die in love, in ecstasy, dancing, is to know how to be reborn on a higher plane. And each time you die a higher plane is reached.

When you can die ultimately and utterly, not holding back even a little bit of yourself, then that very death takes you into God. That is resurrection.

The third question:

Osho,
Why are you not consistent in your statements?

I cannot be. The purpose of my statements is totally different than that of ordinary statements. I am not telling the truth, because truth cannot be told. Then what am I doing here?

If you take my statements as true or untrue, you will miss the whole point. I am using the statements to awaken you. They are neither true nor untrue. They are either useful or useless. But they have nothing to do with truth. They have a certain utility.

It is just as if you are fast asleep and I start ringing a bell, there is nothing of truth or untruth in ringing the bell. To ask the question would be utterly irrelevant. But there is something useful in it: if it helps you wake up, it has been useful.

Buddha is reported to have said, "Truth is that which has utility." Truth is a device, it does not state anything about existence. It is just a device to provoke something which is fast asleep in you.

Now I cannot be consistent, because I have to provoke so many people – different types of minds, different types of sleep are there. I can ring a bell: it may help somebody to wake up, to somebody else it may look like a lullaby and he may fall asleep even more deeply. To somebody it may be a provocation into being awake, to somebody else it may simply give a beautiful dream: that he is in a temple and bells are ringing and he is enjoying, and the prayer is going on and the incense is burning. He has created a dream, he has not come out of his sleep. He will need something else – maybe a hit on the head, or cold water thrown on him, or a good shaking. Different people need different approaches to be provoked, to be awakened.

My statements are not about truth. I am not a philosopher! I am not trying to give you any philosophy. I'm just trying all possible ways to wake you up. If one way fails, I try another – but I cannot leave you alone. So one day I will say one thing, another day I may say another thing. You miss the point if you don't understand the purpose of my statements.

Just the other day I had answered Habib's two questions about Carl Gustav Jung. He missed the whole point. I felt sorry for Habib: he missed the whole thing, he felt offended. And he could not even wait and meditate for a few hours: I finished at 9:45 and he wrote a letter at 9:55. He could not wait a single minute to meditate over it. He thought I am against Jung. Why should I be against Jung? – he has not done anything wrong to me.

But poor Habib; he missed the point. He thinks I am against Jung, so he has to defend Jung. He wrote in the letter that he would like to have a public or private discussion with me, a debate.

Now you cannot discuss with a madman! It will be utterly useless, Habib. It will be pointless. It will drive you crazy.

I have heard…

Once it happened, an Egyptian king went mad. He was a great chess player. All medicines were tried, all physicians worked on him, but nothing, no help. And he was drowning and drowning in madness.

Then one fakir came, a Sufi mystic, and he said, "Wait! If you can bring a great chess player to us here, it will be of great help. He has to stay and play chess with this mad king."

Now who would like to play chess with a madman? But the king was ready to offer as much money as was asked for. A chess player was ready – so much money! And the mystic was right: after one year the king was perfectly sane. But the chess player went mad.

So if you have a discussion with me, beware – you will go mad! – because I am not a consistent man, I am not logical either. I am absurd.

And Habib missed the point. If he was a Freudian I would have attacked Freud, if he was a Marxist I would have attacked Marx, and if he was an Oshoite, I would have attacked Osho! It is not a question of Jung! Jung comes nowhere into it. The attack is on Habib's ego! Because the ego is Jungian, so poor Jung has to be attacked.

Now tomorrow somebody comes and he is a Freudian, and I will attack Freud. And I will say, "He is nothing compared to Jung – a pygmy!" And then naturally I become inconsistent, because you miss the whole point! I have nothing to do with Freud or Jung. Who cares? My effort is to provoke you, to show you the point. It is not that Habib is feeling offended because I have criticized Jung; he is feeling offended because his ego is hurt. If he can see it, then my statements were useful. If he cannot see it, then the arrow missed the point. Then I will have to use some other device.

I have to destroy your ego-structures. Hence, don't ask me again and again why my statements are not consistent. I have only one consistency: that is of being inconsistent. I am consistently inconsistent, that's the only consistency that I have. And I have infinite freedom because a consistent man cannot have infinite freedom. I can play, I can joke, I can enjoy shattering your egos, destroying your structures. I'm not serious about these things. I dare to play, to try first one thing, then another. My statements are like the actors on the stage: let them contradict each other; they are not there to tell the truth, but to provoke it, to discover it.

And I would like to tell you too: do not do anything merely for the sake of consistency. That is the shelter for fools and philosophers – which are the same people. Never do anything just for the sake of consistency. This is undesirable since it limits experimentation and exploration. Action, so as to be consistent with the past, develops into a programmatic addiction. It freezes you into stasis, halting the evolutionary march of becoming. You should retain all power over current behavior. None should be yielded to the past. Acting consistent with precedent is a form of death and destroys all potential to grow into understanding.

Remember, what is consistency? It means my today has to be obedient to my yesterday – that is consistency. My present has to be obedient with my past – that is consistency. But then how am I going to grow? Then how am I going to move? If I remain consistent with the past, then there is no growth possible.

Growth means inconsistency: your today has to go beyond your yesterday, has to be inconsistent with it, has to use it as a stepping-stone, has not to be confined by it, and your tomorrow has to go beyond your today. If each day you go on moving away from your past, you will be growing, you will be reaching, achieving higher peaks.

Consistent people are stupid people. Their life is stagnant. They stink of death, they are like corpses: they go on rotting, they don't live. Life is basically not a logical phenomenon but a dialectical phenomenon. Dialectics means thesis, antithesis, synthesis: your yesterday was a thesis, your today will be its antithesis and your tomorrow will be a synthesis. Your tomorrow will create a thesis and the next day an antithesis and then synthesis – and so on it goes. You go on in a dialectical way. Life is a dialectical process; it is not a linear, logical process.

Life is a contradictory process. That's why I cannot define myself – today's definition won't be applicable tomorrow. I cannot define myself because it is like defining a cloud or an ocean or a growing tree or a child. I constantly change, because change is the very soul of life. Except change, nothing is eternal.

I am committed to change. Change is my God, because that is the only unchanging phenomenon in life. Hence I call it God. Everything else changes: life changes, death changes – only change remains. I worship change. I am in love with it. I cannot define myself once and forever. I have to define myself each moment of my life; and one never knows what each next moment is going to bring.

To be with me is to be in a constant flux, in a constant movement. Those who are not daring enough, sooner or later have to drop out of this journey that I am taking you on. Those who are not courageous enough and who don't have guts to accept the unknown future and to remain available to the unknowable and the mysterious, and who are in a hurry to have a dogma, a belief system, a philosophy – so that they can stop growing, so that they can cling to the dogma, so that they can become fanatics about the dogma – those who are constantly in search of a certain orthodoxy in which nothing will ever change, these are the dead people, cowards. They can't become my people.

I'm bringing you a totally different kind of religion. It has never happened before in the world. All the religions in the world were believers in permanence, I believe in change. All the religions of the world were dogmatic, I am absolutely nondogmatic, antidogmatic. All the religions of the world were reduced into philosophical statements. When I will be gone, I will leave you in such a mess, nobody will ever be able to reduce what I was saying, really. Nobody will be able to reduce it into a dogma.

You cannot pinpoint me, you cannot fix me. I am not a thing. I am a river, a cloud which is constantly changing its form. My idea of consistency is rooted in this continual change, this dynamic dance called life. Yes, to me God is a dancer: constant movement, that is the beauty of God. In fact I would not like to call God a dancer but dance itself, because even the word *dancer* would be false. It gives an idea of a certain entity. But just dance, just cloud…

There is an ancient Christian mystic treatise, *The Cloud of Unknowing*. No other book has such a beautiful title: *The Cloud of Unknowing*. That is the definition of God: "cloud" and "of unknowing."

You cannot make knowledge out of the experience of God. In fact, the more you experience God, the less and less you will know. The day God has happened to you totally, you will not be found there: the knower has gone, disappeared, the dewdrop has slipped into the ocean, or…the ocean has slipped into the dewdrop.

I am not burdened by my yesterday. It has already been changed by today. I live in the present because there is no other way to live. All other ways are ways of death.

So please, don't ask about consistency. You have to learn, you have to understand my inconsistency. You have to understand my contradictions.

The basic thing is that my statements are not saying *anything* about truth. My statements are just provocations. I am urging you to discover, I am not delivering you the truth! Truth is not a thing to be given to you, it is not a commodity. It is untransferable. I am simply creating a desire and a longing, an intense longing in you to search and seek and explore. If I am very consistent, you will stop seeking.

You will think, "What is the need? Osho knows, I can believe in him." That's what Christianity has been doing, Buddhism has been doing, Jainaism has been doing. "Buddha knows, so what is the need? We can believe. He is not deceiving, he cannot lie. He has stated the truth. What further truths are we going to discover? He has stated the truth; we can believe in it." You need not worry about your own exploration. And this is one of the most fundamental things about truth: that unless it is *yours*, it is not. My truth cannot be your truth. There is no way. My truth cannot be transferred to you.

Truth is absolutely individual. All the buddhas have wanted to give it to you, I want it to be given to you, but there is no way. All that can be done is to provoke an inquiry in you, such a tremendous desire to know that you drop all your luggage, unnecessary luggage, and you start moving into the journey, that you gather courage to come out of your securities, conveniences, ideologies, philosophies, orthodoxies; that you gather courage to come out of your mind and to go into the unknown. The cloud of existence, one has to disappear into it.

So I am not going to oblige you by giving you a dogma. No. I will go on contradicting myself each day, every moment. Slowly slowly you will see there is no point in clinging to any of my ideas. And in that very moment you will become aware: there is no need to cling to *any idea whatsoever* – mine, Buddha's, Jesus', anybody's. All ideas have to be dropped.

And when there is no idea in your mind, you will find God there. When all philosophies have disappeared, then religion wells up in your being like a spring.

The fourth question:

Osho,
Why is it so difficult to ask the real question? And why do I feel so
stupid about this and any other question?

The real question cannot be asked. Only unreal questions can be asked. That's why whenever you will ask a question you will feel a little bit stupid – because deep down you will know it is unreal. And only the unreal can be asked!

The real question cannot be asked. Why? – because to find the real question you will have to go so deep into your being, you will have to go to the very center of your being. Unreal questions exist on the periphery, unreal questions are millions. The real question is only one, but it exists at the center. If you want to ask the real question you will have to go to the center of your being. And the problem is: when you are at the center of your being, you know the real question, but immediately you know the real answer too.

The real question contains the real answer in it. They are instant, together, simultaneously they happen. So that's why the real question can never be asked. If you don't know the real question, how can you ask? If you know the real question immediately you know the real answer too. They are not two separate things but two aspects of the same coin: on one side the real question, on the other side the real answer.

But one has to ask many unreal questions before one becomes aware of this. You should feel blessed that you are aware of the phenomenon that the real question is so difficult to ask, *impossible* to ask. This is a good sign, a milestone. Even to ask "Why is it so difficult to ask the real question?" shows that you are moving in the direction of the real question. It shows that now you can detect immediately when you come across a false question. You have become capable of knowing the false as the false; this is the first step towards knowing the true as the true. Before one can know truth, one will have to know untruth, utterly and absolutely.

And that's why you say, "And why do I feel so stupid about this and any other question?"

All questions are stupid questions. But I am not saying don't ask them. Just by not asking you will not become wise. Stupid questions have to be asked so they can be dropped, and dropping stupid questions is dropping stupidity. And slowly slowly, one becomes aware that, "All my questions are useless. Why am I asking? Even if I get the answer, how is it going to change my life?"

Once I was staying in a village. Two old men came to me – one was a Hindu, another was a Jaina. The Jainas don't believe in the existence of God. Both were friends, almost lifelong friends. Both must have been nearabout seventy, and both had quarreled for their whole lives – whether God exists or not? The Hindu insisted that he exists and would quote the Vedas and Upanishads and Gita, and the Jaina would insist that he does not exist and would quote Mahavira and Neminath and Parshwanath and his *tirthankaras*. And they argued and argued to no end, because these questions are so meaningless, so futile, you can go on arguing – *ad infinitum*, there is no end to it. Nobody can prove absolutely, nobody can disprove absolutely either. The questions are so utterly useless. Nothing can be proved definitely this way or that, so the question goes on hanging.

Hearing that I was staying in the guesthouse outside the village, they came to see me. And they said, "Our whole life has been a conflict. We are friends, in every way we are friendly, but about this question of God we immediately start quarreling. And we have quarreled our whole life. Now you are here: give us a definite answer so this quarrel can be stopped, and we can at least die in ease."

I asked them, "If it is proved definitely that God is, how is it going to change your life?"

They shrugged their shoulders. They said, "We will live as we are living."

"Or, if it is proved," I told them, "that God definitely does not exist, how is it going to change your life?"

They said, "It is not going to change our lives at all, because we both live exactly the same life. We are partners in a business. He believes in God, I don't believe in God, but as far as our lives are concerned we have the same pattern. His God does not make any difference, my no-God does not make any difference."

Then I said, "This is a futile question."

Which question is futile? One whose answer is not going to make a change in your life, it is useless. People ask, "Who created the world?" How is it going to change your life? Anybody – A, B, C, D – anybody; how is it going to change your life? "Is there life after death?" – how is it going to change your life?

Can't you see theists and atheists all living the same kind of life, the same rotten kind of life? Can't you see the Catholic and the communist living the same kind of life – the same lies, the same falsehood, the same masks? Can't you see the Protestant and the Catholic living the same life? Can't you see the Hindu and the Mohammedan living the same life, with no difference at all? All differences are only verbal. No verbal difference makes any difference in their existence. They have been discussing about useless questions.

But why do people ask useless questions? – to avoid going in. They pretend that they are great inquirers: they are interested in God, they are interested in the after-life, they are interested in heaven and hell. And the real thing is that they are not interested in themselves: to avoid that, to avoid seeing this fact, that "I am not interested in my own being," they have created all these questions. These questions are their strategies to avoid their central question: "Who am I?"

True religion consists in the inquiry: "Who am I?" And nobody else can answer it. You will have to go digging deeper and deeper into your being. One day, when you have reached the very source of your life, you will know. That day, the real question and the real answer will have happened simultaneously.

The fifth question:

> Osho,
> *I am often able to achieve the state – or what seems like the state –*
> *which you call "being a hollow bamboo" – silent, watching, empty.*
> *The only problem is that there is no bliss in that emptiness: it is just*
> *nothing. Can I expect something to fill it one of these days?*

Mariel Strauss, it is because of this idea that you are missing the whole beauty of nothingness: this desire to fill it. You are not really a hollow bamboo, because in this hollow bamboo this desire is there. And this desire is enough to fill the hollow bamboo, to block its emptiness. This desire to fill it one day, this expectation that, "Someday, God will come and fill my emptiness," this very idea is preventing you from really becoming a hollow bamboo. Drop this desire, forget all about filling your hollow bamboo – then you are a hollow bamboo. And when you are a hollow bamboo, it is immediately full of God. But not that you have to desire it. If you desire it you will go on missing it.

This is one of the basic paradoxes to be understood about religious inquiry. Understand it as deeply as possible, let it sink deeply into your heart, because this is not only Mariel Strauss' problem, this is everybody's problem. Anybody who goes on in the search for truth, for being, for God, or whatsoever you call it, will have to come across it.

You can feel that you are empty, but deep down, lurking somewhere is the desire, the hope, the expectation that "Now, where is God? It is getting late and I have remained a hollow bamboo so long. What is the point? This is just nothingness."

There is condemnation when you say "This is *just* nothingness." You are not happy with this hollow bamboo-ness, you are not happy with this emptiness. There is condemnation. You have managed somehow, because you have heard me saying again and again that the moment you are a hollow bamboo God will descend in you: "Become empty and you will become full." You want to become full, so you say, "Okay, you will become empty. If that is the only way to become full, you will even try that." But this is not true emptiness. You have not understood the point.

Enjoy emptiness, cherish it, nourish it. Let your emptiness become a dance, a celebration. Forget all about God – to come or not is his business. Why should you be worried? Leave it to him! And when you have completely forgotten about God he comes, *immediately* he comes. He always comes when you are utterly unaware of his coming, you don't even hear his footsteps. One moment he was not there, and suddenly another moment he is there. But your emptiness has to be total. And a total emptiness means no expectation, no future, no desire.

You say, "I am often able to achieve the state…"

You must be forcing it, you must be trying hard, you must be cultivating it, you must be imagining it. It is imaginary, it is not true.

"…or what seems like the state…"

And deep down you also know that it is not the real state. You have managed somehow to create a kind of emptiness in yourself. It is a forced emptiness.

"…which you call 'being a hollow bamboo' – silent, watching, empty.…"

It is not what I call the state of being a hollow bamboo. It is not. If it were, then there would be no desire for God, because there is no desire. It does not matter what you desire. God, money, power, prestige, it matters not. Desire is desire, its taste is always the same: desire leads you away from the present, from the here and now into the future, somewhere else; desire does not allow you to relax into the moment. It takes you away from your being.

So what you desire does not matter: you can desire presidency of a country, or you can desire money, or you can desire sainthood, or you can desire God, you can desire truth – desire is desire. Desire means you are torn apart between that which you are and that which you would like to be. This is anguish, this is anxiety, and this anxiety will not allow you to become a hollow bamboo.

To be a hollow bamboo means: a state of desirelessness. Then you are utterly empty, and then that emptiness has a clarity in it, then that emptiness has a splendor in it, a purity in it. Then that emptiness has a holy quality to it. It is so pure, it is so innocent that you will not call it "just emptiness" or "just nothingness." That emptiness is God itself! Once you are empty, once you are in the here and now, with no desire taking you away from your reality, God is. God means "that which is."

God is already the case; your desiring mind does not allow you to see it. Your desiring mind makes you a monkey: you go on jumping from one branch to another branch. You go on jumping, you are never in a state of rest. This desire and that desire, and one desire creates another desire, and it is a continuum. When there is no desire where can you go? When there is no desire where is the future? When there is no desire where is time? Where is past? When there is no desire where is mind? Where is memory? Where is imagination? All gone! Cut one single root which is the chief root of the tree of mind: cut desire, and just be. In that state of being you are a hollow bamboo. And the moment you are a hollow bamboo, reality bursts upon you! As if it has been always waiting but you were not available to it: it floods you!

The last question:

Osho,
Is not life stranger than fiction?

It is. It has to be, because fiction is only a partial reflection of life, a very finite reflection of life. Life is infinitely complex. Life has no beginning, no end; it is always on and on, it is going on and on. It is a pilgrimage with no goal.

Fiction is just a reflection of a small part of it. Fiction is like a small window in your room. Yes, when the sky is full of stars, you see a part of the sky through the window, but the sky becomes framed by the window. The sky itself has no frame to it – it is infinite, it knows no boundaries – but your window gives a frame to it. A fiction is a framed part of the sky. Howsoever strange, mysterious, unbelievable the fiction may be, it is very pale compared to real life.

Real life is the mystery of mysteries…never possible to explain it. And the fiction arises out of the human mind. The mind is a mirror: it reflects a few things. If you have a good mirror, a creative mirror, you can create poetry, you can create music, you can create fiction, you can write, you can paint. But all that you will paint and all that you will create and all that you will write will remain a very tiny atomic part of reality – and not really a part but a *reflection* of the part, in your mind.

To see life as it is, is mind-blowing. To see life as it is, is psychedelic. To see life as it is, is to become expanded in consciousness.

The fiction has to begin somewhere. Of necessity, it has to begin somewhere. It will have the first page and somewhere it has to end, it cannot go on and on. You can lengthen it, make it very long, like Tolstoy's *War and Peace* – it can go on and on and on, and it is very very tiring and lengthy. But still a moment comes when you have to put the last full stop. You cannot go on forever.

But life goes on forever. One wave turns into another wave, one tree creates other trees, one man gives birth to children – it goes on: there is no beginning and there is no end.

Art is only a poor imitation. Hence the artist remains in imagination, the artist remains in dreams. He is a dreamer, a good dreamer – a dreamer who dreams in color, not just black and white – but still a dreamer.

A mystic is one who has dropped all dreams, who has thrown away this mirror of the mind and who looks directly into life, without any medium interfering. Then he sees the eternal progression, then in a single moment he sees all eternity, and in a single atom he can see the whole reflected.

Just think: you contain your mother, your father, your father's father, your mother's mother, and so on and so forth. You contain Adam and Eve – if there was a time when things began... I don't think there was a time when things began. "Adam and Eve" is again a fiction, a religious fiction. Things never began, things have always been.

You contain the whole past. All the dreams of your father and your mother are contained in your cells, and all the dreams of their fathers and their mothers, and so on and so forth – all the dreams of the whole of humanity have preceded you. And not only of humanity but all the animals that have preceded humanity, and not only all the animals but all the trees that have preceded all the animals, and not only the trees but all the rocks and all the mountains and rivers that have preceded trees – you contain all of that in you. You are vast!

And so is the case with the future – you contain the whole future too: the children that will be born and the poems that will be written – not only by the Shakespeares of the past but the Shakespeares of the future too, the dreams that have been seen and the dreams that will be seen. All the poets and all the painters are in you, ready to be born, all the scientists, all the mystics – the whole future, the eternal future.

So you contain the whole past, you contain the whole future. The whole converges upon this small, tiny moment. And so is the case with space, as it is with time: you contain the whole of space in you, all the trees and all the stars.

A great Indian mystic, Swami Ramateerth, when he attained to enlightenment, started saying things which look mad. People started thinking that he had gone bizarre, because he started saying, "I see stars moving within me, not outside, but inside. When I see the morning sun rising, I see it rising in me, not outside."

Now this looks like a kind of madness. It is not. He was saying something tremendously significant. He was saying: I am part of the whole and the whole is part of me. So everything is within that is without, and everything is without that is within. All that has happened is in me, and all that is going to happen is in me, and all that is happening is in me.

To feel this, to see this, is to be in prayer, in awe, in wonder. Will you not be grateful to be part of this mysterious existence? Will you not feel grateful to have something to do with this splendor? Will you not feel grateful, thankful for all that surrounds you and all that is contained in you?

To see this mysterious existence, to feel it in the deepest core of your heart, and immediately a prayer arises – a prayer that has no words to it, a prayer that is silence, a prayer that doesn't say anything but feels tremendous, a prayer that arises out of you like fragrance, a prayer that is like music with no words, celestial music, or what Pythagoras used to call "the harmony of the stars," the melody of the whole. When that music starts rising in you, that's what the *Secret of the Golden Flower* is all about: suddenly a flower bursts open in you, a golden lotus. You have arrived, you have come home.

This is what I am provoking you towards, this is what I am trying to awaken in you – this desire, this longing, this thirst, this appetite. Once you are possessed by this hunger, for the first time you will become aware of the benediction and the supreme blessedness of existence. You will not feel meaningless, you will not feel accidental. You will not feel at all as Jean-Paul Sartre says, that "Man is a useless passion"; no, not at all. You will feel yourself tremendously significant, because you are part of an infinite significance, and you are to contribute something by your being here.

You will become creative, because that is the only way to be really thankful to God – to be creative, to make this existence a little more beautiful than you had found it. The day you leave, this will be your only contentment: if you have made the existence a little more beautiful.

When a buddha leaves he leaves in tremendous contentment because he knows he is leaving the existence behind with a little more poetry in it, with a little more awareness in it, with a little more prayer in it.

Remember that when you leave the world, you can die in contentment only if you have made this world a little more worth living in, a little more meaningful, with a little more dancing, celebrating. If you have added a little festivity to it, a little laughter, a little sense of humor, if you have been able to light a small lamp of light and you have been able to disperse a little darkness from the world, you will die in utter joy – you are fulfilled, your life has been of fruition and flowering. Otherwise people die in misery.

Jean-Paul Sartre is right for the majority of the people, but that majority is living in ignorance, unconsciousness. That majority is not really yet able to declare its humanity. Only a Buddha or a Krishna or a Zarathustra or a Jesus can claim that they are human beings. They are human beings because they have bloomed: their whole beings have come to flowering. Once they have blossomed nothing is left, all is fulfilled.

Create this longing, this thirst. You have the seed, all that you need is a thirst. That thirst will become the occasion for the seed to sprout. You have the potential, all that you need is a tremendous longing. If you become aflame with longing you will be purified. The baser metal of your life will be transformed into a higher metal, into gold. This is all that alchemy is about. And the *Secret of the Golden Flower* is an alchemical treatise.

Enough for today.

CHAPTER 19

The Golden Flower is Opening

Master Lu-Tsu said:

There are many kinds of confirmatory experiences. One must not content oneself with small demands but must rise to the thought that all living creatures have to be redeemed. One must not be trivial and irresponsible in heart, but must strive to make deeds prove one's words.

If, when there is quiet, the spirit has continuously and uninterruptedly a sense of great joy as if intoxicated or freshly bathed, it is a sign that the light-principle is harmonious in the whole body; then the Golden Flower begins to bud. When, furthermore, all openings are quiet, and the silver moon stands in the middle of heaven, and one has the feeling that this great Earth is a world of light and brightness, that is a sign that the body of the heart opens itself to clarity. It is a sign that the Golden Flower is opening. Furthermore, the whole body feels strong and firm so that it fears neither storm nor frost. Things by which other men are displeased, when I meet them, cannot becloud the brightness of the seed of the spirit. Yellow gold fills the house, the steps are of white jade. Rotten and stinking things on earth that come in contact with one breath of the true energy will immediately live again. Red blood becomes milk.

The fragile body of the flesh is sheer gold and diamonds. That is a
sign that the Golden Flower is crystallized.

The brilliancy of the light gradually crystallizes. Hence a great terrace
arises and upon it, in the course of time, the Buddha appears. When
the golden being appears who should it be but the Buddha? For the
Buddha is the golden holy man of the great enlightenment. This is a
great confirmatory experience.

A parable:

One day the lord Vishnu was sitting in a deep cave within a far mountain meditating with his disciple. Upon the completion of the meditation the disciple was so moved that he prostrated himself at Vishnu's feet and begged to be able to perform some service for his lord, in gratitude. Vishnu smiled and shook his head, "It will be most difficult for you to repay me in actions for what I have just given you freely."

"Please lord," the disciple said, "allow me the grace of serving you."

"Very well," Vishnu relented, "I would like a nice cool cup of water."

"At once lord," the disciple said, and he ran down the mountain singing in joy. After a while he came to a small house at the edge of a beautiful valley and knocked at the door. "May I please have a cool cup of water for my master," he called. "We are wandering sannyasins and have no home on this earth."

A wondrous maiden answered his call and looked at him with undisguised adoration. "Ah," she whispered, "you must serve that holy saint upon the far mountain. Please good sir, enter my house and bestow your blessing therein."

"Forgive my rudeness," he answered, "but I am in haste. I must return to my master with his water immediately."

"Surely, just your blessing won't upset him. After all he is a great holy man, and as his disciple you are obligated to help those of us who are less fortunate. Please," she repeated, "just your blessing for my humble house. It is such an honor to have you here and to be enabled to serve the lord through you."

So the story goes, he relented and entered the house and blessed all therein. And then it was time for dinner and he was persuaded to stay and further the blessing by partaking of her food, thereby making it also holy. And since it was so late and so far back to the mountain, and he might slip in the dark and spill the water, he was persuaded to sleep there that night and get an early start in the morning. But in the morning, the cows were in pain because there was no one to help her milk them, and if he could just help her this once – after all, cows are sacred to the lord Krishna and they should not be allowed to suffer or be in pain – it would be so wondrous.

And days became weeks, and still he remained. They were married and had numerous children, he worked the land well and brought forth good harvests. He purchased more land and put it under cultivation, and soon his neighbors looked to him for advice and help and he gave it freely. His family prospered, temples were built through his effort, schools and hospitals replaced the jungle, and the valley became a jewel upon the earth. Harmony prevailed where only wilderness had been and many flocked to the valley as news of its prosperity and peace spread throughout the land. There was no poverty or disease there and all men sang their praises to God as they worked. He watched his children grow and have their own children, and it was good.

One day as an old man, he stood upon a low hill facing the valley, he thought of all that had transpired since he had arrived: farms and happy prosperity as far as the eye could see. And he was pleased.

Suddenly there was a great tidal wave, and as he watched, it flooded the whole valley, and in an instant all was gone. Wife, children, farms, schools, neighbors – all gone. He stared bewildered at the holocaust that spread before him. And then he saw riding upon the face of the waters his master, Vishnu, who looked at him and smiled sadly, and said, "I'm still waiting for my water!"

This is the story of man. This is what has happened to everybody. We have completely forgotten why we are here, why we came in the first place – what to learn, what to earn, what to know, who we are and from whence and to where, what is our source and the cause of our journey into life, into body, into the world, and what we have attained up to now? And if a tidal wave comes – and it is going to come, it always comes, its name is death – all will be gone: children, family, name, fame, money, power, prestige. All will be gone in a single moment and you will be left alone, utterly alone. All that you had done will be undone by the tidal wave. All that you had worked for will prove nothing but a dream, and your hands and your heart will be empty. And you will have to face the Lord, you will have to face existence.

And the existence has been waiting for you – long, long it has been waiting for you – to bring something for which you had been sent in the first place. But you have fallen asleep and you are dreaming a thousand and one dreams. All that you have been doing up to now is nothing but a dream, because death comes and all is washed away.

Reality cannot be washed away by death. Reality knows no death. Reality is undying. Reality is deathless. Reality is eternal. All that dies simply proves by its death that it was unreal, that it was an illusion, maya, a dream – maybe a nice dream, but a dream all the same. You may be dreaming of hell or you may be dreaming of heaven, it does not make much difference. The moment you will be awakened you will find yourself utterly empty – and empty in a negative sense, not in the positive sense as buddhas know it: not empty of the ego but empty of all that your ego has been trying to do; full of ego but empty of any attainment, empty of any realization, empty of any knowledge. And it is not that the ego does not claim knowledge; it claims. The ego is very knowledgeable, it collects information. It is a great collector: it collects money, it collects information, it collects every kind of thing. It believes in accumulation. It is greed and nothing but greed. Ego is another name for greed, it wants to possess. But all that you possess will be gone and all that you have done, you have done in your dream. The moment you will be awakened you will be surprised at how much time has been wasted, at how many lives you have been living in a dream, at how many dreams you have lived.

To be a seeker means to come out of this dream, to come out of this dreaming state of consciousness. To be a seeker means: making an effort to wake up. To wake up is to become a buddha – to be alert, to be conscious, to be full of light within so that all unconsciousness disappears, so that all sleep disappears, so the darkness of sleep is no more inside you and you are fully awake.

It happened:

A great astrologer saw Buddha. He could not believe his eyes – that body, that golden aura around the body, those beautiful eyes, as silent as any lake can be and as deep and as pure as any lake can be, that crystal-clarity, that walking grace. He fell at Buddha's feet and he said, "I have studied astrology, palmistry. My whole life I have been studying types of men, but I have never come across a man like you! To what type do you belong? Are you a god who has descended on the earth? – because you don't seem to belong to this earth. I can't see any heaviness in you. You are absolutely light, weightless. I am wondering how you are walking on the earth because I don't see any gravitation functioning on you. Are you a god who has descended from heaven just to have a look at what is happening on the earth? A messenger from God? A prophet? Who are you?"

And Buddha said, "I am not a god."

The astrologer asked, "Then are you what in Indian mythology is called a *yaksha?*" – a little bit lower than the gods.

And Buddha said, "No, I am not a *yaksha* either."

"Then who are you? What kind of man, what category to put you in?"

And Buddha said, "I am not a man or a woman."

Now the astrologer was very much puzzled, and he said, "What do you mean? Do you mean you are an animal, an animal spirit, or the spirit of a tree, or the spirit of a mountain or the spirit of a river?" – because Indian mythology is pantheistic: it believes in all kinds of spirits. "So who are you, the spirit of a rosebush? You look so beautiful, so innocent."

And Buddha said, "No, I am not an animal, nor the spirit of a tree, nor the spirit of a mountain."

"Then who are you?" The astrologer was puzzled very much.

And Buddha said, "I am awareness and nothing else. You cannot categorize me because all categories are applicable to dreams."

Somebody is dreaming he is a man, somebody else is dreaming she is a woman, and so on and so forth. Categories belong to the world of dreams. When one becomes awakened one is simply that principle of awakenedness, awareness. One is just a witness and nothing else: a pure witness. All clouds have disappeared. The cloud of a man or a woman, animal, god, trees – all clouds, all forms have disappeared. One is just a formless awareness, the pure sky, endless, infinite, vast. This awareness is empty of clouds but full of the sky. This is positive emptiness, this is nirvana.

Then there is a negative emptiness: you are full of clouds – so much so that not even a bit of sky can be seen, you are full of knowledge – so much knowledge not even a little space is left for meditation.

It is said: He who knows not and yet knows that he knows, is a fool – usually called a pundit or a scholar – shun him. He who knows not, and knows not that he knows not, is innocent, a child – wake him. He who knows not, and knows that he knows not, is a buddha – follow him.

To come to this realization: "I am nobody" is the meaning of being a buddha. Buddha is not the name of somebody. Buddha is the name for "nobody-ness." And Buddha is not an entity. Buddha is just space, open space, openness, a name for openness, for open sky.

Watch your mind: how much dreaming continues. And it is not only that you dream in the night, you are continuously in a dream. Even while you think that you are awake, even in the daytime, the continuity is not broken. At any moment close your eyes and relax and you will immediately see dreams floating. They are always there like an undercurrent, they never leave you. They are constantly present and constantly affecting your being. Their existence is subliminal. You may not be alert about them, you may not even suspect their existence but they are continuously there. Even when you are listening to me, there is that movie inside you, continuing, that drama of dreams. Hence you cannot hear what I am saying. First it has to pass through your dreams, and your dreams distort it; you hear something else that has not been said. Your dreams distort, your dreams manipulate, your dreams project, your dreams change things: I say one thing, you hear quite another.

And those dreams are very powerful inside you, and you don't know what to do with those dreams. In fact you have become so identified with the dreams that you don't know that you are separate, that you can watch, that you can be distant, that you can be just an onlooker. You have become too identified with the dreams.

Just the other day I was talking about poor Habib. Now he has become so identified with being a Jungian analyst that he cannot watch what is happening. I had mentioned that just two days before, I had finished my talk at 9:45, and he wrote a letter at 9:55, after just ten minutes. Yesterday he went even further: while I was talking he was writing the letter! While I was discussing him, he could not wait even ten minutes. And that's what I was saying: Wait a little, be a little patient, meditate over it. You cannot understand these things immediately; you are not in that state of understanding, of clarity, of perception. But while I was talking he started writing the letter. At exactly the same time, while I was talking, he was writing the letter. Now what could he write? I had not even talked, I had not even spoken. He must have heard, he must have taken the clue from his own mind. He could not understand a single word. His dream seems to be too strong, he is burdened by his knowledge. And I was saying, "Let your Jungian ego drop."

But do you know what happened? Habib died – he renounced sannyas rather than dropping the Jungian ego. That's what he heard. I was saying, "Drop the Jungian ego!"; he heard something else. He heard, "Then this sannyas is not for me. I cannot drop my knowledge, that's all I have. And how can I drop it? How can one put the mind aside? It is impossible! So it is better to drop sannyas." He dropped sannyas. Now Habib no longer exists, he died a very early death. In fact, he died before he was born.

What happened? Could he not see the point? Who prevented him from seeing the point? His mind must have become much too crowded. All that he has been reading, accumulating – he has become overly attached to it. He had come here to seek and search. What kind of search is this if you are not ready to leave anything of your ego? What kind of inquiry is this?

People usually think they are spiritual seekers if they can add something more to their egos. Your so-called spiritual trips are nothing but subtle trips of the ego. People want more gratification for the ego, more strength for the ego, more vitality for the ego. They want a holy aura around the ego, and the holy aura arises only when the ego is gone. They cannot co-exist.

And it is very rare to come across a teaching which can awaken you. It is very rare to come across a master who can shake you up into wakefulness, who can pull you out of your long long, deep-rooted dreams. It is a rare phenomenon to come across a master, it is very easy to miss. It is easy to miss because the basic fundamental of being with a master is to put your head in front of him so that he can crush it with his sledgehammer. A master is a sledgehammer. People search for a different kind of situation where the master – they think he is the master if he buttresses their egos – says to them, "Good! You are a great spiritual seeker."

That's what the late Habib wanted: he wanted me to say that he is a great spiritual seeker, that whatsoever he has done is perfectly beautiful, the right foundation for the temple, that he is almost ready, just a little bit has to be added to him and all would be perfect. That's what he wanted. That is not possible – because first I have to destroy you. Only through your utter destruction is the possibility of your awakening. And destruction is hard, painful.

A great Hassidic saying says: God is not nice, God is not an uncle. God is an earthquake!

So is a master! A master is not an uncle, a master is not nice, a master is an earthquake. Only those who are ready to risk all, in toto, who are ready to die as egos, can be born. This is what Jesus means when he says, "You will have to carry your cross on your own shoulders. If you want to follow me, you will have to carry your cross on your own shoulders."

Kabir has said, "If you really want to follow me, burn your house immediately!" What house was he talking about? The house of dreams in which you have lived has to be utterly burned so that you can be under the open sky again and the stars and the sun and the moon, so you can be in the wind again, in the rain, so you can be available to nature once more – because God is nothing but the hidden-most core of nature. God is not a kind of knowledge, God is innocence. You know God not by knowledge but by becoming utterly innocent.

But it is very difficult for the ego…even to hear these words is difficult. And the ego will immediately distort them, manipulate them, change them, color them, paint them and make them in such a way that they support the ego rather than destroying it.

One story reflecting this observation concerns a man who had an obsession that he was dead. He went to a psychiatrist for help. The psychiatrist used all the known techniques at his command, but to no avail. Finally, the psychiatrist tried appealing to the patient's logic.

"Do dead men bleed?" asked the doctor.

"No, of course not," answered the patient.

"All right," said the doctor. "Now let us try an experiment." The doctor took a sharp needle and pricked the man's skin and the patient began to bleed from his wound profusely.

"There! What do you say now?" asked the psychiatrist.

"Well, I will be darned!" answered the patient. "By gosh! Dead people *do* bleed!"

That's how the ego functions, the mind functions: it turns things into proofs, supports, food for itself. The ego is very subtle and its ways are very cunning, and it can convince you that you are right. It will try in every way, in every possible way to try and convince you that it is right and anything that goes against it is wrong. Remember, the ego is *never* right! And if something does oppose it, don't miss the opportunity: use that occasion to destroy your ego. The moment you can destroy your ego will be the moment of great blessing because when you are not, God is, and *when you are not, you are.* This is the greatest paradox of life and existence: when you are not, you are.

That's why Vishnu was not willing… Vishnu said to his disciple, "It will be most difficult for you to repay me in actions for what I have just given you freely."

Why? Why would it be most difficult? Because the master knows that the disciple is still in dreams, he is still in his ego. In fact, the very idea that, "I want to repay you, I want to do something for you because you have done so much for me," is an ego-idea. When the disciple has dropped the ego, who is there to repay? Who? Who is there even to thank? There is nobody. There is utter silence. And in that utter silence the master is happy: the disciple has repaid – through this utter silence.

A man came to Buddha and he wanted to do something for humanity. He was a very rich man. And he asked Buddha, "Just tell me what I can do for humanity? I have much money, no children, the wife has died, I am alone. I can do much."

Buddha looked at him with very sad eyes and remained silent. The man said, "Why are you silent? Why don't you speak? You always talk about compassion, and I am here ready to do something. Whatsoever you say I will do. Don't be worried – I have enough money! Just ask me to do any task and I will do it."

Buddha said, "I understand what you are saying, but I am feeling sad: you cannot do a thing because you still are not. Before one can do something, one has to be. It is not a question of money – that you have – but that *you* are not!"

That quality of compassion is a shadow of being, and the being is missing. The ego can never be compassionate, the ego is cruel. Even in its games of compassion it is cruel. And when the ego is gone, even if the egoless person looks to you to be very cruel, he is not, he cannot be. Even his cruelty must be a deep compassion.

When a Zen master hits the disciple's head with his staff it is not cruel, it is tremendous compassion. When a Zen Master jumps on his disciple and beats him it is not cruel, because sometimes it has happened that with the hit of the master, the disciple has become enlightened – in a single moment, in a single lightning experience.

Buddha said, "You cannot do anything. I know about your money, I have heard about you, but when I look into you I feel very sad for you. You want to do something, but the element that can do something is missing. All that you can do is dream."

That's why Vishnu says, "It will be most difficult for you to repay me in actions what I have just given you freely." That's what George Gurdjieff used to say to his disciples. The first thing that he had said to P.D. Ouspensky was this, exactly this.

Ouspensky was a great seeker, a seeker of knowledge. When he had gone to see Gurdjieff for the first time, he was already a world famous mathematician, philosopher, thinker. His greatest book had already been published, *Tertium Organum*. It is a rare book – also rare because the man was not awakened. How could he manage to write such a beautiful piece? Only an awakened man can see a few faults, otherwise it is very difficult to find any fault in it. It is almost perfect, as if a buddha has written it.

But when George Gurdjieff looked into the book, he just turned here and there and threw it out of the room. And he said, "All nonsense! You do not know anything! And how can you know? Before one can know one has to be!" And Ouspensky had traveled all over the East in search of a master. It is a beautiful story, almost a parable.

He had traveled in India, he had gone to Ceylon, to Burma. He had lived in monasteries, in Himalayan caves. He had met lamas and swamis and many Hindu mystics, but nobody could satisfy him. Why? – because all that they said was nothing but a repetition of the scriptures that he had already studied. Not a single word was their own. Frustrated, he went back – back to Russia, to Petrograd where he used to live. In Petrograd, in one coffee house, he met Gurdjieff. And just the first meeting, and the master's look at him...and the revelation: "This is the man I have been searching for. This is the town I have lived in my whole life, and this is the coffee house I have been visiting for years, and this man is sitting here in the coffee house! And I have been searching for him in Ceylon, in Nepal, in Kashmir, in faraway places."

The first thing that Gurdjieff said to Ouspensky was, "Unless you are, you cannot know a thing. Unless you are, you cannot do a thing."

And the paradox is that you are only when you have disappeared, when the word "I" is no longer relevant. These sutras are the keys to create that state of buddhahood – when you are just awareness and nobody, full of light but utter emptiness.

The sutras:

> Master Lu-Tsu said:
> There are many kinds of confirmatory experiences.

A confirmatory experience means that you are coming closer to home. One has to understand, one has to be aware of confirmatory experiences, because that gives courage, hope, that gives vitality. You start feeling that you are not searching in vain, that the morning is very close by. Maybe it is still night and dark, but the first confirmatory experience has started filtering in. The stars are disappearing, the East is becoming red, the sun has not arisen, it is early dawn – confirmatory that the sun is not far away. If the East is becoming red, then soon, any moment, the sun will rise on the horizon. The birds have started singing, the birds are praising the coming morning. Trees look alive, sleep is disappearing, people are waking up. These are confirmatory experiences.

Exactly like that, on the spiritual path there are experiences which are very confirmatory. It is as if you are moving towards a beautiful garden you cannot see; but the closer you come to the garden, the breezes are cooler – that you can feel. The farther away you go, the more the coolness disappears; the closer you come, the more the coolness appears again. The more close you come, the more the breeze is not only cool, but there is fragrance too, the fragrance of many flowers. The farther away you go, the more the fragrance disappears. The closer you come the more you can hear birds singing in the trees. The trees you cannot see, but the song of the birds – a distant call of a cuckoo, there must be a mango grove…you are coming closer. These are confirmatory experiences. Exactly the same happens when you move towards the inner garden, towards the inner source of life, of joy, of silence, of bliss. When you start moving towards the center a few things start disappearing and a few new things start appearing.

> One must not content oneself with small demands but must rise to
> the thought that all living creatures have to be redeemed.

And remember, when confirmatory experiences start appearing, don't be satisfied too soon. The cool breeze has come, and you sit there and you think that you have arrived. The coolness is beautiful, the coolness is blissful, but you have to go far. Don't be satisfied with small things. Feel happy that they have started happening, take them as milestones, but they are not goals. Enjoy them, thank God, feel gratitude, but go on moving in the same direction from where the confirmatory experiences are coming.

And don't be contented with small demands. For example, peacefulness is a small demand, it can be easily attained. The state of a non-tense mind can easily be attained, it is not very difficult. To be happy and cheerful can easily be attained, it is not much. To be at ease, unanxious, without anxiety is not something very great. Then what is great and what should one keep in mind, that this is the goal?

> One must rise to the thought that all living creatures have
> to be redeemed.

You will be surprised to know that this is the criterion, and this has always been the criterion. In Buddhism it is called "the principle of bodhisattvahood."

The closer you are coming to your own inner center, the more you will start feeling the suffering of all beings of the world. On the one hand you will feel very calm and quiet, and on the other hand you will start feeling a deep sympathy for all those who suffer. And there is suffering and suffering and suffering, the whole place is full of suffering. On the one hand you will feel great joy arising in you, and on the other hand a great sadness too, that millions are suffering – and ridiculously suffering, for no reason suffering! This is their birthright, to attain to this blissfulness that is coming to you.

And don't become satisfied that you have become blissful, so all is finished. If you become blissful, all is not finished. Really, now the journey takes a new turn. When you have attained to buddhahood, when you have come home, now the real work starts. Up to now it was only a dream. Now the real work starts: help others to come out of their dreams. When the disciple has attained, he has to become a master.

This is what in Christianity is called "the principle of christ-consciousness." Christians have not really been able to understand it, they have misunderstood it. They think that Jesus is the only christ.

The word *christ* comes from Krishna. It is a principle. The principle is that when you are redeemed, you have to redeem all. To be redeemed from misery is blissful, but nothing compared to when you start redeeming others from their misery. To redeem oneself from misery is still selfish, self-oriented. Something of the self still lingers, you are only concerned with yourself. And when the self disappears and you are redeemed, how is it possible to stop the journey? Now, you have to redeem others. That's why Jesus is called "the Redeemer." But he is not the only christ. There have been many before him, there have been many after him, there will be many in the future. Whoever becomes a buddha has to become, *of necessity,* a redeemer of all.

One's joy, one's peace, one's blessings are small things. Don't be contented with them. Remember always that one day you have to share, one day you have to help others to be awakened. This seed must be planted deep in your heart, so that when your buddhahood blooms you don't disappear from the world.

Buddhists have two words; one is *arhat*. Arhat means: the person who has become enlightened but thinks all is finished, his work is complete – he disappears. The other is called *bodhisattva:* he has become enlightened but he does not disappear – he insists on being here, he prolongs himself to be here, as long as it is possible.

The story is that when Buddha reached the doors of nirvana the doors were opened, celestial music was played, golden flowers showered, angels with garlands were ready to receive him, but he refused to enter. He turned his back to the door.

The angels were surprised, they could not believe it. They asked him again and again, "What are you doing? Your whole life – not only one but many lives – you have been searching for *this* door. Now you have arrived and you are turning your back to the door? And we have been waiting for you! And the whole paradise is full of joy – one more person has become a buddha. Come in! Let us celebrate your buddhahood together."

But Buddha said, "Unless all those who are in suffering are redeemed, I'm not going to enter. I will have to wait. I am going to be the last. Let others move first."

And the beautiful story says that he is still waiting at the door. The door is open because the angels cannot close it – any moment he may want to enter, that is his right to enter. So the door is open, and he's keeping the door open, and the celestial music continues, and the flowers are still being showered, and the angels are waiting with garlands, and he's standing outside the door. And he's calling people forth; he's calling, challenging, he's provoking. He's telling people, "The doors are open, don't miss this opportunity. Come in! And I am going to be the last. Now the doors shall never be closed. They will be closed only when everybody is redeemed and enlightened."

This is just a parable, tremendously significant. Don't think of it as history, otherwise you will miss the point. There is no door, no angels, no garlands, no celestial music. And Buddha, the moment he became enlightened, has disappeared – how can he stand and keep his back to the door, who is there to stand? But the principle: the energy that Buddha released into existence is still functioning, that energy is still available to those who are *really* searching. The energy goes on and on working, and it will go on working for eternity.

Jesus is no more, but his christ-consciousness has entered into the new sphere. Mahavira is no more, but his consciousness has entered into this oceanic life. These people have become part of existence; they vibrate. That is the meaning of the parable: they still provoke you, and if you are ready to receive their message they are still ready to take you to the other shore.

The moment a master dies he becomes part of that infinite energy in which Buddha has joined, Mahavira has joined, Zarathustra, Lao Tzu, Jesus, Mohammed. Whenever a master dies, more energy is redeemed – and it is becoming a tidal wave. So many enlightened people have existed, it is becoming a continuous tidal wave. You are fortunate: if you really long, if you really desire, this tidal wave can take you to the other shore.

Keep it in your deepest heart: don't be satisfied with small things. Many things happen on the Way, many *miraculous* things happen on the Way, but don't be satisfied with anything. Remember, you have to become a christ-consciousness, a bodhisattva – less than that is not going to make you contented. This is divine discontent.

> *One must not be trivial and irresponsible in heart, but must strive to make deeds prove one's words.*

And this life of a seeker should not be that of trivia, because each small thing that you go on doing wastes time, energy, life.

The seeker cannot waste. His whole life has to be devoted and dedicated to one single point. He cannot waste here and there, he cannot go and sit in the coffee house and gossip unnecessarily, he cannot read that which is not going to help. He's not going to do a single thing which is not going to help his journey, and he's not going to collect a single thing that will become a burden later on and will have to be dropped. He remains simple. This simplicity has nothing to do with asceticism. This simplicity is simply scientific. He does not accumulate garbage because then you have to carry it: he remains unburdened. And the greatest garbage is that of knowledge, because all other garbage is outside you, knowledge gets inside; it makes your head very heavy, and the head should be very light.

Have you watched, or have you seen a Japanese doll called *daruma*? Daruma is the Japanese name for Bodhidharma. The doll is beautiful: it represents the enlightened man, the daruma doll. It's beauty is that you can throw it any way but it always sits back in full lotus posture. You throw it, you cannot topple it – it again comes back. Its bottom is heavy, its head is light, so you cannot put it upside down. It is always rightside up.

Just the opposite is the case with human beings: they are upside down. Their heads are very heavy, they are top-heavy. They are standing on their heads. A man who is knowledgeable stands on his head. He is in a continuous *sirshasana*, a headstand.

The man who has no knowledge in the head, whose head is empty, silent, is rightside up. He is in a lotus posture, he is a daruma doll. You cannot topple him, there is no way – he will always come back. You cannot disturb him, there is no way – his undisturbedness remains continuous.

> *One must not be trivial and irresponsible in the heart...*

What is responsibility? Ordinarily the meaning of the word has become associated with wrong things. The real responsibility is towards God and towards nobody else; or, the real responsibility is towards your own nature and to nobody else. You are not responsible to the society or to the church or to the state. You are not responsible to the family, to the community. You are responsible only to one thing: that is your original face, your original being. And in that responsibility all other responsibilities are covered automatically. Become natural.

And the man who is natural is responsible – because he responds. The man who is not natural never responds, he only reacts. Reactions mean being mechanical, response is nonmechanical, spontaneous.

You see a beautiful flower and you suddenly say something: "It is beautiful." Watch whether it is a reaction or a response. Go deep into it, scrutinize it. What you have said – that "The flower is beautiful" – is it your spontaneous response to this moment, here and now? Is this your experience, or are you simply repeating a cliché because you have heard others saying that flowers are beautiful? Observe the moment in depth – are you voicing the words of someone else? Maybe it is your mother... You can remember the day, for the first time she had taken you to the garden, the public gardens, and she had told you, "Look at this rose. How beautiful it is!" And then the books that you have been reading, and the films that you have been seeing, and the people you have been talking to – and they all have been saying, "Roses are beautiful." It has become a programmed thing in you. The moment you see the rose flower your program says, "It is beautiful," not you. It is just a gramophone record, it is a tape. The rose outside triggers the tape and it simply repeats. It is reaction.

What is response? Response is unprogrammed: experiencing in the moment. You look at the flower, you really look at the flower, with no ideas covering your eyes. You look at *this* flower, the *thisness* of it; all knowledge put aside, your heart responds. Your mind reacts. Responsibility is of the heart. You may not say anything; in fact, there is no need to say, "This is beautiful."

I have heard...

Lao Tzu used to go for a morning walk. A neighbor wanted to be with him. Lao Tzu said, "But remember, don't be talkative. You can come along, but don't be talkative."

Many times the man wanted to say something, but knowing Lao Tzu, looking at him, he controlled himself. But when the sun started rising and it was so beautiful, the temptation was so much that he forgot all about what Lao Tzu had said and he said, "Look! What a beautiful morning!"

And Lao Tzu said, "So, you have become talkative. You are too talkative! You are here, I am here, the sun is here, the sun is rising – so what is the point of saying to me 'The sun is beautiful'? Do you think I can't see it? Am I blind? What is the point of saying it? I am also here."

In fact, the man who said, "The morning is beautiful", was not there. He was repeating, it was a reaction.

When you respond, words may not be needed at all or sometimes they may be needed – it will depend on the situation. But they will not necessarily be there: they may be, they may not be.

Response is of the heart. Response is a feeling, not a thought. You are thrilled: seeing a rose flower something starts dancing in you, something is stirred at the deepest core of your being, something starts opening inside you. The outer flower challenges the inner flower, and the inner flower responds – this is response-ability of the heart. And if you are not engaged in trivialities, you will have enough energy, abundant energy, to have this inner dance of the heart. When energy is dissipated in thoughts, your feelings are starved.

Thoughts are parasites: they live on the energy which is really for the feelings, they exploit it. Thoughts are like leakages in your being: they take your energy out. Then you are like a pot with holes – nothing can be contained in you, you remain poor. When there are no thoughts your energy is contained inside, its level starts rising higher and higher, you have a kind of fullness. In that fullness the heart responds. And then life is poetry, then life is music, and then only can you do the miracle of making deeds prove your words, not before it. Then you don't only say "I love you," your very existence proves the love. Then your words are not impotent words, they have a soul to them. And to live like that is the only life worth living: when your words and your deeds correspond, when your words and deeds are not opposites, when your words are full of your sincerity, when whatsoever you say you are.

Before that, you live in a kind of split: you say one thing, you do another. You remain schizophrenic – the whole humanity is schizophrenic – unless you come to this point where words and deeds are no more separate, but two aspects of the same phenomenon. You say what you feel, you feel what you say, you do what you say, you say what you do: one can simply watch you and will see the authenticity of your being.

If, when there is quiet, the spirit has continuously and
uninterruptedly a sense of great joy as if intoxicated or freshly bathed,
it is a sign that the light-principle is harmonious in the whole body;
then the Golden Flower begins to bud.

When there is quiet – a great confirmatory sign – then *the spirit has continuously and uninterruptedly a sense of great joy.* For no reason at all you suddenly feel yourself joyous. In ordinary life, if there is some reason you are joyful. You have met a beautiful woman and you are joyous, or you have got the money that you always wanted and you are joyous, or you have purchased the house with a beautiful garden and you are joyous – but these joys cannot last long, they are momentary. They cannot remain continuous and uninterrupted.

I have heard…

Mulla Nasruddin was sitting, very sad, in front of his house. A neighbor asked, "Mulla, why are you looking so sad?"

And Mulla said, "Look! Fifteen days ago my uncle died and he left me fifty thousand rupees."

The neighbor said, "But this is no reason to be sad! You should be happy."

Mulla said, "First you listen to the whole story. And seven days ago my other uncle died and left me seven thousand rupees. And now, nothing. Nobody is dying, nothing is happening. The week is passing by, and I am really sad."

If your joy is caused by something it will disappear, it will be momentary. It will soon leave you in deep sadness. All joys leave you in deep sadness. But there is a different kind of joy, that is a confirmatory sign: that you are suddenly joyous for no reason at all. You cannot pinpoint why. If somebody asks, "Why are you joyous?" you cannot answer.

I cannot answer why I am joyous. There is no reason. It's simply so. Now *this* joy cannot be disturbed. Now whatsoever happens, it will continue. It is there day in, day out. You may be young, you may be old, you may be alive, you may be dying – it is always there. When you have found some joy that remains – circumstances change but it abides – then you are certainly coming closer to buddhahood. This is a confirmatory sign.

If joy comes and goes, that is not of much value, that is a worldly phenomenon. When joy abides, remains, uninterrupted and continuous – as if you are intoxicated, without any drug you are stoned, as if you have just taken a bath, fresh as morning dewdrops, fresh as new leaves in the spring, fresh as lotus leaves in the pond, as if you have just taken a bath – when you remain continuously in that freshness that remains and remains and nothing disturbs it, know well you are coming closer to home.

It is a sign that the light-principle is harmonious in the whole body.

Now your whole body is functioning as a harmonious unity. Your whole body is in accord. You are no more split, you are no more fragmentary. This is individuation: you are one whole, all parts functioning and humming together, all parts functioning in an orchestra of being, nothing is out of tune. The body, the mind, the soul, the lowest and the highest, from sex to *samadhi* – all *is* functioning in a tremendous harmony and an incredible unison.

> *...then the Golden Flower begins to bud. When, furthermore, all openings are quiet, and the silver moon stands in the middle of heaven, and one has the feeling that this great Earth is a world of light and brightness, that is a sign that the body of the heart opens itself to clarity. It is a sign that the Golden Flower is opening.*

Then, furthermore, when all openings, all senses are quiet, not only the mind... Mind is your inner sense, that has to be made silent first. Then there are five senses which are mindfeeders: your eyes, your ears, your nose, all the senses.

They continuously bring information from the outside and they go on pooling the information inside, in the mind. When they are also quiet, not bringing anything, they are utterly silent, passive – eyes look but don't bring anything in, ears hear but don't cling to anything heard, the tongue tastes but hankers not for the taste, when all your senses *...are quiet and the silver moon stands in the middle of heaven* – the silver moon represents the feminine principle.

When *...the silver moon stands in the middle of heaven* – when all senses are passive, mind is passive and quiet – that means you have attained to the feminine principle of passivity, awaiting. You have become a womb.

It is a full moon night, all is cool and silent and passive, nothing stirs – the joy is infinite!

> *...and one has the feeling that this great Earth is a world of light and brightness...*

And it is not only that you feel it within. When it is within, you immediately start feeling it without too – that this whole earth is a world of light and brightness.

> ...that is a sign that the body of the heart opens itself to clarity.

You are becoming transparent, clear, clean, perceptive.

The feminine principle brings clarity because it is a passive principle. It brings rest, utter rest. You are simply there doing nothing, all is clear, all clouds gone. You can see through and through into reality. Inwards there is silence and joy, and outwards there is silence and joy.

> It is a sign that the Golden Flower is opening.

First, it was just beginning to bud, now it is opening. One more step has been taken.

> Furthermore, the whole body feels strong and firm so that it fears
> neither storm nor frost.

As your silence and joy deepen, you start feeling that there is no death for you. In death only the persona dies, the personality. The essence never dies. When you know something abiding in you, something that never changes – the joy that continues irrespective of conditions – then you know for the first time that something is deathless in you, something in you is eternal. And that moment is the moment of strength, potentiality, fearlessness. Then one is not afraid. Then trembling disappears. For the first time you look into reality without fear. Otherwise your so-called gods are just out of fear: you have created them to console yourself, you have created them as props for your fear, as protection, as armor. You are afraid, you need somebody to cling to. These are false gods, these are not true gods. Out of fear how can you find the true God?

And the so-called religious people are known as God-fearing. The real religious person has no fear, neither of the world nor of God. In fearlessness a totally different vision of God arises.

> Things by which other men are displeased, when I meet them, cannot
> becloud the brightness of the seed of the spirit.

Now nothing clouds, nothing can overwhelm you and distort your clarity. Your vision remains intact. Somebody insults you but it doesn't become a cloud. Somebody is angry, you can see through and through: you really feel compassion for the angry person because he's unnecessarily burning in a fire. You shower your bliss, your peace, your love on him. He is a fool, he needs all compassion.

Yellow Gold fills the house…

Now the second principle starts functioning: the masculine principle, Yellow Gold. Moon represents the feminine – anima; and the sun, the Yellow Gold represents the male principle – animus. The moon is yin and the sun is yang.

First, you have to become a silent, passive, feminine principle. Only out of the womb of the feminine the masculine will arise, only out of passivity the action will arise, and then the action will not have restlessness in it. Then the action will be simply a flowering. It will not have anxiety as its shadow, it will not come out of desire. It will come out of abundant energy. It will come because there is so much energy and you have to dance.

Yellow Gold fills the house, the steps are of white jade.

That white jade means the feminine, the steps are yin. The ladder is feminine. But when you have reached, suddenly passivity blooms into action.

Yellow gold fills the house, the steps are of white jade. Rotten and stinking things on earth that come in contact with one breath of the true energy will immediately live again.

And if you can come in contact with such a man whose inner steps are of white jade – whose inner sky is full of the moon and whose inner house is full of yellow gold – if you can come in contact with such a man, even if you are dead, you will immediately revive. That is the meaning of the story of Lazarus, Jesus calling Lazarus forth out of his grave. All buddha's have been calling people forth out of their graves.

I am calling you out of your graves, because the way you have lived is not the true Way: you have become concerned with trivia and you have forgotten the essential, you are just collecting seashells and colored stones on the sea beach and you have forgotten all about the diamonds which are very close by, you are collecting rubbish which will be taken away by death. I am calling you forth to attain treasures which no death can take away from you: Lazarus, come out of your grave!

And the one who listens becomes a disciple. The one who listens becomes a sannyasin. The one who listens starts moving into the inner world. His journey is totally different from other people's journey: he may live in the world but he's no longer there, his concern is utterly different.

Red blood becomes milk.

This is the meaning of the famous parable about Mahavira. It is said that a snake, a very dangerous snake, attacked Mahavira, bit his foot, but instead of blood, milk started flowing. Now Jainas take it literally, and then they become a laughing stock. It is not a literal message, it is a parable. Red blood represents violence and milk represents love.

The moment the child is born, the mother's breasts become full of milk – out of love, out of feeling for the newborn babe, suddenly her blood starts changing into milk. Suddenly a miracle starts happening in the chemistry of the mother: up to now she had been just a woman, now she is a mother. When a child is born, two persons are born – on the one hand, the child, on the other hand, the mother. The mother has a different chemistry from the woman, the miracle has happened: out of love, blood starts turning into milk. It is symbolic: blood is violence, milk is love.

When a person reaches to this state, all violence disappears: he's all love – love and nothing else.

The fragile body of the flesh is sheer gold and diamonds.

And those who can see, those who have eyes to see, will be able to see in the body of the Buddha not fragile flesh, but sheer gold and diamonds. That's why disciples are not believed by others. Others think the disciples have become hypnotized because they start seeing things which nobody else can see, which are available only to the close disciples. They start seeing, in the ordinary physical body, something else – another body, the body of gold and diamonds, the body of eternity. This body of flesh is the body of time. Hidden behind it is the body of eternity. But for that one needs eyes to see…and only love and surrender can give you the eyes to see.

That is a sign that the Golden Flower is crystallized.

But when one is moving into this inner journey and one can see one's own body as gold and diamonds, then one can be certain that the Golden Flower is crystallized. First it was just budding, then it was opening, now it is crystallized.

> *The brilliancy of the light gradually crystallizes. Hence a*
> *great terrace arises, and upon it, in the course of time,*
> *the Buddha appears.*

Now you can be certain: the Buddha is not far away, the dawn is close by, the night is over. On the terrace of this vision of gold and diamonds, of the eternal body – as this brilliance crystallizes a terrace arises – in the course of time, the Buddha appears.

One cannot do anything beyond this point. When the Golden Flower has crystallized, when the lotus has crystallized, you cannot do anything beyond this point. Now one has simply to wait: sitting silently, doing nothing, and the spring comes, and the grass grows by itself. One moment,

> *…in the course of time…*

When the spring comes…

> *…Buddha appears. When the golden being appears who should it be*
> *but the Buddha?*

In the East we have called it Buddha, in the West you have called it Christ – it is the same principle.

> *For the Buddha is the golden holy man of the great enlightenment.*
> *This is a great confirmatory experience.*

And when you have seen within yourself a terrace of brilliancy, a crystallized light and on the terrace of it Buddha appearing, when you have seen the Golden Flower open, bloomed, and on the golden lotus Buddha appearing, you have come home.

This is the ultimate goal. This has to be found. This can be found. This is your birthright. If you miss, only you will be responsible, nobody else. Risk *all*, but don't miss it! Sacrifice *all*, but don't miss it!

Enough for today.

CHAPTER 20
Words Cannot Contain It

The first question:

Osho,
I love you. I also love your jokes. I am very serious these days. This
whole enlightenment game is too heavy. Please tell more jokes.

Enlightenment, the very idea of enlightenment, is the greatest joke there is. It is a joke because it is trying to get something which is already there. It is trying to reach somewhere where you are already. It is trying to get rid of something which is not there at all. It is an effort which is ridiculous.

You are enlightened from the very beginning. Enlightenment is your nature. Enlightenment is not something that has to be achieved, it is not a goal. It is your source, it is your very energy.

But once you start thinking about enlightenment as a goal, you will become serious, you will be in tremendous trouble – and absolutely unnecessarily, of your own creation. And you will never succeed either, because to think of enlightenment as a goal is already to miss the whole point. It is not there to be sought, it is in the seeker. The seeker cannot seek it! If the seeker tries to seek it, he will never find it. It is as if somebody is trying to find his glasses and the glasses are on his nose; he's trying to find the glasses with the help of the glasses, and he is not aware. It is ridiculous!

You are creating a serious trip for yourself. You are making it a goal and it is your source. You are making it your ambition – and it is already the case! From the very beginning, nobody is unenlightened. Then what has happened to people? Why are they searching? Why do they go on searching? Why do they make a goal out of it?

In life, everything else has to be found – except enlightenment. If you want money, it has to be a goal; otherwise you will not find it. You have to work hard for it, you have to put your whole energy into the ambition, then only will you find. Then too it is not absolutely certain – you may find, you may not find. If you want power you will have to seek and search in every possible way – legal, illegal, right, wrong. In life, everything has to be found because you don't bring money with you and you don't bring power with you, and you don't bring palaces with you. You come naked, empty-handed, and you go naked and empty-handed. You don't bring a thing of this world – and all those things are needed, and you rush and you try to achieve this and that.

Slowly, slowly the idea arises in you that all these things will be taken away from you, death will come and will annihilate everything: you become frightened, fear arises. Out of fear, you start thinking to search for something which will not be taken away from you: God, truth, enlightenment, nirvana, or you can give it any name. Now you start seeking nirvana, enlightenment, God, *samadhi* in the same way as you have been seeking money, power, fame – because you have learned a logic, you have learned a program. Now the program says, "You cannot get money without seeking for it, how can you get enlightenment without seeking for it? So seek, search, fight, struggle." And there is the whole crux of the matter – and you become ridiculous.

Money has to be sought if you want to have more money, but enlightenment is already there. You bring it with you. It is your original face. It is your emptiness, your consciousness. It is your being. When you die, everything else will die except your enlightenment, except your consciousness. Nobody can take it away from you.

But the logic that you have learned in the world drives you crazy. It is very logical to search, seek money, power, name, fame; it is very illogical to seek enlightenment. And then it becomes a heavy trip, very serious. That's why a lot of religious people look so serious. Religious people cannot think somebody is religious if he is not serious. Seriousness has become almost synonymous with religiousness – sad, long faces. Do you see your saints laughing? That's why the Indian so-called saints are against me: they cannot believe that an enlightened person can tell jokes. They cannot believe!

My own experience is that only an enlightened person can tell jokes. What else is left? He has seen the greatest joke of it all: he has seen the whole absurdity of searching for enlightenment.

One finds enlightenment not by searching, but by one day coming to such a point of desperation that one drops all effort. In that very moment one becomes aware of it: when searching stops, desiring disappears, you are left alone with your being – nowhere to go, you are in.

The inward journey is not really a journey. When all journeys disappear – nowhere to go, no interest in going, you have searched in every direction and every direction has failed you – in *utter* desperation you simply stop, you collapse. But that very collapse is the moment of the transformation. If you're going nowhere, you are in. Not seeking anything, only the seeker is left. Not trying to catch anything, you become aware of the catcher. Not being interested in any object – money *or* enlightenment *or* God – only subjectivity is there. You are back home…and a great laughter, because you have always been there.

It is said that when Bodhidharma became enlightened he did not stop laughing for seven years. There is another story, in Japan, of the laughing buddha, Hotei.

His whole teaching was just laughter. He would move from one place to another, from one marketplace to another marketplace. He would stand in the middle of the market and start laughing – that was his sermon. His laughter was catching, infectious; a *real* laughter, his whole belly pulsating with the laughter, shaking with laughter. He would roll on the ground with laughter. People who would collect together, they would start laughing, and then the laughter would spread, and tidal waves of laughter, and the whole village would be overwhelmed with laughter.

People used to wait for Hotei to come to their village because he brought such joy, such blessings. He never uttered a single word, never. You asked about Buddha and he would laugh, you asked about enlightenment and he would laugh, you asked about truth and he would laugh. Laughter was his only message.

Now on the opposite extreme, Christians say Jesus never laughed. Christians must be misrepresenting Jesus. If Christians are right, then Jesus was not enlightened – and I would rather prefer Jesus to be enlightened than Christians to be right. So I say to you, he laughed! He *must* have laughed. Only such people can laugh. Their whole energy becomes a bubbling joy. Their whole being wells up into celebration. Laughter is celebration. Jesus must have laughed. My own feeling is that his laughter must have offended the serious so-called rabbis of his day.

He must have told beautiful jokes. He was a Jew, and Jews have the best jokes in the world. And he was not a man who could be believed to be so serious that he never laughed. A wrong impression has been created by Christianity. Jesus is painted as crucified – that gives the wrong impression. For his whole life he was not on the cross. My own understanding is that on his cross also he must have laughed, because only a man of great laughter can say to God, "Father, forgive these people, because they don't know what they are doing." He was not serious, he was not sad, even the cross was a celebration.

Animals can play, at the most, but no animal can celebrate. It is given only to human beings. It is their privilege, prerogative, to celebrate. And laughter is the best celebration. To laugh is your fundamental human quality. If you come across a buffalo laughing, you will go mad. No other animal can laugh, only man. It is something special, a gift of God. And naturally, when one becomes enlightened, one will be able to have a total laughter. You need reasons to laugh; he will not need any reasons to laugh. Laughter will be just his natural quality.

That is the meaning of the story that Bodhidharma never stopped laughing for seven years. There was no reason – just the whole ridiculousness of the thing: so many buddhas and everybody believing that he is not a buddha and trying to attain buddhahood.

You are all buddhas. Whether you know it or not, it doesn't matter – your buddhahood is not affected by it, you still remain a buddha. You can believe that you are not a buddha; your belief is not going to transform your nature. You can believe anything! Your belief remains superficial. At the very core of your soul, you are a buddha.

The moment you are not in desire, you will become aware of your innermost center. Desire takes you away from yourself. And that is the problem, you must be too desirous of enlightenment, hence you are becoming serious. Otherwise there is nothing serious in enlightenment.

The second question:

Osho,
Why is truth inexpressible? Why can't it be told?

Truth is an experience of thoughtlessness. Truth is an experience of wordlessness. You come to experience truth only in utter silence. It is utter silence, hence it is impossible to reduce it to sound, to word, to thought. Its intrinsic nature is without thought. To express truth in words would be like expressing the sky through the clouds. The sky is not expressed through the clouds. The sky, covered with clouds, disappears, you cannot see it. The more clouds there are the less the sky is available, and the less clouds there are the more sky is available, no clouds and the whole sky is available. You cannot express the sky through the clouds. They are the hindrances. So are thoughts.

Truth is your consciousness, thoughts are clouds in the sky of consciousness. You cannot express through thoughts. Your thoughts can, at the most, indicate – like fingers pointing to the moon. But remember, fingers are not the moon and don't start worshipping the fingers. That's what has happened in the world: somebody is worshipping one finger, somebody else some other finger – Christians, Mohammedans, Hindus, Buddhists. What are Buddhists doing? – worshipping Buddha. This is just a finger pointing to the moon. Where is the moon? They are sucking the finger and have completely forgotten the moon.

That's why I say to you: Don't start biting *my* finger! Don't become too much interested in what is said. That which is said is only pointing a finger to that which cannot be said. So all words are, at the most, arrows. That's why they can be misunderstood, easily misunderstood: fingers you are acquainted with, the moon you have never seen, and when I show the moon with the finger it is more possible to become interested in the finger than to look away from it and see the moon. To see the moon you will have to look away from the finger, you will have to become completely oblivious to the finger.

"To tell the truth," said Oscar Wilde, "you have to wear a mask."

All words are masks, all theories, dogmas, philosophies are masks, all religions, all theologies are masks. He's right: to tell the truth, you have to wear a mask. You cannot tell it straight, there is no way. To bring the word in simply means: now you cannot be straight, a medium has come in. Now the expression is through the medium, the medium will bring its own distortions into it. If you have a colored glass before your eyes, you will see the world in the same color. Now words will become like glasses on your eyes: they will color your world. That's why different people look at the world in different ways – because they have been conditioned differently.

A Hindu looks at the world differently from the Christian. A Hindu can worship the tree and the Christian will think, "What nonsense! Worshipping a tree?" The Christian will think, "This man has to be brought to his senses, converted. This man is a pagan. Make efforts to bring him to the true religion. This man is primitive" – because the Christian has a different upbringing, a different conditioning. Ask the Hindu: he has a different mind. He says, "The whole existence is divine. The tree is also divine. And the question is not what you are worshipping, the question is that you are worshipping. What you worship makes no difference." And the Hindu will say, "You go on worshipping a dead cross – it is made of wood – and I am worshipping an alive tree, and you think I am foolish? Who is foolish? The tree is alive and life is flowing, and the tree is green and the tree is in blossom. God is still flowing in it as green juice. Your cross is dead. It is better to worship the tree," the Hindu will say, "than to worship the cross."

The Hindu worships Krishna – dancing, playing on his flute – and the Christian cannot believe it because the world is in suffering: "And how can this man be so cruel that he is playing on his flute? The world needs to be redeemed and he is dancing with girls! What is he doing? What kind of religion is this?" He has a conditioning that the man of God has to die for the world so that the world can be redeemed, the man of God has to become a sacrifice, he has to be a martyr – not a singer, not a musician, not a dancer, but a martyr.

A Hindu has a different conditioning: he thinks if Jesus is crucified then he must have been suffering from bad karma from his past life – otherwise why should he be crucified? Crucifixion is not a good thing. It means he must have committed some bad things in his past life, because "as you sow, so you reap." "He cannot be the man of God. If he is the man of God then crucifixion is simply impossible." They have a different vision and different conditioning: the man of God has to sing the song of God, the celestial song, Bhagavad-Gita. He has to dance and sing in praise of God. The world need not be redeemed, the world has only to be enlightened, helped – to laugh, to love, to be.

Now it depends, it is according to your conditioning. Once you drop all conditionings you will be able to understand all kinds of minds very easily, and you will be able to see their benefits and their harms. You will be able to see what is beautiful in a certain conditioning and what is ugly. Yes, the Hindu has something lovely to say: "God is there and we have to praise God." Right! But the world is suffering too, and something has to be done for the world, for its sufferings. And the Christian is not absolutely wrong: just the flute won't do, it has not done much for India. India is terribly poor, starving. Life is ugly. People are somehow pulling, dragging themselves. It has not been helped by the flute. Something more is needed, just dancing won't do. Schools will be needed and hospitals will be needed and food will be needed.

Christianity is not all wrong, but again it makes only a half-statement. When the food is there, when the house is there, when the medicine is there, when the education is there, then what? Then just crucify yourself? What else is left? Where is the flute?

The West is suffering from affluence: all is there now, but nobody knows what to do. They have worked for three hundred years, hard work, to make everything right. Now everything is right: the house is ready, food is available, technology has provided for all needs – now what to do? Except to commit suicide life seems meaningless, because the flute is missing.

In the East man has lived with a half-vision: God is beautiful, and life is beautiful, but then he has been avoiding the ugly part of it and not trying to transform it at all. The East has lived in a very unrevolutionary way, an *anti-*revolutionary way. It has lived a very reactionary life – orthodox, conventional, conformist. Revolution is something Western, revolution is something Christian. The world has to be transformed as much as the consciousness has to be transformed.

But when you put *all* conditionings aside you will be able to see that the world needs a totally different kind of vision. It needs a *total* vision – neither Christian nor Hindu nor Mohammedan. It needs a total vision. All these are aspects of that total vision: Mohammed is one door, Christ is another, Krishna is still another, and Buddha too. All are different doors to the same temple and all doors are needed, only then will the temple be rich. And even if all the doors are accepted, then truth has not been told in its fullness – because it is infinite. You can put Buddha, Christ, Zarathustra, Lao Tzu, Mahavira, Mohammed together: still truth has not been told in its totality. It can never be told. It is infinite. All words are small, all human efforts are limited.

And then it cannot be told straight. It can be communicated straight, but it cannot be told straight – and that is the difference between a thinker and a meditator. The thinker goes roundabout because he has to go through thought. He searches for the sky through the clouds and gets lost in the clouds, may never reach the sky: the thinker gets lost in thoughts. The meditator starts by dropping thoughts. He starts by dropping thinking itself, and a moment comes when there is no thought: then there is immediacy, then there is nothing between you and that which is. Then there is nothing at all – you are bridged with reality. But that is an experience and whenever you would like to tell that experience to somebody else you will have to use words – out of necessity – and words cannot contain it.

For certain purposes you can say the truth straight – for certain purposes. "The cat sat on the mat": either the cat did it, he did sit there, or he did not. But there are other kinds of truths which you cannot catch hold of so easily. This is a fact, not a truth. So remember the difference: if some truth can be said through language, then it is a fact. "The cat sat on the mat" – now there is an objective way of knowing whether this is true or not. If it is true it is a fact, if it is untrue it is not a fact, it is a fiction. But there are other kinds of truth which cannot be said so easily. You cannot catch hold of them.

Language is riddled with all kinds of ambiguity. If anyone says God, love or freedom, you need to know exactly what he means when he is saying it. These are big words – *God*. Now a Hindu means something, a Mohammedan means something else, a Christian means something else. There are three hundred religions in the world, so there are three hundred meanings to the word *God*. Even those three hundred meanings don't exhaust it because new religions are being created every day, and they will go on being created. There can be as many religions as there are people in the world. Each man can have his own religion.

Then what is the meaning of the word *God*? It becomes vaguer and vaguer and vaguer. It becomes a chaos. You cannot pinpoint anything about it. And if you try to pinpoint you destroy its beauty, because you destroy its unlimitedness. If you fix it, you have killed it.

A butterfly on the wing is one thing, and a butterfly killed and pinned down in an album is a totally different thing. It is not the same butterfly. Where is the life? The moment you pin the butterfly down in an album, it is just a corpse.

When Buddha says, "God," it is a butterfly on the wing: when you catch hold of the word, you pin it down in a book, you think you know, you think you have understood; all that you have got is just a corpse, the life has flown away.

The life is an experience! Words cannot carry the experience. When I say something…unsaid, when it is throbbing in my heart, it is alive. The moment it has left my lips it is no more the same thing: life is left behind in my heart, it goes on throbbing there, and only the word – dead, corpse-like – moves into the air. Just a sound, a ripple, reaches to you. It is not the same thing as it was unsaid.

And then more complexities arise: the moment the sound reaches your mind you start giving your meaning to it – and your meaning may be just the opposite of my meaning because it will depend on your experience. If you meditate, then maybe your meaning will come closer and closer to me. If you have come to a point where you can stop all thinking and get in tune so deeply with yourself that there is absolute silence, then you will come closest to the meaning of what has been said to you. In fact, then there will be no need to even say it. I can just look into your eyes and you will understand, I can just sit by your side and hold your hand and you will understand. Then understanding is a transfer, a transmission – beyond words, beyond scriptures. The higher up you go, the thicker grows the mystery.

The lower kinds of facts can be relayed through words because we have all experienced them. When I say "a tree" you understand exactly what I mean, but when I say "nirvana" you only hear the word, you don't understand what I mean – because as far as the tree is concerned, it is a common experience – my experience, your experience. If I say "a rock," immediately it is understood. It is a mundane fact. But when I say "love," it is a little more difficult. And when I say "nirvana," even more difficult – because the higher the truth, the fewer are those who will be able to understand it.

Jesus was misunderstood. Out of misunderstanding he was killed. He was talking of the Kingdom of God, and the Roman rulers became suspicious. They started thinking, "He is a politician and he wants to rule the world. He wants to create his own kingdom" – because he was talking continuously and saying to people, "I have come to establish the Kingdom of God." He was saying one thing, the politicians were interpreting something else. He was not talking of the kingdom of this world, he was talking of the kingdom of the other world, the invisible. He was not concerned with politics at all.

It has always happened: the higher you go the more dumb you feel, and whatsoever you say you can *immediately* see it has been misunderstood.

Lao Tzu has said, "If I say something and people understand it, then I know it was not really worth saying. But if I say something and people don't understand, then I know that there must have been some truth in it."

We must learn to live with this, this mystery of higher truths. Music is one way of doing it, far better than language, because music has no words, so it cannot tell anything – truth, untruth – so it can tell no truth or lies. It says nothing, it simply shows – and that is the beauty of music. You don't think whether music is true or untrue; that is irrelevant. You simply listen to it, you become overwhelmed by it, you are possessed by it, you fall in tune with it, you are transported to some other realm, to some other vision of reality. You are not in the mundane world: music takes you to the higher peaks of life and existence. It simply takes your hand and leads you, very politely, very lovingly, into the mysterious.

Music was born as part of religion. Music was born in temples, music was born in the mystery schools, in the esoteric schools of seekers of truth. It was born as an effort to convey something which cannot be conveyed through words. Music can bear witness to the mystery, and that is all.

If you love a Master, you start hearing his music, the music of his being. Even through his words you start hearing the wordless message, you start hearing... listening to the gaps between the words, you start reading between the lines.

Slowly slowly words become transparent; then they don't hide, they reveal. But for that, trust and love are needed. For that, disciplehood is needed.

Just the other night a new sannyasin was here, Kavio – a beautiful man with great potential. He has come here with his beloved. She's also a beautiful woman. She wants to look into my eyes, and she is not a sannyasin yet. Kavio asked me about it, and I had to say that unless she is a sannyasin, even if she looks into my eyes she will not be able to see anything.

To be a sannyasin means to be ready to receive. I will be giving, but she will not be able to receive – because she is not ready to pay anything to receive it. She should take the jump into sannyas. Sannyas means surrender, surrender creates receptivity. Surrender means you become vulnerable, open, you don't defend. Surrender means now you put your arms away, now you drop your armor. Now even if the Master wants to kill you, you will be happy to be killed by the Master.

I have heard...

One day Hassan of Busra and Malik, son of Dinar, and Sakik of Bulk, came to see Rabiya el-Adawiya when she was ill.

Rabiya is one of the greatest woman mystics of the world, and these three saints came to see her because she was ill.

Hassan said, "None is sincere in his claim to the love of God unless he patiently endures the blows of his Lord."

Rabiya said, "This smells of egoism."

Sakik said, "None is sincere in his claim unless he give thanks for the blows of his Lord."

Rabiya said, "This must be still bettered. Still something of egoism is there."

Malik, son of Dinar, said, "None is sincere in his claim unless he delights in the blows of his Lord."

Rabiya said, "Good, but still needs to be improved. A very subtle ego is still hiding there like a shadow."

Then they all said, "Please do speak. You yourself say."

She said, "None is sincere in his claim unless he forgets the blows in beholding his Lord."

Let me repeat it: "None is sincere in his claim unless he forgets the blows in beholding his Lord."

Even when the Master hits, you feel tremendously happy. And the Master has to hit to make openings in your being. You have grown a hard crust around yourself, that was necessary for survival; otherwise you would not have survived at all. You had to protect yourself against so many dangerous situations. You have become afraid, frightened; you have created a Great Wall of China around you.

When you come to a Master you have to drop that armor. And the armor may have gone so deep that you cannot drop it, then the Master has to hit you, the Master has to use a sledge-hammer! He has to cut many chunks of your being because they are not really part of you. They are part of the armor which has become too much identified with your being. And when those chunks are removed and cut, it is painful, it hurts – but only then the Master can pour himself into you.

One has to pay for it. And by paying I mean: one has to be ready to drop all defenses. That's what sannyas is all about; only in a master-disciple relationship can truth be conveyed, because only in that relationship are words not needed.

I use words to persuade you to become a disciple. Words cannot convey the truth, but words can convey this approach: that there is a possibility of being in a certain love-relationship with a Master, there is a possibility of coming closer to somebody who has seen who he is. You are also that, but you have not seen it yet. Coming closer to somebody who has known, one day his vibe starts triggering a process of knowing in your being. That is the transfer.

Kavio's woman has some longing to be connected with me, to be related with me, but still wants to be related to me as an outsider – is afraid of getting involved, is afraid of being committed. But that very fear will not allow her to receive what I want to give. I am ready to give to anybody! It is *not* a condition from *my* side that you have to be a sannyasin, that only then will my energy be flowing towards you. This is my observation and experience: that only a sannyasin receives it, the others are not ready to receive.

The music of silence, the music of a loving surrender, the music of the being of a Master – that is the way to relate, to convey.

Music, in a sense, is absolutely silent. Sounds are there but those sounds only make the silence deeper: they help the silence, they are not against silence – that is the difference between noise and music. Noise is just sound which does not lead you to silence, music is a sound that becomes a door to silence. Modern music is not much of a music, it is noise; it does not lead you to calm or silence. Classical music is real music. The definition of real music is: that sound which leads you into silence.

Music, in a sense, is absolutely silent. Even song is not pure music, because a song has words in it. It is a compromise with language, it is halfway to music.

It is better than ordinary language. Poetry is better than prose, poetry is a little closer to music, and the closer the poetry is to music the more poetic it is. Hence the highest form of poetry comes very close to music: it does not have much meaning but it contains much silence, it provokes silence.

The being of a Master is the being of music, poetry, song. But they all lead to silence, and truth can only be conveyed in silence. Have you not observed the fact that whenever you are in love you can be silent easily? You need not talk, you can just sit together with the person you love. There is nothing to say. Just to be together is more than enough, more than one can ask. Just to be together is such a contentment. There is no need even to say that "I love you." That would be a kind of disturbance, that would be utterly superfluous. That would not say much. In love, you can be silent.

Sannyas is a love affair, and you can be silent only as the love deepens – and then the truth can be transferred. But it is a transfer of energy, of music, of love. It is not verbal, it is not a philosophy.

The third question:

> Osho,
> Why won't you leave India? Those dim-witted politicians in New
> Delhi will be the last people in the world to understand what is going
> on here.

It is difficult for me to leave India. India has something tremendously valuable: it has the longest, deepest search for truth. Many buddhas have walked on this land, under these trees – the very earth has become sacred. To be here is totally different than to be anywhere else. And what I am trying to bring to you is more easily possible here than anywhere else.

India has fallen from its peaks. It is no longer its past glory. It is one of the ugliest spots now on the earth, but still, because a Gautam Buddha walked, and a Mahavira and a Krishna, and millions that no other country can claim....

Jesus is very alone in Jerusalem, Mohammed is very very alone in the Arabian countries, Lao Tzu has a very small company – Chuang Tzu and a few others. They tried hard to create something, but India has the longest spiritual vibe. At least for five thousand years the search has gone on deepening, and still the waters are flowing.

Indians themselves have forgotten about them. In fact they are no longer interested in their own heritage. They are no longer interested in those living waters. They have deserted them. But for whomsoever wants to seek and search and be, India still provides the best climate – spiritual climate, I mean.

Indians have become very materialistic, that is true. But with so many buddhas the release of their energy still pulsates, in spite of the Indian materialism. Indians have become *really* materialistic, far more materialistic than any country in the world. And great hypocrisy exists, because they go on claiming to be religious, and they are no more. My own observation is that now the Indian mind is more and more materialistic, more gross than any other mind. Their whole interest is in money, in power-politics, in material things.

Just a few days ago I told Laxmi to purchase the most costly car possible in the country. One thing good about Laxmi: she never asks why. She purchased it. It worked – it was a device.

Laxmi was knocking on the doors of the banks to get money for the new commune – we need much money, nearabout five crore rupees will be needed. Who is going to loan that much money to me? The day she purchased the car, seeing that we have the money, banks started coming to her office, offering, "Take as much money as you want." Now she is puzzled: from whom to take? Everybody wants to give on better terms, and they are after her.

I have been working in India for twenty years continuously, thousands of people have been transformed, millions have listened to me and many more have been reading what I am saying, but the *Times of India*, the most conventional newspaper of India, still the most British, has not published a single article about me or my work. But the day Laxmi purchased the car there was a big article – on the car, not on me!

Now they are all interested. The news of the car has been published all over the country – in all the newspapers, in all the languages. Now what kind of people are these? Their interest is not in me, not in meditation, not in the thousands of people who are meditating here; they are completely unaware of what is happening here. But they became interested in the car.

They come here – many people come to the office – not to see me or to see you. They inquire, "Can we see the car?" Laxmi says to them, "You can come in the early morning discourse, and you can see the car too." And poor fellows – they have to come and listen for ninety minutes just to see the car. What a torture! And these are rich people, educated people. But can you think of a country that is becoming more and more materialistic? And they are very worried, and editorials have been written on the car and they ask, "Why?" – why can't I live a simple life?

My life is absolutely simple: so simple really, that I am always satisfied with the best kinds of things. It is absolutely simple! What more simplicity is possible? The best things can be expressed in a single sentence. There is no complexity about it: I like quality. I'm not interested in how much it costs but in the quality. I like quality in people, not quantity. I like quality in everything, not quantity. We could have purchased thirty Indian cars instead of this one, but that would have been quantity – and even thirty wouldn't have been of any use.

But their puzzle, why they can't understand it, is that they pretend to be religious, but deep down their whole obsession is materialistic. They carry a hypocrisy, and to fulfill their hypocrisy the whole Indian religious world has to compromise. If somebody wants to become a saint he has to live in utter poverty. It is almost a kind of masochism: he has to torture himself. The more he tortures himself, the more people think he is religious: "See how religiously he is living!"

To live religiously means to live joyously. To live religiously means to live meditatively. To live religiously means to live this world as a gift of God. But their minds are obsessed and they can't understand.

Once the purpose of the car is served, it will be gone. The purpose is almost served, but it can show you... I can even come in a bullock cart. That would not be much. It would be even more colorful, and I would enjoy the ride more.

They come here and they look, and their whole point is, "Why such a beautiful ashram?" They want something dirty, shabby, a sloppy place, and then it is an ashram. They cannot believe that the ashram can be clean, beautiful, with trees and flowers, and comfortable. They cannot believe it. And not that they don't want comforts for themselves; they are hankering for it. They are, in fact, jealous. The Indian mind has become materialistic, grossly materialistic.

A spiritual mind makes no distinctions between matter and spirit. It is undivided. The whole existence is one: that is the spiritual mind. The materialist, even if he loves a woman, reduces her to a thing. Then who is a spiritualist? A spiritualist is a person who, even if he touches a thing, transforms it into a person. You will be surprised by my definition. A spiritual person is one who, even if he drives a car, the car becomes a person. He feels for the car, he listens for its humming sound. He has all affection and care for it. Even a thing starts becoming a person, alive; he has communion with the thing too. And a materialistic person is one who, even if he loves a man or a woman, a person, immediately reduces them into a thing. The woman becomes a wife – the wife is a thing; the man becomes a husband – the husband is a thing – an institution and all institutions are ugly, dead.

You ask me, "Why won't you leave India?"

This India that you see in the newspapers, this India I have already left. The India that you know, I have already left. Have you ever seen me going out of the gate? I live in my room. Whether this room is here or anywhere else, I will live in the room; it will be the same. I have left this India already. I am not concerned with this India that you come to know through radio, television, newspapers – the India of the politicians, of the hypocrites, of the masochistic mahatmas. I have left it already.

But I cannot leave. There is a hidden India too, an esoteric India too – where buddhas are still alive, where you can contact Mahavira more easily than anywhere else, where the whole tradition of the awakened ones is like an undercurrent. I can't leave that. For me, there is no problem; I can leave, I will be the same anywhere. But for you it will not be the same.

I want to use that undercurrent for your transformation. It will be easier. Unknowingly, unawares, but you will be surrounded by the Buddha-vibe. And once the new commune is established, you will see miracles happening, because I can make that undercurrent available to you in its totality. That would not be possible anywhere else.

Nowhere else has religion lived so tremendously as it has lived in this country. Just as science is a Western by-product, religion is an Eastern by-product. If you want to learn science you have to go to the West, because the sources are there. The whole Western mind is such that science comes out of it very easily. That was the case, as far as religion is concerned, in the East, and the East is synonymous with India.

You are not aware, you cannot be aware of what I am intending to do. These are all devices, so never start making a conclusion just by seeing something: you may not be aware of its background, you may not be aware of the intention, and you may not be aware of what is going to happen through it.

Now Laxmi knows that the car has helped her tremendously. Once its work is finished it can be gone. Never take anything on its face value here, things have hidden meanings. They are devices.

The new commune is going to become a river of all the buddhas. You will be able to use all that great energy easily. We will make a great reservoir of it. You will be able to live and breathe in it, and you can ride on those tidal waves and move to the unknown.

So I cannot leave India.

And you say: "Those dim-witted politicians in New Delhi will be the last people in the world to understand what is going on here."

Politicians are politicians. They are all alike everywhere; maybe a little bit different on the surface, but deep down they are the same people because politics is politics. I know Indian politics has become the dirtiest in the world. That too is part of Indian hypocrisy. Even Indian politicians try to prove that they are mahatmas, even Morarji Desai tries to prove that he is a super-mahatma. A politician and a mahatma? Because of this hypocrisy Indian politics has become the most dirty game.

If things are clear, if somebody says, "I am ambitious and I want to be on the top," at least he is sincere. But in India the politician says, "I am the humblest man, and I don't want to be on the top. What is there? There is nothing. My search is for God, but just to serve people I have to go. I am obliging you by becoming the Prime Minister of the country." Now this hypocrisy is making things very dirty.

Just a few days ago Indian politics took a change, and it was hoped that it would be for the better. But it is proving just the opposite: the change has been for the worse. And now it seems clear that the man who has been responsible for this change, J. Prakash Narayan, will not be forgiven by the future, because he has given power to the most reactionary section of the country. He has given power to a bunch of power-hungry wolves, and now he himself is feeling impotent and cannot do anything. Once they are in power they don't care anything about him. Now the whole Indian scene is nothing but politics: how to reach power and how to exploit, how to have more money and how to have more power, and how to remain in power longer.

But this is so everywhere, more or less. And politicians will create trouble everywhere for me and for my people, because I stand for a totally new vision of life. I stand for a revolution in human consciousness. Politics always supports the vested interest – it has to support it – so everywhere the trouble will be the same.

One thing more will be difficult: from any other country I can be thrown out immediately, here they cannot do that. And it is not that this has only been so with me, it has always been so.

Gurdjieff was not allowed to enter England, he was not allowed to settle in many countries. For his whole life he was moving from one country to another. He could not do his work. How could he do the work? The work needs a kind of settlement. He would gather his disciples and then the country had to be left and the disciples would be scattered again. Again he would gather, he would spend a few years in gathering, and by the time the disciples had gathered, the politicians were against him and he had to leave the country, and again everything was disturbed.

This continued for his whole life. He could not help – not a single person could become enlightened through him, and many would have become. He had the potential. He was a rare genius, a rare Master – but the situations wouldn't allow.

If I leave India that will be the situation again and again. Whenever my people will gather in one country, there will be trouble. And here they can create trouble for you – that can be managed easily – but they cannot create trouble for me. At least they cannot throw me out of the country! They would like me to go, they will do everything so that I leave, because my presence is becoming difficult, very difficult for them. The more I am here and the more my people are growing and the more the commune will become an established fact, the more I am going to shatter all their values, all their hypocrisies.

So I cannot leave India. And I know the Indian politicians will be the last people in the world to understand what is going on here. They will not even be the last – they will never understand.

The politician cannot understand religion. It is impossible. The language of politics is just the opposite of the language of religion. Religion is non-desiring, non-ambitiousness, non-possessiveness. Religion is living in the here and now. Politics is ambition, desire, always in the future, tomorrow. Religion is to accept oneself, to accept whatsoever one is and to relax with it. Politics arises out of inferiority complex, out of comparison. Compare yourself with others and you are always feeling inferior. Somebody is more beautiful, somebody is more knowledgeable, somebody is more intelligent – and you are suffering from an inferiority complex. You want to prove yourself.

Now, if you are not intelligent, what can you do to become intelligent? It is impossible. If you don't have a musical genius, what can you do? There is no way to do anything about it. If you are not beautiful, you are not beautiful. But then only one thing is left: you can become a politician. That is the last resort of all the people who suffer from an inferiority complex: there, anybody, whosoever has violence enough, brutality enough, whosoever has the animal alive in him, can rush. No other talent is needed, no kind of genius is needed. In fact the less intelligence you have, the better will be your chances of succeeding.

I have heard...

Mulla Nasruddin suffered very much because people thought he was an idiot. Finally he decided to go to the brain surgeon and let him transplant another brain. So he went to the surgeon, and the surgeon said, "But Mulla, there are brains and brains. You come in and you see." And there were many brains.

Mulla said, "What is the difference – because I see different prices written on every case? On one case the price is only twenty-five rupees and on another it is twenty-five thousand rupees." Mulla asked, "What is the difference?"

The surgeon said, "Mulla, the first, which is priced at only twenty-five rupees, belongs to a great scientist. And the second, which is twenty-five thousand rupees, belongs to a politician."

Mulla said, "Do you mean to say that the politician's brain is far more superior to the scientist's?"

The surgeon said, "No, don't misunderstand me. It is priced more because it has never been used. It is absolutely unused, brand new. The scientist's has been used too much. It is finished, it is burnt out."

In politics you don't need brains, you don't need intelligence, you don't need sensitivity, you don't need awareness, you don't need love, you don't need compassion. These are all barriers! In politics you need just the opposite qualities. Disqualifications everywhere else are qualifications in politics. All that is needed is a mad hunger for power – and that is created by an inferiority complex.

The religious man has no inferiority complex. Only the religious man has no inferiority complex because he never compares, and without comparison you cannot be superior or inferior. So the religious man is neither superior nor inferior, he is simply himself. He accepts the way God has made him and he enjoys the way God has made him. He's utterly happy. Just because he *is*, he is grateful. His every moment is one of gratitude. He does not want to become anybody else, he is utterly contented. He knows he is unique – neither inferior nor superior. He knows everybody is unique, because two persons are not alike.

So politicians can never understand what religion is. They never understood Buddha, they never understood Christ, they never understood any religious phenomenon that has happened on the earth. They were always against it. The presence of the religious person is a danger to the politician.

And I know you are right: "Those dim-witted politicians in New Delhi" will never understand me. That's true. But we are not worried. I am not in any way concerned that they should understand me. They need not. All that I am concerned with is: that they leave me alone, and my work alone – that's enough. And sooner or later they will have to leave it alone, because they cannot argue with me, they have nothing to say. They have not answered me. I have been criticizing them for twenty years: they have not answered, they *cannot* answer. What I am saying they also feel, deep down, is right.

Politicians personally come to me and they say, "Osho, whatsoever you say is absolutely right, but we cannot confess that 'it is what is happening there in New Delhi' publicly."

Privately they always say, "You are right," but publicly they cannot say it, because if I am right, if they say it publicly, the crowd, the mob will go against them. They have to depend on the crowd, they have to depend on it continuously for votes. They have to go on supporting all kinds of stupid ideas and superstitions of the mob. Their dependence is tremendous.

For twenty years I have criticized Mahatma Gandhi and his philosophy. No Gandhian has answered. Many Gandhians have come to me and they say, "Whatsoever you say is right, but we cannot say it in public, because if we say that whatsoever you say about Mahatma Gandhi is right, we will lose." The public believes in Mahatma Gandhi, so utter nonsense has to be supported because Gandhi was anti-technological. Now this country will remain poor if this country remains anti-technological, this country will never be in a state of well-being. And there is no need for technology always to be anti-ecology. There is no need: a technology can be developed which can be in tune with ecology, a technology can be developed which can help people and will not destroy nature. But Gandhi was against technology.

He was against the railway, he was against the post office, he was against electricity. He was against machines of all kinds. They know this is stupid, ...but they go on saying so, and they go on paying homage to Mahatma Gandhi because they have to get the votes from the people, and the people worship the Mahatma – because the Mahatma fits with their ideas of how a mahatma should be.

Mahatma Gandhi fits with the Indian mob. The Indian mob worships him. The politician has to follow the mob. Remember always: in politics the leader follows the followers. He has to! He only pretends that he is leading. Deep down he has to follow the followers. Once the followers leave him, he is nowhere. He cannot stand on his own, he has no ground of his own.

Gandhi worshipped poverty. Now if you worship poverty you will remain poor. Poverty has to be hated. I hate poverty! I cannot say to worship it – that would be a crime – and I don't see any religious quality in just being poor. But Gandhi talked much about poverty and its beauty – it helps the poor man's ego, it buttresses his ego, he feels good. It is a consolation: that he is religious, simple – he may not have riches but he has some spiritual richness.

Poverty in itself is not a spiritual richness; no, not at all. Poverty is ugly and poverty has to be destroyed. And to destroy poverty, technology has to be brought in.

Mahatma Gandhi was against birth control. Now if you are against birth control this country will become poorer and poorer every day. Then there is no possibility.

One day Mulla Nasruddin was saying to me, "Osho, it seems that soon everybody will be reduced to beggars. All will be begging!"

I asked him, "Nasruddin, from whom?"

The country is going to such poverty that even to exist as beggars will not be possible, because from whom will you beg? And when there is poverty there is crime. Poverty is the source of all crime – not the source of religiousness, not the source of spirituality.

Richness is the source of spirituality and religiousness, because religion is the ultimate luxury. It is the highest art, the greatest music, the profoundest dance. When you have everything else, only then do you start looking for God. When you are finished with everything else, when you have seen everything and you have found that you are not satisfied, you start searching for God.

A poor man has no idea of God. His God is nothing but a support: he clings, leans upon the idea of God.

This happens every day: when a poor man comes to me he never comes with the problems which are religious. He says, "My wife is ill. Osho, can you bless her? My son is not getting employment. Can you help?" Now these things have nothing to do with religion at all. But he never comes with the problem of meditation or love; those are not his problems at all. His problem is bread, shelter. Life is in such a state that he is trying to survive somehow. When a man is drowning in the river, will he ask, "What is meditation?" Or, will he ask, "What is love?" He wants to be helped to come out of his situation first. He is drowning, life is disappearing – who bothers about meditation?

A hungry man cannot be interested in meditation. But Gandhi thinks that poverty has something spiritual in it. It is just ugly. It is the most unspiritual thing in the world, because it is the source of all crime and sin.

I have heard…

There were reports of people claiming to have seen the spirit of Diogenes stalking the streets of many capitals of the world again. The learned Greek was first spotted in Paris. Some people approached the lamp-bearing philosopher: "Diogenes, what are you doing in Paris?"

Diogenes laughed a hearty laugh, he was very very happy, and he said,

"Messieurs, I am searching for truth." There was joy, there was dance, there was hope in his eyes.

And then it was heard that he was seen walking in London. Some bobbies again found him with his lamp: "Diogenes, what are you doing in London?"

Now he was not so joyous. He tried to smile but it came only with an effort. He said, "Gentlemen, I am searching for truth." Hope was disappearing from his eyes, sadness was settling.

And then he was seen in New York. Hope had completely disappeared, he was utterly sad, but he still repeated, almost mechanically, parrot-like, "I am searching for truth."

And then inevitably he was reported to have been seen in New Delhi. One Gandhian politician, clad in pure white khadi, approached him and asked, "Diogenes, what are you doing in New Delhi?"

And he was very angry, almost in a rage, and he said, "Netaji, I am searching for my lamp!"

In New Delhi you cannot save your lamp.

The country is falling into deeper and deeper misery every day. The misery is creating more misery. It always happens: if you have you get more, if you don't have, even that which you have starts disappearing. And the Indian politician is responsible for all this nonsense because he goes on preaching high ideals. The Indian politician only talks, empty and shallow promises – nothing is ever fulfilled. He cannot fulfill because his beliefs are stupid; or maybe he has to believe in those stupid superstitions.

For example, they still talk about celibacy – not birth control but celibacy: people should be celibate so that the population can be reduced. Now this is nonsense. How many people can be celibate? And this is not a way to reduce the population. And they still think in terms of no-technology, no-machines.

The whole country has become like a wound, a cancer.

I see all this. That's also why I don't want to leave this country. I want to create a small oasis of my commune, which will be absolutely technological and still ecological. It has to be a model so that we can say to the whole country that if this can happen with five thousand sannyasins in a small place, why can't it happen on a higher scale, a greater scale, to the whole country?

My commune can become an example. It will be simple and rich. It will be technological and not against ecology. It will be absolutely scientific and yet human. It will be a totally different kind of communism. It will be a commune not for something from the outside or from the top, but because people love each other – they have created a family, they want to live together. We will be doing farming, collective farming, with all the technology possible. The commune will be made absolutely independent, with no need to go outside. And my effort is that we will not be bringing anything inside, we will produce everything. It can become a great oasis in this desert country. It can be of much help, it can create great inspiration.

So I am not going to leave it. The country will need me, and you too.
Enough for today.

CHAPTER 21
The Spirit Returns and Touches Heaven

Master Lu-Tsu said:

Now there are three confirmatory experiences which can be tested. The first is that, when one has entered the state of meditation, the gods are in the valley. Men are heard talking as though at a distance of several hundred paces, each one quite clear. But the sounds are all like an echo in a valley. One can always hear them, but never oneself. This is called: "The presence of the gods in the valley."

At times the following can be experienced: as soon as one is quiet, the light of the eyes begins to blaze up, so that everything before one becomes quite bright as if one were in a cloud. If one opens one's eyes and seeks the body, it is not to be found any more. This is called: "In the empty chamber it grows light." Inside and outside, everything is equally light. That is a very favorable sign.

Or, when one sits in meditation, the fleshly body becomes quite shining like silk or jade. It seems difficult to remain sitting: one feels as if drawn upward. This is called: "The spirit returns and touches heaven." In time, one can experience it in such a way that one really floats upward.

And now, it is already possible to have all three of these experiences.
But not everything can be expressed. Different things appear to each
person according to his disposition. If one experiences these things, it
is a sign of a good aptitude. With these things it is just as it is when
one drinks water: one can tell for oneself whether the water is warm
or cold. In the same way a man must convince himself about these
experiences, then only are they real.

Master Lu-Tsu said:
When there is a gradual success in producing the circulation of the
light, a man must not give up his ordinary occupation in doing it.
The ancients said: When occupations come to us, we must accept
them; when things come to us, we must understand them from
the ground up. If the occupations are properly handled by correct
thoughts, the light is not scattered by outside things, but circulates
according to its own law. Even the still invisible circulation of the
light gets started this way; how much more, then, is it the case
with the true circulation of the light which has already manifested
itself clearly.

When in ordinary life one has the ability always to react to things
by reflexes only, without any admixture of a thought of others or of
oneself, that is a circulation of the light arising out of circumstances.
This is the first secret.

If early in the morning, one can rid oneself of all entanglements
and meditate from one to two double hours, and then can orientate
oneself towards all activities and outside things in a purely objective,
reflex way, and if this can be continued without any interruption,
then after two or three months all the perfected ones come from
heaven and approve such behavior.

It was a beautiful morning. It must have been a morning like this. The breeze was
cool and full of the sweet smell of the wet earth. The birds were singing and the sun
was rising on the horizon. The dewdrops were shining on the grass leaves like pearls.
It is always beautiful. All that is needed is eyes to see it. The birds are there,

singing every morning, but who is there to listen? And the trees are blooming, but who is there to appreciate? The aesthetic heart is absent, only the calculating mind is functioning. Hence you live in an ugly world.

I am relating to you an ancient story:

Gautam Buddha's sannyasins were meditating under the mango trees....

Morning is the best time to meditate. After the whole night's rest you are very close to the center of your being. It is easier to move into the center consciously, early in the morning, than at any other time – because for the whole night you have been there at the center, you have just left it. The world of a thousand and one things has not yet arisen. You are just on the way, moving towards things, moving into the outside world, but the inner center is very close, around the corner. Just a turning of the head and you will be able to see that which is: truth, God, enlightenment. You will be able to see that into which you had gone when dreams had stopped and sleep was profound. But then you were unconscious.

Deep sleep rejuvenates because although unconsciously you enter into the core of your being, but you still enter – and all the tiredness of the outside world is taken away, and all the wounds are healed, and all the dust disappears. You have taken a bath, you have dived deep into your own being.

That's why Patanjali says: Deep, dreamless sleep is almost like *samadhi* – but almost, not exactly samadhi. What is the difference? – only very small or very great – but this much difference is there: in sleep you are unconscious, in samadhi you are conscious. But the space is the same.

So in the morning when you have just awakened and you are very close to the center – soon the periphery will take you, will possess you, you will have to go into the world of occupations – before you go into that external journey, have a look, so that consciously you can see who you are. This is what meditation is all about. Hence, down the ages, in the morning, early morning – when the earth is awakening and the trees are awakening and the birds are awakening and the sun is awakening – when the whole atmosphere is full of awakening, you can use this situation. You can ride on this tide of awakening and you can enter into your own being, awake, alert, aware, and your whole life will be transformed. And your whole day will be transformed because then you will have a different orientation.

Then you can go into the marketplace and still you will remain in contact with your inner core. And that is the greatest secret, the *Secret of the Golden Flower*. Buddha's sannyasins were meditating under the mango trees that morning...

As you have gathered around me, thousands had gathered around Buddha. There was nothing else to learn other than to meditate.

Buddhas don't teach, they only share. They don't give you a doctrine, they certainly give you a discipline. They don't give you beliefs, they certainly give you a taste of trust. And just a drop of the taste of trust and life is transmuted. And to connect with an awakened being, the only way is to become a little bit awakened on your own part too, because the like can meet the like. To be with a Buddha is to be a little bit more alert than life generally requires you to be. Life wants you to be automatic, robot-like. When you go to a Master, he requires that you drop your automatism, that you de-automatize yourself, that you become a little more alert, that you don't go on looking at things...also remember your being.

So Buddha's disciples were meditating... Such a beautiful morning is not to be missed! And when birds are praising the morning sun, you have also to praise God. And when trees are swaying in the wind, you have also to participate in this eternal dance, you have also to celebrate. Another day is born – forget the past, die to the past – be born anew.

Buddha had a disciple named Subhuti... Buddha was a very fortunate Master: he had tremendously potential disciples. A few of them were really rare beings. Subhuti is one of those rare beings who was just on the verge of buddhahood – just one step more and he would be a buddha. He was coming home, every moment coming home, closer and closer to the center – where ego disappears and God is born, where you die and the whole is born. When the part disappears into the whole, when the cosmos takes place and then you are no more a separate entity, trembling, afraid of death, then you are part of this eternal play of existence. He was just on the verge.

He was one of the *most* silent of Buddha's disciples. So silent was he that the scriptures say that he had almost become absent. He would come and nobody would take note of him. He would pass and nobody would become aware that he had passed.

He was a very silent breeze... Ordinarily you want to be noticed. If you are not noticed, you feel hurt. You want attention. *Who* wants attention? Attention is the requirement of the ego, the ego feeds on it. So if attention is not given to you, if you come and nobody notices you, you pass and nobody says, "Good morning. How are you?" – as if you had not passed – you will feel wounded. You will start thinking, "So, I am thought to be a nobody, and I will show these people who I am!"

The ego always hankers for attention.

Subhuti was so silent... His desire for attention had disappeared. And the moment desire for attention disappears, all politics disappears from your being. Then you are religious. Then you are perfectly at home with your nobodiness. Then you live a totally different life. Then you live so silently that you don't make any fuss, that you don't make any ripples, that you come and you go as if you had never come and you had never gone.

He was, and yet he was not... In fact, the moment you *really* are, you drop all ideas of your ego. People carry the idea of the ego because they are not. Try to understand this paradox: those who are not, they brag about themselves – they have to brag, they have to prove to the world. They are constantly performing. They know if they don't perform they are nobodies. They have to perform, they have to shout, they have to make noise, they have to force others to take note. Adolf Hitlers and Genghis Khans and Tamerlanes and all the stupid lot of politicians down the ages – all that they have been doing is to make more and more people take note of them. These are the people who are not.

The people who are, are so contented with their being, who cares whether anybody takes note or not? They are so much to themselves, enough unto themselves.

So this is the paradox: the man who is *not* tries, pretends that he is much, somebody special, and the man who *is* pretends not, brags not, becomes a very silent existence.

He existed as an absence... And only in absence does real presence arise: the person disappears but presence arises.

He had melted slowly and disappeared as a person... And when that happens, when that miracle happens, the very absence becomes a radiant presence.

Subhuti was also sitting under a tree, not even meditating.... Others were meditating, he was simply sitting there doing nothing. That is the highest form of meditation. To *do* meditation is to be just a beginner. The beginner has to *do* the meditation. But one who has understood meditation cannot even think in terms of doing, because the moment that you do something you are stirred, the moment that you do something you are tense, the moment that you do something the ego enters again from the back door – because with the doing comes the doer. Meditation is a state of non-doing. Certainly in the beginning one has to do, but slowly slowly – as meditation deepens, understanding arises – doing disappears. Then meditation is being, not doing.

Doing is part of the world of having. Doing is another aspect of having. You have to do if you want to have, if you want to have you will have to do. And millions of people remain in the world of doing and having. Beyond these two there is another world, the world of being, where you don't have anything and you are not a doer either – all is utterly silent, all is absolutely passive, not even a ripple.

So he was not doing meditation, remember. He was just sitting and doing nothing, and then suddenly, flowers began to fall around him. And those were not ordinary flowers – not of this world, not earthly – they were not falling from the trees. They were falling from the sky, from nowhere, out of the blue. He had never seen such beauty and such freshness and such fragrance. Those were the flowers of the beyond, Golden Flowers. He was naturally in awe and wonder. And then he heard the gods whispering to him, "We are praising you for your discourse on emptiness…"

Now he was really puzzled. "Discourse on emptiness? But I have not spoken of emptiness," said Subhuti.

"You have not spoken of emptiness, we have not heard emptiness," responded the gods. "This is true emptiness."

And blossoms showered upon Subhuti like rain.

This is one of the most beautiful stories I have ever come across. A great meaning is hidden there: if you are silent, if you are utterly silent, existence starts showering on you – blessings shower on you like rain. If you are silent, if you are in the state of meditation, just being and doing nothing, the whole existence converges upon you with all its grace, with all its beauty and benediction.

This is the state Jesus calls the state of beatitude. For the first time you become aware of the splendor of existence. Each moment is an eternity then, and even to breathe is such a joy, such a celebration. Misery disappears the moment you disappear. Misery is the shadow of the ego. And blessing is a natural phenomenon: it happens on its own the moment you are empty – the whole existence rushes in, explodes. Ludwig Wittgenstein has said, "The mystical is not the 'how' of the world, but that it exists."

Just that it exists is the mystery. There is no need to go anywhere else. The mystery is not hidden, the mystery is all over the place. Just that it exists is the mystery of it! You need not dig deep to find the mystery. Mystery is everywhere, on the surface as much as in the depth. All that is needed is a heart that feels. All that is needed is a being that is available, open. All that is needed is alertness – alertness without any effort and tension. All that is needed is a state of meditation, and then favors from existence start showering like rain.

The sutras:

> Master Lu-Tsu said:
> Now there are three confirmatory experiences which can be tested.
> The first is that, when one has entered the state of meditation, the
> gods are in the valley. Men are heard talking as though at a distance
> of several hundred paces, each one quite clear. But the sounds are all
> like an echo in a valley: one can always hear them, but never oneself.
> This is called: "The presence of the gods in the valley."

Lu-Tsu is talking about three confirmatory signs. The first he calls *the gods are in the valley*. Those who are moving – and you all are moving towards meditation – are going to come across these strange but tremendously beautiful spaces. The first sign that meditation has started becoming a crystallized phenomenon in you is *the presence of the gods in the valley*.

What does this metaphor mean? It means the moment meditation starts happening in you, the whole existence becomes a valley and you are at the top of a hill. You start rising upwards and the whole world becomes a valley, far away, deep down there – and you are sitting on a sunlit hilltop. Meditation takes you upwards – not physically, but spiritually – and the phenomenon is very clear when it happens. These will be the signs.

When you are moving inwards in the meditation, suddenly you will see a great distance arising between you and the noises around you. You may be sitting in a marketplace and suddenly you will see a gap is arising between you and the noises. Just a moment before those noises were almost identified with you, you were in them; now you are getting away from them. You are there physically as you had been before, there is no need to go to the mountains. This is the way to find the real mountains of the within, this is the way to find the Himalayas within. You start moving into deep silence and suddenly, all the noises that were so close to you, and such a turmoil that was there, start going far away, receding backwards. Everything is as it was before, on the outside nothing has been changed, you are sitting in the same place where you had started meditating – but as meditation deepens this will be felt: you will feel distance arising from outside things.

> *Men are heard talking as though at a distance of several*
> *hundred paces...*

As if suddenly the world has gone away from you or you have gone away from the world, but each thought is quite clear; whatsoever is being said outside is quite clear, in fact, more clear than it was before. This is the magic of meditation.

You are not becoming unconscious, because in unconsciousness also you will see that noises are disappearing. For example, if you have been given chloroform you will feel this same phenomenon happening: noises start going away, away, away...and they are gone – but you have fallen unconscious, you cannot hear anything clearly. Just the same happens in meditation, but with a difference: the noises start going away from you, but every noise becomes distinctly clear, more clear than it was before, because now a witnessing is arising.

First you were also a noise in all the noises, you were lost in it. Now you are a witness, an observer, and because you are so silent you can see everything distinctly, clearly. Although noises are far away, they are more clear than ever before. Each single note is heard.

If in meditation you are listening to music this will happen. First you will see the music is going far away, and the second thing, simultaneously will also be felt: each note is becoming so clear and so distinct as it has never been before. Before, those notes were mixed with each other, overlapping into each other. Now they are all clearcut individuals, atomic. Each single note is separate.

> *Men are heard talking as though at a distance of several*
> *hundred paces, each one quite clear. But the sounds are all like*
> *an echo in a valley.*

And the third thing will be felt: that they are not heard directly but as if indirectly; as if they are echoes of the real sounds, not the sounds themselves. They become more insubstantial, their substance is lost. They become less material, their matter disappears. They are no more heavy, they are light. You can see their weightlessness – they are like echoes. The whole existence becomes an echo.

That is why Hindu mystics call the world maya, illusion. Illusion does not mean unreal, it simply means shadow-like, echo-like. It does not mean non-existential, it simply means dream-like. Shadow-like, dream-like, echo-like – that will be the feeling: you cannot feel that these things are real. The whole existence becomes a dream – distinct, you are alert – and very dream-like because you are alert. First you were lost in the dream: not alert and you were thinking that this is reality. You were identified with your mind, now you are no more identified with the mind; a separate entity has arisen in you: the watchfulness, *sakshi*.

One can always hear them, but never oneself.

And the fourth thing in it will be felt: you can hear the whole existence around you – people talking, walking, children laughing, somebody crying, a bird calls, a car passes by, an airplane, the train. You will be able to hear everything. Just one thing, you will not be able to hear yourself: you have completely disappeared, you are an emptiness – you are becoming a Subhuti. You are just not there at all. You cannot feel yourself as an entity. All the noises are there, just your inner noises have disappeared. Ordinarily there are more noises inside you than on the outside – the real turmoil is within you, the real madness is there – and when the outer madness and inner madness both meet together, hell is created.

The outer madness is going to continue, because you have not produced it and you cannot destroy it. But you can destroy your inner madness very easily, it is within your capacity. Once the inner madness is not there, the outer madness becomes insubstantial; it loses all reality, it becomes illusory – you cannot find your own voice, there is no thought arising in you so no sound. This is called *the gods are in the valley* – you have become empty and everything has gone deep down in the valley – only echoes are heard. And when echoes are heard, certainly you are not affected.

Just the other day a madman tried to rape Anuradha. He was caught before he could do any harm. I asked Anuradha to come to me, just to see whether she is affected by it or not – and I was tremendously happy that she is not affected at all – not at all, not even a trace. That's the beauty of growing meditation: even if you are murdered you will remain unaffected.

Now, the effort to rape her was murderous. And let Morarji Desai know that this is the true image of his India – an Indian tried it! And this is not a single case, it has been happening almost regularly. It has become so dangerous for my sannyasins to move outside. This ugly India is not my India. This ugly India belongs to Morarji Desai and Charan Singh and Mr Advani, and company. I simply disown this ugly India.

But there is another India: the India of the buddhas, the eternal India. I am part of it, you are part of it. In fact, anywhere, wherever meditation is happening, that person becomes part of that eternal India. That eternal India is not geographical – it is a spiritual space – and to become part of that eternal India is to become a sannyasin.

And I was happy, tremendously happy, seeing Anuradha: she had remained absolutely unaffected, not a ripple of fear, nothing – as if nothing had happened, as if the attempt was made in a dream. This is how one grows slowly slowly into meditation: all becomes insubstantial, one can see everything.

She fought back – she was courageous and brave, she did whatsoever was needed to be done, she didn't yield – but the inner consciousness remained unaffected.

This is called: "The presence of the gods in the valley."

At times the following can be experienced: as soon as one is quiet the light of the eyes begins to blaze up, so that everything before one becomes quite bright as if one were in a cloud. If one opens one's eyes and seeks the body, it is not to be found any more. This is called: "In the empty chamber it grows light." Inside and outside, everything is equally light. That is a very favorable sign.

Now, the second sign is called *In the empty chamber it grows light*.

Unless you become empty, you will remain dark, you will remain darkness. *In the empty chamber it grows light* – when you are utterly empty, when there is nobody inside you, then light happens. The presence of the ego creates darkness. Darkness and ego are synonymous. No-ego and light are synonymous.

So *all* methods of meditation, whatsoever their orientation, finally merge in this empty chamber of your inner being. Just a silent space is left, and in that space you find great light arising, without any source. It is not like the light that you see when the sun rises, because the light that comes from the sun cannot be eternal; in the night it will disappear again. It is not like the light that needs fuel, because when the fuel is finished the light will disappear.

This light has a very mysterious quality: it has no source, no cause. It is not caused, hence once it appears it remains, it never disappears. In fact, it is already there, just that you are not empty enough to see it. And when this light starts growing in you these will be the experiences, *as soon as one is quiet* – the moment you sit silently and you become quiet, still, unmoving within and without *the light of the eyes begins to blaze up*. Suddenly you will see your light is pouring through your eyes.

This is an experience that science has not yet become aware of. Science thinks that light gets into the eyes, but never otherwise. Light comes from the outside, gets into the eyes, enters into you – this is only half the story. The other half is known only by the mystics and the meditators. This is only one part: the light entering into you. There is another part: the light pouring out of your eyes. And when the light starts pouring out of your eyes *the light of the eyes begins to blaze up, so that everything before one becomes quite bright,* then this whole existence brightens up.

Then you see that trees are more green than ever, and their greenness has a quality of luminosity in it. Then you see the roses are rosier than ever. The same roses, the same trees, but something from you is pouring into them, revealing them more clearly than ever. Then small things have such beauty. Just colored stones are more beautiful to a buddha than the Koh-i-Noor diamond to Queen Elizabeth. To Queen Elizabeth, even the Koh-i-Noor, the greatest diamond in the world, is not so beautiful as an ordinary stone is to a buddha. Why? – because a buddha's eyes can pour light and in that light ordinary stones become Koh-i-Noors, ordinary people become buddhas. To a buddha, everything is full of buddhahood. Hence Buddha has said, "The day I became enlightened, the whole existence became enlightened. The trees and the mountains and the rivers and the rocks – all became enlightened." The whole existence was raised to a higher plenitude.

It depends on you: how much you can put into existence, only that much will you get. If you don't put anything into it you won't get anything out of it. First you have to put into it to get out of it. That's why creative people know more beauty, more love, more joy than uncreative people, because creative people put something into existence – existence responds…and responds generously.

Your eyes are empty: they don't give anything, they only take. They are hoarders, they don't share. So whenever you will come across eyes which can share, you will see a tremendously different quality, a tremendous beauty, silence, power, potential. If you can see those eyes which can pour their light into you, your whole heart will be stirred.

But even to see that light you will have to be a little more alert than you are. The sun may be rising and it may be morning, but you may be fast asleep – but then no sun is rising for you, and there is no morning; you may be lost in a dark night, in a nightmare. You have to be a little more wakeful…but this happens! In the modern consciousness an experience of this kind has come through psychedelics – a little bit. It is forced, it is violent – it is not natural, you are raping your chemistry – but the experience has happened. And many people have come to meditation through drugs because the drug has made them aware of something they were never aware of.

When you have taken some drug, the world looks more beautiful, ordinary things look extraordinary. What is happening? The drug is forcing some inner light from your eyes to fall onto things – but it is a forced phenomenon, and dangerous – and after each drug-trip you will fall into a deeper darkness than before. And in the person who has been taking drugs long, you will find his eyes *utterly* empty – because he has been pouring light out of his eyes and he does not know how to create it. He does not know how to make his inner light circulate so that more light is created; he simply pours. So a man who takes drugs, by and by, loses the vitality of his eyes, the youth of his eyes. His eyes become dull, dark, black holes.

Just the opposite happens through meditation: the more quiet you become, the more light is created – and it is not a forced phenomenon. You have so much that it starts overflowing from your eyes – it simply starts overflowing. Because you have too much it has to be shared, like when the cloud is full of rain it has to rain. You are full of light and more light is coming in, streaming in every moment, and there is no end to it – now you can share: you can share with the trees and with the rocks and with people, you can give to the existence. This is a very favorable sign.

But don't be deceived by drugs. Drugs give you only false experiences, forced experiences, and any forced experience is destructive to your inner ecology, your inner harmony, and finally you will be a loser, not an achiever.

> At times the following can be experienced: as soon as one is quiet, the
> light of the eyes begins to blaze up...

You will see it! – your eyes are becoming aflame. And with the eyes becoming aflame the whole existence is taking a new color, a new depth, a new dimension, as if things are no more three-dimensional but four-dimensional. A new dimension is added: the dimension of luminosity.

> ...the light of the eyes begins to blaze up, so that everything before
> one becomes quite bright, as if one were in a cloud.

As if the sun is shining on the cloud and the whole cloud is afire, and you are in the cloud and the cloud is just fire reflecting the sun, one starts living in this cloud of light. One sleeps in it, one walks in it, one sits in it; this cloud continues. This cloud has been seen as the aura. Those who have eyes to see, they will see a light around the saints – a light around their heads, around their bodies. A subtle aura surrounds them.

Now even science is agreeing with it. Particularly in Russia, Kirlian photography has come to very significant conclusions. One of them is that everything is surrounded by a subtle aura – we just need eyes to see – and in different states the aura changes. Now these are scientific conclusions. When you are ill you have a different aura – dull, sad, lusterless. If you are going to die, within six months your aura disappears. Then your body has no light around it. And if you are happy, joyous, fulfilled, contented, then the aura grows bigger and stronger, becomes more and more bright.

Of course Kirlian experiments have not been done on any buddha yet – and it is very difficult to find a buddha in Soviet Russia, particularly now. It is unfortunate, because the whole country has fallen into a trap of utter nonsense. The whole country has fallen into the trap of materialism. Never before has any country been ruled by materialists. Materialism has always persisted, but never has a country been ruled by materialists. Never has a country been conditioned to be materialistic like Soviet Russia. Children are taught there is no God, no soul; man is just a body. There is no question of prayer, no question of meditation, no question of becoming silent.

If Kirlian photographers come across a man like Jesus or Buddha or Subhuti, then they will know the miracle. Then they will come across the purest light, the coolest light – which is light, which is life, which is love.

If one opens one's eyes and seeks the body...

In this moment, when you are full of light inside and your eyes are afire and the whole existence is aflame with new life, if you then open your eyes and try to find your body, you will not find it. In these moments matter disappears. In fact, modern physics says that there is no matter at all; it is an illusion, there is nothing solid in your body. Deep down, modern physics says, your body is constituted of electrons. Electrons mean light-atoms, atoms of light. So when this inner fire burns bright, it is *really* there, and when you open your eyes, you will not find your physical body. Not that it is not there – it is there – but you won't see it as you had seen it before. It will be just a cloud of light, you will see the aura. The gestalt has changed. Now you will see something which you had never seen before, and all that you had seen before has disappeared. It depends on your vision. Because you don't have a vision to see the spirit, you can only see the body, the physical. To see matter, nothing is needed – no intelligence, no meditativeness, no prayer. To see matter is very gross, to see spirit is very subtle.

Once you are capable of seeing the spirit, you will be able to see that matter has disappeared. You cannot see both together. That's why – again let me repeat – Hindu mystics have called the world illusory, because they have come to a point when they have seen: matter does not exist, and all that exists is God, all that exists is consciousness.

Matter is just a mistake. You have not seen rightly, that's how matter arises. It *is* consciousness. For example, when I see you I see you as consciousness, not as matter. When I touch you I don't touch your body, I touch you in your innermost core – I touch your energy! When I look into your eyes I am not looking into your physical eyes, I am trying to contact your spiritual eye. It is there! To you it is not there yet, for me it is already there. And if you listen to me, and if you try to understand what is being shared with you, soon it will become a reality for you too.

Either God is or the world is; both are never found together. Those who see the world never see God, and those who have seen God, for them the world has disappeared, "the world" was just a misunderstanding. It is just like you can commit a mistake while counting or doing arithmetic: two plus two, and you make five, then the whole thing will go wrong. When you go back and you find the mistake and you correct it and two plus two becomes four again, the whole thing changes. Exactly like this, matter is a mistake of vision.

It is just like Hindu mystics say: a rope seen in darkness and you have thought it is a snake – and because you thought it is a snake you start running, your heart is pounding, and you are out of breath, and you are trembling, and it is a cool night but you are perspiring – you may even have a heart attack, and for no reason at all! And in the morning, when it is found to have been just a rope, it will look very ridiculous.

Once I was staying in a house with a friend. There were so many mice in the house, and rats. It happened that night that a rat must have entered into the bed of my friend when we were asleep. The rat was just going to bite, just going to bite his foot, and he was awakened. He jumped out of the bed, screamed; the rat must have escaped. Nothing was harmed – he was just going to bite – but he became very much afraid. He was afraid that maybe it was a snake. And I said, "You are a fool! There is no snake, nothing" – and we looked around – "and we know that there are so many rats in your house. It must have been a rat." So he was satisfied, we went to sleep. Everything was perfectly good.

We went to the river, we swam in the river, we came back. After lunch a snake was found in the house, and immediately my friend became unconscious – the very idea! And I tried hard, but now he was already unconscious, so what to do?

For one and a half hours he remained unconscious, in a kind of coma. Doctors were called, they checked. They said, "There is no problem, no poison, nothing. Even the rat has not done any harm, and there is no question of any snake." But still injections were given to bring him back…just the idea! But the idea can create a reality.

When you see a rope and you start running, your running is a reality, and your heart pounding is a reality. And you may have a heart attack, you may even die – this is a reality! But the snake was not there. That was just an idea.

The mystics say the world is just idea: you are unnecessarily afraid, unnecessarily running away, unnecessarily worried – it is just an idea, a mistake. There is no world, there is only God – the whole consists only of consciousness.

> If one opens one's eyes and seeks the body, it is not to be found any
> more. This is called: "In the empty chamber it grows light." Inside
> and outside, everything is equally light. That is a very favorable sign.

These have to be understood because these are going to happen to you too, and the understanding will help; otherwise one day you open your eyes and you don't find your body there, you may go crazy. You will certainly feel something has gone wrong: either you are dead or mad – and what has happened to the body? But if you understand these sutras, they will remind you in the right moment. That's why I am talking on so many scriptures: to make you aware of all that is possible, so when it happens you are not taken aback. You know, you can understand. You have maps already; you can figure out where you are and you can rest in that understanding.

> Or when one sits in meditation, the fleshly body becomes quite
> shining like silk or jade. It seems difficult to remain sitting: one feels

as if drawn upward. This is called: "The spirit returns and touches heaven." In time, one can experience it in such a way that one really floats upward.

The third sign: *The spirit returns and touches heaven.*

This happens very soon. It starts happening in the very early stages. Sitting silently, suddenly you feel you are a little higher than the ground – maybe six inches higher. With great surprise you open your eyes and you find you are sitting on the ground, so you must have been dreaming, you think.

No, you have not been dreaming. Your physical body remained on the earth. But you have another body, the body of light, hidden inside it. Call it the astral body, the subtle body, the vital body, any name you want – that body starts rising higher – and from the inside you can feel only that body, because that is your inside. When you open your eyes your material body is sitting on the ground, perfectly in the same way as it was sitting before. Don't think that you have been hallucinating – not at all, it is a real fact: you had floated a little – but in your second body not in your first body.

...the fleshly body becomes quite shining like silk or jade.

And simultaneously, whenever you will feel that you have risen above the ground, as if gravitation affects you no more, as if a different law has started working on you, I call that law "the law of grace." One law is the law of gravitation: it pulls you down. I call another law, "the law of grace": it pulls you up. And certainly, sooner or later, science has to discover it, because every law has to be complemented by its opposite. No law can exist in aloneness. Gravitation must have its complementary. Just as day has night and summer has winter and man has woman and love has hate and life has death and the negative has the positive, so, exactly so, there *must* be a law which has to compensate, complement from the other extreme. That law I call "the law of grace": it pulls you upwards. This experience of your fleshly body becoming *quite shining like silk or jade*, happens simultaneously whenever you start feeling that it is...

...difficult to remain sitting: one feels as if drawn upward.
This is called: "The spirit returns and touches heaven."

Now the upward journey is starting. And remember, the upward and inward are synonymous, outward and downward are synonymous. The more in you go, the more up you go. The deeper you reach upwards, the deeper you reach inwards. They are the same, one dimension; two aspects of the same dimension.

> *In time, one can experience it in such a way that one really*
> *floats upward.*

And that too happens: when this inner body starts rising so high and has tremendous power, then even the physical body can start floating with it. It is possible, but there is no need to make it happen. That is foolish. If it happens one day of its own accord, enjoy it and don't take much note of it. These confirmatory signs have to be understood, not bragged about. Don't talk to anybody about them, otherwise the ego will come back and will start exploiting these experiences. And once the ego comes, experiences will disappear. Never talk about them! If they happen just understand them, take note of them, and forget all about them.

> *And now, it is already possible to have all three of these experiences.*
> *But not everything can be expressed.*

These three experiences *are* possible, and even if you have experienced them, you will not be able to express them. And whatsoever is said here is only just symbolic, because the real experience cannot be said. All that is said becomes a lie: say it and you have falsified the truth. Truth cannot be said, but still we have to say something. Hence these metaphors have been developed: *gods in the valley, in the empty chamber it grows light, the spirit returns upward,* or *the spirit returns and touches heaven.* These are just symbols, metaphors – to indicate something. But the experience is vast!

> *Different things appear to each person according to his disposition.*

And this too has to be remembered: they all may not happen to you, or may happen in a different order, or may happen in different ways. And there are a thousand and one things too which are possible because people are so different. To somebody these experiences may not happen the way they have been described.

For example, to somebody it may not happen that he is rising upward, it may happen that he is becoming bigger – becoming bigger and bigger, the whole room is full of him. And then he goes on becoming bigger and bigger, now the house is inside him. And it is very puzzling. One wants to open one's eyes and see what is happening – "Am I going mad?" And a moment is possible when one sees that, "The whole existence is inside me. I am not outside it, it is not outside me. It is inside me and the stars are moving within me." Or to somebody it may happen that he becomes smaller and smaller: becomes a molecule, almost invisible, then an atom, and then disappears. That is possible. Patanjali has catalogued all the experiences that are possible.

People have different dispositions, different talents, different potentials, so to everybody they are going to happen in a different way. These are just to indicate that things like this happen – don't think that you are going mad or something appears bizarre to you.

> With these things it is just as it is when one drinks water: one can
> tell for oneself whether the water is warm or cold.

It is an experience. When you drink water, only you know whether it is cold or warm. And if you are thirsty, only you know whether it is quenching your thirst or creating more. Nobody else sitting outside watching you can know what is happening inside – if the thirst is quenched or made more, if the water is cool or warm – nobody can see from the outside. Even if they can see you drinking water, they cannot experience your experience. People are able to see you meditating, but they cannot see what is happening inside.

Many people come here and they ask me for permission to watch people meditating. And I say, "How will you watch? Nobody has ever been able to watch. You can see people sitting or dancing or singing, but that is *not* the real thing. Meditation is happening inside them. Nobody can see except them. So if you really want to see, you will have to participate. You will have to become a meditator – that is the only way. You cannot borrow, nobody can inform you." So those who come here as spectators just waste their time. These are things which can be known only through participation.

> In the same way a man must convince himself about these
> experiences, then only are they real.

And don't start believing because Lu-Tsu is saying so. Just try to understand him, keep it stored in your memory. There is no need to believe in these things, no need to disbelieve either. Just let them be in your memory so whenever the time is ripe and something starts happening you will be able to understand. These are just giving you maps so you are not lost – because even in the inward journey there are many points from where one can be lost; one can misunderstand, one can become afraid, frightened. One can escape from the inside into the outside world.

And these experiences are *not* frightening. But your interpretation can make them frightening. Just think, one day you open your eyes and you don't see your body – your interpretation can be frightening: "This is certainly a sign of madness." You will stop meditating, you will become afraid of meditation, because who knows now what will happen next time, and where you are moving, where you are going? You will become suspicious of the whole experience. You will think you are becoming neurotic.

Every day people come to me with their experiences. When they relate their experiences, I can see their fear, their faces, their eyes – they are afraid. When I say that these are good signs, immediately the climate changes. They start laughing, they are happy. If they can hear me saying that "This is beautiful", "I am happy with you", "You are growing well", *immediately* there is a great change. From sadness they jump to great joy. Nothing has changed, their experience is the same; I have just given them a different interpretation. They were frightened because they knew not.

These things have not to be believed or disbelieved, but just kept stored in the memory so if the time arises you will be able to interpret rightly – and right interpretations are of *great* significance; otherwise the inner journey becomes very difficult. There are many points from where one wants to return and go back into the world and be normal.

One starts feeling something abnormal is happening, and "abnormal" is a condemnatory word. And if you talk to other people who have never meditated they will say, "You go to the psychoanalyst or the psychiatrist. Better that you be checked. What nonsense are you talking – that you become bigger? Have you lost all reason? You say that you go upward and gravitation disappears? Or that you become smaller and smaller and smaller and you disappear? You are hallucinating, you have become a victim of illusions. You go to the psychiatrist – he will put you right, he will fix you."

And if you go to the psychoanalyst or the psychiatrist, they *are* going to fix you: they will hammer on your head with their so-called knowledge. They don't know a thing about meditation! Meditation has not entered in their consciousness yet. They don't know anything about the experiences that happen on the Way, but they know much about mad people. And there is one thing to be taken note of: that there are many experiences which are similar – which happen to a meditator and also happen to a madman – which are so similar that the psychiatrist is *bound* to think that you need treatment, that something has to be fixed in you. And he will treat you as a madman – he will give you drugs or injections or electro-shocks to bring you back to your normal mind. He may destroy your whole possibility for meditation.

This is now a great danger in the West: people learning meditation go back to the West, and if something happens which is not within their comprehension, and they talk to the priest – and the Christian priest knows nothing about meditation – he will send them to the psychiatrist. And if they talk to the psychiatrist, he knows only about madmen, he knows nothing about buddhas – and a few of their experiences are similar. He is bound to interpret that you have fallen below normality, you have to be pulled back, and whatsoever he will do will be destructive, will be harmful to your body, to your mind. The harm can be so much that never again will you be able to go into meditation – he can create *such* barriers.

So if something happens sometimes, always go to people who meditate. That's why I am insisting so much to open centers all over the world so sannyasins can meditate, and if something happens they can meet sannyasins, they can go and share their experiences. At least there will be somebody sympathetic, at least there will be somebody who will not condemn you, who will respect your experience, who will accept your experience, who will give you hope and inspiration, and who will say, "Good. You go ahead. Much more is going to happen."

A Master is needed only because of this – somebody whom you can trust and who's simply saying, "It is good, and you can go ahead," and you *can* go ahead. The journey is hazardous.

> *Master Lu-Tsu said:*
> *When there is a gradual success in producing the circulation of*
> *the light, a man must not give up his ordinary occupation in*
> *doing it.*

That's my insistence too: that a sannyasin should not renounce the world. Your meditation *should* grow *in* the world. It should be part of the day-to-day existence. You should not become an escapist. Why?

The ancients said: When occupations come to us, we must accept them; when things come to us, we must understand them from the ground up. If the occupations are properly handled by correct thoughts, the light is not scattered by outside things, but circulates according to its own law. Even the still invisible circulation of the light gets started this way; how much more, then, is it the case with the true circulation of the light which has already manifested itself clearly.

First, whatsoever situation you are in is a God-given situation: don't reject it. It is an opportunity, an occasion to grow. If you escape from the opportunity, you will not grow. The people who go to the Himalayan caves and start living there and become very much attached to the caves remain ungrown-up. They remain childish. They have not become seasoned. If you bring them to the world they will be shattered, they will not be able to bear it.

Just a few days ago one sannyasin came after three months of living in the Himalayas and she said, "But now it is difficult to be here. I want to go back." Now this is not gaining in maturity. Now the Himalayas will become her obsession, and whatsoever she is thinking is her meditation, her silence, is not hers; it is just a by-product of the Himalayan silence. I told her, "You be here for three weeks and then you tell me what happens to your silence and your meditation. If it disappears, then it has nothing to do with you. And then it is better not to go to the Himalayas. Grow in meditation here! If you can be meditative here, in the marketplace, and then you go to the Himalayas, your meditation will be enhanced a thousandfold. But don't cling there, always come back to the world. It is good as a holiday."

Yes, it is good once in a while to move into the mountains, it is beautiful. But to become addicted, to start thinking of renouncing the world is utterly wrong – because it is in the storms of the world that integrity arises, it is in the challenges of the world that you crystallize.

Lu-Tsu says: Accept the situation you are in; it must be the right situation for you, that's why you are in it. Existence cares for you. It is given to you not without any reason. It is not accidental, *nothing* is accidental. Whatsoever is your need is given to you. If it were your need to be in the Himalayas, you would have been in the Himalayas. And when the need arises, you will find that either you go to the Himalayas or the Himalayas come to you. It happens: when the disciple is ready the Master arrives, and when your inner silence is ready God arrives. And whatsoever is needed on the path is *always* supplied. Existence cares, mothers.

So don't be worried. Rather, use the opportunity. This challenging world, this constant turmoil on the outside, has to be used. You have to be a witness to it. Watch it. Learn how not to be affected by it. Learn to remain unaffected, untouched by it – like a lotus leaf in water. And then you will be grateful, because it is only by being watchful of all the turmoil that one day, suddenly, "the gods are in the valley" – you see the marketplace disappearing far away, becoming an echo. This is *real* growth.

And if you can rightly be meditative in the ordinary occupations of life, there is nothing which cannot happen to you. The light will start circulating, you just be watchful.

Meditate in the morning and then keep close to your center. Go into the world but keep close to your center; go on remembering yourself, remain conscious of what you are doing.

> *When in ordinary life one has the ability always to react to things*
> *by reflexes only, without any admixture of a thought of others or of*
> *oneself, that is a circulation of the light arising out of circumstances.*
> *This is the first secret.*

And when things arise, act, but don't get identified in the act. Remain a spectator. Do whatsoever is needful, just like a reflex. Do whatsoever is needful, but don't become a doer, don't get involved in it. Do it, and be finished with it – like a reflex.

> *If early in the morning, one can rid oneself of all entanglements*
> *and meditate from one to two double hours, and then can orientate*
> *oneself towards all activities and outside things in a purely objective*
> *reflex way, and if this can be continued without any interruption,*
> *then after two or three months all the perfected ones come from*
> *heaven and approve such behavior.*

Behave in an objective way. Take note of the situation, and whatsoever is needful, do it. But don't become attached to the doing, don't become worried about it, don't think of the result. Just do the needful and remain alert and aloof and distant and faraway in your center, rooted there. But every early morning, orient yourself towards the inner center so you can remember it your whole day.

Two times are the best. The first best time is the early morning: orient yourself to the center so you can live on the circumference but yet with full remembrance of the center. And the second time is before you go to bed: orient yourself again to the center, so in your deep sleep also – even while you are dreaming, while you are unconscious – you can remain more and more, closer and closer to the center. These two times are the best. And if you can meditate these two times, you need not go anywhere else. You need not go to any monastery, to any cave, and you need not renounce the world – and one day suddenly you will see blossoms showering on you and gods whispering in your ear.

The whole existence celebrates the moment when one soul arrives home. What happened to Subhuti can happen to you. Aspire to it. It is your birthright, it can be claimed.

Enough for today.

CHAPTER 22

Aloneness is Ultimate

The first question:

> *Osho,*
> *After the tidal wave of events and with the memory of a profound*
> *experience, I face new aloneness. Efforts to share or escape into*
> *distractions have bad results. Why do I cling to this habit of escaping*
> *aloneness? A few comments may help me for the task ahead.*

Aloneness is ultimate. There is no way to be anything other than alone. One can forget it, one can drown oneself in so many things, but again and again the truth asserts. Hence, after each profound experience you will feel alone. After a great love experience you will feel alone, after a deep meditation you will feel alone.

That's why all great experiences make people sad. In the wake of a profound experience, sadness always settles. It is because of this phenomenon that millions of people don't hanker after profound experiences, they avoid them. They don't want to go deep in love, sex is enough, because sex is superficial: it will not leave them alone. It will be fun, an entertainment, for a moment they will enjoy it and then they will forget all about it. It will not bring them to their own center. But love brings you to your center: love is so profound that it leaves you alone.

This will look very paradoxical, because ordinarily people think love will make you aware of togetherness. That is utter nonsense. If love is deep it will increase your awareness of aloneness, not togetherness, because whenever anything goes deep, what happens? – you leave the periphery of your being and you fall into your center, and the center is all alone. There only you are, or not even you, but only a consciousness – with no ego in it, with no identity in it, with no definition in it – an abyss of consciousness.

After listening to great music, or after penetrating into the meaning of great poetry, or seeing the beauty of a sunset, it always happens: in the wake of it you will feel sad. Seeing this, millions have decided not to see beauty, not to love, not to meditate, not to pray – to avoid all that is profound. But even if you avoid truth, truth stikes you sometimes. Unawares, it possesses you.

You can distract yourself for the moment, but no distraction is going to help. Aloneness has to be accepted because it is ultimate. It is not an accident, it is the very way things are. It is Tao. Once you accept it, the quality changes. Aloneness is not creating sadness. Your idea that you should not be alone, that is creating sadness; your idea that to be alone is to be sad is creating the problem. Aloneness is utterly beautiful because it is profoundly free. It is absolute freedom – how can it create sadness?

But your interpretation is wrong. You will have to drop your interpretation. In fact, when you say, "I face new aloneness", you really mean you face new loneliness. And you have not seen the distinction between loneliness and aloneness. You need to understand the difference between the two.

Aloneness, misinterpreted, looks like loneliness. Loneliness means you are missing the other. And who is the other? – any excuse that helps you to drown your consciousness, any intoxicant. It may be a woman, a man, a book, anything – anything that helps you to forget yourself, that takes away your self-remembrance, that unburdens you from your awareness. You mean loneliness really.

Loneliness is a negative state: the other is missed and you start searching and seeking for the other. Aloneness is immensely beautiful. Aloneness means a moment when the other is no longer needed, you are enough unto yourself – so enough that you can share your aloneness with the whole existence, so inexhaustible is your aloneness that you can pour it unto the whole existence and it will still remain there. You are rich when you are alone, you are poor when you feel lonely.

The lonely person is a beggar, his heart is a begging bowl. The alone person is an emperor. Buddha is alone...

And, what has happened to you has been aloneness, but your interpretation is wrong. Your interpretation is coming from your past experiences, from your past mind. It is from your memory. Your mind is giving you a wrong idea. You drop the mind, you go into your aloneness: watch it, taste it. All the aspects of it have to be looked into. Enter into it from all the possible doors. It is the greatest temple there is. And it is in this aloneness that you will find yourself – and to find oneself is to find God. God is alone.

And once you have looked into it without the mind interfering you will not want to be distracted at all. Then there is nothing to distract, then there is no need to be distracted. Then you would not like to escape from it because it is life, it is eternal life. Why should one want to escape from it? And I'm not saying that in this aloneness you will not be able to relate. In fact, for the first time you will be able to relate.

A lonely person cannot relate because his need is so much, he clings, he leans upon the other. He tries to possess the other because he is constantly afraid: "If the other goes, then what? I will be left lonely again." Hence, so much possessiveness exists in the world. It has a reason. The reason is simple: you are afraid – if the other leaves, then you will be left alone, utterly lonely. And you don't like that, and you feel miserable even with the idea of it. Possess the other, possess the other so totally that there is no possibility of the other escaping from you. And the other is also doing the same to you: the other is trying to possess you. Hence love becomes a miserable thing. Love becomes politics, love becomes domination, exploitation. It is because lonely people cannot love.

Lonely people have nothing to give. Lonely people exploit each other. And naturally, when you have nothing to give and the other starts exploiting, you feel offended. You want to exploit the other and not be exploited. That's where politics enters in: you want to give as little as possible and get as much as possible – and the other is doing the same to you, and both are creating misery for each other.

I have heard…

A man stopped his car deep down in the woods and started being very loving to the woman who was sitting by his side. But the woman said, "Stop! You don't really know who I am. I am a prostitute, and my fee is fifty dollars."

The man gave the woman fifty dollars, made love to her. When it was finished he sat silently at the steering wheel without moving.

The woman asked, "Now why are we waiting here? It is getting late and I want to go back home."

And the man said, "Sorry, but I must tell you, I am a taxi driver…and the fare back is fifty dollars."

This is what is happening in your love-relationship: somebody is a prostitute, somebody is a taxi driver. It is a bargain, it is tit-for-tat. It is continuous conflict.

That's why couples are continuously fighting. They cannot leave each other; although they go on fighting they cannot leave. In fact that's why they are fighting – so that nobody can leave. They cannot be at ease because if they are at ease then they will be at a loss and the other will exploit more. Once you see the point you will understand the whole misery of marriage. The whole foundation of it is there.

One wonders why people don't leave each other if they are not happy with each other? They cannot leave! They cannot live together, they cannot separate either. In fact, the very idea of separation is creating the conflict. They cripple each other so the other cannot escape, even if he or she wants to escape. They burden each other with such responsibilities, such moralities, that even if the other leaves he or she will feel guilty. His own conscience will hurt, will pinch him – that he has done something wrong. And together, all that they do is fight. Together, all they do is a continuous haggling for the price. Your marriage, your so-called love, is a marketplace. It is not love. Out of loneliness there is no possibility of love.

Out of loneliness people start meditating; out of loneliness there is no possibility of meditation either. They are feeling lonely and they want something to stuff themselves with. They need a mantra, Transcendental Meditation or all that kind of nonsense. They would like something to stuff themselves with because they are feeling empty and lonely. Repeating "Ram-Ram, Krishna-Krishna" or "Ave Maria" or anything will help them to at least forget themselves. This is not meditation! This is just covering up loneliness, emptiness. This is just covering up a black hole in yourself.

Or, they start praying in the churches and in the temples and they start talking to God. Now God is their imagination. They cannot find the other in the world because it is too costly to find the other in the world and it takes so much trouble, so now they create "the other," high there in heaven – they start talking to God. But they cannot live without the other, the other has to be there. They may escape into the desert, but even in the desert cave they will be looking at the sky and talking to the other. This is fantasy and nothing else. And if you go on talking for long, you may start hallucinating that the other is there.

Your need is such that you can create the other through imagination. That's why the so-called religions have tried to take you away from the others that are ordinary and available. They would like you not to get married – why? – because if you are married and you have a woman, a man, you don't need a God. It is a strategy: they will not allow you to be in the marketplace because then you are occupied and you will not feel your loneliness. Then why should you talk to God? You can talk to people. They will take you to the Himalayan caves, to the monasteries, so that you are left so lonely that out of the misery of loneliness you have to talk to God, you have to create a God to your heart's content. And then the deeper your starvation for the other is, the more is the possibility of visions of God. And those visions are nothing but illusions, dreams seen with open eyes. It is like when a person is put on a long fast, he may start imagining food, he may start seeing food.

I have heard about a poet who was lost in a forest for three days, hungry, and then came the full moon night. He looked at the moon and he was surprised, because all his life, whenever he had seen the full moon he had always remembered beautiful faces of women, his beloved, things like that. But that day, after three days of starvation – tired, hungry, thirsty – he looked at the moon and he saw white bread, a *chapati*, floating in the sky above the clouds. He could not believe his eyes: "What kind of poetry is this? A great poet, and the full moon looks like a chapati!"

And you all know that if you are starved of something too much, you will start substituting it with imagination. If you have lived in a forest, alone for many days, and you have not seen a woman, even the ugliest woman in the world will look like Cleopatra.

Mulla Nasruddin goes to a hill station. He has a bungalow there. Sometimes he says, "I am going for three weeks," but by the second week he is back, or even after seven days or ten days.

I asked Nasruddin, "Many times you say, 'I am going for three weeks and four weeks,' then you come within two weeks or even earlier. What is the matter?"

He said, "There is something in it. I have kept a woman there to look after the house. She is the ugliest woman – horrible she is, repulsive she is! Just to look at her and one feels like vomiting."

I asked then, "But what has she to do with it, with your coming early?"

He said, "There is a story in it. When I go to the hill station, she looks horrible. But slowly, slowly after four, five days, she is not so horrible. Then after eight, ten days, I start seeing some beauty in her. The day I start seeing beauty in her is the day I escape, because that means enough is enough! I have lived away from the world too much, away from my woman; now even this horrible woman has started looking beautiful! That simply means I have starved myself too much. So that is the criterion: whatsoever I say – three weeks, four weeks – is not the point. The real criterion is: the day I see the woman is beautiful and I start fantasizing about her, then I pack up my things and I escape. I know the woman is horrible, and if I stay one or two days more, then there is going to be danger – I may fall in love with this horrible woman!"

Loneliness cannot create love. It creates need. Love is not a need. Then what is love? Love is luxury. It comes out of aloneness: when you are tremendously alone and happy and joyous and celebrating, and great energy goes on storing in you. You don't need anybody. In that moment the energy is so much, you would like it to be shared – then you give. You give because you have so much, you give without asking anything in return – that is love.

So very few people attain to love, and those are the people who attain first to aloneness. And when you are alone, meditation is natural, simple, spontaneous. Then just sitting silently, doing nothing, and you are in meditation. You need not repeat a mantra, you need not chant any stupid sound. You simply sit, or you walk, or you do your things, and meditation is there like a climate surrounding you, like a white cloud surrounding you. You are suffused with the light, you are immersed in it, bathed in it, and that freshness goes on welling up in you. *Now* you start sharing. What else can you do?

When a song is born in your heart you have to sing it. And when love is born in your heart – love is a by-product of aloneness – you have to shower it. When the cloud is full of rain, it showers and when the flower is full of fragrance, it releases its fragrance to the winds. Unaddressed, the fragrance is released and the flower does not wait to ask, "What is coming back to me in return?" The flower is happy that the winds have been kind enough to relieve him of a burden. This is real love – then there is no possessiveness. And this is real meditation – then there is no effort.

What has happened to you is something immensely valuable, just your interpretation is wrong.

You say, "After the tidal wave of events and with the memory of a profound experience, I face new aloneness."

Please don't call it aloneness, or if you call it aloneness then try to understand its nature.

"Efforts to share or escape into distractions have bad results."

They are bound to have bad results – because it is aloneness, really aloneness. You will miss something if you escape from it. It is escaping from your own innermost treasure, it is escaping from your richness, from your own kingdom. The result will be disastrous. Don't escape; dig deep into it, dive deep into it, forget all escaping. That's what, you have been doing your whole life. This time, no! This time you have to go into it. This time you have to taste it in its totality. You have to become it, you have to see what it is, root and all. And once you have seen it and lived it, you will come out of it a totally new person – reborn.

I have been watching you: since the day you have come here, I have continuously been watching you. I have been around you, I have been looking into your eyes, your face – something profound *has* happened. But *much more* is going to happen! If you escape you will miss that "much more" that is on the way. No! This time, no! Many times you have been doing it, for many lives you have been doing it. This time drop all fear, drop all memories – go into the new face of aloneness. It is really aloneness, it is not loneliness. You need not escape. If you escape from loneliness you will feel good. If you escape from aloneness you will feel bad.

"Efforts to share or escape into distractions have bad results."

Don't share right now. Let it gather, let it become a cloud full of rainwater, then the sharing will happen of its own accord, there will be no effort to share. Right now if you start sharing, it will be again just a way of finding the other in the name of sharing. It will be escape. Sharing has to be allowed to happen on its own. You just go on gathering this aloneness and one day you will see: the fragrance is released to the winds. One day you will see: the sharing has started – you will be a witness to it. You will not be a doer, but only a witness.

"Why do I cling to this habit of escaping aloneness?"

Because you have not yet understood it as aloneness! You go on interpreting it as loneliness. And I can understand it. This is how everybody does it. When you feel aloneness for the first time you interpret it as loneliness because that is a known phenomenon, you have felt it all your life. The moment the child leaves the mother's womb, the first experience is of loneliness, he starts feeling lonely: he had to leave his home.

The greatest trauma that happens is when the child has to leave the womb. He wants to cling to the womb, he does not want to go out of it. For nine months he has lived there, he has loved the space, the warmth, and he has been so beautifully taken care of, with no responsibility, no worry. Why should he leave? He is being thrown out, expelled. He does not want to go out. Life

– we call it birth – but the child thinks it is going to be death. It is death to him, because it is the end of the life that he has known for nine months. He is shocked, he feels punished. And he cannot think yet, so the feeling goes very deep in the body. It is a feeling of his total being, not a thought, hence it permeates every cell of his body and remains there. That is the first experience of being lonely. And then again and again many more experiences will come.

One day the mother takes the breast away and the child is again lonely. Someday the child is removed from the mother and the nurse starts taking care – again lonely. One day he is not allowed to sleep in the mother's room, he is given a separate room – again lonely. Remember the day in your childhood when you had to sleep alone in a room for the first time – the darkness, the coldness, nobody there surrounding you. And it had never been so before; the mother's warmth, her soft body, had always been available. Now the child clings to a toy, a teddy bear – but is it a substitute? Or he clings to the blanket – but is it a substitute? A poor substitute, but somehow, he manages. He feels very lonely, dark, left, thrown away, rejected. These are the wounds that go on gathering and go on making the idea of loneliness deeper and deeper. Then one day he has to leave the home and go to the hostel with strange people, unknown. Just remember all these wounds, they are there! And it goes on and on: your whole life is a long process of feeling lonely.

And then by chance some profound experience happens to you and because of that profound experience you have a glimpse of your being – but your whole mind knows only loneliness, so it transforms the experience of aloneness into loneliness. It labels it as loneliness, the experience of solitude is defined as solitariness.

That's where, you are missing. Forget the interpretation. This is really something new that is happening. It is new, so you cannot figure out what it is. The only way to know is to go into it, to be acquainted with it. Just as Master Lu-Tsu said, "It is like when you drink water – only you know whether it is cool or warm."

Now drink this aloneness. This fresh energy that is welling up in you: drink it, taste it. And you will be surprised: it is nothing like what you have known before. It is freedom, freedom from the other. It is what in the East we call *moksha,* utter freedom. And after this freedom love will become possible, after this freedom sharing will happen, after this freedom your life will have a totally different significance, a totally different splendor to it. Your hidden splendor will be released.

The second question:

Osho,
Why do revolutions fail?

Firstly, because they are not revolutions. Revolution can only possible occur in the individual soul. The social revolution is a pseudo phenomenon, because the society has no soul of its own. Revolution is a spiritual phenomenon. There can be no political revolution, no social revolution, no economic revolution. The only revolution is that of the spirit; it is individual. And if millions of individuals change, then the society will change as a consequence, not vice versa. You cannot change the society first and hope that individuals will change later on.

That's why revolutions have been failing: because we have taken revolution from a very wrong direction. We have thought that if we change the society, change the structure – economic or political – then one day the individuals, the constituent elements of the society will change. This is stupid. Who is going to bring about this revolution?

For example, in 1917 a great so-called revolution happened in Russia. But who is going to take charge of this revolution? Who is going to become powerful? Joseph Stalin became powerful. Now Joseph Stalin had not gone through any revolution himself; he is a by-product of the same society that he had changed or was trying to change. He proved a far more dangerous czar than the czars that he had destroyed, because he was created by those czars, he was a by-product of a feudal society. He tried to change the society, but he himself was a dictatorial mind. He imposed his dictatorship on the country, revolution became counter-revolution – and this has been the misfortune of all the revolutions that have happened in the world because the revolutionary is the same type of person. He has been created by the past, he is not new. What is he going to do? – he will repeat the past, labels will be new. He will call it communism, socialism, fascism – that doesn't matter, you can have fancy names. Fancy names only befool people.

Mulla Nasruddin went to a doctor, told him to check him and said, "Please, tell me in plain language. I don't want any of the abracadabra of medical science. You simply tell me plainly what the problem is with me. Don't use big names in Latin and Greek. Simply say in plain language what exactly is the matter with me."

The doctor checked and he said, "If you want to know exactly, in plain language: there is nothing wrong with you, you are simply lazy."

He said, "Good. Thank you. Now give it a fancy name to tell my wife. And the bigger the name, the better. Make it as difficult as you can."

We go on giving fancy names, but deep down the reality remains the same.

Nothing happened in 1917. One czar was replaced by another czar, and of course, more dangerous. Why more dangerous? – because Stalin had destroyed the czar, he was a stronger man – certainly, more cunning. He knew how the czar had been destroyed, so he had all the ideas of how to protect himself so he would not go the same way. He created a greater slavery in Russia than there was before because he was afraid that sooner or later he would be thrown away. So he had to break all the bridges and he had to throw all the ladders that he had used and he was more cautious. The czar himself was not so cautious because he was a born czar: he had got it through inheritance, he had taken it for granted. Stalin had worked his way himself and it had been a torturous way and a long journey, and he had to destroy many enemies.

After the revolution he started destroying and killing all those people who could be, in some way, competitors with him. Trotsky was murdered because he was the next man, very close, and in fact more influential in Russia than Joseph Stalin because he was an intellectual Jew, was a greater orator, had more mass appeal. Stalin was nothing intellectually compared to Trotsky – he had to be killed. And there are possibilities that even Lenin was poisoned through his doctors. And then the years that Stalin remained in power, he destroyed all potential competitors. One by one, all the members of the Politburo were killed – he must have been the strongest man in the whole history of humanity – and he turned the whole country into a big prison.

This is how revolutions fail – the first reason: because we try from the wrong end.

Secondly, once a revolution has succeeded we have to destroy the revolutionaries because the revolutionaries *are* dangerous people. They have destroyed the first society, they will destroy the second – because they are addicted to revolution. They know only one thing, they are experts only in one thing: in overthrowing governments. They don't care what government. Their whole expertise and their whole power is in overthrowing governments. Once a revolution succeeds the first work of the people who come in power is to destroy all the remaining revolutionaries – and they had succeeded because of them! So each revolution turns into counter-revolution because the people who had brought them into power are more dangerous people.

Try to understand. The mind of a revolutionary is a destructive mind: he knows how to destroy, he does not know how to create. He is very capable of provoking people into violence, but he is absolutely incapable of helping people to become calm and quiet and go to work and create. He does not know that language: his whole life he has been a revolutionary, his whole work, his whole expertise, was to provoke people, to destroy. He knows only that language and you cannot hope to change his whole life pattern at the end of his life.

So those who are in power have to destroy all the remaining revolutionaries. Each revolution kills its own fathers – it has to be done – and once those fathers are killed, the revolution has turned into a counter-revolution. It is no more revolutionary, it is anti-revolutionary.

Just now it has happened in India. Jayprakash Narayan led a great upheaval, helped the country to change its government. And the people who came into power, Morarji Desai and others, came into power because of Jayprakash Narayan. But once they came into power they started getting out of the hands of Jayprakash Narayan. They started reducing him. They became afraid: "This man is dangerous and this man has influence over the masses – again he can prove a great problem. The man has to be reduced, utterly reduced."

This happened when the British government was thrown out of this country. Mahatma Gandhi was the man who did that. Once the power came to Indian hands, they started neglecting Mahatma Gandhi. His last words were, "Nobody listens to me. I am the most useless person." And the people who were in power were in power because of him, but nobody listened to him. There is every suspicion that the people he had put into power were involved in his murder, directly or indirectly. Maybe they were not involved directly, but indirectly: they were fully aware that he was going to be murdered but they didn't take any precautions. This is indirect support.

Morarji Desai was in power. He was informed that some conspiracy was on, but he didn't take any notice of it – as if deep down they all wanted to get rid of the Mahatma, because now he was a continuous difficulty because he had the old idea – in the same way he continued, he had his old expertise. Morarji had always been against the government, he was still against the government. Now the government was his but he went on saying things, criticizing and the government was feeling very embarrassed. They all felt relieved. Although they wept, cried and they said, "A great misfortune has happened," but deep down they all felt relieved.

The same is the situation with Jayprakash Narayan: now he is feeling utterly left behind, nobody cares. In fact, the people who are in power will be praying that if he dies soon, it will be good. And he is very ill – half the week he is on dialysis. He cannot work, his body is getting weaker every day. And they must be feeling very happy that soon he will be gone, so there will be nobody who is more powerful than they are.

I would like to tell Jayprakash…

I love the man. He is a good man – so good that it was not his destiny to be in politics – he is a non-politician. He is a poet, a dreamer, a utopian, a good man – as all dreamers are good men.

I would like to tell him: Apologize to the country before you die. Tell the country that in your name a gang of power-hungry politicians has cheated you and the country both, that you have been deceived and the country has been deceived. Tell the country that the revolution has failed! But don't only tell the country that the revolution has failed. Remember to tell this too, that all revolutions will go on failing in the same way, because their very foundation is wrong.

Revolution cannot be imposed from above. Who will impose it? The people who will impose it will be part of the past, they will continue the past. Tell the people that there is no future for political revolutions. Only one kind of revolution is possible and that is spiritual revolution: each individual has to change in his being. And if we can change millions of people then the society will change. There is no other way, there is no shortcut.

And this too has to be understood: it is an inherent characteristic of any developing system that heroes emerge and are heroes only in the context which stimulated their creation. As these heroes overcome and change such contexts, the heroes themselves become the context to be changed.

A certain hero is born in a certain situation. For example, Mahatma Gandhi was born because of the British Empire. He was meaningful only in the context of the British Empire. Once the British Empire died Mahatma Gandhi was meaningless. The context was not there, from where can you get the meaning? So once the context is changed, then the hero himself becomes a useless burden.

Lenin became a burden to those who came into power, Gandhi became a burden to those who came into power, Jayprakash has become a burden right now to those who are in power – and this is the history, the whole history.

But there is a fundamental law working: It is an inherent characteristic of any developing system that heroes emerge and are heroes only in the context which stimulated their creation.

Political leaders are temporary leaders. They exist in a certain context, when the context is gone they are gone. That is where buddhas are different: their context is eternity. Their context is not a part of time. This is where Jesus, Zarathustra, Lao Tzu, remain eternally meaningful: because they are not part of time, their message is eternal. Their message exists in the context of human misery, human ignorance. Unless the whole existence becomes enlightened, Buddha will not become irrelevant. That's why I say political leaders come and go, they are on the stage just for a few moments. Only spiritual beings remain, abide. Buddha is still meaningful and will remain meaningful, forever and forever, because enlightenment will always be a need.

Politicians don't make the real history of humanity, they only create noise. The real history is something else that runs like an undercurrent, the real history has not yet been written because we become much too engrossed in the temporal things. We become much too obsessed with the newspaper which is only relevant today, and tomorrow it will be meaningless. If you have eyes to see, see the point: become interested in the eternal.

Old, ancient societies were not interested in the day-to-day too much. Their interest was deeper. They were not brought up on the newspaper, radio and television. They recited the Koran, they meditated on the Gita, they chanted the Vedas, they contemplated on the statues of Buddha and Mahavira. These are eternal phenomena.

That's why I say the events that happen every day are almost meaningless, because the moment they happen, immediately they disappear because their context changes. Political revolutions have been happening and disappearing; they are bubbles, soap bubbles. Maybe for a moment they look very beautiful, but they are not eternal diamonds.

The eternal diamond is the inner revolution. But the inner revolution is difficult because the inner revolution needs creativity and the outer revolution needs destructiveness. Hate is easy, love is difficult. To destroy is easy, to create a Taj Mahal takes years. It took forty years and fifty thousand persons working every day. But how many days would it take to destroy it? Just take a bulldozer and within a day the land will be flat. To destroy is very easy, so people become very interested in destruction; they think this is a shortcut. To create is very difficult.

And again I will remind you: because all political revolutions are destructive – they are capable in destroying – they can provoke people into destruction. It is very easy to provoke people into destruction because people are frustrated, people are in misery; you can provoke them into any revolt. But the moment they have destroyed, the problem arises: "Now what to do?" They don't know how to create, and your so-called revolutionaries don't know what to do now. Then everybody is at a loss. The misery continues, sometimes even becomes deeper, uglier. After a few years, again people forget and again they start thinking in terms of revolution – and the political leader is always there to lead you into destruction.

My work here is of creativity. I am not provoking you into any destruction, I am not telling you to blame others for your misery. I am telling you, you are responsible, so only those who have the guts to take this responsibility can be with me. But this is a real revolution. If you take the responsibility for your life you can start changing it. Slow will be the change, only in the course of time will you start moving into the world of light and crystallization, but once you are crystallized you will know what real revolution is. Then share your revolution with others. It has to go that way: from heart to heart.

Governments, social structures, have been changed many times, but nothing really changes. Again the same thing is repeated. That's why I don't call my sannyasins revolutionary but rebellious – just to make the differentiation. Revolution has become too contaminated with the social idea. Rebellion is individual.

Rebel! Take responsibility for your life. Drop all that nonsense which has been put inside you. Drop all that you have been taught and start learning again from *ABC*. It is a hard, arduous journey.

And remember one thing more: coping systems and governments, begin as useful and gradually become counter-productive. This is the nature of the evolutionary process. Whatsoever happens on the outside may look in the beginning as if it is very productive, soon it becomes counter-productive – because life goes on changing. Your structures always lag behind and each structure in its own turn becomes a grave. It has to be broken again.

But I am showing you a way where there is no need for any structure inside. Consciousness can remain unstructured. That is the meaning of the word *freedom*. There need not be any structure, any character to consciousness – it can live moment-to-moment without any structure, without any morality, without any character, because consciousness is *enough*. You can respond, and your response will be good and virtuous because you responded consciously.

Live consciously, without any structure, so you will never be caught in a counter-productive system. Otherwise that too happens: you learn one thing, it is beautiful, but only for a few days will it remain beautiful; soon it will become a habit and again you will find yourself surrounded by a habit, encaged.

Real life has to be lived without habits. You have heard, again and again you have been told, "Drop bad habits." I tell you: Drop habit as such! There are not good and bad habits: all habits are bad. Remain without habits, live without habits, then you live moment-to-moment out of freedom – and this is the life of a revolutionary.

And remember also: So in the light of their past service, do not blame any program for being counter-productive as you remove it. Housecleaning should be guiltless. You will remove a program as it no longer fits your developing gestalt. But avoid the temptation to be harsh with the program you remove, because they were necessary stepping-stones to get to where you are now. Love them for this while defusing their power over you for upcoming phases.

Whatsoever you do will become a habit, sooner or later. The moment you see it has become a habit, drop it – it is counter-productive now, it is counter-revolutionary now. It will pull you backwards, it will not allow you to move forwards. It will keep you tethered to the known, it will not allow you to go into the unscheduled, unmapped, unmeasured. So whenever you remove a habit don't feel guilty – "Housecleaning should be guiltless" and it should not be harsh either. When you remove a habit, howsoever good it has been, when you remove it don't feel guilty. Don't think, "My mother taught me this. If I am removing it I am betraying her."

People write letters to me: "How can I take sannyas? My parents have taught me to be a Catholic Christian. Will it not be betraying them?" "I have been brought up as a Mohammedan. Would I be going against the people who have taught me with such love, with such care, to be a Mohammedan?" Guilt arises.

If you are feeling flowing, free, in being a Catholic, there is no need to change. But the desire to change is there. That simply shows you are feeling confined. Yes, your mother taught you something that she knew, that she felt would be good for you, but the context has changed. You are living a totally different life than your mother lived. How can she remain a teacher to you forever?

Don't feel guilty when you drop a program, and don't feel harsh either – because these are the two extremes. Either people feel guilty or they feel very harsh, antagonistic, angry. There is no need to even feel angry, because whatsoever the poor old woman knew and thought would be good for you she taught you. It served its purpose. In fact, who knows? – if you were not a Catholic Christian you may not have come to me. It has brought you here. So whatsoever has happened in the past has been used as a stepping-stone: feel grateful to it. No need to feel guilty, no need to feel harsh.

Whenever you remove a program, remove it just as you remove your clothes. When your body grows, your clothes become small. You don't feel guilty because you are removing pajamas your mother had given you that don't fit you anymore. You have to remove them! And you don't feel angry either. You need not first beat them and throw petrol on them and burn them and make such fuss about it. You don't do that either, because you know they have served their purpose.

Man is a growing gestalt. Every day new things are to happen, every day you have to absorb the new. And make a place for the new, the old has to be gone, the old has to be said goodbye to – with all thankfulness. If you can remember these two things – never feel guilty when you remove an old program and never feel harsh when you remove an old program – you will be moving towards the revolution I am intending you to understand.

A revolutionary is not really angry. Why should he be? There is no reason. Whatsoever your parents could do they did, and they did it with all good wishes. It is another matter that whatsoever they were doing was not useful, was not making you free. But that was not their intention. Their intention was good and they could not have done otherwise. They had lived in a different world.

So remember, when you bring up your own children, remember: don't give them programs, give them understanding. Don't give them fixed rules, just offer them the vision to see things so they can find their own rules. Don't give them knowledge, just give them awareness. That's what I would like my sannyasins to do with their own children: give them awareness whenever and wherever they are.... And remember, they will not be in the same world in which you are living and you have lived. They will have their own world: you cannot dream about it, you cannot think about it. They will never repeat the same life-pattern as you. They will have their own lifestyle.

Give them awareness: wherever they are they can find a way. Give them light, give them eyes to see, to understand, and give them courage to be free. Give them enough courage so that whenever they find something is not right in their program they can put it away, they can drop it. This is love.

Don't enforce any pattern on them. They will be living in a totally different world, so give your love but don't give your knowledge. The world is changing so fast that whatsoever you give will be out of date soon and will become a burden on them, and they will feel guilty if they drop it. Or if they really want to drop it they will have to be angry with you. In both ways it is not good, so don't create that situation for your own children.

Live a life of revolution and impart revolution to your children. Live a life of revolution and impart revolution to all those you love. Only this revolution will never fail...but this revolution has not been tried yet.

Jesus was talking about this, but it has not been tried. Buddha talked about this, but it has not been tried. I am talking about this; it depends on you whether it will be tried or not. The revolution that can succeed has not been tried, and the revolutions that have been tried have all failed.

The third question:

> *Osho,*
> *You are known throughout the world as the Tantra Master or the sex guru, yet in the three years I have been in your ashram, not only have I had less sex than ever before in my life, but thought and heard less about it as well. Will you explain this discrepancy?*

Just the other day in a magazine, *Cine Blitz,* I came across a headline, and they say I am the Hugh Heffner of the spiritual world. And what are they talking about?

Yes, I teach you how to go deep in love. I teach you how to go deep in sex too, because that is the only way to go beyond. To go through it is the only way to go beyond it – but my goal is to take you beyond. Now this is a problem and I am going to be misunderstood again and again all over the world.

People have become accustomed: they think religious people have to be against sex, and those who are not against sex, how can they be religious? These have become *deadly* settled categories. I am unsettling all those categories and I don't expect the world immediately to change so much from its settled patterns of mind. So I don't expect them to understand me either. When they misunderstand, I perfectly understand their misunderstanding. I have no false hopes, it will take years or centuries for them to understand me. But this always happens.

I am creating a new vision of life. The vision is so new that they don't have any category for categorizing it, so all are angry. Mahatma Morarji Desai is angry. He is angry because he is sexually repressed, utterly repressed, with no understanding. He has just repressed his sexuality.

The story is that when Morarji Desai was young – it is sixty years back when he was young – in his village a man raped his sister. That shocked him very much, and he thought that it was sex that was the cause of such a great crime. In fact, repression may have been the cause; otherwise who wants to rape one's own sister? In fact, sisters don't look very appealing at all. One has lived with them, one has grown up with them: unless a person is very repressed it is very difficult to fall in love with his own sister, almost impossible.

Love always happens with the unknown, with the unacquainted. Familiarity breeds contempt. How can one love one's own sister? But the man must have been living in a deep repression – maybe he had never known any woman? He must have been desperate. But what Morarji concluded out of it was this: that sex is the root cause of all crime. If it can drive people mad and they can rape their own sisters, this is the root cause of all crime. He decided never to go into sex again – not for any religious reason, not for any spiritual reason – and since that time he has been repressing.

And the same was true about his guru, Mahatma Gandhi. It was also a trauma that created his lifelong celibacy. His father was dying and he was massaging his father's feet, and the doctors had said that this might be the last night, he might not see the morning again. But at twelve o'clock in the night when the father fell asleep, he went back and started making love to his wife. He went back to his room, and when he was just in the middle of the act, somebody knocked on the door and said, "What are you doing? Where are you? Your father is dead."

It shocked him. It was a trauma, a great trauma that transformed his whole life – not for the better, but for the worse. He felt guilty. He concluded that it was the lust, the sex, that had driven him at the last moment when his father was dying. He had committed a crime, a sin. He could never forgive himself so he renounced sex and for his whole life he suppressed sex. Only in the end, in the last years of his life, did he become aware of the suppression because the sexual fantasy continued to the very end. Then he started trying some Tantra experiments so that before he died he could get rid of sex – but it was too late.

These people cannot understand. They will think that I am a sex guru, that I am teaching you sex, that I am teaching you indulgence. These people cannot understand. Hugh Heffner cannot understand either, because he will ask why am I talking about meditation, why am I talking about spirituality? Spirituality, meditation, *samadhi* – these things will look like nonsense to him. So both Morarji Desai and Hugh Heffner will misunderstand me. I am going to be misunderstood by the so-called spiritualists and by the so-called materialists. That is my fate. I can only be understood by a *new* kind of being who has seen this totality: that man is both body and soul and that life matures only through experiences.

Sex can become a stepping-stone towards samadhi. If you understand it deeply, if you experience it deeply, you will be free of it. But that freedom will have a totally different quality: it will not be a repressed sex. A repressed sex continues underground, goes on in your unconscious, on and on, and goes on affecting your life.

I have heard…

Once a wealthy old religious woman caught a burglar ransacking her things. She had lived her whole life as a celibate, almost like a nun.

"Listen lady, keep quiet if you don't want to be hurt. Just tell me where your jewels are."

She said, "I don't keep them here. They are stored away in the bank in the safe-deposit vault."

"Where is all your silver then?"

"I am sorry, but it is all out, being cleaned and polished."

"Give me your money then."

"I tell you," she said, "I don't keep any cash on hand."

"Listen lady, I am warning you – give me your money or I will rip it off you." And he started feeling her up and down.

"I keep telling you," she said, "I don't have any money. But if you do that again I will write you a check."

I have also heard another story…maybe it is about the same burglar!

In the middle of the night a phone call came through at the police station. Somebody was in need of immediate help. The voice on the phone said desperately, "Come soon! Come immediately! A burglar is trapped in an old woman's room!"

The police inspector on duty said, "We will be there within five minutes. But who is calling?"

And the voice said, "It is the burglar."

If you repress, you will carry the wound for your whole life – unhealed. Repression is not the way.

The radical change comes through understanding, and understanding comes through experience. So I give you total freedom to experience all that your mind, your body want to experience, with just one condition: be alert, be watchful, be conscious.

If you can make love consciously, you will be surprised: love has all the keys to samadhi. If you go deeply into love with full consciousness, alert and aware, you will see that it is not love that attracts you, but that in the highest peak of love, in the orgasmic explosion, your mind disappears, your thoughts stop, and that is from where the nectar flows into you. It is not really sex that gives you that beautiful experience. Sex simply helps, in a natural way, to come to a point where mind is dissolved – of course, for a moment. The clouds disperse and you can see the sun. Again those clouds will be there and the sun will be lost and again you will start fantasizing about sex. If you go unconscious, then you will miss this whole secret again and again. It is not sex that is keeping you tethered to the world, it is unconsciousness!

So the question is not how to drop sex; the question is how to drop unconsciousness. Be conscious and let your natural being have its whole flow. And sex is a natural part: you are born of it, every cell of your body is a sexual cell. Repressing it is against nature.

But there is a transcendence which is a totally different matter. If you are alert and aware in your orgasmic moment, you will see time disappears, for a moment there is no time – no past, no future, you are utterly in the here and now – and that is the beauty. It is because of that, that you feel such joy, so much blessing showers on you.

Now these two secrets have to be understood: one, the disappearance of the mind for a moment, and the disappearance of time for a moment. And these are two aspects of one phenomenon: one aspect is time, the other aspect is mind. When these two disappear you are in utter bliss, you are in God. And meditation is a way to let these disappear without going into sex.

When you go into meditation one day you will recognize the truth that in meditation it also happens – mind disappears, time disappears – and that day will be the day of great realization. That day you will see why you were so interested in sex, and that very day all interest in sex will disappear. Not that you will have to drop it by effort, it will simply disappear, just like dewdrops in the morning sun disappear – with no trace, with no wounds. If you can create it through meditation, it is far easier to create it – because you do it alone. The other is not needed, you need not depend on the other.

Secondly, if you can do it meditatively, no energy is lost. On the contrary you become more vital because energy is saved.

Thirdly, if you can do it meditatively, then you can remain in it as long as you want, it is not momentary: you can by and by learn how to remain in it for twenty-four hours. A buddha lives in the orgasmic state for twenty-four hours, day in and day out. Between the day Gautama Buddha became enlightened and the day he died there is a distance of forty-two years. For these forty-two years he was utterly in an orgasmic state. Just think! Those few moments you have are nothing compared to a Buddha's.

I am teaching you a new kind of synthesis. I am all for that transcendence that brings you to buddhahood, but it is transcendence, not repression. Through repression nobody ever transcends. Through repression one goes on moving and moving in the same rut. Repressing, you have to repress every day. To the very last moment of your death, sex will haunt you. If you really want to get rid of it…and I want you to get rid of it! But I am not against sex, because those who are against sex can never get rid of it. Hence the paradox of my teachings.

Only those who are really ready to understand will be able to understand; otherwise I am going to be misunderstood. The crowd, the mass, is going to misunderstand me. But I don't expect either, that they should understand. I feel sorry for them, but there is no expectation either, so I never feel offended. I know that the teaching is so new that it will take centuries to create criteria on which it can be judged. Criteria are not there.

It is said when a poet is really great his poetry cannot be understood; because all the old poetry is different from it. The great poet has to create his own criteria on which his poetry can be judged. So is it the case with a great painter: you cannot judge a great painter by the old painters and the old masters. He has such a new message that no old valuations will be of any help, so he has to create new values also. It takes time. And if it is so with poetry and painting and sculpture, what to say about enlightenment? That is the greatest art, the art of all the arts. It takes centuries.

The last question:

Osho,
I am very much afraid that something unexpected is going to happen
to me. What should I do?

It is good that something unexpected is going to happen to you. In fact, if only the expected happened, you would be utterly bored. Just think of a life in which only that which you expect always happens. What would you do with such a life? There would be no joy in it, it would be sheer boredom. You expect a friend and he knocks on the door, you expect a headache and it is there, you expect your wife to leave and she leaves – you expect and it happens: within twenty-four hours you would commit suicide! What will you do if all that happens, happens just by your expectation and according to your expectation?

Life is an adventure because the unexpected happens. The greater would be the adventure if more and more unexpected things happened to you. Feel blissful! The unexpected happens – be ready for it, make way for it. Don't ask for the expected. That's why I say remain empty for the future. Don't project, let the future happen on its own, and you will be continuously in joy. You will have a dance in your being, because each thing that will happen will be so unexpected. And when it is unexpected, it has a mystery in it...

I have heard about a clairvoyant little boy. It seems this boy had premonitions. Once while reciting his prayers he said, "God bless mommy, God bless daddy, God bless grandma, goodbye grandpa." The next day grandpa died of a stroke.

Then later on the little boy said, "God bless mommy, God bless daddy, good-bye grandma." Then grandma was hit while crossing the street.

Sometime later in his prayers, he said, "God bless mommy, good-bye daddy." The father was really upset. He had himself driven to the office, but he could not work there at all. Finally he decided to come home early, but he was afraid to drive back so he took a taxi home and rushed in.

He was greeted by his wife, who said, "What do you think happened today, dear? The most awful thing! The milkman dropped dead on the back porch!"

Enough for today.

CHAPTER 23
The Moon Gathers Up the Ten Thousand Waters

Master Lu-Tsu said:
Four words crystallize the spirit in the space of energy.
In the sixth month white snow is suddenly seen to fly.
At the third watch the sun's disk sends out blinding rays.
In the water blows the wind of the Gentle.
Wandering in heaven, one eats the spirit-energy of the Receptive. And
the still deeper secret of the secret: The land that is nowhere, that is
the true home…

These verses are full of mystery. The meaning is: the most important
things in the great Tao are the words: action through non-action.
Non-action prevents a man from becoming entangled in form and
image (materiality). Action in non-action prevents a man from
sinking into numbing emptiness and dead nothingness. Heretofore
we have spoken of the circulation of the light, indicating thereby the
initial release which works from without upon what lies within. This
is to aid one in obtaining the Master. It is for pupils in the beginning
stages. They go through the two lower transitions in order to gain the
upper one. After the sequence of events is clear and the nature of the
release is known, heaven no longer withholds the Way, but reveals the
ultimate truth. Disciples, keep it secret and redouble your efforts!

The circulation of the light is the inclusive term. The further the work advances, the more does the Golden Flower bloom. But there is a still more marvelous kind of circulation. Till now we have worked from the outside on what is within; now we stay in the center and rule what is external. Hitherto it was a service in aid of the Master; now, it is a dissemination of the commands of the Master. The whole relation-ship is now reversed. If one wants to penetrate the more subtle regions by this method, one must first see to it that the body and heart are completely controlled, that one is quite free and at peace, letting go of all entanglements, untroubled by the slightest excitement, and with the heavenly heart exactly in the middle. When the rotating light shines towards what is within, it does not develop a dependence on things, the energy of the dark is fixed, and the Golden Flower shines concentratedly. This is then the collected light of polarity. Related things attract each other. Thus the polarized light-line of the Abysmal presses upward. It is not only the light in the abyss, but it is creative light which meets creative light. As soon as these two substances meet each other, they unite inseparably and there develops an unceasing life; it comes and goes, rises and falls of itself, in the house of the primal energy. One is aware of an effulgence and infinity. The whole body feels light and would like to fly. This is the state of which it is said: Clouds fill the thousand mountains. Gradually it goes to and fro quite softly; it rises and falls imperceptibly. The pulse stands still and breathing stops. This is the moment of true creative union, the state of which it is said: The moon gathers up the ten thousand waters. In the midst of this darkness, the heavenly heart suddenly begins a movement. This is the return of the one light, the time when the child comes to life.

There was once a king who had three sons. Desiring to determine the fitness of each of them in order to determine the most suited for the prospective job of ruling the kingdom, he hit upon a strange test.

The king ordered his sons to accompany him, with bows and arrows, on a ride into the country. Pausing at a spot beside the road near an open field, the king pointed out a vulture sitting on a tree limb, within easy bow shot.

"I wish you to shoot at that vulture," said the king to his eldest son. "But tell me first, what do you see?"

Wonderingly, the prince replied, "Why, I see grass, the clouds, the sky, the river, a tree, and…"

"Enough!" said the king, and beckoned the second son to make ready to shoot. The latter was about to do so when his father again said, "Tell me first, what do you see?"

"Ah, I see the horses, the ground, a field of wheat, and an old dead tree with a vulture on it," answered the youth.

"Never mind shooting it," the king said, and turning to his youngest son, ordered him to hit the vulture, and again repeated the question, "First, what do you see?"

The youth replied deliberately, not taking his gaze for an instant from his intended victim as he drew taut the bowstring and aimed the shaft, "I see," he said, "the point where the wings join the body…." And the young man let fly the arrow and the bird tumbled to the ground.

The third son became the king.

The kingdom belongs to those who can work in a concentrated way – and the kingdom of the within, more so. The way of moving in life with a direction – with a goal, with a clearcut vision – crystallizes your energies. The goal is just an excuse. The direction is just a device.

Ordinarily you are scattered all over the place – one part going in this direction, another part going in another direction. Ordinarily you are many, a mob, and each fragment of your being is constantly contradicting the other fragment. How can you achieve anything in life? How can you feel fulfilled? If misery becomes your whole story, and if life proves to be nothing but a tragedy, there is no need to wonder. Except you, nobody else is responsible.

You have an inexhaustible source of energy, but even that can be wasted. If your fragments are in a kind of civil war you will not achieve anything worthwhile – to say nothing about God, to say nothing about truth. You will not achieve *anything* worthwhile, because all realization, either of the without or of the within, needs one thing absolutely: that you be one – so that your whole energy can pour into your work, so that your whole energy can become a quest.

Questions you have many; that is not going to help – unless all your questions are together and create a quest in you. When your life becomes a quest, when it has a direction, it starts moving towards fulfillment. Then it will have crystallization. Crystallization means: slowly slowly you become one piece, slowly slowly individuation arises in you. And the ultimate realization of truth is nothing but the ultimate realization of unity within your being. That is the meaning of the word *God*. God is not there somewhere in the heavens, waiting for you. God is waiting within you, but you can find him only if you are one – because only the one can find the one.

Remember the famous words of the great mystic, Plotinus: "Flight of the alone to the alone." First you have to become alone. That's what I was saying yesterday to Amrito: become alone. Alone means: become all one. This aloneness, or all-oneness, this inner unity, releases immense power because all dissipation stops. You stop leaking. The ordinary man is like an earthen pot which is leaking from everywhere and has many holes in it: you can go on filling it again and again, but again and again you will find it is empty. Your effort will not bring any fruition; first the holes have to be stopped.

Think of your life as a great occasion to become one. Once you start moving in one direction – you pull yourself together – something in you starts settling, a center arises. And that center is the door to God.

These sutras are of immense value. They are very mysterious too, because when one starts imparting truth one has to use the language of poetry, parable, mystery. There is no other way. The language of mathematics is inadequate; one has to be very metaphorical.

Before we enter into the sutras, listen to this small story.

The great Zen Master, Nansen, was getting very old and was waiting for his successor to arrive. In fact, he was ready to leave the body but was just hanging around for the successor to come so he could transfer whatsoever he had attained, so he could give the key.

Now he had many disciples, so it looks very strange. He had thousands of disciples: why could he not give his key to one of these thousands of disciples? He had great scholars around him – very skillful, very logical, efficient, intellectual – but he had to wait. These people were able to understand logic but they were not able to understand love. And love speaks a totally different language. These people were capable of understanding mathematics but were absolutely incapable of understanding the language of metaphor. These people were perfectly able to understand prose but were not available to the mysteries of poetry – so he had to wait.

He was lying down on his bed in his chamber, sick, old, and hanging around the old body somehow, managing somehow. It was on that day that for the first time he saw his successor, Joshu, coming into the room. His very coming...not a single word had been uttered. Neither had the Master spoken nor the disciple, the future disciple. He was a stranger, but the way he entered the room was enough.

The Master asked him, "Where have you come from?"

For days the Master had not spoken: he was so sick, so old, he was preserving his energy in every way. He was not even speaking. After many days, these were his first words – to Joshu, "Where have you come from?"

Joshu said, "From Zuizo Temple." Zuizo means figure of bliss.

Nansen laughed – he had not laughed for many months – and asked, "Have you seen the figure of bliss?"

Joshu said, "The figure of bliss, I have not seen. A lying Buddha, I have seen."

At this Nansen stood up – he had not been out of his bed for almost a year. At this Nansen stood up and asked, "Do you have a Master already?"

Joshu answered, "I have."

Nansen asked, "Who is your Master?" as if all sickness had disappeared, as if he were young again. His voice was clear, youthful, vigorous, vital: "Who is your Master?!"

Joshu laughed and said, "Although winter is past its peak it is still very cold. May I suggest, my Master, that you take good care of your body?" And that was that.

And Nansen said, "Now I can die peacefully. A man has arrived who can understand my language. A man has arrived who can meet not on the surface but in the depth."

Joshu said, "My Master, take good care of your body." Just saying that, the initiation had happened. And the way Joshu said, "Although winter is past its peak, it is still very cold," he knows how to speak in metaphors. He knows the way of poetry. And he knows the way of love. That's why he said, "May I suggest, my Master, that you take good care of your body. Please lie down. You need not jump out of your bed. You are my Master! I have not seen bliss yet, but I have seen a Buddha."

The Master recognized the disciple, the disciple recognized the Master – in a single split moment. What transpired? That which transpired is beyond language. But still that, *even that,* has to be told in language. Even this story has to be related to you in language. There is no other way.

These words of Master Lu-Tsu are very mysterious. Try to understand them through your heart in a very loving, sympathetic way.

There are two ways to listen to a thing. One is the way of the critic who is constantly inside criticizing, judging, evaluating – whether it is right or wrong, whether it fits with me or not, whether it agrees with my knowledge or not. He's constantly comparing, criticizing. That is not the way to understand these beautiful sutras. These sutras are beyond the critical mind. They are available only to one who is sympathetic; or, even better, to one who is empathetic – who can fall in tune, who can become just open and listen totally – so it is not only the physical heart but the deep, hidden spiritual heart that is stirred by them.

Master Lu-Tsu said:
Four words crystallize the spirit in the space of energy.

You have the energy, you have all that you will ever need. Still you are poor, still you are a beggar. You have not used your energy. You have not opened your treasure yet. You have not even looked at what God has given to you. Without looking in you are rushing out, hence the misery. And the misery is going to remain, because you cannot find anything in the outside world that can satisfy you. Nobody has ever found anything in the outside world, not even the great Alexander. You can have the whole kingdom of the earth. You can become a *chakravartin,* the ruler of the whole earth, of all the seven continents.

You will be surprised: modern geography says there are only six continents, but the ancient Indian geography says there are seven continents. It must be Atlantis that they count in. And a person who rules over all the seven continents is called a chakravartin. Even if you become a chakravartin you will remain poor, you will not gain anything. In fact, you will have lost much, because your whole life you will have been struggling for the trivial, for the mundane, for the meaningless, for the futile – which is going to be taken away by death any moment. Unless you have something of the within, you are not going to become rich.

Only the kingdom of the within makes one rich, because even death cannot take it away. It cannot be robbed, it cannot be destroyed, it cannot be taken away. Once you have known it, it is yours forever.

You have the inner space, you have the inner energy. All is available, just that you have not looked into it. You have the beautiful veena but you have not even touched it, you have not even seen what music it contains. In fact, you have almost become oblivious to it.

Lu-Tsu says, *Four words…* only four words can crystallize your being, can create an emperor in you, can make you a Buddha or a Christ or a Krishna. What are those four words?

Now try to understand these four metaphors.

First:

In the sixth month white snow is suddenly seen to fly.

Second:

At the third watch the sun's disk sends out blinding rays.

Third:

In the water blows the wind of the Gentle.

Fourth:

Wandering in heaven, one eats the spirit-energy of the Receptive. And the still deeper secret of the secret: the land that is nowhere, that is the true home...

Now try to decipher these mysterious words, these esoteric statements. They have great hidden beauty and great hidden meaning. Be very sympathetic, because that is the only way to understand something esoteric.

In the sixth month white snow...

The sixth month is the middle of the year. It represents the middle of everything. If you can be in the middle of everything – never leaning to any extreme – you have fulfilled the first requirement. This has immense value for the seeker, on an existential quest: be in the middle. Always remember the middle, "The Golden Mean." Don't eat too much and don't fast too much – neither this way nor that. Don't become too attached to things and don't renounce them either. Be with people but not too much – not so much that you cannot be alone at all. And don't start being solitary, don't become addicted to loneliness – don't avoid people. Be in the world but don't let the world enter in you. There is no need to escape from the world. Never move to the extreme.

This is one of the most fundamental things to be remembered, because the mind always moves from one extreme to another extreme. Mind lives through extremes. Mind dies in the middle – this is the secret.

There are people who will eat too much, and then for few days they will diet. And then after a few days' suffering, the so-called dieting, they will start eating too much again – with a vengeance – and again. This is a vicious circle: from one extreme they will move to the other, from the other again back. Back and forth, like a pendulum of an old clock they go on moving, and they don't know that because the pendulum moves, the clock remains alive. It is a beautiful metaphor, the clock. If the pendulum stays in the middle, the clock stops; so is the mind.

If you move from one extreme to another extreme, mind continues, time continues – mind and time are synonymous. The moment you stop in the middle, time disappears, the clock stops; mind disappears, the mind stops. And in that moment, when there is no mind and no time, suddenly you become aware for the first time of who you are. All clouds have disappeared and the sky is open and the sun is shining bright.

In the sixth month white snow...

And in China, in the part where these sutras were written, it is the sixth month of the year when the snow appears. It is the middle path – when coolness appears in your being. And white snow represents a few things: whiteness, purity, coolness, tranquility, virgin freshness, beauty and grace.

Be in the middle and you will see that your inner being is becoming like the Himalayas: Himalayan peaks covered with virgin snow, and all is cool, and all is utterly silent, and all is utterly fresh, all impurities gone.

The impurity is of the mind. When there is no mind, no thought, there is no impurity. It is thought that pollutes your being.

In the sixth month white snow is suddenly seen to fly.

And it happens suddenly. Just be in the middle, and out of nowhere, out of the blue, the white snow starts appearing. You try it, this is an experiment. It is not a philosophy to be understood, it is an experiment to be done. Try to be in the middle of anything and you will see great coolness, calmness, collectedness arising in you.

At the third watch the sun's disk sends out blinding rays.

And the second metaphor is the third watch. Man has three layers: first is the body, second the mind, third is the soul. If you have fulfilled the first requirement, then the second will be possible. You cannot do the second before doing the first, so you will have to move methodologically. You cannot start from the middle, you cannot take any step from anywhere. There is a sequence. First attain the middle of everything, and the whole day watch whether your mind is going to extremes. Avoid the extremes and then the second thing will become possible. When you mange to avoid the extremes you will become aware of three things in you: the body – the gross part of you; the mind – the subtle part of you; and the soul – the beyond.

Body and mind are two aspects of matter. Body is visible matter, mind is invisible matter. And when you see the bodymind both, you, the seer, are the third. That is the third watch: the watcher, the observer, the witness.

At the third watch the sun's disk sends out blinding rays.

And then when you are attuned to your watching, one with your witness, suddenly, as if in the middle of the night, the sun rises and there is great light. You are full of light within and without, the whole existence becomes aflame.

And the third:

In the water blows the wind of the Gentle.

Water, in Taoism, represents the ultimate course of things. It represents the Tao itself. Lao Tzu has called his path "The Watercourse Way" for many reasons. First, the water is soft, humble, seeks the lowest place. Just as Jesus says, "Those who are the last in this world will be the first in my kingdom of God, and those who are the first will be the last," water seeks the lowest place, the lowest level. It may rain on Everest but it doesn't remain there. It starts running towards the valley. And in the valley too, it will reach to the deepest part. It remains the last, it is non-ambition. It has no ambitions to be the first.

And to be water means to be a sannyasin: to be water-like means to be utterly happy in your being a nobody.

And secondly, water means movement. It is always moving. And whenever it is not moving it becomes dirty, impure, even poisonous. It dies. Its life is in movement, in dynamism, in flow. The whole life is a flow, nothing is static.

The scientist, Eddington, is reported to have said that the word *rest* is utterly meaningless, because in existence, there is never anything at rest. It corresponds to no reality, to no fact. Everything is growing, moving, on the way: life is a pilgrimage. In life, nouns are false, only verbs are true. In language we have created nouns. Those nouns give a very false impression about life. They are not right. Someday, in future, when language will become more existential, nouns will disappear and will be replaced – *all* nouns will be replaced – by verbs. There is nothing like river, but rivering; there is nothing like a tree, but treeing – because never for a moment is the tree static. It is never in a state of is-ness. It is always becoming, flowing, going somewhere. Existence is fluid, hence the metaphor of water, *in the water.*

If you have seen the witness, then the third thing becomes possible: you will see the beauty of the flow. You will not hanker for security and you will not hanker for things to remain as they are. You will start moving with the river, you will become part of the river of existence. You will start enjoying change.

People are *really* afraid of change, *very* afraid of change. Even if the change is for the better, they are afraid. They are afraid of the new because the mind becomes very clever with the old and is always embarrassed with the new, because with the new the mind has to learn again from *ABC* – and who wants to learn? The mind wants the world to remain static. It is because of the mind that societies are conformist, orthodox. Millions of people in the world are conventional. Why? There must be some deep investment in it. This is the investment: nobody wants to learn, nobody wants to grow, nobody wants to be acquainted with the new. People want to go on moving in the old rut, and then naturally they are bored. Then they say, "Why are we bored?" and "How to drop boredom?" – and they are creating the boredom, and they don't see the mechanism of how they create it.

Many people come to me and they say they are bored: "How to get out of boredom?" Boredom is not the problem, boredom is a by-product. Deep down the problem is: are you ready to explore the new? Are you ready to go for an adventure? Adventure means risk: one never knows – it may turn out better, it may turn out worse than you had known before. One can never be certain about it. The only certainty in life is uncertainty. One can only be certain about uncertainty and about nothing else.

The new makes people very apprehensive. They cling to the old. Hence the conventional people in the world – and they are the dead weight, because of them the world remains static. They will go on insisting on their old patterns. For example, in India, people have lived for almost five thousand years with the same structure that Manu created. It may have been good in those days, must have been of some significance. But five thousand years have passed and still in India, the untouchable exists. There are people who cannot even be touched, they are not human beings. The really orthodox will not even touch their shadows. It used to be so, it is still so in a few villages, that when an untouchable, a *sudra,* passes on the street, he has to shout "Please get out of my way. I am coming" – because if his shadow falls on somebody of the high caste, that will be a crime. He can be beaten, beaten to death! Still people are being burned for this crime. And this stupid structure has lived for five thousand years – so inhuman, so undemocratic! That's why in India it seems democracy cannot succeed: the whole Hindu mind is undemocratic. How can you succeed in creating a democratic country if the whole structure of the mind, the conditioning of the mind, is undemocratic?

The basic fundamental of a democracy is that each man is equal, nobody has more value than the other – but that is not acceptable to the Hindu. In fact, the sudra, the untouchable, cannot be counted as a human being. He has to be counted with animals, not with man. The woman cannot be counted with men; she has also been counted with the animals. Now this type of mind – how can it become democratic? So in the name of democracy there is only chaos and nothing else, because there are no foundations for democracy. But for five thousand years this country has lived with this structure and is not ready to leave the structure. What is the beauty of this structure? There is nothing like beauty in it. It is utterly ugly, horrible, repulsive, nauseating! The only thing is, because people have lived so long, they don't want to learn anything else. They want to live with it, they are at ease with it. They abhor any change.

Remember, this tendency is in every human being, more or less: you don't want change. You are afraid to change because with the change new responsibilities, new challenges will arise. And you are afraid whether you will be able to cope with them or not, so it is better to remain with the old because with the old you have become skillful, efficient, with the old you are the master. With the new, who knows? You may be the master, you may not be the master.

Only children are capable of learning. Because they don't have any past, because they don't have anything old to cling to – that's why children are ready to learn. The more they grow the less they learn. Near about the age of thirteen, people stop learning. That remains their mental age.

If you are a seeker you will have to learn continuously. Life is learning. Learning never stops. Even at the moment of death the seeker goes on learning: he learns death. He's always ready to change.

Water represents the changing element, the eternally changing, flux-like phenomenon. Those who are ready to change, and forget and forgive the past, and are ready to go with the moment, are the *real* human beings because they are the adventurers. They know the beauties of life and the benedictions of life. And life reveals its mysteries only to these people, and *only* to these people – because they are worthy, they have earned it. By risking, they have earned. They are courageous.

In the water blows the wind of the Gentle.

And the third metaphor: if you become a water-like phenomenon – changing, constantly changing, moving, flowing, never clinging to the past and the old, always searching for the new and always enjoying the new – then *the wind of the Gentle* blows, then grace descends. Then beatitude descends in your being. Then the first dance of the divinity in you…that is called "the wind of the Gentle."

God is very gentle. He never knocks on your doors. You never hear his footsteps. When He comes, He comes so silently, without making any noise. Unless you are water-like, the breeze of God will never dance on you. First become fluid.

That is my message too, to my sannyasins: remain fluid.

And remember, the future belongs to those who are ready to change, constantly, because now the world is changing so fast that the people who cling to the old are going to suffer very much. In the past they have not suffered very much. On the contrary, the people who were ready to change have suffered very much.

In the future, just the reverse is going to be the case: the future belongs to those who will love change and who will be dancingly ready to change when the moment arises, who will celebrate change. And whenever there will be an occasion to change, they will never miss it. The future is going to be with them. History is taking a great turn. It is moving on another plane. That's why my insistence is always that whenever something is changing, don't prevent it.

If your relationship with your woman is changing, don't prevent it. Allow it, let it have its own course. Even if you have to separate, don't be worried. That clinging mind will keep you miserable. If it is changing, it is changing! Enjoy the change, enjoy the new. Receive the new, welcome it. And soon you will see that if you become capable of receiving the new without any fuss about the old, your life will start having an elegance, a grace, a gentleness. You will become like a soft flower.

This is the moment when a seeker starts dancing. This is the moment when celebration starts. And remember, porpoises and chimpanzees may play, only man celebrates. Celebration is utterly human. You have heard many definitions: somebody says man is the rational animal, and somebody says something else. I say: man is the celebrating animal. That is where he is different from all other animals.

But how can you celebrate if you are clinging to the old? Then you live in your grave because you live in the past, you live in the dead, and you don't allow life to reach you. It is as if a rosebush has become addicted to the old roses which are dead, dried up, and it goes on collecting those petals that have fallen – and is afraid of new buds and new flowers, and is afraid of the spring.

This is the situation of millions of people, the majority of people: they remain clinging to the dead petals, dried. They go on collecting them, they live in their memories. They call it nostalgia; it is stupidity, nothing else.

A real man has no nostalgia at all. He never looks back because it is no longer there. He lives in the moment and remains open for the future. The present is his, and the present makes him more aware and capable of receiving the future. His doors are always open for the wind, for the rain, for the sun. He is an opening.

In the water blows the wind of the Gentle.

And this is the moment one becomes aware of God, not before it.

First, you start balancing yourself in the center. Second, you start becoming aware of the witness, the soul. And third, you start becoming aware of the presence – some unknown mysterious presence, *the wind of the Gentle.*

Wandering in heaven, one eats the spirit-energy of the Receptive.

And the fourth metaphor is when you have started becoming aware of the presence of God, your duality, your fundamental polarity starts disappearing. Then you are neither man nor woman, neither yin nor yang. Then suddenly your man eats your woman, your woman eats your man. At this point, the Hindu concept of *ardhanarishwar* becomes significant. Then you are both and neither. You have transcended the duality of the positive and the negative.

Wandering in heaven...

But this is possible only when you have known the gentle breeze, the subtle dance, the presence of God, and you have started wandering into the open sky. You are no more clinging to anything, you are no more crawling and creeping on the earth. You are not in your grave. You have opened your wings, you are on the wing in the sky, available to existence and all its challenges – no longer orthodox, no longer conventional, no longer conformist. You are a rebel. And only the rebellious spirit starts feeling the presence of God. This is heaven! – the presence of God.

Then the fourth miracle happens which crystallizes you absolutely: your duality disappears. Otherwise, deep down, you remain split. If you are a man you go on repressing your woman. You have to. The society teaches you, "Remember, you are a man." If you cry and weep, somebody is bound to comment, "What are you doing? It is okay for women to cry and weep, but you are a man. You are not expected to weep." And immediately your tears dry, you pull them back, you hold them back. You are a man, you are supposed to be a man, and you cannot cry.

If you cannot cry how are you going to laugh? Your laughter will be half-hearted, lukewarm, because you will be afraid that if you laugh too much you may be so relaxed that the tears that you are holding back may start flowing from your eyes.

Have you not watched this phenomenon? If somebody laughs too much, he starts crying. Why? Why do eyes become tearful when you laugh too much? – because laughter means you are allowing. And if you are allowing, you are allowing everything. You cannot allow one thing and prevent another thing; that is not possible. If you have to repress one thing you will have to repress *all* things. This is something very basic to be learned: repress one thing and your whole personality has to be repressed to the same extent. If you cannot weep, you cannot laugh. If you cannot laugh, you cannot weep. If you cannot be angry, you cannot have compassion. If you cannot be compassionate, you cannot be angry either. Life maintains a certain level: whatsoever you allow to one thing you will have to allow the same amount to other things in your life. You cannot do one thing: "I will hold my tears back but I will laugh whole-heartedly." This is impossible.

Man is taught to become more and more masculine. Small boys – we start changing their basic, fundamental balance and forcing them towards one polarity. The boy has to be forced to be a man, so a few things are allowed to him. If he fights we say it is perfectly okay: he has to fight for his whole life. If he plays with guns and pistols and kills and reads detective novels, we say it is okay. But, to the girl we don't allow the gun. To the girl we say, "You play with dolls. Arrange marriages. Become a mother. Make a house. Cook food. Play things like that, because this is your life and this is going to be your life: prepare for it." We don't allow girls to climb on the trees, to hang on the branches upside-down. We just don't allow it. We say, "You are a girl. This is not supposed to be done. This is not graceful for you."

Slowly, slowly we emphasize the polarity, one polarity, and the other polarity is repressed utterly. This is the basic schizophrenia. And everybody suffers from it because the society has not yet been able to accept your whole being.

Moving towards reality you will have to accept yourself. You are man/woman together, woman/man together. Nobody is just man and nobody is just woman. And this is beautiful that you are both, because that gives richness – to your life, to your being. It gives you many colors. You are the whole spectrum, the whole rainbow. You are not a single color. All colors are yours.

At the fourth, when you start moving into the divine presence, all schizophrenia disappears – and there is no other way for the schizophrenia to disappear. Psychoanalysis is not going to help much. In fact, it goes on emphasizing your polarity. Psychology has yet to come to a point where it is not male-dominated, otherwise stupid things go on in the name of psychology.

Sigmund Freud says that women suffer from penis-envy. Utter nonsense! He never says that men suffer from breast-envy. This is male-oriented. In fact, women never suffer from any envy. On the contrary, man suffers very much because he cannot reproduce, he cannot create a child. Because he cannot create a child he moves into many other creativities as substitutes: he writes poetry, he paints, he sculpts, he makes architecture. These are substitute creations, because deep down he knows one thing: that he cannot produce life. But Freud never talks about that. That would have been truer. He says women suffer from penis-envy. This is utter nonsense. Psychology is still carrying the same division between man and woman. The human being is both, but this ultimate integration happens only at the fourth stage.

Wandering in heaven, one eats the spirit-energy of the Receptive.

The Receptive means the female. One eats one's opposite. And remember, eating means absorbing. That's why there are ancient sayings that each disciple has to become a cannibal – because he has to eat his Master. Don't take it literally. It is just a metaphor, but very significant, because eating means you absorb, you digest. The Master becomes part of you, is no more separate. That's what Jesus says at The Last Supper when he is taking leave of his disciples. He breaks bread and gives the bread to his disciples and says, "This is me. Eat it, this is my flesh," pours wine and gives it to his disciples and says, "This is me. Drink it, this is my blood." Again this is a metaphor. He is saying to his disciples, "Become cannibals. Eat your Master, digest your Master, so there is no division between you and your Master."

The same is true about this fourth statement: you have to eat the other polarity in you. Lu-Tsu must have been speaking to his male disciples, because down the ages it is the man who has been more adventurous, more in quest. The woman seems to be more settled, at home. So there must have been male disciples, he must have been talking to male disciples. That's why he says, "Eat your woman." But the same is true about women disciples: they have to eat their man. Inside, the other has to be absorbed so the duality disappears.

And once these four words have been fulfilled, then the greatest secret of all becomes available to you.

> *And the still deeper secret of the secret: The land that is*
> *nowhere, that is the true home...*

And now, for the first time you will become aware that you are not, but your non-existence does not mean mere emptiness. The person in you disappears, but presence appears. Separation from existence in you disappears, but the whole starts abiding in you. You are no more an island. Now there is no way to locate where you are. Hence:

> *The land that is nowhere, that is the true home...*

Now you cannot say where you are, who you are...and this is the true home. This word *nowhere* is really beautiful.

A great Indian mystic, Swami Ramateertha, used to say again and again that he had a friend who was a Supreme Court advocate, and he was utterly atheistic, continuously arguing against God. He had written on the walls in his drawing room in capital letters: "God is nowhere" – to provoke somebody. Whosoever would come to see him or visit him would first have to see "God is nowhere." And he was always ready to jump upon you if you said, "God is."

Then his child was born and the child started learning language. The child was just at the beginning and one day the child was sitting in the lap of the father and he started reading. Now "nowhere" is a big word and the child could not read it, so he split it in two and he read: God is now here. Nowhere can be split into two words: *now*, *here*. And the father was surprised, because he had written those words but he had never read it that way. The meaning was diametrically changed: God is now here… He looked into the eyes of the child, those innocent eyes, and for the first time he felt something mysterious. For the first time he felt as if God had spoken through the child. His atheism, his lifelong atheism, disappeared because of the statement of the child. And Ramateertha says that when he died he was one of the most religious persons he had known in his life. But the change happened through the child, just by mistake – because the child could not read the word *nowhere* together, as one word.

This word *now-here*, *nowhere*, is beautiful. When you know God is now-here, then you know God is nowhere – both are the same. God is *not* somewhere, that is true, so you cannot say where he is, you cannot locate, you cannot pinpoint.

Nanak has said that to ask where God is, is utterly wrong; ask where he is not. And if he is everywhere, to say God is everywhere or to say God is nowhere means the same – because when he is everywhere, there is no point in saying where. He just is.

"The land that is nowhere" is now-here.

Now is the only time, and here, the only space. And if you cannot find God now-here, you will not be able to find him anywhere else. This moment, *this very moment*…

If three steps have been fulfilled and the fourth achieved, this will happen, this is the secret of the secrets: that God is not a person sitting somewhere. God will never be known as a person, has never been known as a person – and those people who have known God as a person were simply befooled by their own imaginations. If you see Christ, it is your imagination. You are creating it. If you see Krishna, it is your imagination. You can cultivate your imagination, you can practice it, but you are creating a dream, you are projecting a dream. It is your dream-mind functioning.

Truth is not a person and truth is not *there*, not outside. It is not found as an object. It is your witnessing subjectivity. And that is possible only when your man and woman have disappeared into one.

As the French say: There are three sexes – men, women, and clergymen. They say it jokingly but it has something significant in it. There *are* three sexes:

men, women and the buddhas.

The buddha cannot be called a man or a woman. Although he has a certain body – it may be of man or woman – but a buddha is no more identified with his body He's just a pure witness. He's as away from his body as you are away from his body, as distant as you are distant from his body. You are standing there outside looking at his body, he's standing deep down inside looking at his body. But the distance from you to his body and from his body to himself is the same. He is no more identified with his body. You cannot call him a man or a woman. The buddha is simply beyond.

And when this beyond has opened,

The land that is nowhere, that is the true home...

You have come home.

These verses are full of mystery. The meaning is: the most important
things in the great Tao are the words: action through non-action.

Only when you have come home will you know the ultimate meaning of the words *action through non-action*. But from the very beginning you have to keep moving in that direction, only then one day the ultimate happens.

What is the meaning of action through non-action? It is very easy to be active, it is very easy to be inactive. There are people who are active, continuously active, restless, day in, day out. That's what has happened in the West: people have become super-active. They cannot sit in rest even for a single moment. Even sitting in their beautiful, comfortable chairs, they are fidgeting, they are changing their posture. They cannot be at rest. Their whole life is a turmoil, they need something to keep them occupied. They are driving themselves mad through activity.

In the East people have become very inactive, lazy. They are dying out of their laziness. They are poor because of their laziness. They go on condemning the whole world, as if they are poor because of the world, because of other people. They are poor because they are lazy, utterly lazy. They are poor because action has completely disappeared – how can they be productive? How can they be rich? And it is not that they are poor because they have been exploited. Even if you distribute all the money that the rich people in India have, the poverty will not disappear. All those rich people will become poor, that is true, but no poor persons will become rich. Poverty is there, deep down, because of inaction. And it is very easy to choose one polarity: action is male, inaction is female.

Lu-Tsu says,

One has to learn action through non-action.

One has to learn this complex game. One has to do, but not become a doer. One has to do almost as if one is functioning as an instrument of God. One has to do and yet remain egoless. Act, respond, but don't become restless. When the action is complete, you have responded, go into rest. Work when it is needed to work, play when it is needed to play. Rest, lie down on the beach, when you have worked and played. When you are lying down on the beach under the sun, don't think of work – don't think of the office, don't think of the files. Forget all about the world. Lying in the sun, lie in the sun. Enjoy it. This is possible only when you learn the secret of action through inaction. In the office do whatsoever is needed, in the factory do whatsoever is needed, but even while you are doing remain a witness: deep down, in deep rest, utterly centered, the periphery moving like a wheel, but the center is the center of the cyclone. Nothing is moving at the center.

This man is the perfect man: his soul is at rest, his center is absolutely tranquil, his periphery in action in doing a thousand and one things of the world. This is my concept of a sannyasin. That's why I say don't leave the world. Remain in the world, act in the world, do whatsoever is needful, and yet remain transcendental, aloof, detached, a lotus flower in the pond.

Non-action prevents a man from becoming entangled in form and image.

If you remember that your deepest core is in non-action you will not be deceived, you will not be entangled by form and image. That is materiality. You will not become worldly.

Action in non-action prevents a man from sinking into numbing emptiness and dead nothingness.

And the other danger is: you can regress into a kind of numbness, deadness, dullness, a negative kind of emptiness, nothingness. That too has to be avoided. Action in non-action will prevent this. Action will keep you positive, inaction will keep you negative. Action will keep you male, inaction will keep you female. If both are balanced then they cancel each other and the beyond opens, and suddenly you see Buddha arising in you.

> *Heretofore we have spoken of the circulation of the light, indicating thereby the initial release which works from without upon what lies within. This is to aid one in obtaining the Master.*

The first two words:

> *In the sixth month white snow is suddenly seen to fly...*

And the second:

> *At the third watch the sun's disk sends out blinding rays...*

These are the lower steps, and the second two are the higher steps:

> *In the water blows the wind of the Gentle...*

And the fourth:

> *Wandering in heaven, one eats the spirit-energy of the Receptive.*

The first two are the lower steps. They help you to find the Master. If you come across a Master you will recognize him only if these two steps have been taken before. Otherwise you can come across a buddha and you can pass a buddha without ever becoming aware of what you have missed. Someday, later in life, when you will have attained these two steps, then you will weep and cry and repent because then you will remember a buddha had passed you on the Way. Then you will feel great guilt at how you could miss.

The first two help to find the Master. With the first two, you have to work from the without towards the within. The work is to start from without – because it is there where you are – and you have to start moving inwards.

With the second two: you have found the Master, the Master has found you. Now the second two are to fulfill his commandments. The process is reversed: now the within starts working on the without. With the first two you were cultivating, practicing, meditating, you were working, searching, groping in the dark. With the second two you have found the Master, you have heard his voice, you have seen his eyes, you have felt his heart. His presence has permeated your being. Trust has arisen. Now you simply follow, you simply fulfill his commandments – and in fulfilling those commandments is your fulfillment.

> *It is for pupils in the beginning stages. They go through the*
> *two lower transitions in order to gain the upper one. After*
> *the sequence of events is clear and the nature of the release is*
> *known, heaven no longer withholds the Way, but reveals the*
> *ultimate truth. Disciples, keep it secret and redouble*
> *your effort!*

The first two will need great concentrated effort on your part. You will have to be consciously working, deliberately working. It is arduous. The first two steps are arduous because your eyes are closed, your heart is not beating. The second two steps are easy because now your eyes are open: you have recognized the Master, you have heard the message, now things are clear. Now you can see. Even if the Himalayan peak is far away, you can see it. Maybe it is a thousand-mile journey yet, but now you can see it. Even from far away you can see the sunlit peaks of the Himalayas, you know they are there. Now it is only a question of time. And now you know a guide is with you who has been coming down and up on those peaks again and again. Now you can listen and you can follow.

The first two steps are in great doubt: one has to struggle. Every possibility is there that one may go astray. Small things can lead people astray, very small things. When they will think later on, they will know the ridiculousness of them – very small things, of no meaning at all – but they can prevent you. The seeker has to be very alert. In the first two steps he has to be very cautious, only then can he fulfill the lower steps. The lower fulfilled, the higher becomes available.

> *…heaven no longer withholds the Way…*

Through the Master, heaven starts opening the Way.

> *…but reveals the ultimate truth. Disciples, keep it secret and*
> *redouble your efforts!*

The circulation of the light is the inclusive term. The further the work advances, the more does the Golden Flower bloom. But there is a still more marvelous kind of circulation.

Up to now we have talked about the circulation of the light that *you* do, that *you* have to manage, practice. But there is a still more marvelous kind of circulation. That need not be practiced, it happens of its own accord. It is a gift, it is a grace.

When you have fulfilled the first two steps, the Master arrives. When you have fulfilled the second two higher steps, God arrives.

And the fifth secret, the secret of the secrets is that now things start happening on their own. You need not do anything. In fact, if you do anything it will be a hindrance. Now everything is spontaneous, on its own. Tao has taken possession of you – or call it God: you are possessed! You have disappeared utterly. Now only God is in you. Just as he blooms in flowers and the trees, he will bloom in you in the Golden Flower. Now it is up to him, now it is none of your concern. Now it is his will, your will has done its work.

In the first two steps, great will was needed. In the second two steps, a willing surrender was needed. And after the four steps are finished there is no need of will, there is no need of surrender either. Remember, surrender is also just to drop the will. In the first two steps you cultivate the will, in the second two steps you have to drop the will – that is surrender, and when will has been dropped by surrender, the ultimate secret of secrets is neither will nor surrender. Again, will is man, surrender is woman; with the fourth crossed, you have crossed man and woman both: will gone, surrender too, gone. Now you are not there. You are nowhere to be found. There is nobody, nothingness, nirvana, and Tao now fulfills its own work. Just as spring comes and trees bloom and rains come and clouds gather and morning comes and the sun rises, and in the night the sky is full of stars – all goes on without any effort anywhere. The sun is not making any effort to rise in the morning, neither do the stars struggle to shine in the night, nor do the flowers have to make great effort to bloom. You have become part of the ultimate nature.

But there is a still more marvelous kind of circulation. Till now we have worked from the outside on what is within; now we stay in the center and rule what is external. Hitherto it was a service in aid of the Master; now it is a dissemination of the commands of the Master.

*The whole relationship is now reversed. If one wants to penetrate
the more subtle regions by this method, one must first see to it that
body and heart are completely controlled, that one is quite free and
at peace, letting go of all entanglements, untroubled by the slightest
excitement, and with the heavenly heart exactly in the middle. When
the rotating light shines towards what is within, it does not develop
a dependence on things, the energy of the dark is fixed, and the
Golden Flower shines concentratedly. This is then the collected light
of polarity. Related things attract each other. Thus the polarized light-
line of the Abysmal presses upward.*

If you are divided in two – into man and woman, negative-positive, darkness-light, mind-heart, thought-feeling – if you are divided in two, your energy will be going downward. Division is the way of the downward. When you are undivided, one, you start moving upward. To be one is to move upward, to be two is to move downward. Duality is the way to hell, non-duality is the way to heaven.

*Thus the polarized light-line of the Abysmal presses upward. It is not
only the light in the abyss, but it is creative light which meets creative
light.*

And when this unity has happened within you, great creativity explodes. One never knows what potential one is carrying about: there may be a poet waiting, or a painter, or a singer, or a dancer. One never knows who is waiting inside you. When your man and woman will meet, your potential will be released. It will become actual. That's how the Upanishads were born, and the Koran, and the Bible, and Khajuraho, and Konarak, and the Taj Mahal, and Ajanta and Ellora. All this creativity is totally different from the so-called creativity that you know in the modern age. Picasso is a totally different kind of creator from the man who conceived the Taj Mahal.

The man who conceived the Taj Mahal – his polarity had disappeared. He was a Sufi mystic. It was his vision, it was out of deep meditation. Still if you meditate on the Taj Mahal on a full moon night you will be surprised: something deep inside you will start rising up, will start moving upwards. If you meditate deeply on the Taj Mahal for one hour on a full moon night, sitting there, just looking at it, something will become cool in you. Snow, coolness, freshness will appear within you. Or the statues of Buddha that were carved by the great Buddhist mystics – just meditating, looking at the statue, something settles inside you.

Look at a Picasso painting and you feel it will drive you mad. If you go on looking at it for one hour, you will feel nausea. It is more like vomiting, not like creativity – as if Picasso is pouring his neurosis on the painting. Maybe paintng relieves him of *his* neurosis. That's what psychologists say too. Many times it has been found that a madman was given color and canvas and was told to paint, and the moment he started painting his madness started disappearing. So now there are schools in psychoanalysis; they say: psychotherapy through painting, therapy through painting. Yes, it is possible, it releases: what has been going on inside you is poured onto the canvas, you are relieved.

It is just the same kind of relief that you feel when your stomach is disturbed, you are feeling sick, and you vomit. After vomiting you feel relieved. But what about the people who will look at the vomit? But who cares about them? And foolish people are always there: if you tell them that this is modern art – it may be just vomit – they will appreciate. They will say, "If critics are saying this is modern art, it must be."

I have heard...

There was an exhibition of a modern painter, and people were standing in front of a painting and appreciating greatly. Great critics had gathered and they were also applauding it. Then the painter came and he said, "Wait! The painting is hanging upside-down."

Nobody had seen that the painting was hanging upside-down. In fact, because it was hanging upside-down, it was looking more mysterious.

People are just stupid: in anything, they follow the fashion. This is not creativity. This is neurosis, or a neurotic kind of creativity. There is another kind of creativity, what Gurdjieff used to call "the objective art."

When the inner polarity is no longer polar, when your inner divisions have disappeared and you have become one, then creativity is released. Then you may do something that will be of immense help to humanity, because it will be coming out of your wholeness and out of your health. It will be a song of wholeness. It will be like the Song of Solomon – of immense beauty, of immense splendor.

Related things attract each other.

When you are *really* one, God is attracted towards you – because the one is attracted towards the one – "the flight of the alone to the alone." You start flying towards God and God starts flying towards you.

> *It is not only the light in the abyss, but it is creative light which meets creative light. As soon as these two substances meet each other, they unite inseparably, and there develops an unceasing life; it comes and goes, rises and falls of itself, in the house of the primal energy.*

And when your creativity is fully released the creativity of God descends in you and there is a meeting between these two creators. Only a creator can meet the creator, only the creator is worthy of meeting the creator. And when these two creativities, human and divine, meet…

Remember, there are two meetings. The first meeting is the meeting of the man and the woman within you; and the second, ultimate meeting is the meeting of you as a human being – total, whole – with the whole; the meeting of the human with the divine, the ultimate meeting. That is eternal. Once that has happened you are beyond death. It cannot be undone again.

> *One is aware of effulgence and infinity. The whole body feels light and would like to fly. This is the state of which it is said: Clouds fill the thousand mountains.*

Now you are infinite, like…

> *…clouds fill the thousand mountain. Gradually it goes to and fro quite softly: it rises and falls imperceptibly. The pulse stands still and breathing stops. This is the moment of true creative union, the state of which it is said: The moon gathers up the ten thousand waters. In the midst of this darkness, the heavenly heart suddenly begins a movement. This is the return of the one light, the time when the child comes to life.*

And when does it happen? This meeting of the creator within you with the creator of the whole – when does it happen? It happens when you are so silent, so totally silent, so absent that the pulse stands still and breathing stops.

> *This is the moment of true creative union, the state of which it is
> said: The moon gathers up the ten thousand waters.*

You know that when the moon is full, sea water starts rising towards the moon, wants to go to the moon. Exactly like that, man wants to reach to God. But unless you create this capacity in you, this utter emptiness in you, you will rise a little and you will fall again. But when you have become an absence – an absence but not negative, an absence of utter positivity – then *the moon gathers up the ten thousand waters.* Then you rise and you go on rising, and the meeting with the moon…

> *In the midst of this darkness, the heavenly heart suddenly begins
> a movement.*

And when your ordinary heart has stopped and your ordinary pulse has stopped, then for the first time you feel a totally different quality starting. You again breathe, but the breathing is no more the same. Your pulse again starts pulsating, but it is no more the same pulse. Now God lives in you. Now you are not there, only God is.

That's why we call Buddha "Bhagwan": a moment came when God started living in him – the man disappeared. Then the man was just a hollow bamboo and the song of God started flowing through him. This is the ultimate goal.

Enough for today.

CHAPTER 24

I Sure Dig You, Man

The first question:

Osho,
What exactly is intelligence, and what is the relation
of the intelligence of the heart to the intelligence of
the mind?

Intelligence is the inborn capacity to see, to perceive. Every child is born intelligent, then made stupid by the society. We educate him in stupidity. Sooner or later he graduates in stupidity.

Intelligence is a natural phenomenon – just as breathing is, just as seeing is. Intelligence is the inner seeing, it is intuitive. It has nothing to do with intellect, remember. Never confuse intellect with intelligence. They are polar opposites. Intellect is of the head: it is taught by others, it is imposed on you, you have to cultivate it, it is borrowed. It is something foreign, it is not inborn. But intelligence is inborn. It is your very being, your very nature. All animals are intelligent. They are not intellectuals, true, but they are all intelligent. Trees are intelligent, the whole existence is intelligent, and each child born is born intelligent. Have you ever come across a child who is stupid? It is impossible! But to come across a grown-up person who is intelligent is very rare. Something goes wrong in between.

I would like you to listen to this beautiful story. It may help. The story is called "The Animal School."

The animals got together in the forest one day and decided to start a school. There was a rabbit, a bird, a squirrel, a fish and an eel, and they formed a Board of Directors. The rabbit insisted that running be in the curriculum, the bird insisted that flying be in the curriculum, the fish insisted that swimming had to be in the curriculum, and the squirrel said that perpendicular tree-climbing was absolutely necessary to the curriculum. They put all of these things together and wrote a curriculum guide. Then they insisted that *all* of the animals take *all* of the subjects.

Although the rabbit was getting an *A* in running, perpendicular tree-climbing was a real problem for him. He kept falling over backwards. Pretty soon he got to be sort of brain-damaged and he could not run anymore. He found that instead of making an *A* in running he was making a *C*, and of course, he always made an *F* in perpendicular climbing. The bird was really beautiful at flying, but when it came to burrowing in the ground he could not do so well. He kept breaking his beak and wings. Pretty soon he was making a *C* in flying as well as an *F* in burrowing, and he had a hell of a time with perpendicular tree-climbing.

The moral of the story is that the person who was valedictorian of the class was a mentally retarded eel who did everything in a half-way fashion. But the educators were all happy because everybody was taking all of the subjects, and it was called a "broad-based education."

We laugh at this, but that's what it is: it is what you did. We really are trying to make everybody the same as everybody else, and hence destroying everybody's potential for being oneself.

Intelligence dies in imitating others. If you want to remain intelligent you will have to drop imitating. Intelligence commits suicide in copying, in becoming a carbon copy. The moment you start thinking, "How to be like that person?" you are falling from your intelligence, you are becoming stupid. The moment you compare yourself with somebody else you are losing your natural potential. Now you will never be happy, and you will never be clean, clear, transparent. You will lose your clarity, you will lose your vision, you will have borrowed eyes. But how can you see through somebody else's eyes? You need your own eyes, you need your own legs to walk, your own heart to beat. People are living a borrowed life, hence their life is paralyzed. This paralysis makes them look very stupid.

A totally new kind of education is needed in the world. The person who is born to be a poet is proving himself stupid in mathematics and the person who could have been a great mathematician is just cramming history and feeling lost.

Everything is topsy-turvy because education is not according to your nature: it does not pay any respect to the individual. It forces everybody into a certain pattern. Maybe by accident the pattern fits a few people but the majority is lost and the majority lives in misery.

The greatest misery in life is to feel oneself stupid, unworthy, unintelligent. And nobody is born unintelligent, nobody can be born unintelligent because we come from God, God is pure intelligence. We bring some flavor, some fragrance from God when we come into the world. But immediately the society jumps upon you, starts manipulating, teaching, changing, cutting, adding, and soon you have lost all shape, all form. The society wants you to be obedient, conformist, orthodox. This is how your intelligence is destroyed.

My whole approach is to take you out of this imposed pattern. This is a prison cell in which you are living. You can drop it. It will be difficult to drop because you have become so accustomed to it. It will be difficult to drop because it is not just like clothing. It has become almost your skin, you have lived with it so long. It will be difficult to drop because this is your whole identity – but it has to be dropped if you really want to claim your real being.

If you really want to be intelligent you have to be a rebel. Only the rebellious person is intelligent. What do I mean by rebellion? – I mean dropping all that has been enforced on you against your will – the morality, the religion, the politics, whatsoever it is. Drop all that has been forced on you against your will. Search again for who you are, start from *ABC* again. Think that your time up to now has been a wastage because you have been following.

No person is similar to anybody else. Each is unique – that is the nature of intelligence – and each is incomparable. Don't compare yourself to anybody. How can you compare? You are you and the other is other. You are not similar, so comparison is not possible. But we have been taught to compare and are continuously comparing. Directly, indirectly, consciously, unconsciously, we live in comparison. And if you compare you will never respect yourself: somebody is more beautiful than you, somebody is taller than you, somebody is healthier than you, and somebody is something else, somebody has such a musical voice... you will be burdened and burdened if you go on comparing.

Millions of people are there: you will be crushed by your comparisons. And you had a beautiful soul, a beautiful being which wanted to bloom, which wanted to become a Golden Flower, but you never allowed it. Be unburdened, put all aside. Regain, reclaim your innocence, your childhood. Jesus is right when he says, "Unless you are born again, you shall not enter into my kingdom of God."

I say the same to you: Unless you are born *again*...

Let your sannyas be a new birth! Drop all the garbage that has been put on you – be fresh and start from the very beginning. And you will be surprised – how much intelligence is immediately released.

You ask, "What exactly is intelligence?"

It is capacity to see, capacity to understand, capacity to live your own life according to your own nature. That is what intelligence is.

And what is stupidity? Following others, imitating others, obeying others, looking through their eyes, trying to imbibe their knowledge as your knowledge: that is stupidity. That's why pundits are almost always stupid people: they are parrots, they repeat, they are gramophone records. They can repeat skillfully, but let a new situation arise, that which is not written in their books, and they are at a loss. They don't have any intelligence.

Intelligence is the capacity to respond moment-to-moment to life as it happens, not according to a program. Only unintelligent people have a program. They are afraid. They know that they don't have enough intelligence to encounter life as it is. They have to be ready, they rehearse. They prepare the answer before the question has been raised, and that's how they prove themselves stupid – because the question is never the same. The question is always new. Each day brings its own problems, its own challenges, and each moment brings its own questions. And if you have ready-made answers in your head you will not even be able to listen to the question. You will be so full of your answer, you will be incapable of listening, you will not be available and whatsoever you will do you will do according to your ready-made answer – which is irrelevant, which has no relationship with the reality as it is.

Intelligence is to relate with reality, unprepared. And the beauty of facing life unprepared is tremendous. Then life has a newness, a youth, then life has a flow and freshness. Then life has so many surprises. And when life has so many surprises, boredom never settles in you.

The stupid person is always bored. He is bored because of the answers that he has gathered from others and goes on repeating. He is bored because his eyes are so full of knowledge, he cannot see what is happening. He knows too much without knowing at all. He is not wise, he is only knowledgeable. When he looks at a roseflower, he does not look at *this* roseflower. All the roseflowers that he has read about, all the roseflowers that the poets have talked about, all the roseflowers that painters have painted and philosophers have discussed, and all the roseflowers that he had heard about, they are standing in his eyes – a great queue of memories, information. *This* roseflower that is there is lost in that queue, in that crowd – he cannot see it, he simply repeats. He says, "This roseflower is beautiful." Those words are also not his own, not authentic, not sincere, not true. Somebody else's voice…he is just playing a tape.

Stupidity is repetition, repeating others. It is cheap – cheap because you need not learn. Learning is arduous. It needs guts to learn. Learning means one has to be humble. Learning means one has to be ready to drop the old, one has to be constantly ready to accept the new. Learning means a non-egoistic state.

And one never knows where learning will lead you. One cannot predict about the learner. His life will remain unpredictable. He himself cannot predict what is going to happen tomorrow, where he will be tomorrow. He moves in a state of no-knowledge. Only when you live in a state of no-knowledge, a *constant* state of no-knowledge, do you learn. That's why children learn beautifully; as they grow old they stop learning, because knowledge gathers and it is cheap to repeat it. Why bother? It is cheap, simple, to follow the pattern, to move in a circle. But then boredom settles. Stupidity and boredom go together.

The intelligent person is as fresh as dewdrops in the morning sun, as fresh as the stars in the night. You can feel his newness, so new, like a breeze. Intelligence is the capacity to be reborn again and again. To die to the past is intelligence, and to live in the present is intelligence.

And, you also ask, "What is the relationship of intelligence of the heart to the intelligence of the mind?"

They are diametrically opposite. The intelligence of the head is not intelligence at all. It is knowledgeability. The intelligence of the heart is the intelligence, the only intelligence there is. The head is simply an accumulator. It is always old, it is never new, it is never original. It is good for certain purposes: for filing it is perfectly good and in life one needs this – many things have to be remembered. The mind, the head, is a bio-computer. You can go on accumulating knowledge in it and whenever you need you can take it out. It is good for mathematics, good for calculation, good for the day-to-day life, the marketplace. But if you think this is your whole life then you will remain stupid. You will never know the beauty of feeling and you will never know the blessing of the heart. And you will never know the grace that descends only through the heart, the God that enters only through the heart. You will never know prayer, you will never know love.

The intelligence of the heart creates poetry in your life, gives dance to your steps, makes your life a joy, a celebration, a festivity, a laughter. It gives you a sense of humor. It makes you capable of love, of sharing. That is true life. The life that is lived from the head is a mechanical life. You become a robot, maybe very efficient – robots are very efficient, machines are more efficient than man. You can earn much through the head, but you will not live much. You may have a better standard of living but you won't have any life. Life is of the heart.

Life can only grow through the heart. It is the soil of the heart where love grows, life grows, God grows. All that is beautiful, all that is really valuable, all that is meaningful, significant, comes through the heart. The heart is your very center, the head is just your periphery. To live in the head is to live on the circumference without ever becoming aware of the beauties and the treasures of the center. To live on the periphery is stupidity.

You ask, "What is stupidity?" To live in the head is stupidity. To live in the heart and *use* the head whenever needed is intelligence. But the center, the master, is at the very core of your being: the master is the heart, and the head is just a servant. This is intelligence. When the head becomes the master and forgets all about the heart, that is stupidity. It is up to you to choose.

Remember, the head as a slave is a beautiful slave, of much utility, but as a master is a dangerous master and will destroy your whole life, will poison your whole life. Look around! People's lives are absolutely poisoned, poisoned by the head: they cannot feel, they are no more sensitive – nothing thrills them. The sun rises but nothing rises in them; they look at the sun empty-eyed. The sky becomes full of the stars – the marvel, the mystery! – but nothing stirs in their hearts, no song arises. Birds sing, man has forgotten to sing. Clouds come in the sky and the peacocks dance; and man does not know how to dance – he has become a cripple. Trees bloom; man thinks, never feels, and without feeling there is no flowering possible.

The Golden Flower that we have been talking about this whole month is there in you, waiting – waiting for centuries, for lives. When are you going to give attention to it so that it can bloom? And unless a man becomes a Golden Flower – what the yogis have called "the one-thousand-petaled lotus," *sahasrar* – unless your life becomes an opening, one thousand petals open and the fragrance is released, you will have lived in vain – "a tale told by an idiot, full of fury and noise, signifying nothing."

Watch, scrutinize, observe, have another look at your life. Nobody else is going to help you. You have depended on others so long, that's why you have become stupid – now take care. It is your own responsibility. You *owe* it to yourself to have a deep penetrating look at what you are doing with your life. Is there any poetry in your heart? If it is not there, then don't waste time: help your heart to weave and spin poetry. Is there any romance in your life or not? If there is not, then you are dead, then you are already in your grave. Come *out* of it! Let life have something of the romantic in it, something like adventure. Explore!

Millions of beauties and splendors are waiting for you. You go on moving around and around, never entering into the temple of life. The door is the heart.

So I say: the real intelligence is of the heart. It is not intellectual, it is emotional. It is not like thinking, it is like feeling. It is not logic, it is love.

The second question:

> Osho,
> What is it in the make-up of someone like Eva Renzi that makes her
> tell such outrageous lies about a community like ours?

I feel sorry for Eva Renzi. She was really in great need. She has missed an opportunity. She must be suffering from a split personality: she is not one, she is two. She is schizophrenic. That's why she had come in search, to find some clarity, some integration.

She has been in psychotherapy, she has been psychoanalyzed, but the psychoanalysis has not been of much help. That's why her husband suggested that she come here. The husband also has not been able to live with her. They are separated.

And just the other day I was reading a statement by one of the directors – she is a film actress – and the director remembers that ten or twelve years ago he was directing a film and she was the heroine in the film. They had booked a beautiful castle somewhere in Germany for only one day, and the whole crew waited and all the actors waited – and Eva Renzi never turned up! Almost in tears, everybody left. And in the evening she turned up, laughing, smiling. And the director says he became so crazy that he hit her with a chair. And then he felt bad too. He had a heart attack. For three, four months he had to rest. He says that anybody who can live for one hour with Eva Renzi will hit her!

Now the poor woman must have been in deep suffering. She *is* crazy! She would have been immensely helped if she had been a little patient, if she had been here a little longer. But these patterns go very deep. These patterns go so deep that it is almost impossible to help such people. She was in one group, the Centering group – she created trouble there – and she was creating so much trouble that the whole group was disturbed. And you cannot allow one hundred and twenty-five people to be disturbed for one person. So Prasad, the group leader, had to tell her that if she was so angry, in such a rage, so much in violence, that it would be better that she participate in the Encounter group where she could release her anger, her rage, as a means of catharsis, but the Centering group was not for her.

She immediately left and entered into the Encounter group, and within hours she was gone – because there also she created much trouble, provoked everybody to fight. The Encounter group is meant for release, and when people started fighting with her she left the group – now the other personality must have taken possession of the poor woman.

She did not report to the police here in Pune. If there had been something wrong with her she should have gone to the police. She went to police in Bombay and reported that she had been beaten – so much so that the room was full of blood – her clothes had been torn apart and she had to go out of the ashram naked to the hotel! Now, do you think a beautiful woman like Eva Renzi walking naked on the Pune streets would have survived? Nobody remembers a naked woman in the Blue Diamond, bleeding and going there. Nobody had seen her and there are thousands of people here the whole day. But noone recalled seeing her going and leaving, naked, bleeding, shouting, crying. Nobody had seen her. She reported to the police in Bombay, not here. And the police came and searched, and found the whole thing was a lie.

But I don't think that she is lying. It is her other personality, her other self: the other person had taken possession of her, not that she was lying knowingly. When the other person takes possession, it becomes impossible – you don't know what you are saying, why you are saying it.

The people who are split function almost like two persons. When they are in one personality they are one person, when they are in another personality they are a different person, and both personalities never meet.

Now she has created much fuss in Germany, in the newspapers, but I feel real compassion for her. I invite her again. I have not seen her. All this happened within just a day, I have not seen her. I would like to see her and help her. She needs help. And she has gone so deeply into this schizophrenia that I don't think she can be helped anywhere else. If she comes back it will be good: those two personalities can be welded again. But it will need patience. If she had come with her husband or some friends it would have been better. They would have prevented her from escaping so soon.

A little time will be needed. A lifelong pattern can't be changed in one day.

And the schizophrenics have their own ideas about things. They are so full of their own madness that they think everybody else is mad. Their projections are such, they feel that they are being persecuted, everybody is going to murder them or kill them.

Once it happened:

I had to live in the same room with a professor for a few months. He was a schizophrenic. When he was good he was utterly good, a really nice fellow, but when he was bad he was really bad. And it was very difficult to know when he was going to be good, when he was going to be bad. In the middle of the night he would start shouting or would start provoking me to fight with him. If you didn't fight, you didn't honor him. If you didn't start fighting, then he would be angry. If you fought him you unnecessarily got into trouble with him, and then the neighbors would come, and he would shout and he would make such fuss. And by the morning he would have forgotten everything! If you reminded him he would say, "No, you must have dreamt it." If you called the neighbors he would say, "They must have been dreaming, because I have slept so well the whole night." It was so difficult. I would go to the university to teach, when I would come home all my things would be gone!

He had two personalities. The other personality was really something! He would store everything in his suitcases and lock them. When he was good he would be very generous, he would give his things to me. I enjoyed living with him for a few months because it was such a surprise – you never knew what was going to happen today. And when he was in his bad personality, in the neurotic, he was so afraid that anything…and he would think the murderer was coming or the police were coming to catch hold of him. And he would imagine a jeep passing by in the middle of the night – he would wake me up. He would say, "Look, the police are reaching, the jeep has come. Now I will be caught. And I tell you that I am innocent! And I have not done anything wrong – you are my witness!" Just the whistle of the police in the night and he would be alerted.

These people are in deep suffering. They have their own ideas, and they are so clouded in their ideas that they don't see the reality.

Now I don't think she is aware at all of what she is saying, of what she is reporting to the newspapers. She says one man, an old man, a Dutchman – he is none other than the famous author, Amrito – tried to rape her. Now he will be the last man to think of rape – she is just like a daughter to him – and he is such a nice, loving person. But somehow she had got the idea that there was an old Dutchman in the Encounter group who wanted to rape her. Now she is going around telling people, the newspapers. But the idea had got into her, and newspapers are always ready to exploit anything.

A man came home to find his wife having a nervous breakdown, screaming and banging her head on the wall.

"What is the matter, darling?" said the worried husband.

"I am homesick!" sobbed the distraught woman.

"But you are at home, darling," said the husband.

"Exactly!" said the wife, "I am sick of home!"

When you have your ideas, your own interpretations, things start appearing like that. And you can always find explanations, excuses, you can always find arguments. And remember, neurotic people are very argumentative because they are hung-up in the head.

So don't feel angry with Eva Renzi, not at all. And don't be worried about what is happening in Germany. It is going to help my work tremendously! I know my business and how to do it. Don't be worried about it.

Now it is all over Germany, everybody knows my name – this is something great – and everybody is asking about me, "Who is this man?" Sannyasins who have come from Germany just a few days ago report that even taxi drivers ask, "Are you going to Pune? I am also thinking of going! What is happening there?"

Now many people will be coming because of Eva Renzi. And remember, there is always a balance, otherwise life would collapse. Her negative statements started creating positive statements. That's how it always happens. That's what I mean when I say I know my business. Now this director has come to defend me. He does not know me, but he says that if it has happened to Eva Renzi it is perfectly good – she needed it, she deserved it! He says all the people who knew her will be happy, particularly her husband. Now more and more positive statements will be coming.

Just create the negative and the positive starts coming. Create the positive and the negative starts coming. They always balance, otherwise life would collapse. So never be worried about negative things. It is always like that.

Do you know who created Christianity? – not Christ, but the people who crucified him. If they had not crucified him there would have been no Christianity, you would never have even heard of Jesus. It is the people who crucified him.

Now crucifixion is such a negativity that the positive is bound to happen – somebody is bound to start worshipping. Life always balances.

So the poor woman is in suffering but it is good for my work. Nothing is wrong in it. Those lies that she is telling will be refuted, people will come up on their own from many unknown quarters. And many people will come just out of curiosity. Many more lies will follow and many more truths to balance them. Now because she started the thing, many newspapers have come to Pune. Since she started the ball rolling, many newspapers, many journalists have come – a few have written against, a few have written for.

One journalist seems to be really very inventive. He writes that he reached to the ashram-gate door at five thirty, early in the morning. He knocked on the door: a great beauty, a blonde, opened the door – at five thirty! – and welcomed him with an apple, or something like an apple. He said, "I don't know what fruit it was. She gave the fruit to me and she said, 'You are welcome in the Garden of the Master. Come in!' And I asked, 'What is this apple?' and she said, 'You eat it. It will give you sexual energy.'"

Now the taxi drivers are asking, "Are there such types of fruits in the garden? We would like to come." Who would not like to come! Let these people work. They are helping my work. Nothing to be worried about. I always rejoice!

The third question:

> *Osho,*
> *What is your message, Osho? I don't understand you.*

My message is that there is no message. I am not here to give you a message, because a meaning will become knowledge. My purpose here is to impart something of my being. It is not a message, it is a gift. It is not a theory, it is not a philosophy. I want you to partake of my being. It cannot be reduced into a dogma. You cannot go back and tell people what you have learned here. You will not be able to. If you have learned anything, you will not be able to relate it to anybody – although your whole being will show it. You will not be able to say it but only to show it. Your eyes will show it, your face will beam, your whole energy will have a different vibe.

I am not functioning here as a teacher. This is not a school. I don't teach you a thing. I simply want you to participate with me, in this mystery that has happened to me. Fall in tune with my energy, vibrate with me, pulsate with me – and you will know something which is beyond words, which no message can contain.

Once the great Master Joshu was asked for his word. Joshu said, "There is not even half a word."

When he was asked further, "Master, but are you not here?" he said, "I am not a word."

He is right. A master is not a word, a master is a door. A master is not a message but a medium. It is a link, a bridge. Pass through the door, pass through the bridge, and you will come to know exactly what life is all about. If you can dive deep into the Master you will start feeling the presence of God – but it is not a message.

And you say you don't understand me? I know why you can't understand me: because whatsoever I am saying is so simple, that is why. Had it been complex you would have understood it. You are accustomed to complexity. The more complex a thing is, the more your intellect starts working on it – the challenge to the ego.... My communion with you is so simple, so utterly simple that there is no challenge for the ego. That is the reason why you can't understand me.

What I say is simple and absolutely clear. I don't use any jargon. I am simply using the language that you use in your day-to-day work, in your day-to-day life. Maybe that is the reason for your not understanding me: the obvious is what I say and teach – yes, the obvious – but the obvious sounds bizarre because you have become so accustomed to the complexities that the mad mind goes on spinning and weaving around you.

And moreover, always keep in mind that what I say is said for no particular reason, there is no motive behind it – just as they say "art for art's sake." What I am saying to you has no particular reason behind it, no motive, but a sheer joy of being together with you, a sheer response to your questions. Not that my answers will solve your questions; no, not at all. If my answers can solve your questions, then it becomes a message. My answers will only help you to understand your questions – and when a question is understood, it dissolves. No question is ever solved. If you understand a question rightly it dissolves, it is not solved. It becomes insignificant, trivial and false – like a dry leaf from the tree, it loses all meaning. I am not going to give you answers, I am going to take away your questions.

And when the mind has no question to ask, in that utter silence where no question is present, you come to know that which is – call it God, call it Tao, truth, nirvana, or what you will.

That's why I say there is no particular reason in my saying whatsoever I say to you. There is no particular motive behind it, it is a simple response to your being. I am only being a mirror, hence there is no particular need to understand me. Don't try to understand me. There is nothing to understand. Just be with me and understanding will come on its own. And these are two different types of understandings. When you try to understand me you will miss, because while I am imparting something to you, you are engaged and occupied in understanding it. You will miss it.

Don't try to understand it, just listen! Just as I am talking to you without any motive, listen on your part without any motive – and the meeting is bound to happen. When I am without motive and you are without motive, what can hinder, what can obstruct the meeting? Then the meeting is going to happen. And in that communion there is understanding, in that communion is light, clarity, and transparency.

So rather than trying to understand me, celebrate me, rejoice in me – and you will understand, and without any effort to understand.

Nobody ever understands through effort. What effort do you make when you listen to music? Do you try to understand it? If you try to understand it, you will miss the whole joy of it. The music has to be rejoiced in. Do you try to understand a dance? Then you will miss it. The dance has to be celebrated. Do you try to understand the roseflowers and the songs of the birds in the morning? There is no need! Just be with the roseflower, just see the bird on the wing – don't let anything hinder – and suddenly, understanding arises. And that understanding arises straight from the heart, straight from your intelligence. It is not of the head.

And then the understanding has a totally different flavor, a totally different fragrance to it. Then it has beauty – because it comes out of effortlessness, it comes out of love. If you try to understand me, logic will be there, mind will be there. If you don't try to understand me, if you just listen for the sake of listening, then slowly, slowly something starts opening in you, arising in you, awakening in you.

Let me be a provocation, not a message. Let me be an alarm to wake you up, not a message. If you think in terms of a message you will create a wall between me and you. Just be here. Just as I am with you, you be with me: for no particular reason – just for the sheer joy of this silence, this presence that surrounds me and you, that joins me and you, this meditativeness, this grace, this moment of sheer beauty and benediction.

And your heart will understand. Whether your mind understands or not is of no significance.

The fourth question:

Osho,
Morarji Desai says that students should not take part in politics.
What do you say about it?

Remember always: whatsoever the politicians say, it is always politics. Whenever a politician reaches to power he always starts telling the students not to participate in politics – but only when he is in power. When he is not in power he is all in favor – students *should* participate in politics.

How has Morarji reached to power? Basically, it was a students' movement in Gujarat and Bihar. On that tidal wave of the youth movement he has reached to power. Now he must be afraid: now if students continue to participate in politics he can be toppled.

This is something beautiful to be understood: whenever politicians are out of power they provoke the students; the same politicians, when they reach to power, they start telling the students, "Please, this is not your work. You should go to the colleges, to the universities. Politics has to be avoided. Don't be distracted by politics!" Because that is the bridge, that bridge has to be broken; otherwise others will be coming. And students cannot be befooled so easily as others can be befooled.

Youth cannot be befooled as easily as others can be befooled because youth is still not involved in the vested interests of the society. The older you grow the more your investment is in the status quo. You cannot go against it. You are married, you have children, you have a job, you have to look after the family, and there are a thousand and one responsibilities on you. You would like everything to remain as it is. You will be afraid of any change. Who knows? – your job is lost, and what is going to happen to your children?

Students prove to be the most revolutionary part of the society – for the simple reason that they have no investment, for the simple reason that they can ask for, demand change. And of course they are young; their eyes can still see a little bit, they can still feel, and of course they are going to live in the future. The past is not their world, but the future. The older you grow the less future you have and the more past. A man of seventy has very little future and a very long past. And the man who is only twenty has very little past and a long future – his orientation is the future. And whenever the future is the orientation there is rebellion, revolution. And the people who are in power are always afraid of any kind of rebellion, of any kind of revolution.

So remember, when politicians say, "Participate in politics," then too it is politics. When they say, "Don't participate in politics," then too it is politics. They always speak politics. Even in their sleep, if they start saying something, it is politics – don't believe them! Even in their dreams they remain politicians.

But they are cunning people, shrewd people: whenever there is a revolution, whenever there is some change, some movement, and the youth is stirred, the shrewd politicians simply ride on the wave.

Now this revolution that happened just one and a half years ago was created by the youth, and the power went into the hands of the very rotten old. This is strange that the stir was of the youth but the people who came into power are all above seventy, and a few are even above eighty. One sometimes wonders why dead people can't get out of their graves and become prime ministers and presidents...they will prove to be even better!

I was reading a story:

Three old friends met for lunch one day. Well advanced in years, they met periodically to keep up to date on each other. The youngest of the three told his news first. His wife had just given him a baby girl – and he was almost seventy-nine years old!

The second man spoke. He was eighty-three years of age and his wife had just had a son. The two fathers were proud as peacocks.

Then the third man offered some food for thought. "My friends," he said, "let me tell you a story. I am eighty-eight. Used to hunt a lot, but I am too old for that nonsense now. But last week I was strolling in the park and a cottontail came bounding out of the bushes. True to an old instinct, I raised my walking cane to shooting position, cried, 'Bang! Bang!' and the rabbit rolled over dead!

"A few minutes later I spied another cottontail. Again I simulated a rifle with my cane and cried 'Bang!' Again the rabbit dropped dead!

"What necromancy, what strange spell is this? I wondered aloud. Then, gentlemen, I glanced behind – ten paces to the rear was a young boy shooting with a real rifle!"

Morarji Desai should ponder over it: your "Bang! Bang!" has not done anything, just the youth of the country have been shooting behind you. But now, naturally, once you have reached to power you become afraid.

But you ask me, "What do you say about it?"

I also say to you to avoid politics, don't take part in politics – not for the same reason, of course. First, I am not a politician. Second, I am not in power. I have nothing to be afraid of in your taking part in politics. So, the reason why Morarji Desai says, "Don't participate in politics," is because of something else. The reason why I say to you, "Don't participate in politics," is totally different. The reason is: leave politics for the stupid people, the utterly stupid who cannot do anything else. First try to be a scientist, a poet, a painter, an architect, a musician, a novelist, a potter, a weaver, a carpenter – something intelligent, something creative. If you find that you cannot create anything, when you have looked around and tried everywhere, and everywhere you get "F," then go into politics – that is the last resort of the stupid and the scoundrels – never before. First try. There are beautiful experiences in life. Politics is destructive, it is the most ugly phenomenon. Leave it to others who cannot do anything else. And remember, if you don't leave it to others who cannot do anything else, those others will become criminals.

The criminal and the politician are the same type of people. If the criminal becomes politically successful he is a great leader. If the politician cannot succeed in being in power he becomes a criminal. They are destructive people: their whole effort is to dominate others.

The really creative person is not interested in dominating anybody. He is so utterly rejoicing in life, he wants to create, he wants to participate with God. Creativity is prayer. And whenever you produce something, in those moments you are with God – you walk with God, you live in God. The more creative you are the more divine you are. To me, creativity is religion. Art is just the entrance to the temple of religion. Create something!

When you fail everywhere, then politics. It is not for the intelligent people, it is for the utterly unintelligent and stupid. And of course, they also need somewhere, some place, to do some nonsense of their own. They need parliaments to quarrel in and go mad. Leave it to them!

I also say to students: Don't participate in politics unless you have failed everywhere else. First try other dimensions of life, far richer. But my reason is totally different.

And if you become interested in politics too early you will remain retarded for your whole life. When are you going to read Kalidas and Shakespeare and Milton and Tennyson and Eliot and Pound? When are you going to see the great painters, learn their art? When are you going to meditate in Khajuraho, Konarak? When are you going to dream great dreams of creating a Taj Mahal or a painting or poetry? When? There is great literature, great painting, great poetry. You must watch your steps.

Politics seems to be attractive for only one single reason, and that has to be understood.

The English word *self-consciousness* has to be understood. That will help you. It has two meanings. One is the meaning which Buddha preaches and Gurdjieff preaches and I preach: it means to become conscious of yourself, become alert. Gurdjieff used the word *self-remembering*, and Buddha uses the words *sama smrati* – mindfulness, consciousness. Krishnamurti uses the word *awareness* – become fully alert and aware. This is the one meaning of the word *self-conscious*. The word is very ambiguous.

The other meaning is when you stand on a stage and you become self-conscious, and you start trembling. The other meaning is pathological. The first meaning means you are conscious of yourself – you are not a robot, you function out of awareness. The second means that you are aware that *others* are conscious of you, that others are watching you, that you are an object of others' consciousness – and you become afraid. So many people watching, if something goes wrong, and they will laugh and they will think you are a fool or ridiculous – and you become afraid. Others are watching you – you are an object. You become conscious of this phenomenon: conscious that others are conscious of you – then fear arises. But joy too arises: "So many people watching me." So you repress your fear, you stand there on the stage without trembling: "So many people watching me…." The fear is: "If something goes wrong they will think you are a fool." The joy is: "If nothing goes wrong, and I can perform well, then so many people will think, 'Look! What a great man! What a great artist, actor, speaker, orator!' If I can succeed in performing something, so many people will look towards me, upwards at me, and will enhance my ego."

The politician lives in this. He wants many people to look up to him so his ego is enhanced. He is afraid of going within because he knows there is nothing, emptiness. He does not know who he is. He collects his information about himself from other people's eyes, from what they say. If they say, "You are a great man" he believes he is a great man – he rides on the winds. If they say, "You are a mahatma" he feels happy, his ego is fulfilled. He is attaining a kind of identity – now he knows who he is. But this is not true self-knowledge; others can take it away at any moment. And they always take, because sooner or later they can see that you have not fulfilled your promises, that your performance has been bogus.

You can see Morarji Desai's great ego eroding by and by. You can see the same with Jimmy Carter – the smile becoming smaller and smaller, disappearing – because you cannot fulfill the promises that you have made to the people. And you always make big promises: without making big promises you will not reach to power. So you give fantastic promises that you know you cannot fulfill – but who cares! Once you are in power, then we will see: then we will see how they can take you out of power. You will cling, and you will have all the powers to cling, and the whole bureaucracy and the whole government machinery will be with you. Once you are in power who cares about the promises? The leaders forget all about their promises. And don't remind them! They feel hurt and annoyed.

But people start seeing that the promises are not being fulfilled: "These people have cheated us!" The image starts falling, the person becomes smaller. That hurts.

The politician is continuously in search of enhancing his ego. He needs others people's attention. Millions of people have to feed his ego. The artist, the mystic, the musician, the dancer – if they are also asking for others' attention, then they are politicians. Then they are not real artists, not real mystics.

The real mystic, the real artist, is one who knows the other meaning of self-consciousness: he is simply conscious of himself. He does not need anybody else's attention. He is enough unto himself. He can be silently sitting and enjoying himself, he does not need anybody. His life is of awareness, he moves with awareness, his each step is full of light. Hence he never repents, he never feels guilty. Whatsoever he does, he does with full awareness. All that he can do he does, and whatsoever happens he accepts – because that is the only thing that could have happened. He never looks back. He moves ahead and he lives in the present, but he lives in a very conscious way.

Self-consciousness in the meaning Buddha gives makes you a creator, and self-consciousness the way a politician needs it makes you just an egoist.

I say to you: Don't participate in politics because that is searching for the ego. And to search for the ego is to search for something poisonous that will destroy your whole life. The politician is the poorest man in the world, the most empty man, the most hollow – stuffed with straw and nothing else.

The last question:

Osho,
When can a therapy be called "finished"?

Therapy is the need of the divided person. Therapy is the need of the person who has fallen into fragments. Therapy is complete when you have become a whole, when you are one piece.

But no therapy, as it is known in the modern world, brings you to wholeness. Therapy is at the most, nothing but a rearrangement – maybe a little better than before, but you remain fragmentary. It is the same furniture rearranged in the same room – maybe a little bit more conveniently – but it doesn't make you whole, because when a person becomes whole his life becomes prayer. Prayer is the by-product of wholeness. Wholeness makes you holy. Unless your therapy brings prayer to your heart it is not complete yet. The basic need is that of prayer.

Jung is reported to have said – and his observation is absolutely right – that one half of his patients were in need not of therapy but of religion. He is also reported to have said – and again he is right – that all the patients that went to him who were above forty-two didn't need therapy, but needed prayer. The real need is to have a context in this infinite existence.

The ego makes you separate, prayer dissolves the ego and you become one with existence again. To become one with existence is to attain to bliss. To remain separate, there is conflict. To remain separate means you are fighting with existence, you are not flowing with the river. You may even be trying to go upstream – and going upstream you are going to be frustrated, you are going to fail. Flowing with the river – so much so that you become one with the river, just a part of the river, you don't have any will of your own, you are surrendered to the will of the total – this is prayer. And a therapy is complete, finished, when prayer is born in your heart.

But the prayer has to be true. It should not be a formality, it should not be a repetition, parrotlike. It should arise, it should have roots in your being.

Anutosh has sent me a beautiful joke. Meditate over it.

Every day for six months the kneeling figure, hands clasped in prayer, had intoned the same pitiful story in the shadow of the back pews in his local Catholic church.

"Oh Lord, sure I am only a poor simple fellow. Not even the price of a glass of wine do I have for after mass on Sunday, and I know I am a terribly wicked fellow. I give the missus a clout now and then, and when the kids get too much I have to rebuke them with the back of my hand.

"But I am not asking for much, just a couple of quid in the old wage packet – not for myself, mind, just for the housekeeping to keep the old lady off my back and some sweets for the kids. Maybe the odd drink for me. I would not abuse it though, Lord. Can you help me? It would make an awful lot of difference, and I will ask for nothing more, to be sure. God bless, Hail Mary, Amen!"

Suddenly the door of the church burst open and a smartly dressed West Indian swaggered down the aisle and took a defiant stance in front of the altar, and raising his fist shouted, "Hey dere, Lord. Now you listen here! I dun just got to dis country. I dun got nuttin, and dey ain't about to give me no credit, so I dun come to you. I needs a li'l sugar-mama first. I dun need furs and jewels to dress her in, I needs a big car to drive her in, and I needs money to spend. So I want a big win on de horses and den a good investment, and I needs it double quick. So quit messing around and just get at it. I know you'se can do it Lord, I just knows…"

Turning and striding out, he added, "I sure dig you man, I sure dig you."

Some weeks later the kneeling Catholic is still there, mumbling into his hands, when suddenly the doors burst open and the same West Indian, arms around a gorgeous girl, bops straight down to the altar and grinning from ear to ear, laughs, "I knews you could do it, Lord! I done got a Rolls Royce. I owns de racecourse now. Talk about winning hard, I got my pants full of money here. Say 'thank you' to the Lord, honey."

"Thank you, Lord," said the little honey.

As they walked out he said, "And Lord, any time you want a favor you just come to me, 'cause I just dig you, man!"

Shocked and angry, the little Irishman watched them go, then rushed to the altar and prostrated himself, sobbing. "What have I done that you don't hear my suffering and anguish? How come you don't answer my prayers? I have been asking for months. I don't ask much – he is a foreigner too, and the color of the devil himself! How come you give to him and not so much as answer me? Ah, Holy Mary, have pity and tell me what I'm doing so wrong!"

Suddenly the church went dark, a deathly hush descended all around, a steely blue light appeared above the altar and a voice boomed out: (three finger-clicks) "I guess I just don't dig you, man!"

Prayer has to be of the heart. It has to arise from your total being. It has to be true. Only then, and *only* then, has something happened. God and you should not be on formal terms. You should dig him – only then does he dig you.

Formality has killed all religion. Be informal, be friendly, be relaxed with

God. And the moment you are relaxed with God, therapy is finished: you have entered into the world of religion. Therapy is needed only because people have forgotten how to be religious. Therapy was not needed in the Buddha's time. People naturally knew how to be religious. Therapy is a modern need – people have completely forgotten the ways of being religious. They are Christians, they are Hindus, they are Mohammedans, but not religious.

In my commune I have made it a must that everybody should pass through therapies, because unless you pass through therapies you will not be able to connect yourself with prayer. Therapies will help you to unburden the garbage that has been forced on you by the society, therapies will help you to cathart all the rubbish that you have repressed within yourself. Therapies will clean you. And only in a clean, clear heart is prayer possible. And when prayer arises, the miracle has happened. Prayer is the greatest miracle there is.

Enough for today.

CHAPTER 25

With Emptiness, the Matter Is Settled

Master Lu-tsu said:
When the silence comes, not a single thought arises; he who is looking inward suddenly forgets that he is looking. At this time, body and heart must be left completely released. All entanglements have disappeared without trace. Then I no longer know at what place the house of my spirit and my crucible are. If a man wants to make certain of his body, he cannot get at it. This condition is the penetration of heaven into Earth, the time when all wonders return to their roots.

When one is so far advanced that every shadow and every echo has disappeared, so that one is entirely quiet and firm, this is refuge within the cave of energy, where all that is miraculous returns to its roots. One does not alter the place, but the place alters itself: This is incorporeal space where a thousand and ten thousand places are one place. One does not alter the time, but the time alters itself. This is immeasurable time when all the aeons are like a moment.

As long as the heart has not attained absolute tranquility, it cannot move itself. One moves the movement and forgets the movement; this is not movement in itself. Therefore it is said: If, when stimulated by external things, one moves, it is the impulse of the being. If, when not stimulated

by external things, one moves, it is the movement of heaven. But when
no idea arises, the right ideas come. That is the true idea. When things
are quiet and one is quite firm, and the release of heaven suddenly moves,
is this not a movement without purpose? Action through non-action
has just this meaning.

The deepest secret cannot be dispensed with from the beginning to the
end. This is the washing of the heart and the purification of the thoughts;
this is the bath. Its beginning is beyond polarity and it empties again
beyond polarity.

The Buddha speaks of the transient, the creator of consciousness, as being
the fundamental truth of religion. And the whole work of completing life
and human nature lies in the expression "to bring about emptiness."
All religions agree in the one proposition, the finding of the spiritual
Elixir in order to pass from death to life. In what does this spiritual Elixir
consist? It means forever dwelling in purposelessness. The deepest secret
of the bath that is to be found in our teaching is thus confined to the work
of making the heart empty. Therewith the matter is settled.

It was a full moon night. The earth was looking like a bride. The light was showering like rain, and there was great delight in the sky, in the ocean, in the wind. The trees were swaying in the wind as if drunk, intoxicated, lost, and the faraway mountains with their snow-covered peaks looked like buddhas in deep meditation. The wind passing through the ancient pines was pure music, and the quality of a dancing universe was so solid and so tangible that one could have almost touched it. And on such a night of sheer joy and benediction, something of the beyond descended on the earth: a rare woman, Chiyono, became enlightened – she regained paradise, she came home. What a moment to die in time, and to time, and be born in eternity, as eternity! What a moment to disappear utterly, and be for the first time.

The nun Chiyono studied for years, but was unable to find enlightenment. One night she was carrying an old pail filled with water. As she was walking along, she was watching the full moon reflected in the pail of water. Suddenly, the bamboo strips that held the pail together broke and the pail fell apart. The water rushed out, the moon's reflection disappeared, and Chiyono became enlightened.

She wrote this verse:

This way and that way
I tried to keep the pail together,
Hoping the weak bamboo would never break.
Suddenly the bottom fell out...
No more water,
No more moon in the water,
Emptiness in my hand.

Enlightenment happens when it happens: you cannot order it, you cannot cause it to happen. Still, you can do much for it to happen, but whatsoever you do is not going to function as a cause. Whatsoever you do is not going to bring enlightenment to you, but it prepares you to receive it. It comes when it comes. Whatsoever you do simply prepares you to receive it – to see it as it arises, to recognize it when it comes.

It happens...but if you are not ready you go on missing it. It is happening every moment. Every breath that goes in and comes out brings enlightenment to you, because enlightenment is the very stuff the existence is made of. But to recognize it is the problem, to see that it is there is the problem.

God is. There is no question of God's being. The question is: we cannot see him, we don't have eyes. All the meditations and the prayers and the purifications only help you, make you capable of seeing. Once you can see, you will be surprised – it has always been there. Day in, day out, year in, year out, it was showering on you, but you were not sensitive enough to catch hold of it, you were not empty enough to be filled by it. You were too much full of your own ego.

If one comes to fundamentals then this is the most fundamental thing: the moment you are not, enlightenment is. With emptiness, the matter is settled.

If you continue you will remain ignorant and full of darkness. *You* are darkness, your presence is the "dark night of the soul." When you are, you are separate from existence. That's what darkness consists of – the idea of separation – that "There is a gap between me and the whole. Then I am left alone, then there is misery because fear surrounds me: I am so alone, and I am so tiny, and sooner or later death will come and destroy me, and I have no way to protect myself against death." Hence one lives in trembling and fear. But *we* create the trembling and the fear, we cause it – by the very idea of being separate from existence.

The moment you drop this separation, the moment you see that you are not separate, that you *cannot* be separate, that there is *no way* to be separate, that you are part of the whole, intrinsic to the whole, that you are in the whole and the whole is in you, the matter is settled, and settled forever. Death disappears, fear disappears, anguish disappears, and the whole energy that is involved in fear, in anxiety, in anguish, is released. That same energy becomes the celebration of the soul.

What *is* enlightenment? – the capacity to see oneself *as one really is*. We are utterly empty of the ego. The ego is just a make-believe. We have created it, we have projected it, it is our illusion, our dream – it exists not, in itself it is not there. So the more one becomes aware and looks within, the more one finds oneself not. The more you become aware, the less you are. And the moment awareness is full, you have disappeared – no more water, no more reflection of the moon in the water, emptiness in your hands. And it is emptiness…"therewith the matter is settled."

This happened to Chiyono: she had studied for years, she had practiced all kinds of meditations, she had cultivated all kinds of techniques but was unable to find enlightenment.

You cannot cause it. It is beyond you. If you could cause it, it would be below you. If you could cause it, then it would be again nothing but a new decoration for your ego. You cannot cause it. You cannot make it happen. You have to disappear for it to be.

So you can study all the scriptures of the world: you will become very learned, knowledgeable, but you will remain unenlightened. In fact, you will become more unenlightened than you were before because the more knowledge you have the more ego you have, the more you practice ascetic techniques the more your ego is strengthened: "I am doing this and I am doing that, and I have done so much – so many fasts, so many bows." The more you do, the more you feel that now you are worthy and you can claim enlightenment.

Enlightenment cannot be claimed. One has to utterly disappear for it to be. The mind has to cease for God to be. Call it God or enlightenment – it is the same thing.

"Chiyono studied for years but was unable to find enlightenment."

Enlightenment is not something that you can find by searching; it comes to you when all search proves futile. And remember, I am not saying don't search, because unless you search you will never come to know that search is futile. And I am not saying don't meditate; if you don't meditate you will never come to understand that there is a meditation which you cannot do but which comes to you.

Your meditations will simply cleanse your eyes, will make you more perceptive. Your heart will become more alert, aware, loving, sensitive. Your being will start seeing things you had not seen before. You will start exploring new spaces within your being. Something new will happen every day, every moment. Your meditations are like a bath: they will give you a freshness – but that freshness is not enlightenment. That only prepares the way. You never reach to enlightenment. It is always the other way round: enlightenment reaches to you.

Prepare the way for God so that he can reach you. You cannot find Him. You can only wait, in deep trust, so that *he* can find you.

That's how Chiyono was missing: she was searching, seeking, she was *much* too involved in this inquiry. But this inquiry will also feed your ego, that "I am a seeker," that "I am no ordinary man," that "I am spiritual," that "I am religious," that "I am holy." And if that attitude of "holier than thou" arises, you are lost forever. That is the greatest sin you can commit in your life, the greatest fall. If the idea arises in you that, "I am holier than others" that "I am a saint and others are sinners," that "Look at my virtuous life," if you become righteous you are lost, because this righteous ego will be the most subtle ego and it will be very difficult for you to drop it. It is easier to drop iron chains. But if you can have golden chains studded with diamonds, it will become more and more difficult to drop them because they will not look like chains, they will look like valuable ornaments.

It is easy to get out of a dirty prison cell, but if it is a palace, who wants to get out of it? Really one wants to get into it, not out of it. The sinner is closer to God than the saint, because the sinner wants to get out of his bondage and the saint is enjoying an ego-trip.

Chiyono was a nun. She must have been enjoying subtle, righteous attitudes – knowledgeability, virtue – her renunciation was great. It is said that she was one of the most beautiful women, so beautiful that when she went into one monastery they refused her, because to have such a beautiful woman in there would create trouble for the monks. Then she had to disfigure her face to enter into another monastery. She must have been a very beautiful woman, but just think…she disfigured her face, made it ugly, but deep down she must have been thinking, "Look at my renunciation. I was one of the most beautiful women, I have disfigured my face – nobody has done this before, or since. Look at my renunciation, look at my detachment from the body: I don't care a bit about beauty, I am bent upon finding enlightenment, whatsoever the cost." And she continued missing.

But one full-moon night it happened. It happened out of the blue, suddenly. It always happens out of the blue, it always happens suddenly. But I am not saying that it could have happened to anybody else – it happened to Chiyono. All that she had done had not caused it, but all that she had done had caused one thing in her: the understanding that whatsoever you do you fail, that man cannot succeed.

She must have come to a state of utter hopelessness. That hopelessness can be felt only when you have done all that you can do. And when that hopelessness comes, hope has arrived – because in that hopelessness the ego is shattered to the ground. One no longer claims.

The ego disappears only from the peak, when it has come to its crescendo. You cannot drop a lukewarm ego. No, that is not possible, because it still hopes. It says, "Who knows? – a few efforts more, a few more practices, a little more renunciation… Who knows? We have not looked in all the directions yet, there is still a possibility" – and the ego lingers. But when you have explored, searched – in all possible directions – and you have always failed, nothing but failure has been your experience, how long can you continue searching, seeking? One day, searching and seeking drop.

So remember this paradox: enlightenment is possible only to those who stop seeking. But who can stop seeking? – only one who has searched deeply enough. This is the paradox. This is one of the great secrets to be understood. Let it sink into your heart.

There is every possibility of choosing one. There are people who say, "Seek, and ye shall find" – that is only half the truth. Just by seeking nobody has ever found. Then there are people who say, "If by seeking, God cannot be found, then why seek at all? Wait. It will happen through his grace." It never happens that way either. You have been waiting for centuries, for lives, and it has not happened: it is enough to prove that it doesn't happen that way. Then how does it happen? It happens to a seeker when he drops his seeking.

It happens to one who has searched with his total potential and has failed, utterly failed. In that failure, the first ray of light, and then it takes you by surprise! When you are completely feeling hopeless, when you are thinking to forget all about enlightenment, when the search has stopped, when even the desire to be enlightened has left you, suddenly it is there…and "therewith the matter is settled."

That's how it happened to Chiyono, that's how it happened to Buddha, that's how it always happens.

Buddha worked for six years – hard work. I think nobody else has done such hard work. He did whatsoever he was told, whatsoever he heard could be done, whatsoever he could gather from anywhere. He went to every kind of Master and he did real, arduous work – sincere, serious. But then one day, after six years of wastage, he realized the fact that it was not going to happen that way, that "The more I work for it, the more I am."

That day he relaxed. He dropped the whole search. And that very night... and again it was a full-moon night. The full moon has something to do with it: the full moon affects your heart as deeply as it affects the ocean. The full moon stirs you towards beauty and beatitude. It creates something in you...an elixir. It makes you so sensitive that you can see things you had never seen before.

It was a full-moon night. Buddha relaxed, utterly relaxed, slept for the first time – because when you are searching for something how can you sleep? Even in sleep the search continues, the desire goes on creating dreams. Now all had failed. He had seen the world, the kingdom, the joys and the miseries of love and relationship, the agony and the ecstasy of the body, of the mind; and then he had been an ascetic, a monk, followed many paths – that too he had seen. He saw the so-called world and he had seen the so-called other-worldly world, and both had failed. Now there was nowhere to go, not even a single inch to move. All desire disappeared. When one is so hopeless, how can one desire? Desire means hope. Desire means that still something can be done.

That night Buddha came to know that *nothing* can be done, nothing at all. Just see the point, it is of tremendous beauty: nothing can be done, nothing at all. He relaxed. His body must have been in a let-go, his heart in a let-go. No desire, no future – this moment was all.

And it was a full-moon night, and he slept deeply, and in the morning when he woke up he not only woke up from his ordinary sleep, he woke up from the metaphysical sleep we all are living in. He became awakened.

He used to say to his disciples, "I worked hard and could not attain, and when I had dropped the very idea of work, then I attained."

That's why I call my work "the play." You have to be in a paradoxical state. That is the meaning of the word *play*. You work very seriously, as if through work something is going to happen, but it never happens through work. It happens only when work disappears and playfulness arises, relaxation arises; and not a cultivated relaxation either, but a relaxation that comes out of the understanding that: "In all that I can do, my 'I' will go on persisting; all that I can do will go on feeding my ego, and the ego is the barrier. So my doing is really my undoing." Seeing this, doing evaporates. And when there is no doing, how can the doer

exist? Doing gone, the doer follows it just like a shadow. And then you are left –
total, whole, in the whole, part of this cosmic play. That is enlightenment.

These sutras are of tremendous value. Meditate over them.

> Master Lu-tsu said:
> When the silence comes, not a single thought arises; he who is
> looking inward suddenly forgets that he is looking.

There are two kinds of silences: one is that which you cultivate, the other is
that which arrives. Your cultivated silence is nothing but repressed noise. You can
sit silently, and if you sit long and you continue the practice for months and years
together, slowly slowly you will become capable of repressing all noise inside. But
still you will be sitting on a volcano – it can erupt any moment, any small excuse
will do. This is not real silence, this is just imposed silence.

This is what is happening all around the world: the people who try to
meditate, the people who try to become silent, are only imposing a silence upon
themselves. It can be imposed. You can have a layer of silence around yourself,
but that is just deceiving yourself and nothing else. That layer is not going to help
you or anybody else around you.

Unless silence arises from your very being – not imposed from the without
on the within but comes just the other way round, comes, wells up from the
within towards the without, rises from the center towards the circumference...
that is a totally different phenomenon.

Lu-tsu said, *When the silence comes*. Remember, not brought, not forced, but
when it comes – *not a single thought arises*. Then you are not sitting on a volcano.
That's why my whole approach is: rather than cultivating silence, cathart your
inner noise, throw it out.

People become very puzzled when they come to me for the first time. If
they have been with some Buddhist master, then they were doing vipassana,
sitting, forcing themselves into a certain static posture. Why the static posture?
– because when the body is forced to remain in one posture, mind also is
forced to remain in one posture. Body and mind function together.

Mind is the inner aspect of the body. It is a material phenomenon, it has
nothing to do with your being. It is as much matter as your body. So if you
do something with the body that automatically happens to the mind. Hence
down the ages people have been cultivating postures – sit in a lotus posture,
force your body to be like a statue, a marble statue. If your body is *really* still,

forced, you will see your mind falls into a kind of silence, which is false, which is not true. He has just been forced to be silent by the body posture. You try it: just make the posture of anger – with your fists, your face, your teeth, just go into the posture of anger – and you will be surprised, you start feeling angry. That's what the actor does: he moves the body into the posture, and following it, mind comes in.

Two great psychologists, James and Lange, discovered a very strange theory at the beginning of this century. It is known as the James-Lange theory. They said something very uncommon which goes against the whole common sense of the ages. Ordinarily we think that when a man is afraid he runs away, in fear he starts running. James and Lange said it is not true – because he runs, that's why he feels fear.

It looks absurd, but it has some truth in it – half. The common sense truth was half, this too is another half of the same whole. If you start laughing, you will find yourself feeling a little less sad than you were before. You just go and sit with a few friends who are laughing, telling jokes, and you forget your sadness, your misery – you start laughing and once you start laughing you are feeling good. You started with the body....

Try it! If you are feeling sad, start running, go running around the block seven times, breathing deep breaths, in the sun, in the wind, and after seven rounds, stand and see whether your mind is the same. No, it can't be the same. The bodily change has changed the mind. The body chemistry changes the mind. Hence the yoga postures: they are all postures to force the mind into a certain pattern. That is not real silence.

The real silence has to be a silence that comes on its own. My suggestion is: don't force your body. Rather, dance, sing, move, run, jog, swim. Let the body have all kinds of movements so your mind also has all kinds of movements, and through all those kinds of inner movements, the mind starts catharting, releasing its poisons.

Shout, be angry, beat a pillow and you will be surprised – after beating a pillow you feel very good: something in the mind has been released. It does not matter whether you were beating your wife, your husband, or the pillow. The pillow will do as perfectly well as and better than beating the wife or husband, because the body does not know whom you are beating. Just the very posture of beating and the mind starts releasing its anger. Mind and body collaborate.

Start with catharsis, so that you become empty of all the rubbish that has been accumulating in you from your very childhood. You were angry but you could not be angry because the mother becomes mad if you become angry – so you repressed it. You were angry, you wanted to shout, but you could not shout, rather, on the contrary, you smiled – *all that* is accumulated in you. It has to be thrown out, and then wait...and a silence starts descending in you. That silence has a beauty of its own. It is totally different – its quality is different, its depth is different.

When the silence comes, not a single thought arises

Not that you force your thinking not to arise, not that you keep watch, not that you become very tight and you won't allow a single thought to pass. You are not struggling, you are in a let-go, but nothing arises – that is beautiful, when no thought arises, when thoughts disappear of their own accord. Then you are utterly silent. And this silence is positive, the forced silence is negative.

He who is looking inward suddenly forgets that he is looking.

And in this experience this will happen:

He who is looking inward suddenly forgets that he is looking.

This is *real* inward looking – when you forget that you are looking inwards. If you remember that you are looking inward, that again is a thought and nothing else. First you were looking outward, now you are looking inward, but the ego is there. First it was extrovert, now it is introvert, but the ego is there. First you were looking at the trees, now you are looking at the thoughts; first you were looking at the objects, now you are looking at the subject – but the whole thing remains the same: you are still divided in two – the looker and the looked upon, the observer and the observed, the subject and the object. The duality persists.

This is not real silence, because when there are two there is bound to be conflict. Two cannot be silent. When you are one, then there is silence because there is no possibility of any conflict.

Allow silence to descend on you rather than forcing it. The forced silence is artificial, arbitrary. That is one of the great changes that I am trying to make here with you, with my people. All the old methods are basically of enforcing something. My own understanding is: never enforce anything. Rather, throw out all junk that you have been carrying, become more and more empty, become more roomy, create a more space in you. And in that space the silence comes.

Nature abhors emptiness, and if you can throw all the junk out and you are empty, you will see something from the beyond starts descending in you: a dancing energy enters in you, in your every cell you are full of song – wordless, soundless – a divine music. In this music there is nobody who is looking. In this music there is nobody who is looked at. The observer is the observed, the dancer has become the dance, and all duality has disappeared.

This non-duality is the only real silence.

At this time, body and heart must be left completely released.

And in such moments you should remain in a let-go. Forget all your postures. Forget everything that you try to do. Don't try to do anything, be in a state of non-doing – just relaxed, utterly relaxed, doing nothing – because the more relaxed you are the more silence can penetrate into your being – just open, vulnerable, relaxed.

All entanglements have disappeared without trace.

And then you will be surprised – all those desires that you have been trying to drop and were unable to drop have disappeared on their own. All entanglements, all occupations of the mind, all those thoughts, all that traffic of the mind is no more there. You will be surprised – where have all those people gone? You were trying hard, and not even a single thought can be forced out when you try. You can do it: if you want to throw out a single thought, you will be an utter failure. You will not be able to throw it out. The more you will throw it out, the more it will bump in, rebound in.

Just sit silently and try not to think of a monkey, and you will see – it is a simple experiment – not one, but many monkeys will start coming, and they will make faces at you. And the more you push them away the more they will knock on your doors, and they will say, "We want to come in." And monkeys are not so polite: they may not even ask, they may simply jump in – you will be surrounded by monkeys and monkeys. The more you try to forget them the more they will be there, because to try to forget something is nothing but remembering it. It is another way of remembering. You cannot forget by making efforts.

When silence descends, then suddenly all entanglements disappear – and without a trace! They don't even leave a trace behind. You cannot believe that all that noise…where has it gone? You cannot believe that it ever existed in you. You cannot believe that it still exists in others. This is one of the basic problems every realized person has to face.

When you come to me with all your problems you don't understand my difficulty. My difficulty basically is: how can you manage so many problems, how do you go on managing? You are doing something really incredible, something impossible! – because even if I try to hold to a thought, it slips away. I cannot hold it, it wants to get out. And you say that you want to stop your thoughts and you cannot stop, and you are tired and you are weary and you are fed up and bored. You are really doing something impossible!

And the day silence will descend on you, you will understand…not even a trace. You cannot believe that they had ever existed in you. They have simply disappeared. They were just shadows. Thoughts are not substantial, just shadows. When a shadow disappears it doesn't leave a trace. You cannot find the footprints of a shadow, because in the first place it was nonsubstantial. So are your thoughts, so is your mind.

> *Then I no longer know at what place the house of my spirit and*
> *my crucible are.*

And when this state happens, silence descends in you and you are overwhelmed by it, and you don't know whether you are looking in or out, you don't know who is the looker and who is the looked upon.

> *Then I no longer know at what place the house of my spirit and*
> *my crucible are.*

Then you cannot say who you are. You are, in fact for the first time you are – but who, what? No answer will be coming.

Bodhidharma was an outrageous man and annoyed the Emperor Wu greatly. Bodhidharma was extremely blunt, he would call a spade a spade and nothing else. The Emperor asked Bodhidharma, "I have done many virtuous deeds. What will be my reward in heaven?"

Bodhidharma looked with great contempt at the Emperor and said, "Reward? You will fall into hell! What heaven are you talking about?"

The Emperor said, "For my virtuous deeds I will fall into hell? And I have made so many temples and thousands of Buddha-statues, and thousands of Buddhist monks are maintained, monasteries are maintained from the treasury, and I am doing so much service to Buddha's *dhamma*, his message. The whole country is becoming Buddhist. People are meditating, worshipping, scriptures are being translated, thousands of scholars are working on the translations, and you think there will be no reward? Are not my acts holy?"

And Bodhidharma said, "Holy? There is nothing holy in the world. There is nothing holy, nothing unholy. But mind you," he said, "drop this idea of being a virtuous man, drop this idea of doing great things, otherwise you will fall into the seventh hell."

Naturally the Emperor was annoyed, irritated...must have been a very polished and cultured man, otherwise he would have been violent with Bodhidharma. But even he could not resist the temptation: annoyed, angry, he asked, "Then who are you standing before me? Nothing holy, nothing unholy, no virtue? Who are you standing before me?"

Bodhidharma laughed and said, "I don't know, sir."

But the Emperor could not understand. You also would have missed.

Ordinarily people think that a man who has arrived knows who he is – we call him the man of self-knowledge – and Bodhidharma says, "I don't know." This is the highest peak of self-knowledge, this is *real* self-knowledge. One has disappeared: who is there to know? Knowing means the knower and the known, there is no duality anymore: who is there to know? There is just silence, *tremendous* silence, no division, indivisibility: how could Bodhidharma say "I know"?

If he had said, "Yes, I know that I am an eternal soul," that would have been very ordinary. Maybe Wu would have been more convinced, but Bodhidharma would have lost face. He was true. He said, "I don't know." Who follows a man who says, "I don't know who I am"?

Wu dropped the idea of following this man. And when Emperor Wu could not understand Bodhidharma, Bodhidharma said, "If even the Emperor cannot understand me, then what about others?"

So he went into the mountains and sat for nine years, facing a wall. When people would come and ask, "Why do you go on facing a wall?" he would say, "Because if I face people they also look like walls. It is better to face the wall. I will face a person only when I see that he is not a wall, that he can respond, that he can understand."

His statement that "I don't know" is of immense beauty, grandeur.

Then I no longer know at what place the house of my spirit and
my crucible are. If a man wants to make certain of his body,
he cannot get at it.

In this moment, when silence overwhelms you, encompasses you, if you want to make sure about your body you will not be able to get at it. There is no body anymore, or, the whole existence is your body because you are not separated anymore. You cannot define, you cannot draw a line that "This is my body." The whole existence is your body, or, there is no body at all.

This sometimes can drive you crazy. Beware! Don't be worried if sometimes it happens that you open your eyes and you cannot find your body, that you cannot see it at all.

Just the other night a sannyasin was asking me, "When I stand before a mirror I feel very puzzled, because I cannot see that this reflection is mine." Now it is puzzling. He avoids the mirror because whenever he looks into the mirror this problem arises: "Who is this fellow?" He cannot feel that "This is me." Now it can drive you crazy, and he was very disturbed because of it.

But this is a beneficial sign, a confirmatory sign. Something really good is happening: he is becoming disidentified with the body. It is good, he is on the right way. I told him to look into the mirror as much as possible: whenever he has time to just sit before the mirror, see the body reflected in the mirror and go on feeling that "This is not me." There is no need to repeat "This is not me" because that would be false. Just feel! And it is happening to him of its own accord, so there is no problem. This will be his natural meditation. This is enough. Slowly slowly, one day, the moment will arrive when he will not be able to see the reflection in the mirror. That is even more disorienting.

It happened to Swabhava. I had given this meditation to him. For months he did it, and then one day he was standing before the mirror and the reflection disappeared. He rubbed his eyes: what is happening? Had he gone mad? The mirror was there, he was standing before the mirror, and the reflection had disappeared. And that day became a great day of transformation for his being.

Now Swabhava is a totally different person, utterly different. When he had come to me for the first time, he was just ego and nothing else – and a Punjabi ego, which is the most dangerous in India. In fact he was trapped because of his Punjabi ego. He wanted to know about truth, and I asked him, "Are you ready to risk?" Now that was a challenge to his ego: "Are you courageous enough to risk all?" He could not say no, he could not withdraw. He said, "Yes." He looked a little frightened – who knows what will be expected of him? – but he took the jump. And the day it happened in the mirror that his reflection disappeared, something very deep inside him changed, moved.

Now you can see Swabhava in a totally different way. He has become so simple, so humble, goes on working in the Vipassana godown. He is a rich man, a millionaire. He was a boss in a big factory, his own factory. Hundreds of people were working under him. Now he is working like a laborer in the ashram but has never been so happy as he is now, has never been so blissful as he is now.

This moment may come to you one day: that meditating, silence descends and you cannot find your body, if you want to look in the mirror, you cannot see your face. Don't be worried. Take it as a very confirmatory sign. Something beautiful is on the way: your old identity is eroding, your old idea of yourself is disappearing, and you have to disappear totally before God can take possession of you.

> *If a man wants to make certain of his body, he cannot get at it. This*
> *condition is the penetration of heaven into Earth…*

When you cannot see your body, when you cannot feel your body, you cannot touch your body, this is *the penetration of heaven into Earth* – paradise is descending, God is coming to you – God has reached! His heart is with your heart, his hand is in your hand. That's why you have disappeared: the part has become the whole.

> *…the time when all wonders return to their roots.*

And now your whole life will be nothing but wonder. Each moment will be a unique moment. Each experience will be incredible, just far out. Your life from now onwards will be sheer poetry. From now onwards you will never be bored, each moment life is so new, how can one be bored? People are bored because they go on carrying their old, dead, dull ego. When there is no ego there is no boredom. Then life is delight! Then each single thing that happens is a gift from God. One feels constantly like bowing down, one feels constantly in gratitude…

> *…the time when all wonders return to their roots.*

> *When one is so far advanced that every shadow and every echo*
> *has disappeared…*

You must remember that first Lu-tsu says: A moment comes when gods are in the valley. You feel yourself sitting on a hilltop and the whole world is in the valley, you can hear the sounds – and very clearly, and very distinctly – but they are faraway, distant, like echoes in the valley. Now even those echoes disappear. All shadows are gone.

Remember Chiyono? She wrote these words in celebration of her enlightenment:

This way and that way
I tried to keep the pail together,
Hoping the weak bamboo would never break.
Suddenly the bottom fell out...
No more water,
No more moon in the water,
Emptiness in my hand.

All reflections, shadows, echoes are gone. Only that which is remains, and the utter beauty of it.

> ...*so that one is entirely quiet and firm, this is refuge within the cave*
> *of energy, where all that is miraculous returns to its roots.*

The whole life outside becomes a constant wonder. You are again a child on the seabeach, running in the wind and in the sun, and collecting seashells and colored stones as if you have found a mine of diamonds. The whole existence outside takes the quality of wonder. And what happens inside?

> ...*that is miraculous returns to its roots.*

And in the deep insight, parallel to the outside wonder, the *miraculous returns to its roots.*

What is the miracle? To *be* is the greatest miracle, just to be. You need not be rich to feel it, you need not be educated to feel it, you need not be famous to feel it. Just to be! That you are is the greatest miracle there is, the greatest mystery. Why are you? There is no reason. You have not earned it, you had not even asked for it. It has simply happened.

So outside there is wonder, inside the world of miracles – this is how the enlightened person lives. And now these things start happening.

One does not alter the place, but the place alters itself.

Now you need not go to the Himalayas, you need not renounce the marketplace. You are in the marketplace, but the place is no more the same – the place alters itself. Even the marketplace becomes so beautiful that the Himalayas are nothing compared to it. The ordinary reality becomes suffused with *extraordinary* beauty. The same trees that you had been passing every day and had never looked at, were always oblivious of, suddenly burst forth in bloom, suddenly burst forth on your consciousness with all their flowers and fragrance. Life becomes very colorful, psychedelic, and things change themselves – just because you have come to this inner silence, this egolessness.

One does not alter the place, but the place alters itself.

That's why I insist again and again that my sannyasins are not to leave the world. Let this be the criterion of your enlightenment: that the world has to change itself when you are enlightened – it *has* to change.

And by escaping from the world you will not be going anywhere: wherever you go you will create the same world again, because the blueprint for creating it is within you. You can leave one woman thinking that because of this woman the problems arise – the children are there, and the house, and all the responsibilities that you have accumulated throughout your life. You can leave this woman and these poor children and you can escape – many have done that down the ages – but you had fallen in love with this woman, that possibility to fall in love again is within you. You will fall in love again…with some other woman. And sooner or later – and it is going to be sooner than later – another family will arise, another man, another woman, children, responsibilities.

You cannot change life easily. You only change the context, but deep down you carry the blueprint. The context was created by the blueprint. It is like a seed: you destroy the tree but you carry the seed; wherever the seed will fall into the soil again, the tree will be back. The seed has to be burned.

Then wherever you are this miracle will be felt.

One does not alter the place, but the place alters itself.

This very world becomes paradise, this very world nirvana, this very body the body of Buddha.

> *This is incorporeal space where a thousand and ten thousand places*
> *are one place. One does not alter the time, but the time alters itself.*
> *This is immeasurable time when all the aeons are like a moment.*

You don't alter anything. And these two are the constituents of the world. Just see, what Lu-tsu is saying is now perfectly collaborated by modern physics. Albert Einstein says that the world consists only of two things, time and space. And in fact they are not two, but one, so he has to coin a new word. He does not call it time and space, he calls it "spatiotime": one word with not even a hyphen needed between the two, because time is the fourth dimension of space. You need not change space, you need not change time. They change of their own accord. *Just change yourself.* With the change in the heart, the whole existence changes.

Heaven is not somewhere else, neither is hell somewhere else. It is within you, both are within you. You create them. But people go on doing stupid things.

Just a few days ago a man wrote me a letter: "What is happening?" He has changed wives four times. This is now the fourth time he has got married, this is the fourth woman he is living with. And now he says, "What always happens? In the beginning everything seems to be beautiful, and within six months it is the same all over again." It will happen the same all over again, because you are the same. And there are complexities.

For example, you are fed up with your wife – mind is always hankering for the new, something new, sensational. You have seen the woman, you are acquainted with her whole topography. Now you know her geography, nothing more is left to explore. You become interested in some other woman. When you become interested in some other woman, your woman will start creating more trouble for you. Seeing that you are not interested in her but in somebody else, jealousy will arise. She will create much trouble – she will nag you, she will become nasty, and the more she will nag the more you will be repelled by her.

Now see the vicious circle: she wants you to be with her, but whatsoever she is doing has repelled you. She will become more and more possessive and more and more jealous, and life in the home will become impossible to live. It will be hell. You will avoid her as much as you can. You will work late in the office, even if there is no work you will go on sitting in the office, because to go home means to face your woman, and again the same misery. And what does she actually want? She wants you to be with her. But whatsoever she is doing is just the opposite: she is driving you away. And the more she will drive you away, the more the other woman will look beautiful, fantastic. The more the other woman will look fantastic and beautiful, the more you would like to be with her and she would like to be with you. And soon she will start saying, "Leave the other woman if you want to be with me."

Now she does not know that the beauty that the man is finding in her will disappear the moment he leaves the other woman, because ninety percent of the beauty that he is seeing in this woman depends on the other woman. She thinks the other woman is her enemy, she is not. In fact it is because of the other woman that this man has fallen in love with her. These are unconscious ways. Seeds that you don't see and they go on working. And she will feel very happy. And the more she will feel happy and the more you would like to be with her, the more your woman will look ugly in comparison. Soon you would like to live with this woman forever. You leave the other woman, you start living with this woman. The day you leave the other woman the whole context has changed: now you will be with this new woman but she will not look so beautiful, so alluring. The hypnosis will start disappearing because there is nobody else to repel you.

Within six months the hypnosis has disappeared: this woman is as the other was. Now the geography explored, you are finished. And the woman cannot believe what has happened – "This man was so much in love. What happened?" She destroyed it herself. And this man cannot believe what happened – "This woman was so incredible, and has proved so ordinary." Again the movement, the same movement, the same vicious circle with the same seed deep in the unconscious, he will start falling in love with somebody else. People fall in love and fall out of love unconsciously. They go on changing partners but they don't change themselves. They go on changing the outside but they remain the same.

You can go on changing – that's what you have been doing for many many lives, the same repetition. It is a vicious circle that goes on moving. It is a wheel: the same spokes come on the top and go down, and again come on the top and go down. It is the wheel that goes on moving, and you are caught in the wheel.

Become aware. You need not change the place, you need not change time, you need not change anything on the outside. The outside is as perfect as it can be. There is just one thing you have to do – you have to become more conscious, more alert, more aware, more empty, so there is nothing to project on the outside. You have to burn all the seeds inside, you have to burn the whole blueprint inside. Once that blueprint is burnt, seeds are burnt, and you have thrown all that was inside and you are just empty, something from the beyond enters in you – paradise penetrates into the earth – and at that point is the moment of transformation.

With this change, the whole existence is totally different. The same woman, the same children, the same people, the same office, the same marketplace, but it is no more the same because you are no more the same. This is the right way of transformation: never start from the without, start from the within.

> As long as the heart has not attained absolute tranquility, it cannot move itself. One moves the movement and forgets the movement; this is not movement in itself. Therefore it is said: If, when stimulated by external things, one moves, it is the impulse of the being. If, when not stimulated by external things, one moves, it is the movement of heaven.

Remember, let heaven move you, allow God to move you, surrender to the total. Otherwise you will go on reacting to situations, and the situations will go on functioning on you, on your unconscious, and you will remain the same. You can change women, you can change men, you can change jobs, you can change houses, you can go on changing things but nothing will really ever change. Unless the whole takes possession of you and your heart is no more moved by outer things, but is moved by the innermost core of your being – call it God, heaven, Tao – when you are not moving it, when you are just an instrument in the hands of the total, this is what Jesus means when he says, "Thy kingdom come, thy will be done." That is his way of saying, a Jewish way of saying the same truth. This is a Chinese way of saying it: "Let heaven move your heart".

> But when no idea arises, the right ideas come.

And this is the miracle: when *no* ideas arise then whatsoever you do is the right thing. There is no question of deciding what is right and what is wrong. When the mind is silent and the heart is moved by God, whatsoever happens is right.

It is not that if you do right things you will become a saint. If you are a saint, then whatsoever you do is right. If you are trying to become a saint by doing right you will simply become repressed and nothing else. You will go on repressing the wrong and you will go on pretending the right. You will be a hypocrite.

Don't try to become a saint. Let God take possession of you. You just be empty, surrendered, in a state of let-go: let him move your heart, and then all is beautiful. Then whatsoever happens is virtuous, then wrong is not possible. In short, whatsoever comes out of the ego is wrong. That's why Bodhidharma said, "You will go into hell. Although you have been doing things which look *apparently* virtuous, religious, but deep down you are feeling a gratification in the ego." Whatsoever comes out of the ego is going to take you into misery.

Drop the ego, and then let things happen. Just as when the wind comes and the trees sway and the sun rises and the birds sing, let the whole possess you, don't live a private life, on your own. Let God live through you, then all is good. All that is out of God is good.

> *That is the true idea. When things are quiet and one is quite firm, and the release of heaven suddenly moves, is this not a movement without purpose?*

Now there is no purpose in your life because there is no private goal.

> *Action through non-action has just this meaning.*

One lives because God wants to live through one, one does because God wants to do something through one, but one is not interested this way or that. Whatsoever role is given to you, you go on playing it. It is his drama, he is the author of it and the director of it – you do your act as perfectly as you can. Whatsoever act is given to you, you perform it.

If you are a householder then be a householder, if you are a businessman then remain a businessman. There is no need to change these things. All that is needed is to drop the idea that you are the doer, drop the idea that you have to attain to some goal, drop the idea that you have to reach somewhere. Let him take you wherever he wants – you be just a dry leaf in the wind – and then all is good, and then life is blissful.

There can't be any tension now, can't be any anxiety. You cannot fail, you can never feel frustrated, because in the first place you were not expecting anything. This is living a purposeless life.

> *Action through non-action has just this meaning.*
> *The deepest secret cannot be dispensed with from the beginning to the end. This is the washing of the heart and the purification of the thoughts; this is the bath.*

Lu-tsu says: This we call "the bath" – God showers on you and you are cleansed, utterly cleansed. God floods you, and you are not left anywhere, not even in a corner somewhere in the unconscious. No nook or corner is left without God: he fills you totally. God is light, and when *he fills you* totally this is called enlightenment: you are full of light.

> *Its beginning is beyond polarity and it empties again*
> *beyond polarity.*

And now you have come home. Now again you are one as you were before you were born, as you were before the beginning. Zen people call it "the original face." The original face is one, single – neither man nor woman, neither positive nor negative. The moment you are born, the moment you enter into the manifested world, you become two.

When you enter meditation again deep silence descends, suddenly the two have disappeared – you have become one again. In the beginning you are beyond polarity, in the end you are again beyond polarity. Only in between the two are you divided. In the middle is the world. In the beginning is God, in the end is God. The source is the goal. Either fall back into the source or disappear in the goal; it is saying the same thing in different ways.

> *The Buddha speaks of the transient, the creator of consciousness,*
> *as being the fundamental truth of religion. And the whole work of*
> *completing life and human nature lies in the expression "to bring*
> *about emptiness."*

The whole of religion can be reduced to a simple phenomenon, *to bring about emptiness* – be empty and you will be full, remain full and you will remain empty. Be utterly absent and the presence of the beyond will penetrate you. Go on holding yourself, clinging to yourself, and you will remain just an emptiness, a shadow, a reflection, not a reality.

> *All the religions agree in the one proposition, the finding of the*
> *spiritual Elixir in order to pass from death to life.*

And this is the Elixir all the religions have been searching for: the secret of being utterly empty. Then you cannot die because there is nobody to die, you have already disappeared. Now there is no possibility of death, you have already died! The man who has died as an ego has attained eternal life.

> *In what does this spiritual Elixir consist? It means forever dwelling in*
> *purposelessness.*

Now when the ego is no more there and you are empty, and the silence has descended in you, how will you live? You will live eternally in purposelessness.

Is there any purpose when a rosebush blooms? Is there any purpose when a bird starts singing in the morning? Is there any purpose when the sun rises? Is there any purpose in this existence at all?

This existence is not a business, hence there is no purpose. It is sheer joy, playfulness, what the Hindus call *leela*. It is just delight in energy. Energy is there and energy is dancing and delighting. When you have energy you delight in it: you run, you sing, you dance, you swim, you play. Energy delights in expression. You become creative – you paint, you write poetry, you compose music – out of sheer energy. Existence is energy and the energy wants to dance, for no purpose at all. Dance for dance's sake, art for art's sake, love for love's sake...existence for existence's sake.

> *It means forever dwelling in purposelessness. The deepest secret of the*
> *bath that is to be found in our teaching is thus confined to the work*
> *of making the heart empty.*

Do only one thing: pour out all that you are carrying in the heart – throw it out – and you have done the only fundamental thing that is needed to be done.

> *Therewith the matter is settled.*

A tremendously beautiful statement: *Therewith the matter is settled.* Nothing else is needed. No scriptures are needed, no temples are needed, no priests are needed – *therewith the matter is settled.* Only one thing is needed: become empty so God can flow in you. Make space for him. Be a hollow bamboo so he can make a flute out of you. And when he sings there is beauty, when he sings there is ecstasy, when he sings there is laughter.

When you sing there is only misery, and tears, and agony, because the ego is a very small thing. It cannot contain ecstasy, it can only contain agony. To contain ecstasy you will have to become infinite because ecstasy is infinite. If you want to contain the ocean you will have to become vast.

By being empty one becomes vast, by being empty one becomes spacious – you become ready. And God can become a guest if the host is ready. By being empty you also become the host. Become a host: God has been waiting at your door for long, knocking, but you don't listen.

There is so much noise within you – how can you listen to the knock? You are so preoccupied with your own foolish things, how can you see the sheer beauty of purposelessness? You are worried about how to have a bigger bank balance, you are worried about how to succeed in politics, you are worried about how to become a little more famous, and God goes on knocking on your door. He is ready to pour himself into you but you are not ready to receive him.

Yes, Lu-tsu is right: the most fundamental thing of all the religions is to bring about emptiness. The whole work of all the yogas, tantras, of all the alchemical systems – Tao, Sufi, Hassid – consists in only one thing: making the heart empty.

Therewith the matter is settled.

I will repeat this beautiful story:

The nun called Chiyono studied for years but she was unable to find enlightenment. One night, she was carrying an old pail filled with water to her house. As she was walking along, she was watching the full moon beautifully reflected in the pail of water. Suddenly the bamboo strips that held the pail together snapped and broke and the pail fell apart. And as the water rushed out, the moon's reflection disappeared, and Chiyono became enlightened.

She wrote this verse:

This way and that way
I tried to keep the pail together,
Hoping the weak bamboo would never break.
Suddenly the bottom fell out.
No more water,
No more moon in the water,
Emptiness in my hand.

And *therewith the matter is settled…*
Enough for today.

CHAPTER 26

Because of Love, We Are Together

The first question:

Osho,
Can you give me a message to take to the Western world so that
people there might understand you and your followers?

My message is very simple. That's why it is difficult to understand. I teach the obvious, it is not complex at all. Because it is not complex there is nothing much to understand in it. It has to be lived, experienced. My message is not verbal, logical, rational. It is existential. So those who want to understand it intellectually will only misunderstand it.

Still, there are a few fundamentals I would like to tell you. One: up to now man has lived only half-heartedly. In the East, in the West, man has remained lopsided. Neither has the Eastern man been whole nor has the Western man been whole. The West has chosen the body, is body-oriented; the East has chosen the soul, is soul-oriented; and man is both, a great harmony of both. Man is both and a transcendence. Neither in the East nor in the West has man been accepted totally. We have not yet dared to accept man in his totality.

That is one of the most fundamental things I want everybody to understand about my teaching: I teach the whole man. The very idea of East and West is nonsense. That too is because of the ancient division. All divisions have to be dissolved. I teach one world. East and West have to disappear. Both are schizophrenic. The West is right-handed, the East is left-handed; the West is active, the East is passive; the West is extrovert, the East is introvert – but man is both and beyond both.

To be total, one has to be as capable of being extrovert as of being introvert. To be total, one has to be capable of breathing out and breathing in. Inhalation is as much needed as exhalation. In fact, they are not two: exhalation-inhalation is *one* process.

The West has chosen the outside world – matter – has become very scientific, has created great technology, but man is crushed underneath that technology because man has not grown simultaneously. Man is lagging far behind, science has gone far ahead, and the science that man has created is now destroying man himself.

Man's inner world has remained poor in the West, man is spiritually starved in the West. And the same has happened in the East from the other extreme: man has completely denied his body, his world. The East has insisted on denying all that is outside you, renouncing the manifested world and just going in, remaining at your center. The East is spiritually rich but materially very poor and starved. The East has suffered, the West has suffered.

My message is: now it is time that we should drop this division of the outer and the inner, of the lower and the higher, of the left-handed and the right-handed. We should drop this division between man and woman, between East and West. We should create a whole man who is capable of both.

That's why I am going to be misunderstood everywhere. The Eastern religious person is angry with me because he thinks I am teaching materialism, and the Western rational thinker is angry with me because he thinks I am teaching spiritual mumbo jumbo. *Everybody* is angry at me – and that is natural, I can understand it.

I am teaching the whole man, from the lowest rung of the ladder to the highest rung – from sex to *samadhi*, from the body to the soul, from matter to God. My trust is total.

I would like to tell you that up to now man has not trusted. Not even in the East has man trusted. In the East man has doubted the world, hence in the East the world is called illusory, maya. In the West man has doubted God, soul. They are thought to be just hallucinations, pathologies. To the really Western mind Jesus looks like a neurotic, psychologically ill, in need of psychiatric treatment. To the East the West looks animalistic – "Eat, drink and be merry" – that seems to be the understanding of the East about the West. That that is the only Western philosophy: be like animals, gross. The West has doubted the inner world, the

East has doubted the outer world. Both have lived in doubt and their trust has been half-hearted.

My trust is total. I trust the outer, I trust the inner – because outer and inner are both together, they cannot be separated. There is *no* God without this world, there is no world without God. God is the innermost core of this world. The juice flowing in the trees is God, the blood circulating in your body is God, the consciousness residing in you is God. God and the world are mixed together just like a dancer and his dance: they cannot be separated, they are inseparable. So I don't say the world is illusion – that is nonsense. The world is as real as consciousness. Neither do I say that the inner world is neurosis, madness, hallucination. It is not. It is the very foundation of reality.

I teach the whole man. I am not a materialist, nor a spiritualist. My approach is holistic – and the whole man can only be holy.

Because of this there is going to be great misunderstanding about me, and anybody can pick things, find faults with me, and it is very easy. The spiritualist can call me Epicurean, a follower of Charvaka – and he is not absolutely wrong because half of me is Epicurean. I accept Epicurus and Charvaka because they teach the body and the joys of the body and the exhilaration of the body. And there is exhilaration in the body, and the moment you drop that, you become serious and sad.

That's why the Eastern saint looks so sad, no joy. They talk about bliss but it doesn't show on their faces. They look utterly miserable. They look utterly dead – because they are afraid of the outer, and one who is afraid of the outer will be afraid of love because love is an outgoing process. Love means the other, love means relating, love means communicating with the other. Love means the relationship between I and thou. The East denies the other, hence the East is against love. And if you are against love you will lose dance.

Without love, there is no dance in life and no song. Without love there is no poetry. Life becomes dull, a drag. Without love you can live, but only at the minimum. It will be almost like vegetating. And that's what is happening to the Eastern spirituality; go into the monasteries, go into the ashrams....

That's why my ashram looks so utterly different – because people are dancing, singing, holding hands, hugging, loving, joyous. This is not the Eastern concept of an ashram. An ashram has to be absolutely joyless, it has to be more like a cemetery than like a garden, because the moment you stop love, all that is flowing in you stops, becomes stagnant. You cannot celebrate without love. How can you celebrate without love? And what will you celebrate, and with what?

Mulla Nasruddin was saying to me one day, "I have lived a hundred years. I have celebrated my hundredth birthday, and I have never chased a woman in my life, and I have not ever been drinking. I have never played cards, gambled, I don't smoke, I eat simple, vegetarian food."

I asked him, "But then how did you celebrate your hundredth birthday? How can you celebrate? With what? And for what? Just living for a hundred years can't be a celebration. You have not lived if you have not loved!"

The East is against love. That's why Eastern spirituality is sad, dull, dead. No juice flows through the Eastern saint. He is afraid of *any* flow, any vibration, any pulsation, any streaming of his energy. He is constantly controlling himself, repressing himself. He is sitting upon himself, on guard. He is against himself and against the world. He is simply waiting to die. He is committing a slow suicide.

That's why my ashram is going to be misunderstood. This will look like the ashram of a Charvaka, this will look like the garden of Epicurus.

The Western man has loved – there is laughter and there is dancing and there is song – but the Western man has lost *all* idea of who he is. He has lost track of consciousness, he is not aware. He has become more and more mechanical because he denies the inner. So laughter is there but laughter cannot go deep, because there is no depth. The depth is not accepted. So the West lives in a shallow laughter and East lives in a deep sadness. This is the misery, the agony that has happened to man.

My message is: it is time now, man is mature enough to come out of these half-hearted, lopsided patterns. These programs have to be dropped and changed. One should accept the outer and the inner both, and totally, and with no conditions at all. Then there will be consciousness and there will be love, and they will not be contradictory to each other but complementary. Love will give you joy, consciousness will give you crystallization. Consciousness will make you aware of who you are, and love will make you aware of what this world is. And between these two banks, the river of life flows. I teach the whole man.

This is one of the most fundamental things to be understood – then all else will become easy, then things will be simple. This is the base. I teach the world and I teach God, and I teach them in the same breath. I want to bring Epicurus and Buddha as close as possible. Buddha is sitting under his tree; you cannot conceive of Buddha dancing. Epicurus is dancing in his garden; you cannot conceive of Epicurus sitting silently under a tree, meditating. I would like Epicurus and Buddha to become one.

Life should be a rhythm of dance and silence, of music and sound and silence. Life should be a rhythm of going out as far as possible and going in as far as possible, because God is both. Close your eyes and you see God, open your eyes and you see God, because God is all there is.

You ask me, "Can you give me a message to take to the Western world so that people there might understand you and your followers?"

The people who are with me are not my followers. They are my lovers, but not my followers. They are my friends, but not my followers. They are my disciples, but not my followers.

And what is the difference between a disciple and a follower? A follower believes: whatsoever is said, he makes a dogma out of it. The disciple listens, learns, experiments, and unless he finds the truth himself he remains open.

I am not giving any dogma to my friends here, to my sannyasins. All that I am doing here is helping them to understand themselves. All I am doing here is helping them to be themselves.

A follower imitates. A Christian has to imitate Christ and a Buddhist has to imitate Buddha – and all imitators are pseudo. I want my friends to be authentic. How can you follow me? I am so different from you and you are so different from me. You are so unique. There has never been a person like you and there will never be again. God only creates one person once. He is very innovative, he does not repeat. He does not make man on an assembly line. It is not like Fiat cars or Ford cars: you can see thousands and thousands alike, exactly alike. God always creates the unique. Go into the garden: you will not find two grass leaves the same. Not even identical twins are the same. So how can you follow anybody? All following is wrong.

So my second message: man has not to follow anybody. Understand certainly, learn certainly, listen certainly, remain open, but follow your own inner spontaneity, follow your own being. I help people here to be themselves. Just as in my garden I help the roses to be roses and the lotus to be a lotus. I don't try to help the lotus to be a rose. The world is rich because there is variety. The world would be ugly if only roses grew and no other flower. Thousands of flowers grow, and the world is beautiful. Each person has to be authentically himself, utterly himself.

So the sannyasins who are here with me are not my followers. They love me, through their love they have come close to me. Their love has brought me here, their love has brought them here – because of love we are together – but I am not the leader and they are not the followers. And I am not creating a cult, I am not creating a church. The sannyasins are just a commune of friends, not a church. We don't have any dogma that everybody has to believe in. There is nothing to be believed in, but millions of things to be experimented with. My ashram is a lab, we experiment here. That too is creating great trouble, because man has forgotten to experiment.

We are experimenting in a multi-dimensional way. We are experimenting with Tao, we are experimenting with Sufism, we are experimenting with Jainism, Hinduism, Islam, Christianity, we are experimenting with Tantra, Yoga, alchemy. We are experimenting with all the possibilities that can make the human consciousness rich and a human being whole. That is creating trouble, because when the follower of Yoga comes he cannot understand why Tantra should be experimented with; he is against Tantra. When the follower of Tantra comes he cannot see why Yoga should be experimented with; he is against Yoga.

I am not against anything. I am for all. I am *utterly* for all. I claim the whole human heritage, and whatsoever is good in any tradition is mine, and whatsoever can make man richer in health and wealth is mine. I don't belong to any tradition, all traditions belong to me.

So this is a new experiment. It has never been done before in such a way: this is the synthesis of all the paths. So I am teaching a synthesis. And my feeling is that the man who has only been experimenting with Yoga will remain partial, will grow only in part – as if a man's hand has become too big and the whole body remains small. He will be a monster...unless he can experiment with Tantra also, because Tantra is complementary to Yoga.

Remember, this is one of my basic insights: that in life there are no contradictions, all contradictions are complementaries. Night is complementary to the day, so is summer to winter, so is death to life. They are not against each other. There is nothing against, because there is only one energy – it is one God. My left hand and my right hand are not against each other, they are complementary. Opposites are just like wings of a bird, two wings – they look opposite to each other but they support each other. The bird cannot fly with one wing.

Tantra and Tao have to be experimented with together.

Now Yoga has a great insight into discipline, and Tao has a great insight into spontaneity. They are opposite, on the surface. But unless your discipline makes you more spontaneous and unless your spontaneity makes you more disciplined, you will not be whole. Yoga is control, Tantra is uncontrol, and both are needed. A man has to be so capable of order that if the need arises he can function in utter order. But order should not become a fixation, otherwise he will become a robot. He should be able to come out of his system, his discipline, whenever the need arises, and he can be spontaneous, floating, in a let-go. That he can get only through Tantra, from nowhere else.

I am bringing all the opposites into my sannyasins' lives as complementaries. Yogis will be against me because they cannot see how sex and love can be a part of a seeker's life. They are afraid. They are afraid of sex because sex is the most spontaneous thing in your life – it has to be controlled. They know that once sex is controlled, everything else is controlled, so their basic attack is on sex. Tantra says if your sex is not spontaneous your whole life will become robot-like. It has to be in freedom. And both are right, and both are right together! – this is my approach. I will look absurd because my approach is very illogical. Logic will always insist: either be a Yogi or be a Tantrika. I believe in life, I don't believe in logic – and life is both together.

A great discipline is needed in life, because you have to live in a world with so many people, you have to live in discipline; otherwise life would become a chaos. Life would become impossible if you couldn't live in a discipline. But if you only live in discipline and you forget spontaneity and you become the discipline and you are not capable of getting out of it, then again life is lost, you have become a machine. Now, these are the two alternatives that have been available to man up to now: either become a chaos – which is not good, or become a machine – which is not good either.

I want you to be alert, conscious, aware, disciplined, and yet capable of spontaneity. When you are working, be disciplined. But work is not all. When you are playing, forget all discipline.

I used to stay in a Calcutta house with a High Court judge. His wife told me, "My husband only listens to you. You are the only person who can bring something into his life. Our whole family is tired with his attitude. He remains the magistrate even in the house." She said, "Even in bed he remains the judge of the High Court. He expects me to call him, 'My Lord'. He is never spontaneous, and in everything he makes rules and laws. The children are tired. When he enters into the house the whole house falls silent, all joy disappears. We all wait for him to go to the court."

Now I know that man: he is a good judge, a very conscientious magistrate, very sincere, honest – and these are good qualities – but he has become a machine. If he comes home and remains the magistrate, that is not good. One has to relax too. One has to play with children, but he cannot play with children;

that would be coming down too much. Even with his wife he remains on the high pedestal, far away – he still remains the magistrate.

This is what has happened to the followers of Yoga: they cannot be playful, they cannot rejoice in anything, they cannot participate in celebration – because they cannot relax.

And Tantra alone creates chaos. Tantra alone makes you very, very selfish. You don't care about anybody. You forget that you are part of a great whole, that you belong to a society, that you belong to existence and you are committed to this existence, without it you will be nowhere: you have to fulfill some demands from the side of existence, from the side of society. If you become utterly chaotic, then you cannot exist. Then nobody can exist.

So there has to be a great understanding between chaos and mechanicalness, and exactly in the middle there is a point where I would like my sannyasins to be: exactly in the middle, capable of going to both the extremes when needed, and always capable of moving away from there. I teach this fluidity, I teach this liquidity.

I don't teach fixed life patterns, dead gestalts. I teach growing life syntheses, growing patterns, growing gestalts, and always capable of comprehending the other, the opposite. Then life is beautiful.

And one can know truth only when one has been able to transform the opposites into complementaries. Then only is one's life symmetrical. There is balance – positive and negative are both equally balanced. In that balancing is transcendence. In that balancing one knows the beyond, one opens up to the beyond: the Golden Flower blooms.

The second question:

> Osho,
> *What should I do? – follow the path of action or the path of knowledge or the path of devotion?*

Follow all three. Act with love and awareness. Love with awareness, and let your love be creative. Bring awareness not against love, but full of the juice of love. And let your awareness participate in existence, let it be creative. These three are part of your being.

This is the real trinity, and if you avoid one then something in you will be denied and will remain stuck. And remember that you can grow only as a total being. If you want to come to me you can come only if your whole being comes here. Your one hand cannot come, your one leg cannot come.

I have heard about a villager. He went to the capital city of his country for the first time and he asked the taxi driver to take him to a certain place. Now it was a big place. The taxi driver asked, "Which part?" And the villager said, "Part? I want to go whole."

You cannot go in parts. You can go only when you are whole. Now action is a must. So is awareness, so is love. Why should you choose? – there is no need. All choosing will be committing suicide. Let all the three mix and meet and merge and become one. Be this trinity, be this *trimurti*. These are the three faces of God.

Mulla Nasruddin's mother-in-law died far away in Brazil. Telegraphically he was asked how the remains should be disposed of. He replied, "Embalm, cremate, bury. Take no chances."

The third question:

> *Osho,*
> *As you call yourself "God," what is the meaning of this word?*
> *And are there more gods? Who are they?*

Joey, I am God because I am not. And the moment you are not, you are also a God. God is not something special; God is our very being, God is our very existence. When I say I am God I am simply saying I exist. Existence and God are synonymous in my language. I say the trees are also God, and so are the rocks, and so are you.

Yes, Joey, even a journalist is a God! He may not know. You may not be aware of your godliness. I am aware of it! And the moment I became aware of my godliness I became aware of everybody else's godliness. So it will be difficult for me to tell you how many gods there are. Infinity…all beings are gods at different stages of recognition, realization, awareness. But I can understand your problem: Joey is a Dutch journalist.

People coming from the West cannot understand a few things, because their idea of God is the very limited idea that Christianity has given to them. Their idea of God is a very limited idea.

In India we have three words for God – no other language has such richness, and certainly – because we have been working on the inward for centuries, thousands of years have been devoted to it. Naturally we have followed all the possibilities of God's existence. It is just like I have heard that Eskimos have an unusually large number of names for snow because they know different kinds of snow. Now no other language can have so many names for snow; we never come across it as much. Now the West has all the words for science, in the East we have to coin words for scientific terminology, we don't have it. But as far as religion is concerned the whole world will have to follow the East, because we have worked deep down into the interiormost being.

We have three words for God. The first is *Brahma*. It means the one, the undivided one, when the creator and the creation were asleep in each other. Now Christianity has no word for it. God created the world, Christianity says. So one day – it must have been Monday – God created the world. Just that the working week starts on Monday, and he rested on Sunday, just a holiday. Theologians have even been searching for an exact date, and they have found one: four thousand and four years before Jesus, on a certain Monday, God created the world. Before that, where was the world? And before that, who was God? – because he had not created, so he was not a creator. God means "the creator." But before creation, how could he be a creator?

So creation was latent, potential, unmanifest in the creator. The creator and the creation were together, one. Christianity has no word for it. We have; we call it Brahma. It is the state when the dancer has not started dancing; the dance and the dancer are one. When the dancer has started dancing, now there is a division. The singer has not sung his song yet, the song is fast asleep in the singer; the moment he sings the division starts. The painter, once he paints, is separate from the painting.

The second word in India is *Ishwar*. Ishwar means the creator: the unity has broken in two, the duality has arisen. Now the world is separate and the creator is separate. Now Brahma, the one absolute, has become two.

The third word is *Bhagwan*. It means *anybody* who has again seen the unity – of the dancer and the dance, of the painter and the painting, of the poet and the poetry, of the creator and the creation. One who has seen the unity again, one who has comprehended the unity again in his being, he is called Bhagwan. Literally the word means "the blessed one," it does not mean God. But because of the poverty of Western languages there is a problem: you have to translate

"Brahma" also as "God," you have to translate "Ishwar" also as "God," you have to translate "Bhagwan" also as "God." This is simply a poor language, nothing else. Bhagwan literally means "the blessed one."

Who is the blessed one? – one who has known the unity again, one who has reached to the original source again, he is called Bhagwan. That's why we call Krishna "Bhagwan," and Buddha "Bhagwan." And you will be surprised to know: Buddha never believed in any God.

Certainly Bhagwan cannot mean God. Buddha never believed in any God, he never believed in any creation or any creator. Still, Buddhists call him "Bhagwan," "the blessed one," because he understood. Whatsoever the truth is – you call it God, creator, truth, nirvana, enlightenment – that is not the point. He understood, and in that understanding blessings showered on him. He became Bhagwan, the blessed one.

Now this is going to be a constant problem: I declare myself to be the blessed one, I have seen, those flowers have showered on me. By declaring myself Bhagwan I am not saying that I have created the world – I don't take that responsibility! By declaring myself Bhagwan I am simply saying that I have been blessed by existence, the grace has descended into me – I have seen. And the moment seeing happens you disappear, you are no more. The blessed one is one who is no more. I am not, God is: this is the *experience* that makes one blessed.

Now the paradox has to be understood. Man never meets God, man can only dissolve, disappear, then God is: in your absence God's presence descends. The whole work of religion is nothing but helping you to disappear as an ego. And the moment you look into yourself and there is no I, no ego to be found, but only utter silence, utter emptiness is present, "therewith the matter is settled" – you are God. You are God not against others – not that others are not God and you. You are God because then only God is!

So I am not saying I am God and you are not God. In declaring myself, I am also declaring you divine, and not only you – the animals, the birds, the trees, the rocks, the whole existence consists of God and nothing else. I am not saying I am holier than you. I am not saying I am more special than you. All that I am saying is that I have disappeared, and in that disappearance grace has showered, ecstasy has arisen – I am utterly gone, and gone forever – and in this space that is left behind there is nothing else but God.

In fact, when you say "I am" you are uttering a falsehood, because you are not. The moment you say "I am" you are separating yourself from existence, and this is absolutely false, a lie. You are not separate from existence, you are not capable of being yourself apart from existence – not even for a single moment can you exist. No man is an island. The moment you see it, separation disappears, suddenly you are one with the trees and with the stars, and that moment is the moment of blessings: you have come home.

That's all that is meant by "Bhagwan": the word simply means "the blessed one."

The fourth question:

Osho,
Why am I so afraid of women? And why am I so bored with my wife?

All men are afraid of women, and all women are afraid of men. They have good reasons to mistrust each other, since they have been trained from early years to be enemies of each other. They are not born to be enemies, but they achieve enmity. And after about twenty years of such training in being afraid of each other they are supposed to marry one day and find complete trust in each other. All this for a five rupee marriage license?

Twenty years training of being afraid of each other, in a lifetime of around sixty to seventy years, that is one third of your life, and the most delicate and sensitive part of your life, because psychologists say a man learns fifty percent of his whole life's learning by the time he is seven. In the remaining sixty-three years he will learn only fifty percent more. Fifty percent is learned by the time you are seven. By the time you are twenty almost eighty percent is learned. You have become fixed, hard. Distrust has been taught to you.

The boys have been told, "Avoid girls, they are dangerous." The girls have been told, "Avoid boys, they are nasty, they will do something evil to you." And then after this complete conditioning of twenty years – just think, twenty years of constantly being taught by the parents, by the school, by the college, by the university, by the church, by the priest – one day suddenly how can you drop this twenty years of conditioning?

This question arises again and again. So many people come and tell me that they are afraid of women. Women tell me they are afraid of men. You were not born afraid; otherwise no man would enter into a woman's womb, if he was really afraid. Then no woman would be conceived, because she can be conceived only through a man. You were not afraid in your beginnings. A child is born simply unafraid. Then we teach him fear and we condition his mind.

This has to be dropped. This has driven people almost neurotic. Then people fight, then they are constantly fighting – husbands and wives constantly fighting – and they are worried about why they go on fighting. And all relationships turn sour. Why does it happen? You have been poisoned, and you have to consciously drop that conditioning, otherwise you will remain afraid.

There is nothing to be afraid of in a man or a woman. They are just like you – just as much in need of love as you are, hankering just as much to join hands with you as you are hankering. They want to participate in your life, they want others to participate in their lives, because the more people participate in each other's lives, the more joy arises.

People are looking very sad. They have become very lonely. Even in crowds people are lonely because everybody is afraid of everybody else. If people are sitting close to each other, but they are holding themselves – holding so much so that their whole being becomes hard, a hard crust surrounds them, an armor arises around their being. So even when they meet there is no real meeting. People hold hands but those hands are cold, no love is flowing. They hug each other: yes, bones clash with each other, but the heart remains far away.

People have to love. Love is a great need, just as food is a need. Food is a lower need, love is a higher need, a much higher-order value.

Now psychologists have been doing much research work on children who were brought up without any love. Almost fifty percent of children die if they are brought up without love; within two years they die. They are given good food, nourishment, every scientific care, but mechanically. The nurse comes, gives them a bath, feeds them, *every* care is taken, but no human love. The nurse will not hug them close to her heart, the nurse will not give her warm body to the child. Warmth is not given, within two years fifty percent of those children die. And this is strange, because there is no visible reason why they die. They were perfectly healthy, the body was going perfectly well, they were not ill or anything, but suddenly, for no reason at all, they start dying.

And the remaining fifty percent are in more trouble than those who die. Those who die are more intelligent. Those who survive become neurotic, schizophrenic, psychotic, because no love has showered on them. Love makes you one piece. It is like glue – it glues you together. They start falling into fragments, there is nothing to hold them together – no vision of life, no experience of love – nothing to hold them together, their lives seem meaningless. So many of them turn neurotic, many of them become criminals, because love makes a person creative. If love is missing then a person becomes destructive. Had Adolf Hitler's mother loved him more, the world would have been totally different.

If there is no love the person forgets the language of creativity, becomes destructive, so criminals, politicians are born – they are the same types of people. There is no difference in them, no qualitative difference. Their faces differ, their masks are different, but deep down they are all criminals. In fact, you have been reading the history of human crimes and nothing else. You have not yet been taught the real history of humanity, because the real history consists of buddhas, christs, Lao Tzus. That's what I am trying to do here, now talking about Lu-tsu. You may not even have heard his name.

Now talking on this tremendously beautiful book, *The Secret of the Golden Flower,* I am trying to make you aware that a totally different human history exists which has been kept out of the schools. History takes note only of crimes, history takes note only of destruction. If you kill somebody on the streets you will be in the newspapers, and if you give a roseflower to somebody you will never be heard of again. Nobody will know about it.

If love is missing in childhood the person will become either a politician or a criminal, or will go mad, or will find some destructive way because he will not know how to create. His life will be meaningless, he will not feel any significance. He will feel very very condemned, because unless you have been loved you cannot feel your worth. The moment somebody loves you, you become worthy, you start feeling you are needed – existence would be a little less without you. When a woman loves you, you know that if you are gone somebody is going to be sad. When a man loves you, you know that you are making somebody's life happy – and because you are making somebody's life happy, great joy arises in you. Joy arises only in creating joy for others; there is no other way. The more people you can make happy, the more you will feel happy.

This is the real meaning of service, this is the real meaning of religion: help people become happy, help people become warm, help people become loving. Create a little beauty in the world, create a little joy, create a little corner where people can celebrate and sing and dance and be, and you will be happy – immense will be your reward. But the man who has never been loved does not know it. So the fifty percent that survive prove to be very dangerous people.

Love is such a basic need, it is exactly the food for the soul. The body needs food, the soul also needs food. The body lives on material food, the soul lives on spiritual food. Love is spiritual food, spiritual nourishment.

In my vision of a better world children will be taught to love each other. Boys and girls will not be put apart. No division, no disgust with each other should be created. But why has this disgust been created?– because there has been a great fear of sex. Sex is not accepted – that is the problem, because sex is not accepted children have to be kept apart. And humanity is going to suffer unless it accepts sex as a natural phenomenon. This whole problem of man/woman arises because sex is condemned. This condemnation has to go – and now it can go.

In the past I can understand. There were reasons for it. For example, if a girl became pregnant, then there would have been problems. Parents were very much afraid, the society was very much afraid, people lived in fear. The boys and girls had to be kept apart, great walls had to be raised between them. And then one day, after twenty years, suddenly you open the door and you say, "She is not your enemy, she is your wife. Love her!" and, "He is not your enemy, he is your husband. Love him!" And what about those twenty years when he was the enemy? And what about those twenty years' experiences? Can you suddenly drop them so easily? You cannot drop them. They linger on, they hang around you – your whole life.

But now there is no need. In my understanding, the greatest revolution in the world has been that which is created by "the pill." Lenin and Mao Tse Tung are nothing compared to the pill. The pill is the greatest revolutionary. This is going to create a totally different world because fear can be dropped, now there is no need to be afraid. The fear of pregnancy has been the cause of condemning sex. Now there is no need to condemn it at all. It can be accepted.

Science has prepared the ground for a new culture, and I am heralding *that* future! That's why all those who are burdened with their pasts are going to be against me. They cannot understand me, because I *see* into the future, what is going to happen in the future, and I am preparing the way for it. Man and woman have to be brought as close as possible. And now there is no fear.

In the past, I understand the fear was there. I can forgive those people in the past, because they were helpless. But now you cannot be forgiven if you teach your children to be separate and antagonize them against each other. There is no need. Now boys and girls can mix and meet and be together, and all fear about sex can be dropped. And the beauty is that because of the fear and because of the condemnation and because of the denial, sex has become so important; otherwise it is not so important.

Try to understand a simple psychological law: if you deny something too much it becomes very important. The very denial makes it important. You become *obsessed* with it. Now girls and boys have to be kept apart for twenty years – they become *obsessed* with each other, they only think of the other. They cannot think of anything else.

I have heard of an incident that happened to former Ambassador Ellis while he was an envoy to Greece. Both he and his secretary had been preoccupied by an approaching deadline. He had to fly to Rome to give a report before a European security conference. She, a healthy, buxom lass of twenty-three, was two days away from her wedding to a handsome Marine guard after a six-month engagement. Naturally, her mind was on the state of her trousseau rather than on the state of the Greek government. Ambassador Ellis was trying to finish up his paper on Greece before rushing to the airport. He had entitled his study – a report saying that the political situation was more shaky than the economic – "Man Shall Not Live By Bread Alone." Before he had a chance to really go over the copy, he had to race to the Athens airport. He left word that the speech should be teletyped to the Rome Embassy so they could type it for distribution for the next day's conference.

When he arrived in Rome he was met by a group of foreign service officers who were to take him to the hotel to deliver the speech. They were a bit puzzled by the printed title of the report. Ambassador Ellis looked at one of the mimeographed copies. The bride-to-be's rendition of the Ambassador's dictated Biblical saying came out not "Man Shall Not Live by Bread Alone" but "Man Shall Not Love in Bed Alone."

The mind can become preoccupied. Twenty years' training in anti-sexual teachings makes the mind preoccupied, and all kinds of perversions arise. Homosexuality arises, lesbianism arises, people start living in fantasies – pornography arises, dirty films, "blue films" arise – and this whole thing goes on because of the nonsense that you do. Now you want pornography to stop; it cannot stop. You are creating the situation for it. If boys and girls could be together, who would bother to look at a nude picture?

You go and meet some aboriginal tribe in India who live naked and you show your *Playboy* magazine to them and they will all laugh. I have lived with them, and I have talked with them, and they all laugh. They cannot believe: "What is there?" They live naked, so they know what a woman looks like and they know what a man looks like.

Pornography is created by your priests – they are the foundation of it – and then all kinds of perversions, because when you cannot actually meet the other pole for which the attraction is natural, you start fantasizing. Then a greater problem arises: twenty years of fantasies and dreams, and then you meet a real woman and she falls very low, very low from your expectations – because all those fantasies! You were completely free to fantasize – no real woman is going to satisfy you! Because of your fantasies and dreams you have created such ideas about a woman which no woman can fulfill, and you imagined such ideas about men which no man can fulfill. Hence the frustration, hence the bitterness that arises between couples, because the man feels cheated. "This is not the woman" – because he was thinking, dreaming, and he was free to create whatsoever he wanted in his dream, and this woman looks very poor compared to his fantasy.

In your fantasy women don't perspire – or do they? And they don't quarrel with you, and they don't nag you, and they are just golden, just sweet flowers. And they always remain young, they never become old, and they don't get grumpy. Because they are your creations, if you want them laughing, they laugh. Their bodies are made not of this world.

But when you meet a real women she perspires, her breath smells, and sometimes it is natural to be grumpy. And she nags, and she fights, she throws pillows and breaks things, and she won't allow you a thousand and one things, she starts curbing your freedom. Your fantasy women never curbed your freedom! Now this woman seems to be like a trap. And she is not as beautiful as you had been thinking. She is not a Cleopatra. She is an ordinary woman, just as you are an ordinary man. Neither you are fulfilling her desire nor she is fulfilling your desire. Nobody has the obligation to fulfill your fantasies! People are *real* people. And because this twenty years' starvation creates fantasy, it creates trouble for your future life.

You ask me, "Why am I afraid of women? And why am I bored with my wife?" You must have fantasized too much. You will have to drop your fantasies. You will have to learn to live with reality. You will have to learn to see the extraordinary in the ordinary. That needs great art. A woman is not just her skin, not just her face, not just her body proportion. A woman is a soul! You have to be intimate with her, you have to get involved in her life, in her inner life. You have to merge and meet with her energies. And people don't know how to meet and how to merge; they have never been taught. The art of love has not been taught to you, and everybody thinks that they know what love is. You don't know. You come only with the potential of love but not with the art of it.

Fifty years ago, near Calcutta, in a jungle, two girls were found, Kamala and Vimala. They were brought up by wolves. Maybe they were unwanted children and the mother had left them in the forest. It has happened many times, almost in every part of the world: once in a while, a child has been found who has grown up with the animals.

Those two girls were absolutely inhuman. They walked on all fours, they could not stand on two feet. They learned from the wolves to walk on all fours. They howled like wolves, they could not speak Bengali. And they were very dangerous – they ran like wolves. No Olympic champion would have defeated them, they were so quick and fast. And if they jumped, if they became angry, they would tear you in parts. They looked human, but their whole training had been that of the wolves.

You are born with a capacity to learn language, but you are not born with a language itself. Exactly like this, you are born with the capacity to love, but you are not born with the art of love. That art of love has to be taught, has to be imbibed.

And just the opposite is happening: you have been taught the art of hate and hatred, not of love. You have been taught how to hate people. Christians have been taught to hate the Mohammedans, Mohammedans have been taught to hate the Hindus, Indians have been taught to hate the Pakistanis. Hate has been taught in many ways. Man has been taught to hate the woman, the woman has been taught to hate the man, and now suddenly one day you decide to get married, and you get married – to your *enemy!* – and then the whole turmoil starts. Then the life becomes just a nightmare.

You are bored with your wife because you don't know how to enter into her soul. You may be able to enter her body, but that is going to become boring very soon because that will be the repetition. The body is a very superficial thing. You can make love to the body once, twice, thrice, and then you become perfectly acquainted with the body, its contours. Then there is nothing new. Then you start becoming interested in other women: you think they must be having something different from your wife – at least behind the clothes it appears they must be having something different. You can still fantasize about them.

Clothes have been invented to help your sexual desire. A naked woman leaves nothing to your fantasy. That's why naked women are not so attractive, neither are naked men. But when a woman or a man is hidden behind clothes, they leave much to your fantasy. You can fantasize about what is behind it.

Now you cannot imagine about your wife, that is the trouble. You can imagine about your neighbor's wife, she looks attractive.

I have heard…

A man had a severe coronary and was told that if he wanted to live he had to completely cut out drinking, smoking and all forms of physical exertion. After six months he went into the doctor's office for a check-up. After he was told he was progressing fine, he said to the doctor, "You know, sometimes I want a drink so much – not a lot, just a taste of it. Could I not have just one drink or two, maybe once a week on a Friday or Saturday night?"

"No," the doctor said, "but I will tell you what. I will allow you one glass of wine with your evening meal."

Some months later he was back for another physical. This time he told the doctor, "You know, doctor, sometimes I just crave for a cigarette. If I could just puff one when I wake up and another after each meal."

"No," said the doctor. "You would soon be smoking a pack a day. But if you want you can smoke one cigar a week, perhaps after your Sunday dinner."

Months went by, and our friend's health as well as state of mind improved. There was only one thing that gnawed at him. When he went to the doctor again he came out with it very bluntly. "Doctor, it is not normal to go without sexual relations. Surely I am healthy enough to be able to resume that."

"No," said the doctor. "The physical exertion as well as excitement could just be too much. But I will tell you what: I will allow you once a week to have sex – but only with your wife."

People feel bored with their wives and with their husbands. The reason is: they have not been able to contact the other's real soul. They have been able to contact the body, but they have missed the contact that happens heart to heart, center to center, soul to soul. Once you know how to contact soul to soul, when you have become soul-mates, then there is no boredom at all. Then there is always something to discover in the other because each being is an infinity, and each being contains God himself. There is no end to exploring.

That's why I say Tantra should become a compulsory phenomenon for all human beings. Each school, each college, each university, should teach Tantra. Tantra is the science of contacting souls, of going to the deepest core of the other. Only in a world which knows the art of Tantra will this boredom disappear; otherwise it cannot disappear – you can tolerate it, you can suffer it, you can be a martyr to it. That's how in the past, people have been martyrs. They say, "What to do? This is fate. This life is finished. Next life we will choose some other woman or some other man, but this life is gone, and nothing can be done. And there are children and a thousand and one problems, and the prestige and the society and the respectability...." So they have suffered and they have remained martyrs.

Now they are no longer ready to suffer so they have moved to the other extreme: now they are indulging in all kinds of sex, but that too is not giving any contentment. Neither the Indian is contented nor is the American. Nobody is contented, because the basic thing is missed by both. The basic thing is unless you become capable of decoding the inner mystery of your woman or your man, sooner or later you will get fed up, bored. Then either you become a martyr – remain with it, suffer it, wait for death to deliver you – or you start indulging with other women. But whatsoever you have done with *this* woman will be done with the other, and you will get fed up with the other, and with the other, and your whole life will be just changing partners. That is not going to satisfy either… unless you learn the secret art of Tantra.

Tantra is one of the most important secrets ever discovered. But it is very delicate because it is the *greatest* art. To paint is easy, to create poetry is easy, but to create a communion with the energy of the other, a dancing communion, is the greatest and the most difficult art to learn.

People are against me because I am telling people how to love: I am telling people how to make love a prayer, I am telling people how to love so deeply that love itself becomes your religion – that your woman one day disappears and you find God there, that your man one day disappears and you find God there, that one day – in deep communion, in deep orgasmic experience, in that ecstasy – for a moment you both disappear and there is only God and nothing else.

You have been taught down the ages to be against sex, and that has made you very sexual. Now this paradox has to be understood. If you want to understand me, this paradox has to be understood very very deeply, clearly: you have been made sexual by all the condemnation of sex.

Just the other day one government officer came to look around the ashram, because the government is very worried: "What is going on here?" – what am I teaching people? And he kept a very haughty posture. Sheela took him around the ashram, Sheela was walking with him. He started moving closer and closer to Sheela, he started touching her body. So she would keep aloof, but he would come close again. And Sheela was worried, "What to do with this man?" And she was worried – she could have hit him. And I have told her that next time it happens, give him a good beating – he needs it, he deserves it.

He had come to find out what was going on here – particularly about sex. And when he found Sheela alone – she was taking him around – he came close, perspiring, and asked, "Can I kiss you?" Now this man is sent here to inquire about what is happening here.

Remember it: next time you find a government official here, give him a kiss of death!

And in the office he again became very holier-than-thou.

This repressed sexuality...

I have heard of the visit of J.P. Morgan to the home of Dwight Morrow. The great American financier was noted, among other things, for a bulbous red nose of unsurpassing ugliness.

"Remember, Anne," Mrs Morrow kept saying to her daughter, "you must not say one word about Mr Morgan's red nose. You must remember that you must not even look at it very much."

Anne promised, but when Morgan arrived her mother watched and waited tensely. Anne was as good as gold, but Mrs Morrow dared not relax. Turning to the financier with a gracious smile, she prepared to pour tea and said, "Mr Morgan, will you have one or two lumps in your nose?"

That's what has happened to the whole humanity: repressed sex has become the obsession.

People think I am teaching sexuality? I am teaching transcendence. Soon this will be the only place where nobody will be obsessed with sex. It is already the experience of hundreds of sannyasins. Every day I receive letters: "What is happening, Osho? My sex is disappearing. I no longer find much interest in it" – men and women both.

That interest is a pathological interest that has been created by repression. Once repression is taken away that interest will disappear, and then there is a natural feel – which is not obsessive, which is not pathological. And whatsoever is natural is good. This interest in sex is unnatural. And the problem is, this is being created by the priest and by the politician, by the so-called mahatmas. They are the culprits – and they go on creating it, and they think they are helping humanity to go beyond sex. They are not! They are throwing humanity into this whole mess.

If you understand me rightly, then you will be surprised by the experience that you will go through in this commune: soon you will find sex has become a natural phenomenon, and finally, as your meditations will deepen, as you will start meeting with each other's souls more and more, the body contact will become less and less. A moment comes when there is no need for sexuality to be there, it has taken a new turn – the energy has started moving upwards. It is the same energy. At the lowest rung it is sex, at the highest rung it is *samadhi*.

I have written one book – not written, my discourses have been collected in it – it is called *From Sex to Superconsciousness*. Now fifteen years have passed. Since then nearabout two hundred books have been published, but nobody seems to read any other book – not in India. They all read *From Sex to Superconsciousness*. They all criticize it also, they are all against it. Articles are still being written about it, books are still being written against it, and mahatmas go on objecting to it – and I have written two hundred books, and no other book is mentioned, no other book is looked at.

Do you understand? – "Mr Morgan, will you have one or two lumps in your nose?"– as if I have written only one book.

People are suffering from a wound. Sex has become a wound. It needs to be healed. Remember, there is no need to be afraid of women, no need to be afraid of men. We are all alike, the same God. We have to learn how to love each other, we have to come closer to each other because that is the only way to come close to God. Love is one of the greatest doors to God, just as awareness is another.

The East has followed the way of awareness and become lopsided. The West has followed the way of love and has become lopsided. I teach you both: a loving awareness, a conscious love. And with this you will become integrated, you will attain individuation.

Enough for today.

CHAPTER 27

The Contemplation of Emptiness

Master Lu-tsu said:

If you are not yet clear, I will make it clear to you through the threefold Buddhist contemplation of emptiness, delusion, and the center.

Emptiness comes as the first of the three contemplations. All things are looked upon as empty. Then follows delusion. Although it is known that they are empty, things are not destroyed, but one attends to one's affairs in the midst of emptiness. But although one does not destroy things, neither does one pay attention to them; this is contemplation of the center. While practicing contemplation of the empty, one also knows that one cannot destroy the ten thousand things, and still one does not notice them. In this way the three contemplations fall together. But, after all, strength is in envisioning the empty. Therefore, when one practices contemplation of emptiness, emptiness is certainly empty, but delusion is empty too, and the center is empty. It needs great strength to practice contemplation of delusion; then delusion is really delusion, but emptiness is also delusion, and the center is delusion too. Being on the way of the center, one also creates images of the emptiness; they are not called empty, but are called central. One practices also contemplation of delusion, but one does not call it delusion, one calls it central. As to what has to do with the center, more need not be said.

A Zen Story...

Just before the Zen Master, Ninakawa, passed away, another Zen Master, Ikkyu, visited him. "Shall I lead you on?" Ikkyu asked.

Ninakawa replied, "I came here alone and I go alone. What help could you be to me?"

Ikkyu answered, "If you think you really came and you are really going, if you think that you come and go, that is your delusion. Let me show you the path on which there is no coming and no going."

With his words Ikkyu had revealed the path so clearly that Ninakawa smiled, and without saying a single word, nodded and passed away.

This is a beautiful story. A few things have to be understood about it. They will help you to enter into the sutras of Lu-tsu.

First: to a man who is in search of truth even death is an occasion, to the man who is not in search even life is not an occasion to learn. People live their lives without learning a thing at all. They pass through life but without gaining any maturity through it. They remain almost asleep.

People live like sleepwalkers. They remain drunk – they don't know what they are doing, they don't know why they are doing, they don't know where they come from, they don't know to where they are going. They are simply like driftwood, at the mercy of the winds. Their lives are accidental. Remember that word *accidental*.

Millions of people live only accidental lives, and unless you take hold of your life and start changing it from the accidental to the existential, there is going to be no transformation.

That's what sannyas is all about: an effort to change the accidental into the existential, an effort to change the unconscious life into a conscious life, the effort to wake up. And then life is learning, and so is death. Then one goes on learning. Then each moment, each situation, comes as a gift. Yes, even suffering is a gift from God, but only for those who know how to learn, how to receive the gift. Even blessings are not gifts for you because you don't know how to receive them, you don't know how to absorb them. Your life is lived in a robot-like way.

I have heard...

A man came home very late in the night. The excuse that he gave to his wife for coming home too late was this...

In fact, the poor man had imbibed a bit too freely, but told his angry wife that he had taken the wrong bus.

His wife said, "That's easy to understand considering the shape you are in, but how did you know you were on the wrong bus?"

The husband said, "Well, it seemed strange when I stood on one corner for a couple of hours, but what finally convinced me was the fact that people kept coming in and ordering hamburgers and coffee."

It was not even a bus!

The life that you are living is not even a life. It can't be. How can it be life if there is no light in you? How can it be life if there is no love in you? How can it be life if you function mechanically? Only with consciousness does life arrive – not by birth but by consciousness. It is only a meditator who starts beginning to live. Others are befooling themselves, they are not really living. They may be doing a thousand and one things – they go on doing, and to the very end they go on doing. Accumulating wealth, achieving power, fulfilling this ambition and that, they go on and on. But still, the total, the sum total of their lives is nil.

Interviewing the sixty-year-old rodeo champion in Austin, Texas, the New York newspaperman remarked, "You are really an extraordinary man to be a rodeo champion at your age."

"Shucks," said the cowboy, "I am not nearly the man my Pa is. He is still place-kicking for a football team and he is eighty-six."

"Amazing!" gasped the journalist. "I'd like to meet your father."

"Can't right now. He's in El Paso standing up for Grandpa. Grandpa is getting married tomorrow. He's a hundred and fourteen."

"Your family is simply unbelievable," said the newspaperman. "Here you are, a rodeo champion at sixty, your father is a football player at eighty-six, and now your grandfather wants to get married at a hundred and fourteen."

"Hell, mister, you got that wrong," said the Texan. "Grandpa does not want to get married. He *has* to."

This way life goes on and on to, the very end. This is not real life. You are just a victim – a victim of your unconscious instincts, a victim of biology, a victim of physiology, a victim of nature. This is the bondage. To be free of all this unconsciousness is liberation. To be free of the bondage of your body chemistry, to be free of the bondage of the program that nature has put in your body cells, to be free of all that is unconscious in you, to be on your own, to be a conscious light – that is the beginning of real life. Count your age only from the moment when you start living consciously, fully alert, meditatively. When each act has the flavor of consciousness, then you are coming closer to home; otherwise you are going farther and farther away.

And life gives you many opportunities to wake up. But rather than waking up, rather than using those opportunities, you start searching for even deeper drugs to drown you in unconsciousness. When suffering comes, that is an occasion to wake up, but then you start searching for a drug. The drug may be sex, may be alcohol, may be LSD, the drug may be money, may be power-politics – the drug can be anything. Anything that keeps you unconscious is a drug. Anything that keeps you engaged in the non-essential is a drug. Drugs are not only sold at the chemist. Drugs are available everywhere. Your schools, your colleges, your universities sell drugs because they create ambition, and ambition keeps people unconscious. Ambition keeps them running, chasing shadows, illusions, dreams. Your politicians are the greatest drug-peddlers: they continuously go on creating a powerlust in you, a hunger, a greed for power, that keeps you occupied.

To be ambitious, to be competitive, is to be alcoholic. And this is a deeper alcohol. The ordinary alcohol can be prohibited. This alcohol is so tremendously available from every nook and corner – from parents, from priests, from politicians, from professors. Your whole society lives in this drugged state. If you have something to run after, you feel good. The moment you have nothing to run after, you feel lost. You immediately create some new occupation.

The observation of the buddhas down the ages is that when suffering comes it is a hint from God that it is time – "Wake up." But you drown the agony in a drug.

Your wife dies – you start drinking too much, or you start gambling. It was an opportunity to see that this life is not going to last forever. This house is made on the sands, this life is a paper boat – it will be drowned any moment. Any whim of the winds and the life will be gone. Wake up! Your wife is dead, you are going to be dead because you are standing in the same queue, and the queue is coming closer and closer to the window called death.

But you don't wake up; you start searching for another wife. You go bankrupt but you don't wake up. You are defeated but you don't wake up. You start searching – with more vigor, with more vengeance.

A woman went to one of those health clinics where they have about seven doctors. After twenty minutes in one doctor's office she ran screaming down the hall. Another doctor who finally got the story out of her called the first doctor. "What is the idea of telling that patient she is pregnant? She is not! You nearly frightened her to death."

"I know," the first doctor said, "but I cured her hiccups, didn't I?"

If you listen, if you watch, you will see that every suffering that happens in your life is a blessing in disguise: it can cure you of your hiccups. It is a shock...and you need shocks – because you have grown many buffers around yourself, you have grown many shock absorbers around yourself. They have to be broken. Unless they are broken you will live in a dream. And remember, in a dream the dream looks real. And you know it perfectly well, you dream every night: in a dream the dream looks absolutely real. And you can always find reasons and logic to support your dreams. Even when the dream is broken you can find reasons to support the dream which was absolutely false.

I have heard...

A man woke up one morning in a state of shock. He woke his wife and said, "Darling, I had a terrible dream last night. I dreamt I was eating a ten kilo marshmallow, and on top of that, I can't find my pillow anywhere."

Even when you wake up you may find some support. You may look around, and you can *always* find support. Your mind is very cunning, your mind plays many games upon you, many tricks upon you, and it can look very logical. It can appear very convincing.

A Frenchman came home and was startled to find his son in bed with his grandmother...

Now it can happen only in France!

"Son," he said, "how can you do this?"

"Well," said his son, "You sleep with my mama, I sleep with your mama. *C'est logique!*"

You can prove things are logical, even absurd things. Be alert. Your mind is all in favor of dreams, your mind is the source of dreaming, hence it has a duty, an obligation, to support those dreams. If you are not very alert you will be deceived and tricked and trapped by your own mind again and again, in the same stupidities that you have come across many times and you have repented for many times and you have decided many times, taken a vow, "Never again!" But the mind will come with subtle allurements. The mind is the greatest salesman. The mind is very persuasive. And because the mind is always helping your unconscious desires, the body also supports the mind.

The effort to wake up is really arduous. This is the greatest challenge that a man can encounter in life – and only a *man* can encounter it, a courageous man: it needs guts to accept the challenge to wake up. This is the greatest adventure there is. It is easier to go to the moon, it is easier to go to Everest, it is easier to go to the depths of the Pacific Ocean. The real problem arises when you go into your own self, the real problem arises when you start waking up. Then your whole past is against it, your whole past then hangs around your neck like mountains – it pulls you down. It does not allow you to fly into the sky, into the infinite, into eternity, into God, into nirvana.

This beautiful parable, that one master is dying and another master comes to say good-bye to him – but what a way to say good-bye! The opportunity of death is used. Yes, only very conscious people can use the chance that death makes available. Death looked at unconsciously is the enemy, death looked at consciously is the greatest friend. Death looked at unconsciously is just a shattering of all your dreams, of all your life patterns, of all the structures that you have been raising, of all that you have invested in – an utter collapse. But death looked at consciously is the beginning of a new life, a door to the divine.

Ninakawa is dying and Ikkyu asks, "Shall I lead you on?"

He is saying that death is a beginning, not an end. "Shall I lead you on? Do you need my help in any way? You are going to learn a new way of being, a new vision is going to arise; you are entering into a new dimension, a new plenitude – shall I lead you on? Is my help in any way needed?"

Ninakawa replied, "I came here alone and I go alone. What help could you be to me?"

Yes, we come alone and we go alone. And between these two alonenesses we create all the dreams of togetherness, relationship, love, family, friends, clubs, societies, nations, churches, organizations. Alone we come, alone we go. Aloneness is our ultimate nature. But in between these two, how many dreams we dream! One becomes a husband or a wife, a father or a mother, one accumulates money, power, prestige, respectability – and knowing perfectly well that you come empty-handed and you go empty-handed, you cannot take a thing from here. Still one goes on accumulating, still one goes on becoming attached, more and more attached, more rooted in this world from where we have to leave.

Use this world as a caravanserai, don't make a home in it. Use it, certainly, but don't be used by it. There is no point in possessing anything because the moment you start possessing something you are possessed by it. The more you possess the more you are possessed. Use! – but remember: be watchful that death is coming, it is always on the way. Any moment it may knock on the door and you will have to leave *everything* as it is. And it is *always* in the middle that you have to leave. One cannot complete anything in life.

Ninakawa replied perfectly well: "I came here alone and I go alone. What help could you be to me? How can you help me in death? Maybe in life we can have the illusion of being helped, of being helpers, but how in death?"

He's telling a great truth, but there are truths and truths and greater truths. Ikkyu answered with an even higher truth.

Remember this: the conflict is not between the untrue and the true. The real conflict is between the lower truth and the higher truth. The untrue is untrue: what can it do, what harm can it do to truth? The problem is never of a choice between the untrue and the true. The problem is always between a lower truth and a higher truth.

What Ninakawa said is a *great* truth – that we come alone and we go alone. But there is still a higher truth.

Ikkyu answered, "If you think you really come and go, that is your illusion." Who comes? Who goes? All is as it is. Coming and going is also a dream.

For example, in the night you fall asleep, a dream arises. In the morning the dream disappears. Do you think you had gone somewhere and you have come back? You find yourself in the same room, on the same bed – and all that dreaming? You may have traveled to faraway places – you may have visited the moon, the planets, the stars – but in the morning when you wake up you don't wake up on a star. You wake up in the same place where you had slept.

Life is a dream! We are where we are. We are that which we are. Not for a single moment have we moved, and not a single inch have we moved from our true nature! This is the ultimate statement of truth.

Yes, Ninakawa was saying something significant, very significant – "Alone we come, alone we go" – but Ikkyu is stating something even far more profound. He says, "What going? What coming? You are talking complete nonsense!

Who comes? Who goes?"

Waves arise in the ocean and then disappear in the ocean. When the wave arises in the ocean it is still the ocean, as much as it was before it had risen, and then the wave disappears back into the ocean. Forms arise and disappear, the reality remains as it is. All changes are only appearances. Deep, at the deepest core, nothing ever changes. There it is all the same. Time is a peripheral phenomenon. At the center there is no time, no change, no movement. All is eternal there.

Just see the point – and this dialogue happening at the moment when Ninakawa was dying. These are not the things to be discussed at the time of death. At the time of death people try to help the person, console him, "You are not dying. Who says you are dying? You are going to live." Even when they know – the doctor has said, "Now all is finished and nothing can be done anymore" – then too the family goes on pretending that you are not going to die. The family goes on helping the dream to remain a little longer, and the family goes on hoping some miracle will happen and the person will be saved.

This dialogue is immensely beautiful: when somebody is dying, it is better to make him aware that death has come. In fact it is better to make everybody aware – whether the death has come today or not, whether it is going to come tomorrow or the day after tomorrow doesn't matter: it is going to come. One thing is certain, that it is going to come. In life only one thing is certain, and that is death, so it is better to talk of it from the very beginning.

In the ancient cultures every child was made aware of death. Your very foundation should be made on that awareness of death. The man who is aware of death will certainly become aware of life, and the man who is unaware of death will remain unaware of life too – because life and death are two aspects of the same coin.

Ikkyu said, "If you think..." – but remember, he uses the word *if* because he knows, he knows this man, Ninakawa. He can see through and through, the man is transparent: he knows that he has arrived. Maybe he is just provoking Ikkyu to say something beautiful, to say something of truth. Maybe his provocation is just a trick, he is playing a game. That's why he says, "If you think you really come and go, that is your delusion. Let me show you the path on which there is no coming and no going."

What is that path on which there is no coming and no going? Yes, there is a place inside you, that is your eternal home, where nothing ever happens, where nothing ever changes – no birth, no death, no coming, no going, no arising, no disappearing. All is always the same.

With his words Ikkyu had revealed the path so clearly that Ninakawa smiled, nodded and passed away.

It can't be said in a better way – that's why Ninakawa didn't utter a single word anymore. But he smiled…because that which cannot be said can be smiled, that which cannot be said can be nodded, that which cannot be said can be shown. He showed it with his face: he recognized, he nodded, he said to Ikkyu, "Right, absolutely right. So you have also come home."

The dialogue between two masters is very rare, because when two masters meet, ordinarily they remain silent – there is nothing to say. But whenever it happens that two Masters say something to each other, it is a great play. There is a playfulness. It is not an argument, remember. It is a dialogue. They are provoking each other to say it in a better way. And Ikkyu has said it, Ninakawa is satisfied, utterly satisfied.

What has Ikkyu said? – that the life that we think is, is not, and we have not looked at that which is at all. We have become much too occupied with the illusory, and we go on remaining occupied with the illusory to the very end.

I have heard….

A man was very worried about his widowed mother-in-law. The widow was eighty-two years old and in much agony. One night, just to get her out of the house, the man arranged a date for her with a man who was eighty-five years old. She returned home from the date very late that evening and more than a little upset.

"What happened?" the man asked.

"Are you kidding?" she snapped, "I had to slap his face three times!"

"You mean," asked the man, "he got fresh?"

"No!" she replied. "I thought he was dead!"

But even up to that point people go on making dates. If there are really ghosts, they must be doing the same things you are doing…the same things. And it continues, life after life.

I have heard about a couple. They were in deep love with each other and they were both spiritualists. They believed in Christian Science. Just one day, talking to each other about death and profound subjects like that, they decided that if one of them died he had to contact the other on the thirtieth day after death, and the other would be open, receptive and would call on the thirtieth day at a particular time.

As it happened, the man died in a car accident. The woman was eagerly awaiting. The thirtieth day came, the right fixed time came. She closed the doors, put the light off, and asked, "John, are you there?" half believing, half not-believing. But she could not believe it when she heard John's voice.

John said, "Yes, darling. I am here."

The woman asked, "How are you? Are you happy there?"

And he said, "I am very happy. Look at this cow – how beautiful she looks."

"Cow?" the woman said, "What are you talking about?"

"Yes," he said, "such a beautiful cow. Such big tits, such a beautiful, young body, such proportion."

The woman said, "Have you gone mad?! I am dying to hear something more about heaven and you are talking about a foolish cow!"

And he said, "What heaven are you talking about? I have become a bull in Koregaon Park, Pune!"

It continues – the same stupidity, life after life. Unless you become conscious you will go on moving in this wheel, and this wheel goes on mercilessly repeating itself. It is very boring, and it is utterly stupid to continue it. But to become aware needs great effort. To become aware, you will have to go into a long struggle with your own sleep, with your own unconscious states. You will have to fight your way. The struggle is hard and arduous and the path is uphill.

Now the sutras. These sutras can immensely help you to awaken.

> Master Lu-tsu said:
> If you are not yet clear, I will make it clear to you through the
> threefold Buddhist contemplation of emptiness, delusion, and the
> center.

The compassion of the master is infinite. He makes things clear again and again, knowing perfectly well that your sleep is deep: you may not have heard the first time – he says it again; you may not have heard the second time.

Buddha lived for forty-two years after his enlightenment, saying the same thing morning, evening, day in, day out, for forty-two years – the same thing continuously – because one never knows in what moment you will be able to understand, one never knows when you may be receptive. One never knows when a small window will open in your heart and the guest will be able to enter and the ray of light will penetrate you.

In twenty-four hours' time you are not always the same. Sometimes you are very hard and it is very difficult to penetrate. Sometimes you are very deaf – you hear and yet you hear not – but sometimes you are a little more open, more vulnerable, more loving, more capable of listening, less argumentative. Sometimes you are soft, feminine. Sometimes you are masculine and hard. It is a rhythm that goes on changing. You can watch it, and you will soon become aware that there are moments when you are more understanding and there are moments when you are less understanding. You are not the same for twenty-four hours. You are constantly changing, you are in a flux, hence the Master has to go on speaking. One never knows when the right moment for you is, so he goes on repeating. Whenever the right moment comes the transformation will happen. A single hit in the heart and you will be a totally different person after that. You will never be the same again.

Lu-tsu has been saying.... We are coming closer and closer to the end of this beautiful book, *The Secret of the Golden Flower*. Again he says, *If you are not yet clear...* He has made everything clear, but...

> *If you are not yet clear, I will make it clear to you through*
> *the threefold Buddhist contemplation of emptiness, delusion,*
> *and the center.*

And what is clarity? Clarity is a state of mind when there are no thoughts. Thoughts are like clouds in the sky. And when the sky is full of clouds you cannot see the sun. When there are no clouds in your sky, in your inner sky, in your consciousness, there is clarity.

Clarity does not mean cleverness, remember. Clever people are not clear people. To be clever is easy because to be clever is nothing but another name for being cunning, a good name for being cunning. Clever people are cunning people but they are not clear people. To be an intellectual is not to be intelligent, remember. To be intellectual is easy: you can gather information, you can acquire knowledge and you can become a great intellectual, a scholar, a pundit – but that is not clarity and that is not intelligence. Intelligence is just the opposite. When there is no knowledge moving in the head, when there is no cloud passing in the inner sky, when there is no calculation, no cleverness, or cunningness, when you are not thinking at all but you are just there like a mirror reflecting whatsoever is – that is clarity. Clarity means a mirrorlike quality. And to be clear is to face God.

God cannot be known by knowledge, God is known by clarity. God is not known by cleverness, not by cunningness, but by innocence. Innocence is clarity. That's why Jesus says, "Unless you are like small children, you will not enter into my kingdom of God." What does he mean? He simply means that unless you are as clear as a small child whose inner sky is yet unclouded, whose mirror is still without any dust on it, whose perception is absolutely pure – he can see things as they are, he does not distort them, he has no investment in distorting them, he does not project, he simply sees whatsoever is the case, he is a passive mirror – that is clarity. Lu-tsu said: *If you are not yet clear, I will make it clear to you through the threefold Buddhist contemplation...* This threefold Buddhist contemplation is one of the greatest devices of meditation. Remember, it is a device, it is not a philosophy. If you think it is a philosophy you have missed the point totally.

And that's what has happened: down the ages great treatises have been written on Buddhist philosophy, and that is just nonsense because Buddha is not a philosopher. He has not taught any philosophy at all. He was really very anti-philosophical.

It was his usual procedure: whenever he would enter into a town, that his disciples would go in front of him declaring to the people, "Please don't ask philosophical questions of the Buddha." He had made a list of eleven questions; in those eleven questions the whole of philosophy is contained: about God, about creation, about reincarnation, about life after death and all that. In those eleven questions the whole possible philosophy is contained. You cannot ask any question if you look at that list of eleven questions. That list was declared in the town: "Please don't ask those questions of the Buddha, because he is not a philosopher, he is not a metaphysician, he is not a thinker! He has come here as a physician, not as a philosopher. If your eyes are blind, he has some medicine. If your ears are deaf, he's a surgeon."

Buddha has said again and again, "I am a physician," but great philosophy has arisen in his name, and the words that he used as devices have become philosophical tenets. For example, emptiness: now there are Buddhist schools which say that this is a fundamental principle – that all is empty. It is simply a device, it says nothing about existence. It simply says something about your mind. It helps you to become clear, that's all. Buddha is not concerned about existence, Buddha is concerned about your clarity, because he says, "If you are clear you will know what existence is." And what is the point in talking about existence? It is utterly futile. It is as if you are talking about light and colors and the rainbows and the flowers to a blind man: it is utterly absurd.

You cannot talk about the sunrise to the blind man and you cannot talk about the silver light of the moon in the night to a blind man. You cannot tell him that trees are green, because green will make no sense to him. He will hear the word – just the way you hear the word *God*, he will hear the word *green*: neither you understand nor does he understand. Just by hearing the word again and again don't get the idea, the stupid idea, that you understand what God is. God has to be seen to be understood. There is no other way. And green has to be seen to be understood. There is no other way.

Ramakrishna used to tell:

A blind man was invited by his friends. They prepared *kheer,* a delicacy made out of milk. The blind man loved the kheer very much and he asked, "What exactly is it? And how does it look?"

Sitting by his side was a great philosopher, and as philosophers are prone to – they cannot miss an opportunity to teach, to philosophize – he immediately started telling the blind man how the kheer was made, how it looked. And when he said, "It is pure white", the blind man said, "Wait! That word does not make any sense to me. What do you mean by 'pure white'? Will you be kind enough to explain it to me?"

And as philosophers are, without ever seeing that the man was blind, he started explaining what pure white was. He said, "Have you seen white swans, white cranes? Yes, it is just like a pure white crane, or a white swan, or a white flower."

"Crane?" the poor blind man said, "You are making it more and more mysterious. I don't understand what white is. Now the problem arises: What is this crane? I have never seen it."

And still the philosopher was not aware that this man could not see, so whatsoever he said was going to be irrelevant. And he started explaining what a white crane was. And then he invented a device: he gave his hand to the blind man and told him to touch it. And he said, "Look, the way my hand is bent, this is how the neck of the crane is."

And the blind man laughed joyously and was very happy, and he thanked him from the very bottom of his heart and said, "Now I understand what kheer is – like a bent hand? Now I understand. I'm so grateful to you."

Then the philosopher became aware of what he had done.

You cannot explain whiteness to a blind man, there is no way at all. Yes, you can help him: you can treat his eyes, you can send him to Dr. Modi's eye camp

– Dr. Modi sometimes comes here – he needs surgery. The day he's able to see, no explanation will be needed – he will know what white is, what green is. So is the case with God, so is the case with existence.

So remember, the first thing is that this is just a device: emptiness, delusion, and the center. This is not a philosophical statement. Buddha is not saying that "I am proposing a system of thought." He is simply saying that "I am creating a device."

Another story so it becomes clear to you:

A man came home from the market. Suddenly he saw his house on fire. His children were playing inside, small children. He shouted from the outside because he was afraid to go in himself. He shouted, "Children, come out! The house is on fire!" But the children were so engrossed in their games, they wouldn't listen. Then he devised: he shouted loudly, "Do you hear me or not? I have brought many toys for you from the market!" and they all rushed out – and he had not brought a single toy.

But those children had told him, "You are going to the market, so bring some toys for us." Outside, seeing no toys, they said, "Where are the toys?"

The man started laughing and he said, "It was a device to bring you out of the house which is on fire. Tomorrow I will bring toys for you."

These are devices. Remember, a device is neither true nor untrue. A device is either useful or useless, but never true or untrue. Those words are not relevant to a device. The meditations that you are doing here are all devices – neither true nor untrue. They are useful or useless, certainly, but there is no question of truth. I'm giving you toys so that you can come out of the house which is on fire. When you are out you will understand – even those children understood: when they saw the house on fire they forgot all about toys and they understood the love of the father. He must have loved those children immensely, that's why he could even lie. It was a lie.

You will be surprised to know that Zen Masters have been saying down the ages that Buddha was the greatest liar. But his compassion was such that he lied. He created devices. This is a device – three things to be contemplated: emptiness, delusion, and the center.

Emptiness means: this whole world outside, the objective world, is utterly empty. Think of it as empty, contemplate on it as empty and you will be surprised: the moment you start getting into this idea of the emptiness of the whole world, many things will start changing of their own accord. You will not be greedy – who can be greedy when things are empty? You will not be ambitious – how can you be ambitious when things are empty? If you know that the president's chair is just empty, who bothers? Because you give it too much substance – you make it much too real – you become ambitious. When you know that money is empty, who bothers? One can use it, but there is no question of worrying about it.

Start thinking that all this world that surrounds you is empty...forms and forms, like dreams.

Gurdjieff used to say to his disciples, "Walking on the street, remember that you are in a dream, and the people that are passing you are just dream phenomena. The shops are dreams." And meditating on this for three months it starts happening. A *great* explosion happens: suddenly everything becomes empty. Shops are there, people are walking, people are purchasing and the people who are passing you by are there. Nothing has changed on the surface, but suddenly you see just empty forms.

You go to a movie house and you know perfectly well that on the screen there is nothing but empty forms, but you are befooled by those empty forms. Sitting in a movie house you pass through all kinds of emotions. Some tragedy is happening and you start crying. Maybe that's why a movie house has to be kept in darkness, otherwise it would look so stupid and silly. If somebody – your wife, your friend sitting by your side – comes to know that you are crying, they will laugh. They will say, "What are you doing? There is just an empty screen, nothing else, and a projected film, just a game of white and black" – or maybe it is technicolor – "but it is all shadows." But one can become so involved in the shadows that the shadows start looking substantial.

Just the other way round is the device of the Buddha. Buddha says: These people who are looking so substantial to you, just think that they are a dream, empty. And one day you will be surprised: the whole world has become a white screen and only shadows are passing. And when only shadows are passing you will find a great detachment arising in you. You will be aloof, far away. Then nothing matters.

The second is delusion.

When you see, when you meditate, contemplate continuously that the whole world is empty, just a dream, the second phenomenon will start happening. Just by thinking that it is a dream it is not going to disappear, remember. Don't fall into that fallacy. Don't think, "If I think for long that the world is a dream, it will disappear." It is not going to disappear. You can go on knowing perfectly well that the film on the movie screen is just a projection, but still it continues. Just by your thinking, it will not disappear. It is not possible that for the meditator sitting in the cinema the film will disappear, that others will be able to see and he will not see, that he will see only the white screen, no. He will also see the film but with a difference: knowing that it is a dream. The world does not disappear, the world remains, but its significance is gone, its substance is gone.

It is like when you put a straight stick into water. The moment it enters into the water it looks bent. You take it out, you know it is not bent. You put it in again, but in the water it looks bent. Now you know perfectly well that this is a delusion – it only appears bent, it is not bent. But just by understanding that it is a delusion, the bentness will not disappear.

So the first thing is to meditate that the world is empty. Then the second thing will arise: the world still remains but now it is a delusion. Now it has no substance in it. It is the same stuff dreams are made of. The first unconscious perception of the world looked very substantial – it was very objective, it was *there*. After meditating on emptiness, it is still there but it is no longer substantial, it is only a mind game. It is like a dream.

That's what Hindus mean when they say, "The world is maya." It does not mean that for the saint it disappears. It simply means: now there is no value in it; it has become valueless, *utterly* valueless.

And the third thing is the center.

When the world is no longer substantial – the objective world disappears and becomes subjective delusion – then a new experience arises in you: for the first time *you* become substantial. Ordinarily you are projecting substance in the objective world. When you take it away from there, you become substantial. When the world is real, you are unreal. When the world becomes unreal, you become real. Let me explain it again through the movie.

If you become aware that there is only screen and shadows passing by, you will suddenly become aware that you are – those shadows are false but you are real. When you become completely lost in the shadows you become unreal – you forget yourself completely. In a dream, you forget yourself completely; the dream becomes real. Your whole reality is exploited by the dream. The dream takes all the reality and leaves you just hollow. When you have taken away the reality from the dream, you become real – a center arises in you, you become integrated. This is what is called individuation, crystallization. Either the world can be real or you can be real. Both cannot be real together.

Remember it: both cannot be real together. It is a change of gestalt. When you take reality out of the world, you start becoming real – you attain to being. And there are only two types of people: the people who are interested in having and the people who are interested in being.

The people who are interested in having, believe that the world is real – "Have more money, have more power, have more name, fame." They are unreal people: they have lost their center completely, they don't know who they are – the self has become a shadow. And the other kind of people, whom I call the religious people, are those who take the reality from the outside world and put it back where it belongs: they start gaining substance, they start gaining being – they have *more* being. And whenever you come across a person who has more being, you will feel a magnetic force. If Buddha attracted thousands of people it is because of this substantial being.

You can see it: if you look into the person who has political power you will find him just hollow, stuffed with straw and nothing else. The man who has much money and thinks that he has something, look into him and you will find just a black hole – a poor man is hiding behind, a beggar.

When a man has being then he may be an emperor or he may be a beggar – he's always an emperor. He may be a beggar like Buddha or he may be an emperor like Janak, it makes no difference: he's always an emperor, *wherever* he is. His kingdom is of the within, he has become substantial. He *is!* You are not. You have things, you don't have being – and you are using things as a substitute. The more objects you have, the more you can believe that you are, hence the hunger, the greed, the ambition: have more and more and more, because that is the only way you can deceive yourself that "I am somebody."

But the person who has being is unconcerned. Having is not his game. That does not mean that he leaves the world and renounces the world. If somebody renounces the world that simply shows that he still thinks the world is very real. Otherwise why should you renounce? You don't go shouting around the neighborhood in the morning after you get up, saying, "I have renounced my dreams. I was a king in the dream, and I have renounced the kingdom." People will think you have gone mad, they will inform the police. They will tell you to go to a psychiatrist, that you need some psychological treatment: "Are you mad? If it is a dream, how can you renounce it?"

Buddha renounced because he was living in a dream, thinking it very substantial. He became enlightened in the forest. Remember, when he renounced he was ignorant. Had he become enlightened before renouncing the world, he would never have renounced – there was no point! Janak became enlightened when he was a king in the palace, hence he never renounced it – there was no point. Krishna never renounced, there was no point. How to renounce something which is a shadow? Buddha renounced, Mahavira renounced because they were not yet enlightened.

What I am trying to say is this: people have renounced the world only in ignorance. Even Buddha, when he was ignorant, renounced the world. When he became enlightened he came back into the world. He had to come, because he knew that there are many other people who were fast asleep and thinking that their dreams are real: he had to wake them up.

The center arises only when you have taken all the reality from the outside world.

You have given your reality to things, you have poured your reality into things. You can watch it – people are in deep love with things, they have poured their souls into things and they have completely forgotten who they are – they are lost in their things.

Come back home, take your reality back. Things are only as real as you make them: it is your projection; otherwise they are empty, just white screens, of no significance at all – neither to be indulged in nor to be renounced. Both are irrelevant.

Emptiness comes as the first of the three contemplations. All things are looked upon as empty. And then follows delusion. Although it is known that they are empty, things are not destroyed, but one attends to one's affairs in the midst of the emptiness.

Listen to it deeply, because the people who are miserable in the world almost always start thinking of renouncing the world – as if the world is the problem! The world is never the problem, *you* are the problem, and wherever you go you will create the problem. You are the projector: You can renounce the world – the world is just a white screen – but the projector is within you. You can go anywhere and you will start projecting your film there, onto something else. It may not be a palace, then it may be a small hut – but that hut will become your kingdom. It may not even be a hut....

Wandering in the Himalayas I have come across many people. Once I came across a saint – a so-called saint – who had lived for at least thirty years in a cave. I liked the cave and I had two or three friends with me, so we stayed overnight in the cave. He was very angry. He said, "What do you mean? This is *my* cave!"

I said, "But you have renounced the world. How can this cave be yours?"

He said, "This is *mine!* I have lived for thirty years here."

"You may have lived here for thirty lives. But what is the meaning of renunciation? Why did you leave your wife? Why did you leave your house? What was the problem there? The problem was 'mine'. Now this cave is yours; now the problem has come with the cave, now the possessiveness has become attached to the cave."

It doesn't matter where you go; it is not so simple to change your life. You have to change your perception, your gestalt, your very being. You have to change the inner mechanism.

Lu-tsu said, *Things are not destroyed, but one attends to one's affairs in the midst of the emptiness.* One knows that all is empty but one continues to attend to one's affairs. There is no need to go anywhere. Where can you go? The whole world is empty! The Himalayas are as empty as the shops on M.G. Road, and the trees and the animals in the Himalayas are as much shadows as the people that live in Pune. It does not make any difference. The difference has to happen in your center, in your inner being.

> But although one does not destroy things, neither does one pay
> attention to them…

This is the change: one does not destroy, renounce, but one does not pay attention to them; one takes away one's attention. Attention is food – that's how you become attached to things. If a woman attracts you, you want to look at her again and again and again: you are feeding, you are projecting. If you love a thing, you pay attention to it. By paying attention you become attached to it. Attachment is through the bridge of attention. There is no need to renounce anything, just cut the bridge: live in the world without paying attention to things, go on moving as if you are moving in emptiness.

> …this is contemplation of the center.

And if you can do this, a center will arise in you. If you can live in the world as if you are not in it, if you can live in the world as if the world is just a dream, then suddenly a great energy will crystallize in you – the whole energy that was being dissipated. In a thousand ways you have been dissipating your energy, in every direction you are leaking. Your attention is a leaking point. When you are not leaking anymore, when your attention is no more moving, when your attention is gathering inside, accumulating inside, crystallizing inside, the center arises.

> *While practicing contemplation of the empty, one also knows that*
> *one cannot destroy the ten thousand things, and still one does not*
> *notice them.*

One knows that this dream has to continue. This is a beautiful dream too. There is nothing to be worried about in it. No need to renounce, no need to destroy, no need to fight with it. You don't fight with your shadow – you know it is a shadow. You don't want to destroy it either because you know it is a shadow. You are not worried about it because it goes on following you, it never leaves you alone, because you know it is a shadow. To know that the world is a shadow – a reflection of the real but not the real itself, the moon seen in the lake but not the moon itself – then one is at home even in the world. Without taking any notice of the world one goes on doing one's duties, goes on doing one's work, goes on living in a very detached way.

> *In this way the three contemplations fall together.*

Then the three contemplations are no longer three, it becomes one single contemplation. You are gathering at the center and you become aware of the center. This is what Gurdjieff calls self-remembering and Buddha calls *sammasati*, mindfulness, and Mahavira calls *vivek*, discrimination. Now you have seen what is unreal, you have discriminated the unreal from the real. Now you have seen what is shadow and what is substance.

You have seen the real moon and you have seen the reflection in the water. Now…the reflection continues! Just by knowing that it is a reflection it is not going to disappear. It continues, and there is no problem – it is beautiful! You can sit by the side of the lake and see the reflection – it is beautiful, there is no problem out of it – but you know it is not real.

> *But, after all, strength is in envisioning the empty.*

But remember, the whole integration, crystallization, arises out of *envisioning the empty*. That is the beginning of meditation.

Therefore, when one practices contemplation of emptiness, emptiness
is certainly empty...

Now you will have to go into a little more depth. When you know that all
is empty, there is a problem. You may start thinking that emptiness is something
very real – that is the problem – because the mind always gets caught in words.

There is a small story in the beautiful book *Alice in Wonderland*:

Alice reaches to the king. The king is waiting eagerly for some love-letter to
arrive. He's asking everybody, "Have you seen the messenger?" He asks Alice
also, "Did you see some messenger coming towards me?"

Alice says, "Nobody, sir," and the king thinks she has seen somebody whose
name is Nobody.

The king says, "But it seems Nobody walks slower than you, otherwise he
would have reached. Because I have been hearing the news again and again:
many people have arrived and they all say 'Nobody, sir,' and Nobody has not
reached yet! So it seems Nobody walks slower than you."

And Alice thought, "What is he saying? – nobody walks slower than me?" She
retorted back. She said, "Nobody walks faster than me!" She felt offended.

The king said, "Nobody walks faster than you? Why has he not arrived yet?"

Alice realised what the problem was. She said, "Sir, Nobody is nobody."

And the king said, "Of course. Nobody has to be Nobody. But where is he?"

And in this way it went on.

Even emptiness can become a thing. That's what happened in Buddhist
philosophy: philosophers started talking about emptiness as if emptiness were
God, as if emptiness were the very substance of life. They started talking of
nothing as if nothing were something. Nothing is only a word. In nature, no does
not exist. No is man's invention. In nature, everything is yes. In nature, only the
positive exists. The negative is man's invention.

For example, this chair is just a chair. In nature the chair is just a chair – it is
what it is – but in language we can say, "This is not a table. This is not a horse.
This is not a man" – and all those statements are right, because the chair is not
the table, and the chair is not the horse, and the chair is not the man. But these
are just linguistic negatives. In nature, in existence, the chair is simply the chair.
In nature the negative does not exist, but only the positive. But in language
the negative exists, and because of the negative great philosophies have arisen:

nothingness becomes a thing in itself, absence is talked about as if it were some kind of presence. So beware of it.

To make you alert, Master Lu-tsu says, remember:

> ...*emptiness is certainly empty, but delusion is empty too...*

Don't start thinking that delusion is real at least as a delusion. The delusion is also empty, just nothing in itself. For example, you see a snake in a rope: when you look, it is there, when you bring the light it is not there. Now the question can arise, "Where has the snake gone? From where had it come?" It never came, it never went away, it never existed. In nature the rope was always a rope. It was your illusion. You created, you projected the snake – a mind phenomenon.

Remember:

> ...*emptiness is certainly empty, but delusion is empty too, and the center is empty.*

This is the greatest contribution of Buddha.

The Hindus say: The world is illusion. The Jainas say: The world is illusion, the mind is also illusion. Buddha says: The world is illusion, the mind is illusion, and the center too. His insight is tremendous. He says if the seen is illusion, how can the seer be a reality? This is the profoundest statement of nirvana: if the dream is illusion then the dreamer is illusion too, if the dance is illusion, then the dancer is illusion too.

What is he trying to say? He's trying to say: first leave the world, then leave the illusion of the mind, and then leave the idea of the center too, of the self too; otherwise ego will persist. In a new name, in a subtle way, ego will persist. Let that too be gone, let everything be gone. Let there be simply emptiness, nothingness – and in that nothingness is all, in that utter absence is the presence.

Buddha never talks about that presence, because he says that has to be known, that should not be talked about, because mind is so cunning – if you talk about that presence it starts becoming greedy for that presence. If you talk about God, the mind starts thinking how to attain to God? Buddha never talks of or discusses God, not that God is not – who else can know that God is other than a buddha? But he never talks, for a very certain reason: the talk of God can create desire for God, and if desire is there you will never attain God. All desire has to disappear. Only in a state of desirelessness, God arrives.

> *It needs great strength to practice contemplation of delusion; then*
> *delusion is really delusion, but emptiness is also delusion, and*
> *the center is delusion too. Being on the way of the center, one also*
> *creates images of the emptiness.*

These images of emptiness are just helps. First, to take you out of the world Buddha says the world is empty. Now the delusion becomes true. Then he says the delusion is also empty. Now the center becomes true. Now he says the center is also empty. All has disappeared with no trace, utter silence – and in that utter silence is benediction, is God.

> *One practices also contemplation of delusion, but one does not call*
> *it delusion, one calls it central. As to what has to do with the center,*
> *more need not be said.*

And what will happen when all has gone – the world, the mind, the self? Master Lu-tsu is right. He says, *More need not be said* – because to say more will be dangerous, to say more will be giving you an object to desire – and the desire comes, and the whole world comes in.

This is a great device. If you can meditate over it, you will attain to the infinity, to the eternity, to the timeless – to the real life.

Enough for today.

CHAPTER 28

Tao is Already Happening

The first question:

> *Osho,*
> *Yes! Yes! Wake me up! This silly, multi-schizophrenic, leaking,*
> *watering can has been deeply affected by these lectures – but one*
> *thing lately is, I am feeling more and more gross. Osho, I want my*
> *lotuses to bloom, to feel Tao, be worthy of Tao, to be Tao.*
>
> *I want to fall into love! Will it, can it really happen? Can this real,*
> *beautiful soul inside burst into being?*

Tao, that's why I have given you the name Tao: there is a message for you in it. Tao means spontaneity, nature. Tao is not a practice, it is not effort, it is not cultivation. It is patience, it is trust, it is waiting for things to happen, even if one has to wait for eternity.

Tao needs no work on your part. All that you can do will be an undoing, because the moment the doer comes, nature disappears. The moment the doer takes hold of you, you are possessed by the idea of the ego. And then there is a wall between you and Tao – or call it Existence.

The doer has to dissolve, and you cannot do anything to dissolve it. How can you do anything to dissolve the doer? Whatsoever you do will go on feeding it. Just a simple understanding that all is taken care of… Trees are growing – not that they are making any effort to grow. Birds are singing – not that they go to some music school. Rivers are flowing – nobody has taught them how to reach to the ocean. They don't carry any map, they don't know any path, they don't have any scriptures, still every river reaches to the ocean.

Just look around! This immense universe is functioning so perfectly well that nothing can be added to it. It needs no improvement. Seeing this, one relaxes. If stars can go on dancing and flowers can go on blooming and birds can go on singing, why not you? You also belong to this universe. You are part of it. In fact, you are the most valuable part of it, the greatest flowering is going to happen in you – the flowering of consciousness, the golden flower of being. You are not neglected, you are taken care of.

To understand life is to relax.

Yes, only understanding is needed, not cultivation, not practicing. You don't need to become virtuous, religious. The people who try to become virtuous and religious become simply egoistic and nothing more.

Drop this hankering, Tao, to be something other than you are. This is the moment! Just be in it! Be utterly one with the whole. And it need not be practiced because it is already the case! All that is needed is a little bit of understanding, a vision, and then all starts happening of its own accord.

That's why I have given you the name Tao. The message is that you are not to create a character around you, that you are not to manufacture a certain personality in you, that you are not to think of future, of nirvana, of enlightenment, of God. God is not in the future, neither is God in the past. God is here and now, always here and now. God is *this* very condition.

People always think of God as the source, the original cause. They miss the point. God is not the original cause somewhere back, far, far away. God is not the original cause. Or, there are people who think of God as the ultimate goal, again far, far away in the future. Either in the past or in the future – and that's how you go on missing. And God knows only one tense, and that is present. The now is another name for God. He is *this* very condition! *This moment,* within and without, God is.

And God is not something sacred, holy, far away again in heaven. God is all the conditions – and when I say all, I mean all: the sacred, the profane; the body, the soul; the matter, the consciousness. The lowest of the low is God and the holiest of the holy is God, and there is not any difference between the two. Judas is as much God as Jesus, because there cannot be anything else. These are just roles, just acts played on the stage, in a drama.

To understand it is to relax. Then there is nowhere to go, then there is nothing to do. Then what is left is celebration, then what is left is to live joyously, rejoice moment-to-moment, and don't divide things. Don't say "I am going to the temple"; don't say that this is something sacred, holy. Drinking tea is as sacred as doing yoga. Sleeping silently, relaxed, is as sacred as prayer. Looking at a tree, talking to a friend, walking early in the morning, working in the factory or in the office, is as holy as anything else. This is the understanding that is needed for Tao to happen.

Tao is already happening – just your misunderstanding… Tao is already showering – in the sunrays, on the green trees. But you just think, "This is just the sun and these are just the trees – where is God? These are just people – where is God?" You want God to be something specific, and that's why you miss. God is not something special, not a particular being. God is all these conditions. God is this totality. This moment – my talking to you, your listening to me, this communion, this silence, this bridging – yes, this is God, this is Tao. So forget all about achieving. Don't become an achiever.

My sannyasins have to drop all kinds of ambitions – material, worldly and spiritual – all. To be ambitious is to be stupid. That's why I say politicians are stupid, because they are the most ambitious people in the world. The more ambitious you are the more stupid you will be.

Ambition makes you stupid. Why? – because intelligence is of the here and now and ambition is of the future, intelligence blooms *this* moment, and ambition always thinks of faraway lands. Ambition is of the tomorrow, and because of ambition you go on missing the intelligence that is just now showering, welling up within you.

I have heard…

It was decided to send a monkey and a politician to the moon. Their instructions on what to do after landing were sealed into pockets in their suits. As soon as they had touched down on the lunar landscape, the monkey opened his set of instructions.

It read:

Check all fuel tanks.

Check computer and re-program the same.

Take samples of rock, sand and air.

Check oxygen levels and density.

Check landing craft for damage.

Check stabilizers and anti-gravity devices.

Then send radio message down to Earth reporting position.

Then the politician opened his sealed instructions.

It said in big letters: Feed the monkey!!!

Ambition makes a person really stupid – even a monkey is more intelligent. Don't be ambitious! And remember, mind is very cunning: you drop ambition in one direction and the mind starts creating the same ambitious trap in another direction. Running after money, one day you understand that it is futile – even if you attain it, death will take it away. You start dropping that ambition. But then you start thinking "How to have more virtue?" It is the *same* game – "How to have more money" – now you say, "How to have more virtue, more *punya.*"

Do you know, the name of this town, Pune, comes from the Sanskrit root punya? Punya means virtue. Do you see any virtuous people in Pune?

In fact, the virtuous person cannot be religious, because he has allowed ambition to enter from the back door – again he has started accumulating, acquiring. Somebody is on a power trip in the world, and then one day, seeing the futility of it.... And one day everybody comes to see the futility of it, even the mediocre mind comes to see the futility of it. It is so futile! If you fail you fail, if you succeed you fail – it is so futile!

If you fail, certainly you fail, and there is frustration. If you succeed, then too deep down you fail, because you see you have succeeded and nothing has happened through your success. You remain the same kind of empty, hollow, ugly beggar – nothing has happened. All the money has accumulated around you, you are sitting on the throne of a president, and deep down the same beggar, the same ugly face, the same monster, the same horrible mind. So failing you fail, succeeding you fail – this is the futility.

Then the mind starts thinking of having something in paradise. But that is again the same game, played with different names, in different times, in different spaces – but the same mind projecting.

My teaching to you is: live in the *here and now!* Drop *all* kinds of ambitions – this is sannyas. Drop *all* kinds of ambitions, and see the miracle happening: once you drop all ambitions you will have so much energy left that there will be no way other than to celebrate. You will have so much energy in you – all the energy that is involved in ambitions is released because ambitions have been dropped – and energy becomes an oceanic experience within your soul. That is paradise, that is God. God is not a goal, but an experience of a non-ambitious mind.

Tao has not to be achieved! The achievers go on missing it. The non-achievers suddenly realize that they have always lived in paradise, but because of their ambitions they were not able to see it.

So Tao, just try to understand what I am sharing with you. I am sharing with you this moment, this space. I am not giving you any goals. I am not driving you crazy for some achievement in the future. I am not inspiring you to run and chase some shadows. I am simply imparting to you what has happened to me, I want it to be shared with you: dropping all ambition, I have arrived.

Drop all ambitions and just be, and see the beauty and the benediction of existence. It is incredible, it is simply far-out! You have never dreamt about it, how beautiful it is. You *could not* have dreamt about it, it surpasses all your imaginations and fantasies. Its beauty is unbelievable, and the grace that is showering on you is just showering for no reason at all. It is *very* unreasonable! God does not give you because you are worthy. God gives you because he has so much, he cannot contain it!

Try to see my vision – it is totally different from your so-called religions. Your so-called religions are very miserly and very economical. Your so-called religions believe in the laws of economics: you do this and God will do this to you, be worthy and he will make you happy, do something wrong and you go to hell – a very simple mathematics, as if your God is nothing but a magistrate who goes on looking into the books of laws and goes on sending people to hell or heaven.

God does not believe in your economics. God believes in love, God is love – not economics. He does not give you because you are worthy, he gives because he has! Remember the famous Jesus parable? – and Jesus has told the most beautiful parables ever told in the world. Nobody has ever been able to surpass him.

The parable is:

A man, a very rich man, has a great garden, the grapes are ripe. He sends his manager to the marketplace to bring a few laborers – those grapes have to be collected now, otherwise they will start falling, they will start rotting. A few laborers come and they start working. By the afternoon it is realized that these people are not enough, so more are called. When the sun is almost setting it is realized that even this will not do, so more laborers are called. And then the sun sets and the darkness descends and they all gather…and the owner of the garden gives everybody the same amount of money – to those who had come in the morning and to those who had come in the afternoon, and even to those who had just come and had only worked not more than half an hour.

Naturally, the people who had come in the morning became annoyed, irritated, angry. They said, "What is this? This is unfair! We worked the whole day and we get the same amount of money for our work. And these people have just come, they have not even worked at all – they are also getting the same amount of money? This is unfair!"

And the master started laughing and he said, "Just think of one thing: whatsoever you have got, is it not enough for your labor?"

They said, "It is enough. It is in fact double what we ordinarily get from somebody else."

The master said, "Then why are you worried about others? This is my money. You have got double of what you would have got anywhere else, but you are not happy – you are being miserable because I have given to others. This is my money and I have so much to give: my treasures are full, I am burdened. I give to these laborers not because they have worked, but because I have so much that I don't know what to do with it! Why are you angry?"

Jesus tells this parable in reference to God. And he says, "When you are facing God he will give you not because you have done this or you have done that – not because of your worth – but because he has *so* much, he is burdened. He is burdened like a cloud full of rain: it *has* to rain – not because the earth is worthy. Have you not watched? – the clouds come and they rain on all kinds of soil. They rain on stones, rocks, they rain on fertile soil, and they rain also on wastelands where nothing grows and nothing will ever grow.

Exactly like that, when a flower opens up, its fragrance is released to the winds, to all the directions, to whomsoever passes by the road it is available. It makes no distinction between the worthy and the unworthy. That's what I want to relate to you...

Somebody else has asked one question: "Osho, I have listened this whole month. You have not even mentioned once the law of karma."

I cannot mention it because it is part of economics. It is part of human cunningness and cleverness. It has nothing to do with real religion.

The law of karma says you will get only that which you earn. And I want to say to you: you don't get according to your worth, you get according to God's abundance – sinners and saints, good and bad. The only thing that is needed is: Are you ready to receive it? I am not talking about worthiness. I am simply saying: Are you open to accept it? Are you ready, available, vulnerable, so when it showers on you, you can let it soak in?

Who is available? One who lives in the present, moment-to-moment, is available to God. And this I am saying to you because this has been *my* experience. I am not talking philosophy to you; simply stating what I have experienced. God gives out of his abundance. But you are not available. You are in the past or in the future. The future is not yet, the past is no more: you move in shadows.

Come to the real! And the real is always the here and now. God knows only one time and that is now, and only one space, that is here.

The second question:

> Osho,
> You said meditation is "non-doing." But to lose oneself in an activity,
> is it not required to focus, choose, will?

If you focus, you will remain; if you choose, the chooser will be there; if you will, the ego cannot disappear. If you really want to get lost in any kind of activity you have to be a non-chooser, you have to drop your will.

Your will simply means you don't trust God's will yet. Your will simply means you are still fighting, struggling with God. Your will simply means you are trying to push the river, you are not ready to go with the river. Your will simply means you are trying to conquer something, you are violent, you are aggressive.

To be lost in any activity – it may be cleaning the floor or dancing or painting or loving, it may be anything – to be lost in it, you have to drop your will. You have to simply be like a dead leaf in the wind, so wherever the wind blows the dead leaf moves with it: to the south it says yes, to the north it says yes, if the wind leaves it on the ground it says yes. It knows only *yes*, it knows no *no* – it is a yes-saying – and that is the moment of benediction, of bliss. Then you will never be frustrated because there is nobody to be frustrated. Frustration comes out of expectations. Out of will is your defeat.

And see people's faces: they are all looking defeated, sooner or later. Except for small children, you will find everybody defeated. And small children are still laughing and smiling because they don't know what is going to happen. Soon their laughter will disappear, soon their smiles will be gone, soon they will become dry, desert-like, just as everybody else has become. Look at the old people, how they are living: disillusioned they are. They had great dreams, all dreams have failed, all gods have failed – they are utterly frustrated, their root and all. Now they have only one climate around them – that of frustration.

That is why old people are so chronically irritated – life has been cheating them. With what great fantasies they had started the journey, with what beautiful dreams! – and slowly, slowly all dreams have turned into dust, and they have only one taste in their mouths – that of dust. And nothing else. How can they avoid not being irritated? They are annoyed – not towards somebody in particular; they are simply in rage! They lived in vain! Seventy years, eighty years have passed, they passed through all kinds of turmoil, they suffered all kinds of anxieties and nightmares, and for what? – "a tale told by an idiot, full of fury and noise, signifying nothing"?

And when a man comes to see that this whole affair of life has been a kind of idiocy, he really feels frustrated: "What kind of joke is this?" God does not look to be benevolent, he seems to be a kind of sadist, torturing people: giving them great ideas and then frustrating them continuously. As you grow up you grow deeper and deeper into frustration. Soon your life is nothing but a tragedy.

This happens because of your dreams, expectations, ambitions, your will. You wanted to do something in the world and you could not, hence the impotence.

My teaching is: please, don't try to do anything in the world – let things happen – and you will never be frustrated, and your life will remain fresh, as fresh as ever, and you will be able to smile even at the very last moment. You will die smiling. You will be a conqueror without any effort to conquer, because all efforts to conquer lead to defeat. The real conquerors are those who never try to conquer. This is the paradox to be understood: the real gainers are those who had never thought of gaining anything, who simply lived moment-to-moment, enjoyed the morning and the afternoon and the evening.

When the great Zen Master, Joshu, was asked, "What is your fundamental teaching?" he said, "When it is hot it is hot, and when it is cold it is cold."

The man who was asking was a great philosopher. He said, "Are you kidding me? This is your philosophy – 'When it is hot it is hot, when it is cold it is cold'? What kind of philosophy is this?"

Joshu said, "This is the whole of what I have been teaching to my disciples: just live in the moment, whatsoever it is – if it is hot it is hot – accept it and don't desire the opposite."

That is what will is – it is hot and you want it to be cool, it is cool and you want it to be hot. That is will. Will means desiring something which is not. Desiring against reality is will. When young be young, when old be old.

Another Zen Master was asked, "How do you live? What is the secret of your constant joy?"

He said, "Not much of a secret, a simple phenomenon: when I feel hungry I eat and when I feel tired I sleep."

This is living will-lessly: when hungry one eats, when tired one sleeps. This is living moment-to-moment – with no plan, with no program, with no desire to impose your will upon existence. The very effort to impose your will on existence is *violent*. The really non-violent person is one who does not impose his will upon existence. He takes things as they come and he is always surprised that whatsoever comes brings a treasure with it.

But you are constantly desiring something else, so whatsoever comes never fulfills you. And what you desire is not going to come because this whole, this immense whole, has no obligation to fulfill your desires. You can be with it, you can be against it. If you are against it you will live in hell, if you are with it you will live in heaven. That's my definition of heaven and hell: to be with the whole is heaven, to be against the whole is hell.

You ask, "You said meditation is 'non-doing.'"

Yes. I am not saying that a meditator will become lazy, indolent. No! He will do a thousand and one things but he will not be the doer of it, that is to be remembered.

It happened: a Zen Master was chopping wood. A man had come to inquire. He had heard the name of the Zen Master. It had been a long journey to come to the mountains where the Master lived with his disciples. He asked this woodcutter – because he could not think that the Master would be chopping wood – he asked this woodcutter, "I have heard about a great Zen Master who is enlightened. Where is he?"

And the Master said, "Look at me! I am that!"

The seeker thought this man to be mad. Still, to be polite with him – and it is better to be polite with a madman…. And he had a great axe in his hand, and who knows? And he looked so ferocious….

And he said, "I am that! What do you want?"

He said, "So you are that great Master! What did you do before your enlightenment?"

He said, "I used to chop wood and carry water from the well."

"And now what do you do?"

He said, "I chop wood and carry water from the well."

And the man said, "Then what is the difference? Then what is the point of your enlightenment if you still chop wood and carry the water from the well?"

And the master laughed…and the mountains must have laughed with him, and the trees. It is said, around that monastery, that still, after thousands of years, sometimes that laughter is heard. He laughed and said, "You fool! Before enlightenment *I* used to chop wood, *I* used to carry water. Now water is carried, wood is chopped. I am not the doer, that is the difference."

I am not saying that a meditator has to become lazy, I am not saying that a meditator has to become dull and dead. In fact the meditator will have more energy than the non-meditator can ever have, and the energy will have its own dance: it will chop wood, it will carry water from the well.

A meditator is bound to become very creative – only a meditator can be creative – because all the energies converge on the moment. He has so much that it starts overflowing. His cup is small and his energy is so much that it starts overflowing. But he is a non-doer: his action has no will in it. He dances because he finds dance happening, he loves because he finds love happening.

Observe the fact: can you will love? Can you will it if you are ordered to "love this woman!" or "love this man!"? You can only go through empty gestures of loving. You may hug the woman, you may kiss the woman, but can you love? It is impossible to will love. There is no way! You can be forced, you can be ordered: "See the beauty of the roseflower!" and if somebody is standing behind you with a gun and he says, "Look at the beauty of the flower, otherwise you will be killed," you will look and you will say, "Yes, so beautiful, so tremendously beautiful."

It happened…an ancient Sufi story….

When Tamerlane conquered the town of Mulla Nasruddin, he had heard many stories about Mulla, many mysterious stories: of his occult powers, esoteric powers, and all that.

The first thing he did was, he asked Mulla to come to the court. He told Mulla, "I have heard many stories of your occult power, esoteric experiences. Are they true? And don't try to lie to me. And you know that I am a dangerous man. If you lie your head will be cut off immediately." And he took his sword out of the sheath – a naked sword in the hands of Tamerlane who used to cut people as if there was no life in them, and he used to enjoy cutting people.

Mulla looked down and said, "See, I can see hell there – deep down in the earth – and devils are torturing people and great fire is burning." And then he looked up and he said, "Look, I can see heaven, God sitting on a great golden throne and angels dancing and singing and praising him."

Tamerlane said, "How do you manage to do these miracles? How can you see? I don't see anything! What is your secret?"

Mulla said, "No secret – it is just fear – I don't see anything either! You put your sword back into the sheath and then all these visions will disappear. It is just fear, nothing else."

You go on living a life of fear, desire, ambition, greed. And out of your fear you create heaven and hell, and out of your greed you create heaven and hell, out of your ambition you create heaven and hell – but these are all your creations. Out of your greed you create great philosophies. Your God is nothing but your fear personified, and your prayers are nothing but your tremblings; you are afraid.

What I am saying to you is: no other prayer is needed, no hell and heaven are needed – all is available right this very moment. You just drop all this nonsense of willing. Let God will through you, let God *live* through you – and it is not that you will become lazy. You will become very, very creative: great poetry will be born out of you and great music will arise in your being. But one thing is certain, you will not look at it as if it is your creation, you will know it is God's – he has spoken through you, he has painted through you, he has loved through you.

You cannot will love. You can be ordered to love, and that is what is happening: millions of couples in the world have been ordered to love, because "She is your wife – love her!" And "he is your husband – love him!" And now what can you do? – because the police are there and the court is there and the government is there, and if you don't love you will be in trouble. Out of fear you try to manage – you pretend. And naturally, pretensions cannot make you happy.

And the same way, you go to the church and to the temple and to the mosque to pray – because you have been ordered to pray. If you don't pray you will fall in hell, and who wants to suffer in hell? Is this life not enough of a suffering? Who wants to go to hell? Enough is enough! One wants to avoid hell, so it is better to go and pray. But it is out of fear, and anything that is out of fear is false. You cannot will prayer and you cannot will love and you cannot will the experience of beauty. It is not possible. Nothing that is of any value is possible through willing. All that is beautiful and great happens when your will disappears.

Focusing is not needed, because focusing means concentration, concentration means tension. Non-focusing is needed, a state of utter distraction is needed so that you are open and available to all the sides, to the whole existence. And the difference is great: when you concentrate you are focused on one thing, but closed to everything else.

For example, if you are listening to me you can listen in two ways. One is the way of concentration that has been taught to you in the schools, colleges, universities. If you concentrate on me, then you will be sitting here very tense and you will feel tired. Then you cannot listen to this airplane passing by, and the birds chirping, and the wind blowing through the trees. No, all that has to be excluded from your consciousness. You have to narrow down your consciousness, and narrowing down your consciousness is great effort, tiring.

There is another way of listening, and that is my way of listening: you are simply open, available. I am speaking, the airplane passes by, you hear that noise too; the birds sing, you hear that noise too – and this is not a distraction. In fact, what I am saying becomes more beautiful because it partakes of many other things too. The birds singing around add something to what I am saying: it becomes more total, it is not taken apart from life. It represents the whole life then. Then the trees are a part of it, and the wind and the rain and the sun – all are a part of it. And then you are not tired after one hour, you will feel refreshed, relaxed. You may not be able to remember exactly what I have said, but that is not needed at all. You will have absorbed it. It will have its impact on your being forever, it will have become part of you, you will have digested it.

One needs to memorize something if one does not understand it. If one understands it, it is finished; there is no need to carry it as a memory. You need to memorize something because you don't understand it – out of fear: maybe sometimes in future it will be needed, so you have to program your mind. But it is a tiring business. Focusing is concentration, concentration is tiring.

I teach you meditation, not concentration. And this is the difference: meditation is just an open, relaxed being, availability – to all that is happening – and then suddenly silence descends, the beyond penetrates you, the heaven penetrates the earth. Then God is very close by: he is hand in hand, you breathe him.

I want you to experience God with me. I don't want you to practice experiencing God later on. That is nonsense! If you cannot experience it here with me, where are you going to experience it? Sitting in your room in a lotus posture, looking silly, you will experience God? Experience it this very moment! *This* is a state of non-doing – I am not doing anything. Talking to you is not an act for me, it is just a response. It is natural. Your presence provokes it. And I am not there willing it – it is happening. And your listening to me need not be in any kind of will – you also let it happen. Then there will be meeting, communion.

There is no need to focus, no need to choose, no need to will. These are the ways of the ego, and the ego has to be utterly dropped. Then you live in a totally different way, an egoless way. And that is the way of Tao.

The third question:

Osho,
Why do I always fall asleep during the discourse?

This is a very ancient religious practice. This is not new. You are not doing something special. Religious people have always been doing it. So take it as a confirmatory sign! You must be becoming religious.

I have heard…

During the Second World War the pastor at a church was asked how many persons could sleep in the church building in the event of an attack.

"I don't know," replied the pastor, "but we sleep four hundred every Sunday morning."

This is perfectly good. You enjoy your sleep! Don't feel guilty about it. Sleep is as much a spiritual activity as anything else. Let it happen. Don't be worried about it, otherwise you will start fighting with your sleep. What will you do – you start feeling sleepy and you will not sleep?

I don't give you any commandment. I don't give you any orders. I don't say, "Don't sleep. This is bad-mannered, this is a sin." No! What can you do? If sleep comes, sleep comes. Let it come. Fall into it easily, totally, and you will be surprised – soon it will disappear. Or a new phenomenon will arise in you: that you will become able to sleep and yet absorb me.

We have a special term for it in India – no other language of the world has such a term because no other people have gone so deeply into these spaces. We have a special term; we call it *yoga nidra,* a meditative sleep. If you listen to me totally, you can relax. And the relaxation will take you into a kind of sleep which is not ordinary sleep. You will not hear exactly what I am saying, but still, you will find that something has been constantly happening to you. So nothing to be worried about.

And there can be many reasons. Maybe your sleep is not deep enough in the night. And remember, I am not against sleep at all, no. I am not against anything.

If your sleep is not good in the night, maybe in the morning, feeling love for me, feeling warmth for me, being together with me, you start almost feeling like you are cuddled, and you go into sleep. It is perfectly good, it is healthy. And if you can sleep deeply here, soon you will be able to sleep deeply in the night too. Then it will disappear. If it is an ordinary sleep it will disappear. If it is yoga nidra, a meditative sleep, it will become deeper and deeper. But you will not be missing anything.

And one thing is very good about it – don't feel guilty, because I say this is a very ancient religious tradition. In fact doctors have been known to send people to religious discourses when they suffer from insomnia.

It reminds me of an atheist who often got into discussions with the minister. After much urging the atheist finally agreed to attend a church service the following Sunday. The minister prepared a masterly discourse to appeal specially to his friend's appreciation of logic.

When the two met the next day, the atheist conceded, "I will say this for your Sunday sermon – it kept me awake until the early hours of the morning."

The clergyman beamed. "I am happy that I succeeded in making you doubt the wisdom of your convictions."

"Ah," said the other, "it was not that. You see, when I nap in the daytime I can't sleep at night."

Remember perfectly well that with me all is allowed. Never feel guilty. If there is anything I want you to get rid of, that is guilt; otherwise small things start becoming wounds in you. You feel guilty – "What will others think? You have fallen asleep!" This has nothing to do with anybody else. Fall asleep! Waking also, you are not very awake, so I don't think you will be losing anything. What is your wakefulness? Just your eyes are open, that's all. And one can sleep perfectly well with open eyes – just a little practice is needed.

That's what happens in many car accidents. Many car accidents happen somewhere in the night nearabout between two and four, and the reason is that the driver is trying hard to keep his eyes open; by and by, he becomes capable of keeping his eyes open, and still he falls asleep. He keeps his eyes open and falls asleep with open eyes. Now this is a scientific finding. And that worsens the whole problem, because he thinks he is awake, so he goes on driving because his eyes are open – but the sleep has taken possession of him, he is no longer aware of his surroundings or dangers.

When you are awake, there is not much wakefulness; just a small part of you is awake. So you are not a loser, don't be worried. Whenever sannyasins come and ask me, "What should we do?" I tell them: Don't fight, otherwise you will miss me and you will miss the sleep too. That will be really unnecessary trouble. If you fight with your sleep you cannot understand what I am saying and you cannot sleep either. At least save one – sleep. If it is physical sleep it will help you: soon you will be able to sleep deeply in the night, because you learn the art of sleeping. If you can sleep here while I am shouting at you, then who can keep you awake in the night? Or, if it is yoga nidra, then it is a tremendously beautiful space.

There are a few people who fall into yoga nidra: Sheela is one, Mukta is one, Arup is one. They fall into yoga nidra. That is good! They become so utterly silent that it *looks* like sleep. They also feel asleep, but something starts entering into them. Yoga nidra is more like a hypnotic sleep.

You can go to Santosh, our hypnotist – he will tell you more about it. In a hypnotic sleep something tremendously beautiful is possible. What happens in a hypnotic sleep? The person becomes asleep to the whole world, but not to the hypnotist's voice. He goes on listening to it, one window remains open. That is why the hypnotist can order. He can tell the hypnotized person, "Stand up!" and he immediately stands up. If somebody else orders him he will not listen, he will remain asleep. In yoga nidra that happens.

Being with the master you become so relaxed – where else can you be so relaxed? Where else are you so accepted and so welcomed, so loved, so cherished? You start falling into a kind of sleep.

In fact, the word *hypnos* means nothing but sleep. The meaning of the word *hypnos* is sleep. You start falling into a kind of relaxed state, deep relaxation, but still my voice is being heard. Your intellect may not understand but your heart goes on absorbing it. And then it goes very deep, sometimes deeper than you can hear it while awake.

I have heard…

Herb McGlinchey, a Philadelphia ward leader, was once followed around by a reporter who was trying to write a feature story on how a busy politician spends his time. Now McGlinchey's drinking abilities were legendary. By the end of the day McGlinchey was still fresh and dapper, but the reporter who followed McGlinchey back to the bar at the forty-second ward clubhouse was soaked to the gills and was taking a nap sitting at the bar with his head resting on his folded arms. McGlinchey was whispering into his ear, "McGlinchey is the greatest. McGlinchey is terrific."

"What are you doing, Herb?" an aide asked.

"Shut up!" McGlinchey is reported to have said. "I am talking to his subconscious. We are going to own this guy!"

When you fall into yoga nidra, your conscious mind goes into sleep, but your unconscious is very alert and goes on absorbing. And that absorption is very deep, it goes to your very roots.

So don't be worried about it. If you fall asleep, fall asleep. Hungry, eat; tired, sleep. And when it is hot, it is hot, and when it is cold, it is cold. This acceptance is trust.

The fourth question:

Osho,
How do you feel when somebody leaves sannyas?

I feel great! – because unless I leave, you cannot leave sannyas. And when I see that it is almost impossible to work upon you, when I see that you are not going to be available to me – in this life at least – I start taking myself away from you. You can't be aware of it, because you are not even aware that I had got involved with you. If you were aware of my involvement with you, then there would be no need for me to drop you. I start taking away, because the same energy can be used by somebody else, the same time can be used by somebody else who has more potential, more receptive.

And you will need another Buddha in some other time, in some other life. This is not the time for you, this is not the life for you. But because you are not aware of anything, one day you think you are leaving sannyas. Before you leave, I have left you – in fact, long before. Sometimes it has happened that I have left the man two years before, and after two years' time he leaves sannyas. It takes him two years because people go on postponing, postponing, postponing. But I always give him the feeling – so that he feels good – that it is he who is leaving sannyas. I don't expel anybody from sannyas, at least not directly. I always give the feeling to the person that he is leaving it; at least he will feel good that he has done something.

But I always feel great, because I feel unburdened. If a person is rock-like, to carry him is a burden. And if he does not cooperate, then it is utterly useless to go on working on him. There is a certain time limit. I work, I do whatsoever can be done, but if I see it is an impossible case – and there are impossible cases – then he has to be left for somebody else in some future life.

And certainly, many more buddhas will be coming in future and they will need disciples, so I cannot finish all! Gautama the Buddha took care of me, I have to take care of other buddhas who will be coming.

It reminds me of what happened to a Presbyterian minister.

One summer the Baptists and the Methodists agreed to stage an evangelical revival week. The Presbyterians reluctantly agreed to go along with it. And at the end of the week the ministers got together to discuss the results of the camp Bible session.

The Methodist said, "We won four new members."

The Baptist said, "We did even better. Six people became converts to the Baptist faith."

They both turned to the Presbyterian and asked him how he did.

The parson answered, "We did best of all. We did not add any but we got rid of ten."

The work consists of two things: I have to help people to become sannyasins – seeing their possibilities, potentialities, hoping for them; but when I see that a person is impossible – that the more I give to him the less he receives, the more I give to him the more closed he becomes, as if he is obliging me – when this feeling becomes settled.... And it is not that I take a hasty decision about it. I give all the opportunities and occasions for the person, but if it is impossible, then it is impossible – then I withdraw myself from his being. Once I have withdrawn, sooner or later he will have to drop sannyas.

It functions both ways. The moment you take sannyas, you think *you* are taking sannyas. In the majority of cases I have chosen you – that's why you take sannyas; otherwise you would not have been able to take such a risk. And it also works the second way: when you drop sannyas, I have chosen you and I help you to drop it, because left to yourself you may go on postponing for your whole life. When you take sannyas, then you postpone for a long, long time. When you want to drop it, then too you postpone for a long, long time. You cannot do anything immediately. You cannot live the moment in its totality.

And this too I have felt: once you have left sannyas there is a possibility you may come back – because then you will miss me and then you will understand what was being showered on you. Then you will miss the nourishment, then you will miss the contact. When you are getting it you start taking it for granted. Sometimes it is good to take it away so real thirst and an appetite arises in you and you start seeing.

But next time when you come for sannyas, it is not going to be that easy. I will not initiate you so easily; then you will have to earn it. Once you drop sannyas, coming back is going to be difficult. I will create all kinds of barriers. Unless you transcend those barriers you will not be accepted again.

That too is to help you, because there are people who can enjoy things only if they are difficult. If things are very simple and easy they cannot enjoy them. They need long, hard, arduous ways.

Sannyas is a simple phenomenon because the whole foundation of it is to relax and live in Tao, relax and let God take care of you. It has to be very simple – it is simple – but your mind understands difficult things more easily: if you have barriers to cross you become challenged.

When Hillary reached the Everest peak, do you know what he said? He was asked, "Why? Why did you take such a risk? – because there is nothing. You went there and you came back, there is nothing to get! Why did you take such a risk? And many people have died before: for almost seventy years people have been trying to reach Everest."

And do you know what Hillary said? He said, "It was such a challenge! Just the presence of Everest, unconquered, was a great challenge. It had to be conquered! There is nothing, I know, but that is not the point. Unconquered, and Everest is standing there, proud? Man has to conquer it!"

This is how man's mind functions.

So next time when a person comes back – and many want to come back – then it is going to be difficult. Then I am going to create all kinds of difficulties for you, for your sake. That too is a help for you.

The last question:

> *Osho,*
> *I wonder why you don't hit me on the head as you hit the others.*

I will tell you a small story.

The question reminds me of the flies that those expert Japanese Samurai wielders can cut in mid-air. An American tourist heard of the incredible swordsmanship of the cultists of the ancient rite. While in Tokyo he made inquiries as to where the best swordsman was. The best was not available, neither was the second best, but the American got a chance to see Japan's number-three Samurai wielder. The swordsman let a fly out of the bottle. While it was in flight he struck with the sword – Swish! – the fly was cut in half.

The American was impressed. He could not see that anyone could do better than that. But a little later he wangled an invitation to the number-two man. Again a fly was released from the bottle. The Japanese expert made two swishes with the sword. Incredibly the fly was hacked and quartered in mid-air.

Now he could not see how number-one could do better than that. Finally his place on the waiting list went to the top. He was ushered into the presence of the best swordsman in Japan. Once again there was the ritual of opening the bottle with the fly. While it was buzzing above, the swordsman wielded a great chop. To the American's surprise the fly kept in flight. The American said, "I don't see why you are number one. The number-three sliced the fly in two, and then I saw the number-two cut it to quarters in two passes. But you missed completely."

"Miss, did I?" said the number-one swordsman. "I assure you, that fly will never propagate again!"

Enough for today.

CHAPTER 29

Where the Positive and Negative Meet

The Tao, the undivided, great One, gives rise to two opposite reality principles, the dark and the light, yin and yang. From yin comes the receptive feminine principle; from yang comes the creative masculine principle; from yin comes ming, life; from yang, hsing or human nature.

Each individual contains a central monad, which, at the moment of conception, splits into life and human nature, ming and hsing.

In the personal bodily existence of the individual they are represented by two other polarities, anima and animus. All during the life of the individual these two are in conflict, each striving for mastery.

If the life-energy flows downward, that is, without let or hindrance into the outer world, the anima is victorious over the animus; no Golden Flower is developed. If the life-energy is led through the "backward-flowing" process, that is, conserved, and made to "rise" instead of allowed to dissipate, the animus has been victorious. A man who holds to the way of conservation all through life may reach the stage of the Golden Flower, which then frees the ego from the conflict of the opposites, and it again becomes part of the Tao, the undivided, great One.

The old pond
Frog jumps in
The sound of water

This is one of the most famous haiku by Matsuo Basho. It has that special flavor that only awakened people are aware of. Its beauty is not only aesthetic but existential. Its fragrance is that of buddhahood.

Tao simply means that which is, with no qualification, with no adjective. Tao means: just so.

The old pond
Frog jumps in
The sound of water

Haiku is not ordinary poetry. The ordinary poetry is of imagination. The ordinary poetry is a creation of the mind. Haiku simply reflects that which is. Consciousness becomes a mirror and reflects that which confronts it. The mirror remains untouched by what it reflects.

An ugly person passes before a mirror – the mirror does not become ugly, the mirror remains in its sameness. A beautiful person passes by, the mirror does not become beautiful either. And when there is nobody to reflect, the mirror is still the same. Reflecting, not reflecting, reflecting good, reflecting bad, the mirror remains virgin. So is the consciousness of one who has awakened.

Basho was a disciple of the Zen Master, Buko. The time this incredibly beautiful haiku was born, he was living in a small hut by the side of an old pond. One day, after a brief rain, Master Buko visited Basho and asked, "How is your understanding these days?"

Remember, the Master has not asked, "How is your knowledge?" He has asked, "How is your understanding?"

Understanding is totally different from knowledge. Knowledge is borrowed, understanding is one's own. Knowledge comes from without, understanding wells up within. Knowledge is ugly, because it is secondhand. And knowledge can never become part of your being. It will remain alien, it will remain foreign, it cannot get roots into you. Understanding grows out of you, it is your own flowering. It is authentically yours, hence it has beauty, and it liberates.

Truth can never be borrowed from anybody, and the borrowed truth is no longer truth. A borrowed truth is already a lie. The moment truth is said, it becomes a lie. Truth has to be experienced, not to be heard, not to be read. Truth is not just going to be a part of your accumulation, part of your memory. It has to be existential: each pore of your being should feel it. Yes, it has to be a feeling: each breath should be full of it. It should pulsate in you, it should circulate in you like your blood. When truth is understood, you become it.

Hence the Master Buko asked his disciple, "Basho, how is your understanding these days?" And don't forget those two beautiful words, "these days."

Truth is always growing. Truth is a movement. It is not static, it is dynamic. It is a dance. It is like growing trees and flowing rivers and moving stars. Truth is never at any point, a static phenomenon. It is not a stasis; it is utterly dynamic, it is movement. To be alive it has to be moving.

Only death is static, only death is stagnant. Hence the people who are dead may look alive on the surface, but if their truth is no longer growing they are dead – their soul is no longer growing. Truth is not an idea but your very being, your very soul.

Hence the Master asked, "How is your understanding *these* days?" He is not asking about the past. Knowledge is always about the past, imagination is always about the future. He is asking about the present, he is asking about the immediate.

Basho responded,

Rain has passed
Green moss moistened.

Just a few moments before it was raining: the rain has passed, green moss moistened. It is good, but not *very* good. It is already past. It is no longer immediate. The moment a memory already, it is no longer experiencing. Buko was not contented – the answer was good but not great. And a Master is never contented unless the answer is absolute, unless the answer is really as it should be – and certainly not with the potential of a man like Basho.

Now nobody knows about Buko, his Master. He is known only because of Basho. The disciple had infinite potential, the Master cannot be contented so easily. Remember it! – the more potential you have, the more you will be put to hard tasks. The Master will be severe with you. He is going to be very hard on you.

The answer was good if it had come from somebody of lesser potential than Basho – the Master might have nodded his head in consent – but not to Basho. Even a gap of a few minutes is enough. The rain is no more there, the clouds have dispersed, it is already sunny, the sun is shining all around, on the old pond, on the hut…

He said, "Say something more!"

And when the Master says, "Say something more," he does not mean talk a little more about it, he does not mean "more" in a quantitative sense. He means: say something deeper, say something more intense, say something more existential, say something more – qualitatively!

At that instant Basho heard the plop of a frog jumping into the pond. He said,

Frog jumps in
The sound of water

Now, this is Tao: the immediate, that which is, alive, throbbing, this very moment. Tao knows no past, no future. Tao knows only one kind of time, that is present. Tao knows only the here and now. Just let your mind disappear and then there is no past and no future. Past and future are mind creations. In reality, there is only present. And when there is no past, no future, how can you even call it present? – because present has meaning only in reference to past and future. The present is sandwiched between past and future. If you have taken away past and future, the present also disappears.

That is the moment of Tao: when time disappears, when one is in utter immediacy, when one is utterly in the here and now, neither roaming somewhere in the ghosts of the past nor in the unborn images of the future. This is the moment of enlightenment: when time is not, and when you are utterly here and nowhere else. And when there is no time, there is no mind. Mind and time are synonymous. The more mind you have, the more you are conscious of time. That's why in the Western world a great time-consciousness has arisen: it is because of the cultivation of the mind.

Go to the primitive people living in the mountains or in the jungles, go to the aboriginals and there is no time-consciousness, because the mind has not been cultivated yet. And it again happens – when through understanding one drops all the nostalgia for the past and all the fancies for the future, time disappears again. And with the disappearance of time, suddenly mind is no more found. And when there is no mind there is silence. In that silence the beyond penetrates the earth, in that silence the unknown descends into you. In that silence, the meeting with God, in that silence, the benediction, the blessing. In that silence is the Kingdom of God.

Basho said,

Frog jumps in
The sound of water.

This is a statement of Tao. This is Tao – simple, pure, nude.

At this response the Master was immensely delighted. The Master is always delighted whenever a disciple comes back home. The delight of the Master knows no bounds, as if he becomes enlightened again! More perfection is added to his already perfect being. He needed nothing to be added to him, but each time a disciple flares up into awareness, becomes aflame, the Master feels as if he has again become enlightened.

The Master was immensely delighted, and the very delight of the Master became the occasion of Basho's enlightenment. Seeing the delighted face of the Master, seeing the aura of his joy, the nod of his consent – or maybe he said nothing – his silence showering on the disciple as grace, Basho became enlightened! What a moment to become enlightened! Thousands of people have become enlightened in the past, but the way Basho became enlightened is simply unique. Because the Master was delighted, his very delight penetrated his heart like a sword. Flowers showered on him, because the Master must have smiled… The unheard music was heard because the Master must have looked at him with joy, with blessing.

I don't know, but Buko must have danced or done something crazy like that. The enlightenment of a disciple is no small matter.

Later on, Basho continued to polish the haiku like a diamond. For his whole life he continued to polish it – because this is a rare phenomenon, this small haiku:

The old pond
Frog jumps in
The sound of water.

It was because of this that his own process of enlightenment was triggered. He continued to polish it like a diamond. He continued to cut it and give it more and more depth. He added: The old pond. The first statement was only:

Frog jumps in
The sound of water.

Later on he added: The old pond. My feeling is that the old pond must have insisted on being included. And the old pond had every right to be included – without the old pond there would have been no frog, no jumping in, no sound of water – Basho owed much to the old pond. He included it.

Now the haiku became:

The old pond
Frog jumps in
The sound of water.

And still later on, he dropped the words "of water."

Now the haiku was not so perfect as before, but more complete than before. Now it was:

The old pond
Frog jumps in
The sound

It is not so perfect as before, but it is more complete. What do I mean when I say it is more complete?

Now it is a growing phenomenon, it does not require a full stop. Before there was a full stop, it was a finished product; you could not have added anything to it. It didn't leave anything for you to meditate upon. But just "the sound," and it opens a door. There is no full stop anymore. It becomes a quest. So now it is more complete but less perfect. Now it is utterly complete, complete in the sense that it is growing. Now it is a tree growing, unpredictable. Now one has to meditate over it. And this became one of the great meditations for the seekers who were to follow Basho. Now it has more beauty than before.

Always remember, anything complete, anything absolutely complete, loses something from it – it becomes dead. All the great painters know this. And the greatest paintings are those which have been left a little bit incomplete, the last touch has not been given to them. And the greatest poems are those which have been left incomplete – so a door remains open for you to enter, so your being can have a communion with the incomplete poetry, so your being can complete it, so it can be completed in your existence.

Now it was,

The old pond
Frog jumps in
The sound

Still later, he dropped a few more things. Now it became,

The old pond
Frog jumps in
Plop!

Now this is getting to the crescendo: just "plop!" This is truer – truer to the frog, truer to the pond, truer to reality. The reality knows only "plop!" and it simply leaves you there – to wonder, to inquire, to meditate.

Somebody asked Basho, "Why have you dropped the words 'of water' and finally even 'the sound'?"

Basho said, "I want you to hear what kind of sound it is. I don't want to say, I want you to hear what kind of sound it is."

The old pond
Frog jumps in
Plop!

You are left in a new kind of meditative space. Suddenly the old pond becomes a reality very close by. You can feel it, it is here. And the frog jumps in: it is not a frog of the past. And "plop!" – you can hear it again, it becomes a reality. This is great art, that what the artist lived through, he can create again in somebody who is receptive, who is available, who is ready to go on the journey of exploration.

This is the way of all the buddhas. Their statements are nothing but triggering points of a certain process in you called meditation. This is the way of Tao: to bring you to that which is. This is my way too: to help you to fall utterly in the moment. *This* moment! This is it!

Tao is not a doctrine. It is a special way of becoming aware. It is the way of awakening, the way of enlightenment, the way of coming back home. Tao simply means "the Way." And remember, it does not mean it in the ordinary sense of the word. Whenever you hear the words "the way" you start thinking of a goal somewhere faraway, of where the way leads you. No. Tao means "the Way," but not in reference to a goal. Then what does it mean? It means "the way things are." It simply means the way things are, already are, just so: nothing has to be achieved, all is showering on you. Just be here and now and celebrate.

My definition of religion is celebration.

But there are people who would not like such a simple phenomenon as Tao: their egos do not feel challenged enough, they are always interested in the hard way. They are always interested in difficulties. If there are not difficulties, they will create them. They cannot do things in a simple way. They are almost incapable of being simple, and to be simple is the only way to be in God. God is simplicity, innocence.

God is as simple as the rosebush and the call of the cuckoo from the mango grove. God is as simple as the giggle of a girl. God is as simple as a leaf falling from the tree. God is as simple as the gentle and cooling breeze passing through the ancient pine trees.

But there are people who would not like God to be so simple. These are the people who create theologies, these are the people who create difficult, abstract speculations about God, who make the whole thing so difficult that it becomes almost incomprehensible. And God is very simple.

The old pond
Frog jumps in
Plop!

Yes, God is like that...

It has to be remembered again and again by you, because your ego will play tricks on you. That is how people go on missing the simple way of Tao. Christianity has so much of a following, Buddhism has a great following, Islam has a great following, but Tao is still not a church – never has been a church, never became an organization. Individuals have existed, individuals have followed it, individuals have attained through it, but it never became the way of the masses. Why? – because it is available only to those who are ready to drop the ways of the ego, who are ready to be simple, innocent, childlike.

There are some people who always look for the difficult side of the problem. To them the easy solution never appears. They always have to think of the most complicated one.

I recall a young man who was applying for admission to one of the most exclusive country clubs in Newport. The rather reserved, unimpressive-looking young man was notified that he must play a round of golf with the club officers as a prerequisite to his acceptance.

On the appointed afternoon he met them on the first tee equipped with a hockey stick, a croquet mallet and a billiard cue. The officers looked him over incredulously but nevertheless proceeded to tee off. To their dismay the young man coolly drove off 275 yards with the hockey stick, gracefully arched his second shot to the green with the croquet mallet and sank a twenty-foot putt with a billiard cue.

After soundly drubbing the baffled officers with a subpar 68, the applicant retired with them to the club bar. There he ordered a Scotch and soda, and when it arrived he mixed the drink himself by tossing the contents of the shot glass over his shoulder into the waiting soda behind him on the bar. This further display of the young man's incredible physical coordination was too much for the officers of the club.

"You are miraculous!" they exclaimed. "What is the story behind these fantastic talents of yours?"

"All my life," the man explained, "physical activity of any sort has been child's play for me. To overcome the boredom that has resulted from my monotonous mastery of everything, I try to do almost everything the most difficult way possible. Thus I play tennis with a ping-pong paddle, ping-pong with a tennis racket, and so on."

"Wait a minute," interrupted one of the club officers. "If it is true, as you say, that you do everything physical in the most difficult manner possible, I have one question…"

"I know," said the young man, smiling. "Everyone asks me the same thing, and I don't mind telling you – standing up, in a hammock."

This is the way of the ego.

Tao is simple, utterly simple. You don't have to stand up in a hammock. The most fundamental thing about Tao is that it is a child's play. But to be a child seems to be almost impossible for people. Who wants to be a child? Jesus says, "Unless you are like small children, you will not enter into my Kingdom of God." But it seems nobody wants to be a child; that is where our misery lies.

All these days we have been going deeper and deeper into the world of Tao. Today are the last sutras, the concluding remarks by Master Lu-tsu. They are simple. You just have to be simple to understand them. There is not much knowledge in them, but certainly much insight. They will not make you well-informed. In fact, they will take all knowledge away, they will make you ignorant! But if a man can be ignorant, can be courageous enough to drop all his knowledge and can live in a state of not-knowing, then there is no barrier between him and God, no barrier between him and existence. Knowledge creates the barrier.

Adam has been expelled from the Garden of Eden because he has eaten the fruit of the Tree of Knowledge. That fruit has to be vomited. Once knowledge is vomited out, you are clean. And in that cleanness, all is available. All is already available – just because you are not clean and stuffed with knowledge, you cannot see it.

The sutras:

> *The Tao, the undivided, great One, gives rise to two opposite reality*
> *principles, the dark and the light, yin and yang. From yin comes*
> *the receptive feminine principle; from yang comes the creative*
> *masculine principle; from yin comes ming, life; from yang, hsing*
> *or human nature.*

This is the concluding part of *The Secret of the Golden Flower.* This is summarizing of the whole treatise, so that you can remember.

> *The Tao, the undivided, great One, gives rise to two opposite reality*
> *principles…*

First, what is Tao? – that which is, unnamed, unqualified, simply that which is. It contains all. It contains the trees and the stars, it contains you and me and the animals and the birds. It contains all that is. And that which is, contains all that has ever been, and that which is, contains all that is ever going to be.

Tao cannot be said just because it encompasses all – and no word can contain all. The very purpose of a word is to denote. The very purpose of a word is to classify. A table is a table and not a chair, and a chair is a chair and not a dog, and a dog is a dog and not a man. The word is meaningful only because it has a definite boundary around it: it excludes everything out of it, it includes only something tiny and excludes the whole existence.

Tao includes all, excludes nothing. That's why Tao cannot be said. It can be shown but not said. The man of Tao can give you a taste of it if you are ready to go into him and let him come into you. The man of Tao can give you a glimpse, a lightning glimpse of the totality of existence…but you may become frightened. That's what happened in the great song, *Bhagavad-Gita.*

The disciple Arjuna asked Krishna his master, his friend, his guide, "You say great things. You argue well. Your proofs are very convincing, yet doubt persists deep down within me. The doubt is because I have not experienced what you are saying to me. Why don't you give me a little experience of it? – just a little taste on the tip of the tongue will do. There is no need to go on arguing about it so long, there is no need to produce so many proofs for it. Just a little taste and I will be convinced and my doubts will disappear."

Krishna said, "Okay."

And then it happened, one of the most beautiful stories that has ever happened between a Master and a disciple: Krishna became huge and Krishna became infinite and worlds started rotating within him, and Arjuna was frightened: the millions of hands of Krishna and all the stars and all the planets within him, and life and death within him, all polarities meeting and merging in him – it was a chaos. Arjuna thought he must be going mad. He closed his eyes in fear, and he cried and shouted, "Come back! Come back to your ordinary form with two hands. Be my old friend again. This is too much!"

Krishna came back and he said, "I knew it. You are not yet ready to have the taste of the totality."

Totality will frighten you. Its sheer vastness is such, it is going to frighten you out of your wits. It is abysmal, and you will start disappearing into it like a soap bubble. It is so vast that you will lose all orientation of who you are.

That's what happened to Arjuna. And he said, "Yes, I was feeling as if I was going to die, or as if I was going to be mad, or as if I had already gone mad. Thank you for coming back to your original form."

And Krishna said, "This is not my original form. That was my original form."

Tao is infinity. Tao is totality. Tao is all that is, hence it cannot be said. But in the deep intimacy of a Master and a disciple, something of it starts pulsating. There are moments when you become available to the whole, when you don't function as a separate entity, when you lose the idea of separation for a few moments, when you are one and united. When the drop disappears into the ocean – even for a single moment – then you know what Tao is.

So Tao cannot be said but can be portrayed. That's what I have been trying to convey to you here.

This is not a school of philosophy. I'm not teaching you any philosophy at all. This is an existential school. I am teaching you existence as it is. And existence is already here; you just have to become a little more courageous to open up, to allow it in. It is knocking on your doors!

Jesus says, "Knock and the door shall be opened unto you. Ask and it shall be given. Seek and ye shall find."

I would like to say just the opposite to you: God is knocking on your doors, has been knocking for millennia, hear! – He's knocking on the door…open your doors. Listen! – He's asking you to come out of your self-imposed prison. He is seeking you – let him seek you, help him seek you! He is searching for you – and you are escaping, and you have been escaping for lives together. And you are miserable, and still you go on escaping. And whenever his hand comes close to you, you become frightened. And I understand. The fear is natural. What is the fear? The fear is: if God is, then you cannot be.

Friedrich Nietzsche has said, "If God is, then how can I be? Then how I can be…? So, I decide that there is no God; *then only* can I be."

And that's how millions of people have decided: they have denied God in order to be. If there is no God, ego is possible. If there is God how can the ego be supported? By what? Then you are no more there, that is the fear. God is the death of the ego.

Tao can be tasted, Tao can be experienced, but one condition has to be fulfilled: you have to be so simple that you don't have any ego, you have to be so silent that there is no idea of "I."

> *The Tao, the undivided, great One, gives rise to two opposite reality principles…*

This is the very fundamental of the Taoist approach: that the one becomes two – because then only is the play possible. The one has to become two, and the two have to be opposites to each other – then the game starts.

The ancient Hindu scriptures say God was alone and was feeling really very very lonely. He decided to create the other. That's why Hindus say the existence is *leela,* a play: God created the other just to have a little fun.

Tao is one, but the moment it becomes manifested it has to become two. Manifestation has to be dual, it cannot be one. It has to be two, it has to split into two. It has to become matter and consciousness, it has to become man and woman, it has to become day and night, it has to become life and death. You will find these two principles everywhere. The whole life consists of these two principles, and behind these two principles is hidden the One. If you continue to remain involved between these two dualities and the polar opposites, you will remain in the world. If you are intelligent, if you are a little more alert, and if you start looking deeper, into the depths of things, you will be surprised – these opposites are not really opposites but complementaries and behind both is one single energy: that is Tao.

> Tao...gives rise to two opposite reality principles, the dark and the
> light, yin and yang. From yin comes the receptive feminine principle;
> from yang comes the creative masculine principle; from yin comes
> ming, life; from yang, hsing or human nature.

Basically, the polarities can be named man/woman: the masculine, the feminine. And it is closer to our human reality to understand it that way. We can call it negative and positive, but that would be a little far away. To call it yin and yang, Shiva and Shakti, man and woman, brings it very close to our heart – we know this duality.

Man is attracted towards the woman, the woman is attracted towards the man, and yet they constantly fight. They cannot live separately and they cannot live together either. Attraction is tremendous, repulsion too. When you are with your woman or with your man you start thinking of how to be alone, you start thinking of freedom, of being alone, and the beauty and the silence and all that. When you are alone you simply start feeling lonely and you start hankering for the other, and you start thinking of those loving spaces, warmth and all that. When alone you want to be together, when together you want to be alone. Watch it, it has a great message for you.

It simply says: you are half and the woman is half, together you become one. But then a problem arises. In that moment of oneness you are ecstatic, you rejoice, but then the problem arises: this oneness, is it man or woman? Which is the dominating factor? That is the conflict. Man and woman want to be one, but man wants to remain the dominating factor in that oneness, the woman should surrender, submit. And the same is the desire from the woman's side, that the man should surrender and submit. Both want to be one, but that oneness has to be "mine." If I am man then that oneness has to be man's; the woman has to disappear into the man. If I am a woman then it has to be that of woman; the man has to disappear into the woman. Hence the conflict – the attraction and the repulsion – and the whole comedy and tragedy of life.

The feminine principle is receptive and the masculine principle is creative, and both can only go together. Separate, they both suffer. Then the woman has nothing to receive and feels empty. And if there is nobody to receive, the man's creativity is lost because there is nobody to appreciate, inspire. The woman receives, inspires and helps the man to flow in his creativity. Man's creativity helps the woman to flow into her receptivity. This receptivity of the woman is not only biological, it is spiritual too. Behind all great poets you will find the inspiration of a woman. The women have not themselves been great poets – they need not be – but no great poetry is ever born without a woman. She functions as a lighthouse. Men have been great poets, but without a woman the poetry simply dies and withers away.

Receptivity and creativity are two wings of the bird. This flight towards the unknown can be completed only with both of the wings. With one wing the bird is not going to go anywhere. And remember, creativity is not more valuable than receptivity – they are equal, they are utterly equal. No wing, right or left, is greater than the other, cannot be. They are equal. They are not similar but they are equal to one another.

Now there is a great desire in women's hearts to be creative – for a certain reason: because creativity is praised. Nobel Prizes are given only to creators, not to those who show tremendous receptivity. Now this is an ugly situation which creates an obsessive desire to be creative, because the receptive person is not appreciated at all, is not valued at all, is not talked about at all. So all over the world the woman wants to be creative, but the moment she wants to be creative she starts losing her femininity, her grace. She starts becoming more and more masculine, because the creative is the masculine principle. She starts becoming more and more hard. She loses softness and roundness, starts growing corners, starts fighting. You can see the shouting Lib Movement women – their shouts are ugly. And I know their fight is right, but fighting is not the way of woman! – the very fight will destroy their womanhood. It has to be done in some other way. In fact, man should fight for woman's equality.

The people who can understand, the people who can think, the people who are intelligent, should create a man's movement for women's liberation. They should fight! It is their imposed slavery on woman – they should feel guilty, they should undo whatsoever they have done. But if the woman starts fighting – and then naturally she starts thinking to be creative, paint, dance, sing, sculpt, compose – very unconsciously she is imitating man. And remember, woman imitating man will always be a second-rate man. That is ugly and the very effort of being equal is lost. The woman can only be a first-rate woman. If she wants to be a man, she will only be a second-rate man. It is just the same way if a man wants to be receptive: he can't have that natural receptivity of a woman. He will become a second-rate woman. To be first-rate you have to follow your nature.

Never imitate. Follow your own intrinsic nature, your own built-in nature, because only from the fulfillment of that nature does one arrive to a state of bliss, fulfillment, contentment.

Woman creates life: life in general, life as a universal phenomenon. Man, or the male element, creates human nature. Man is particular, woman is universal. Man goes into details of things. Man becomes a specialist. That's why male-dominated fields all become fields of specialization sooner or later. That's what is happening in science: everything slowly, slowly becomes a specialization, and new branches arise, branches out of branches. And now the whole thing seems to be a very absurd situation.

Man has created much knowledge and has gone into deep detail, but now there is nobody to make a whole out of that knowledge. Nobody knows how to create a synthesis. That synthesis is possible only through a woman, not through a man, because woman is a universalizing principle.

Man dissects. woman unites. That's why a woman feels closer to religion than a man, and has always felt closer to religion than a man. You may not have observed the fact. The fundamental fact is: that religion thinks in terms of one, wholeness, totality. That's what Tao is, or God, or whatsoever you will. Science dissects and goes on splitting and has reached to the electron, to the smallest particle. These are polar-opposite ways. Religion goes on joining things together, together, together, and comes to the ultimate Tao which contains all – it is the ultimate unity, and science goes on splitting and splitting, specializing and more specializing. They say specialization means to know more and more about less and less.

I have heard…

It is the twenty-first century, and a man goes to a doctor. He is troubled by his eyes; he is getting old. And the doctor asks the man, "Which of your eyes is causing you trouble?"

And he says, "My right eye."

The doctor says, "Sorry, you will have to go to somebody else, because I only specialize in left eyes."

It is going to happen. It is already happening.

Man is no longer one unity; there are so many specialists. Nobody thinks about the man as a whole, as a totality. That is one of the greatest problems that medical science is facing and has to face and find a solution for – because the patient is not thought of as one unity. If his head is in trouble, then the head has to be taken as a separate part and just give some medicine – aspirin or something. Nobody bothers about the whole system – because the aspirin will first go into the stomach, it can't go directly to the head. What is going to happen to the stomach? – that is nobody's concern.

Man is a unity. You cannot treat him like a machine. If something is wrong with your car you go to the garage, he changes the part, because the machine has no soul – it is only the sum total of its parts. And what is a soul? Soul means that something more is there than the sum total of its parts: there is a unity behind. Modern medical science is facing it tremendously, and the reason is because all of these sciences have been developed by men. The impact of the woman is missing, because the woman always universalizes. She thinks in terms of unities, she never thinks in terms of parts.

A woman is never mathematical, she cannot be. Her whole approach is holistic. That is the meaning of this statement made twenty-five centuries ago. It is yet contemporary.

> The Tao, the undivided, great One, gives rise to two opposite reality
> principles, the dark and the light, yin and yang. From yin comes
> the receptive feminine principle; from yang comes the creative
> masculine principle; from yin comes ming, life; from yang, hsing
> or human nature.

> Each individual contains a central monad, which, at the moment of
> conception, splits into life and human nature, ming and hsing.

Each individual comes as a single unit, unitary, and then is split. It is just like a ray passing through a prism is split into seven colors. Conception functions like a prism: the one white ray splits into seven colors. The one Tao splits into two opposite polarities: man and woman. Remember that no man is man alone – the woman is behind, hidden in him – and so is it with the woman. Both are bisexual.

If the conscious mind is man, then the unconscious is woman. If the conscious mind is woman, then the unconscious is man. It has to be so. And the desire to meet with the woman or with the man on the outside is not going to fulfill you – unless you know how to meet the inner man and the inner woman. The outer woman can give you only a few glimpses of meeting – beautiful moments, but at a great cost. And all lovers know that yes, there are a few ecstatic moments, but one has to pay a great price for them: one has to lose one's freedom, one has to lose one's own being, and one has to become dependent and one has to compromise in a thousand and one ways, which hurts and wounds. The meeting with the outer woman or the outer man is going to be only momentary.

But there is another meeting, and that is one of the secret messages of Tao: that you can find your inner woman – where your conscious and unconscious meet, where your light and darkness meet, where your earth and sky meet, where your positive and negative meet. And once that meeting has happened within you, you are whole. This is what is called the man of Tao. The man of Tao is neither man nor woman. He has come back to his oneness. He is alone: all one.

You cannot call Lao Tzu a man or a woman, or Buddha a man or a woman, or Jesus a man or a woman. Biologically they are, spiritually they are not. Spiritually they have gone beyond. Buddha has no unconscious in him, no division. He is undivided. And when you are undivided all conflict within you ceases. Otherwise you are in a constant civil war: you are not only fighting with the outer woman, you are fighting continuously with the inner woman too. And you know those moments.

A moment comes when you want to cry, your inner woman is ready to shed tears, but your man stops it. Your man says, "What are you doing, man? Are you mad? People will think that you are being very feminine. Stop your tears! This is not right for a man like you. It is okay for women, let them cry and weep, but you have to keep a face – hard, strong, invulnerable. Hold your tears back!" And the fight has started.

And the same happens to the woman. You would like to climb a tree, and it is so beautiful, and the highest branches of the tree are playing with the clouds. Who would not like to climb? But your inner woman says, "Wait! This is allowed only to men, not to you. You are a woman. You have to think of what is right for a woman and what is not right. You have to follow certain manners, etiquette." And you repress it.

This goes on continuously: man represses his woman, woman represses her man, and the repressed part starts taking revenge in subtle ways. It starts coming from the backdoor, it starts poisoning you. So there are moments when the woman becomes very hard, cruel, nagging, fighting, ugly: that is the man taking revenge. Climbing on a tree would have been beautiful, but that you denied. Now the man comes through the backdoor and you start screaming at your husband or at your children, and you start throwing things. Now this is ugly, this is pathological. It was good to cry. Tears are beautiful because they are part of life. It was good to cry, there was no need to hide those tears. If you hide your tears, you will not be able to laugh either. You will always be afraid – if you laugh too much, you may feel so relaxed with the laughter that the repressed tears may start coming up.

Nietzsche has said, "I laugh just to keep my tears hidden, because I am afraid if I don't laugh I may start crying."

Now this is one aspect. One can go on smiling, this is not real laughter. One can go on smiling – this is diplomatic – so that nobody can see tears ready to come from your eyes. People become engaged in your smile and don't look at your eyes. This is one way. The other way is to keep a very hard face – don't even laugh, don't even smile. Let people know that you are a man of steel. That is the meaning of the word *stalin*: man of steel. It is said that Stalin never used to laugh. How could he laugh? – a man of steel. Steel men cannot laugh.

But this is ugly, this is becoming mechanical. This is dehumanizing. Either one becomes false, pseudo, or one becomes very hard, has to grow a hard crust to keep oneself in constant control.

Tao says there is no need to deny the opposite polarity of your being. Accept it, it is you! Both these rays are you. Let them meet and merge! Let them dance together! Let them become one so deeply that again you can have the vision of one – Tao, the great One, undivided.

> In the personal bodily existence of the individual they are
> represented by two other polarities, anima and animus. All during
> the life of the individual these two are in conflict, each striving for
> mastery.

Drop fighting for mastery! That is your inner politics. Both are equal and nobody can ever be the master. Both are needed and equally needed. Accept both – although it is very difficult, logically very difficult to accept both, because they are diametrically opposite. But logic is not true to life itself. More true to life is what is known as dialectics.

Logic is not true to life. Logic is linear. It does not contain the opposite. Tao says the opposite is always there, running parallel to it. The process is not logical but dialectical. Thesis is opposed by antithesis: man is opposed by woman, and out of this opposition, out of this conflict, out of this challenge, energy is released. And that energy can either be dissipated – if you are foolish, or can be accumulated – if you are wise. If dissipated you will remain in constant conflict, a civil war. Your life will become schizophrenic. Or, if you are wise, intelligent, and you know how to contain the opposites together in a deep friendly embrace, then thesis opposed by antithesis will create a new phenomenon in your being: synthesis. On a higher plane you will arise, in a deeper way you will be united. And then again the synthesis functions as a thesis, creates its antithesis, and again, on a higher plane, synthesis. It goes on and on, waves upon waves, higher and higher. There are planes upon planes, and one can go on reaching. The ultimate plane is the total synthesis of your life: all conflict disappears – is not dropped, but disappears of its own accord.

This is Tao, the Tao, the undivided, the great One.

> *If the life-energy flows downward, that is, without let or*
> *hindrance into the outer world, the anima is victorious over*
> *the animus; no Golden Flower is developed.*

If energy flows downward and outward, your energy becomes reproductive, sexually reproductive. A great phenomenon! That's how you were born, that's how everybody else was born – a Buddha, a Jesus, a Krishna. If energy flows downward, it creates new people, new forms for God to embody. But the Golden Flower does not bloom. You produce somebody else – a child, a beautiful child: life continues, life goes on moving, remains flowing, but the Golden Flower cannot bloom this way.

How does the Golden Flower bloom?

> *If the life-energy is led through the "backward-flowing" process,*
> *that is, conserved, and made to "rise" instead of allowed to*
> *dissipate, the animus has been victorious.*

These are the two possibilities: energy flowing downward becomes sexuality, energy flowing upward becomes spirituality. Energy flowing downward is reproductive, energy flowing upward is creative. Energy flowing downward creates new life, energy flowing upward gives *you* a new birth. That's what Jesus means when he says, "Unless you are born again" – not from a father and mother, but by your own upward movement – unless you become a *dwija*, a twice-born "you will not enter into my kingdom of God."

The Golden Flower is waiting at the highest peak of your being. In the yoga map it is called *sahasrar,* one-thousand-petaled lotus. It is the seventh chakra – in your head. The lowest is the sex chakra, *muladhar,* and the highest is the seventh chakra, sahasrar. From the lowest chakra, energy moves downward, creates new life. If the energy is conserved, helped to move upwards, it reaches one day to the sahasrar – and the Golden Flower blooms. Of course, it needs energy. It is there only as a potential, as a possibility. Unless energy becomes available for it, it will not become actual.

It is like when you don't give water to a tree: the tree is waiting, the water is not coming. The green juice is not flowing upwards, how can it bloom into a thousand and one flowers? – impossible. It will remain sad, it will almost remain dying. It will be a slow suicide. By and by the leaves will also wither away, by and by the branches will die, and ultimately, the roots. It needs a constant upward flow of energy.

Just as the green sap moves in a tree, man is also a tree. And this is not a new symbol that I am using – of man as a tree – it is one of the most ancient symbols. It has been used in the Jewish mystical schools: it is called the Tree of Life. Just as Buddhism has reached to its crescendo in Zen, and Islam in Sufism, Judaism has reached its ultimate peaks in the Kabbala. The Kabbala says that man is a tree, and it needs great energy for the flowers to bloom.

But remember, to conserve energy does not mean to repress energy. That's where many people become misguided. To conserve energy does not mean to repress. The processes are absolutely different.

Repression means you are continuously repressing at the lowest center and where it becomes too much at the lowest center it will create perverted sexuality. If you don't allow it a natural let-go and the energy accumulates at the lowest center too much, it will find some way or other. It can become perverted, it *will* become perverted! It will create pathology. Ask the psychiatrists, psychologists, psychoanalysts – they say: "Out of a hundred percent, ninety-five percent of the psychological cases are because of sexuality. Somewhere or other, sex is involved." This is too big a number, ninety-five percent. And the people who never go to the psychiatrists and the psychoanalysts are not in a better position either – everybody is suppressed.

Suppression is not transformation. Let it be understood once and for all: repression can never become a transformation. Then what is transformation? And what is conservation of energy? Conservation of energy is a meditative process. It is not moralistic.

I will suggest a small method to you that will be of immense help. It has been used by Taoists down the ages. It is given only from the Masters to the disciples, that's why it has not been written in the books. But now the time has come that it should be given, because now millions of people are working on their spiritual search *through* books. Masters are not so available either.

This is a simple method of transforming your energy and leading it upwards. And always remember, Taoist methods are very simple, so don't think, "How can such a simple thing be of such great importance?" Practice it, experiment with it and you will know.

The process is:

At least twice a day – the best times are early in the morning, just before you get out of your bed. The moment you feel you are alert, awake, do it for twenty minutes. Do it first thing in the morning! – don't get out of the bed. Do it there, then and there, immediately! – because when you are coming out of sleep you are very very delicate, receptive. When you are coming out of sleep you are very fresh, and the impact will go very deep. When you are just coming out of your sleep you are less in the mind than ever. Hence some gaps are there through which the method will penetrate into your innermost core. And early in the morning, when you are awakening, and when the whole earth is awakening, there is a great tide of awakening energy all over the world. Use that tide, don't miss that opportunity.

All ancient religions used to pray early in the morning when the sun rose, because the rising of the sun is the rising of all the energies in existence. In that moment you can simply ride on the rising energy wave; it will be easier. By the evening it will be difficult, energies will be falling back. Then you will be fighting against the current, in the morning you will be going with the current.

So the best time to begin is in the early morning, immediately, just when you are half-asleep, half-awake. And the process is so simple. It needs no posture, no *yogasana*, no bath is needed, nothing.

You simply lie down, as you are lying down in your bed, on your back. Keep your eyes closed.

When you breathe in, just visualize great light entering from your head into your body, as if a sun has risen just close to your head – golden light pouring into your head. You are just hollow and the golden light is pouring into your head, and going, going, going, deep, deep, and going out through your toes. When you breathe in, do it with this visualization.

And when you breathe out, visualize another thing: darkness entering through your toes, a great dark river entering through your toes, coming up, and going out through the head. Do slow, deep breathing so you can visualize.

Go very slowly. And just out of sleep you can have very deep and slow breaths because the body is rested, relaxed.

Let me repeat: breathing in, let golden light come into you through your head, because it is there that the Golden Flower is waiting. That golden light will help. It will cleanse your whole body and will make it absolutely full of creativity. This is male energy.

Then when you exhale, let darkness, the darkest you can conceive, like a dark night, river-like, come from your toes upwards – this is feminine energy: it will soothe you, it will make you receptive, it will calm you, it will give you rest – and let it go out of the head. Then inhale again, and golden light enters in.

Do it for twenty minutes, early in the morning.

And then the second best time is when you are going back to sleep, in the night.

Lie down on the bed, relax for a few minutes. When you start feeling that now you are wavering between sleep and waking, just in that middle, start the process again, and continue for twenty minutes. If you fall asleep doing it, it is the best, because the impact will remain in the subconscious and will continue working even though you are not awake.

And after a three-month period you will be surprised: the energy that was constantly gathering at the *muladhar,* at the lowest, the sex center, is no more gathering there. It is going upwards.

Just the other day somebody had asked a question. He said that he has seen the most beautiful women around here that he has ever seen anywhere else, but they are non-erotic.

Why is it so? It is so, his observation is right. If you meditate deeply you will become non-erotic. You will have a different kind of beauty, but it will not be erotic. It will start having the flavor of spirituality. It will start having the subtleness of grace, not the grossness of sexuality.

Sex is gross because it is the lowest rung of your ladder. As energies move upwards, a totally different kind of beauty and grace arises in you, which is divine. You become less and less of the body and more and more of the spirit. If you do this simple method for three months, you will be surprised: there is no need to repress, transformation has started happening.

> *A man who holds to the way of conservation all through life may*
> *reach the stage of the Golden Flower…*

And if you can go on doing this for your whole life, one day it is going to happen.

The Master Lu-tsu says "your whole life" so that you remain patient. It can happen any day, it can happen today, or tomorrow, or the day after tomorrow. It depends with what intensity, with what sincerity you work for it, with what longing, what totality you go into it. And the day the Golden Flower blooms in you is the day of buddhahood. You have attained the greatest treasure there is.

> A man who holds to the way of conservation all through life may
> reach the stage of the Golden Flower, which then frees the ego from
> the conflict of the opposites, and it again becomes part of the Tao, the
> undivided great One.

From Tao to Tao, from One to One – as Plotinus says, "The flight of the alone to the alone."

Enough for today.

CHAPTER 30
This Very World, the Paradise

The first question:

Osho,
Your dancing meditations seem to be bringing forth an overwhelming
sensuousness. All that has not been taken, all that has not been given is
revealed then… The play of nature on my whole being, all the beauty that
I behold, all the music that enchants my ears and my soul, all seem to be
expressed in voluptuousness. Even when I close my eyes in silent sitting,
this tangible presence is felt.

I welcome and enjoy this growing sensitivity, an "orgasmic" affair with
life. I cannot imagine God descending upon me but as the ultimate lover
when I will be turned inside out, totally open and as readable as the
glorious moon.

Can I trust this feeling? And is it of any meaning with regard to being
with you and growing through you?

I have not been blessed with transcendental experiences. All I know and
all that seems to be my lot to know is this joy, ever-increasing and fresh, to
be part of the cosmic play and to be able to transmute it in my daily living

– in all kinds of creative fashions, from cooking to dancing and praying.
Can you please advise me.

This is what I am teaching here. I don't teach the transcendental, I teach the immanent – because the immanent is the transcendental. I don't teach the ultimate, I teach the immediate – because the immediate is the body of the ultimate. If you enter into the immediate you will find the ultimate pulsating there. The ultimate is the heartbeat of the immediate.

This is my fundamental teaching: that there is no division between this and that. That is contained in this, the other shore is contained in this shore. You need not go anywhere. If you can be joyous, flowing, alive, sensitive, orgasmic, *this* very shore immediately is transformed into the other shore…*this* very world the paradise, *this* very body the Buddha.

Remember it, because down the ages religions have been teaching a dichotomy between this and that. Religions have been teaching a kind of schizophrenia, a split, between the body and the soul, between the lower and the higher, between the outer and the inner, and so on and so forth.

All divisions are false, reality is one. There is nothing lower and nothing higher, and there is nothing outer, nothing inner. There is no body, no soul. It is all one. The body is the soul visible, and the soul is the body invisible. There is no creator other than this very creation. The creator and the creation are not separated, they are as one as the dancer and the dance. They cannot exist apart, they can only exist as one. You cannot take the dancer apart from his dance; if you take him, he is no more a dancer. You cannot take the dance apart from the dancer, there is no possibility. They are utterly one, expressions of the same energy, the same phenomenon.

So what is happening to you, is *exactly* what should happen. This is what I am desiring, longing, praying for you. This is the way you are coming closer and closer to me. Forget all about transcendental experiences. All those so-called transcendental experiences are nothing but bullshit. *These* are the real experiences: *this* sensitivity that is growing in you, this receptivity that is becoming deeper and deeper every moment, this joy of existence, of life, of being, of love.

Don't think of seeing some spiritual visions – God sitting on a golden throne. Those are all fantasies of starved minds, of mediocre minds. Don't think about something extraordinary, because the extraordinary is desired only by the very ordinary – that is the desire of the inferior. If you are intelligent, if you are alert, the ordinary becomes the extraordinary. And that is the magic I teach you.

I am giving you an alchemy. Yes, cooking can become prayer. Only then are you religious. If cooking can become prayer, only then. If cleaning the floor can become meditation, only then.

This ordinary life is ordinary only because you are dull, because you are asleep, because you are thick. It is ordinary only because you don't have perception to see its depth. You can't see the colors of life and the beautiful forms of life and the eternal benediction that goes on showering each moment of it. It is a continuum. Because you can't see the beauty of a rising sun and you can't see the beauty of the stars in the night, and because you can't see the beauty of human eyes, hence out of this poverty arises the desire for some transcendental experience – experiencing God, heaven, paradise, experiencing the arousal of the serpent power in your spine. Experiencing these things or desiring to experience these things are all mind-games. The true religion is always of the here and the now.

Yes, that's what I want you to become, sensuous, because if you are not sensuous you can never be spiritual. If you cannot enjoy the small things of life, if you cannot sip your tea with celebration, you are not religious at all. You can go to Kaaba or to Jerusalem or you can go to Kashi, you will never be religious anywhere if you cannot sip tea with utter gratitude. And the aroma of the tea, and the beautiful smell that is arising – if you cannot feel it, if you are not sensuous enough to feel it, you will not be able to feel God, because God is the center of everything.

God is not the original cause and God is not the ultimate goal. God is the center of every condition that you come across every moment of your life: God is the center of the woman you have fallen in love with, God is the center of the man you have become friendly with. God is the center of everything that you come across. God means the center, and the world means the periphery, the circumference. And they are never separate. And the center is hidden in the circumference.

To be sensuous means to become aware of the circumference, and to be spiritual means to become aware of the center. Sensuousness is the beginning of spirituality. Become more and more sensuous; that is the way of being alive.

But your old religions have been teaching you just the opposite: they teach you a kind of bodily death, they teach you to make your body more and more insensitive. That is a cheap trick: make your body more and more cold so that you can pretend a kind of aloofness, so that you can say, "Nothing affects me." Because you are carrying a dull and dead body around yourself, naturally nothing affects you. But this is not growth.

Real growth is: you are open, vulnerable, you are affected by everything and yet nothing affects you. You are in the midst of situations and yet not part of them. You are on the circumference of everything and yet the center is never forgotten.

You say, "Your dancing meditation seems to be bringing forth an overwhelming sensuousness."

You are blessed. Allow it, don't become afraid, and don't let your old conditionings interfere.

That's why I teach dance, I teach music, I teach singing: I want your body to vibrate at the optimum, I want your body to become a pulsating, streaming phenomenon, not a stagnant pool, but a running, rushing river to the ocean.

"All that has not been taken, all that has not been given is revealed then…."

Yes, when you are sensuous God is available; all the mysteries are close by, because that is the only way to know the mysterious. Sensuousness means you are open, your doors are open, you are ready to throb with existence. If a bird starts singing, the sensuous person immediately feels the song echoed in his deepest core of being. The non-sensuous person does not hear it at all, or maybe it is just a noise somewhere. It does not penetrate his heart. A cuckoo starts calling – a sensuous person starts feeling as if the cuckoo is not calling from some faraway mango grove, but from deep down within his own soul. It becomes his own call, it becomes his own longing for the divine, his own longing for the beloved. In that moment the observer and the observed are one. Seeing a beautiful flower bloom, the sensuous person blooms with it, becomes a flower with it.

The sensuous person is liquid, flowing, fluid. Each experience, and he becomes it. Seeing a sunset, he is the sunset. Seeing the night, dark night, beautiful silent darkness, he becomes the darkness. In the morning he becomes the light. He is *all* that life is. He tastes life from every nook and corner, hence he becomes rich. This is real richness. Listening to music he is music, listening to the sound of water he becomes that sound. And when the wind passes through a bamboo grove, and the cracking bamboos, and he is not far away from them: he is amidst them, one of them – he is a bamboo.

A Zen Master told one of his disciples who wanted to paint bamboos, "Go and first become a bamboo."

He was an accomplished painter. He had passed all the art examinations, and with distinction. His name had already started becoming famous. And the Master said, "You go to the forest, live with the bamboos for a few years, become a bamboo. And the day you can become a bamboo come back and paint, not before it. How can you paint a bamboo if you have not known what a bamboo feels like from within? You can paint a bamboo from the outside, but that is just a photograph."

And that is the difference between photography and painting. A photograph can never be a painting. Howsoever skillfully, artfully done, it remains only the reflection of the circumference of the bamboo. No camera can enter into the soul.

When for the first time photography was developed, a great fear arose in the world of painting that maybe now painting would lose its old beauty and its old pedestal, because photography would be developed more and more every day and soon it would fulfill its requirement. That fear was absolutely unbased. In fact after the invention of the camera, photography has developed tremendously, but simultaneously painting has learned new dimensions, new visions, new perceptions. Painting has become richer, it had to become. Before the invention of the camera the painter was functioning as a camera.

...The Master said, "You go to the forest." And the disciple went, and for three years he remained in the forest, being with the bamboos in all kinds of climates. Because when it is raining the bamboo has a different joy, and when it is windy the bamboo has a different mood, and when it is sunny, of course everything changes in the being of the bamboo. And when a cuckoo comes into the bamboo grove and starts calling, the bamboos are silent and responsive.

He had to be there for three years, and then it happened. One day it happened, sitting by the side of the bamboos, he forgot who he was: and the wind started blowing and he started swaying – like a bamboo! Only later on did he remember that for a long time he had not been a man. He had entered into the soul of the bamboo – then he painted the bamboos.

Those bamboos certainly have a totally different quality which no photograph can ever have. Photographs can be beautiful, but dead. That painting is alive because it shows the soul of the bamboo – in all its moods, in all its richness, in all its climates. Sadness is there and joy is there, and agony is there and ecstasy is there, and all that a bamboo knows – the whole biography of a bamboo is there.

To be sensuous is to be available to the mysteries of life. Become more and more sensuous, and drop all condemnation. Let your body become just a door. All your senses should become clear doors, with no hindrances, so that when you hear you become the music and when you see you become the light, and when you touch you become that which you have touched.

You say, "I welcome and enjoy this growing sensitivity, an 'orgasmic' affair with life. I cannot imagine God descending upon me but as the ultimate lover when I will be turned inside out, totally open and as readable as the glorious moon."

You have understood me rightly. This is my message in short: God comes always as a lover, God is the immediate and the ultimate Beloved. And if you know God in some other way, remember, that God is your mind creation, it is not the true God. And because religions arose around untrue gods they have been unable to help humanity to become more loving. On the contrary, they have filled the whole world with hatred, with violence. The true religion can only conceive of God as the Beloved.

You are on the right track. Your past will pull you back: the priests, the parents, the conditionings in your mind, will pull you back. Beware. Drop all that. Trust this growing sensitivity, this orgasmic openness. This is the door to the divine. Trust it, and go headlong with it.

The second question:

> Osho,
> When you say "Good!" does it mean "good" or does it sometimes
> mean "don't bother me with your nonsense"?

First meditate on this small anecdote:

I recall the time a man gave a speech at a Rotary Club on the subject of journalism and journalists. One of the tenets of the Rotarians is not to swear or use cusswords. But the speaker, not being a Rotarian himself, did not know this, and in his talk he used a profanity he should not have used in that particular hall to that particular audience. At the end of the meeting a local minister in the audience approached the speaker and dressed him down for having used the language he did. The speaker apologized profusely, and the minister went on about how Rotarians, to say nothing of the church, strongly disapproved of bad language. He then walked away. He got about ten feet down the corridor, then turned around and approached the speaker again. "Off the record," he said, "and just between us, any time you want to call a journalist a son-of-a-bitch, it is okay with me."

So on the record, "good" simply means good. Off the record, it means "don't bother me with your nonsense."

The third question:

Osho,
Watching the energy changes that are constantly happening in me,
suddenly the question arises: What is that which is watching and in
what sense is it different from the observed energy?

Kosha, this is a beautiful space to enter into, when the question arises for the first time: What is the observed and who is the observer? This is a beautiful space to enter into – when the question becomes relevant.

Now, on each step you will start losing the duality of the observer and the observed. The observer and the observed, in the ultimate sense, in reality, are one. They are two only because we have not yet been capable of seeing the One.

Remember *The Secret of the Golden Flower.* It says: Tao is one, then it divides itself into two – yin and yang, darkness and light, life and death. But the reality *is* One. It looks like two. It looks like two because we see it through the prism of the mind. The twoness of it is a creation of our minds. It is not there.

It is just like when on a full moon night you look at the moon and then press your eyelid – and suddenly you see two moons. And you know the moon is one. But go on pressing the eye – and you know perfectly well the moon is one – but now you can see two moons. That's exactly what is happening. Mind is creating duality, because mind cannot conceive the One. There is an intrinsic impossibility for the mind to conceive the One. Try to understand why the mind cannot conceive the One.

Mind needs distinctions, the One is distinctionless. The whole purpose of the mind is to demark things, the whole purpose of the mind is to particularize things – this is a woman and that is a man, this is a friend and that is an enemy, this is food and this is just stone, this is a chair and that is a table, this is the door and this is the wall. This is the function of the mind: the whole purpose of the mind is to make distinctions. It is very utilitarian, it has to be used. But in the ultimate sense, it becomes the barrier. That which is a help on the circumference becomes a hindrance at the center.

Mind has no truth, but only utility. Just as a child is born, no child brings a label with himself, a nameplate or anything: he simply comes. You don't ask him, "Who are you, and what is your name, and from where are you coming?" The child will simply look at you and will think you are stupid: "What nonsense you are talking!" You start giving him a name, an identity, and you know that name is false – although useful but false, untrue but utilitarian. He will need that name.

There are millions of people. If he falls in love with a woman and she wants to write a letter to him, how is she supposed to write a letter to a man who has no name? How can the letter be delivered to him?

It has utility in the world. We give him a name and slowly, slowly we completely forget that the name is just a utilitarian device. It has no truth about it. You can change the name. You can go to the court, declare that you drop your old name and you will be a new name. You can change as many times as you want.

Exactly like that, mind is a device, a natural device to help you function in the world, to find you things. If you drop the mind all is blurred into one reality. Then it will not be possible to make any distinction between what is a marshmallow and what is a pillow. You may start sleeping with the marshmallow underneath your head and you may start eating the pillow.

So I am not saying mind is not useful. Mind is useful, but its very usefulness is based on creating distinctions. When you start moving in meditation, you are moving beyond mind. You are moving beyond utility into truth. And then you are trying to see that which is, not that which is useful. Then slowly, slowly the duality will disappear.

And, Kosha, this is just on the threshold – when the observer and the observed disappear. And I have been watching you, Kosha – you have been growing so beautifully.

Kosha is a well-educated woman. She is a PhD, although here she just cleans the toilets. But that has been of immense help, PhDs need that; otherwise they remain hung-up in the head. It has been a device. Deliberately, I have put Kosha into cleaning work, and she has proved really beautiful. She has completely forgotten her PhD, her education, her career, her name, etcetera – all forgotten. She has just become involved in the work that has been given to her – utterly. And that utterness, that totalness, is bringing this great fruit into her being.

Now this is not a philosophical question that she is asking. Philosophy has disappeared from her mind. Now this is an experience, something existential. Now she is really faced with a problem: Who in this situation is the observer and who is the observed?

Now you will have to drop that idea also. The observer will be the observed. Now there will be no distinction between the two: the seer will be the seen and the knower will be the known and the lover will be the beloved. It is very strange when for the first time it starts happening: it blurs you, your whole mind structure simply shatters. It looks almost as if you are going mad – or what?

Just think: seeing a bamboo, and you forget who is the bamboo and who is the seer – it will look insane. And when you come back into your normal, utilitarian world, you will become suspicious, distrustful, doubting: "What is happening? This is dangerous! How can I be the bamboo?" But this is true. We are all part of one reality.

I am in my right hand, I am in my left hand. I am in my body, but my body is joined with the earth and the sun and the moon. We are all joined together, interlinked. Nobody is independent, we are all interdependent.

When slowly, slowly the mind takes a leap from you – you say good-bye to the mind and the no-mind opens its infinity – then you are the bamboo, then you are *in* the bamboo, *as* the bamboo, the observer has become the observed. And the tremendous benediction of it! And the great transformation that comes through it!

And this will be happening, Kosha, more and more. You have earned it. Don't be afraid! It will appear like insanity and the mind will condemn it like insanity.

This is the point when you have to listen to the Master, not to the mind. I say to you: go ahead. You have risked a lot, now risk a little more. Let this distinction also disappear, and with its disappearance, the satori!

The fourth question:

> Osho,
> *Cannot the teaching of being here and now be sometimes dangerous,*
> *in the hands of fools of course?*

In the hands of the fools anything can be dangerous, anything whatever! The Koran is dangerous, the Bible is dangerous, the Gita is dangerous – and you know it. The whole history is full of proofs. Such beautiful statements, so crystal clear, but in the hands of the fools something goes wrong – and the nectar becomes poison.

And just the reverse is the case: if you are intelligent, wise, even poison becomes medicine.

One day a man came to me. He was very worried because he had been following J. Krishnamurti for almost twenty years. Then he had a chance, accidentally, to fly with Krishnamurti from Delhi to Bombay.

And then he saw…and what he saw shocked him, shook him completely. He could not sleep. Why had he wasted time with this man for twenty years?

So he came to me and said, "What should I do now? My twenty years have been wasted!"

I said, "What actually has happened?"

He said, "I saw him reading a detective novel!"

I said, "In the hands of J. Krishnamurti a detective novel becomes a Koran. And in your hands, a Koran becomes just a detective novel."

It depends. It *all* depends on you.

I have heard....

A man asked his psychoanalyst after many days of psychoanalysis...nothing was happening. Both were getting worried. He was paying so much and nothing was coming out of it.

Finally he blurted out. He said, "I think the real problem is not my mind, the real problem is the people with whom I work – my manager, my treasurer, the clerks. The people with whom I work are the real problem. So just psychoanalyzing *my* mind is not going to help."

The psychoanalyst asked, "What exactly is the problem with the people that you work with?"

He said, "They are all utterly lazy. Nobody wants to work, they just all go on postponing their duties."

The psychoanalyst said, "You do one thing: you make beautiful boards. Write on the boards in capital letters: Do it now! Tomorrow never comes! Tomorrow is death, life is today. And put this board everywhere in your office, so wherever they look they will find it. This will have some impact on them."

After the third day the psychiatrist phoned his patient. His wife was on the phone and she said, "He is in the hospital because he has been beaten badly by his people."

He said, "Why?"

The woman said, "I think it is because of your advice."

So he rushed to the hospital. The man was really in pain, he was fractured all over the body.

He asked, "What happened?"

The man said, "It is you and your stupid advice. The treasurer immediately escaped with all the cash – Do it now! Tomorrow never comes! Tomorrow is death! He simply wrote a note: 'I have been thinking of escaping with the cash for many years, but if it is so – tomorrow is death – then this is the time.' My manager has escaped, eloped with my typist. And the other workers just jumped upon me and started beating me. They said, 'We had always wanted to beat you, and we were postponing'."

You ask me, "Cannot the teaching of being here and now sometimes be dangerous?"

It can be if you work in such an office, or if you have such people inside your head.

I have heard…

At the time of the Wilson government in England, George Brown – always drunk – is Foreign Secretary. A reception is held on the visit of the French President, Pompidou.

Madame Pompidou is seated next to Brown, who starts the conversation drunkenly. "What do you want out of life, Madame?"

Madame Pompidou replies, "All I want is happiness." She added as she felt Brown's hand traveling up her thigh, "But not before the soup."

I teach you to be here and now, but you will have to take care of many things – "not before the soup"!

To be here and now needs great intelligence. It is not the message for the stupid, for the mediocre. When I say to you to be here and now I am giving great respect to your intelligence. This is my way of showing respect towards you. You have to be worthy of it.

To be here and now means to be very alert, aware, conscious, so that this moment is no more burdened with past, no more burdened with future, so the present is unburdened of all garbage and is clear, pure, innocent. And in that innocence you will find the door into God.

But remember always: you can turn, change the meaning, impose your own ideas on the greatest of teachings and destroy them. All depends on you.

The fifth question:

> Osho,
> Why is feminine energy the "darkness" principle? Does this
> mean that there is supposed to be something sinister about it?
> The author of The Secret of the Golden Flower seems a little male
> chauvinistic sometimes.

The question is from Ma Ananda Prem.

Ananda Prem, you are a female chauvinist! Rather than thinking about the author of *The Secret of the Golden Flower,* think about yourself.

Master Lu-tsu is saying something just factual. Who has given you the idea that darkness symbolizes something sinister? That is your idea! Darkness is as beautiful as light, equally beautiful and as valuable as light. Do you think night has less value than the day? In fact, it may have more value than the day, but not less. It is the day that tires you, exhausts you, it is the night that rejuvenates you, replenishes you. It is the day that kills you, it is the night that refreshes you again, prepares you for tomorrow, keeps you young. What is sinister in darkness? Darkness is vast. Light is never so vast. Light is always limited, darkness has no limitations. Light is shallow, darkness has depth.

That's why we have not painted Krishna as white but as black. One of his names is Shyam; "shyam" means the black one. Why? – just to give a sense of depth. Whiteness is a little shallow. Hence in the West, so much craze for a suntan, because the white face does not give the feeling of depth. Lying on the sun-beach under the sun, to get a little brown, and it starts having a depth and a beauty of its own.

And darkness is cool, and darkness makes you feel alone. It is very meditative. You cannot sleep in the light, you need darkness to sleep. And sleep and *samadhi* are very similar. In darkness you can enter into no-mind very easily.

Who has given you the idea, Ananda Prem, that darkness is sinister? It must be your own female chauvinistic mind.

Nothing is wrong in darkness. Darkness is the energy of the earth and light is the energy of the sky, and the meeting of the earth and the sky is the whole secret of existence. Man is a meeting of the earth and the sky, and they both have to be in balance. If your light and darkness principle are balanced, if your male and female principles are in deep harmony, you will attain to One.

Lu-tsu is simply stating a fact. The woman is more restful than man. Light is the principle of restlessness. That's why in the morning as the sun rises you have to awake, you cannot rest anymore. As the sun sets you start feeling sleepy, now you are getting ready to rest – fall into tremendously deep oblivion. Light will bring you back to the circumference, to the day-to-day affairs, the routine world. Darkness takes you far far away from this world. You forget all the turmoil and the anxiety and the worry and the hurry.

The woman has the same quality of giving you rest. If you love a woman, just being with her is restful.

Only a person who has come to meet with his inner woman can live without a woman. Then there is no necessity, because he is rested, he has found an inner shelter. But till you find an inner shelter, you will have to find an outer shelter – it is absolutely necessary. The woman gives you rest, hence Lu-tsu calls her dark.

The moment you are in the embrace of your woman or in her lap, you are again a child and she is your mother. She may be your wife, but she again becomes your mother. Again she overwhelms you like darkness: she makes you cool, she takes away all the heat that has been generated by the day. It is easier to fall in deep sleep with your woman. She is the principle of the dark. And the woman is as vast as darkness.

Man is very particular, woman is universal. That's why man is tired sooner, the woman has more capacity to resist. Women live longer than men. Women suffer less from illnesses than men. Women go mad less than men. Women commit suicide less than men. She is restful, cool, calm and collected, and she has that vastness.

The woman is always generous. She gives and does not ask in return. She protects, she nourishes – not only the child: she nurses the child with her milk, she nurses her beloved with love – which is a higher-value food, which is a deeper food, a nourishment for the soul.

Who has given you, Ananda Prem, the idea that darkness is sinister? There is nothing sinister. But I can understand from where this idea must be coming.

The Western mind has lived on duality and has never been able to penetrate to the One. The Jewish heritage is of duality, and because of Judaism, Christianity and Islam also became dualistic. Ananda Prem carries a Jewish heritage.

The Jewish heritage is that God is good. But then where to put all the badness that you come across in the world? So as a scapegoat the Devil has been created. The Devil is all bad, God is all good – to protect God from badness. Otherwise you will have to put badness somewhere or other. And if there is only one God, that means good and bad both are contained in him. Then he is both.

Jews have never been that courageous. They were afraid to put good and bad both in the same God, so the only possible way out was to create two Gods, a God of good and a God of bad. Hence the God-and-Devil duality. Then God is light and the Devil is dark. Then the Devil is always painted as dark, animal-like, with horns and a tail and hooves, and with a dark color, like a dark night, sinister. That's from where Ananda Prem gets the idea of darkness being sinister. And the same has penetrated into Christianity and into Islam. Both these religions are by-products of Judaism.

There have really been only two religions, Judaism and Hinduism. Christianity and Islam belong to the Judaic tradition. Jainism and Buddhism belong to the Hindu world, the Hindu vision. The Hindu vision is totally different. In the Hindu vision there is no Devil. It is non-dual, God is both: God *has* to be both. But both are so balanced in God that they cancel each other, and God is beyond. God is *both,* that's why God is beyond, because they cancel each other.

This is the Eastern concept of the transcendental, the non-dual. So you will see Eastern gods painted black and you will see Eastern goddesses looking very devilish. Just think of Kali, the Mother, with a garland of human skulls! No Jew can conceive that God is God with human skulls – and with a fresh head just recently cut, blood dripping, in her hand. And not only that, she is dancing on the chest of her husband...must be a real woman! And with all this, and a sword in hand, she is so beautiful, so utterly beautiful. Look into her eyes – the tremendous depth and beauty and compassion and love and warmth.

Now the Western mind is simply baffled: "What nonsense is this? If this woman is God then who is the Devil?" They cannot understand, because we have been trying to bring both the polarities together. They have both been brought absolutely together in Mother Kali. "Kali" means the black.

And the word *kal* is very significant: it means three things. First, it means black; second, it means time; third, it means death. The Mother Kali represents all these three things. She is time, the eternal movement of time, this infinite movement, change, flux. And she is death too, and she is black – and yet, look deep into her and see the beauty and the benediction and the compassion and the love and the warmth. She is life and she is death. She is black *and* she is white. She is the meeting of the polar opposites.

Lu-tsu is not a male chauvinist. Be a little more careful when you start talking about people like Lu-tsu. Be a little more alert. People like Lu-tsu or Lao Tzu or Chuang Tzu, or Buddha or Krishna or Christ are neither men nor women. They have gone, gone beyond. They have transcended all dualities. And still, both dualities are in them, but so balanced, in such harmony – sound and silence in such harmony – that great music is created; black and white in such harmony that the whole panorama of existence is created; life and death in such deep embrace, that eternity arises out of it.

The sixth question:

Osho,
Do you believe in the Second Coming of Christ?

And who do you think I am?

Christ is not a person, Christ is a state of consciousness. There have been Christs before Jesus, there have been Christs after Jesus. Jesus is only one of the many different Christs that have existed. Buddha is a Christ, Mahavira is a Christ, Lu-tsu is a Christ, Zarathustra is a Christ. Christ simply means the ultimate state of consciousness; it is equivalent to Buddha.

Buddha is not the name of any person, it is a happening. So is Christ – it is not Jesus' name! His name was Jesus. One day Jesus disappeared and the Christ-consciousness descended in him. He was no more the ego, he became the vehicle of the whole. He could say, "I and my Father in heaven are one." This is Christ-consciousness; it has nothing to do with Jesus.

If you are waiting for Jesus' second coming, then you are waiting in vain. But if you are waiting for Christ's coming, Christ has always been coming: Christ is in front of you, you are listening to him – not to Jesus, certainly, not to Gautama Siddhartha, certainly. But you are facing a buddha, just as you are facing a Christ.

You remind me…

I have heard of an editor of an upstate small-town newspaper. For years he had cherished a set of old-fashioned wooden scarhead type of some sixty-point size. On more than one occasion his assistants had tried to induce him to use it, but he always firmly vetoed the idea.

One summer the old man went away for a short fishing trip. In his absence a cyclone struck the town, tore the steeple off the church, unroofed several houses, sucked a couple of wells dry, and scattered a few barns around. No bigger catastrophe had hit the town in years. So, figuring, "Now is our chance," his assistants got down the sixty-point type from the shelf and set up a sensational front-page headline with it.

Two days later the editor came storming into the office. "Great Jehosaphat!" he shouted. "What do you mean by taking down that type for a cyclone? All these years I have been saving that type for the second coming of Christ!"

Then you will be waiting in vain.

Don't think that Christ and Jesus are synonymous. That's where the error lies in two thousand years of the Christian Church. Many have come in this time – this has been a long period – many have come out of the Christian fold, and a few have come even in the Christian fold itself. Meister Eckhart was a Christ, so was Jakob Boehme, so was Saint Francis. These were in the same fold, but still

Christianity missed them because they were waiting for Jesus – the same body, the same form. That is utter nonsense. It is not going to happen again. Jesus cannot be repeated.

To repeat Jesus you will have to repeat the whole history that preceded Jesus, and that is impossible. Jesus cannot be repeated, because for Jesus to be here you will need Mariam, you will need Joseph the Carpenter, you will need the whole two-thousand-year-old world of Jerusalem. You will need Herod the King, and Pontius Pilate the Governor General. You will need the whole structure, because Jesus came as part of it. No, Jesus cannot be repeated. There is no way. But Christ can descend, Christ can descend in anybody.

When John the Baptist baptized Jesus in the River Jordan, the story says a great white dove came from heaven, out of the blue – nobody had seen such whiteness, such purity – and he descended into Jesus and disappeared into Jesus.

This is just symbolic. This is symbolic of christhood: Jesus became enlightened...something of the beyond. As Master Lu-tsu would like to say, "Heaven penetrated the earth." These are just symbols, metaphors: a white dove descending from heaven, entering into Jesus and disappearing. And since that moment Jesus is no longer Jesus, he is Christ. The same happened to Buddha under the bodhi tree: something descended in him, and after that he was not Gautama Siddhartha, he was the Buddha.

Don't wait for Jesus' coming. And if you wait for Jesus' coming you will be wasting your time. He is not going to come, he cannot come. But if you are waiting for Christ's coming then there is no need to wait – Christ is already here! And those who have waited for Christ – not for the particular form, but the consciousness, the essence of it – have always found Christ somewhere or other. Thousands of Masters have existed in the same consciousness.

It is said...

A Christian missionary went to see a Zen Master. The old Zen Master had never heard of Christ. He lived in a faraway mountain cave. The missionary really took much trouble in reaching there. It was a hard and arduous journey, hazardous and dangerous too. He carried his Bible – he wanted to convert the old Master because his name was all over the country, and millions loved him and traveled to his cave.

So he went there and he told the Master, "I would like to read a few sentences to you." And he opened the Bible and started reading the Sermon on the Mount: "Blessed are the meek, for theirs is the Kingdom of God," and so on and so forth.

Only a few sentences, and the old Master said, "Wait! Whosoever said this was a buddha! *Whosoever* said this was a Buddha. No need to read further. I have also experienced this. No need to read further. Yes, blessed are the meek for theirs is the Kingdom of God. Look at me! It has happened to me!"

Now this poor missionary had come to convert. He had come to convert this Christ into a Christian. He wanted to convert a Christ into a Christian! The utter stupidity of it! But he could not understand yet.

He said, "Let me read the whole thing. You will be very impressed."

But the old man said, "There is no need to read it. Whosoever said it is a buddha. He knows as much as I know. We are the same. You look at me!"

But the Christian was too much of a Christian; he went back with his Bible thinking this old man was crazy, "Calling himself Christ? How can he be a Christ?" He was thinking in terms of Jesus, he does not know the meaning of Christ.

Christ is the Western equivalent of Buddha, the Awakened One, the Blessed One. That is actually the meaning of Christ. The meaning of Bhagwan is the meaning of Christ – the Blessed One.

And the last question:

> *Osho,*
> *I have fallen in love many times in my life, but it has always been*
> *very frustrating. What is the cause of it?*

Love is almost an unknown phenomenon, so you must have fallen into something else. And if you fall into something else, sooner or later you have to fall out of it. Love is a very rare experience. Don't call it love. It is your desire, it is your fantasy that you call love. It is your need, it is your fear of being lonely. You feel lonely and empty and you want to fill yourself with somebody else, and nobody can fill himself with somebody else, so sooner or later, frustration.

Frustration is bound to happen to your so-called love. And then when you fall in love, what do you really start doing? You start fantasizing, expecting too much. Because you expect too much, too much frustration follows. This is something new in this age, and more so in the West than in the East. The East has been very pragmatic about love, very realistic. Not much frustration happens in the East because people never expect much out of it – so what frustration? Marriage comes first in the East, and then living together with a woman or man, slowly slowly you start becoming friendly, you start liking each other, you start helping each other, and a kind of love grows. But there is no romance in it, hence no frustration.

In the West love has to happen first, and love drives you crazy. It is a hormonal disease that you call love, it is something chemical. And in that chemical impact, as if you are under a drug, stoned.... Actually, it is that: the drug has been released by your own hormones so you don't know it, when you inject a drug, you know. It is a biological drug, nature has been using it to propagate. Otherwise, just think – if there were no intoxicant inside you...just think for a moment that there is no intoxication with love, no desire to propagate – who will propagate? For what? The world would stop. Nature has befooled you: it has put a built-in program in you, it triggers a process of hormones in you, and suddenly you start seeing dreams and small things start looking very great.

I have heard...

A lovely but rather flat-chested young woman visited a physician for her periodic physical examination.

"Please remove your blouse," the doctor told her.

"Oh no," the young lady protested. "I just couldn't!"

"Come, come," the doctor replied to the young lady. "Let us not make mountains out of molehills."

But in love that is what happens – people start making mountains out of molehills. And then when frustration sets in, they start making molehills out of mountains. Everything looks beautiful when you are in that drugged state. That's why in all the languages of the world the phrase is "falling in" – you fall from your consciousness, you lose your consciousness, you are almost a drunkard. Then an ordinary woman looks so beautiful, so angelic, an ordinary man looks like Hercules. Everything looks so great and so big, and this is nothing but a projection of your desire.

And sooner or later it will clash with reality – and Hercules will come down, and Cleopatra will come down. And then you are sitting face to face with an ordinary man, an ordinary woman, wondering what you are doing there, wondering how you got there. And if there are a few children also playing around, then finished! Then just because of these children now you have to be together. Hercules is dead, Cleopatra is dead; just two ordinary, silly-looking people taking care of the children, because they have to be educated. And they will do the same, sooner or later.

Your expectations are so great, hence the frustration.

Meditate over this. Go very very slowly.

The lady of the house called down to her butler, "Smithers, come up to my bedroom, please."

When he came through the door, she said, "Now Smithers, the time has come. Take off my shoes." So Smithers took off her shoes.

"Now take off my stockings." So he took off her stockings. "Now Smithers, take off my dress." So he took off her dress.

"Now Smithers, take off my brassiere." So off comes her bra. *"Now* Smithers, take off my knickers. And if I ever catch you wearing my clothes again, you will have to find yourself another job!"

Now this is what happens – you were expecting, expecting, expecting…and the frustration!

Enough for today.

CHAPTER 31
The Festive Dimension

The first question:

> *Osho,*
> *One of the controversial issues about your Ashram concerns*
> *indulgence in sex and what are being condemned as sexual*
> *perversions or orgies. We would like Osho to give us his views*
> *on sex and its role in transcendence.*
> *–R.K. Karanjia, Editor, Blitz*

My dear Karanjia, the way I teach is the way of life-affirmation. I teach people life in its totality. In the past, religions have been life negative: they have denied life, destroyed life, they have been antagonistic to life, their God was against life. To me, life and God are synonymous, there is no other God than life itself – I worship life –and if life is God, then love is his temple.

These three Is are the fundamentals of my teaching: life as God, love as the temple, light as the experience. If you have learned these three Is, you have learned all.

But because the religions have remained antagonistic to life and love, it is natural that a great controversy will arise around me. I cherish it – it is natural. I am not worried by the controversy. I would be worried if it didn't arise. It is absolutely expected, it is absolutely according to my plan of work.

Why have the religions been life-negative in the past? In the name of religion man has been exploited – exploited by the priest and by the politician. And the priest and the politician have been in deep conspiracy against man. In this century, just fifty years ago, the Nizam of Hyderabad had five hundred wives and was still thought to be a very religious man because he followed all the rituals.

The priest and the politician have both been doing all that they have been telling the people not to do, sometimes openly, sometimes from the back door.

I have heard...there is an old saying, "Fool me once, shame on you. Fool me twice, shame on me."

But the priests have been fooling you down the ages, and they have fooled you so long that it is now almost an accepted phenomenon. It has been so ancient that we take it for granted – nobody thinks that they are being fooled.

It reminds me of a church a friend of mine went to which runs raffles. Once a year they get three automobiles, and they put them up in front of the church, and they sell the chances. Last year they raffled off a Cadillac, a Mercury, and a Plymouth. Three days after the raffle the pastor was walking down the street, and he bumped into my friend coming out of a thirst parlor.

My friend looked at him and said, "Can you tell me who won the automobiles? Who won the Cadillac?"

And the priest said, "Why, the Cardinal did. Wasn't he lucky?" And my friend said, "Who won the Mercury?"

"Why, the Monsignor did. Wasn't he lucky?"

And my friend said, "Well, tell me, who won the Plymouth?" And the priest said, "Why, Father Murphy. Wasn't he lucky?"

At that moment my friend started to go back in and get another drink. The priest grabbed him and said, "By the way, how many tickets did you buy?"

And my friend said, "I didn't buy a damned one! Wasn't I lucky?"

The priests have tremendously harmed the human heart, human consciousness. They have put this poisonous idea in man that life is something ugly. They have been teaching people how to get rid of life. I teach my people to get deeper into it. They have been teaching how to be free of life. I teach how to make your life free. They have been teaching how to end this life, and I am teaching you how to move into it for eternity, on and on, how to live life abundantly, hence the controversy. It is bound to be there. My vision is just the opposite to what has been taught in the name of religion.

I am bringing a new vision of religion to the world. This is the boldest attempt ever made: to accept life in its multidimensions, to enjoy it, to celebrate it, to rejoice in it. Renunciation is not my way, but rejoicing. Fasting is not my way, but feasting. And to be festive is to be religious. My definition of religion is the festive dimension.

No other animal can be festive, no other animal knows anything about festivals. Porpoises can play, chimpanzees can play, only man celebrates. Celebration is the highest growth of consciousness, expression, manifestation, flowering of the Golden Flower.

I teach you celebration. Celebration is my key.

And I teach you: celebrate your sex, it is a God-given gift; celebrate your body, it is God's grace. Celebrate each moment that has been given to you, each breath, each heartbeat. It is such a benediction. Live God right now! I don't give you God as a goal, I make God available to you right now, this very moment. Celebrate, and you are in God.

The old religions were sad. The old religions were serious. My religion is that of playfulness: everything has to be taken into the mood of playfulness. Don't take life seriously. It is fun. And to take it as fun is to be prayerful. Then there is no complaint, then there is only gratefulness.

The question is important. A few things would be helpful.

There are people who are pathological, and the pathological mind has dominated in the past. Those people cannot enjoy, they don't know how to enjoy. Because they are incapable of enjoying, they make a great virtue out of it. Non-enjoyment becomes virtue.

Everybody is born with the capacity to enjoy, but not with the art. People think just because they are alive and they breathe and they exist, so they know how to enjoy. That is sheer stupidity. Enjoyment is a great art, it is a great discipline. It is as subtle a discipline as music or poetry or painting. It is the greatest creativity.

People are born and they start thinking that they are ready to enjoy life, and they cannot enjoy because they don't know how to enjoy it. They make a mess out of their lives, and sooner or later, when-you are making a mess, there are only two possibilities. One is: think that you are being stupid with life – that hurts the ego. The other is: that life is worthless, that life is misery – "There is no joy in life, that's why I am not enjoying it. Nothing is wrong with me. If there is something wrong, it is in the very structure of life itself." This has been the approach in the past: "If I cannot see light, then there is no light" – not that I am blind. "If I cannot hear sound, then there is no sound" – not that I am deaf.

This has been very, very helpful to the egoist. He tries, and then he finds he cannot enjoy; finding that he cannot enjoy, he starts condemning. He starts condemning those who can enjoy too. He feels jealous, he feels disturbed. Out of his jealousy, out of his disturbance, he poisons people's minds. If you are enjoying he says, "Look, you will suffer in hell. You are doing a crime! Celebrating, dancing, singing, loving?" Life is a punishment for him, and you are taking it as a reward? And these pathological people have dominated in the past.

Once, a friend of mine was alone on a dreary night in a lounge of an intercontinental hotel. Hoping to strike up a conversation with a distinguished-looking man sitting nearby, he said, "May I buy you a drink?"

"No," said the man coolly. "Don't drink. Tried it once and did not like it."

Nothing daunted my friend, so he offered him a cigar, saying he had just picked up a good one.

"No, don't smoke. Tried it once and did not like it."

"Then how about a little game of rummy?"

"No. Don't play cards. Tried it once, but did not like it. But my son will be dropping by after a bit. He might want to play."

My friend settled back in his chair and said, "Your only child, I presume."

These are the potential priests: they tried once and they didn't enjoy – as if enjoyment is their birthright.

It has to be earned, it is an art. One has to imbibe it. It takes years of preparation, it takes years of cleansing. To hear classical music just for the first time and to think that you don't enjoy it, "so forget all about it," would be stupid. Your ears need a certain discipline, only then can they understand the subtle. The gross is available, it is easy to be with the gross, because it is animal. But to move into the deeper realms of life one needs great discipline, great meditativeness, great prayerfulness, great gratitude. And the basic thing to remember is: "If life is not becoming a celebration, then something is wrong with me, not with life itself."

The old religions said life is wrong. I say, if something is not happening to you, you are wrong. I make you responsible, not life. Life is God. And from there the whole process changes: then something has to be cleaned in you, something that is hanging around you has to be cut, chunks of conditioning have to be dropped. You have to go through a surgery.

That's what this Ashram is all about: it is a surgical place. It is no ordinary ashram like the thousands there are in India. It is a great existential experiment: we are creating a future here, a new kind of man with a new responsibility. We are laying the foundation stones of a new day, of a new sunrise. We are opening new doors to possibilities which have remained closed in the past. And because of this, humanity has suffered in the past, suffered a lot, and unnecessarily suffered. And the more people suffered, the more they thought, "The priests are right – life is wrong!" And the priests were creating more and more negative attitudes in people.

Moe went to a department store to buy himself a suit. He found the style he wanted, so he took the jacket off the hanger and tried it on.

A salesman came up to him. "Yes, sir. It looks wonderful on you."

"It may look wonderful," said Moe irritably, "But it fits so terribly. The shoulders pinch me."

The salesman did not bat an eye. "Put on the pants," he suggested. "They will be so tight, you will forget all about the shoulders."

That has been the common practice of the priest: if something hurts, he gives you an even more tight structure, more tight and dead and dull, a character. If something hurts, he makes you hurt more so you forget all about the old hurt. It always happens: if you have a headache and your house catches fire, you will forget about the headache. Who can afford to think about a headache when the house is on fire?

The priest goes on inventing more and more tortures for you. He has not allowed you to enjoy anything. Taste is wrong; you should eat food without tasting. If you taste you are committing a crime. Dance is wrong – why? – because it is bodily, and the body is the enemy. Music is wrong because it is sensuous. *All* is wrong!

You have to go on cutting yourself. Rather than expanding, the priest has been trying to shrink you. In the modern age the psychoanalyst is called the "shrink," but the priests have been doing that down the ages – they have been shrinking people – and when you have shrunk so much that it hurts all over, that you are almost in a prison cell, so small that you cannot move, that has been called character. Then naturally, one wants to get rid of life. One prays to God for only one thing: relieve me, redeem me.

Your priests have been against God! – let me say it that way – because God creates existence and your priests create only such structures around you so that you cannot live existence. Your *mahatmas* are against God.

I am all for God – and God means life.

You have asked, "One of the controversial issues about your commune concerns indulgence in sex..."

This is the only place where there is no indulgence in sex, but it will surprise you.

Indulgence needs repression. The more repressed a person is, the more he wants to indulge. It is like, if you have been fasting for a few days and then you relax, you start eating too much, you indulge. Indulgence is a by-product of repression. For thirty days you fasted, you repressed, you fought with yourself, you lived in a kind of hell. Then after thirty days you start moving in the opposite direction, to the opposite extreme: you start indulging. Indulgence is the absolute opposite extreme of repression.

Because I am against repression, how is indulgence possible in my place? I cut the very root of it. If a man is healthily eating, he does not indulge in eating. If he is enjoying his food he does not indulge, he does not eat too much. In fact because he loves his body, he loves his food, he remains very careful. To stuff the body too much is not the sign of a lover of the body, it is a sign of the enemy. There are two ways that the body can be killed: either by starvation or by over-stuffing it – but both are the ways of enmity. The lover of the body, one who respects his body as God's gift, cannot do either. He will neither fast nor will he indulge in food. And the same is true about sex and about everything.

Indulgence is created by the priests because they create repression. Once you create repression people start indulging. The more a desire is repressed, the more it wants to assert. It becomes mad, it becomes aggressive! When it is allowed its natural flow, when it is accepted, when there is no fight with it, there comes a balance.

So let me tell you, sir, that this is the only place – maybe the *only* place in the whole of the world – where indulgence is impossible.

Yes, when people come, in the beginning, for a few days they indulge – but I am not responsible for it. The priests, the politicians, the puritans, the moralists – Morarji Desai, etcetera – they are responsible for it. I have not been teaching people to repress; the people who have been teaching repression are responsible for it. And when people come to me they come with all those conditionings, so when I say relax, naturally they start indulging a little bit. But how long can one indulge? When you really relax, sooner or later the balance is achieved. The moment balance is achieved there is no repression, no indulgence.

But I can understand the question: for the so-called religious, my balanced, normal, natural people will look as if they are indulging. Just think of a man who is fasting, and you are taking your breakfast, and he passes by – the aroma of the coffee and the smell of the bread and the butter, and the joy on your face – what do you think he thinks about you? He thinks you are indulging, you will suffer in hell: "You can go on indulging a few days more, then I will see. When you will suffer in hell, then you will know. You will have to pay very badly for what you are doing." These are the thoughts in his mind. These are the ways he protects himself, these are the ways he represses himself. It is out of his unnaturalness that he starts thinking you are unnatural. Now, enjoying one's breakfast is not unnatural at all!

And the man who enjoys his food never eats too much – he *cannot,* it is impossible. Have you ever come across wild animals who are fat? Now, nobody is teaching them naturopathy and nobody is teaching them dieting or fasting. You never come across a fat wild animal.

I am deliberately saying *wild* animal, I am not talking about the zoos, because it is different in zoos – animals start imitating man. In zoos you can find fat animals, ugly, but not in the wild state. Why? – because an animal simply loves, enjoys his body, eats to the point where the body is satisfied, not a bit more.

And yes, sometimes it happens that the animal fasts too, but not according to Jainism. If he feels that the body is in such a state that it cannot take food – he is ill, and it is harmful to load the body – these are *natural* instincts, he does not eat. Sometimes even the animal may try to vomit, to unburden. A dog will go and eat grass, that helps him to vomit. And you cannot persuade him to eat till he becomes healthy again. These are natural instincts.

Priests have contaminated man so much that he has forgotten all his natural instincts. Now he lives by ideas. He has to fast because he follows a certain philosophy of fasting. He does not listen to the body; the body is hungry and he fasts. And then sometimes the body is not hungry at all and he eats. He goes on losing contact with his body.

I want you to come down from your mind to your senses. Enter back into your senses.

I teach you the body: the body is beautiful, divine. Come back to the body, let the body become alive again, and it will take care. You need not worry about it. The body has a built-in program to keep you healthy, to keep you alive, to keep you vibrant, to keep you young, fresh. The body has a built-in program: you need not learn anything about it from books and teachings.

So when people come to me in the beginning, sometimes they may indulge – but I am not responsible for their indulgence. The priests, the people who have conditioned them, they are responsible. If these people can be here with me for a few days, sooner or later the balance is restored. And with balance comes tranquility, calmness, a subtle joy and a subtle naturalness.

Sex has four stages. Those stages have to be understood. Only at the fourth stage does sex become the Golden Flower. Not to understand those four stages is dangerous, and the whole tradition has been keeping you unaware of those four stages.

The first stage is autosexual.

When the child is born he is a narcissist. He loves his body tremendously, and it is beautiful. He knows only *his* body: just sucking his own thumb, and he is in such euphoria. You see the child sucking his own thumb – what euphoria is on his face. Just playing with his own body, trying to take his toe into his mouth, making a circle of the energy. When the child takes his toe into the mouth a circle is created and the energy starts moving in a circle. The light circulates naturally in the child and he enjoys, because when the light circulates there is great joy inside.

The child plays with his own sexual organs – not knowing they are sexual organs. He has not yet been conditioned, he knows his body as one whole. And certainly, the sexual organs are the most sensitive part of his body. He utterly enjoys touching them, playing with them.

And here is where the society, the poisonous society, enters into the psyche of the child: "Don't touch!" "Don't" is the first dirty, four-letter word. And out of this one four-letter word, then many more come: can't, won't – these are all four-letter words. Once the child is told "Don't!" – and the angry parent, mother or father, and the child's hand is taken away from his genital organs, which are naturally very enjoyable, he really enjoys it. And he is not being sexual or anything: it is just the most sensitive part of his body, the most alive part of his body, that's all. But our conditioned minds…. He is touching a sexual organ, that is bad: we take his hand away, we create guilt in the child. Now we have started destroying his natural sexuality. Now we have started poisoning the original source of his joy, of his being. Now we are creating hypocrisy in him, he will become a diplomat: when the parents are there he will not play with his sexual organs. Now the first lie has entered. He cannot be true. Now he knows: if he is true to himself, if he respects himself, if he respects his own joy, if he respects his own instinct, then the parents are angry and he is helpless against them – he is dependent on them, his survival is with them – if they renounce him, he will be dead. So the question is of choosing what? – whether you want to live, and the condition is that if you want to live you have to be against yourself. And the child has to yield.

The child is the most exploited phenomenon in the world. No other class has been so exploited as the child. He cannot do anything: he cannot make unions to fight with the parents, he cannot go to the court, he cannot go to the government. He has no way to protect himself against the parental attack.

And when the parents stop him, they are stopping him because of their own conditioning; their parents had done the same to them. They are very much embarrassed by the child's touching his own genital organs and playing with them, and so unashamedly.

Now the child knows nothing of shame. He is innocent. The "don't" has entered, the energy recoils – the first trauma has happened. Now the child will never be able to accept his sexuality naturally, joyously – repression has happened – and the child is divided in two, his body is no more whole. Some part of the body is not acceptable, some part of the body is ugly, some part of the body is unworthy to be part of him – he rejects it. Deep down in his psychology he starts castrating himself – and the energy recoils: energy will not be flowing as naturally as it used to flow before this "don't" happened.

And the natural outcome of this stupidity that has been perpetually practiced on humanity is: first, the child is no more a natural being, hypocrisy has entered – he has to hide something from the parents, or he has to feel guilty.

This is the autosexual state. Many people remain stuck there. That's why so much masturbation continues all over the world. It is a natural state, it would have passed on its own. It was a growing phase, but the parents disturbed the energy's growing phase. The child becomes stuck. He wants to play with his genital organs and he cannot: repressing, repressing, one day it is too much and he is *possessed* by the sexual energy. And once he has started masturbating, it may become a habit, a mechanical habit, and then he will never move to the second stage. And the people who are responsible are the parents, the priest, the politicians – the whole social mind that has existed up to now.

Now this man may remain stuck at this stage, which is very childish. He will never attain to full grown-up sexuality. He will never come to know the blissfulness that can come only to a grown-up sexual being. And the irony is that these are the same people who condemn masturbation and make much fuss about it, and they make such statements which are very dangerous. They have been telling people that if you masturbate you will go blind, if you masturbate you will become a zombie, if you masturbate you will never be intelligent, you will remain stupid. And now all the scientific findings are agreed upon one point: that masturbation never harms anybody – but *these* suggestions harm. Now this is an absolute agreement, there are no two opinions about it.

All the psychological researches agree that masturbation never harms anybody, it is a natural outlet of energy. But these ideas – that you will go blind

– may make it dangerous to your eyes, because again and again you will think that you will go blind, that you will go blind, that you will go blind…. So many people are using glasses, and the reason may not be in the eyes, the reason may be just somewhere else. So many millions of people are stupid, and the reason may not be that they are stupid – because no child is born stupid, all children are born intelligent – and the reason may be somewhere else: in these techniques you will remain ill, you will lose self-confidence. And so many people are afraid, trembling continuously, have no trust, no self-confidence, are continuously afraid, because they know what they have been doing.

Now thousands of letters come to me: "We are caught up in this trap. How can we come out of it?"

And let me repeat: masturbation has never harmed anybody.

But the moment when a person masturbates is a very sensitive and delicate moment – his whole being is open and flowing. In that moment if some suggestion is dropped in his mind – and he himself will drop the suggestion, "Now what if I go mad? if I go blind? if I remain always stupid?" – these constant autohypnotic suggestions are the cause of a thousand and one illnesses, of a thousand and one psychological problems, perversions. Who is responsible for this?

And people who come to me come with all these perversions. I try to help them – and *many* are helped and many grow beyond it – but the society thinks I am teaching people some perversions. This is just unbelievable! I am helping you to grow beyond your perversions; the society has given you perversions – and you live in a perverted society!

If the child is allowed the natural phase of autosexuality, he moves on his own to the second phase, the homosexual. But very few people move to the second phase. The majority remain with the first phase, and even while making love to a woman or a man you may not be doing anything else but just a mutual masturbation. Because very few people attain to orgasmic states, very few people come to the glimpses that are bound to be there if your sexuality is mature. Very few people come to know about God through their lovemaking – which is a natural phenomenon!

In lovemaking, meditation happens naturally. But it doesn't happen. And the reason is that millions, the majority, are stuck at the first stage. Even if they have got married and they have children, but their lovemaking is not more than mutual masturbation. It is not real lovemaking. Lovemaking is an art, a great art: it needs great sensitivity, needs great awareness, meditativeness, it needs maturity.

The second phase is homosexual.

Few people move to the second phase. It is a natural phase. The child loves his body. If the child is a boy, he loves a boy's body, *his* body. To jump to a woman's body, to a girl's body, would be too much of a big gap. Naturally, first he moves in love with other boys. Or if the child is a girl, the first natural instinct is to love other girls because they have the same kind of body, the same kind of being. She can understand the girls better than the boys. Boys are a world apart.

So the homosexual phase is a natural phase. But then their society helps people to remain stuck again – because it creates barriers between man and woman, girls and boys. If those barriers are not there, then soon the homosexual phase fades away, the interest starts happening in the heterosex, the other sex. But for that, society does not give chances – a great China Wall exists between the boy and the girl. In the schools they have to sit apart or they have to be educated separately, in the colleges they have to live in separate hostels. Their meeting, their being together, is not accepted.

That is one of the problems that is happening to me and to my people in this so-called educated city. If this city is educated, then I wonder what city can be called uneducated? The only problem to the Puneites is that my people are moving together, man and woman. It should be a natural phenomenon! People should be happy that men and women are moving together, creating a love-vibe around. But they have never moved together, they start feeling disturbed, they start feeling jealous, they start feeling angry, because who are these people to enjoy what has not been given to them? If it has not been their joy they will not allow anybody else to have it either.

But they will not say it that way: they will talk great philosophy, they will hide their jealousies behind great words of morality, of religion, of culture – and they don't know anything of morality or religion or culture, because all culture, all religion, all morality has to be based on love. If it is not based on love it is not there at all. It is just a game, a pseudo-game that you go on playing on the surface and deep down you remain just the opposite of it.

Homosexuality is perpetuated by the society and condemned by the same society. These strategies have to be understood. The same society condemns the homosexual, calls him perverted, criminal. There are still countries where homosexuality is punished – you can be sent to jail for ten years. There have been countries where a homosexual could have been sentenced to death! And it is the same society that creates it!

You divide man and woman apart for so long that you create watertight compartments – and when the man wants to love he cannot find the woman, and the woman wants to love and she cannot find a man, then, whatsoever is available.

She starts falling in love with a woman, he starts falling in love with a man, and it is not satisfying either, but it is better than nothing. Nature has to find its way. If you don't allow the natural course, it will find some roundabout way. Otherwise homosexuality is a natural phase: it passes by itself.

And the third phase is heterosexual.

When a man is really out of autosex, homosex, then he is capable and mature, for falling in love with a woman – which is a totally different world, a different chemistry, a different psychology, a different spirituality. Then he is able to play with this different world, this different organism. They are poles apart, but when they come close – and there are moments when they are really close and overlapping – first glimpses, lightning glimpses of *samadhi* are attained.

Because it does not happen, many people think that I am just talking something like poetry. It is not poetry! I am not talking fiction. I am talking reality. What I am saying is an existential phenomenon. But the need is that the man and the woman must be mature, they must have gone beyond the first two stages – only then can this happen. And very rarely, *very* rarely, are there people who are mature men and mature women, so nothing happens. They make love, but that love is only superficial. Deep down they are autosexual, or at the most, homosexual.

To love a woman or to love a man, a new kind of being is needed, which can accept the polar opposite. And only with the polar opposite – just as with negative and positive electricity meeting, electricity is born. Just like that, when life electricities meet – man and woman, yin and yang, Shiva and Shakti, when that meeting happens, that merger, that total oblivion, that drunkenness, when they have disappeared as separate entities, separate egos, are no longer there separate but are throbbing as one, two bodies in one soul – that is the first experience of no-mind, no-ego, no-time, and that is the first experience of samadhi.

Once this has been experienced, then a desire arises: how to attain this samadhi so that it can become a natural state of affairs and you need not depend on a woman, you need not depend on a man? – because dependence brings slavery. Only out of the experience of heterosexual orgasm does a person start searching for ways, means, and methods – Yoga, Tantra, Tao – so that he can attain the same state on his own or on her own.

And yes, it can be attained, because deep inside each man is a man and a woman – half comes from his father, half comes from his mother – and each woman is half woman, half man. So once you have known it happening through the outside of the woman, you will have the first glimpse that it can happen within too. The outer woman simply triggered it, the outer man simply acted as a catalytic agent – now you start meditating.

Then the fourth phase, the ultimate phase comes, which is *brahmacharya,* which is *real* celibacy, not the celibacy of the monks – that is not celibacy at all – but the celibacy of the buddhas.

It is brahmacharya: sex has disappeared. You don't need the outer woman, you don't need the outer man. Now your inner man and woman have fallen in a togetherness, and this togetherness is not momentary. This is real marriage: you are welded together. Now to be orgasmic is your natural state. A Buddha lives in orgasm continuously, he breathes in and out, in orgasm.

These are the four stages of sex.

My effort here is to take you to the fourth. But people who come to me come to me corrupted, crippled by the society, poisoned by the society: I have to take much poison out of them, I have to take much pus out of their beings, and only if they are courageous enough to be with me long enough, ready to risk, does this transformation become possible.

And the people who live on the outside and just hear rumors about what is happening here are bound to have stupid notions – that indulgence is happening, that orgies are happening, that violence is happening. It is as if in a surgery you come to know that that surgeon is very dangerous because he cuts people's parts, he opens their stomachs, much blood comes out – "That doctor is very dangerous. Never go to him!"

I am a physician, or better, I am a surgeon, and this place is a place for spiritual surgery. It is an alchemical experiment in transforming your energies. The ordinary masses *cannot understand it,* hence so much misunderstanding is bound to remain about me. It will go slowly, slowly. It may take centuries. And the people who have so much repressed sexuality in their beings can't have understanding of what is happening here. Their repression makes their eyes blind, they start projecting their ideas.

For example, a man who has repressed all his sexuality for his whole life will go mad seeing a naked woman, because it will be like an explosion in his being. But a man who has not repressed any sexuality will not even take any note of seeing a naked woman. Or he may simply think, "What a beautiful body!" – and that is that. He does not want to grab it, he does not want to possess it. Just as you look at a roseflower: the rose flower is naked, you don't put clothes on the rose flower. You don't put clothes on the animals. There are a few ladies in England who try to put clothes on their dogs, because "naked" dogs...

Now these old ladies must be dirty! What kind of mind is this?

So if in some of my groups nudity happens – which is a natural part of the group process – and some people, some sly people, can sometimes take photographs with small, automatic cameras, and then those pictures are published all over the world and it is thought that orgies are happening here… Something totally different is happening here.

Twenty nuns were on a pilgrimage to Lourdes when their plane crashed. They all, of course, went to heaven where they were met by Saint Peter and the recording angel.

"Welcome ladies," he said. "Just a pure formality: will all those who are virgins take one step forward." There was an embarrassed silence as only nineteen stepped forward.

The recording angel put down his pen, turned to Peter and said, "Excuse me, but what shall we do with the deaf one?"

Whom do you think you are deceiving with your repressions? Your repressions are bound to take revenge on you from the back door.

The whole hypocrisy can disappear from the world if sex is accepted naturally. Ninety-nine percent of hypocrisy is dependent on sex-repression.

Now, religions go on giving you double-binds. They first say, "Be authentic, be true," and all that they teach makes you inauthentic, untrue, hypocrites. This is a double-bind. They say, "Believe in truth, believe in God" – now this is a double-bind: belief simply means you don't know and still you are believing – it is untrue. If one has to be true, one has to seek and search and only then believe. But they say, "First believe in God, and then you will be able to find him." To begin with belief is to begin with a lie. And God is truth, and you begin in lies. Life is truth, and you begin in hypocrisy. If you go on missing, it is no wonder. You are bound to miss all joy.

In the past, this antagonism towards sex has been exploited for one more reason. First, the priest exploited it to make you afraid, to make you tremble. Then he became very high, holier than you; he dominated you. And the politician exploited it in another way, for some other reason: if sex is repressed, man becomes violent. Now, this is a scientific finding again: violence is a perversion of sexual energy. Now the politicians needed armies, violent people, murderers. The only way to get so many murderers was to repress sex. If you don't repress sex, who wants to kill? For what?

The sword, the dagger, the bayonet are nothing but phallic deep down. The man wanted to penetrate the woman's body and it would have been a beautiful phenomenon if it had happened in love. But it could not happen, it was not allowed. Now he is mad, he wants to enter anybody's body, in any way – with a dagger, with a sword, with a bayonet.

Sex has been repressed, the politician exploited it in his own way. He needed armies, he needed slaves ready to die or to kill. The person who has not lived his life in celebration is ready to die for anything. He is ready to become a martyr for any stupid idea, ideology, scripture, religion.

The man who has lived the joy and the blessings of a life will not be so easily ready to die. He will say, "Why? Life is so precious. I cannot sacrifice my life just for a piece of cloth called the national flag." "I cannot sacrifice my life," he will say, "just because somebody has burned the Koran. So what? Print another." "I cannot sacrifice my life because somebody has burned a temple. So what? My life is more precious than your temple, because it is the alive temple of God." But a man who has not loved and who has not lived is always ready.

I have heard:

A great British politician went to see Adolf Hitler. They were standing on the fourth story and talking to each other, and Adolf Hitler was bragging about his power and he was saying, "It is better that you yield without fighting. Otherwise we will destroy your whole country. You don't know what kind of men I have got." And to show, he just ordered a soldier who was standing on guard, "Jump!" And the soldier didn't say a thing, he simply jumped. He did not even hesitate for a single moment. The English politician was really impressed. And to impress him still more, he ordered the second soldier to jump, and he also jumped.

By the time he ordered the third, the Englishman could not contain himself; he rushed and caught hold of the third. He said, "Are you mad? Why are you jumping like that?"

The man said, "Leave me alone. Let me jump! It is better to die than to live with this man."

When life is misery it is better to die. Any excuse is enough.

The politician needed violence, so he exploited others. The priest needed power, so he exploited others.

I am neither a priest nor a politician. I am just a human being, as you are. And I can see humanity – how much it has suffered. I feel for it because it is me, it is you – and I want to have a totally different future for humanity, for the children to come, for the people who will come on the earth. If we can create a different future for them, that will be the only revolution. Up to now no revolution has happened, because ninety-nine percent of hypocrisy, untruth, exploitation, violence depends on sexual repression, and no sexual revolution has yet happened.

I am trying to create that situation. It is going to be against the society, it is going to make me very controversial, but it is natural. I want the controversy to spread all over the world, because only through that controversy the people who have intelligence, the people who have any kind of understanding, are bound to come to me. These repressed people cannot understand. Their minds are full of holy cow dung.

I have heard about a Boston priest who had volunteered to work part-time in a peace group protesting the war in Vietnam. Doing some writing as well as organizing, he would scurry in and out of the storefront headquarters among the motley assembly of bearded students, jeans-clad coeds, and young mothers with babies in papoose sacks or strollers. Once when he had to make an important phone call, he found all the phones taken. Knowing there was a pay-phone in the basement, he rushed downstairs. There at a table was a barebreasted mother who had just finished giving lunch to her baby. In great embarrassment, the girl crossed her arms over her chest and said, "I beg your pardon, father."

The priest smiled, "Don't be embarrassed, young lady. We priests may be celibate, but in our work we grow accustomed to a great many things. I assure you your condition does not trouble me in the least. In fact, you can perhaps do me a favor: Could you give me a dime for two nipples?"

A repressed mind is an obsessed mind. He cannot see reality as it is. It is impossible. Before he can see reality as it is, he will have to drop all kinds of repressions. A clean mind is needed, an innocent mind is needed.

The actor Charles Coburn told how his father warned him about the evils of certain types of theaters. His father was a very, very religious man.

"What kind of theaters, father?" he asked.

"Burlesque theaters, son. Don't ever go in one."

Immediately Coburn asked, "Why not?" And his father answered, "Because you will see things in a burlesque theater that you should not see."

That, of course, aroused his curiosity. Not many days passed before he took in his first burlesque. Coburn remarked, "And I found out my father was right. I did see something I should not have – I saw my father there."

Man has lived with hypocrisy. I want you to be authentic human beings – true to nature, true to your being, respectful. Have some dignity: you have been chosen by God. It is a great gift, just this life. Make it a festival, celebrate it. Love deeply, and deep love will release your intelligence. Love deeply, because only embedded love will give you first glimpses of meditation and will release your prayer. Drop all the taboos.

You will have to risk much – that's what sannyas is all about: the art of risking – because you will be moving into the unknown, you will be moving into the unfamiliar, unacquainted, uncharted. The society gives you a map, a clear-cut style of life to live. I give you only freedom. The society gives you character, I give you only consciousness. The society teaches you to live a conformist life. Of course, if you live a conformist, conventional life you will be more secure, but more dead too. I give you an invitation to go on an adventure.

Live in insecurity! Live in revolution! Be a rebel! Risk, because nothing is ever attained in life without risk. The more you risk, the closer you are to God. When you can risk all, all is yours.

And don't be a hypocrite, and don't compromise.

The situation recalls an incident around the turn of the century in a Baptist church. A young soprano in the choir loft got so carried away with her solo that she fell out. Breaking her fall, the singer caught herself in the chandelier – and there she was suspended upside-down. The fiery Baptist minister was equal to the occasion. He said, "Speaking on my very sermon subject of 'Hell and Damnation,' I tell you that he who looks with lust in his heart shall be blinded."

An old codger in the front pew said, "Reverend, with such a great opportunity, is it all right to risk one eye?"

That's what people have been doing – risking one eye. I tell you, risk both! Don't compromise. Risk all. Let life be a play, a risk, a gamble. And when you can risk all you will attain to a sharpness in your being: your soul will be born. The Golden Flower can bloom in you only if you are courageous, daring. It blooms only in courage.

And remember, sex may look like mud, but it contains the lotus flower in it. This is one of my fundamentals: the lowest contains the highest, and the highest is nothing but the manifestation of the lowest. The seed contains the flowers and the flowers are nothing but expressions of the seed. Sex contains samadhi, because life contains God.

Move from sex to samadhi, from sex to superconsciousness – this is the only natural and rightful way. Don't get stuck anywhere in sex. I teach you sex and transcendence together, because the transcendence is possible only *through* it. And the people who are teaching repression are not teaching transcendence. In fact, they go on pouring more mud on you. They go on forcing you deeper in the mud because there is no possibility of transcendence if you have not moved through these sexual stages of autoeroticism, of homoeroticism, of heteroeroticism, and then to transcendence – and the lotus blooms, the one-thousand-petaled lotus. You are containing it in yourself. Avoid the priests and the politicians and you can achieve it. They are standing in the way.

But they always wanted it this way. It is good for them, it is not good for anybody else. They have diverted your love. They have taken its natural object from you; then love can be diverted. Now there are people who are in love with the motherland – what foolishness! What do you mean by "motherland"? There are people who are in love with the fatherland – still more foolish. There are people who are in love with countries, ideologies – communism, fascism, Hinduism, Christianity.

Your natural object of love has been taken away; now your love is frantically searching for anything to become tethered to.

A great scientist was working on animals; he calls it "imprinting." He says when the animal comes out of the egg, whatsoever he comes across, he immediately becomes attached to it. He becomes attached to the mother because the mother is almost always there. Giving warmth, taking care of the egg, the mother is there. The moment the child opens his eyes, comes out of the egg, looks around at the world, the first thing he comes across is the mother. He becomes attached to the mother.

One scientist was trying to change the subject, and he succeeded. He removed the mother. When the child was coming out of the egg, he removed the mother; he sat there himself. Then he was in trouble, because the child would continuously follow him. And not only that, when the child became a grown-up, became sexually mature, he liked to make love to his feet. He would come to his feet and would try to make love to the feet – because that was the first thing he had seen.

Mother is your first love. It is because of the mother that you will fall in love with a woman someday. And, almost always, you will fall in love with a woman who looks in some way like your mother.

"Psychiatry is a lot of junk," said one man to another.

"Oh?" said his companion. "Why do you say that?"

"Well, today my psychiatrist told me that I am in love with my umbrella. Have you ever heard of anything so silly?"

"It does sound rather daft."

"I mean, me and my umbrella certainly have a sincere affection for each other. But *love?* That is just ridiculous!"

If your natural object of love is taken away, you will love money…you may even love your umbrella. You may start falling in love with things: you may start falling in love with flags, countries, and all kinds of nonsense is possible once your natural love is distracted.

Bring your love to its natural object, let it have a spontaneity of its own. Allow it to take possession of you, and you will be transformed through it.

Love is the key, love is the secret.

The last question:

> *Osho,*
> *Yesterday you so lovingly transmitted the spirit of Tao. Throughout this series I have been bathing rapturously in these waters. All that you have ever said is coming true. I begin to feel surrender as the natural climate of the flower growing toward the sun. The beauty is here, is here….*

The old pond,
Samarpan jumps in,
the sound.

Enough for today.

Resources

In this work Osho comments on selected excerpts from:

In chapters 1, 3, 5, 7, 9, 11, 13, 15, 17, 21, 23, 25, 27, 29
Wilhelm, Richard (Ed.), *The Secret of the Golden Flower (A Chinese Book of Life)*, London: Kegan Paul, Trench & Trübner, 1931

In chapter 8
Lathem, Edward (Ed.), *The Poetry of Robert Frost, The Collected Poems, Complete and Unabridged,* New York: Holt, Rinehart & Winston, 1969

Williams, Margery, *The Velveteen Rabbit*, New York: Henry Holt and Company Inc.

In chapter 18
Gibran, Kahlol, *The Prophet*, London: Wilhelm Heinemann Ltd, 1926

In chapter 25
Zen Buddhism, New York: Peter Pauper Press, 1959

In chapter 27
Reps, Paul, *Zen Flesh, Zen Bones*, Japan: Charles E Tuttle Co. Inc., 1957

In chapter 29
Aitken, Robert, *A Zen Wave Basho's Haiku and Zen,* by Robert Aitken, New York: John Weatherhill Inc., 1978

www.OSHO.com

A comprehensive multi-language website including a magazine, OSHO Books, OSHO TALKS in audio and video formats, the OSHO Library text archive in English and Hindi and extensive information about OSHO Meditations. You will also find the program schedule of the OSHO Multiversity and information about the OSHO International Meditation Resort.

Websites:

http://OSHO.com/AllAboutOSHO

http://OSHO.com/Resort

http://OSHO.com/Shop/en

http://www.youtube.com/OSHO

http://www.oshobytes.blogspot.com

http://www.Twitter.com/OSHOtimes

http://www.facebook.com/OSHO.International

http://www.flickr.com/photos/oshointernational

To contact OSHO International Foundation:

www.osho.com/oshointernational, oshointernational@oshointernational.com

OSHO International Meditation Resort

OSHO International Meditation Resort

Each year the Meditation Resort welcomes thousands of people from more than 100 countries. The unique campus provides an opportunity for a direct personal experience of a new way of living – with more awareness, relaxation, celebration and creativity. A great variety of around-the-clock and around-the-year program options are available. Doing nothing and just relaxing is one of them!

All of the programs are based on Osho's vision of "Zorba the Buddha" – a qualitatively new kind of human being who is able both to participate creatively in everyday life and to relax into silence and meditation.

Location

Located 100 miles southeast of Mumbai in the thriving modern city of Pune, India, the OSHO International Meditation Resort is a holiday destination with a difference. The Meditation Resort is spread over 28 acres of spectacular gardens in a beautiful tree-lined residential area.

OSHO Meditations

A full daily schedule of meditations for every type of person includes both traditional and revolutionary methods, and particularly the OSHO Active MeditationsTM. The meditations take place in what may be the world's largest meditation hall, the OSHO Auditorium.

OSHO Multiversity

Individual sessions, courses and workshops cover everything from creative arts to holistic health, personal transformation, relationship and life transition, transforming meditation into a lifestyle for life and work, esoteric sciences, and the "Zen" approach to sports and recreation. The secret of the OSHO Multiversity's success lies in the fact that all its programs are combined with meditation, supporting the understanding that as human beings we are far more than the sum of our parts.

OSHO Basho Spa

The luxurious Basho Spa provides for leisurely open-air swimming surrounded by trees and tropical greenery. The uniquely styled, spacious Jacuzzi, the saunas, gym, tennis courts … all these are enhanced by their stunningly beautiful setting.

Cuisine

A variety of different eating areas serve delicious Western, Asian and Indian vegetarian food – most of it organically grown especially for the Meditation Resort. Breads and cakes are baked in the resort's own bakery.

Night Life

There are many evening events to choose from – dancing being at the top of the list! Other activities include full-moon meditations beneath the stars, variety shows, music performances and meditations for daily life. Or you can just enjoy meeting people at the Plaza Café, or walking in the nighttime serenity of the gardens of this fairytale environment.

Facilities

You can buy all of your basic necessities and toiletries in the Galleria. The OSHO Multimedia Gallery sells a large range of OSHO media products. There is also a bank, a travel agency and a Cyber Café on campus. For those who enjoy shopping, Pune provides all the options, ranging from traditional and ethnic Indian products to all of the global brand-name stores.

Accommodation

You can choose to stay in the elegant rooms of the OSHO Guesthouse, or for longer stays on campus you can select one of the OSHO Living-In program packages. Additionally there is a plentiful variety of nearby hotels and serviced apartments to choose from.

www.osho.com/meditationresort
www.osho.com/guesthouse
www.osho.com/livingin

WATKINS

Sharing Wisdom Since
1893

The story of Watkins Publishing dates back to March 1893, when
John M. Watkins, a scholar of esotericism, overheard his friend and
teacher Madame Blavatsky lamenting the fact that there was nowhere
in London to buy books on mysticism, occultism or metaphysics. At that
moment Watkins was born, soon to become the home of many of the
leading lights of spiritual literature, including Carl Jung, Rudolf Steiner,
Alice Bailey and Chögyam Trungpa.

Today our passion for vigorous questioning remains resolute. With over
350 titles on our list, Watkins Publishing continues to be at the cutting
edge. Our books reflect the development of spiritual thinking and new
science over the past 120 years, and we stay committed to publishing
titles that change lives.

DISCOVER MORE...

Read our blog   Watch and listen to   Sign up to our
our authors in action   mailing list

JOIN IN THE CONVERSATION

f WatkinsPublishing   @watkinswisdom

WatkinsPublishingLtd   +watkinspublishing1893

Our books celebrate conscious, passionate, wise and happy living.
Be part of the community by visiting

www.watkinspublishing.com